CourseCompass

Learning just got more exciting!

Welcome, Karen!
Courses you are taking
The Struggle for Democracy

What is CourseCompass?

CourseCompass is a nationally hosted, dynamic, interactive online learning environment powered by state-of-the-art Blackboard™ technology. With CourseCompass, you can access materials designed specifically to go with this textbook, participate in online discussions, take quizzes and tests online, and submit homework electronically. You can also do some cool stuff like keep a personal calendar, take notes with the Electric Blackboard, and create your own homepage that other students in your course can view.

How will CourseCompass help me?

CourseCompass makes it easy to find and organize all your course materials. Your instructor can post announcements, the course syllabus and schedule, lecture notes, homework assignments, articles and links to relevant web sites, and more. All this content is available all the time; you can access it with just a few clicks of the mouse!

CourseCompass also lets you:

- Communicate online with your instructor and other students
- Hand in and pick up assignments electronically
- Check your scores on quizzes and tests
- Keep track of personal appointments, your "to do" list, and course events
- Store information about classmates and friends

Turn the page to get your Student Access Code!

CourseCompass

Your personal
Student Access Code
below!

Go to http://students.pearsoned.com

What are these words?

The string of six words is your unique **CourseCompass** *Student Access Code*. This code is your personal passport to a wide array of resources available to you in CourseCompass including your instructor's syllabus, online quizzes and tests, additional reading assignments, and more! Use this code to register as a CourseCompass student, following the CourseCompass registration directions provided on page 2 of *Using Course Compass*. You will only enter this Student Access Code once in order to set up your personal subscription to the online learning environment.

Your Student Access Code is:

LSCCDH-ABUZZ-AZOLE-TIGON-PUVIS-TOUSE

IMPORTANT

This Student Access Code is non-transferable and can only be used by one student. If you have purchased a used textbook, this Student Access Code will no longer be valid and you will have to purchase a new Student Access Code through your local bookstore.

Technical Support

If you experience technical problems or have questions about using your personal Student Access Code, you can reach the CourseCompass Customer Support center at any time by:

1 Calling 1-800-677-6337, or
2 Sending email to support@coursecompass.com

A Customer Support representative will respond during business hours (9:00 AM to 6:00 PM, Eastern Standard Time).

The use of CourseCompass requires an Internet connection. Internet connectivity is provided by your local Internet service provider and requires either Microsoft Internet Explorer or Netscape Navigator Version 4.0+.

Important: Please read the License Agreement located on the Log In screen before using CourseCompass. By using the website, you indicate that you have read, understood, and accepted the terms of this Agreement.

Using CourseCompass

CourseCompass

How do I get started with CourseCompass?
Turn the page to learn how to:

- Register, enroll in your course, and log in to CourseCompass (see page 2)
- Get around in CourseCompass (see page 4)
- Use the tools on the My CourseCompass page (see page 5)
- Explore the content in your course (see page 7)
- Take a test online (see page 11)

For more information, you can always look in the online Help.

 Look for this symbol to learn about cool stuff you can do with CourseCompass!

Registering and logging in

To open your CourseCompass course, you need a *student access code* and a *course ID*. You can find your Access Code on the first page titled "Student Access Code." Your Instructor will give you the **Course ID**.

Once you have both your access code and the course ID, you can register in CourseCompass and enroll in your course. To do so, follow these general steps:

1   Go to http://students.pearsoned.com.

2   Click 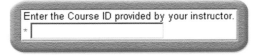 .

3   Enter your six-word student access code when prompted. Type one word in each of the boxes provided. Do not type the hyphens.

Enter your access code here:

4   If you already have a login name and password for another Pearson Education product, type them in. If you don't have a CourseCompass login and password, just skip this step!—you'll create them in step 9.

5   When asked, enter the course ID your instructor gave you.

Enter the Course ID provided by your instructor.
*

6   Enter the personal information requested.

Make sure you provide an email address that you check regularly because this is where CourseCompass sends registration information.

7   Enter your school's zip code.

8   Click the name of your school in the list provided. If the name of your school doesn't appear in the list, click Other and enter its city and state (or country).

9   Enter the login name and password you want to use for CourseCompass. You'll also be able to use this login name and password for other Pearson Education products.

Tip To see examples of login names and passwords, click **Need help?** link. Because login names must be unique, you may need to add one or more numbers to the end of your first choice.

10 Just in case you ever forget your login or password, select and answer the question you want CourseCompass Customer Support to use to verify your identity.

11 Review the **License Agreement**, which displays in a separate window. To confirm your agreement with the terms and conditions in the license, return to the registration page and click the **I agree** box.

12 Review the information in the Summary on the left. If you need to change it, click your browser's Back button. If it's OK, click **Finish Registration.**

13 CourseCompass confirms your registration. Print a copy of this page, which includes your *summary information, login name,* and *password.*

14 Click **Log In Now**.

15 Type your **login name** and **password** in the appropriate boxes, and then click the ▶ LOGIN button to see your customized My CourseCompass page.

Congratulations! You've registered in CourseCompass and enrolled in this course. To enter this course from now on, just go to http://students.pearsoned.com and log in to CourseCompass.

Getting started in CourseCompass

Now that you've enrolled in your online course and logged in, you can begin exploring CourseCompass.

When you enter your course, you see the **My CourseCompass** page. This page contains lots of information that's already customized for you—such as your name and the title of this course. You can make other customizations yourself, such as changing the color scheme of the page.

Header —
Tabs —

Your courses —

Tools area —

Search the web —

 ## Header

In the header area, which is always visible in CourseCompass, you can click:

- **Home** to return to your starting point within CourseCompass
- ⑦ **Help** to open CourseCompass online student Help
- **Logout** to exit from CourseCompass

Tabs

In addition to the My CourseCompass page, there are other main pages in CourseCompass. To access one of these pages, click its tab.

- The **Courses** page lists all the online courses you are taking. You click the title of a course to go directly to it.
- The **Services** page tells you how to contact CourseCompass Customer Support.

Tools area

The **My CourseCompass** page also has a Tools area with links to announcements for all your online courses, a personal "To Do" list, your grades on home-work and tests, and an Address Book. You can even send email and search the web right from CourseCompass!

Modules

The main part of the My CourseCompass page contains boxes, called *modules*, that give you access to CourseCompass courses, features, and information. These modules might include:

* **Courses**, which lists and lets you link to all the courses you are taking
* **Announcements**, which displays system-wide announcements and announcements for all your courses
* **News from Pearson Education**, which shows you updates about Pearson Education products and services
* **Learning with CourseCompass**, which links to resources to help you work in CourseCompass
* **Services and Support**, which tells you how to contact CourseCompass Customer Support

Picking your own colors for the **My CourseCompass page**

You can change the color of the text and the background of the module title bars on the My CourseCompass page:

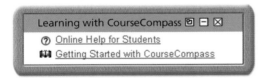

To customize the colors:

1 Click (**Colors**) in the upper-right corner of the My CourseCompass page.

2 To change the color of the module title bars on the My CourseCompass page, click (🎨 **Pick**) next to Select Module Banner Color. Click a color in the ColorPicker.

3 To change the color of the text in the module headers, click (🎨 **Pick**) next to Select Banner Text Color. Click a color in the ColorPicker.

4 Click (**Submit**).

CourseCompass displays the My CourseCompass page with the new color scheme:

Exploring your course

Now you're ready to check out your course! You can open your course in two ways:

- Click the course title on the My CourseCompass page:

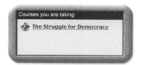

or

- Click the **Courses** tab and then click the course's title on the Course List page.

Viewing course announcements

The **course announcements** page shows you any announcements from your instructor. You can view all the announcements related to this course, or you can view course announcements for a limited period of time by clicking one of the tabs in the announcements area.

Adding your friends to your **Address Book**

To add a contact to your Address Book:

1 Click **Address Book** in the Tools area on the My CourseCompass page.

2 Click [Add Contact].

3 Under Personal Information, enter the person's first name (required), middle name, and last name (required), title, email address, school, address, URL, and phone numbers.

4 Click (**Submit**), and then click OK.

Viewing course information

You access different areas in your course by clicking the buttons on the left side of the page. Your instructor can store course materials in any of the CourseCompass content areas represented by these navigation buttons.

These are some of the buttons you might see:

Course Home	Links to outline of course
Announcements	Links to announcements for your course
Course Information	Links to logistical info for your course, such as a syllabus
Staff Information	Links to information about your instructor
Course Documents	Links to course materials, such as lecture notes
Assignments	Links to homework
Books	Links to the electronic textbook, if available
Communication	Links to communication tools, such as Discussion Board
External Links	Links to relevant web sites
Tools	Links to other tools, such as the Digital Drop Box
Resources	Links to the Blackboard Resource Center
Course Map	Links to an outline of each content area

Your instructor might have changed the names of some of these buttons or added new ones. In any case, clicking navigation buttons is one way to get to content in your course.

Adding events to your
personal calendar

CourseCompass automatically creates a calendar for each course, which you can view within your course. Alternatively, you can click Calendar in the Tools area on the My CourseCompass page to see scheduled events for all your courses. You can also add your own personal appointments to this calendar. To do so:

1 Click **Calendar** in the Tools area on the My CourseCompass page.

2 Click [Add Event] .

3 Fill in the event information, time, and date.
Click (Submit) , and then click OK.

Your calendar appears, with the event you just added. Depending on the date of your event, and how you are viewing your calendar—by day, week, or month—you may have to click another calendar tab to see your event.

Viewing and printing your course syllabus

One of your first tasks in CourseCompass will be to find and print your course syllabus. If your instructor has not told you where to locate the syllabus, look in Course Information. To do so:

1 Click your course's title on the My CourseCompass or Course List page.

2 Click **Course Information** .

3 Click the syllabus link, if one appears, as shown here:

Depending on how your instructor created the course syllabus, clicking the syllabus link either displays the syllabus in CourseCompass or opens another application to display a linked syllabus file.

4 If your computer is connected to a printer, you can print the syllabus. To do so, click **File** and then **Print** on your browser's menu.

If you didn't find a syllabus in the Course Information area, click the Course Documents button or open the course map to see whether you can find a link to the syllabus. If all else fails, you can email your instructor!

Delivering an assignment using the Digital Drop Box

You can deliver completed online assignments using the Digital Drop Box. You can upload and send the file all at once, or you can post the file and send it later. To do so:

1 Click your course's title on the My CourseCompass or Course List page.

2 Click **Tools** .

3 Click the Digital Drop Box link.

4 Click **Add File** to upload the file but not send it to your instructor right away.

or

Click **Send File** to upload the file and send it now.

5 Type the assignment title.

6 Click 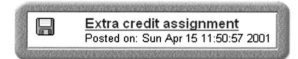 and find the directory on your computer where you saved your assignment. Click the file name and click Open.

7 Optionally, type additional information or instructions in the Comments box.

8 Click (**Submit**), and then click OK.

Your file appears in the Digital Drop Box:

> 💾 **Extra credit assignment**
> Posted on: Sun Apr 15 11:50:57 2001

Note To send a file at a later date, go to the Digital Drop Box, click 📑 **Send File** , click the arrow at the edge of the Select file box, and click the name of the file you want to deliver to your instructor.

 ## Participating in a Discussion Board

Your instructor can set up Discussion Board forums to let you hold course-related discussions with other students outside of class time. A Discussion Board forum is like a string of email messages. Unlike a chat session, you can participate in a Discussion Board forum at any time.

Within a forum, CourseCompass groups related messages into threads. Depending on how your instructor set up your course, you can create a message to start a new thread or reply to existing messages.

To participate in a Discussion Board forum:

1 Click your course's title on the My CourseCompass page.

2 Click **Communication** .

3 Click the Discussion Board link.

4 Click the title of the Discussion Board forum you want to enter:

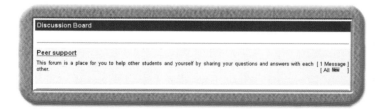

5 Click ⬚ Add New Thread to begin a new conversation thread.

or

Click the title of a message to which you want to reply, and click (**Reply**) .

6 Type a subject for the message. If you are replying to an existing message, the subject box already contains text that you can replace if you want.

7 Type the message or reply.

8 If the forum allows anonymous postings and you want to hide your identity, click the box next to Post Message as Anonymous.

9 Click Browse... to attach a file, if that option is available.

10 Click (**Preview**) if you want to see how your message will look.

11 Click (**Submit**) .

The Discussion Board page appears, with your message or response.

Taking tests online

Your instructor may assign assessments for you to complete online. These assessments can range in length and complexity from pre-class exercises, to short quizzes, to full-length exams. To complete any type of online assessment:

1 Click your course's title on the My CourseCompass page.

2 Click **Assignments** or **Course Documents** and find the assessment.

Note Your instructor can place assessments in any content area of CourseCompass. If you don't find your course assessments in the Assignments or Course Documents area, use the Course Home page to quickly locate them.

3 Click the **Take quiz** link below the assessment you want to take, and then click OK.

4 Click or type an answer to each question.

5 Click (**Submit**) at the bottom of the page, and then click OK.

Using Your Course Documents

In your textbook you will find references to the Course Documents section of your course. Within this section, you will find two types of links to web resources that have been developed for use with your book:

| **Course Documents** | —— | Web Explorations |
| | | LongmanParticipate |

The Web Explorations are critical thinking exercises that ask you to investigate, analyze, and enjoy the rich material that can be found on the Internet. These activities begin in your book and then take you, via your Course Documents, out to the many resources on the World Wide Web.

The LongmanParticipate exercises all take you to a distinctive web site for American government students. This web site contains an exciting array of in-depth activities that will help you understand the most important concepts in your course – and make learning them fun! The site contains 95 different activities (simulations, visual literacy exercises, interactive timelines, participation exercises, and comparsion activities), along with a

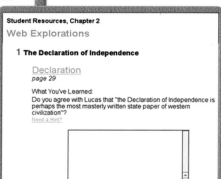

wealth of additional resources to help you succeed in your course.

When you click on "LongmanParticipate" in your Course Documents section, you will be taken to the main login page of **LongmanParticipate.com**.

On your first visit, click "Register Here" and follow the instructions. **Since you have already established a login name and password for your CourseCompass course, you can use these during your registration on LongmanParticipate.com.**

Each time you see a "LongmanParticipate" icon in your book, you are being asked to go to **LongmanParticipate.com** through your Course Documents. Beneath each icon you will find a specific activity type and title listed. Once you pass through the main login page of **LongmanParticipate.com** (you will need to pass through it each time you use the site), use the type and title to find the appropriate exercise.

Taking notes with the **Electric Blackboard**

The Electric Blackboard is like an online memo pad. You can use it to take and store notes in CourseCompass.

1 Click your course's title on the My CourseCompass or Course List page.

2 Click **Tools** .

3 Click the Electric Blackboard link.

4 Type your notes in the large box.

5 Click (**Submit**), and then click OK.

6 Close the Electric Blackboard by clicking the X in the upper-right corner of the window.

When you come back to the Electric Blackboard, your notes will still be there.

Checking your grades

You can see how you're doing in your course by checking your grades online in CourseCompass. CourseCompass lists your scores and also shows you your current standing in the course compared to your classmates.

To check your grades:

1 Click your course title on the My CourseCompass or Course List page.

2 Click .

3 Click the **Check Grade** link.

4 Examine the user statistics, your scores, and, for comparison, the class average on each assessment.

Creating your own **"to do"** list

You can use the Tasks list in CourseCompass to keep track of all the stuff you need to do. You can even prioritize each task so you can stay focused on what's most important.

To create your Tasks list:

1 Click Tasks in the Tools area on the My CourseCompass page.

2 Click Add Task .

3 Under Task Information, type a title and description for the task.

4 Next to Due Date, click the arrows to select the month, day, and year by which the task must be completed.

5 Next to Priority, click the arrow and select Low, Normal, or High. CourseCompass displays a different symbol, depending on your choice.

6 Next to Status, click the arrow and select Not Started, In Progress, or Completed. CourseCompass displays a different symbol, depending on your choice.

7 Click (**Submit**), and then click OK.

CourseCompass adds your task to the list:

Sending email from **CourseCompass**

You can send email to your classmates right from CourseCompass.

To send email:

1 Click **Send email** in the Tools area on the My CourseCompass page and click the appropriate course title.

or

Click your course title on the My CourseCompass or Course List page, and then click [Communication].

2 Click Select Users.

3 Click ☑ next to the name of each person you want to email.

4 Enter the subject and message of the email.

5 Select Send Copy of Message to Self to receive a copy of the email.

6 If you want to attach a file to the message, click (**Add**). Click [Browse...], find the directory on your computer where you saved the file, click the file's name, click Open, and then click (**Submit**).

7 Click (**Submit**), and then click OK.

Tip For information about sending email to all students or small groups in your course, see online student Help.

 ## Technical support

The CourseCompass Customer Support Center is open weekdays from 9 AM to 6 PM Eastern Standard Time. You can contact Customer Support by:

1 Calling **1-800-677-6337** during the above service hours

2 Sending email to **support@coursecompass.com** with a detailed description of your computer system and the technical problem. Our Customer Service Support Center will get back to you promptly.

3 Clicking the link to **Feedback Form** on the Services page

Getting help

To find out more about what you can do in CourseCompass, you can explore the online student Help provided.

1 Click ⑦ **Help** in the CourseCompass header area.

2 CourseCompass student Help opens in a separate window so you can read Help as you work with CourseCompass.

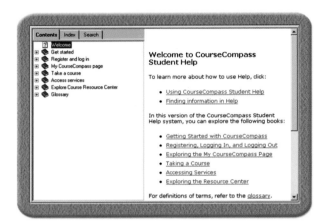

Tip Because Help contains a lot of information, it can take a little while to open. You might want to open the Help window when you start CourseCompass, and leave it open so you can quickly access Help topics as you need them.

The Help window has three tabs:
- **Contents** displays Help books and their pages. To open a book and show its pages, click the plus sign (+) to the left of the book icon. To close a book, click the minus sign (-). Click a page to view the corresponding topic.
- **Index** provides a list of keywords. Doubleclick a keyword to view the corresponding topic. If several topics reference the same keyword, click the title of the topic you want to view.
- **Search** lets you type a word or phrase you want to locate and then click Find. A list of all relevant topics appears. Doubleclick a topic to display it.

A topic might include additional links, which appear underlined in blue. You can click links to display more detail.

You can also click **Related Topics** at the end of a topic to display a list of other relevant topics.

The Struggle for Democracy

The Struggle for Democracy

Fifth Edition

CourseCompass™ Edition

Edward S. Greenberg
University of Colorado

Benjamin I. Page
Northwestern University

Longman

New York   San Francisco   Boston
London   Toronto   Sydney   Tokyo   Singapore   Madrid
Mexico City   Munich   Paris   Cape Town   Hong Kong   Montreal

PUBLISHER	Priscilla McGreehon
SENIOR ACQUISITIONS EDITOR	Eric Stano
DEVELOPMENT EDITOR	Janice Wiggins-Clarke
MARKETING MANAGER	Megan Galvin-Fak
SUPPLEMENTS EDITOR	Jennifer Ackerman
MEDIA SUPPLEMENTS EDITOR	Patrick McCarthy
PRODUCTION MANAGER	Valerie Zaborski
PROJECT COORDINATION, TEXT DESIGN, AND ELECTRONIC PAGE MAKEUP	Elm Street Publishing Services, Inc.
TECHNICAL DESKTOP MANAGER	Heather A. Peres
COVER DESIGN MANAGER	Nancy Danahy
COVER DESIGNER	Keithley & Associates, Inc.
COVER PHOTO	© New York Stock Photo
ART STUDIO	Elm Street Publishing Services, Inc.
PHOTO RESEARCHER	Julie Tesser
SENIOR MANUFACTURING BUYER	Dennis J. Para
PRINTER AND BINDER	Quebecor World–Taunton
COVER PRINTER	Coral Graphic Services

For permission to use copyrighted material, grateful acknowledgment is made to the copyright holders on pp. C-1 and C-2, which are hereby made part of this copyright page.

Library of Congress Cataloging-in-Publication Data
Greenberg, Edward S., 1942–
    The struggle for democracy / Edward S. Greenberg, Benjamin
  I. Page.—5th ed.
     p. cm.
    Includes bibliographical references and index.
    ISBN 0-321-05265-X (hardcover)—ISBN 0-321-08420-9 (softcover)
    1. United States—Politics and government. 2. Democracy—United States.
  I. Page, Benjamin I. II. Title.
  JK271 .G73 2001
  320.473—dc21   00-057556

Please visit our website at http://www.ablongman.com/greenberg

ISBN 0-321-09764-5

1 2 3 4 5 6 7 8 9 10—RNT—04 03 02 01

Brief Contents

Detailed Contents

> **Note:** Each chapter ends with the following sections: Summary, Suggestions for Further Reading, Internet Sources, and Notes. Red bullets designate special features within the chapter.

Part Three Political Linkage   115

Chapter 5   Public Opinion   116

Chapter 6   The Mass Media   148

Part Four   Government and Governing   303

Chapter 11   Congress   304

List of Features

Using the Framework

How Democratic Are We?

The Struggle for Democracy

CourseCompass

Web Explorations

Web Explorations (continued)

Preface

"Critical Thinking" and *The Struggle for Democracy*

The watchword for this fifth edition of *The Struggle for Democracy* is "critical thinking." Critical thinking has always been at the heart of this book, but its sharp edge has gradually, if almost unconsciously, been blunted slightly with each revision as material has been added to answer first one perceived need then another. With this revision, we are resharpening the edge, getting it back to where it is supposed to be. Every element in this version of *The Struggle for Democracy* is designed to serve the "critical thinking" objective. We have pared away any and all materials that do not help students think critically about American government and politics and about their roles as citizens. There are no extraneous or distracting "bells and whistles" in these pages, only text narrative and features that pull in a single direction, with the intention of helping teachers to be better teachers and students to be better learners. In moving in this direction, we are returning to our original vision when we first decided to write this book, responding to what we learned from a multitude of instructors and students about what they want in an introductory textbook, and conforming to what we know, as experienced teachers, works in the classroom. We have created a textbook that treats students as adults, engages their intellectual and emotional attention, and encourages them to be active learners.

The critical thinking orientation of this edition of *The Struggle for Democracy* is organized around two principal themes: *Using the Democracy Standard* and *Using the Framework*. The first helps students come to grips with American government and politics in normative or value terms. The second helps students cut through the jumble of information about government and politics and bring some order out of the confusion, helping them make sense of why things happen. We have also created a rich set of Web Explorations and other interactive activities that can be found in the online course that accompanies this text. We encourage students to do assignments on the Internet where they hone their evaluative and analytical critical thinking skills and, at the same time, have some fun.

Using the Democracy Standard

Throughout the pages of this textbook, we help students think about the system as a whole, as well as particular political practices and institutions, using a clearly articulated democracy evaluative "yardstick" for reaching judgments about the degree to which we have become, or are becoming, more or less democratic.

We develop this "evaluating democracy" theme in a number of places:

- Democracy is carefully defined in Chapter 1, and students learn there how they might use democracy to evaluate the performance of the

American political system. The definition of democracy is broad and inclusive, built on the concepts of popular sovereignty, political equality, and liberty.

- In the opening pages of each chapter, students are reminded about the democracy "yardstick" and how it might be used to think critically about the subject matter to follow.

- Discussion of the relative democratic performance of the American political system, using the Chapter 1 definition as the yardstick, is laced throughout the text narrative.

- A chapter-ending box, "How Democratic Are We?," helps students think through the democracy issue once again, only this time they have the capacity to bring information and insights to bear that they have gained from reading the chapter, attending class and joining its discussions, and doing the Web Explorations. This feature is organized in the following way. It opens with a strongly stated proposition about the relative democratic character of the particular political or governmental institution under consideration in the chapter. The proposition is answered by two opposing views, brief but fairly stated "agree" and "disagree" statements. Finally, we the authors respond to the proposition, sometimes aligning with the "agree" position, sometimes with the "disagree" position, but usually incorporating elements of each into a more subtle and balanced argument. This feature helps students to understand the complexity of many of the issues addressed in the book and to learn how to formulate intellectually compelling arguments.

- A "Struggle for Democracy" box appears in about one-half of the chapters as a way to highlight the dramatic story of peoples' efforts throughout our history to make our politics and government more democratic. It helps remind students that evaluating our political system is not a dry, intellectual activity of the mind alone, but one that engages the heart and the emotions, sometimes compelling people to act for change. It helps remind students, as well, that the kind of political system we have is open-ended, not fixed, and that their actions can matter.

Using the Framework

In Chapter 1 we also provide a simple but powerful analytical framework that helps students understand how our complicated political system works. The framework makes clear that government, politics, and the larger society are deeply intertwined in recognizable patterns; that understanding what is going on requires a holistic focus; and that what might be called "deep structures"—the economy, society, culture, technology, and the constitutional rules—are particularly important for understanding how our system works. These deep structures have a great deal to do with the creation of the problems to which government must attend, the level of resources that is available to solve problems, the ideas that citizens and elected officials have in their heads as they go about using government to address problems, and the distribution of political power in society among individuals, groups, and organizations.

The framework appears in *The Struggle for Democracy* in the following places:

- The framework is discussed in detail in Chapter 1, and students are shown how it can be used to order the large amounts of material they will encounter in the course of their reading. A powerful graphic associated with the discussion makes the framework more understandable and compelling.

- In the opening pages of each chapter, students are reminded about the framework and how it can be used to understand how government and politics work in the United States.

- Chapters in Part Two examine the nature of American society, culture, and economy, the United States's position in the world, and our constitutional rules, and why these issues matter for how government and politics work.

- Concepts and insights from the framework, as well as materials from the chapters in Part Two, are used throughout the text narrative.

- A "Using the Framework" box appears in each chapter. The purpose of the box is to show students how the framework might be used to answer questions they might have about why things happen in American government and politics. Concepts and insights from the framework, as well as a graphical reminder, are used to provide the tools to answer questions that students are interested in, such as "Why is out-of-state tuition more costly than in-state tuition?" and "Why can't we seem to get big money out of politics?"

CourseCompass™ Features

We have designed two features that appear several times in each chapter and take advantage of both the online course available with the text and the critical thinking opportunities held by the Internet. In the "Web Explorations" we identify websites for students to visit, giving them questions or issues to investigate, and ask them to report the results. The students are not casual visitors to these sites; they are investigators and analysts using their critical thinking skills. With the "LongmanParticipate" icons we ask the students to participate in a number of different exercises—simulations, visual literacy exercises, interactive timelines, participation and comparison activities—that allow students to experience first-hand the concepts they might normally only read about.

Organization and Coverage

Part One contains the introduction to the textbook, and focuses primarily on describing the critical thinking tools to be used throughout: democracy and the analytical framework. Part Two covers the structural foundations of American government and politics and addresses, in addition to subjects such as the economy, culture, and international system; the constitutional framework of the American political system; and the development of the federal system. Part Three focuses on what we call *political linkage* institutions, such as parties, elections, public opinion, social movements, and interest groups, that serve to convey the wants, needs, and demands of individuals and groups to public officials. Part

Four concentrates on the central institutions of the national government, including the presidency, Congress, and the Supreme Court. Part Five describes the kinds of policies the national government produces and analyzes how effective government is in solving pressing social and economic problems.

Although all of the standard topics in the introductory course are covered in the text, our focus on using democracy as a measuring rod to evaluate our system of government, and on using an analytical framework for understanding how things work, allows us to take a fresh look at traditional topics and to pay attention to topics that are not covered in detail in other textbooks.

- We pay much more attention to *structural factors*, which include the American economy, social change in the United States, technological innovations and change, the American political culture, and changes in the global system, and examine how they affect politics, government, and public policy. These factors are introduced in Chapter 4—a chapter unique among introductory texts—and are brought to bear on a wide range of issues in subsequent chapters. For example, our discussion of interest group politics includes relevant information about how the distribution of income and wealth affects the ability of different groups to form effective lobbying organizations.

- We attend very carefully to issues of *democratic political theory*. This follows from our critical thinking objective, which asks students to assess the progress of and prospects for democracy in the United States, and from our desire to present American history as the history of the struggle for democracy. For instance, we examine how the evolution of the party system has improved democracy in some respects in the United States but hurt it in others.

- We also include more *historical information* than is common among introductory texts, because the best way to understand the struggle for democracy and evaluate the progress of democracy in the United States benefits from a historical perspective. We show, for example, how the expansion of civil rights in the United States has been associated with important historical events and trends.

- We also include substantial *comparative information,* because we believe that a full understanding of government and politics and the effect of structural factors on them is possible only though a comparison of developments, practices, and institutions in the United States with those in other nations. We understand better how our system of social welfare works, for example, when we see how other rich democratic countries deal with the problems of poverty, unemployment, and old age.

- Our approach also means that the subjects of *civil liberties* and *civil rights* are not treated in conjunction with the Constitution in Part Two, which is the case with many introductory texts, but in Part Five, on public policy. This is because we believe that the real-world status of civil liberties and civil rights, while partly determined by specific provisions of the Constitution, is better understood as the outcome of the interaction of structural, political, and governmental factors. Thus, the status of civil rights for gays and lesbians depends not only on constitutional provisions but also on the state of public opinion, degrees of support from elected political leaders, and the decisions of the Supreme Court. (Instructors who prefer to introduce their students to civil liberties and civil rights immediately after considering the Constitution can simply assign the liberties and rights chapters out of order.)

What's New in This Edition

A number of important changes have been made in this edition. They include the following:

- To reiterate a point already made: the most important change in this fifth edition of *The Struggle for Democracy* is the renewed focus on critical thinking as the central organizing template. To get there, we have considerably refined and strengthened our discussions of democracy as a tool of evaluation and of the framework as a tool of analysis and understanding, paid special attention to drawing out these themes in every chapter, and created a series of web exercises tied to your CourseCompass™ course to enable students to be active critical thinkers.

- This edition of *The Struggle for Democracy* pays more attention to "marginalized" groups in American society, including Hispanics and gays and lesbians. Combining this enhanced attention to marginalized groups with *The Struggle for Democracy*'s traditionally strong coverage of African-Americans and women means that the current edition of this textbook reflects much of the cultural richness, diversity, and complexity of American society itself. These new materials are found throughout in the text narrative, in chapter-opening vignettes, and in boxed features. For example, one Struggle for Democracy box focuses on women's gains in state legislatures, and the vignette in Chapter 4 features the rising electoral power of Hispanic voters in states such as California. Chapter 16 discusses the current status of gay rights legislation in the states.

- We have expanded our coverage of Web sites in the Internet Sources sections and integrated them more tightly with *The Struggle for Democracy* home page. This is in addition to the very strong Internet presence found in the CourseCompass™ features distributed throughout. Together, these will allow both students and instructors to have better access to timely information and alternative perspectives.

- Information has been updated throughout. There is not a single page in the text without fresh information. Timely subjects, such as the historic 2000 Presidential election, the administration of George W. Bush, and the 107th Congress are covered throughout. In addition, topics such as the affirmative action controversy, changing party alignments, and the effect of global economic and technological change, are given greater attention.

- We have continued our effort to make the text more user-friendly for students by paying more attention to the layout of text and the highlighting of key points, better defining technical terms, presenting more detailed captions that explain tables and graphs, and providing more information in photo captions. Most importantly, we have tied the chapters together with critical thinking guideposts, exercises, and concluding observations.

Supplements

Longman Publishers provides an impressive array of text supplements to aid instructors in teaching and students in learning. Each item in this extensive package works together to create a fully integrated learning system. Great care was taken to provide both students and professors with a supportive supplements package that accurately reflects the unique spirit of *The Struggle for Democracy.*

For Qualified College Adopters

CourseCompass™   combines the strength of Longman content with state-of-the-art eLearning tools! CourseCompass™ is a nationally-hosted, dynamic, interactive online course management system powered by BlackBoard, leaders in the development of Internet-based learning tools. This easy-to-use and customizable program enables professors to tailor content and functionality to meet individual course needs! Every CourseCompass™ course includes a range of pre-loaded content such as testing and assessment question pools. This special CourseCompass™ edition of *The Struggle for Democracy* also covers features printed in the text that are tied to your online course. Links to "Web Explorations" and LongmanParticipate.com can be found in the "Course Documents" section. Instructor's can redeem pin codes and set up access at www.coursecompass.com. Students can set up access to their course at http://students.pearson.com. For more information, see the insert in the front of this textbook.

American Government Presentation Library CD-ROM   This complete multimedia presentation tool provides a built-in presentation maker, 20 video clips, 200 photographs, 200 figures and graphs from Longman texts, 20 minutes of audio clips, and links to more than 200 Web sites. Media items can be imported into *PowerPoint®* and *Persuasion®* presentation programs.

The Struggle for Democracy Online (http://www.ablongman.com/greenberg)   Designed to support
instructors and students who are using *The Struggle for Democracy,* this Web site includes summaries, Web Explorations, and practice tests for each chapter for students. For instructors, there are downloadable art and images for each chapter, the *Instructor's Manual,* and a group of teaching links. A link to this site can be found in your CourseCompass™ Course.

Instructor's Manual   Written by Todd M. Schaefer of Central Washington University, this comprehensive manual is designed to help instructors prepare lectures, classroom activities, and assignments. The manual features chapter outlines and summaries, a broad range of teaching suggestions, ideas for student research, and suggestions for discussion that complement text themes.

Test Bank   Prepared by Michele Zebich-Knos of Kennesaw State University, this manual is designed to reinforce and test students' knowledge of the themes and concepts of the text. The test bank contains hundreds of multiple-choice, short-answer, true/false, and essay questions with an answer key.

Test Gen EQ Computerized Testing System   This flexible, easy-to-master computerized test bank includes all the test items in the printed test bank. The software allows professors to edit existing questions and to add their own items. Tests can be printed in several different formats and can include features such as graphs and tables. It is available for Windows and Macintosh computers.

***PowerPoint*® Presentations**   This CD-ROM, available for both Windows and Macintosh platforms, contains about 20 slides per chapter. Written by Dewey M. Clayton of the University of Louisville, these slides can also be easily modified using *PowerPoint*® software.

Transparencies   This acetate package is comprised of 40 images drawn from the text.

Interactive American Government Video   Contains 27 video segments on topics ranging from the term limit debate, to Internet porn, to women in the Citadel. Critical thinking questions accompany each clip, encouraging students to "interact" with the videos.

***Politics in Action* Video**   Eleven "lecture launchers," covering broad subjects such as social movements, conducting a campaign, and the passage of a bill are examined through narrated videos, interviews, edited documentaries, original footage, and political ads. *Politics in Action* is accompanied by an extensive user's manual, which provides background on the segments, links topics to textbooks, and discussion questions.

Longman American Government Video Archive   These videos from a broad range of sources include famous debates, speeches, political commercials, and congressional hearings. The archive also includes series such as "Eyes on the Prize" and "The Power Game." Ask your local sales representative for more information.

Active Learning Guide   This guide is designed to get students actively involved in course material and encourage them to evaluate and defend viewpoints. Included in this guide are role-playing exercises, debates, and Web-based group projects.

For Students

CourseCompass™   See description in the insert at the front of this textbook or under "For Qualified College Adopters" for more information.

Interactive Edition CD-ROM   This unique CD-ROM offers students a complete multimedia learning experience. It contains the full text of the book with hyperlinks to video clips, photos, figures, maps, Web links, practice tests, and primary sources. The easy-to-use navigation makes it simple to search the text, take notes, and highlight key sections. It is FREE when ordered packaged with the text.

Study Guide   Written by James Lance Taylor of the University of San Francisco, this study guide aids students' comprehension of the material covered in the textbook and includes chapter outlines, summaries, term identification, research topics, self-evaluation questions, and multiple-choice and essay questions with an answer key.

Study Wizard CD-ROM   Prepared by David Billeaux of Texas A&M University, this exciting new interactive program helps students learn the major facts and concepts through drill and practice exercises and diagnostic feedback. Study Wizard, which provides immediate correct answers, explanations of answers, and the text page number on which the material is discussed, maintains a running score of the student's performance on the screen throughout the session. Study Wizard also provides a link to the text-specific Web sites in the textbook to offer students additional pedagogical support. It is available in Windows and Macintosh formats.

***The Struggle for Democracy* Online (http://www.ablongman.com/ greenberg)**   Please see description under "For Qualified College Adopters."

CHOICES: An American Government Reader   This exciting new customizable reader allows instructors to choose from an archive of more than 300 readings to create a reader that exactly matches their course needs. Contact your local Allyn&Bacon/Longman representative for more information.

***Voices of Dissent: Critical Readings in American Politics,* Third Edition**   Edited by William F. Grover, Saint Michael's College, and Joseph G. Peschek, Hamline University, this collection of critical essays on American politics goes beyond the debate between mainstream liberalism and conservatism to fundamentally challenge the status quo. *Voices of Dissent* is based on a broad concept that places traditional American political institutions and processes in the context of political economy, ideology, and the state.

10 Things That Every American Government Student Should Read
This reader was compiled by Karen O'Connor, American University. American government instructors across the country voted for the ten things beyond the text—essays, documents, articles—that they believed every American government student should read. The top vote-getters in each of ten categories were put into this unique and useful reader. FREE when ordered packaged with the text.

Getting Involved: A Guide to Student Citizenship   This unique and practical handbook guides students through political participation with concrete advice and extensive sample material—letters, telephone scripts, student interviews, and real-life anecdotes—for getting involved and making a difference in their lives and communities. FREE when ordered packaged with the text.

***A Guide to the Internet for American Government,* Second Edition**
Written by Carol Hays of Southern Illinois University, this guide demonstrates uses of the World Wide Web in the American government course. In addition to explaining links to important sites, the guide includes critical

thinking exercises to get students to apply their knowledge of American government to the Web and use it as a resource for research.

Writing in Political Science, Second Edition

Political science writing requires a distinct set of skills, vocabulary, sources, and methods of inquiry. This guide, by Diane E. Schmidt, takes students step-by-step through all the aspects of writing for political science courses. With an abundance of samples from actual students, the guide also features a section on how to address writing problems and a new section on how to evaluate and cite Internet sources. It is available at a significant discount when packaged with the text.

Discounted Penguin-Putnam Inc. Titles

Longman is offering 22 Penguin titles, including De Tocqueville's *Democracy in America,* Riordan's *Plunkitt of Tammany Hall,* and Iron's *The Courage of Their Convictions,* at more than a 60 percent discount when ordered packaged with *The Struggle for Democracy.*

California State Supplement

This 64-page supplement is a brief primer on state and local issues in California for use in the American government course. It is available free when shrink-wrapped with the text.

Texas State Supplement

This 70-page supplement is a brief primer on state and local issues in Texas for use in the American government course. It is available free when shrink-wrapped with the text.

Newsweek Discount Subscription

Students can receive 12 issues of *Newsweek* magazine at an 80 percent savings off the regular subscription price! Contact your local representative for more information.

Acknowledgments

Writing and producing an introductory textbook is an incredibly complex and cooperative enterprise in which many people besides the authors play roles. We would like to take the opportunity to thank them, one and all. We start with the many wonderful people at Longman who worked on this edition, including development editor Janice Wiggins-Clarke, production manager Donna DeBenedictis, Sue Nodine and her colleagues at Elm Street Publishing Services for design and production work, photo researcher Julie Tesser, and marketing manager Megan Galvin-Fak. Special thanks go to Eric Stano for believing in this project and for helping to put us on the right revision road.

There are many colleagues we want to thank. William "Wild Bill" Haltom of the University of Puget Sound helped with expert advice on the civil liberties and civil rights chapters, as he did on each of the previous editions of *The Struggle for Democracy.* University of Colorado, Boulder, graduate students Dennis Still and Jenny Kehl served as expert research assistants. Jay Zarowitz of Muskegon Community College tested and gave advice on the Web Exploration features. As always, our students in the introductory courses in American government and politics at the University of Colorado and at Northwestern had much to say about what they liked and didn't like in the book, and were more than willing to tell us how it might be improved.

   Over the years, Longman enlisted the help of many political scientists on various aspects of this project. Their advice was especially valuable, and the final version of the book is far better than it would have been without their help. We would like to extend our appreciation to the following political scientists, who gave so generously of their time and expertise through the editions of *The Struggle for Democracy* and its supplements:

Gordon Alexandre, Glendale Community College

John Ambacher, Framingham State College

Jeffrey M. Ayres, Lake Superior State University

Ross K. Baker, Rutgers University

Manley Elliott Banks II, Virginia Commonwealth University

Ryan Barrilleaux, University of Miami

Stephen Bennett, University of Cincinnati

Bill Bianco, Duke University

Melanie J. Blumberg, University of Akron

Joseph P. Boyle, Cypress College

Evelyn Brodkin, University of Chicago

James Bromeland, Winona State University

Barbara Brown, Southern Illinois University–Carbondale

Joseph S. Brown, Baylor University

David E. Camacho, Northern Arizona University

Mary Carns, Stephen F. Austin University

Jim Carter, Sam Houston State University

Gregory Casey, University of Missouri

Carl D. Cavalli, North Georgia College and State University

James Chalmers, Wayne State University

Paul Chardoul, Grand Rapids Community College

Alan J. Cigler, University of Kansas

David Cingranelli, State University of New York at Binghamton

Natale H. Cipollina, CUNY Baruch College

Dewey M. Clayton, University of Louisville

John Coleman, University of Wisconsin

Ken Collier, University of Kansas

Lee Collins, Monmouth College

Edward Collins Jr., University of Maine

Richard W. Crockett, Western Illinois University

Lane Crothers, Illinois State University

Landon Curry, University of Texas

Christine Day, University of New Orleans

Alan Draper, St. Lawrence University

Euel Elliott, University of Texas

Bob England, Oklahoma State University

Robert S. Erikson, University of Houston

Thomas Ferguson, University of Massachusetts, Boston

M. Lauren Ficaro, Chapman University

John Geer, Arizona State University

Scott D. Gerber, College of William and Mary

Thomas Gillespie, Seton Hall University

Doris A. Graber, University of Illinois

John Green, University of Akron

Daniel P. Gregory, El Camino Community College

Eric E. Grier, Georgia State University

Mark F. Griffith, The University of West Alabama

Bruce E. Gronbeck, University of Iowa

Maria Guido, Bentley College

Russell L. Hanson, Indiana University

Valerie Heitshusen, University of Missouri

Richard Herrara, Arizona State University

Roberta Herzberg, Indiana University

Seth Hirshorn, University of Michigan

Eugene Hogan, Western Washington University

Marilyn Howard, Cols State Community College

Ronald J. Hrebnar, University of Utah

David Hunt, Triton College

Jon Hurwitz, University of Pittsburgh

James Hutter, Iowa State University

Gary C. Jacobson, University of California at San Diego

William Jacoby, University of South Carolina

Willoughby Jarrell, Kennesaw State College

Jodi Jenkin, Fullerton College

Christopher B. Jones, Eastern Oregon State University

William Kelly, Auburn University

Fred Kramer, University of Massachusetts

Richard Lehne, Rutgers University

Jan E. Leighley, Texas A&M University

Joel Lieske, Cleveland State University

R. Philip Loy, Taylor University

Stan Luger, University of Northern Colorado

Dean E. Mann, University of California

Joseph R. Marbach, Seton Hall University

Michael D. Martinez, University of Florida

Peter Mathews, Cypress College

Louise Mayo, County College of Morris

Steve Mazurana, University of Northern Colorado

Michael W. McCann, University of Washington

Carroll R. McKibbin, California Polytechnic State University

William P. McLauchlan, Purdue University

Michael E. Meagher, University of Missouri

Charles K. Menifield, Murray State University

Norma H. E. Miller, South Carolina State University

Neil Milner, University of Hawaii

Kristen R. Monroe, Princeton University

Mike Munger, University of Texas

Laurel A. Myer, Sinclair Community College

Albert Nelson, University of Wisconsin, La Crosse

David Nice, Washington State University

Charles Noble, California State University at Long Beach

Colleen M. O'Connor, San Diego Mesa College

Daniel J. O'Connor, California State University at Long Beach

David J. Olson, University of Washington

Laura Katz Olson, Lehigh University

John Orman, Fairfield University

Marvin Overby, University of Mississippi

Elizabeth M. H. Paddock, Drury College

Kenneth T. Palmer, University of Maine

Toby Paone, St. Charles Community College

Arthur Paulson, Southern Connecticut State University

Joseph Peschek, Hamline University

Mark P. Petracca, University of California

Larry Pool, Mountain View College

John D. Redifer, Mesa State College

Richard Reitano, Dutchess Community College

Curtis G. Reithel, University of Wisconsin, La Crosse

Russell D. Renka, Southeast Missouri State University

Richard C. Rich, Virginia Polytechnic Institute and State University

Leroy N. Rieselbach, Indiana University

Sue Tolleson Rinehart, Texas Tech University

Phyllis F. Rippey, Western Illinois University

David Robinson, University of Houston–Downtown

David W. Romero, University of California

Francis E. Rourke, Johns Hopkins University

David C. Saffell, Ohio Northern University

Donald L. Scruggs, Stephens College

Jim Seroka, University of North Florida

L. Earl Shaw, Northern Arizona University

John M. Shebb, University of Tennessee

Mark Silverstein, Boston University

Morton Sipress, University of Wisconsin, Eau Claire

Henry B. Sirgo, McNeese State University

David A. Smeltzer, Portland State University

Neil Snortland, University of Arkansas, Little Rock

C. Neal Tate, University of North Texas

James Lance Taylor, University of San Francisco

Robert Thomas, University of Houston

Richard J. Timpone, State University of New York at Stony Brook

Eric Ulsaner, University of Maryland

Elliot Vittes, University of Central Florida

Charles Walcott, University of Minnesota

Benjamin Walter, Vanderbilt University

Susan Weissman, St. Mary's College of California

Nelson Wikstrom, Virginia Commonwealth University

Daniel Wirls, Merrill College

Eugene R. Wittkopf, Louisiana State University

James Woods, University of Toledo

Jay Zarowitz, Muskegon Community College

Michele Zebich-Knos, Kennesaw State University

Finally, we thank you, the instructors and students who use this book. May it bring you success!

Edward S. Greenberg
Benjamin I. Page

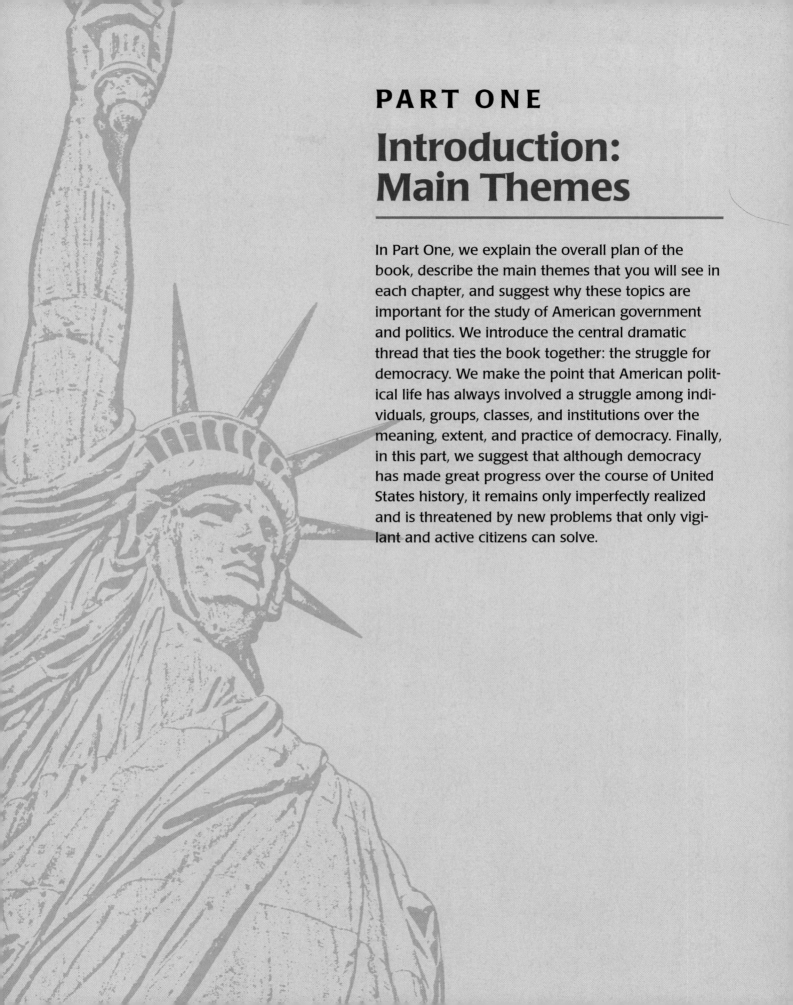

PART ONE

Introduction: Main Themes

In Part One, we explain the overall plan of the book, describe the main themes that you will see in each chapter, and suggest why these topics are important for the study of American government and politics. We introduce the central dramatic thread that ties the book together: the struggle for democracy. We make the point that American political life has always involved a struggle among individuals, groups, classes, and institutions over the meaning, extent, and practice of democracy. Finally, in this part, we suggest that although democracy has made great progress over the course of United States history, it remains only imperfectly realized and is threatened by new problems that only vigilant and active citizens can solve.

CHAPTER 1

Democracy and American Politics

IN THIS CHAPTER

- **Understanding how government and politics work**

- **What democracy means, and how it can be used as a standard to evaluate American government and politics**

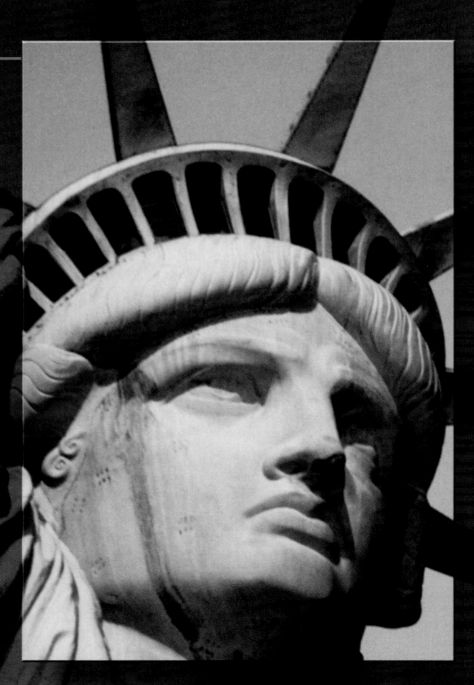

Robert Moses and the Struggle for African-American Voting Rights

The right to vote in elections is fundamental to democracy. But many Americans have won the right to vote only after long struggles. It took more than 30 years from the adoption of the Constitution, for instance, for most states to allow people without property to vote. Women gained the right to vote in all U.S. elections only in 1920, and young people ages 18 to 20 did so only beginning in 1971. As the following story indicates, African-Americans in the South did not have an effective right to vote until after 1965.

In Mississippi in the early 1960s, only 5 percent of African-Americans were registered to vote, and none held elective office, although they accounted for 43 percent of the population. In Amite County, Mississippi, only one African-American was registered to vote out of approximately 5,000 eligible voters; in Walthall County, not a single black was registered, although roughly 3,000 were eligible to vote.[1] What kept them away from the polls was a combination of biased voting registration rules, economic pressures, and physical intimidation and violence directed against those brave enough to defy the prevailing political and social order. In Ruleville, Mississippi, Mrs. Fannie Lou Hamer was forced out of the house she was renting on a large plantation, fired from her job, and arrested, jailed, and beaten by police after she tried to register to vote. In Mileston, after an unsuccessful attempt to register, Hartman Turnbow lost his house to a Molotov cocktail. He was later arrested for arson.[2]

The Student Non-Violent Coordinating Committee (widely known by its initials, SNCC) launched its Voter Education Project in 1961 with the aim of ending black political isolation and powerlessness in the Deep South. Composed primarily of African-American college students from both the North and the South, SNCC aimed to increase black voter registration and to challenge exclusionary rules like the poll tax and the literacy test. SNCC also wanted to enter African-American candidates in local elections. Its first step was to create "freedom schools" in some of the most segregated counties in Mississippi, Alabama, and Georgia to

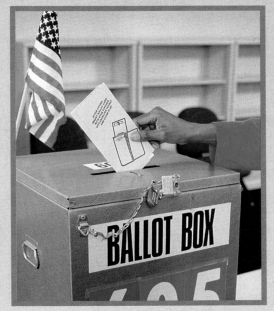

teach black citizens about their rights under the law and to encourage them to register to vote. Needless to say, SNCC volunteers tended to attract the malevolent attentions of police, local officials, and vigilantes.

The first of the freedom schools was founded in McComb, Mississippi, by a remarkable young man named Robert Parris Moses who quit his job as a teacher in order to work with other young people in SNCC. Despite repeated threats to his life and more than a few physical attacks, Moses traveled the back roads of Amite and Walthall counties, meeting with small groups of black farmers and encouraging them to attend the SNCC freedom school. At the school, he showed them not only how to fill out the registration forms but also how to read and interpret the constitution of Mississippi for the "literacy test" required to register to vote. Once people in the school gathered the courage to journey to the county seat to try to register, Moses went along with them to lend support and encouragement.

Moses suffered for these activities. Over a period of a few months, he was arrested several times for purported traffic violations; attacked on the main street of Liberty, Mississippi, by the county sheriff's cousin and beaten with the butt end of a knife; assaulted by a mob behind the McComb County courthouse; hit by police and dragged into the station house while standing in line at the voting registrar's office with one of his students; and jailed for not paying fines connected with his participation in civil rights demonstrations.

Despite the efforts of Bob Moses and other SNCC volunteers and the bravery of African-Americans who dared to defy the rules of black political exclusion in Mississippi, African-American voting registration barely increased in that state in the early 1960s. Black Americans in Mississippi would have to await the passage of the 1965 Voting Rights Act, which provided powerful federal government protections for all American citizens wishing to exercise their right to vote. The Voter Education Project, however, was one of the key building blocks of a powerful civil rights movement (see

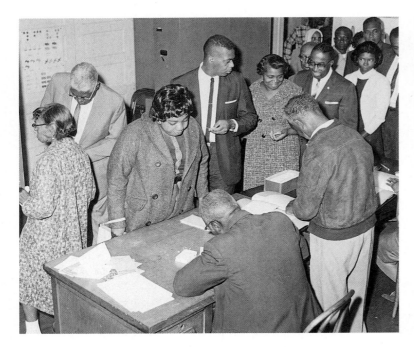

Discriminatory registration restrictions and intimidation heavily curbed African-American voting in the Deep South for almost a century after the end of slavery. It was not until the passage of the 1965 Voting Rights Act that literacy tests, poll taxes, and other devices designed to keep blacks away from the polls were outlawed and African-Americans were able to turn out at the polls in record numbers.

The struggle for democracy has become a global phenomenon. Here, peasants in Guatemala demonstrate for democratic reforms.

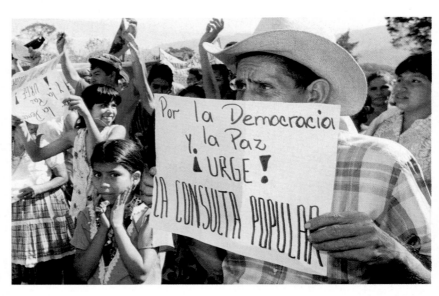

civil rights

Guarantees of equal citizenship to all social groups.

Chapter 8) that would eventually force federal action in the 1960s to support the citizenship rights (or **civil rights**) of African-Americans in the South.

Robert Moses and many other African-Americans in Mississippi were willing to risk all they had, even their lives, to gain full and equal citizenship in the United States. Likewise, throughout our history, Americans from all walks of life have joined the struggle to make the United States a more democratic place. The same thing is happening in many parts of the world today. We live in an age of democratic aspiration and upsurge; people the world over are demanding the right to govern themselves and control their own destinies. And more and more of them are realizing their dream in places such as South Africa, Eastern Europe, and Latin America. Americans are participants in this drama, not only because American political ideas and institutions have often provided inspiration for democratic movements in other countries but also because the struggle for democracy continues in our own society. Although honored and celebrated, democracy remains an unfinished project in the United States. The continuing struggle to expand and perfect democracy is a major feature of American history and a defining characteristic of our politics today. It is a central theme of this book.

Democracy

Why should there not be a patient confidence in the ultimate justice of the people? Is there any better, or equal, hope in the world?

—ABRAHAM LINCOLN, FIRST INAUGURAL ADDRESS

With the notable exception of a handful of **anarchist** philosophers such as Kropotkin, Proudhon, and Wolfe—who believed in the basic altruism and goodness of human beings and their natural ability to cooperate to provide for their mutual needs—virtually all philosophers, political leaders, and ordinary people have agreed over the years that government is both necessary and inevitable. When people live together in groups and communities, it is generally understood that a governmental entity of some sort is needed to provide law and order, to protect against external aggressors, and to provide essential public goods such as roads, waste disposal, and clean water. If government is both necessary and inevitable, certain questions become unavoidable: Who is to govern? How are those who govern to be encouraged to serve the best interests of society? How can governments be induced to make policies and laws that citizens consider legitimate and worth obeying? In short, what is the best form of government? For most Americans—and for increasing numbers of people in other places—the answer is clear: democracy.

The intrinsic attractiveness of democracy's central idea—that ordinary people want to rule themselves and are capable of doing so—is only one reason democracy is so popular. For many political thinkers, democracy is simply superior to every other form of political organization. Some have argued, for example, that democracy is the form of government that best protects human rights because it is the only one based on a recognition of the intrinsic worth and equality of human beings. Others believe that democracy is the form of government most likely to reach rational decisions because it can count on the pooled knowledge and expertise of a society's entire population. Other thinkers have claimed that democracies are more stable and long-lasting because their leaders, elected by their citizens, enjoy a strong sense of

anarchist

A political philosophy which holds that government is both inherently coercive and unnecessary for the provision of public order and services.

WEB EXPLORATION

The Diffusion of Democracy

Issue: Around the world, over the course of the twentieth century, democracy has both advanced and receded in a series of waves.

Site: Go to the Historical Atlas of the Twentieth Century through the "Course Documents" section of your online course. In the "Web Explorations" section for Chapter 1, click on "The Diffusion of Democracy" and then open "Historical Atlas." Under "General Trends," select Government, then look at each decade of the century.

What You've Learned: What conclusions can you make about the spread of democracy over the course of the century? When were the greatest gains made and where? What factors do you think explain the patterns you have discovered?

What is This? When you see a Web Exploration exercise, visit the "Course Documents" section of your online course and follow the directions printed here.

HINT: World wars, the rise and fall of fascism and communism, and the spread of mass communications have all played important roles.

CourseCompass

participation
**You Are Part of
the Political
Landscape**

↑

What is This?
When you see an icon like this,
visit the "Course Documents"
section of your online course,
follow the on-screen instructions, and click on
"LongmanParticipate." Use
the activity type (here: participation) and title (here: "You
Are Part of the Political
Landscape") to find the correct exercise after you have
registered and logged in.

democracy

A system of rule by the people,
defined by the existence of
popular sovereignty, political
equality, and political liberty.

legitimacy. Still others suggest that democracy is the form of government most conducive to economic growth and well-being, a claim that is strongly supported by research findings. Others, finally, believe that democracy is the form of government under which human beings, because they are free, are best able to develop their natural capacities and talents.[3] There are many compelling reasons, then, why democracy has been preferred by so many people.

Americans prefer democracy to other forms of government, and they have helped make the nation more democratic over the course of our history. Nevertheless, democracy remains a work in progress in the United States, an evolving aspiration rather than a finished product. Our goal in this book is to help you think carefully about the quality and progress of democracy in the United States. We want to help you reach your own independent judgments about the degree to which politics and government in the United States make our country more or less democratic. We want to help you draw your own con-clusions about which political practices and institutions in the United States encourage and sustain democracy and which ones discourage and undermine it.

To draw reasonable conclusions about how democratic we are and how democratic we are likely to become and to understand why so many people both in the United States and around the world have struggled so hard to attain it, we first need to be clear about the meaning of democracy. Not everyone uses the term in the same way to mean the same thing. Thus, considerable clarification is required before democracy can be used as a measuring stick to assess American government and politics.

The Democratic Idea

Many of our ideas about democracy originated with the ancient Greeks. The Greek roots of the word *democracy* are *demos,* meaning "the people," and *kratein,* meaning "to rule." **Democracy**, then, is "rule by the people" or, to put it another way, self-government by the *many,* as opposed to the *few* or the *one.* This is similar to Lincoln's definition in his Gettysburg Address: "government of the people, by the people, and for the people."

Most Western philosophers and rulers before the eighteenth century were not friendly to the idea of rule by the *many.* Most believed that governing was a difficult art, requiring the greatest sophistication, intelligence, character, and training—certainly not the province of ordinary people. Most preferred rule by a select *few* (such as an aristocracy, in which a hereditary nobility rules) or by an enlightened *one* (such as a sovereign or a military chieftain). In practice, most governments were quite undemocratic.

The idea that ordinary people might rule themselves represents an impor-tant departure from such beliefs. At the heart of democratic theory is a faith in the capacity of ordinary human beings to govern themselves wisely. As the American philosopher John Dewey put it,

> *The foundation of democracy is faith in the capacities of human nature; faith in human intelligence and in the power of pooled and cooperative experience. It is not belief that these things are complete but that if given a show they will grow and be able to generate progressively the knowledge and wisdom needed to guide collective action.*[4]

Also crucial to the concept of democracy is the idea that it is the purpose of a government to serve *all* of its people and that ultimately none but the people themselves can be relied on to know and hence to act in accordance with their own values and interests. Power in any other hands will eventually lead to **tyranny**, a society where leaders abuse their power.

Direct Versus Representative Democracy

To the ancient Greeks, democracy meant rule by the common people exercised *directly* in open assemblies. They believed that democracy implied face-to-face deliberation and decision making about the public business. **Direct democracy** requires, however, that all citizens be able to meet together regularly to debate and decide the issues of the day. Such a thing was possible in fifth century B.C. Athens, which was small enough to allow all male citizens to gather in one place. In Athens, moreover, male citizens had time to meet and to deliberate because women provided household labor and slaves accounted for most production.

Because direct, participatory democracy is possible only in small communities where citizens with abundant leisure time can meet often on a face-to-face basis, it is an unworkable arrangement for a society such as the United States, which is large and populous and where most people do not have time for continuous involvement in public meetings.[5] Although Thomas Jefferson advocated "direct action of the citizens" as the ideal form of democracy, he lamented that "such a government is evidently restrained to very narrow limits of space and population."[6] He recognized, as we must, that democracy in large societies must take the representative form, since millions of citizens cannot meet in open assembly. By **representative democracy** we mean a system in which the people select others, called *representatives,* to act in their place.

Although representative (indirect) democracy seems to be the only form of democracy possible in large-scale societies, some political commentators argue that the participatory aspects of direct democracy are worth preserving as an ideal and that certain domains of everyday life—workplaces and schools, for instance—could be enriched by more direct democratic practices.[7] It is worth

tyranny

The abuse of power by a ruler or a government.

direct democracy

A form of political decision making in which the public business is decided by all citizens meeting in small assemblies.

representative democracy

Indirect democracy, in which the people rule through elected representatives.

The essence of the classical Greek idea of democracy was face-to-face deliberations among citizens in open assemblies. This is difficult to achieve in societies with large populations where democracy depends instead on the election of representatives.

pointing out, moreover, that direct democracy can and does flourish in some local communities today. In many New England towns, for example, citizens make decisions directly at town meetings. Some observers believe that the Internet will enable more people to become directly involved in political deliberations and decision making in the future.[8]

Fundamental Principles of Representative Democracy

In large societies such as our own, then, democracy means rule by the people, exercised indirectly through representatives elected by the people. Still, this definition is not sufficiently precise to use as a standard by which to evaluate the American political system. To help further clarify the definition of democracy, we add three additional benchmarks drawn from both the scholarly literature and popular understandings about democracy. These benchmarks are *popular sovereignty, political equality,* and *political liberty.* A society in which all three flourish, we argue, is a healthy representative democracy. A society in which any of the three is absent or impaired falls short of the representative democratic ideal. Let us see what each of them means.

popular sovereignty

The basic principle of democracy that the people ultimately rule.

Popular Sovereignty   **Popular sovereignty** means that the ultimate source of all public authority is the people and that government does the people's bidding. If ultimate authority resides not in the hands of the *many* but in the hands of the *few* (as in an aristocratic order) or of the *one* (whether a benevolent sovereign or a ruthless dictator), democracy does not exist.

How can we recognize popular sovereignty when we see it? Four observable conditions are especially important: (1) Government policies reflect what the people want, (2) people participate in the political process, (3) high-quality information and debate are available, and (4) the majority rules.

Democracy requires broad citizen participation in public affairs. Special efforts have been made in recent years—much like these at the University of Texas at Austin—to increase voting registration and turnout among young people, a group with especially low participation rates in American elections.

Government Policies Reflect What the People Want   One sign of popular sovereignty is a close correspondence between what government does and what the people want it to do. It is hard to imagine a situation in which the people rule but government officials make policy contrary to the people's wishes.

This much seems obvious. However, does the democratic ideal require that government always do exactly what the people want, right away, responding to every whim and passing fancy of the people? This question has troubled many democratic theorists, and most have answered that democracy is best served when public officials and representatives respond to what might be called the "deliberative will" of the people: what the people want after they have deliberated about an issue with others. We might, then, want to speak of democracy as a system in which government policies conform to what the people want over some period of time (though not too long).

People Participate in the Political Process   How can the popular will be known, and what makes the people's representatives respect it? Although public opinion polls may convey what the public thinks and wants to political leaders, it is through widespread participation in politics that the popular will is formed, expressed, and enforced. Without widespread participation, what the people want can only be guessed at or approximated. And without participation, nothing guarantees that officials will respond to what the people want. Widespread popular participation—at least voting in elections—is necessary to ensure that responsive representatives will be chosen and that they will have continuous incentives to pay attention to the people. Because widespread participation is so central to popular sovereignty, we can say that the less political participation there is in a society, the weaker the democracy.

High-Quality Information and Debate Are Available   Fashioning an authentic popular will requires that people have access to accurate political information, insightful interpretations, and vigorous debate. These are the responsibility of government officials, opposition parties, opinion leaders, and the mass media. If false or biased information is provided, if policies are not challenged and debated, or if misleading interpretations of the political world (or none at all) are offered, the people cannot form opinions in accordance with their values and interests, and popular sovereignty cannot be said to exist.

The Majority Rules   How can the opinions and preferences of many individual citizens be combined into a single binding decision? Since unanimity is unlikely—so the insistence that new policies should require unanimous agreement for them to be adopted would simply enshrine the status quo—reaching a decision requires a decision rule. If the actions of government are to respond to all citizens, each citizen being counted equally, the only decision rule that makes sense is **majority rule**,[9] which means that the government adopts the policy that the *most* people want. In practical terms, what this means is that the popular will, formed in the best circumstances after careful deliberation, is discovered by ascertaining the positions on public issues of the majority of citizens. The only alternative to majority rule is minority rule, which would unacceptably elevate the *few* over the *many*.

Majority rule has a number of virtues. For one thing, it is the only way to make decisions that is consistent with political equality. This is because it is a form of decision making that recognizes the intrinsic worth and equality of human beings; any other way of making decisions puts a minority of one sort or another at the head of the line and weights the preferences of some people more heavily than those of others. For another thing, majority rule maximizes the

majority rule

The form of political decision making in which policies are decided on the basis of what a majority of the people want.

number of people involved in decision making, enhancing participation, which is important to popular sovereignty. Also, majority rule is more likely (though far from certain) to reach correct decisions because it relies on "pooled judgments"—judgments that take into account a broader range of information, opinions, and expertise than any other way of making decisions. Finally, because more people are involved in making decisions under majority rule, policies that result from such a process are more likely to be accepted by the people than decisions made in other ways.

political equality

The principle that says that each person carries equal weight in the conduct of the public business.

Political Equality   The second fundamental principle of democracy is **political equality**, the idea that each person carries the same weight in voting and other political decision making. Imagine, if you will, a society in which one person could cast 100 votes in an election, another person 50 votes, and still another 25 votes, while many unlucky folks had only 1 vote each—or none at all. We would surely find such an arrangement a curious one, especially if that society described itself as democratic. We would react in this way because equality of citizenship has always been central to the democratic ideal. Democracy is a way of making decisions in which each person has one and only one voice.

Most people know this intuitively. Our sense of what is proper is offended, for instance, when some class of people is denied the right to vote in a society that boasts the outer trappings of democracy. The denial of citizenship rights to African-Americans in the South before the passage of the 1965 Voting Rights Act is such an example. We count it a victory for democracy when previously excluded groups are enfranchised.

Political equality also involves what the Fourteenth Amendment to the Constitution calls "equal protection," meaning that everyone in a democracy is treated the same by government. Government programs, for example, should not favor one group over another or deny benefits or protections to identifiable groups in the population, such as racial and religious minorities. Nor should people be treated better or worse than others by law enforcement agencies and the courts.

Although political equality is a cornerstone of American democracy, the nation's understanding of who is entitled to equal status has changed over the years. The right to vote was granted to all men regardless of race in 1870, although stringent registration rules made it very difficult for nonwhites to exercise that right. It wasn't until 1920 that the Nineteenth Amendment extended the right to vote to women; in 1971, a constitutional amendment lowered the voting age from 21 to 18.

Does democracy require substantial equality in the distribution of income and wealth? Thinkers as diverse as Aristotle, Rousseau, and Jefferson all thought so because they believed that great inequalities in economic circumstances eventually turn into political inequality. Political scientist Robert Dahl describes the problem in the following way:

> *If citizens are unequal in economic resources, so are they likely to be unequal in political resources; and political equality will be impossible to achieve. In the extreme case, a minority of rich will possess so much greater political resources than other citizens that they will control the state, dominate the majority of citizens, and empty the democratic process of all content.*[10]

In later chapters, we will see that income and wealth are distributed in a highly unequal way in the United States and that this inequality is sometimes translated into great inequalities among people and groups in the political arena. In such circumstances, the norm of political equality is violated.

Political Liberty   The third element of democracy is **political liberty**. Political liberty refers to basic freedoms essential to the formation and expression of the popular will and its translation into policy. These essential liberties include the freedoms of speech, of conscience and religion, of the press, and of assembly and association, embodied in the First Amendment to the U.S. Constitution.

Without these liberties (and a few more, including freedom from arbitrary arrest and the right to run for public office), the other fundamental principles of democracy could not exist. Popular sovereignty cannot be guaranteed if people are prevented from participating in politics or if opposition to the government is crushed by the authorities. Popular sovereignty cannot prevail if the voice of the people is silenced and if citizens are not free to argue and debate, based on their own ideas, values, and personal beliefs, and form and express their political opinions.[11] Political equality is violated if some people can speak out but others cannot.

For most people today, democracy and liberty are inseparable. The concept of *self-government* implies not only the right to vote and to run for public office but also the right to speak one's mind, to petition the government, and to join with others in political parties, interest groups, or social movements. For example, the democratic upsurge that swept through Eastern Europe during the early 1990s generated demands not only for elected governments but also for an environment of political freedom that would make such elections meaningful.

Over the years, a number of political philosophers and practitioners have viewed liberty as *threatened* by democracy rather than as essential to it. We will have more to say about this subject later as we consider several possible objections to democracy. But it is our position that self-government and political liberty are inseparable, in the sense that the former is impossible without the latter.[12] It follows that a majority cannot deprive an individual or a minority group of its political liberty without violating democracy itself.

Objections to Majoritarian Representative Democracy

Not everyone is convinced that representative democracy is the best form of government for large societies. Here are the main criticisms that have been leveled against democracy as we have defined it.

political liberty

The principle that citizens in a democracy are protected from government interference in the exercise of a range of basic freedoms, such as the freedoms of speech, association, and conscience.

LongmanParticipate

CourseCompass

simulation
How to Satisfy Aunt Martha

Democracy Leads to Bad Decisions

Majoritarian, representative democracy is not perfect. There is no guarantee that it will always lead to good decisions. A majority, like a minority, can be unwise; it can be cruel and uncaring; it can be carried away by fads and fashions; and it can be misled by unscrupulous or incompetent leaders. Democratic theorist Robert Dahl points out, however, that no other form of government can be shown to consistently lead to better and wiser decisions.[13] The historical record on the results of rule by aristocrats, kings, princes, civil servants, or experts is not encouraging. We would probably do best to stick with majority rule representative democracy despite its faults in light of its many other virtues.

"Majority Tyranny" Threatens Liberty

James Madison and the other Founders of the American republic feared that majority rule was bound to undermine freedom and threaten the rights of the individual. They created a constitutional system (as you will see in Chapter 2) that was in fact designed to protect certain liberties against the unwelcome intrusions of the majority. The fears of the Founders were not without basis. What they called the "popular passions" have sometimes stifled the freedoms of groups and individuals who have dared to be different. Until quite recently, for instance, a majority of Americans were unwilling to allow atheists or communists the same rights of free speech that they allowed others, and conscientious objectors were treated harshly during both world wars.

majority tyranny

Suppression of the rights and liberties of a minority by the majority.

Although there have been instances during our history of **majority tyranny**, in which the majority violated the citizenship rights of a minority—the chapter opening vignette is a good example—there is no evidence that the *many* consistently threaten liberty more than the *few* or the *one*. To put it another way, the majority does not seem to be a special or unique threat to liberty. Violations of freedom seem as likely to come from powerful individuals and groups or from government officials as from the majority.

Political hysteria has periodically blemished the record of American democracy. Fear of domestic communism, captured in this editorial cartoon, was particularly potent in the twentieth century and led to the suppression of political groups deemed threatening by the authorities.

There have been three periods in the history of the United States when liberty was most endangered, and the majority does not figure as the main culprit in any of them:

- In the late 1790s, criticism of public officials was made a crime under the Alien and Sedition Acts.
- After World War I, a "Red scare" swept the nation, highlighted by the infamous antiradical, anti-immigrant, and antiunion raids of Attorney General A. Mitchell Palmer.
- In the late 1940s and early 1950s, another "Red scare," conventionally known as *McCarthyism* (after Senator Joseph McCarthy, who led the attack), was unleashed.

The first two assaults on liberty were initiated by high government officials who acted without any discernible sign of majority pressure to do so. The third, although eventually supported by the majority, was launched not only by people who genuinely feared communism and believed it to be a threat to the United States, but by some who simply wanted to discredit and roll back the liberal policies of the New Deal.[14]

Liberty is essential to self-government, and threats to liberty, whatever their origin, must be guarded against by all who value democracy. But we must firmly reject the view that majority rule inevitably or uniquely threatens liberty. Majority rule is unthinkable, in fact, without the existence of basic political liberties.

The People Are Irrational and Incompetent   Political scientists have spent decades studying the attitudes and behaviors of citizens in the United States, and some of the findings are not encouraging. For the most part, the evidence shows that individual Americans do not care a great deal about politics and are rather poorly informed, unstable in their views, and not much interested in participating in the political process.[15] These findings have led some observers to assert that citizens are ill-equipped for the responsibility of self-governance and that public opinion (the will of the majority) should not be the ultimate determinant of what government does.

In Chapter 5, we will see, however, that this evidence about individuals has often been misinterpreted and that the American public taken collectively is more informed, sophisticated, and stable in its views than it is generally given credit for.

Majoritarian Democracy Threatens Minorities   We have suggested that when rendering a decision in a democracy, the majority must prevail. In most cases, the minority on the losing side of an issue need not worry unduly about its well-being because many of its members are likely to be on the winning side in future decisions. Thus, people on the minority and losing side of an issue such as welfare reform may be part of the majority and winning side on an issue such as educational spending. What prevents majority tyranny over a minority in most policy decisions in a democracy is that the composition of the majority and the minority is always shifting.

What happens, however, in cases that involve race, ethnicity, religion, or sexual orientation, for example, where minority status is fixed? Does the majority pose a threat to such minorities? Many people worry about that possibility. The worry is that unbridled majority rule leaves no room for the claims of minorities. This worry has some historical foundations, for majorities have trampled on minority rights with alarming frequency. Majorities long held, for instance, that Native Americans and African-Americans were inferior to whites and undeserving of full citizenship. Irish, Eastern European, Asian, and Latin American immigrants to our shores, among others, have all been subjected to periods of intolerance on the part of the majority, as have Catholics and Jews. Gays and lesbians have been discriminated against in housing and jobs and have sometimes been violently victimized (the beating death of Mathew Shepard in Laramie, Wyoming, being the most obvious example).

As Robert Dahl points out, however, there is no evidence to support the belief that the rights of minorities are better protected under alternative forms of political government, whether rule by the *few* or by the *one* (fascism, communism, authoritarian dictatorship, theocracy, and the like),[16] and that given the other benefits of majority rule democracy, it is to be preferred.

In any case, democracy, as we have defined it, requires the protection of crucial minority rights. Recall that majority rule is only one of the defining conditions of popular sovereignty and that popular sovereignty is only one of the three basic attributes of democracy, the others being political equality and political liberty. The position of minorities is protected in a fully developed democracy, in our view, by the requirements of equal citizenship (the right to vote, to hold public office, to be protected against violence, and to enjoy the equal protection of the law) and access to the full range of civil liberties (speech, press, conscience, and association). To the extent that a majority violates the citizenship rights and liberties of minorities, society falls short of the democratic ideal.

Democracy as an Evaluative Standard: How Democratic Are We?

After this discussion, it should be easy to see how and why the democratic ideal can be used as a measuring rod with which to evaluate American politics. We have learned that the fundamental attributes of democracy are popular sovereignty, political equality, and political liberty. Each suggests a set of questions that will be raised throughout this book to encourage critical thinking about American political life.

- *Questions about popular sovereignty.* Does government do what citizens want it to do? Do citizens participate in politics? Can citizens be involved when they choose to be, and are political leaders responsive? Do political linkage institutions, such as political parties, elections, interest groups, and social movements, effectively transmit what citizens want to political leaders? What is the quality of the public deliberation on the major public policy issues of the day? Do the media and political leaders provide accurate and complete information?

- *Questions about political equality.* Do some individuals and groups have persistent and substantial advantages over other individuals and groups in the political process? Or is the political game open to all equally? Do government decisions and policies benefit some individuals and groups more than others?

- *Questions about political liberty.* Are citizens' rights and liberties universally available, protected, and used? Are people free to vote? Can they speak openly and freely form groups to petition their government? Do public authorities, private groups, or the majority threaten liberty or the rights of minorities?

These questions will help us assess where we are and where we are going as a democracy. We do not believe that popular sovereignty, political equality, and political liberty are attainable in perfect form. They are, rather, ideals to which our nation can aspire and standards against which we can measure reality.

A Framework for Understanding How American Politics Works

In addition to helping you answer questions about the quality of democracy in the United States, our goal in this textbook is to help you understand how American government and politics work. Things are not as disconnected and random as they may first appear. There are regular tendencies and patterns in our political life, but first we need to know how to organize the flood of information. In this section, we describe a simple way to organize information and to think about how our political system works. Here we set out the basic guidelines that structure how we will talk about and understand government and politics in the United States.

Organizing the Main Factors of Political Life

If we are to understand why things happen in government and politics—for example, the passage of the 1965 Voting Rights Act that Robert Moses and his SNCC colleagues did so much to bring about—we must begin with what biologists call *taxonomy:* placing things in their proper categories. We believe that each and every actor, institution, and process that influences what our politics

WEB EXPLORATION

Understanding What Government Does

Issue: What government does can only be understood by taking into account how government, political linkage, and structural factors interact with one another.

Site: Look at two of the nation's leading newspapers, the *New York Times* and *The Chicago Tribune* through the "Course Documents" section of your online course. In the "Web Explorations" section for Chapter 1, click on "Understanding What Government Does" and then open "newspapers." Select a story about some domestic federal government action (e.g., a new law, a Supreme Court decision, an action by a bureaucratic agency, an executive order, and so on) for each newspaper.

What You've Learned: See if you can organize the story of the government action you have selected according to the categories of the analytical framework explained in this section and shown in Figure 1.1. Does this help you better understand why the government action happened?

HINT: Be sure you have information for each of the categories in the framework. If you do not, this may suggest that the media are not presenting the full story.

African-American combat service in World War II and in Korea helped transform white attitudes about racial equality in the United States and contributed to the emergence of a supportive environment for the civil rights movement. Shown here are six gunners from the 17th Bomb Wing night interdiction team that saw heavy action in Korea.

are like and what our national government does can be placed into four main categories: structure, political linkage, government, and government action.

- *Structure.* This category includes the economy and society, the constitutional rules, the political culture, and the international system, the most fundamental and enduring factors that influence government and politics. They form the foundation upon which all else is built. They determine, to a very large extent, what issues become a part of the political agenda, how political power is distributed among the population, what rules structure how government works, and what values Americans bring to their political deliberations.

- *Political linkage.* This category includes all of the political actors, institutions, and processes that transmit the wants and demands of people and groups in our society to government officials and that together help shape what government officials do and what policies they adopt. These include public opinion, political parties, interest groups, the mass media, and elections.

- *Government.* This category includes all public officials and institutions (Congress, the president, the federal bureaucracy, and the Supreme Court) that have formal, legal responsibilities for making public policy.

- *Government action.* This category includes the wide range of actions carried out by government: making laws, issuing rules and regulations, waging war and providing national defense, settling civil disputes, providing order, and more.

This textbook is organized around these four categories. The chapters in Part Two focus on factors in the structural category. The chapters in Part Three are about political linkage processes and institutions. The chapters in Part Four attend to government institutions and leaders. Finally, the chapters in Part Five examine what government does.

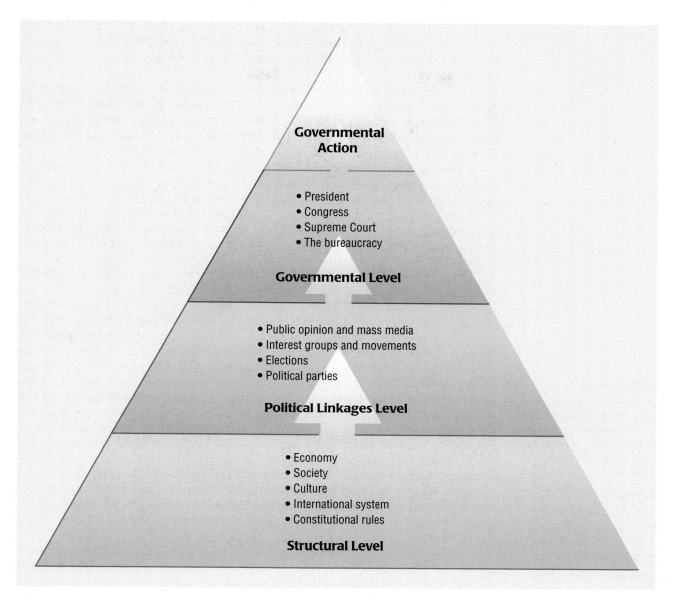

Figure 1.1 ● The Analytical Framework

Various actors, institutions, and processes interact to influence what government does in the United States. Structural factors such as the economy, the culture, the international situation, and constitutional rules play a strong role in political events. They may influence the government directly, or, as is more often the case, through political linkages such as elections, parties, and interest groups. In a democratic society, the policies created by the government should reflect these influences.

Connecting the Main Factors of Political Life

To understand how government and politics work in the United States, we must appreciate the fact that the structural, political linkage, and governmental categories interact with one another in a particular kind of way to determine what actions government takes (see Figure 1.1). The best way to see this is to look at these categories in action, using the passage of the 1965 Voting

Rights Act as an example. The main point of the exercise is to show how connecting and considering together the main factors of political life—structure, political linkage, and government—can help explain why government takes certain actions.

To understand passage of the landmark legislation, we might begin with *government,* focusing our attention on Congress and its members, President Lyndon Johnson (who was the most vigorous proponent of the voting rights legislation) and his advisers, and the Supreme Court, which was becoming increasingly supportive of civil rights claims in the mid-1960s.

Knowing these things, however, would not tell us all that we needed to know. To understand why Congress, the president, and the Court behaved as they did in 1965, we would want to pay attention to the pressures brought to bear on them by *political linkage* actors and institutions: public opinion (increasingly supportive of civil rights), the growing electoral power of African-Americans in the states outside the South, and most important, the moral power of the civil rights movement inspired by people like Robert Moses.

Even knowing these things, however, would not tell us all that we needed to know about why the 1965 Voting Rights Act happened. Our inquiry would have to go deeper to include *structural* factors: economic, cultural, and social change; constitutional rules; and the international position of the United States. For example, economic changes in the nation over the course of many decades triggered a "great migration" of African-Americans from the rural South to the urban North. Over the long run, this population shift to states with large blocks of **electoral college** votes, critical to the election of presidents, increased the political power of African-Americans. Cultural change increased the number of Americans bothered by the second-class citizenship of African-Americans, even as combat service in World War II and the Korean War led many black Americans to insist on full citizenship rights. Finally, the **Cold War** struggle of the United States against the Soviet Union played an important role. Many American leaders, recognizing the contradiction between asking for the support of people of color in Third World countries in the struggle against communism, while treating African-Americans in the United States as second-class citizens, sought an end to the system of official segregation in the South (known as **Jim Crow**).

We see, then, that a full explanation of why the 1965 Voting Rights Act happened (government action) requires that we take into account how governmental, political linkage, and structural factors interact with one another to bring about significant change in American politics.

Understanding American Politics Holistically

This way of looking at things—that what government does can only be understood by considering structural, political linkage, and governmental factors—will be used throughout this book and will help bring order to the information that will be presented. We will suggest throughout that action by public officials is the product not simply of their personal desires (although these are important) but also of the influences and pressures brought to bear by other governmental institutions and by individuals, groups, and classes at work in the political linkage sphere. Political linkage institutions and processes, in turn, can often be understood only when we see how they are shaped by the larger structural context, including such things as the national and global economies and the political culture. This way of understanding how American government and politics work is illustrated in the "Using the Framework" feature on the next page. This feature appears in each of the chapters.

electoral college

Representatives of the states who formally elect the president; the number of electors in each state is equal to the total number of its senators and congressional representatives.

Cold War

The period of tense relations between the United States and the Soviet Union from the late 1940s to the late 1980s.

Jim Crow

Popular term for the system of legal racial segregation that existed in the American South until the middle of the twentieth century.

USING THE FRAMEWORK

The Voting Rights Act

The Voting Rights Act of 1965 transformed the politics of the American South. Under federal government protection, the Act permitted African-Americans to vote and run for elected office in states where a combination of violence, economic pressure, and state and local government rules made political participation difficult if not impossible prior to 1965. We can understand how such a momentous transformation happened by examining structural, political linkage, and governmental factors.

Governmental Action

The Voting Rights Act of 1965

Governmental Level

- The Supreme Court prepared the ground by steadily expanding the reach of the "equal protection" clause of the Constitution.
- A pro-civil rights majority in Congress was responsive to the voting rights issue.
- President Lyndon Johnson pushed hard for federal protection of African-American voting rights.

Political Linkages Level

- The votes of African-Americans proved decisive in several large electoral vote states in the 1960 and 1964 presidential elections.
- Dramatic civil rights demonstrations highlighted the denial of the vote to black Americans in the Deep South.
- Public opinion and the mass media grew more supportive of demands by African-Americans for full citizenship.
- Unions and business organizations endorsed voting rights legislation.

Structural Level

- Industrialization and the rise of manufacturing corporations spurred the "Great Migration."
- Relocation of African-Americans to large states outside the Deep South improved their political, social, and economic standing.
- The Fourteenth Amendment of the Constitution guaranteed "equal protection."
- The struggle against the Soviet Union for the "hearts and minds" of Third World peoples made segregation problematic for the United States in world affairs.

You should also keep in mind that, as in all complex systems, feedback also occurs. That is to say, influences sometimes flow in the opposite direction, from government to political linkage actors and institutions to structural factors. For example, federal tax laws influence the distribution of income and wealth in society, government regulations affect the operations of corporations, and decisions by the courts may determine what interest groups and political parties are able to do. We will want to pay attention, then, to these sorts of influences in our effort to understand how the American political system works.

You need not worry about remembering exactly which actors and influences belong to which of the four categories. That will become obvious because the chapters of the book are organized into sections corresponding to them. Nor do you need to worry about exactly how the people and institutions in the different levels interact with one another. This will become clear as materials are presented and learned and as you become more familiar with the American political process.

LongmanParticipate

CourseCompass

comparative
**Comparing
Political Landscapes**

Summary

The struggle for democracy has played an important role in American history and remains an important theme in our country today, as well as in many other parts of the world. The struggle has involved the effort to make popular sovereignty, political equality, and political liberty more widely available and practiced. Because democracy holds a very special place in Americans' constellation of values and is particularly relevant to judging political processes, it is the standard used throughout this text to evaluate the quality of our politics and government.

The materials about politics and government are organized in a way that will allow us to make sense of the confusing details of everyday events and see *why* things happen the way they do. The organizing framework presented in this chapter visualizes the world of American politics as a set of interrelated *actors* and *influences*—institutions, groups, and individuals—that operate in three interconnected realms: the *structural, political linkage,* and *governmental* sectors. This way of looking at American political life as an ordered, interconnected whole will be used throughout the remainder of the book.

Suggestions for Further Reading

Barber, Benjamin. *Strong Democracy: Participatory Democracy for a New Age.* Berkeley: University of California Press, 1984.
   The case for direct, participatory democracy by a leading contemporary political theorist.

Dahl, Robert A. *Democracy and Its Critics.* New Haven, CT: Yale University Press, 1989.
   A sweeping defense of democracy against its critics by one of the most brilliant political theorists of our time.

Dahl, Robert. *On Democracy.* New Haven, CT: Yale University Press, 1998.
   A brief yet surprisingly thorough examination of classical and contemporary democracy, real and theoretical.

Guttman, Amy, and Dennis Thompson. *Democracy and Disagreement.* Cambridge, U.K.: Belknap Press, 1996.
   A compelling examination of why deliberation is so important to genuine democracy and how more deliberative processes might be incorporated into contemporary democratic societies.

Held, David. *Models of Democracy.* Stanford, CA: Stanford University Press, 1987.
   A highly accessible review of the many possible meanings of democracy.

Putnam, Robert D. *Making Democracy Work: Civic Traditions in Modern Italy.*
Princeton, NJ: Princeton University Press, 1993.
   A brilliant and controversial argument that the success of democratic government depends on the vitality of a participatory and tolerant civic culture.

Wittman, Donald. *The Myth of Democratic Failure: Why Political Institutions Are Efficient.* Chicago: University of Chicago Press, 1995.
   Using economic models of reasoning to argue that democratic institutions are as efficient as economic markets.

Internet Sources

A number of sites on the World Wide Web serve as "gateways" to vast collections of material on American government and politics. In subsequent chapters, we will indicate the location of sites on the Web to begin searches on the specific subject matter of the chapters. Here we concentrate on the general gateways, the starting points for wide-ranging journeys through cyberspace, geared to subjects governmental and political.

For most students, connections to the Internet will be through systems already in operation at most colleges and universities. For some students, connections will be through one of the commercial services such as America Online, CompuServe, or Microsoft Network. As part of its service, each has a browser, a tool used to get around the Internet and find what one wants. University and college systems are likely to have Netscape Navigator or Microsoft Explorer. Whichever browser one uses, simply type in the addresses of the gateways listed here, and the browser will do the rest. Once at the gateway, a simple click on highlighted words and phrases (hyperlinks) will take users to a particular body of information.

Here are the gateways:

Weblinks: A Guide to Internet Resources in Political Science
www.abacon.com/internetguides/pol/weblinks.html

The Jefferson Project   **www.capweb.net/classic/jefferson/**

Internet Public Library   **http://ipl.org/ref/RR/static/gov0000.html**

Yahoo/Government   **http://www.yahoo.com/Government/**

New York Times, Political Points
www.nytimes.com/library/politics/polpoints.html

Notes

1. William H. Chafe, *The Unfinished Journey: America Since World War II* (New York: Oxford University Press, 1986), p. 304; Howard Zinn, *SNCC: The New Abolitionists* (Boston: Beacon Press, 1964), p. 64.

2. Chafe, *Unfinished Journey,* p. 305.

3. Robert A. Dahl, *Democracy and Its Critics* (New Haven, CT: Yale University Press, 1989); and Robert A. Dahl, *On Democracy* (New Haven, CT: Yale University Press, 1998).

4. John Dewey, *The Public and Its Problems* (New York: Holt, 1927), p. 211.

5. See Robert A. Dahl, *After the Revolution: Authority in the Good Society* (New Haven, CT: Yale University Press, 1970); Dahl, *Democracy and Its Critics;* Jane Mansbridge, *Beyond Adversary Democracy* (New York: Basic Books, 1980).

6. Letter to John Taylor, May 28, 1816, in John Dewey, ed., *The Living Thoughts of Thomas Jefferson* (New York: Longmans, Green, 1940).

7. See Benjamin Barber, *Strong Democracy: Participatory Democracy for a New Age* (Berkeley, CA: University of California Press, 1984); Peter Bachrach, *The Theory of Democratic Elitism* (Boston: Little, Brown, 1967); Robert A. Dahl, *A Preface to Economic Democracy* (Berkeley, CA: University of California Press, 1985); Edward S. Greenberg, *Workplace Democracy: The Political Effects of Participation* (Ithaca, NY: Cornell University Press, 1986); C. B. MacPherson, *Democratic Theory: Essays in Retrieval* (Oxford, U. K.: Clarendon Press, 1973); Carole Pateman, *Participation and Democratic Theory* (London: Cambridge University Press, 1970).

8. Esther Dyson, *Release 2.0* (New York: Broadway Books, 1997); Lawrence K. Grossman, *The Electronic Republic: Reshaping Democracy in the Information Age* (New York: Viking Press, 1995).

9. Kenneth May, "A Set of Independent, Necessary, and Sufficient Conditions for Simple Majority Decision," *Econometrica,* 20 (1952), pp. 680–684, shows that only majority rule can guarantee popular sovereignty, political equality, and neutrality among policy alternatives. See also Douglas W. Rae, "Decision Rules and Individual Values in Constitutional Choice," *American Political Science Review,* 63 (1969), pp. 40–53; Phillip D. Straffin Jr., "Majority Rule and General Decision Rules," *Theory and Decision,* 8 (1977), pp. 351–360.

10. Dahl, *A Preface to Economic Democracy,* p. 68.

11. Robert A. Dahl, "On Removing Certain Impediments to Democracy in the United States," *Political Science Quarterly,* 92, No. 1 (Spring 1977), p. 14; Elaine Spitz, *Majority Rule* (Chatham, NJ: Chatham House, 1984), p. 83; Dahl, *Democracy and Its Critics,* p. 170.

12. See Marc Plattner, "Liberalism and Democracy," *Foreign Affairs* (March–April, 1998), pp. 171–180.

13. Dahl, *Democracy and Its Critics,* p. 156.

14. David Caute, *The Great Fear* (New York: Simon & Schuster, 1978); Victor Navasky, *Naming Names* (New York: Viking, 1980); Michael Rogin, *The Intellectuals and McCarthy* (Cambridge, MA: MIT Press, 1967).

15. See Bernard R. Berelson, Paul F. Lazarsfeld, and William N. McPhee, *Voting* (Chicago: University of Chicago Press, 1954); V. O. Key Jr., *Public Opinion and American Democracy* (New York: Knopf, 1961); Herbert McClosky and Alida Brill, *Dimensions of Tolerance* (New York: Russell Sage Foundation, 1983). But see, in rebuttal, James L. Gibson, "Political Intolerance and Political Repression During the McCarthy Red Scare," *American Political Science Review,* 82 (1988), pp. 511–529; Benjamin I. Page and Robert Y. Shapiro, *The Rational Public: Fifty Years of Trends in Americans' Policy Preferences* (Chicago: University of Chicago Press, 1992).

16. Dahl, *Democracy and Its Critics,* p. 161.

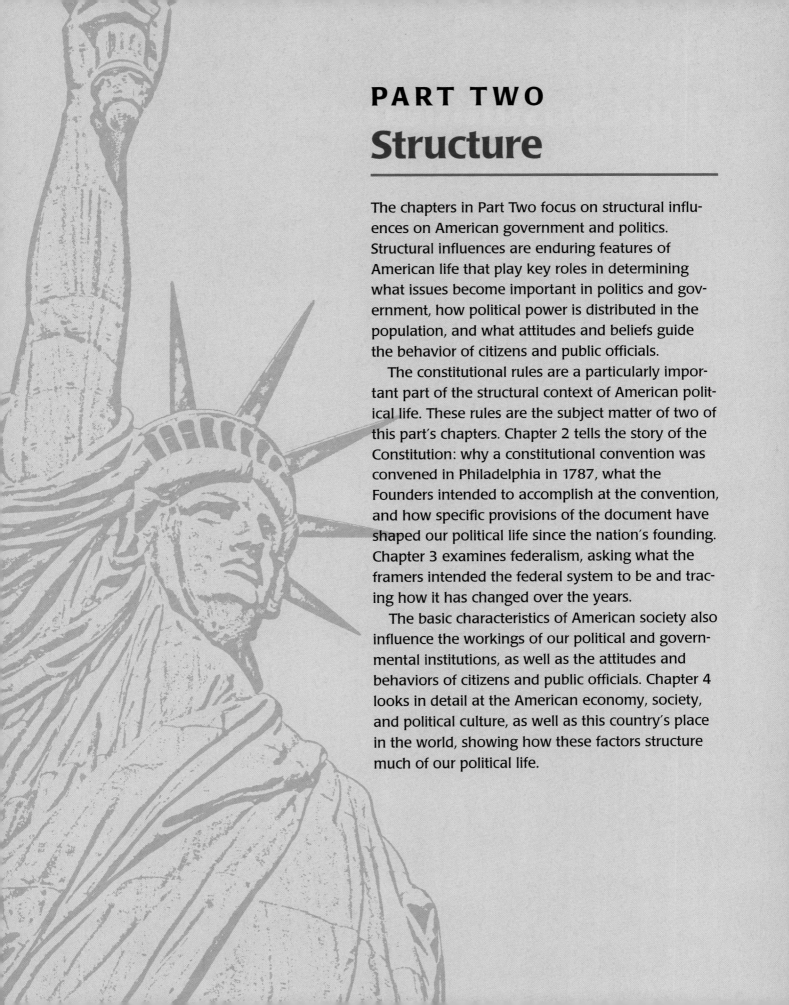

PART TWO
Structure

The chapters in Part Two focus on structural influences on American government and politics. Structural influences are enduring features of American life that play key roles in determining what issues become important in politics and government, how political power is distributed in the population, and what attitudes and beliefs guide the behavior of citizens and public officials.

The constitutional rules are a particularly important part of the structural context of American political life. These rules are the subject matter of two of this part's chapters. Chapter 2 tells the story of the Constitution: why a constitutional convention was convened in Philadelphia in 1787, what the Founders intended to accomplish at the convention, and how specific provisions of the document have shaped our political life since the nation's founding. Chapter 3 examines federalism, asking what the framers intended the federal system to be and tracing how it has changed over the years.

The basic characteristics of American society also influence the workings of our political and governmental institutions, as well as the attitudes and behaviors of citizens and public officials. Chapter 4 looks in detail at the American economy, society, and political culture, as well as this country's place in the world, showing how these factors structure much of our political life.

CHAPTER 2
The Constitution

IN THIS CHAPTER

- The enduring legacies of the American Revolution and the Declaration of Independence
- Our first constitution: The Articles of Confederation
- The Constitutional Convention
- What kind of constitution the framers created
- How the Constitution structures the rules of American politics

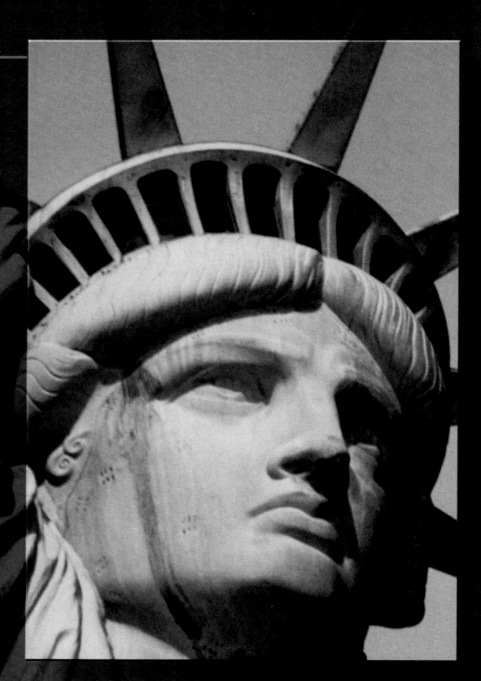

Shays's Rebellion

Artemas Ward, commander of American forces at Bunker Hill, a Revolutionary War hero, and a state judge, could not convince the crowd of several hundred armed farmers to allow him to enter the Worcester, Massachusetts, courthouse. For nearly two hours, he pleaded and threatened, but to no avail. Although most admired him for his achievements, they were determined that he not hold court that day in September 1786, when he was to begin legal proceedings to seize farms for nonpayment of taxes. He left Worcester in a fury, unable to convince the local militia to come to his assistance, and carried word of the rebellion to Boston. Other judges trying to hold court in western Massachusetts in the summer and fall of 1786 had no better luck.[1]

The farmers of western Massachusetts were probably not a rebellious lot by nature, but desperate times pushed many of them to desperate actions. All over the new nation, the end of the Revolutionary War in 1783 brought the collapse of prices for agricultural products and widespread economic distress among farmers. Poor farmers sought relief from their troubles from state governments, and for the most part, political leaders responded. Several states lent money (in the form of scrip, or paper money) to farmers to pay their taxes and debts. Other states passed stay laws, which postponed tax and mortgage payments for hard-pressed farmers.

In Massachusetts, however, the state legislature refused to help. Worse yet, the legislature and the governor decided that all state debts were to be paid off in full to establish the creditworthiness of the state. The state's debt, accumulated to pay the state's share of the costs of the Revolutionary War, was owed primarily to a handful of the wealthiest citizens of the state, who had bought up outstanding notes for pennies on the dollar. To make good on this debt, the legislature levied heavy taxes that fell disproportionately on farmers, especially those in the western part of the state. When taxes could not be paid—a distressingly common circumstance—money could be raised by the state only through foreclosure: the public sale of farmers' lands, buildings, and livestock. Tax foreclosures and imprisonment under harsh conditions for those who could not pay their debts became frequent occurrences. Responding to these dire circumstances, many western Massachusetts farmers took up arms to prevent courts from sitting.

By September 1786, Governor James Bowdoin had seen enough. He issued a proclamation against unlawful assembly and called out the militia to enforce it. Six hundred soldiers were sent to Springfield to ensure that the state supreme court could meet and issue the expected indictments against the leaders of the insurrection. The soldiers were met there by 500 or 600 armed farmers led by a former Revolutionary War officer, Captain Daniel Shays. After a long standoff, the militia withdrew, leaving the rebels in charge and the court unable to meet.

These events only hardened the resolve of the governor to break the rebellion. The armed forces he sent from Boston proved too much for the hastily organized and ill-equipped force under Shays. By the spring of 1787, the Boston militia had defeated the rebels in two pitched battles, one at Springfield and the other at Petersham, and Shays's Rebellion (as it was soon called) ended.

Although the insurrection was put down, most of the new nation's leading citizens were alarmed by the apparent inability of state governments under the Articles of Confederation to maintain public order. Under the Articles, our first constitution (in effect from 1781 to 1788), the national government in Philadelphia was virtually powerless. Responsibility for civil order was mainly in the hands of the states. Shays's Rebellion realized the worst fears of national leaders about the dangers of ineffective state governments and popular democracy out of control, unchecked by a strong national government. George Washington worried, "If government cannot check these disorders, what security has a man?"[2] It was in this climate of crisis that a call was issued for a constitutional convention to meet in Philadelphia to correct the flaws in our first constitution. Rather than amend the Articles of Confederation, however, the men who met in Philadelphia in the summer of 1787 wrote an entirely new constitution.

▶Thinking Critically About This Chapter

This chapter is about the founding of the United States (see Figure 2.1) and the formulation of the constitutional rules that structure American politics to this day.

Using the Framework. You will see in this chapter how structural factors such as the American political culture, economic developments, and the composition of the Constitutional Convention shaped the substance of the Constitution. You will also see how the Constitution is itself an important structural factor for understanding how American government and politics work today.

Using the Democracy Standard. Using the conception of democracy you learned about in Chapter 1, you will be able to see how and why the Framers were uneasy about democracy and created a republican form of government that, although based on popular consent, placed a number of roadblocks in the path of majority rule.   ▶

The Political Theory of the Revolutionary Era

Initially, the American Revolution (1775–1783) was waged more to preserve an existing way of life than to create something new. By and large, American colonists in the 1760s and 1770s were proud to be affiliated with Great Britain and satisfied with the general prosperity that came with participation in the British commercial empire.[3] When the revolution broke out, the colonists at

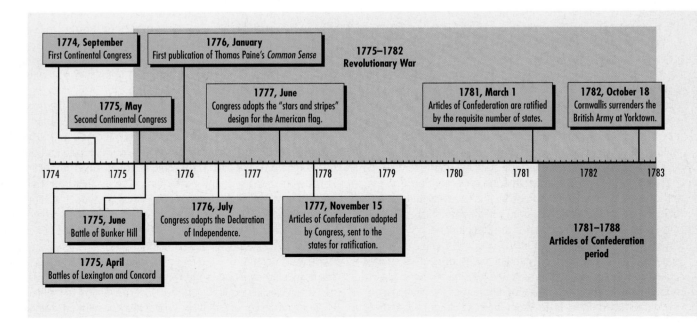

Figure 2.1 ● **Time Line of the Founding of the United States, 1774–1791**

first wanted only to preserve the English constitution and their own rights as British subjects. These traditional rights of life, liberty, and property seemed to be threatened by British policies on trade and taxation. Rather than allowing the American colonists to trade freely with whomever they pleased and to produce whatever goods they wanted, for instance, England was restricting the colonists' freedom to do either in order to protect its own manufacturers. To pay for the military protection of the colonies against raids by Native Americans and their French allies, England imposed taxes on a number of items, including sugar, tea, and stamps (required for legal documents, pamphlets, and newspapers). The imposition of these taxes without the consent of the colonists seemed an act of tyranny to many English subjects in America.

Although the initial aims of the Revolution were quite modest, the American Revolution, like most revolutions, did not stay on the track planned by its leaders. Although it was sparked by a concern for liberty—understood as the preservation of traditional rights against the intrusions of government—it also stimulated the development of sentiments for popular sovereignty and political equality. As these sentiments grew, so did the likelihood that the American colonies would split from their British parent and form a system of government more to the liking of the colonists.

The Declaration of Independence

When the Second Continental Congress began its session on May 10, 1775— the First had met only briefly in 1774 to formulate a list of grievances to submit to the British Parliament—the delegates did not have independence in mind, even though armed conflict with Britain had already begun with the battles of Lexington and Concord. Pushed by the logic of armed conflict, an unyielding British government, and Thomas Paine's incendiary call for American independence in his wildly popular pamphlet *Common Sense,*

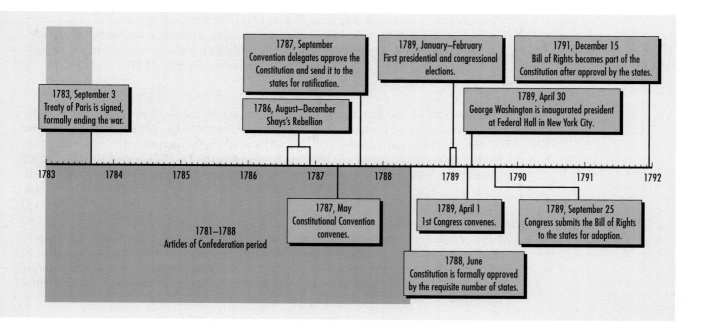

American leaders were reluctant at first to declare independence from Great Britain. One of the things that helped change their minds was Thomas Paine's wildly popular and incendiary pamphlet *Common Sense,* which mercilessly mocked the institution of monarchy.

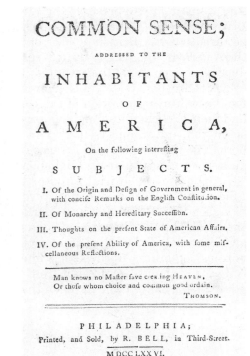

however, the delegates had concluded by the spring of 1776 that separation and independence were inescapable. South Carolina took the first step when it adopted its own constitution and declared itself free from British control. The legislature of Virginia followed suit, its delegates boldly proclaiming that "the United Colonies are, and of right ought to be, free and independent States." In early June, spurred by the examples of these two states, the Continental Congress appointed a special committee, composed of Thomas Jefferson, John Adams, and Benjamin Franklin, to draft a declaration of independence. The document, mostly Jefferson's handiwork, was adopted unanimously by the Second Continental Congress on July 4, 1776.

Key Ideas in the Declaration of Independence   The ideas in Jefferson's Declaration of Independence are so familiar to us that we may easily miss their revolutionary importance. In the late eighteenth century, most societies in the world were ruled by kings with authority purportedly derived from God, subject to little or no control by their subjects. Closely following John Locke's ideas in *The Second Treatise on Government,* Jefferson's argument that legitimate government can be established only by the people and can govern only with their consent seemed outrageous at the time. However, these ideas sparked a responsive chord in people everywhere when they were first presented, and they remain extremely popular all over the world today. Ideas articulated in the Declaration influenced the French Revolution of 1789, the 1991 "velvet revolution" in Czechoslovakia, and many revolutions in between. The argument as presented in the Declaration of Independence goes as follows:

- *Human beings possess rights that cannot be legitimately given away or taken from them.* "We hold these truths to be self-evident, that all men are created equal, that they are endowed by their Creator with certain unalienable Rights, that among these are Life, Liberty, and the Pursuit of Happiness."

● *People create government to protect these rights.* "That to secure these rights, Governments are instituted among Men, deriving their just powers from the consent of the governed."

● *If government fails to protect people's rights or itself becomes a threat to them, people can withdraw their consent from that government and create a new one.* "That whenever any Form of Government becomes destructive of these ends, it is the Right of the People to alter or to abolish it, and to institute new Government, laying its foundation on such principles, and organizing its powers in such form, as to them shall seem most likely to effect their Safety and Happiness."

Omissions in the Declaration   The Declaration of Independence carefully avoided several controversial subjects, including what to do about slavery. Jefferson's initial draft of the document denounced the Crown for violating human rights by "captivating and carrying Africans into slavery," but this was considered too controversial and was dropped. The contradiction between the institution of slavery and the Declaration's sweeping claims for self-government, "unalienable" individual rights, and equality ("all men are created equal")

WEB EXPLORATION

The Declaration of Independence

Issue: The delegates to the Second Continental Congress in Philadelphia did not simply declare independence for the 13 British colonies in North America but gave their reasons for doing so in a document that has influenced people around the world for more than two centuries.

Site: See the Declaration of Independence as eighteenth-century Americans first saw it at the online Exhibition Hall of the National Archives through the "Course Documents" section of your online course. In the "Web Explorations" section for Chapter 2, click on "The Declaration of Independence" and then open "Declaration." Select "Charters of Freedom" then "the Declaration of Independence." Examine the document and then read the online essay, "The Stylistic Artistry of the Declaration."

What You've Learned: Do you agree with Lucas that "the Declaration of Independence is perhaps the most masterly written state paper of western civilization"? This is a very big claim. Has Lucas convinced you that it is true? What is the most memorable and meaningful about the Declaration? What, if anything, is merely mundane and extraneous in Jefferson's document?

HINT: The most stirring and memorable parts of the Declaration come at the beginning and make universal claims about individual rights and the role of government; it is these universal claims, rather than the long list of transgressions by Great Britain that make up the latter part of the Declaration, that have been so influential.

was obvious to many observers at the time and is apparent to us today. (Jefferson, of course, was himself a slaveholder and fathered several children with his slave Sally Hemmings.) Moreover, the Declaration was silent about the political status of women, Native Americans, and African-Americans who were not slaves. Indeed, it is safe to assume that neither Jefferson, the main author of the Declaration, nor the other signers of the document had women, Native Americans, free blacks, or slaves in mind when they were fomenting revolution and calling for a different kind of political society. Interestingly, free blacks and women would go on to play important roles in waging the Revolutionary War against Britain.[4]

The Articles of Confederation: The First Constitution

confederation

A loose association of states or territorial divisions formed for a common purpose.

The leaders of the American Revolution almost certainly did not envision the creation of a single, unified nation. At most, they had in mind a loose **confederation** among the states, a form of government in which the states are virtually independent and hold most governmental powers, while the central government holds almost none. This should not be surprising. Most Americans in the late eighteenth century believed that a government based on popular consent and committed to the protection of individual rights was possible only in small, homogeneous republics, where government was close to the people and where fundamental conflicts of interest among the people did not exist. Given the great geographic expanse of the colonies, as well as their varied ways of life and economic interests, the formation of a single unified republic seemed unlikely.

WEB EXPLORATION

The Articles of Confederation

Issue: The framers met in Philadelphia to amend the Articles of Confederation, but ended up writing an entirely new constitution, judging that the Articles were irretrievably flawed.

Site: Read the Articles of Confederation and the accompanying commentary on their shortcomings through the "Course Documents" section of your online course. Go to the "Web Explorations" for Chapter 2, then click on "The Articles of Confederation" and open "Articles."

What You've Learned: The shortcomings of the Articles are a staple of American history and civics education. Do you agree that they were so flawed that they had to be replaced? Is there anything about the Articles of Confederation, on the other hand, that you find attractive and appealing?

HINT: Your answer will depend on your basic political values. If you believe that government power would better serve the people by being lodged almost solely in the states, then you might not approve of the actions taken by the framers.

Provisions of the Articles

Our first constitution, passed by the Second Continental Congress in the midst of the Revolutionary War in 1777 but not ratified by the requisite number of states until 1781, created a nation that was hardly a nation at all. The Articles of Confederation created in law what had existed in practice from the time of the Declaration of Independence: a loose confederation of independent states, with little power in the central government, much like the United Nations today. Under the Articles, most important decisions were made in state legislatures.

The Articles provided for a central government of sorts, but it had few responsibilities and virtually no power. It could make war or peace, but it had no power to levy taxes (even customs duties) to pursue either goal. It could not regulate commerce between the states, nor could it deny the states the right to collect customs duties. It had no independent chief executive to ensure that the laws passed by Congress would be enforced, nor had it a national court system to settle disputes between the states. The rule requiring that all national laws be approved by 9 of the 13 states made law making almost impossible. And, defects in the new constitution were difficult to remedy because amending the Articles required the unanimous approval of the states.

Shortcomings of the Articles

The Articles did what their authors wanted them to do: preserve the power, independence, and sovereignty of the states and ensure that the central government would not encroach on the liberty of the people. Unfortunately, there were also many problems that the confederation was ill equipped to handle.

Most important, the new central government could not finance its activities. The government was forced to rely on each state's willingness to pay its annual tax assessment. Few states were eager to cooperate. As a result, the bonds and notes of the confederate government became almost worthless, and the government's attempts to borrow were stymied.

The central government was also unable to defend American interests in foreign affairs. Without a chief executive with veto power over actions of the central government in the hands of the states and devoid of a standing military, the confederation lacked the capacity to reach binding agreements with other nations or to deal with a wide range of problems. These included the continuing presence of British troops in western lands ceded to the new nation by Britain at the end of the Revolutionary War, violent clashes with the Native Americans on the western frontier, and piracy on the high seas.

The government was also unable to prevent the outbreak of commercial warfare between the states. As virtually independent nations with the power to levy customs duties, many states became intense commercial rivals of their neighbors and sought to gain every possible advantage against the products of other states. New York and New Jersey, for instance, imposed high tariffs on goods that crossed their borders from other states.

Convening the Constitutional Convention

Historians now generally agree that the failings of the Articles of Confederation led most of the leading citizens of the confederation to believe that a new constitution was desperately needed for the fledgling nation. What is left out of

The Constitution is preserved and on display at the National Archives in Washington, D.C.

many accounts of the convening of the Constitutional Convention in Philadelphia, however, is the story of the growing concern among many of the most influential men in the confederation that the passions for democracy and equality among the common people set loose by the American Revolution were getting out of hand. During the American Revolution, appeals to the people for the defense of freedom and for the spread of the blessings of liberty were often translated by the people to mean their right to better access to the means of government and to the means of livelihood.[5] The common people were convinced that success would bring substantial improvements in their lives.[6]

The Republican Beliefs of the Founders

republicanism

A political doctrine advocating limited government based on popular consent, protected against majority tyranny.

This fever for popular participation and greater equality is not what most of the leaders of the American Revolution had in mind.[7] The Founders were believers in a theory of government known as **republicanism**. Eighteenth-century republicans were most concerned about preventing tyranny, the abuse of power by rulers and the destruction of the liberty of their subjects. They believed that tyranny could be imposed by the *one*, the *few*, or the *many*. That is, tyranny could come from the misrule of a sovereign, a hereditary aristocratic class, or the common people as a whole. Republicans believed that the only way to gain the consent of the governed and to prevent tyranny at the same time was to elect government leaders and limit the power of government. The election of representatives would keep tyrannical kings and others from power while ensuring popular consent. Limiting the power of government, either by stating what government could and could not do in a written constitution or by fragmenting governmental power in the very way government is organized, would prevent tyranny no matter who won control of government.

Although eighteenth-century republicans believed in representative government—a government whose political leaders are elected by the people—they were quite unsympathetic to what we might call popular democracy. For the most part, they thought that public affairs ought to be left to men from the "better" parts of society; the conduct of the public business was, in their view, the province of individuals with wisdom and experience, capacities associated mainly

LongmanParticipate

CourseCompass

participation
**Democracy
and the Internet**

Table 2.1 ○ **Comparing Eighteenth-Century Republicanism and the Democratic Ideal**

Republicanism	Democracy
Government is based on popular consent.	Government is based on popular consent.
Rule by the people is indirect, through representatives.	Rule by the people may be direct or indirect.
The term *people* is narrowly defined (by education, property holding, social standing).	The term *people* is broadly defined.
Elected representatives act as "trustees" (act on their own to discover the public good).	Elected representatives act as "delegates" (act as instructed by the people; accurately reflect their wishes).
Barriers to majority rule exist.	Majority rule prevails.
Government is strictly limited in function.	Government does what the people want it to do.
Government safeguards rights and liberties, with a special emphasis on property rights.	Government safeguards rights and liberties, with no special emphasis on property rights.

with people of social standing, substantial financial resources, and high levels of education.

Nor did eighteenth-century republicans believe that elected representatives should be too responsive to public opinion. Once in office, representatives were to exercise independent judgment, taking into account the needs and interests of society rather than the moods and opinions of the people.

Eighteenth-century republicans, then, did not believe in democracy as defined in Chapter 1. Although republican doctrine allowed the common people a larger role in public life than existed in other political systems of the day, the role of the people was to be far more limited than we expect today (the differences between republican and democratic doctrines are highlighted in Table 2.1). As James Madison put it in *The Federalist Papers,* "[Democracies] have ever been spectacles of turbulence and contention; have ever been found incompatible with personal security or the rights of property; and have in general been as short in their lives as they have been violent in their deaths."[8]

Why the Founders Were Worried

An Excess of Democracy in the States   Worries that untamed democracy was on the rise were not unfounded.[9] In the mid-1780s, popular conventions were created in several states to keep tabs on state legislatures and issue instructions to them on legislation. Both conventions and instructions struck directly at the heart of the republican conception of the legislature as a deliberative body shielded from popular opinion.[10]

The constitution of the state of Pennsylvania under the Articles of Confederation was also an affront to republican principles. Benjamin Rush, a signatory to the Declaration of Independence, described it as "too much upon the democratic order."[11] This constitution replaced the property qualification to vote with a very small tax (thus allowing many more people to vote), created a unicameral (single-house) legislative body whose members were to be elected in annual elections, mandated that legislative deliberations be open to the public, and required that proposed legislation be widely publicized and voted on only after a general election had been held (making the canvassing of public opinion easier).

To many advocates of popular democracy, including Tom Paine, the Pennsylvania constitution was the most perfect instrument of popular sovereignty. To others, like James Madison, the Pennsylvania case was a perfect example of popular tyranny exercised through the legislative branch of government.[12]

The Threat to Property Rights in the States   One of the freedoms that republicans wanted to protect against the intrusions of a tyrannical government was the right of the people to acquire and enjoy private property. Developments toward the end of the 1770s and the beginning of the 1780s seemed to put this freedom in jeopardy. For one thing, the popular culture was growing increasingly hostile to privilege of any kind, whether of social standing, education, or wealth. Writers derided aristocratic airs; expressed their preference for unlettered, plain-speaking leaders; and pointed out how wealth undermined equal rights.[13] Legislatures were increasingly inclined, moreover, to pass laws protecting debtors. Rhode Island and North Carolina issued cheap paper money, which note holders were forced to accept in payment of debts; other states enacted **stay acts**, which forbade farm foreclosures for nonpayment of debts. Popular opinion, while strongly in favor of property rights (most of the debtors in question were owners of small farms), also sympathized with farmers, who were hard-pressed to pay their debts with increasingly tight money, and believed—with some reason—that many creditors had accumulated notes speculatively or unfairly and were not entitled to full repayment. Finally, Shays's Rebellion in western Massachusetts, where armed rebels tried to prevent the state courts from seizing farms for the nonpayment of debts, greatly alarmed American notables.

stay acts
Enactments postponing the collection of taxes or mortgage payments.

The Constitutional Convention

Concerned about these developments and shortcomings in the design of government under the Articles, most of America's economic, social, and political leaders were convinced by 1787 that the new nation and the experiment in self-government were in great peril. These concerns helped convince leaders in the states to select 73 delegates to attend the Constitutional Convention in Philadelphia (only 55 actually showed up for its deliberations). The goal was to create a new government capable of providing both energy and stability.

The convention officially convened in Philadelphia on May 25, 1787, with George Washington presiding. It met in secret for a period of almost four months. By the end of their deliberations, the delegates had hammered out a constitutional framework that has served as one of the structural foundations of American government and politics to the present day.

Who Were the Founders?

The delegates were not common folk. There were no common laborers, skilled craftspeople, small farmers, women, or racial minorities in attendance. Most delegates were wealthy men: holders of government bonds, real estate

Members of the convention sign their names to the Constitution on September 17, 1787. The Constitution did not become the law of the land, however, until the ninth state, New Hampshire, ratified it nine months later.

investors, successful merchants, bankers, lawyers, and owners of large planta-tions worked by slaves. They were, for the most part, far better educated than the average American and solidly steeped in the classics. The journal of the convention debates kept by James Madison of Virginia shows that the delegates were conversant with the great works of Western philosophy and political sci-ence; with great facility and frequency, they quoted Aristotle, Plato, Locke, Montesquieu, and scores of other thinkers. They were also a surprisingly young group, averaging barely over 40 years of age. Finally, they were a group with broad experience in American politics.

Ever since the publication in 1913 of historian Charles Beard's provocative book *An Economic Interpretation of the Constitution,*[14] scholars have debated the framers' intentions. Beard boldly claimed that the framers were engaged in

WEB EXPLORATION

Delegates to the Convention

Issue: The Constitution was made by people who were not much like the average inhabitant of the United States in 1787.

Site: Find out more about the delegates to the Convention by going to the National Archives through the "Course Documents" section of your online course. In the "Web Explorations" section for Chapter 2, click on "Delegates to the Convention" and then open "delegates."

What You've Learned: Select a state and read the biographies of the delegates. How would you describe the average delegate? How repre-sentative do you believe them to have been of the American people of the time?

HINT: There were no women; few artisans and small farmers; and no free blacks, indentured servants, slaves, or Native Americans at the proceedings, who together com-prised the vast majority of the American population.

a conspiracy to protect their immediate and personal economic interests. Those who controlled the convention and the ratification process after the convention, he suggested, were owners of public securities who were interested in a government that could pay its debts, merchants interested in protections of commerce, and land speculators interested in the protection of property rights.

Beard has his defenders and detractors.[15] It is generally agreed that Beard overemphasized the degree to which the framers were driven by the immediate need to "line their own pockets," failed to give credit to their more noble motivations, and even got many of his facts wrong. So a simple self-interest analysis is not supportable. But Beard was probably on the mark in suggesting that broad economic and social-class motives were at work in shaping the actions of the framers. This is not to suggest that they were not concerned about the national interest, economic stability, or the preservation of liberty. It does suggest, however, that the ways in which they understood these concepts were fully compatible with their own positions of economic and social eminence. It is fair to say that the Constitutional Convention was the work of American notables authentically worried about the instability and the economic chaos of the confederation.

Consensus and Conflict at the Convention

The delegates to the convention were of one mind on many fundamental points. They agreed, for instance, that the Articles of Confederation had to be scrapped and replaced with a new constitution.

The delegates also agreed that a substantially strengthened national government was needed to protect American interests in the world, provide for social order, and regulate interstate commerce. Such a government would diminish the power and sovereignty of the states. Supporters of the idea of a strong, centralized national government, such as Alexander Hamilton, had long argued this position. By the time of the convention, even such traditional opponents of centralized governmental power as James Madison had changed their minds. As Madison put it, some way must be found "which will at once support a due supremacy of the national authority, and leave in force the local authorities so far as they can be subordinately useful."[16]

But the delegates also believed that a strong national government was potentially tyrannical and should not be allowed to fall into the hands of any particular interest or set of interests, particularly the majority of the people, to whom Madison referred as "the majority faction." The delegates' most important task became that of finding a formula for instituting republican government based on popular consent but not unduly swayed by public opinion and popular democracy. As Benjamin Franklin put it, "We have been guarding against an evil that old states are most liable to, excess of power in the rulers, but our present danger seems to be a defect of obedience in the subjects."[17]

Instituting republican government, however, would be no easy task because the raw material for republican government—a virtuous people, one that put the common good above self-interest—did not seem to exist in America. As the framers saw it, their task was to try to arrange governmental institutions in a way that would preserve the essentials of republicanism in a society composed of an "immoderate and unvirtuous" people—to find, as James Madison put it, "a republican remedy for the diseases most incident to republican government."[18]

The Great Compromise By far the most intense debate concerned representation in Congress and the relative power of large and small states in the new nation. The **Virginia Plan**, drafted by James Madison, proposed the creation of a strong central government controlled by the most populous states:

Virginia Plan

Proposal by the large states at the Constitutional Convention to create a strong central government with power in the government apportioned to the states on the basis of population.

Virginia, Massachusetts, and Pennsylvania. The Virginians wanted a national legislature with seats apportioned to the states on the basis of population size and with the power to appoint the executive and the judiciary and to veto state laws. The smaller states countered with a set of proposals drafted by William Paterson of New Jersey (thereafter known as the **New Jersey Plan**), whose central feature was a unicameral national legislature whose seats were apportioned equally among the states. The New Jersey Plan envisioned a slightly more powerful national government than the one that existed under the Articles of Confederation, but one that was to be organized on representational lines not unlike those in the Articles, in which each of the states remained sovereign. The Virginia Plan, by contrast, with its strong national government run by a popularly elected legislature, represented a fundamentally different kind of national union, one in which national sovereignty was superior to state sovereignty.

> **New Jersey Plan**
>
> Proposal of the smaller states at the Constitutional Convention to create a government based on the equal representation of the states in a unicameral legislature.

Debate over this issue was so intense that no decision could be reached on the floor of the convention. As a way out of this impasse, the convention appointed a committee to hammer out a compromise. The so-called Committee of Eleven met over the Fourth of July holiday while the convention was adjourned. It presented its report, sometimes called the Great Compromise and sometimes the **Connecticut Compromise** (because it was drafted by Roger Sherman of that state), on July 5, 1787. Its key feature was a bicameral (two-house) national legislature in which each state's representation in the House of Representatives was to be based on population (thus favoring the large states), while representation in the Senate was to be equal for each of the states (thus favoring the small states). The compromise, adopted on July 16, broke the deadlock at the convention and allowed the delegates to turn their attention to other matters.

> **Connecticut Compromise**
>
> Also called the *Great Compromise*; the compromise between the New Jersey and Virginia plans put forth by the Connecticut delegates at the Constitutional Convention; called for a lower legislative house based on population and an upper house based on equal representation of the states.

Slavery   Despite great distaste for the institution of slavery among many delegates, slavery was ultimately condoned in the Constitution, although only indirectly; the word "slavery" does not appear in the Constitution at all. The legal standing of "involuntary servitude" is affirmed in three places. First, the delegates agreed, after much debate, to count three-fifths of a state's slave population (referred to as "three-fifths of all other Persons") in the calculation of

One of the great shortcomings of the framers was their inability or unwillingness to abolish slavery in the Constitution. It would take a great and terrible civil war to rectify their mistake.

USING THE FRAMEWORK

Why Was Slavery Allowed in the Constitution of 1787?

Slavery was allowed in the Constitution until passage, after the Civil War, of the Thirteenth Amendment, which ended involuntary servitude in the United States. Although the words "slave" or "involuntary servitude" never appear in the document, slavery is given constitutional standing in the original document in Article I, Section 2, paragraph 3; Article 2, Section 9; and Article IV, Section 2, paragraph 3. For Americans today, it seems almost inconceivable that such a thing could have happened. Taking a broader and more historical view makes the story clearer, though hardly more acceptable.

Governmental Action

The framers allowed the institution of slavery to continue in Article I, Section 2; Article II, Setion 9; and Article IV, Section 2 of the Constitution.

Governmental Level

- Slaveholders and merchants involved in the slave trade were well represented among the convention delegates.

- Many other delegates, although personally opposed to slavery as an institution, feared that the introduction of a provision to end slavery would cause those states with high numbers of slaves to leave the convention and doom the effort to create a United States of America.

Political Linkages Level

- Slaves and free blacks played no significant political role in America during the Articles of Confederation period. Their concerns about slavery had no political weight.

- Few private organizations—interest groups, churches, or newspapers—were actively pressing for an end to slavery at the time of the constitutional convention.

Structural Level

- Slavery, and the slave trade, was a profitable business in many states.

- For the most part, individuals of European descent in America during the time of the constitutional convention did not believe that people of African descent were equal to whites in any respect nor did they believe that they were beings who possessed basic human rights.

how many representatives a state was entitled to in the House of Representatives (Article I, Section 2, paragraph 3). Much harm was done by this; counting noncitizen slaves for purposes of representation in the House increased the power of the slave states in Congress as well as the number of their electoral votes in presidential elections. This imbalance would continue until 1865, when the Civil War and the Thirteenth Amendment, ratified after the war, ended slavery in the United States. Second, it forbade enactments against the slave trade until the year 1808 (Article I, Section 9). Third, it required nonslave states to return runaway slaves to their owners in slave states (Article IV, Section 2, paragraph 3).

Many Americans today are no doubt bothered by the fact that a significant number of the delegates to a convention whose goal was to build a nontyrannical republic were themselves slaveholders. (Although a few, including George Washington, had provisions in their wills freeing their slaves upon their death). To understand more fully why the delegates did not abolish slavery, see the "Using the Framework" box.

It would finally take a terrible civil war to abolish slavery in the United States. At the convention, Virginia delegate George Mason had a foreboding of such an outcome when he observed about slavery that "providence punishes national sins by national calamities."[19]

The Presidency   The Virginia Plan called for a single executive, while the New Jersey Plan called for a plural executive. In the spirit of cooperation that pervaded the convention after the Great Compromise, the delegates quickly settled on the idea of a single executive. They could not agree, however, on how this executive should be chosen. Both sides rejected direct election by the people of the chief executive, of course, because this would be "too much upon the democratic order," but they locked horns over the Virginia Plan's method of selection: by the vote of state legislatures. The compromise that was eventually struck involved a provision for an **electoral college** that would select the president. In the electoral college, each state would have a total of votes equal to its total number of representatives and senators in Congress. Members of the electoral college would then cast their votes for president. Should the electoral college fail to give a majority to any person, which most framers assumed would usually happen, the House of Representatives would choose the president, with each state having one vote (Article II, Section 1, paragraphs 2 and 3). As we shall see, the system of presidential election did not work out as expected and became far more democratic over the course of our history.

electoral college
Representatives of the states who formally elect the president; the number of electors in each state is equal to the total number of its senators and congressional representatives.

What the Framers Created

To understand American politics today, it is extremely important to understand the Constitution of the United States. Admittedly, the document has evolved. It has been formally amended 27 times, and some very important things in it have changed because of judicial interpretations and political practices. But the major outlines of our present-day government are expressed in and substantially determined by the Constitution that was written in Philadelphia in 1787. The U.S. Constitution is one of the major *structural* factors that has influenced the direction of American government and continues to shape politics today.

What kind of government did the framers create? Let us examine the fundamental design for government laid out in the Constitution.

A Republican Form of Government   Recall that republican doctrine advocated a form of government that, while based on popular consent and some

Table 2.2 ● **Two Systems of Government in the United States**		
	Articles of Confederation	**U.S. Constitution**
Organizing Principle	A loose confederation of independent states, with a weak central government.	A federation of states, with powers divided between states and a central government.
Central Government	No chief executive or national judiciary. Legislature has no power to levy taxes, to regulate commerce between states, or to enforce national policy.	Powers are divided among executive, judicial, and legislative branches, each with certain powers over one another. Central government can levy taxes, regulate commerce and currency, enforce national laws, and raise a military.
State Governments	Sovereign states have veto power over constitutional change, independent power over militia and over commerce between states	States are represented in the national government in Congress and through electoral votes in presidential elections; approval of three-fourths of the states needed to amend the Constitution.

popular participation, places obstacles in the path of majoritarian democracy and limits the purposes and powers of the government in order to prevent tyranny.

Federalism   The Articles of Confederation envisioned a nation structured as a loose union of politically independent units with little power in the hands of the central government. The Constitution fashioned a **federal** system, in which some powers are left to the states, some powers are shared by the component units and the central government, and some powers are granted to the central government alone. As Madison put it in *The Federalist,* No. 46, the state and national governments "are but different agents and trustees of the people, constituted with different powers."

The powers in the Constitution tilt slightly toward the center, however[20] (see Table 2.2). This recasting of the union from a loose confederation to a more centralized federal system is boldly stated in Article VI, Section 2, commonly called the **supremacy clause**:

> *This Constitution and the Laws of the United States which shall be made in Pursuance thereof; and all Treaties made, or which shall be made, under the Authority of the United States, shall be the supreme Law of the Land; and the Judges in every State shall be bound thereby, any Thing in the Constitution or Laws of any State to the Contrary notwithstanding.*

The tilt toward national power is also enhanced by assigning important powers and responsibilities to the national government: to regulate commerce, to provide a uniform currency, to provide uniform laws on bankruptcy, to raise and support an army and a navy, to declare war, to collect taxes and customs duties, to provide for the common defense of the United States, and more (for these provisions, see Article I, Section 8). Especially important for later constitutional history is the last of the clauses in Section 8, which states that Congress has the power to "make all laws which shall be necessary and proper" to carry out its specific powers and responsibilities. We shall see later how this **elastic clause** became one of the foundations for the growth of the federal government

federal

Describing a system in which significant governmental powers are divided between a central government and smaller units, such as states.

supremacy clause

The provision in Article VI of the Constitution that the Constitution itself and the laws and treaties of the United States are the supreme law of the land, taking precedence over state laws and constitutions.

elastic clause

Article I, Section 8; of the Constitution, also called the *necessary and proper clause*; gives Congress the authority to make whatever laws are necessary and proper to carry out its enumerated responsibilities.

in the twentieth century. An example is the military draft. Although it is not mentioned in the Constitution, Congress has instituted a draft several times as a way to carry out its duties to raise an army and a navy.

The Constitution left it up to each of the states, however, to determine qualifications for voting within their borders. This left rules in place in all the states that denied the right to vote to women, slaves, and Native Americans; it left rules untouched in many states that denied the vote to free blacks and to white males without substantial property. Most states removed property qualifications by the 1830s, establishing universal white male suffrage in the United States. It would take many years and constitutional amendments to remove state restrictions on the voting rights of women and racial minorities.

Limited Government   The basic purpose of the U.S. Constitution, like any written constitution, is to define the purposes and powers of the government. Such a definition of purposes and powers automatically places a boundary between what is permissible and what is impermissible. By listing the specific powers (as in Article I, Section 8) of the national government and specifically denying others to the national government (as in Article I, Section 9, and in the first ten amendments to the Constitution, known as the **Bill of Rights**), the Constitution carefully limited what government may legitimately do.

Bill of Rights

The first ten amendments to the U.S. Constitution, concerned with basic liberties.

Checks on Majority Rule   Afraid of unbridled democracy, the framers created a constitution by which the people rule only indirectly, barriers are placed in the path of majorities (see Figure 2.2), and deliberation is prized over conformity to the popular will. As political philosopher Robert Dahl puts it, "To achieve their goal of preserving a set of inalienable rights superior to the majority principle . . . the framers deliberately created a framework of government that was carefully designed to impede and even prevent the operation of majority rule."[21] Let us see how the framers planned to constrain the majority.

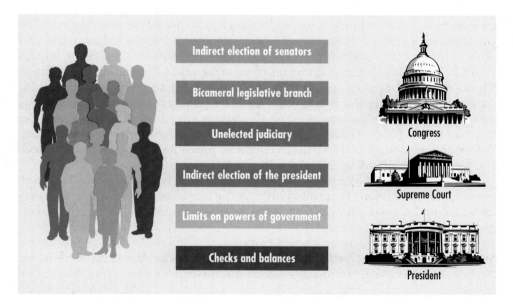

Figure 2.2 ● Limiting the Power of the Majority

The framers of the Constitution were concerned that the unreflective and unstable opinions of the majority might overwhelm the considered judgments of government leaders and lead to tyranny. One antidote was to create mechanisms in the Constitution that, while preserving "the consent of the governed," ensured that the voice of the people would be muted in the councils of government.

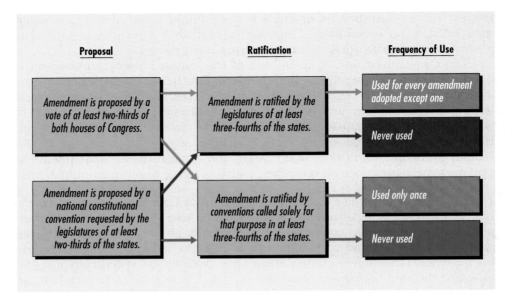

Proposal	Ratification	Frequency of Use
Amendment is proposed by a vote of at least two-thirds of both houses of Congress.	Amendment is ratified by the legislatures of at least three-fourths of the states.	Used for every amendment adopted except one
		Never used
Amendment is proposed by a national constitutional convention requested by the legislatures of at least two-thirds of the states.	Amendment is ratified by conventions called solely for that purpose in at least three-fourths of the states.	Used only once
		Never used

Figure 2.3 ● Amending the Constitution

With two ways of proposing a constitutional amendment and two ways of ratifying one, there are four routes to changing the Constitution. In all but one case (the Twenty-First Amendment, which repealed Prohibition), constitutional amendments have been proposed by Congress and then ratified by the state legislatures.

Of the three branches of government, only a part of one of them is selected by the direct vote of the people: the House of Representatives (Article I, Section 2, paragraph 1). As for the rest of the national government, the president is elected by the electoral college; the members of the Senate are elected by the state legislatures; and judges are appointed by the president and confirmed by the Senate. Representatives, senators, and presidents are elected, moreover, for different terms (two years for representatives, four years for presidents, and six years for senators), from different constituencies, and (often) at different times. These noncongruencies in elections were intended to ensure that popular majorities, at least in the short run, would be unlikely to overwhelm those who govern. Finally, the framers rejected the advice of radical democrats, such as Thomas Paine, Samuel Adams, and Thomas Jefferson, to allow the Constitution to be easily amended. Instead, they created an amending process that is exceedingly cumbersome and difficult (see Figure 2.3).

Thus, the framers designed a system in which the popular will, though given some play (more than anywhere in the world at the time), was largely deflected and slowed, allowing somewhat insulated political leaders to deliberate at their pleasure.

Separation of Powers; Checks and Balances   During the American Revolution, American leaders worried mainly about the misrule of executives (kings and governors) and judges. As an antidote, they substituted legislative supremacy, thinking that placing power in an elected representative body would make government effective and nontyrannical. The men who drafted the Constitution, however, though still leery of executive and judicial power, were more concerned by 1787 about the danger of legislative tyranny. To deal with this problem, the framers turned to the ancient notion of balanced government, popularized by the

French philosopher Montesquieu. The central idea of balanced government is that concentrated power of any kind is dangerous and that the way to prevent tyranny is first to fragment governmental power into its constituent parts—executive, legislative, and judicial—then place each into a separate and independent branch. (In parliamentary systems, these powers are combined in a single body.) In the U.S. Constitution, Article I (on the legislative power), Article II (on the executive power), and Article III (on the judicial power) designate separate spheres of responsibility and enumerate specific powers for each branch. We call this the **separation of powers**.

To further ensure that power would not be exercised tyrannically, the framers arranged for the legislative, executive, and judicial powers to check one another in such a way that "ambition . . . be made to counteract ambition."[22] They did this by ensuring that no branch of the national government would be able to act entirely on its own without the cooperation of the others. To put it another way, each branch has ways of blocking the actions of the others. For instance, Congress is given the chief lawmaking power under the Constitution, but a bill can become a law only if the president signs it. The Supreme Court, moreover, has the power (though it is not specifically mentioned) to reject a law formulated by Congress and signed by the president if it is contrary to the Constitution. What is at work here was described nicely by Thomas Jefferson: "The powers of government should be so divided and balanced among several bodies of magistracy, as that no one could transcend their legal limits, without being effectually checked and constrained by the others."[23] We call the provisions that accomplish this objective **checks and balances**. Figure 2.4 shows in detail how each separate branch of the federal government can be checked by the other two. In this constitutional scheme, each branch has power, but none is able to exercise all of its powers on its own.

The Foundations for a National Free Enterprise Economy

Recall that the framers were concerned that a system based "too much upon the democratic order" would eventually threaten private property. They believed, following eighteenth-century English philosopher John Locke, that the right to accumulate, use, and transfer property was one of the fundamental and inalienable rights that governments were instituted to defend, so they looked for ways to protect property. Recall, also, that the men who wrote the Constitution were concerned that the obstacles to trade allowed under the Articles of Confederation were threatening to block the emergence of a vibrant national economy in which most of them were involved.

Property rights are protected in several places in the Constitution. Article I, Section 10, forbids the states to impair the obligation of contracts, to coin money, or to make anything but gold and silver coin a tender in payment of debts. In other words, the states could no longer help debtors by printing inflated money, forgiving debts, or otherwise infringing on the property of creditors, as had happened in such places as Rhode Island and North Carolina under the Articles of Confederation. Article IV, Section 1, further guarantees contracts by establishing that the states must give "full faith and credit" to the public acts, records, and judicial proceedings of every other state, which meant that one could no longer escape legal and financial obligations in one state by moving to another. In addition, the Constitution guaranteed that the U.S. government would pay all debts contracted under the Articles of Confederation (Article VI, Section 1). Article IV, Section 2, paragraph 3, even protected private property in slaves by requiring states to deliver escaped slaves back to their owners.

separation of powers

The distribution of government legislative, executive, and judicial powers to separate branches of government.

checks and balances

The constitutional principle that government power shall be divided and that the fragments should balance or check one another to prevent tyranny.

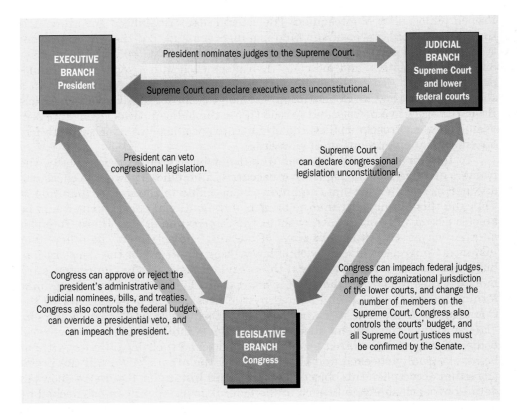

Figure 2.4 ● **Checks and Balances**

The framers of the Constitution believed that tyranny might be avoided if the power of government were fragmented into its executive, legislative, and judicial components and if each component were made the responsibility of a separate branch of government. To further protect against tyranny, they created mechanisms by which the actions of any single branch could be blocked by either or both of the other branches. This system of checks and balances is highlighted in this drawing.

Besides protecting private property, the framers took additional steps to encourage the emergence of a national free enterprise economy. Article I, Section 8, grants Congress the power to regulate interstate commerce (thus ending the chaos of individual states' regulations), to coin money and regulate its value (thus establishing a uniform national currency), to establish uniform laws of bankruptcy, and to protect the financial fruits of invention by establishing patent and copyright laws. At the same time, Article I, Sections 9 and 10, broke down barriers to trade by forbidding the states to impose taxes or duties on other states' exports, to enter into foreign treaties, to coin money, or to lay any imposts or duties on imports or exports.

The Struggle to Ratify the Constitution

Congress had instructed the delegates to the convention to propose changes to the Articles of Confederation. Under the provisions of the Articles of Confederation, such alterations would have required the unanimous consent of the 13 states. To follow such a course would have meant instant rejection of the new constitution, because Rhode Island, never friendly to the deliberations in Philadelphia, surely would have voted against it, and one or two additional states may well have joined Rhode Island. Acting boldly, the framers simply stated that ratification would be based on guidelines specified in Article VII of the unratified document they had just written, namely, approval by nine states meeting in special constitutional conventions. Congress agreed to this procedure, voting on September 28, 1787, to transmit the Constitution to the states for their consideration.

The battle over ratification was heated, and the outcome was far from certain. That the Constitution eventually carried the day may be partly attributed to the fact that the **Federalists** (those who supported the Constitution) did a better job of making their case than the **Anti-Federalists** (those who opposed the Constitution). Their intellectual advantages were nowhere more obvious than in the 85 articles written in defense of the Constitution for New York newspapers, under the name "Publius," by Alexander Hamilton (who wrote the most), James Madison (who wrote the best), and John Jay (who wrote only three). Collected later and published as *The Federalist Papers*, these articles strongly influenced the debate over ratification and remain the most impressive commentaries ever written about the U.S. Constitution (Numbers 10 and 51, written by Madison, are reprinted in the Appendix).

Anti-Federalist opposition to the Constitution was based on fear of centralized power and concern about the absence of a bill of rights.[24] Although the Federalists firmly believed that a bill of rights was unnecessary because of the protection of rights in the state constitutions and the many safeguards against tyranny in the federal Constitution, they promised to add one during the first session of Congress. Without this promise, ratification would probably not have happened. And, they kept their word. The 1st Congress passed a bill of rights in the form of ten amendments to the Constitution (see Table 2.3 and the Appendix), and the amendments were eventually ratified by the required number of states.

Federalists

Proponents of the Constitution during the ratification fight; also the political party of Hamilton, Washington, and Adams.

Anti-Federalists

Opponents of the Constitution during the fight over ratification.

LongmanParticipate

CourseCompass

simulation
**You Are
James Madison**

CourseCompass

WEB EXPLORATION

The Anti-Federalist Case

Issue: History loves winners, so we tend to hear more about the federalists than the Anti-Federalists. Perhaps we have not given the Anti-Federalists a fair hearing.

Site: Read the Anti-Federalist essay number 1 of "Brutus" through the "Course Documents" section of your online course. In the "Web Explorations" section for Chapter 2, click on "The Anti-Federalist Case" and then open "Anti-Federalists."

What You've Learned: Do you think that the Anti-Federalists were entirely wrong or did they point to important flaws and problems in the newly proposed Constitution? After reading this essay, how would you have voted on ratification of the Constitution?

HINT: Your response depends on your political values and beliefs. Much of the Anti-Federalist case sounds very much like contemporary conservative complaints about the federal government.

Table 2.3 ● The Bill of Rights	
Amendment I	Freedom of religion, speech, press, and assembly
Amendment II	The right to bear arms
Amendment III	Prohibition against quartering of troops in private homes
Amendment IV	Prohibition against unreasonable searches and seizures
Amendment V	Rights guaranteed to the accused: requirement for grand jury indictment; protections against double jeopardy, self-incrimination; guarantee of due process
Amendment VI	Right to a speedy and public trial before an impartial jury, to cross-examine witnesses, and to have counsel
Amendment VII	Right to a trial by jury in civil suits
Amendment VIII	Prohibition against excessive bail and fines and against cruel and unusual punishment
Amendment IX	Rights not listed in the Constitution that are retained by the people
Amendment X	States' retention of powers not denied to them by the Constitution or delegated to the national government

Note: See the Appendix for the full text.

Ratification of the Constitution was a close call. Most of the small states quickly approved, attracted by the formula of equal representation in the Senate. Federalists organized a victory in Pennsylvania before the Anti-Federalists realized what had happened. After that, the ratification struggle was very hard. Rhode Island voted no. North Carolina abstained because of the absence of a bill of rights and did not vote its approval until 1790. In the largest and most important states, the vote was exceedingly close. Massachusetts approved by a vote of 187–168; Virginia, by 89–79; and New York, by 30–27. The struggle was especially intense in Virginia, where prominent, articulate, and influential men were involved on both sides of the question. The Federalists could call on George Washington, James Madison, John Marshall, and Edmund Randolph. The Anti-Federalists countered with George Mason, Richard Henry Lee, and Patrick Henry. Patrick Henry was particularly passionate, saying that the Constitution "squints towards monarchy." Although New Hampshire technically put the Constitution over the top, being the ninth state to vote approval, the proponents did not rest easily until approval was narrowly voted by Virginia and New York.

Despite the passions that were unleashed during the debate over the refashioning of the nation's fundamental law, Americans quickly accepted the new order. It is not entirely clear why this happened. Perhaps it was simple weariness from the long effort to win independence and to create a new nation. Perhaps it was because George Washington was elected the nation's first president under the new constitution, lending great legitimacy to the new venture. Perhaps it was because most of the prominent political figures involved in the struggle for independence and in the ratification fight, even those in the Anti-Federalist camp, quickly came to accept and support the new government.

The Changing Constitution, Democracy, and American Politics

The Constitution is the basic rule book for the game of American politics. Constitutional rules apportion power and responsibility among governmental branches, define the fundamental nature of the relationships among governmental institutions, specify how individuals are to be selected for office, and tell how the rules themselves may be changed. Every aspiring politician who wants to attain office, every citizen who wants to influence what government does, and every group that wants to advance its interests in the political arena must know the rules and how to use them to best advantage. Because the Constitution has this character, we understand it to be a fundamental structural factor influencing all of American political life.

Constitutional rules, however, like all rules, can and do change over time. Their tendency to change with the times is why we sometimes speak of the "living Constitution." Constitutional changes come about in three specific ways: formal amendment, judicial interpretation, and political practices.

The Constitution may be formally amended by use of the procedures outlined in Article V of the Constitution (again, refer to Figure 2.3). This method has resulted in the addition of 27 amendments since the founding, the first ten of which (the Bill of Rights) were added within three years of ratification. That only 17 have been added in the roughly 200 years since suggests that this method of changing the Constitution is extremely difficult. Nevertheless, formal amendments have played an important role in expanding democracy in the United States by ending slavery; extending voting rights to African-Americans,

LongmanParticipate

CourseCompass

timeline
The History of Constitutional Amendments

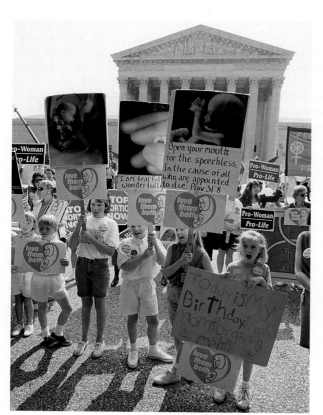

The Constitution has evolved over the years in three ways: through the amendment process, through evolving political practices, and through the Supreme Court's changing interpretation of the Constitution's meaning. Here antiabortion protesters demonstrate in front of the Supreme court building on the anniversary of the Court's *Roe* v. *Wade* decision to demand a reversal of that landmark decision.

women, and young people ages 18 to 20; and making the Senate subject to popular vote.

The Constitution is also changed by decisions and interpretations of the U.S. Supreme Court. For instance, in *Marbury* v. *Madison* (1803), the Court claimed the power of **judicial review**—the right to declare the actions of the other branches of government null and void if they are contrary to the Constitution—even though such a power is not specifically enumerated in the Constitution. In *Griswold* v. *Connecticut* (1965), and later in *Roe* v. *Wade* (1973), the Court supported a fundamental right of privacy even though such a right is nowhere explicitly mentioned in the Constitution.

The meaning of the Constitution also changes through changing political practices. Political parties and nominating conventions are not cited in the Constitution, for example, but it would be hard to think about American politics today without them. It is also fair to say that the framers would not recognize the modern presidency, which is now a far more important office than they

judicial review

The power of the Supreme Court to declare actions of the other branches and levels of government unconstitutional.

HOW DEMOCRATIC ARE WE?

PROPOSITION: The Constitution created a republic, not a democracy.

AGREE: The framers created a republic because they were worried about the possibility of majority tyranny in the new nation. Consequently, they wrote a number of provisions into the Constitution to control the purported excesses of democracy: separation of powers, checks and balances, federalism, an appointed judiciary with life tenure, selection of the president by the electoral college, and election of members of the Senate by state legislatures. Although some of these provisions have not worked precisely as the framers intended, the American system of government remains essentially "republican" in nature, with the majority finding it very difficult to prevail.

DISAGREE: Although the framers had every intention of creating a republic and holding democracy in check, they were unable to do so. Over the years, as the nation became more egalitarian in its cultural, economic, and social life, the tide of democracy transformed the original constitutional design. By formal amendment, judicial interpretations, and changing political practices, government has been fashioned into a highly responsive set of institutions, heeding the voice of the people. Today, the national government does pretty much what the American people want it to do, even if it sometimes takes awhile for it to do so.

THE AUTHORS: You will see throughout this text that the United States is far more democratic than the framers had intended it to be—with much of the credit going to the "struggle for democracy" described in a boxed feature in many of the chapters—but that our system remains very much a republican one. Those pressing for national action to solve any number of problems soon run up against the barriers to decisive action erected by the framers. At almost every point in our system of government, it is easier to block or to veto than to act or enact. There is no denying the fact, however, that elected representatives and executives often try to be responsive to the popular will. Sometimes they are successful; sometimes they are not. There is no denying the additional fact that the framers were successful in creating a governing structure in which political liberty, an important component of democracy, is protected and allowed to flourish. We would call such a system of government a "democrat republic."

envisioned, a change that has been brought about largely by the political and military involvement of the United States in world affairs.

The story of how formal amendment, judicial interpretations, and political practices have changed the constitutional rules in the United States will be told in more detail throughout this text.

Summary

LongmanParticipate

CourseCompass

comparative
Comparing Constitutions

The first constitution joining the American states was the Articles of Confederation. Under its terms, the states were organized into a loose confederation in which the states retained full sovereignty and the central government had little power. Because of a wide range of defects in the Articles of Confederation and fears among many American leaders that democratic and egalitarian tendencies were beginning to spin out of control, a gathering was called in Philadelphia to amend the Articles of Confederation. The delegates chose instead to formulate an entirely new constitution, based on the principles of republicanism (federalism, limited government, the separation of powers, checks and balances, and limitations on majority rule).

The Constitution was ratified in an extremely close vote of the states after a hard-fought struggle between the Federalists and the Anti-Federalists. The Federalists were supported primarily by the economically better-off, urban interests, and believers in a more centralized republicanism; the Anti-Federalists were supported primarily by the economically less well-off, rural interests, and believers in small-scale republicanism. Despite its "close shave," the Constitution became very popular among the American people within only a few years of the ratification fight. Because of the struggle for democracy by the American people, the Constitution has become far more democratic over the years than was originally intended by the framers.

Suggestions for Further Reading

Bernstein, Richard B. *Are We to Be a Nation?* Cambridge, MA: Harvard University Press, 1987.

An accessible, comprehensive, and balanced account of the making of the U.S. Constitution. Includes an extensive collection of documents, drawings, and paintings.

Maier, Pauline. *American Scripture: Making the Declaration of Independence.* New York: Knopf, 1997.

A detailed account of the writing of the Declaration of Independence and its gradual transformation into a revered icon of American democracy.

Rossiter, Clinton, ed. *The Federalist Papers.* New York: New American Library, 1961.

Classic commentaries on the Constitution and its key provisions, written by Alexander Hamilton, John Jay, and James Madison.

Storing, Herbert J. *What the Anti-Federalists Were For.* Chicago: University of Chicago Press, 1981.

The most complete collection available on the published views of the Anti-Federalists. Includes convincing commentary by Storing.

Wills, Gary. *Inventing America: Jefferson's Declaration of Independence.* New York: Random House, 1978.

A different and controversial look at the intellectual origins of the American experiment.

Wills, Gary. *Explaining America: The Federalist.* New York: Doubleday, 1981.

A fresh look at the writing of the Constitution by one of America's most provocative intellectuals.

Wood, Gordon S. *The Creation of the American Republic.* New York: Norton, 1972.
The most exhaustive and respected source on America's changing ideas during the period 1776–1787, or from the start of the American Revolution to the writing of the Constitution.

Wood, Gordon S. *The Radicalism of the American Revolution.* New York: Knopf, 1992.
Examines and rejects the argument that the American Revolution was merely a political and not a social and economic revolution.

Internet Sources

Annotated Constitution   **www.access.gpo.gov/congress/senate/constitution**
An annotation of the Constitution in which each clause is tied to Supreme Court decisions concerning its meaning; done by the Library of Congress.

Biographical Sketches of the Delegates to the Constitutional Convention
http://www.nara.gov/exhall/charters/constitution/confath.html
Profiles of the delegates to the Constitutional Convention.

Cornell University Law School   **http://www.law.cornell.edu/**
Pathways to the full text of U.S. Supreme Court decisions and opinions, articles on constitutional issues, and much more.

Political Science Resources: Political Thought   **http://www.psr.keele.ac.uk/**
A vast collection of documents on democracy, liberty, and constitutionalism.

The U.S. Constitution On-Line   **www.usconstitution.net**
A very rich site that presents material on every aspect of the history and development of the Constitution.

Notes

1. Page Smith, *A People's History of the Young Republic: Vol. 3. The Shaping of America* (New York: McGraw-Hill, 1980), p. 25.

2. Quoted in Jackson Turner Main, *The Anti-Federalists* (Chapel Hill, NC: University of North Carolina Press, 1961), p. 62.

3. Richard Bushman, "Revolution," in Eric Foner and John A. Garraty, eds., *The Reader's Companion to American History* (Boston: Houghton Mifflin, 1991), p. 936; Gordon S. Wood, *The Creation of the American Republic* (New York: Norton, 1972), p. 12.

4. Sarah M. Evans, *Born for Liberty: A History of Women in America* (New York: Free Press, 1997); John Hope Franklin and Alfred A. Moss Jr., *From Slavery to Freedom* (New York: Knopf, 1967).

5. See Hannah Arendt, *On Revolution* (New York: Viking, 1965).

6. Smith, *Shaping of America,* pp. 8–9.

7. Richard Hofstadter, *The American Political Tradition* (New York: Vintage Books, 1948), p. 4.

8. Alexander Hamilton, James Madison, and John Jay, *The Federalist Papers,* ed. Clinton Rossiter (New York: New American Library, 1961), No. 10. (Originally published 1787–1788.)

9. See Gordon S. Wood, *The Radicalism of the American Revolution* (New York: Knopf, 1992).

10. Wood, *Creation of the American Republic,* pp. 311–318.

11. Ibid., ch. 8.

12. Samuel Elliot Morison, *The Oxford History of the American People* (New York: Oxford University Press, 1965), p. 274.

13. See Wood, *Creation of the American Republic,* p. 400.

14. Charles Beard, *An Economic Interpretation of the Constitution* (New York: Macmillan, 1913).

15. See Robert Brown, *Charles Beard and the Constitution* (Princeton, NJ: Princeton University Press, 1956); Hofstadter, *The American Political Tradition;* Leonard Levy, *Constitutional Opinions* (New York: Oxford University Press, 1986); Robert A. McGuire and Robert L. Ohsfeldt, "An Economic Model of Voting Behavior over Specific Issues at the Constitutional Convention of 1787," *Journal of Economic History,* 66 (March 1986), pp. 79–111; James A. Morone, *The Democratic Wish* (New York: Basic Books, 1990); Forrest McDonald, *We the People: The Economic Origins of the Constitution* (Chicago: University of Chicago Press, 1958); Gordon S. Wood, *The Convention and the Constitution* (New York: St. Martin's Press, 1965); Wood, *Creation of the American Republic.*

16. Quoted in Wood, *Creation of the American Republic,* p. 473.

17. Ibid., p. 432.

18. Hamilton, Madison, and Jay, *The Federalist Papers,* Nos. 10 and 39.

19. Max Farrand, *The Records of the Federal Convention of 1787* (New Haven, CT: Yale University Press, 1937).

20. "The Invention of Centralized Federalism," in William H. Riker, ed., *The Development of Centralized Federalism* (Boston: Kluwer Academic, 1987).

21. Robert A. Dahl, "On Removing the Impediments to Democracy in the United States," *Political Science Quarterly,* 92 (Spring 1977), p. 5.

22. Hamilton, Madison, and Jay, *The Federalist Papers,* No. 51.

23. Thomas Jefferson, *Notes on the State of Virginia,* ed. Thomas Perkins Abernathy (New York: Harper & Row, 1964), p. 120.

24. See Main, *The Anti-Federalists;* Wood, *Creation of the American Republic;* Smith, *Shaping of America,* p. 99; Herbert Storing, *What the Anti-Federalists Were For* (Chicago: University of Chicago Press, 1981), p. 71.

CHAPTER 3
Federalism: States and Nation

IN THIS CHAPTER

- What federalism is and why we have it

- Conflicts over the meaning of federalism in the United States

- How our federal system differs from other systems of government

- Advantages and disadvantages of federalism

- The New Federalism and devolution

- Federalism and democracy

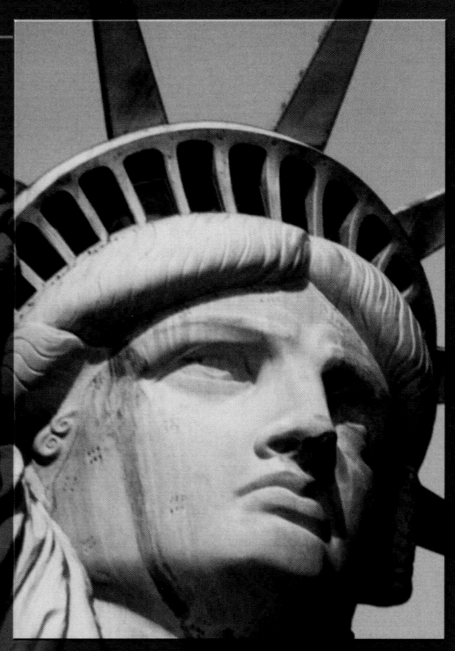

Welfare Reform and the States

Bill Clinton and many Republican and Democratic members of Congress promised to "end welfare as we know it." Long before Congress and the president could agree on a specific plan, however, many state governments—with special permission from Washington—took the lead in trying out their own welfare reforms. This interplay between national and state governments illustrates the dispersion of power in our federal system.

Under the Social Security Act of 1935, the U.S. government established Aid to Families with Dependent Children (AFDC) as an entitlement program for children in poor families. The states administered the program, offering different levels of benefits from one state to another. But the national government, which provided most of the money, also made the rules about who was eligible, for how long, and under what circumstances. It guaranteed that any eligible family in the country would be entitled to benefits.

That pattern of national rule setting began to change around the beginning of the 1990s. New, mostly Republican state governors and legislatures were elected, promising to reform welfare by encouraging work and parental responsibility. Pioneers such as Republican Governor Tommy G. Thompson of Wisconsin, who took office in 1987, came up with many different ideas: requiring efforts to find work; putting time limits on benefits; easing benefit reductions when recipients earned some money working; helping with training, day care, job placement, and community service jobs; requiring young mothers to live with their parents or other adults; paying bonuses for staying in school; and restricting payments for children born to mothers already on welfare.

The Bush administration and especially the Clinton administration granted many "waivers," exceptions to the national rules, so that states could experiment with these ideas. By 1995, 32 states had waivers, affecting about half the nation's 14 million welfare recipients. More than 30 states let recipients earn more and keep assets without losing benefits, 25 states required teenage mothers to live with adults; and more than 20 got waivers to require that welfare recipients find work or to help them do so.

Some of the results were impressive. In Wisconsin, for example, after Thompson took office and persuaded Washington to give him 179 waivers, the welfare rolls dropped by 27 percent, and spending was cut by $210 million per year. The money that was poured into child care and job training seemed to pay off, saving about $2 in welfare costs for each $1 spent. Michigan, under Republican Governor John Engler, cut caseloads to the lowest point in 21 years, led the nation by steering 30 percent of its 190,000 welfare recipients into work, and saved about $100 million a year.[1]

Finally, in 1996, the president and Congress passed the Personal Responsibility and Work Opportunity Act, which made public welfare a state responsibility with federal financial support. The new law ended welfare as an entitlement program, limited recipients to no more than five years of benefits, and imposed work and work-training requirements. Within these general guidelines, states are allowed wide latitude in creating their own welfare programs. Some states remain more generous than others. California, for example, allows recipients to stay on the rolls for five years, provides some benefits for children (using state, not federal, funds) beyond the five-year limit, and only weakly sanctions (with loss of some benefits) individuals who refuse to work or train for work. Florida, by contrast, limits adult recipients to four years, is less generous to children beyond the five-year limit, and cuts off aid to the entire family if the adult fails to comply with work requirements.[2]

▶Thinking Critically About This Chapter

The mixture of state and national action on this issue, and the state experimentation that affected policymaking in the nation as a whole, is characteristic of American federalism. So too is the conflict between national standards and local flexibility. In addition, the shift in responsibility from the national government to the state governments on welfare may portend a change in our long history of enhancing the power of government in Washington, D.C.

Using the Framework. In this chapter, you will learn how and why federalism is one of the most important structural factors that affect American politics and government and shape public policy. You will learn how federalism influences our entire system: from the kinds of political parties we have and the workings of Congress to how domestic programs are affected. You will also learn how federalism itself has changed over time.

Using the Democracy Standard. Using the evaluative tools you learned in Chapter 1, you will be able to judge for yourself whether federalism enriches or diminishes democracy in the United States.   ▶

Federalism as a System of Government

The United States is full of governments. We have not only a federal government in Washington, D.C. (which, to avoid confusion, we will refer to in this chapter as the *national* or *central* government), but also governments in each of 50 states and in each of thousands of smaller governmental units, such as counties (about 3,000 of them), cities, towns and townships, school districts, and special districts that deal with such matters as parks and sanitation.

All these governments are organized and related to each other in a particular way. The small governments—those of counties, cities, towns, and special districts—are legal creations of state governments. They can be created, changed, or abolished by state laws, at the state's convenience. But state governments themselves have much more weight and permanence because of their prominent place in the Constitution. Together with the national government in Washington, D.C., they form what is known as a federal system. The *federal system* is part of the basic structure of U.S. government, deeply rooted in our Constitution and history. It is one of the most important features of American politics, since it affects practically everything else.

The Nature of Federalism

Federalism is a system under which significant government powers are divided between the central government and smaller units, such as states. Neither one completely controls the other; each has some room for independent action. A federal system can be contrasted with two other types of government: a confederation and a unitary government. In a **confederation**, the constituent states get together for certain common purposes but retain ultimate individual authority and can veto major central governmental actions. The United Nations, the European Union, and the American government under the Articles of Confederation are examples. In a **unitary system**, the central government has all the power and can change its constituent units or tell them what to do.

federalism

A system in which significant governmental powers are divided between a central government and smaller units, such as states.

confederation

A loose association of states or territorial divisions formed for a common purpose.

unitary system

A system in which a central government has complete power over its constituent units or states.

Federations are not necessarily forever. The Yugoslav federation of republics, in which each republic was formed primarily on the basis of nationality, could not withstand the dramatic rise in ethnic tensions after the death of Yugoslav leader, Marshall Tito. Here ethnic Serb soldiers and militia escort an elderly Croat from his basement shelter during the battle for Vukovar in 1991.

Japan and France have this kind of government. These three different types of governmental systems are contrasted in Figure 3.1.

Federalism is not a common way of organizing governments around the world. In the early 1990s, 140 (88 percent) of the 159 member countries in the United Nations had unitary rather than federal governments. In the years since the founding of the United States, however, a number of important countries—mostly large and diverse ones—have also established federal systems, often modeling them on the U.S. system.

LongmanParticipate

CourseCompass

comparative
Comparing Federal and Unitary Systems

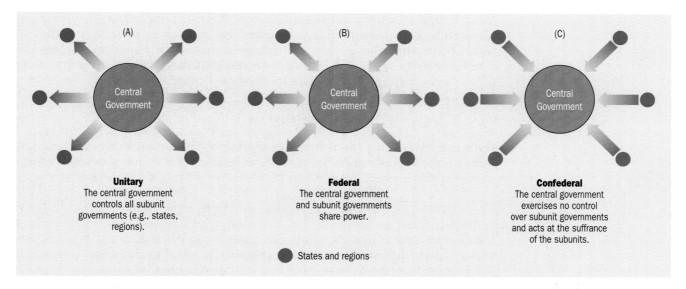

Unitary
The central government controls all subunit governments (e.g., states, regions).

Federal
The central government and subunit governments share power.

Confederal
The central government exercises no control over subunit governments and acts at the suffrance of the subunits.

● States and regions

Figure 3.1 Types of Political Systems

A majority of countries have unitary systems (A), in which the central government controls the state and local governments, which in turn exert power over the citizens. The United States, however, has a federal system (B), in which the central government has power on some issues, while the states have power on others. In a confederation (C), the central institutions have only a loose coordinating role, and all ultimate power stays with the constituent states or units.

The Roots of Federalism

Some of the elements of federalism go back in history at least as far as the Union of Utrecht in the Netherlands in 1579, but federalism as it exists today is largely an American invention.[3]

Historical Origins   American federalism emerged from the particular way in which the states declared independence from Britain—becoming, in effect, separate countries—and then joined together to form a confederation and then a single nation, as discussed in Chapter 2. But we can gain further insight into *why* the United States adopted and has continued a federal system if we look at what other countries with similar systems have in common.

Role of Size and Diversity   Most federal systems around the world are found in countries that are geographically large and have regions that differ from one another in economic activity, religion, ethnicity, and language. In Germany, for example, the conservative Catholics of the south have traditionally been different from the liberal Protestants of the north and east. In Canada, the farmers of the central plains are not much like the fishers of Nova Scotia, and the French-speaking (and primarily Catholic) residents of Quebec differ markedly from the mostly English-speaking Protestants of the rest of the country. India consists of many dramatically different ethnic and religious groups, living far apart in different climates and speaking different languages. Such diverse groups often want the local independence that federalism allows, rather than submitting to a unified central government.

The United States, too, is large and diverse, although it is certainly less regionally diverse than India. From the early days of the Republic, the slave-holding and agriculture-oriented South was quite distinct from the merchant Northeast, and some important differences persist today. Illinois is not Louisiana; the farmers of Iowa differ from defense and electronics workers in California. States today also vary from one another in their approaches to public policy, their racial and ethnic composition, and their political cultures.[4] In *The Federalist Papers,* the Founders argued that this size and diversity made federalism especially appropriate for the new United States.

U.S. Federalism: Pro and Con

Over the years, from the framing of the U.S. Constitution to the present day, people have offered a number of strong arguments for and against federalism, in contrast to a more unitary system. Let us consider some of these arguments.

Pro: Diversity of Needs   The oldest and most important argument in favor of decentralized government is that in a large and diverse country, needs and wants and conditions differ from one place to another. Why not let different states enact different policies to meet their own needs? (See Using the Framework box on why states can set their own tuition levels, including those for out-of-state students.) Federalism may enhance popular sovereignty and majority rule democracy in the sense that distinct majorities in different states can legislate specific policies that they want instead of being subordinated to a single national majority.

Con: The Importance of National Standards   However, the needs or desires that different states pursue may not be worthy ones. Political scientist William Riker has pointed out that, historically, one of the main effects of

USING THE FRAMEWORK

"I Thought That Attending a Public University Would Save a Lot of Money, but It Hasn't Because I Have to Pay Out-of-State Tuition. Why Do I Have to Pay so Much Money?"

All over the United States, students who choose to attend public higher education institutions pay much higher tuition than state residents. Some educational reformers have suggested that the system be reformed so that students might attend college wherever they choose, without financial penalty. They have suggested that, over the long-haul and on average,

such a reform would not have much impact on state budgets because students would randomly distribute themselves across state borders. Such proposals have never gotten very far. Taking a broad view of how structural, political linkage, and governmental factors effect this issue will help explain the situation.

Governmental Action

State legislatures decline to pass uniform tuition legislation.

Governmental Level

- Elected leaders know that voters want access to low cost higher education for state residents; use out-of-state tuition to help subsidize in-state students.

- Elected leaders are not subject to political pressures to change tuition policy.

- Elected leaders are concerned with short-term budget issues; high out-of-state tuition allows them to raise part of the higher education budget out of such revenues.

Political Linkages Level

- Voters in each state insist on access for their children and the children of their neighbors to low-cost higher education.

- There exists little political pressure on elected leaders within the states to lower or eliminate out-of-state tuition, whether from
  Public opinion and voters.
  Parties.
  The mass media.
  Interest groups.
  Social movements.

- Out-of-state students rarely vote in the states where they go to school; politicians have no incentive to think seriously about their tuition concerns.

Structural Level

- The states are mainly responsible for education in our federal system; national tuition reform would require agreements among all the states, something that is highly unlikely.

federalism was to let white majorities in the southern states enslave and then discriminate against black people, without interference from the North.[5] Perhaps it is better, in some cases, to insist on national standards that apply everywhere.

Pro: Closeness to the People   It is sometimes claimed that state governments are closer to the ordinary citizens, who have a better chance to know their officials, to be aware of what they are doing, to contact them, and to hold them responsible for what they do. Thus President Ronald Reagan, in his 1982 State of the Union address, declared, "[My New Federalism] will be designed and administered closer to the grassroots and the people it serves. . . . The programs will be more responsive to both the people they are meant to help and the people who pay for them."[6]

Con: Low Visibility and Lack of Popular Control   However, others respond that geographic closeness may not be the real issue. More Americans are better informed about the *national* government than they are about state governments, and more people participate in national than in state elections. When more people know what the government is doing and more people vote, they are better able to insist that the government do what they want. For that reason, responsiveness to ordinary citizens may actually be greater in national government.

Pro: Innovation and Experimentation   When the states have independent power, they can try out new ideas. Individual states can be "laboratories." If the experiments work, other states or the nation as a whole can adopt their ideas, as has happened on such issues as allowing women and 18-year-olds to vote, fighting air pollution, and dealing with water pollution.[7] As we saw in the opening story, Wisconsin and Michigan took the lead in changing the welfare system in the United States.

WEB EXPLORATION

The States and Term Limits

Issue: One argument in favor of federalism is that it allows the states to innovate and experiment with reforms that may not be possible at the national level. Term limits is one example of this.

Site: Visit the National Council on State Legislatures through the "Course Documents" section of your online course. In the "Web Explorations" section for Chapter 3, click on "The States and Term Limits" and then open "legislatures." Select "public user," then "state legislatures," then choose "about state legislatures" in the dialogue box. Under "contents" select "term limits."

What You've Learned: How many states have term limits? How many do not? How about your own state? Does yours have term limits? What form does it take if you are in such a state? Do you favor term limits or not? Why?

HINT: How you feel about term limits probably depends on whether you believe officials in your state are responsive to the public.

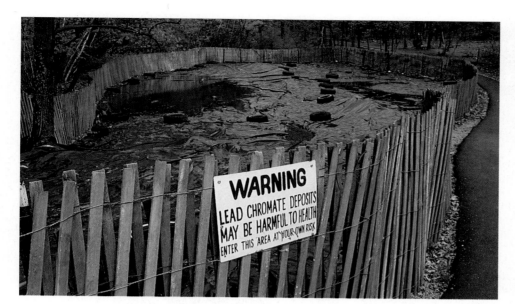

Industrial pollution—here toxic metals seep into the soil and groundwater at an abandoned industrial site—often affects the people of more than one state and requires the participation of the national government to clean up the mess and prevent recurrences.

Likewise, when the national government is controlled by one political party, federalism allows the states with majorities favoring a different party to compensate by enacting different policies. This aspect of diversity in policymaking is related to the Founders' contention that tyranny is less likely when government's power is dispersed. Multiple governments reduce the risks of bad policy or the blockage of the popular will; if things go wrong at one governmental level, they may go right at another.

Con: Spillover Effects and Competition Diversity and experimentation in policies, however, may not always be good. Divergent regulations can cause bad effects that spill over from one state to another. When factories in the Midwest spew out oxides of nitrogen and sulfur that fall as acid rain in the Northeast, the northeastern states can do nothing about it. Only nationwide rules can solve such problems.

Similarly, it is very difficult for cities or local communities in the states to do much about poverty or other social problems. If a city raises taxes to pay for social programs, businesses and the wealthy may move out of town, and the poor may move in, impoverishing the city.[8] Over the last two decades, many firms have moved from the northern Frost Belt to the southern Sun Belt, partly in search of low taxes and a good "business climate," where wages are lower and organized labor is kept at bay by "right to work" laws.

Thus, innovation by state governments may be undercut by competition for investors among communities in the several states. Perhaps only the national government can deal with the aspects of taxes and spending that affect people across state boundaries or that would cause destructive competition among the states.

Pro: Training Ground for Women and Racial Minorities It is in politics at the local and state levels where talented women and minority group members have often been first identified, recruited, and trained for public office (see The Struggle for Democracy box, "Women in State and Local Politics"). And it is their performance on the job and the visibility provided by state and local office

THE STRUGGLE FOR DEMOCRACY

Women in State and Local Politics

Women won the right to vote in 1920, but they have only recently begun to move toward political equality in the sense of holding important political offices. Progress has been greatest in state and local governments.

Just after the 1990 elections—when Kansas, Oregon, and Texas inaugurated women as governors—only 31 women were serving in the U.S. Congress, accounting for just 6 percent of the seats there. But the Center for the American Woman and Politics at Rutgers University found that women constituted 22 percent of state legislators in 1999, up from the 4 percent of 1969. By 1999, the number of women in Congress had jumped to 65 (56 in the House and 9 in the Senate), about 12 percent of the total membership. Women served as majority leaders in nine state legislatures in 1999, as House Speaker in four states, and as minority leaders in eight others. In the state of Washington, women held 12 of the 15 standing committee chairmanships.

Some observers say that there is a long way to go and that progress is much too slow: at the present rate of increase (less than 1 percent per year), it would take 64 years for women to win 50 percent of state legislative seats. But others, pleased that the trend is in the right direction, point out that state legislatures are traditional pipelines to higher office, state or national, and that they handle many important issues. Louisiana, for example, when it had a 97.9 percent male legislature, passed an extremely restrictive abortion law; with more women members, it might have acted differently.

States vary widely in their proportion of women legislators, from Alabama's 3.6 percent to Washington's 41 percent. Most of the lowest proportions are found in

1999: 1,652 women; 22.3% of legislators

Number of Female State Legislators, 1969–1999

Source: National Conference of State Legislators

that often launches women and minorities into national politics. Former Congresswoman Barbara Jordan, an African-American, made her start in Texas politics. Senator Carol Moseley-Braun was a player in Illinois politics before she made her successful run for the Senate (she lost her bid for a second the South; several of the highest are in states like Arizona and New Hampshire, with part-time (and low-paid) legislatures that are easier to get into. The proportion of women working outside the home, the power of political parties, their openness to women, and the extent of legislative turnover in each state also make a difference.

Even more women work in state and local government executive agencies, but they are apparently subject to a glass ceiling. A Rutgers study found that women filled 43.5 percent of lower-level state and local jobs but only 31.3 percent of high-level positions and only 19.8 percent of the very top (cabinet-level) state positions. States generally hire fewer women than

localities, and the percentages of women in high positions varies greatly from state to state. Almost everywhere, however, the trend is up.

Sources: Rutgers Center for the American Woman and Politics, interview (December 17, 1993), Web page (January 1996); Robin Toner, "Women in Politics Gain, but Road Is a Long One," *New York Times* (February 25, 1991), p. A6; "Few Women Found in Top Public Jobs," *New York Times* (January 3, 1992), p. A8; B. Drummond Ayres Jr., "Women in Washington Statehouse Lead U.S. Tide," *New York Times* (April 14, 1997), p. A12; and S.H. Verhovek, "Record for Women in Washington Legislature," *New York Times* (February 4, 1999), p. A14.

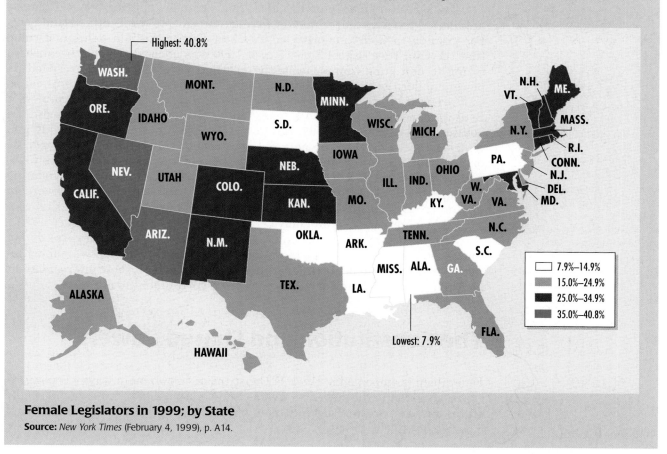

Female Legislators in 1999; by State

Source: *New York Times* (February 4, 1999), p. A14.

term, however). Loretta Sanchez was active in Orange County, California, politics before she won a seat in Congress in 1996. J. C. Watt (R–OK) was elected Oklahoma Corporation Counsel before he won election to the House of Representatives.

What Sort of Federalism?

As the pros and cons indicate, a lot is at stake. It is not likely, however, that Americans will ever have a chance to vote yes or no on the federal system or to choose a unitary government instead. What we can decide is exactly *what sort* of federalism we will have—how much power will go to the states and how much will remain with the national government. Indeed, we may want a fluid system in which the balance of power varies from one kind of policy to another.

The balance of power between states and nation has become a very hot issue in recent years, with most Republicans favoring increasing the power of state governments and Democrats favoring retention of national government programs and standards. The current trend has been toward strengthening state governments' power. President Clinton, former governor of the state of Arkansas and a Democrat, agreed that federalism needed to be reoriented, saying once that he enthusiastically supported "the inexorable move to push more basic jobs of the public sector back to the state level."[9] Republicans in Congress and Clinton joined together to pass two pieces of legislation that significantly changed the course of federalism. The first restricted the use of "unfunded mandates" (to be discussed shortly). The second was the welfare reform discussed in the opening pages of this chapter.

The U.S. Supreme Court has also shown signs of shifting power from the national to the state governments, giving new force to the Tenth Amendment. For example, a Court majority led by Chief Justice William Rehnquist ruled that the Gun-Free School Zones Act of 1990 was unconstitutional because, in trying to ban guns from schools, the national government had exceeded its powers under the commerce clause. Dissenting, Justice Stephen Breyer called this reversal of broad federal powers "extraordinary," and Yale law professor Bruce Ackerman referred to a "constitutional moment," an epochal shift in political philosophy.[10] In 1997, the Court rejected a portion of the Brady gun control law, saying that the national government could not force states to do background checks on gun buyers. In 1999, narrow Court majorities (5–4) decided two cases in which it ruled that states could not be sued for violating federal rules and laws, basing the decision on a concept of "state sovereign immunity" that most constitutional scholars had never heard of and that considerably increased the autonomy of the states.

It is important to keep in mind that arguments about federalism do not concern just abstract theories; they affect who wins and who loses valuable benefits. People's opinions about federalism often depend on their interests, their ideologies, and the kinds of things they want government to do.

The Constitution and Shared Powers

Federalism is embodied in the U.S. Constitution in two main ways: (1) power is expressly given to the states, as well as to the national government, and (2) the states have important roles in shaping, and choosing officials for, the national government itself.

Independent State Powers

supremacy clause

The provision in Article VI of the Constitution that the Constitution itself and the laws and treaties of the United States are the supreme law of the land, taking precedence over state laws and constitutions.

Although the Constitution makes the central government supreme in certain matters, it also makes clear that the state governments have independent powers. The **supremacy clause** in Article VI states that the Constitution, laws, and treaties of the United States shall be the "supreme law of the land," but Article I, Section 8, enumerates what kinds of laws Congress has the power to pass, and the Tenth Amendment declares that the powers not delegated to the central government by the Constitution or prohibited by the Constitution to the states are "*reserved to the states* [emphasis added] respectively, or to the people." This provision is known as the **reservation clause**.

In other words, the U.S. Constitution specifically lists what the national government can do: lay taxes, regulate commerce, establish post offices, declare war, and the like, plus make laws "necessary and proper" for carrying out those powers. The Constitution then provides that all other legitimate government functions may be performed by the states, except for a few things, such as coining money or conducting foreign policy, that are forbidden by Article I, Section 10. The reservation clause is unique to the United States. Other federal systems, such as Canada's and Germany's, reserve to the national government all functions not explicitly given to the states. The Constitution is, thus, not crystal clear on the balance of powers and responsibilities between the state and national governments, leaving ample room for the meaning of federalism to change with the times.

reservation clause
The Tenth Amendment to the Constitution, reserving powers to the states or the people.

The States' Roles in National Government

Moreover, the Constitution's provisions about the formation of the national government recognize a special position for the states. The Constitution declares in Article VII that it was "done in Convention by the unanimous consent of the *states* present" (emphasis added) and provides that it would go into effect not when a majority of all Americans voted for it but when the conventions of nine *states* ratified it. Article V provides that the Constitution can be amended only when conventions in or the legislatures of three-quarters of the states ratify an amendment. Article IV, Section 3, makes clear that no states can be combined or divided into new states without the consent of the state legislatures concerned.

WEB EXPLORATION

State Constitutions

Issue: Although the constitutional organization of state governments are more alike than dissimilar, they do differ in a number of important respects.

Site: You can compare state constitutions through the "Course Documents" section of your online course. In the "Web Explorations" section for Chapter 3, click on "State Constitutions" and then open "State Constitutions." Select the constitution of your own state and those of three others from different geographical regions of the United States.

What You've Learned: How different is the government of your own state from others? Compare the four constitutions on the powers of the governor and on taxation. Are there features of the constitutions of the other states that you prefer to those of your own state? Why?

LongmanParticipate

participation
Explore Your State Constitution

HINT: Some states are much more distrustful than others of executive power and of the legislature's power to tax its citizens.

The states play a central role in the election of the president who is selected for office not by popular vote but by the electoral college vote, assembled on a state-by-state basis. In the end, the disputed 2000 presidential election outcome depended on which candidate would win Florida's 25 electoral votes. Here election officials conduct a hand recount of ballots in Palm Beach County.

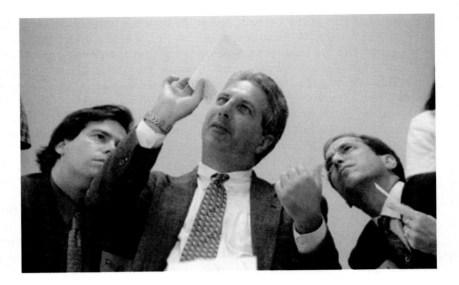

Thus, the state governments have charge of ratifying and amending the Constitution, and the states control their own boundaries.

The Constitution also provides special roles for the states in the selection of national government officials. The states decide who can vote for members of the U.S. House of Representatives by deciding who votes for their own legislatures (Article I, Section 2). Each state is given two senators, who cannot be taken away even by constitutional amendment (Article V), and who until 1913 were chosen by the state legislatures rather than by the voters (Article I, Section 3; altered by the Seventeenth Amendment). And the states play a key part in the complicated electoral college system of choosing a president in which each state has votes equal to the number of its senators and representatives combined, with the president elected by a majority of *electoral* votes, not a majority of popular votes (Article II, Section 1).

Relations Among the States

Our federal system includes a few national provisions (in Article IV of the Constitution) that regulate relations among the states. For example, each state is required to give "full faith and credit" to the public acts, records, and judicial proceedings of every other state. This means, among other things, that contracts signed by individuals or companies in one state must be honored by officials in other states and that decisions by the courts of one state must be recognized by the others.

Under Article IV, moreover, the citizens of each state are entitled to all the "privileges and immunities" of the citizens in the several states. That means that whatever citizenship rights a person has in one state hold in the other states as well. This raises some intriguing questions. One of the most explosive is the following: if a state makes same-sex marriage legal, does the married status of the couple hold if they move to another state? In other words, do all the states have to recognize same-sex marriages if one state makes them legal? After it appeared that the state of Hawaii might approve same-sex marriages in the mid-1990s (Hawaii voters and its state legislature and high court, however, subsequently rejected this possibility), 28 states passed laws to immunize themselves against such a fundamental transformation in marriage law. In 2000, after its Supreme Court ruled that it must either legalize same-sex marriage or fully equalize state benefits to homosexual and hetero-sexual couples, the Vermont legislature equalized benefits. We can see, then, that the nature of American federalism is not set in stone in the Constitution but is strongly influenced by the politics and public sentiment of the times.

Nevertheless, the Constitution remains the starting point for understanding American federalism. Its provisions are summarized in Table 3.1.

The Evolution of Federalism

It took a long time after the adoption of the Constitution for the present federal system to emerge. There were ebbs and flows in the relative power of the states and the federal government. Eventually, however, the national government gained ground. This increase in its power partly reflected trends discussed in Chapter 4: increased industrialization, economic growth, and increasing involvement abroad. In addition, bitter and divisive conflicts over a series of issues, especially slavery, race, and regional economic interests, changed the shape of American federalism, moving us toward the stronger, more unified national government that we have today. Recently, however, there has been a trend toward enhanced power and responsibility in the states.

Table 3.1 ● Constitutional Underpinnings of Federalism

Provisions	Where to Find Them in the Constitution	What They Mean
Supremacy of the national government in its own sphere	Supremacy clause: Article VI	The supremacy clause establishes that federal laws take precedence over state laws.
Limitations on national government powers and reservation of powers to the states	Enumerated national powers: Article I, Section 8 Limits on national powers: Article I, Section 9; Article IV, Section 3; Eleventh Amendment Bill of Rights: First through Tenth Amendments Reservation clause: Tenth Amendment	The powers of the federal government are laid out specifically in the Constitution, as are strict limitations on the power of the federal government. Powers not specifically spelled out are reserved to the states or the people.
Limitations on state powers	Original restrictions: Article I, Section 10 Civil War amendments: Thirteenth through Fifteenth Amendments	The Constitution places strict limitations on the power of the states in particular areas.
State role in national government	Ratification of Constitution: Article VII Amendment of Constitution: Article V Election of representatives: Article I, Section 2 and Section 4 Two senators from each state: Article I, Section 3 No deprivation of state suffrage in Senate: Article V Choice of senators: Article I, Section 3 (however, see Seventeenth Amendment) Election of president: Article II, Section 1 (however, see Twelfth Amendment)	The states' role in national affairs is clearly laid out. Rules for voting and electing representatives, senators, and the president are defined so that state governments play a part.
Regulation of relations among states	Full faith and credit: Article IV, Section 1 Privileges and immunities: Article IV, Section 2	Constitutional rules ensure that the states must respect each other's legal actions

Federalism Before the Civil War

In the late 1790s, during the administration of John Adams, Thomas Jefferson's Republicans deeply resented the Alien and Sedition Acts, which the Federalists used to punish political dissent. The Virginia and Kentucky Resolutions (secretly authored by Madison and Jefferson) declared that the states did not have to obey unconstitutional national laws, leaving it up to the states to decide what was unconstitutional. In this case, the Republicans, representing the more agricultural South, were advocating states' rights against a national government run by the more merchant-oriented Federalists of the Northeast. About a decade later, the merchants of New England used the southerners' own arguments to oppose President Madison's War of 1812 against Britain, which they felt interfered with their trade. Neither of these efforts at **nullification** prevailed, however. Nor did the later attempt by John C. Calhoun and other southern agriculturalists to declare null and void the "tariff of abominations," the high 1833 tariff that raised the prices of imports and hurt southern agricultural exports.

> **nullification**
> An attempt by states to declare national laws or actions null and void.

The Marshall Court   One crucial question about federalism in the early years of the United States concerned who, if anyone, would enforce the supremacy clause. Who would make sure that the U.S. laws and Constitution were actually the "supreme law of the land," controlling state laws? The answer turned out to be the U.S. Supreme Court, but this answer emerged only gradually and haltingly as the Court established its power within the federal system.

Only after the strong-willed and subtle John Marshall became chief justice and, in 1803, established the Supreme Court's authority to declare *national* laws unconstitutional did the Supreme Court turn to the question of national power over the states. In *Fletcher* v. *Peck* (1810), it established the power of judicial review over the states, holding a state law unconstitutional under the U.S. Constitution.[11] Chief Justice Marshall cleverly avoided explicit

WEB EXPLORATION

Regional Variation and Federalism

Issue: Federalism seems most appropriate where there is substantial variation among regions of a nation.

Site: You can examine how much variation exists in the United States by going to the *Statistical Abstracts of the United States* through the "Course Documents" section of your online course. In the "Web Explorations" section for Chapter 3, click on "Regional Variation and Federalism," open "states," and then select "state rankings."

What You've Learned: Compare your own state with three or four others from different geographical regions of the United States on issues such as education, income, population growth, immigration, crime, and the like. Given the profile of your state compared with others, are the differences great enough to support the need for greater autonomy for your state government, or would national rule making and policies make more sense?

HINT: If the differences are significant, from your point of view, federalism would make a lot of sense. Religious differences seem especially important to many people.

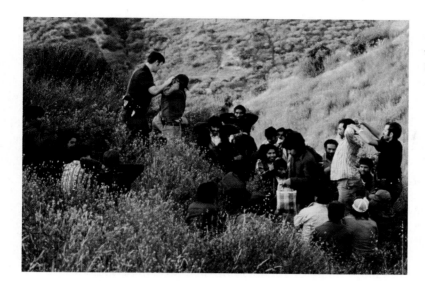

How to control illegal immigration across the U.S.–Mexican border, and what to do about those who make it across, have become contentious issues between several states and the federal government.

discussion of the Court's power of judicial review over state laws. He simply took it for granted and used it.

Afterward, in 1816, the Supreme Court further solidified its position in relation to the states by explicitly upholding as constitutional the Court's use of a "writ of error" to review (and overturn) state court decisions that denied claims made under the Constitution or laws or treaties of the United States. In language important to the interpretation of federalism, Justice Joseph Story declared that the Constitution was the creation of "the people of the United States," not of the individual states, and that the people could—and did—decide to modify state sovereignty.[12]

The Supreme Court also provided crucial legal justification for the expansion of national government power in the important case of *McCulloch* v. *Maryland* (1819). The *McCulloch* case arose because the state of Maryland had imposed a tax on notes issued by the Bank of the United States, which had been incorporated by Congress in 1816. The U.S. government argued that such a tax on a federal entity was invalid. Maryland replied that the incorporation of the bank had been unconstitutional, exceeding the powers of Congress, and that in any case, the states could tax whatever they wanted to within their own borders. But Chief Justice Marshall upheld the constitutionality of the bank's incorporation and its immunity from taxation, and he made a major statement justifying extensive national authority.[13]

In the Court's decision, Marshall declared that the Constitution emanated from the sovereign people. The people had made their national government supreme over all rivals within the sphere of its powers, and those powers must be construed generously if they were to be sufficient for the "various crises" of the age to come. Congress had the power to incorporate the bank under the clause of Article I, Section 8, authorizing Congress to make all laws "necessary and proper" for carrying into execution its named powers. Moreover, Maryland's tax was invalid because "the power to tax involves the power to destroy," which would defeat the national government's supremacy within its sphere. Justice Marshall's broad reading of the **necessary and proper clause** (also known as the *elastic clause*) laid the foundation for an expansion of what the national government could do in the years ahead. He made it clear that states would not be allowed to interfere.

necessary and proper clause
Article I, Section 8, of the Constitution, also known as the *elastic clause*; gives Congress the authority to make whatever laws are necessary and proper to carry out its enumerated responsibilities.

Limiting and Preempting the States

contract clause

The portion of Article I, Section 10, of the Constitution that prohibits states from passing any law "impairing the obligation of contracts."

preemption

Exclusion of the states from actions that might interfere with federal legislation.

Limiting and Preempting the States   At times during the nineteenth century, the Supreme Court limited state government actions based on the Constitution itself, without any legislative action by Congress. (For example, it ruled that the **contract clause** of Article I, Section 10, prevented New Hampshire from changing the Dartmouth College charter.) At other times, the Court ruled that provisions of the U.S. Constitution might actually *exclude* the states from acting in certain areas where they might interfere with federal legislation. This latter doctrine of **preemption**, that when the national government has acted on a certain subject, the states cannot do so, remains with us still.

The Slavery Issue   In the second decade of the nineteenth century, the issue of slavery in the western territories began to dominate disputes about the nature of federalism. As new, nonslave states were settled and sought to join the Union, white southerners feared that their political power in Washington, D.C. (especially in the Senate)—and therefore their ability to protect their own slave system—was slipping away.

The Missouri Compromise of 1820 established an equal number of slave and free states and banned slavery in the territories above a line running westward to the Rockies from Missouri's southern border. But the acquisition of vast new territories in the Southwest through the Mexican War reopened the question of whether new states would be slave or free. The Compromise of 1850 admitted California as a free state and temporarily balanced matters (in white southerners' eyes) by enacting the Fugitive Slave Act, which compelled

The Fugitive Slave Act of 1850, which required that runaway slaves be captured and returned to their owners in the South, inflamed tensions between North and South and helped lead to the greatest crisis of U.S. federalism: the Civil War. This poster was made by abolitionist opponents of the act.

private citizens in the North to help return runaway slaves—legislation that many northerners bitterly resented. The 1854 decision to organize Kansas and Nebraska as territories and let them decide for themselves whether to become slave or free states (even though they were above the Missouri Compromise line and therefore supposed to be free) led to violence between pro- and anti-slavery forces in "bleeding Kansas."

In 1860, the northern and southern wings of the Democratic party split apart over the slavery issue. The old Whig party was destroyed by the issue, and the candidate of the newly formed Republican party, Abraham Lincoln (who opposed slavery in the western territories), was elected president. South Carolina seceded from the Union, soon followed by the other six states of the Deep South, which created the Confederate States of America. When President Lincoln decided to relieve the besieged U.S. garrison at Fort Sumter, South Carolina, the Civil War (the "War Between the States") began.

The Civil War and the Expansion of National Power

The Civil War had profound effects on the relationships between the states and the national government.

Indissoluble Union   The complete northern victory and unconditional southern surrender in the Civil War decisively established that the Union was indissoluble; states could not withdraw or secede. Hardly any American now questions the permanence of the Union, although it is interesting to compare this attitude with our present-day support for the right of new countries to secede from existing countries, as Croatia and Bosnia did from Yugoslavia.

Constitutional Amendments   The Civil War also resulted in constitutional changes that subordinated the states to certain new national standards, enforced by the central government. The Thirteenth Amendment abolished slavery, and the Fifteenth gave former male slaves a constitutional right to vote. (This right was enforced by the national government for a short time after the Civil War; it was then widely ignored until the 1965 Voting Rights Act.)

The Fourteenth Amendment (1868) included broad language going well beyond the slave issue: it declared that *no state* shall "deprive any person of life, liberty, or property, without due process of law; nor deny to any person within its jurisdiction the equal protection of the laws." The **due process clause** eventually became the vehicle by which the Supreme Court ruled that many civil liberties in the Bill of Rights, which originally protected people only against the national government, also provided protections against the states. And the **equal protection clause** was eventually made the foundation for protecting the rights of blacks, women, and other categories of people against discrimination by state or local governments. (These matters are discussed in Chapters 15 and 16.)

Emergency Powers   Still another effect of the Civil War was to set precedents for an enormous expansion of the federal government's power, especially in wartime. President Lincoln exerted extraordinary emergency powers, spending government money without congressional authorization, suspending the writ of habeas corpus (the right of prisoners to demand that reasons be given for their imprisonment) in war zones, and freeing slaves in occupied southern territories. The huge military and industrial effort of waging the war established patterns for future national government action of many sorts.

due process clause

The section of the Fourteenth Amendment that prohibits states from depriving anyone of life, liberty, or property "without due process of law," a guarantee against arbitrary or unfair government action.

equal protection clause

The section of the Fourteenth Amendment that provides equal protection of the laws to all citizens.

Expanded National Activity Since the Civil War

Since the Civil War, the activities of the national government have expanded greatly, so that they now touch on almost every aspect of daily life and are thoroughly entangled with state government activities. During the late nineteenth century, the national government was increasingly active in administering western lands, subsidizing economic development (granting railroads enormous tracts of land along their transcontinental lines), helping farmers, and beginning to regulate business, particularly through the Interstate Commerce Act of 1887 and the Sherman Antitrust Act of 1890. The national government became still more active with Woodrow Wilson's New Freedom domestic legislation in 1913 and 1914, and with the great economic and military effort of World War I.

The New Deal and World War II   Still more important, however, was Franklin Roosevelt's New Deal of the 1930s. In response to the Great Depression, the New Deal created many new national regulatory agencies to supervise various aspects of business, including communications (the Federal Communications Commission, or FCC), airlines (the Civil Aeronautics Board, or CAB), financial markets (the Securities and Exchange Commission, or SEC), utilities (the Federal Power Commission, or FPC), and labor-management relations (the National Labor Relations Board, or NLRB). The New Deal also brought national government spending in such areas as welfare and relief, which had previously been reserved almost entirely to the states, and established the Social Security pension system. National government spending on domestic matters continued to grow in subsequent decades, particularly during and after Lyndon Johnson's Great Society of the 1960s.

Wars were also crucial in the expansion of national government power. The federal government did not spend as much as the states and localities combined until two years after World War I had started and then during World War II, which involved a total economic and military mobilization to fight Germany and Japan.

Ever since World War II, the federal government has spent nearly twice as much per year as all of the states and localities put together, much of the money going in direct payments to individuals (through such items as Social Security benefits). Increasingly, though, the states—and especially local governments—have had many more civilian employees, so there is some ambiguity about which level of government is actually "bigger."[14] (See Figure 3.2)

The Supreme Court's Role   For several decades, beginning in the late nineteenth century, the U.S. Supreme Court resisted the growth in national government power to regulate business. In 1895, for example, it said that the Sherman Antitrust Act could not forbid monopolies in manufacturing, since manufacturing affected interstate commerce only "indirectly." In 1918, the Court struck down as unconstitutional a national law regulating child labor. During the 1930s, the Supreme Court declared unconstitutional such important New Deal measures as the National Recovery Act and the Agricultural Adjustment Act.[15]

After 1937, perhaps chastened by President Roosevelt's attempt to enlarge the Supreme Court and appoint more friendly justices, the Court became a nationalizing force, immediately upholding essential elements of the New Deal, including the Social Security Act and the National Labor Relations Act. Since that time, and until quite recently, the Court has upheld virtually every piece of national legislation that has come before it.

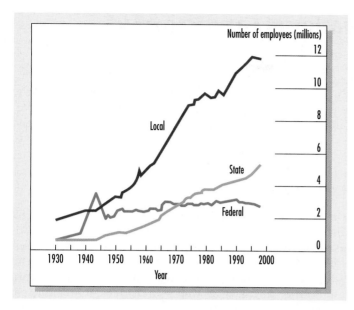

Figure 3.2 ● **Number of Government Employees, by Jurisdiction**

The federal (national) government is now much larger than all the state and local governments put together in terms of the money it spends, but it is much smaller than local government in terms of number of employees.

Sources: U.S. Department of Labor. Bureau of Labor Statistics; U.S. Bureau of the Census.

An important example is the Civil Rights Act of 1964, which rests on a very broad interpretation of the Constitution's commerce clause. In the 1964 act, the national government asserted a power to forbid discrimination at lunch counters and other public accommodations on the grounds that they are engaged in interstate commerce: they serve food imported from out of state. State economies are so closely tied to each other that by this standard, practically every economic transaction everywhere affects interstate commerce and is therefore subject to national legislative power. However, the Court may be rethinking its interpretation of the commerce clause as the basis for a broad grant of national power. In its 1995 decision overturning gun control around schools, a majority of the Court ruled that portions of the Brady bill represented too broad a use of the commerce power. The Court used similar language in 2000 when it invalidated part of the Violence Against Women Act and in 2001 when it did the same to the Americans with Disabilities Act.

"Marble Cake"   Today's federalism is very different from what it was in the 1790s or early 1800s. One major difference is that the national government is dominant in many policy areas; it calls many shots for the states. (Only very recently has some of this dominance been challenged.) Another difference is that state and national government powers and activities have become deeply intertwined and entangled. An old, simple metaphor for federalism was a "layer cake": a system of **dual federalism** in which state and national powers were neatly divided into separate layers. If we stay with bakery images, a much more accurate metaphor for today's federalism is a "marble cake": a **cooperative federalism** in which elements of national and state influence swirl around each other, without any clear boundaries.[16] Much of this intertwining is due to financial links among the national and state governments.

LongmanParticipate

CourseCompass

timeline
**Federalism
over Time**

dual federalism

Federalism in which the powers of the states and the national government are neatly separated like the sections of a layer cake.

cooperative federalism

Federalism in which the powers of the states and the national government are intertwined like the swirls in a marble cake.

The Rise of National Grants-in-Aid to the States

One of the most important elements in modern American federalism is the grant of money from the national government to state and local governments, which has been used to increase national government influence over what the states and localities do. These grants have grown from small beginnings to form a substantial part of government budgets.

Origin and Growth of Grants

National government grants to the states began at least as early as the 1787 Northwest Ordinance. The U.S. government granted land for government buildings, schools, and colleges in the Northwest Territory and imposed various regulations, such as forbidding the importation of any new slaves. During the early nineteenth century, the national government provided some land grants to the states for roads, canals, and railroads, as well as a little cash for militias; after 1862, it helped establish agricultural colleges.

Some small cash-grant programs were begun around 1900 for agriculture, vocational education, and highways. At the beginning of the twentieth century, annual national grants to the states totaled only some $6 million; they grew to about $100 million in the early 1920s and to nearly $300 million toward the end of the 1930s.[17]

However, it was during the 1950s, 1960s, and 1970s, under both Republican and Democratic administrations, that by far the biggest growth occurred. Such programs as President Dwight Eisenhower's interstate highway system and President Lyndon Johnson's Great Society poured money into the states.[18] (See Figure 3.3.)

WEB EXPLORATION

State-National Balance of Payments

Issue: Citizens in the states pay taxes to the federal government, and states receive back federal grants-in-aid to support a range of programs. Some states fare better in this process than others.

Site: Visit the "Course Documents" section of your online course. In the "Web Explorations" section for Chapter 3, click on "State-National Balance of Payments" and then open "taxes." Select the "Balance of Payments," and look at state rankings as well as the profile of your own state.

What You've Learned: Which states fare best in the exchange of funds between the states and the federal government? How does your own state fare? Why do you suppose that some states do better than others?

HINT: Relatively speaking, the poorest states get the most, meaning that a rough sort of regional redistribution is going on.

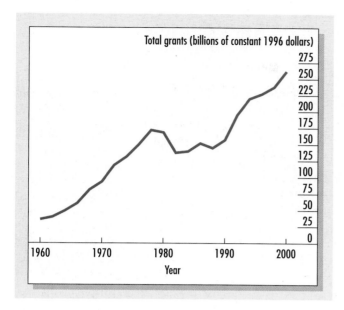

Figure 3.3 ● The Growth of Federal Grants-in-Aid

Federal grants-in-aid to state and local governments grew sharply during the 1960s and peaked at the end of the 1970s. They then declined in the early 1980s but increased again in the 1990s.

Source: Budget of the United States, Fiscal Year 2001, Historical Table.

Reasons for Grants

National grant money to the states increased because Congress sought to deal with many nationwide problems—especially interstate highways, poverty, crime, and pollution—by setting policy at the national level and providing money from national tax revenues while having state and local officials carry out the policies. There were three main reasons for doing things this way.

Externalities   First, the states refused to take responsibility on their own for many of these problems, mainly because of **spillover effects**, sometimes called *externalities,* affecting people outside their borders. The states would not spend their own money if much of the benefit would go to people elsewhere. For example, Wisconsin did not want to pay to clean up its pollution of Lake Michigan when a cleanup would mostly benefit Chicago, Illinois. Also, states were reluctant to spend money to fight poverty if that spending would raise taxes, scare away business investment, and perhaps attract more poor people. To many people, spillovers made national government involvement seem necessary.

spillover effects

Policy effects that go outside the boundaries of the governmental unit making the policy.

Abundant National Government Resources   Second, in the 1960s, when many of these programs were begun, national government tax revenues were abundant. Moreover, revenues came mostly from the progressive federal income tax, meaning that people with high incomes paid a higher percentage of what they earned than people with low incomes did. The federal income tax seemed to many an especially appropriate source of money for combating poverty.

Local Provision   Third, these new programs involved complicated goods and services that required management at the state and local levels. The new programs involved the building of new facilities (such as clinics and sewage treatment plants) and the development of new programs (such as preschool

Lyndon Johnson visits Job Corps sites. The Job Corps was part of Johnson's Great Society of the 1960s, which relied heavily on categorical grants to state and local governments.

education, special education, and job training) that the federal government could not efficiently oversee. Even if the national government was needed to provide money and direction, state and local officials on the scene seemed to be the appropriate people to actually carry out the programs.

Categorical Grants

categorical grants

Federal aid to states and localities clearly specifying what the money can be used for.

Many of the new programs were established through **categorical grants**, which give the states money but clearly specify the category of activity for which the money has to be spent and often define rather precisely how the program should work. For example, the Medicaid program of 1965 and the Clean Air Act of 1970 provided large amounts of money along with specific instructions on how to use it.

As the new programs were developed and enacted, there was much talk about a new system of "cooperative" federalism. Soon, however, conflicts between the national and the state governments emerged. In some cases, when national rules and guidelines were vague, state and local governments used the money for purposes different from those Congress intended. When the rules were tightened up, some state and local governments complained about "red tape." And if state and local governments were bypassed, they complained that their authority had been undermined.

The New Federalism: Block Grants and Revenue Sharing

block grants

Federal grants to the states to be used for general activities.

general revenue sharing

Federal aid to the states without any conditions on how the money is spent.

The Republican Nixon and Ford administrations eased national control, first instituting **block grants** (which give money for more general purposes and with fewer rules than categorical grant programs), then **general revenue sharing**, which distributed money to the states with no federal controls at all. President Nixon spoke of a "New Federalism" and pushed to increase these kinds of grants with few strings attached. They often provided money under an automatic formula related to the statistical characteristics of each state or locality, such as the number of needy residents, the total size of the population, or the average income level.

The states depend on federal aid to help them take care of the homeless. But when 1990 census takers failed to count a large number of homeless people, cities received less money in national grants.

Disputes frequently arise when these formulas benefit one state or region rather than another. Because statistical counts by the census affect how much money the states and localities get, census counts themselves have become the subject of political conflict. Illinois, New York, and Chicago sued the Census Bureau for allegedly undercounting their populations, especially the urban poor, in the 1990 census.

Block grants—and especially revenue sharing—reached a peak at the end of the 1970s, when they constituted about one-quarter of the total grants-in-aid. But then they fell out of favor. Increasing numbers of strings were attached to the money, and general revenue sharing was completely ended in 1987.

One reason for the decline in block grants and revenue sharing was that the strongest backers of the grant programs all tended to distrust state and local governments. The advocates of antipoverty and environmental programs, for example, feared that special interests at the local level would divert money away from its original purposes. So the program backers insisted that the national government impose tight regulations on how the money could be spent.

Thus, the Democrats in Congress defeated most of President Reagan's 1981 effort to consolidate 57 programs into a few block grants. So many restrictions were imposed that the nine new block grants resembled categorical grants. Similar struggles continued in the 1990s as Democrats resisted Republican efforts to transform categorical programs like Medicaid into block grants.

The Slowdown in National Money

At the same time that block grants were falling out of favor in the late 1970s and early 1980s, the flow of federal money to state and local governments began to decline (see Figure 3.3). A number of factors were at work. First, economic problems in the 1970s and 1980s lowered tax receipts and helped contribute to budget deficits. Second, conservative think tanks helped raise public doubts about "big government" in Washington,[19] and its purported inability to run programs that worked.[20] Third and finally, a conservative shift took place in Washington after Ronald Reagan was elected president, and Republicans won a majority in the Senate in the 1980 elections.

During the 1990s, grants-in-aid rose once again (see Figure 3.3). But state populations and state needs were growing, too, and faster than federal

"Sorry, but all my power's been turned back to the states."

By Lorenz; © The New Yorker Magazine, Inc.

government grants. The national government's contribution, as a proportion of the nation's economy, has not returned to the old peak of 3.6 percent of GDP; the figure settled at just 3.0 percent in the mid-1990s.

The Balance of Power and Control

Most contemporary conflicts about federalism concern not just money but also control. The national government exerts a strong influence over many state-administered programs, using a variety of different means, such as mandates and conditions on aid.

Mandates

mandate

A formal order from the national government that the states carry out certain policies.

The government in Washington, D.C., often imposes a **mandate**, or demand, that the states carry out certain policies even when little or no national government aid is offered. (An "unfunded" mandate involves no aid at all, or less aid than compliance will cost.) Mandates have been especially important in the areas of civil rights and the environment. Most civil rights policies flow from the equal protection clause of the Fourteenth Amendment to the U.S. Constitution or from national legislation that imposes uniform national standards. Most environmental regulations also come from the national government, since problems of dirty air, polluted water, and acid rain spill across state boundaries. Many civil rights and environmental regulations, therefore, are enforced by the federal courts.

The courts have, for example, mandated expensive reforms of overcrowded state prisons, most notably in Texas. National legislation and regulations have required state governments to provide costly special facilities for the disabled, to set up environmental protection agencies, and to limit the kinds and amounts of pollutants that can be discharged. The states often complain bitterly about federal mandates that require state spending without providing the money.

Cutting back on these "unfunded mandates" was one of the main promises in the Republicans' 1994 Contract with America.[21] The congressional

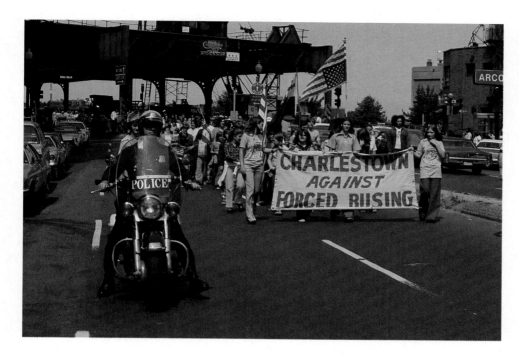

Opposition to federal court-ordered busing—like this demonstration in Charlestown, Massachusetts—formed one element in a conservative turn in U.S. politics at the end of the 1970s.

Republicans delivered on their promise early in 1995 with a bill that had bipartisan support in Congress and that President Clinton signed into law. Because it does not apply to past mandates, however, and because it does not ban unfunded mandates but only regulates them (requiring cost-benefit analyses, for example), it is not yet clear how much effect the legislation will have.

Conditions on Aid

As we have seen, many categorical grant-in-aid programs require that the states spend federal money only in certain restricted ways. Increasingly, even general block grants have carried **conditions**. In theory, these conditions are "voluntary" because the states could refuse to accept the aid. But in practice, there is no clear line between incentives and coercion. Because the states cannot generally afford to give up federal money, they have to accept the conditions.

conditions

Provisions in federal assistance requiring that state and local governments follow certain policies in order to obtain federal funds.

Some of the most important provisions of the 1964 Civil Rights Act, for example, are those that declare that no federal aid of any kind can be used in ways that discriminate against people on grounds of race, gender, religion, or national origin. Thus, the enormous program of national aid for elementary and secondary education, which began in 1965, became a powerful lever for forcing schools to desegregate.

The national government uses its money to influence many diverse kinds of policies. During the energy crisis of the 1970s, all states were required to impose a 55-mile-per-hour speed limit or lose a portion of their highway assistance funds. All states did so (the requirement was finally repealed in 1995). Similarly, in 1984, all states were required to set a minimum drinking age of 21 or have their highway aid cut by 15 percent.

Often the national government entirely preempts state government action in some policy area—that is, it sets up laws and standards that override any state rules—but relies on state enforcement of the national standards. Examples include clean air standards, occupational health and safety rules, and environmental restrictions on surface mining.

Resurgence of the States

A number of indicators demonstrate that the states are becoming more important in the American federal system. First, the states account for an ever-increasing share of public spending in the United States, suggesting that they are becoming more active in providing the wide range of government services the public demands (see Figure 3.4). Second, the states account for an ever-increasing share of public employees in the United States; while state (and local) government employment is growing, federal government employment is shrinking (see Figure 3.2), suggesting again that government service delivery is shifting to the states. Moreover, according to many scholars and political observers, state governments are beginning to capture a rising share of the talented people who enter government service, both in elected office and in state bureaucracies.[22] This would not be happening unless the states were becoming an increasingly important location for policy innovations.

Some have called these developments the "new New Federalism" or "New Federalism II" (recall that Nixon's was the first). What is behind the new vitality of the states within American federalism is the growing national consensus on the virtues of **devolution**. Public opinion surveys, for example, show that a substantial majority of Americans believes that state governments are more effective and more trustworthy than the government in Washington and more likely to be responsive to the people. And Americans say they want state governments to do more and the federal government to do less.[23]

The emerging consensus favoring devolution is also evident in the words and actions of America's political leaders. The Supreme Court, we have seen, has overruled a number of recent federal actions and laws on the ground that the federal government has exceeded its constitutional powers, reversing over half a century of decisions favoring an increased federal government role. President Clinton was also an enthusiastic devotee of devolution as well, freely granting waivers from federal regulations to the states for experimenting with new forms of welfare, boasting of cuts in federal government employment, and touting the benefits of state government. And the Republican majority in the 104th Congress, working with President Clinton (but few from his party), passed legislation restricting "unfunded mandates" and transferring welfare responsibility to the states.

devolution

The delegation of power by the central government to state or local bodies.

LongmanParticipate

CourseCompass

visual literacy
Federalism and Regulations

Defying the expectations of many, Jesse Ventura of Minnesota became a very energetic governor. Here he is on a visit to Japan promoting trade for his state. As the states become more important in national affairs, successful governors are discovering that they must pay attention to a wider range of issues and constituencies than in the past.

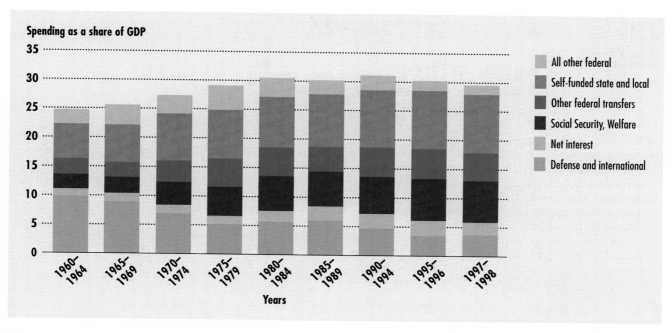

Spending as a share of GDP

Legend:
- All other federal
- Self-funded state and local
- Other federal transfers
- Social Security, Welfare
- Net interest
- Defense and international

Years

Figure 3.4 ● **U.S. Public Spending, 1960–1998**

A steadily increasing share of U.S. public spending is accounted for by state and local governments out of their own revenues. Most of the increase in government spending in recent years has been by the states, suggesting their increasingly important role in our federal system.

Source: Office of Management and Budget, Fiscal 2000 Budget, Historical Table 15.5.

Perhaps not surprisingly, as states take on more responsibilities, state capital politics have begun to take on some of the characteristics of politics in Washington, D.C. Party electoral competition has become more intense, legislative affairs have become more partisan, interest group presence has increased, and campaign contributions have escalated.[24]

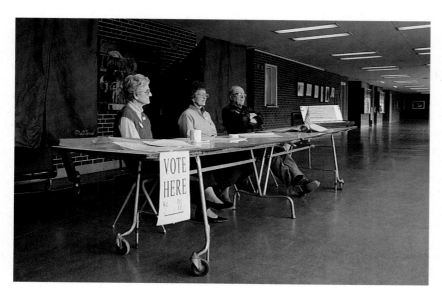

Low voting turnout in state and local elections may mean that a shift of power and responsibility from the federal level to the state level will decrease the quality of American democracy.

HOW DEMOCRATIC ARE WE?

PROPOSITION: Federalism undermines democracy by getting in the way of majority rule and political equality.

AGREE: Federalism adds complexity to policy-making and makes it difficult for citizens to know which elected leaders to hold responsible for government actions. Also, citizens are much less informed about what goes on in state governments where many important policies are made. In state-level politics, popular participation tends to be lower, politics tends to be less visible, and interest groups may have an easier time getting their way. Because the well-organized and the affluent have extra influence, political equality is impaired.

DISAGREE: Federalism promotes popular democracy rather than undermining it. It does so by allowing a majority of citizens in each state to exercise control over a range of policies that directly affect them. This is especially important in a country where the populations of the states vary as widely as they do. With diverse populations, with their diverse needs and interests, federalism allows for diverse policies.

THE AUTHORS: On balance, federalism has served the intentions of the framers by toning down the influence of democracy in determining what the national government does, while maintaining popular consent. There are four ways that federalism constrains democracy. First, many policy areas (such as education) are mainly the responsibility of the states, where policymakers are insulated from national majorities. Second, small-population states play a decisive role in the constitutional amending process. Third, small and large states have equal representation in the Senate, meaning that senators representing a minority of the population can block actions favored by senators representing the majority. Fourth and finally, state politics are much less visible to the public and are especially vulnerable to the influence of special interests. This may well be changing, however; as state governments do more, the media and the public are more likely in the future to pay closer attention.

LongmanParticipate

CourseCompass

simulation
**You Are
a Federal Judge**

Summary

Federalism, a system under which political powers are divided between the state and national governments, is a key structural aspect of American politics. Federalism is most frequently found in large, diverse countries. Arguments in favor of federalism have to do with diversity of needs, closeness to the people, experimentation, and innovation. Arguments against federalism involve national standards, popular control, and needs for uniformity.

The U.S. Constitution specifies the powers of the national government and reserves all others (except a few that are specifically forbidden) to the states. The Constitution also provides special roles for the states in adopting and amending the Constitution and in choosing national officials. The precise balance of federalism has evolved over time, the national government gaining ground as a result of U.S. Supreme Court decisions, the Civil War, expanding national domestic programs, and two world wars.

Contemporary federalism involves complex "marble cake" relations among the national and state governments, in which federal grants-in-aid play an important part. Grants for many purposes grew rapidly but have now slowed down. The national government also influences or controls many state policies through mandates and through conditions placed on aid. The recent trend has been toward a substantial devolution of powers and responsibilities to the states. Federalism has mixed implications for democracy.

Suggestions for Further Reading

Donahue, John D. *Disunited States.* New York: Basic Books, 1997.
  Examines the new vitality of the states in the federal system and raises questions about the costs and benefits of the transformation.

Grodzins, Morton. *The American System.* New Brunswick, NJ: Transaction Books, 1983.
  A classic work that describes and approves of a complex intermingling of national, state, and local government functions.

Hero, Rodney E. *Faces of Inequality: Social Diversity in American Politics.* New York: Oxford University Press, 1998.
  An impressive argument with strong empirical evidence that the racial composition of states matters for patterns of state politics and patterns.

Peterson, Paul E. *The Price of Federalism.* Washington, D.C.: Brookings Institution, 1995.
  Describes modern federalism and argues that the national government is best at redistributive programs, while the states and localities are best at economic development.

Riker, William H. *The Development of American Federalism.* Boston: Kluwer Academic, 1987.
  An influential discussion of what American federalism is and how it came about.

Walker, David B. *The Rebirth of Federalism,* 2nd ed. New York: Chatham House/Seven Bridges Press, 2000.
  Examination of the revitalization of the states and why it has happened.

Internet Sources

Assessing the New Federalism   **http://newfederalism.urban.org/**
  News, essays, and research on the New Federalism and devolution.

National Center for State Courts   **www.ncsc.dni.us/**
  Links to the home pages of the court systems of each of the states.

National Conference of State Legislatures   **http://www.ncsl.org/**
  Information about state governments and federal relations, including the distribution of federal revenues and expenditures in the states.

Publius   **http://www.lafayette.edu/publius/annual.html**
  Home page of the leading academic journal on federalism.

State Constitutions   **www.findlaw.com/**
  A site where the constitutions of all the states may be found.

U.S. Federalism Site   **www.min.net/~kala/fed/**
  As complete a site as one might wish for on the history, philosophy, law, and operation of federalism in the United States.

Notes

1. "Michigan's Welfare System: Praise amid Warning Signs," *New York Times* (October 24, 1995), pp. 1, 12; "Steps Taken on Michigan Welfare," *New York Times* (November 1, 1995), p. 11.

2. Virginia Ellis, "Welfare Reform," *Los Angeles Times* (August 22, 1997), p. 1. We examine the effects of welfare reform on the poor in Chapter 17.

3. William H. Riker, *The Development of American Federalism* (Boston: Kluwer Academic, 1987), pp. 56–60.

4. Rodney Hero, *Faces of Inequality: Social Diversity in American Politics* (New York: Oxford University Press, 1998).

5. William H. Riker, *Federalism: Origin, Operation, Significance* (Boston: Little, Brown, 1964), ch. 6.

6. Quoted in Robert Jay Dilger, ed., *American Intergovernmental Relations Today* (Englewood Cliffs, NJ: Prentice Hall, 1986), p. 188.

7. Jack Walker, "The Diffusion of Innovations among the American States," *American Political Science Review,* 63 (1969), p. 883.

8. Paul E. Peterson, *City Limits* (Chicago: University of Chicago Press, 1981); Paul E. Peterson, *The Price of Federalism* (Washington, D.C.: Brookings Institution, 1995).

9. John D. Donahue, *Disunited States* (New York: Basic Books, 1997), p. 3.

10. "A Gun Ban Is Shot Down," *Time* (May 8, 1995), p. 85.

11. Ibid., pp. 31–34.

12. *Martin* v. *Hunter's Lessee* (1816); see also ibid., pp. 39–42.

13. Robert G. McCloskey, *American Supreme Court,* 2nd ed., ed. Sanford Levinsonn (Chicago: University of Chicago Press, 1994), pp. 43–45.

14. Harold Stanley and Richard Niemi, *Vital Statistics on American Politics,* 4th ed. (Washington, D.C.: CQ Press, 1994), pp. 317, 334.

15. McCloskey, *American Supreme Court,* pp. 97–100, 111–112.

16. Morton Grodzins, *The American System* (New Brunswick, NJ: Transaction Books, 1983).

17. David B. Walker, *Toward a Functioning Federalism* (Cambridge, MA: Winthrop, 1981), pp. 60–63; U.S. Bureau of the Census, *Statistical History of the United States* (Washington, D.C.: U.S. Government Printing Office, 1963), pp. 484–516.

18. Paul E. Peterson, Barry G. Rabe, and Kenneth Wong, *When Federalism Works* (Washington, D.C.: Brookings Institution, 1986), p. 2.

19. Thomas Ferguson and Joel Rogers, *Right Turn: The Decline of the Democrats and the Future of American Politics* (New York: Farrar, Straus & Giroux, 1986); Thomas Byrne Edsall, *The New Politics of Inequality* (New York: Norton, 1984).

20. Jeffrey L. Pressman and Aaron Wildavsky, *Implementation,* 3rd ed. (Berkeley, CA: University of California Press, 1984); Martha Derthick, *New Towns in Town: Why a Federal Program Failed* (Washington, D.C.: Brookings Institution, 1977); Eugene Bardach, *The Implementation Game,* 4th ed. (Cambridge, MA: MIT Press, 1982). In rebuttal, see Peterson, Rabe, and Wong, *When Federalism Works.*

21. Ed Gillespie and Bob Schellhas, eds., *Contract with America: The Bold Plan by Rep. Newt Gingrich, Rep. Dick Armey and the House Republicans to Change the Nation* (New York: Random House, 1994), p. 125.

22. Donahue, *Disunited States,* pp.11–12.

23. Ibid., p. 13.

24. Clifford J. Levy, "More Power Was Supposed to Grease These Skids," *New York Times* (June 27, 1999), p. A5.

CHAPTER 4

The Structural Foundations of American Government and Politics

IN THIS CHAPTER

- How population size, location, and diversity affect American politics

- How the free enterprise economy shapes American political life

- Income and wealth distribution, and why they matter

- How globalization affects the United States and its people

- What Americans believe about people, politics, government, and the economy

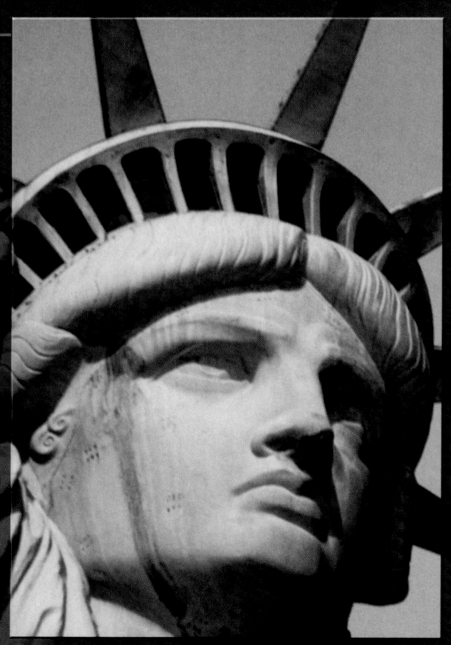

"B-1 Bob" Learns About His District

Bob Dornan and the political establishment were stunned. The nine-term Republican member of Congress from Orange County, California's 46th district had lost his House seat to political newcomer Democrat Loretta Sanchez by a mere 984 votes. Known widely as either "B-1 Bob," because of his staunch support for increased military spending, or "sound-bite Bob," because of the former talk-show host's tendency to attack immigrants, gays, feminists, and liberals with short, savage remarks, Dornan played on his traditional themes during the 1996 congressional election. This tactic had always worked in the past. He saw no reason to change his long-term strategy in his district, he thought, especially against an opponent who had lost her only previous try for elective office.

What Bob Dornan and others learned was that the 46th district, like many others in California and in other states, had experienced enormous demographic changes, and these demographic changes were inevitably going to play themselves out in politics. A bastion of the white middle class for much of the post-war period, by the mid-1990s the district had become mostly working class and minority in composition. In fact, fully 50 percent of the district was Hispanic and 12 percent were Asian. The whites who remained were mainly blue collar and service workers, having migrated to the southern suburbs of Los Angeles over the previous decade. Bob Dornan's oft-repeated campaign themes—increasing military spending, banning abortion, and bashing gays and immigrants—not only failed to resonate with people more concerned about jobs, crime, and education but actively alienated the largest ethnic group in his district.

Loretta Sanchez understood the new math, even if Dornan did not. A former Republican and business consultant, she was also the daughter of Mexican immigrants to the United States and a former Head Start child. She switched her party affiliation, she suggested, because she was angry with the Republican Party, as were many other Hispanics, for sponsoring ballot initiatives attacking affirmative action, bilingual education, and immigrant rights. A moderate Republican turned moderate Democrat, she focused her door-to-door, low-budget campaign on issues more attuned to the interests of potential voters in her district, and spent precious campaign time attending festivities in the Hispanic and Asian communities. Striking back in a way that was typical of his previous campaigns, Dornan attacked Sanchez as "the champion of homosexuals."

Dornan's defeat in 1996—and again in 1998, this time by a landslide margin—was not only the product of the transformation of his district from a predominantly white middle-class one to a working-class and minority-dominated one, but of the general mobilization of the Hispanic vote, especially in California, but elsewhere as well.[1] Dornan was surely smart enough to read the numbers. He surely knew that his district was changing under his feet. But the Hispanic population had always voted in very low numbers before. The Hispanic share of the electorate was always much lower than its share in the population. But the intense support by Gov. Pete Wilson and other Republicans of what appeared to many to be anti-immigrant and antiminority initiatives galvanized Hispanics and pushed them into politics. In Southern California between 1992 and 1996, for example, Hispanic voter registration increased by almost 30 percent, and registered Hispanics came out to vote in higher numbers than before. The results were felt all across the state. By the end of the decade, Hispanic representation in the California legislature had increased by 40 percent, two Hispanics in a row served as Speakers of the California state assembly, and two more Hispanics were added to the state's delegation in the U.S. House of Representatives.

The demographic changes described in this story that are transforming American politics are but the tip of the iceberg of politically relevant changes that are going on in the economy and society. Tracking these many changes, and examining how they are shaping American politics and what government does, is the focus of this chapter.

▶Thinking Critically About This Chapter

Using the Framework. In this chapter, you will learn about the demographic characteristics of the American population (race, ethnicity, geographical location, occupation, income, and the like), the U.S. economy and how it is evolving and changing, and the American political culture. Together with the constitutional rules you learned about in previous chapters, you will see how these structural-level factors have a great deal to do with what issues dominate the political agenda, how political power is distributed in the population, and what ideas Americans bring to bear when grappling with complex public policy issues.

Using the Democratic Standard. Popular sovereignty, political equality, and liberty require a supportive economic and social environment. These include (but are not confined to) such things as a well-educated population, a sizeable middle class with access to resources allowing its members to participate in public affairs, conditions of nondiscrimination against racial and ethnic minorities, and a culture that values and protects liberty. In this chapter you will learn whether or not such an environment exists.   ▶

LongmanParticipate

CourseCompass

simulation
How to Satisfy Aunt Martha

American Society: How It Has Changed and Why It Matters

The typical American today is very different from the typical American of 1950, let alone 1790, when the first census was conducted. Where we live, how we work, our racial and ethnic composition, and our average age and standard of living have all changed substantially. Each change has influenced our political

CourseCompass

WEB EXPLORATION

Immigration and Immigrants

Issue: Immigration, and what to do about it and its social consequences, has become a contentious issue in American politics.

Site: Find out what Americans want to do about immigration by going to Public Agenda On-Line. Visit the "Course Documents" section of your online course. In the "Web Explorations" section for Chapter 4, click on "Immigration and Immigrants" and then open "immigrants." Select "immigration" and look at "people's chief concerns" and "major proposals."

What You've Learned: What are Americans most worried about when it comes to immigration? What do they want to do about it? What policies do Americans favor regarding immigrants who are already in the United States? As you look at each survey question, ask yourself what immigration policies you support. Are your views in line with the majority of Americans, or are you an "outlier"?

HINT: Note that people seem to worry not about immigration as such but about illegal immigration. They strongly support policies that rapidly assimilate immigrants, including a focus on English.

life. This section examines how the American people have changed and why it matters.

Growing Diversity

Ours is an ethnically, religiously, and racially diverse society. The white European Protestants, black slaves, and Native Americans who made up the bulk of the U.S. population when the first census was taken in 1790 were joined by Catholic immigrants from Ireland and Germany in the 1840s and 1850s (see Figure 4.1). In the 1870s, Chinese migrated to America, drawn by jobs in railroad construction. Around the turn of the twentieth century, most emigration was from eastern, central, and southern Europe, with its many ethnic, linguistic, and religious groups. Today most emigration is from Asia and Latin America. The result of this history is substantial diversity in the American population (see Figure 4.2).

The rate of migration to the United States has accelerated in recent decades. If illegal entrants are included in the total, more than 20 million people immigrated to the United States during the 1980s and 1990s, the highest total for any two consecutive decades in American history. As a result, the percentage of foreign-born people resident in the United States has more than doubled since 1970, reaching about 26 million in the year 2000, slightly under 10 percent of the population. Immigration is concentrated in a handful of states, mainly California, New York, New Jersey, Florida, and Texas. In

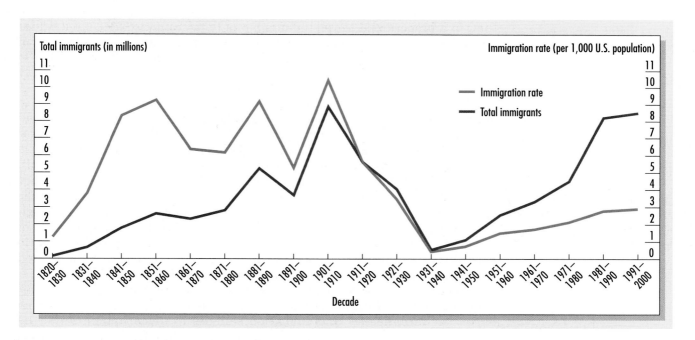

Figure 4.1 ● **Immigration to the United States, by Decade**

Measuring immigration to the United States in different ways gives rise to quite different interpretations of its scale. Measured in total numbers, the high points of immigration were the 1880s, the decade and a half after 1900, and the 1980s and 1990s. Measured in terms of the total U.S. population, however, it is clear that immigration was an important factor in population change for much of the nineteenth century and the early part of the twentieth century but not much after that. Recent immigration, relative to the total U.S. population, remains historically low, although it is on the rise.

Source: U.S. Bureau of the Census.

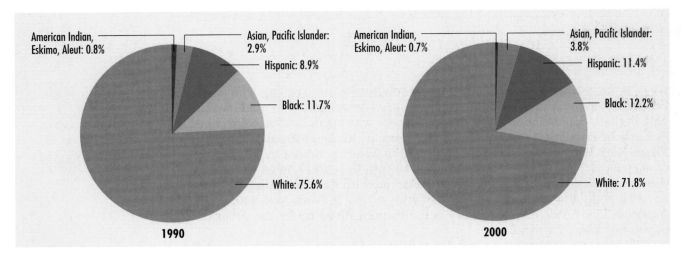

Figure 4.2 ● **Racial Composition of the United States (estimates for 2000)**

The United States is a racially diverse society and is becoming more so every year. Whites remain in the majority by a substantial margin, however.

Source: U.S. Bureau of the Census, 1999.

California, fully 25 percent of the population is foreign-born. Texas is the smallest of the Big Five immigration states, with a total foreign-born population of 11 percent in 1999. Although immigration is substantial, it is worth noting that, in a proportional sense, the number of immigrants to the United States today does not approach historical highs. Thus, immigration as a proportion of the total population was much higher between 1840 and 1920 (refer again to Figure 4.1). For most people, of course, it is what has been happening recently that is most important to them, not historical comparisons.

The most recent wave of immigration, like all previous ones, has added to our rich linguistic, cultural, and religious traditions; it has also helped revitalize formerly poverty-stricken neighborhoods in cities such as Los Angeles, New York, and Chicago. But it has also generated political and social tensions. The arrival of immigrants who are different from the majority population in significant ways has often sparked anti-immigration agitation and demands that public officials stem the tide. **Nativist** (antiforeign) reactions to Irish Catholic migrants were common throughout the nineteenth century. Anti-Chinese agitation swept the western states in the 1870s and 1880s. Alarm at the arrival of waves of immigrants from eastern, southern, and central Europe in the early part of this century led Congress virtually to close the doors of the United States in 1921 and to keep them closed until the 1950s.

The current wave of Spanish-speaking immigration has triggered similar unease. In 1994, for example, California voters approved Proposition 187, which barred welfare, health, and education benefits to illegal immigrants (the Proposition has since been declared unconstitutional by a federal district court). In 1998, California voters approved another proposition that banned bilingual education. In that same year, at the urging of Gov. Pete Wilson, the Board of Regents ended affirmative action programs at the University of California.

Interestingly, national surveys suggest that it is "illegal" immigration that most concerns Americans rather than immigration, per se. They are worried, surveys show, that a majority of "illegals" are on welfare (which is untrue) and that undocumented workers and their families place unjustified burdens on state and local education and health care budgets (which may or may not be

nativist

Antiforeign; applied to political movements active in the nineteenth century.

S. Kelly © 1995 *San Diego Union-Tribune,* Copley News Service

true, depending how one calculates state and local taxes paid by the undocumented). Americans, in the main, support current levels of "legal" immigration, wanting tighter controls imposed only on illegal entry. In addition, substantial majorities report that they are comfortable with the changing racial and ethnic composition of the United States.[2]

Although immigration often triggers an initial negative response from the native population (among all races and ethnic groups, it is important to add), politicians begin to pay attention to immigrant groups as more of their number become citizens and voters. Gov. Pete Wilson of California used the anti-immigrant card as the defining theme of his effort to win the 1996 Republican presidential nomination. He not only failed to win the nomination, but his actions fueled the political mobilization of Hispanic voters in California that resulted in the loss of the legislature and the governorship to the Democratic Party. Candidates for statewide and national office in California today try to avoid Wilson's mistake.

Changing Location

Where the growing population of the United States is located also matters. Although we began as a country of rural farms and small towns, we rapidly became an urban people. By 1910, some 50 cities had populations of more than 100,000, and three (New York, Philadelphia, and Chicago) had more than 1 million. Urbanization, caused mainly by industrialization—the rise of large manufacturing firms required many industrial workers, while the mechanization of farming meant that fewer agricultural workers were needed—continued unabated until the mid-1940s. After World War II, a massive federal and state road-building program and government-guaranteed home loans for veterans started the process by which the United States became an overwhelmingly suburban nation (see Figure 4.3).

This shift in the location of the American population has had important political ramifications. The continued drain of population from rural areas, for instance, has diminished the power of the rural voice in state and national

Extensive suburbanization in the United States has brought its own set of problems. Urban sprawl, affordable housing, and traffic congestion, for example, have recently become important poltitcal issues around the nation.

politics. For their part, central cities, burdened with populations of the poor and the less well-to-do, find it increasingly difficult to provide the level of public services considered normal only a few years ago. Heavily dependent on the assistance of the federal government, poor central-city populations have become even more consistently Democratic in their voting preferences than in the past. Conversely, people living in the distant suburbs, mainly middle-class and working-class homeowners—who increasingly include among their number many members of minority and immigrant groups—have become less willing to support programs for central-city populations. Voters in these

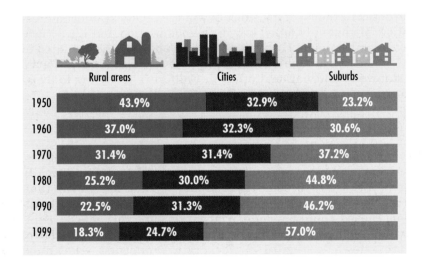

Figure 4.3 ● Population Shift: From Rural to Urban to Suburban

In a relatively short period of time, the United States has changed from a society in which the largest percentage of the population lived in rural areas to one in which the largest percentage lives in suburbs. This development has produced several important changes in American politics and in the fortunes of our political parties.

Source: U.S. Bureau of the Census.

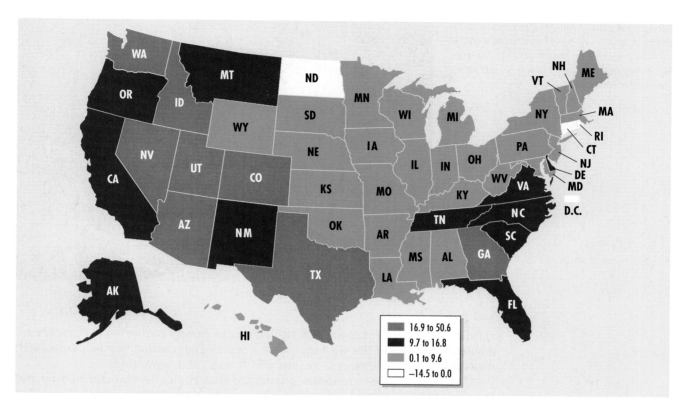

Figure 4.4 ● **Population Change in the States, 1990–2000**

The U.S. Bureau of the Census reports that the relative population sizes of the states changed substantially in the 1990s. For the most part, the Sun Belt states of the South, Southwest, and West gained population, and the states of the Upper Midwest and East lost population. One political outcome of this change is that Sun Belt states gained representatives in the U.S. House of Representatives, while states in the Upper Midwest and Middle Atlantic regions lost representatives.

Source: U.S. Bureau of the Census.

areas have grown less friendly to politicians who promise substantial governmental aid to solve inner-city problems and more friendly to proposals to deal with traffic congestion and sprawl.

The U.S. population has also moved west and south over the course of time. The shift accelerated after World War II as people followed manufacturing jobs to these regions (many companies were attracted to the western and southern states because of their low taxes and antiunion policies). This population shift has led to changes in the relative political power of the states. Following each census from 1950 to 2000, states in the East and the upper Midwest lost congressional seats and presidential electoral votes. States in the West and the South—often referred to as the **Sun Belt** because of their generally pleasant weather—gained at their expense. Figure 4.4 shows the extent of change during the 1990s. Because a majority of Sun Belt states are more conservative than other states, their increasing importance in national politics may have contributed to Republican gains in Congress in the 1990s.

Sun Belt

States of the Lower South, Southwest, and West, where sunny weather and often conservative politics prevail.

Changing Jobs and Occupations

At the time of the first census in 1790, almost three-quarters of all Americans worked in agriculture. Most of the remainder of the population worked in the

Because fewer and fewer families can afford the luxury of having one parent stay home with the children, pressures on government for a longer school day and increased funding for day care are likely to increase.

Industrial Revolution

The period of transition from predominantly agricultural to predominantly industrial societies in the Western nations in the nineteenth century.

blue-collar worker

A skilled, semiskilled, or unskilled worker in industry.

white-collar worker

A person working at a service, sales, or office job.

retail trade, transportation, and skilled trades closely connected to agriculture. About 80 percent of the working, male, nonslave population was self-employed, owning small farms, stores, wagons and horses, and workshops.[3]

The American occupational structure was radically transformed by the industrialization of the United States in the late nineteenth century (often called the **Industrial Revolution**). By 1910, the proportion of the labor force in agriculture had dropped to only 32 percent, and individuals working for others for wages and salaries had swelled to over 69 percent.[4] By 1940, the "typical" American was a skilled, semiskilled, or unskilled **blue-collar worker** in manufacturing.

In 1950, the United States became the first nation in the world in which **white-collar workers** (in clerical, technical, professional, managerial, services, and sales jobs) were in the majority. The recent decline of certain manufacturing industries, the disappearance of the small family farm, and the rapid rise of the high-technology and information sector accelerated the shift of employment from factory and farm to the office. Figure 4.5 shows how the American occupational structure has changed over the years.

For a variety of reasons—technological change, corporate downsizing, the declining power of labor unions, and more—many more Americans are working on a part-time basis, working from their homes for themselves or for companies, or working as independent consultants. A small, undetermined proportion of them receives substantial compensation because the skills and services they offer are highly valued. For many, however, compensation is low, and health and retirement benefits are hard to come by.

Occupational change matters a great deal in our politics. Displaced workers, for example, often ask government to expand welfare and unemployment benefits, job retraining, and programs that encourage economic development.

The shift from manufacturing to service occupations also affects the fortunes of labor unions, to take another example. As heavy industry has become less important in the American economy, the proportion of Americans who belong to labor unions has declined sharply, from approximately 33 percent in the early 1950s to less than 16 percent today. Because unions have always been a strong liberal voice in American politics, support for liberal economic and social policies has grown weaker.

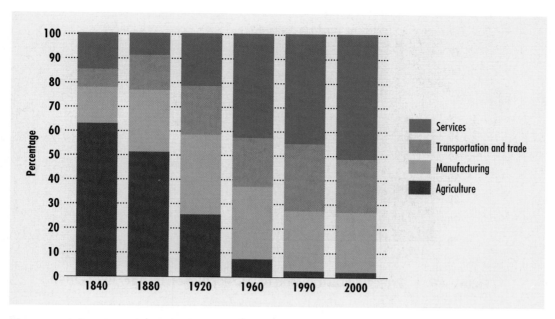

Figure 4.5 ● **Changes in U.S. Occupational Structure**

The United States has been undergoing a long-term transformation in its occupational structure. Most notable has been the rapid decline in the number of Americans working in agriculture, as well as the expansion in the number of those working in service occupations, ranging from sales clerks to financial analysts. Also notable has been the rise and decline in the proportion of Americans in manufacturing occupations.

Source: U.S. Bureau of Labor Statistics.

The expansion of service, clerical, technical, and other kinds of white-collar jobs has coincided, moreover, with a substantial expansion in the number of female workers. The participation of women in the paid workforce has passed 75 percent and is rapidly approaching the participation rate of men. This massive entry by women into working life outside the home has had enormous political consequences. For one thing, paid work has improved women's income (although women still earn only about three-quarters of what men earn) and has increased their influence and self-confidence in many spheres, including politics. These developments very likely contributed to the formation of the women's movement in the late 1960s and early 1970s when women began to reenter the paid workforce in a major way (see Chapter 8). Moreover, because women with young children are now working outside the home in unprecedented numbers—63 percent of married women with children under six years of age are in the paid workforce[5]—we might see strong pressures for government-funded child care and early education and for the extension of the school day.

The Aging of the American Population

One of the most significant demographic trends in the United States and in other industrialized countries is the aging of the population. In 1800, the median age in the United States was just under 16; today it is 35. By 2030, it will be about 38. The proportion of the population over age 65 has been growing, while the proportion between the ages of 18 and 64 has been shrinking. Today 12.7 percent of Americans are elderly. By 2030, this figure is likely to rise to about 20 percent. Meanwhile, the proportion of the population in the prime working years is likely to fall from 61.4 percent today to about 56.5 percent in

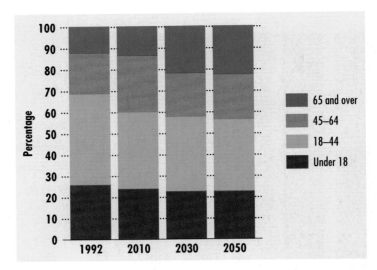

Figure 4.6 ● **Projected Distribution of U.S. Population by Age, 1992–2050**

The American population is gradually aging. The proportion of Americans under the age of 18 has been shrinking, while the proportion over 65 has been growing. Population experts believe the trend will continue.

Source: U.S. Bureau of the Census.

2030 (see Figure 4.6). Moreover, the number of the very old—over age 85—is the fastest-growing age segment of all. Thus, an increasing proportion of Americans is likely to be dependent and in need of services, and a shrinking proportion is likely to be taxpaying wage or salary earners.

Because the population is aging, how to finance Social Security and Medicare is likely to remain an important political question for the foreseeable future. The voting power of the elderly is likely to make it difficult for elected officials to substantially reduce social insurance programs for Americans over age 65. Meanwhile, the tax load on those still in the workforce may feel increasingly burdensome. Also, more and more middle-aged people are trying to figure out how to finance assisted-living and nursing home care for their elderly parents. How these issues will play out in the political arena in the near future will be interesting to follow.

Income, Wealth, and Poverty

The United States enjoys one of the highest standards of living in the world. In terms of gross domestic product (GDP) per capita, the usual measure of a nation's living standards, the United States leads the world. On the UN's Human Development Index—which takes into account education and life expectancy as well as per capita GDP—the United States in 1999 was among the top five nations (with Canada, France, Norway, and Iceland).[6] However, the high standard of living is not shared by all Americans.

Income   After an almost two-decade-long period of stagnation that began in 1973, median household income in the United States began to rise steadily after 1994, coincident with the long economic boom of the mid- and late 1990s. In 1998, median household income surpassed its previous peak (1989), reaching $38,900.[7] In real dollar terms—that is, adjusted for inflation—median

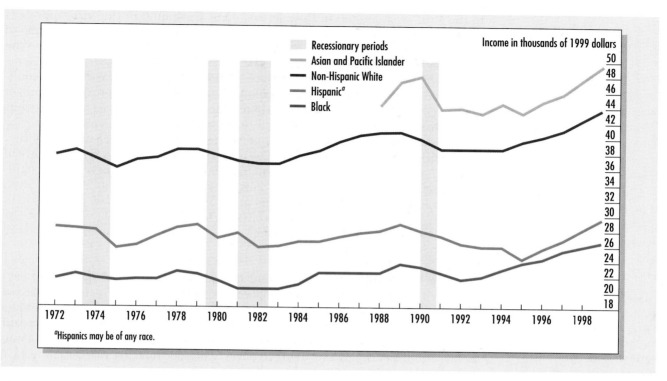

Figure 4.7 ● **Trends in U.S. Median Family Income**

Median family income (controlled for inflation) for all major population groups remained relatively flat from 1973 until the mid-1990s. Median family income then began to rise in response to the strong performance of the U.S. economy.

Source: U.S. Bureau of the Census.

household income was up 21.2 percent from 1967 when the federal government first began to collect this statistic.

Trends in household income vary by group (see Figure 4.7), as one might expect. African-American and Hispanic households have the lowest incomes, while Asian-Americans and non-Hispanic whites have the highest. Note as well that median household incomes for all groups declined in the late 1980s and early 1990s, then began to recover at different times for each group. African-American households recovered first, even as Hispanic households continued to decline. Then white and Asian-American household incomes began to grow. Note, finally, that all groups benefited from the long economic boom, with steady rates of household income growth in the late 1990s.

The long stagnation in median household incomes had important political effects in the United States, creating what some called "the angry middle class." From the mid-1970s to the start of the current economic expansion, in a nation grown accustomed to rising incomes and improvements in the standard of living for each generation, incomes for most Americans stayed flat even though more household members were working than had worked in the past and more people were working longer hours or at more than one job. By the 1980s and early 1990s, political anger had led to frequent outbursts against taxes, immigrants, and welfare recipients and a decline in trust for government and elected leaders. Middle-class anger also had electoral consequences, playing an important role, for example, in the defeat of incumbent president George Bush in the 1992 election and in the success of Pat Buchanan in the early rounds of the Republican presidential primaries in 1996. Middle-class anger, according to most commentators, took aim at congressional Democrats in 1994 and gave the Republicans control of Congress for the first time in 40 years.[8]

Surveys showed that by the end of the 1990s, Americans were again confident about the country's future as well as their own financial prospects.[9] Talk of middle-class anger had largely disappeared, and the usefulness of resentment as a political mobilizing tool seemed to have declined. But no one can say for certain that this contentment is now a permanent feature of American politics. Much will depend on the performance of the economy and the financial fate of households. It would probably not take much of an economic reversal to rekindle anger. After all, even with the long economic boom of the 1990s, median household income levels in real terms are only slightly better than they were in the past. Additionally, while the benefits of the boom seem to have reached virtually every group in the population, some groups have benefited far more than others.

poverty line

The federal government's calculation of the amount of income families of various sizes need to stay out of poverty.

Poverty   In 1955, almost 25 percent of Americans fell below the federal government's official **poverty line**. The percentage dropped steadily until it reached 11.6 in 1973. Beginning in the late 1970s, however, the percentage of Americans classified as poor began to inch upward. It receded a bit in the mid-1980s and started to rise again in the early 1990s, reaching 14.5 percent in 1994. Since then, the percentage of Americans living in poverty has declined; by 1998, it fell to 12.7 percent. The number of Americans living in poverty was 34.5 million in 1998, down from 39.3 million in 1993. Although poverty has declined over the years in the United States, the poverty rate remains very high in absolute terms (34.5 million is a large number) and is substantially higher than poverty in the other rich

WEB EXPLORATION

Comparing Our Standard of Living

Issue: One of the hallmarks of the United States compared with most other countries is our high standard of living.

Site: Compare our standard of living to that of other nations by visiting the Infonation Web site of the United Nations. In the "Course Documents" section of your online course, in the "Web Explorations" section for Chapter 4, click on "Comparing Our Standard of Living" and then open "living standards." From the list of countries, choose the United States, two other rich democracies, and one poor country from each of the following: Latin America, Asia, and Africa. Then choose from among the indicators of quality of life, including per capita income, education and literacy, education of women, life expectancy, and more.

What You've Learned: How does our standard of living stack up? On what indicators are the differences between the rich and poor countries most apparent? Does the United States differ from the other rich countries on any of the indicators? What would you conclude about the American standard of living after reviewing this information?

HINT: Education, the education of women, and homicides are particularly interesting.

USING THE FRAMEWORK

I Keep Hearing About How Well the Economy Is Doing, Yet We Still Can't Seem to Do Anything About Poverty in This Country. Why Is That?

Although the strong economy has caused poverty rates to fall, there is still a surprisingly high number of poor people in the United States. Surveys show that Americans would like to do something to help the poor, although not through the traditional welfare system. But the federal government, with a few exceptions such as the Low Income Tax Credit, has not made the elimination of poverty a major priority. Housing and

Urban Development Secretary Andrew Cuomo attempted to draw public attention to the plight of the poor in poverty pockets such as Benton Harbor, Michigan, and East St. Louis, Illinois, but this attempt failed to spark a reaction. Taking a look at how structural, political linkage, and governmental factors interact on this issue, will help explain the situation.

Governmental Action

The national government provides small safety nets for the poor but does not institute programs to eliminate poverty.

Governmental Level

- Proposals to eliminate poverty do not improve the electoral prospects of public officials at the present time.

- Elected leaders in both parties at the present time support the position that balanced budgets, deregulation, a friendly environment for investors, and encouragement of private enterprise is the best public policy.

- The public overwhelmingly believes that markets rather than government programs are the key to economic prosperity, leaving little sympathy for government-backed poverty reduction.

Political Linkages Level

- Currently, the poor in the United States are politically invisible; they represent a small minority of the electorate, have few organized groups to push their interests, and have not been able to build a social movement.

- Public opinion opposes big federal government programs to redistribute income and is convinced that balanced budgets, deregulation, and privatization have something to do with the good performance of the economy.

- The Democratic Party, historically the party championing the interests of the poor and near-poor, is afraid of being tagged with the "liberal" and "tax-and-spend" labels.

- The media have not paid much attention to the issue of poverty.

Structural Level

- American core beliefs about individualism, initiative, and opportunity make it difficult for proposals to assist the poor to gain recognition.

- The present economic boom, with its record levels of employment, has reinforced the belief that anyone who wants to work, can.

Poverty and homelessness have persisted in the face of strong economic growth. The contrast between rich and poor is evident on the streets of most large American cities.

democracies. In addition, the percentage of Americans who are poor remains higher than it was in 1973.

The distribution of poverty is not random. It is concentrated among racial minorities and single-parent, female-headed households and their children.[10] Roughly 26 percent of black and Hispanic Americans live in poverty, for example

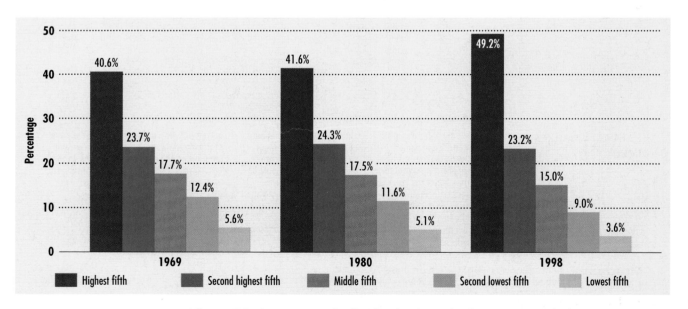

Figure 4.8 ● Income Distribution in the United States, by Quintiles, 1969–1998

Income inequality has been increasing in the United States, reaching levels not seen since the 1920s. A standard way to measure income inequality is to compare the proportion of national income going to each 20 percent (*quintile*) of the population. Especially striking is the shrinking share of the bottom 40 percent and the increasing share of the top 20 percent.

Source: U.S. Bureau of the Census.

(although a sizable middle class has emerged in both communities). More than one in three poor people live in single-parent, female-headed households, and one in five is a child.

Obviously, the extent of poverty is politically consequential. Most importantly, poverty is associated with a range of socially undesirable outcomes, including crime, drug use, and family disintegration,[11] all of which eventually draw the attention of other citizens who want government to do something about it. Additionally, societies with large concentrations of the poor are susceptible to disruption and social turmoil, so governments in such societies must eventually attend to the social control of the poor.

Inequality   Income and wealth are distributed in a highly unequal fashion in the United States, and the economic boom of the 1990s has done nothing to make it less pronounced. Income inequality increased dramatically during the 1980s and early 1990s, reaching its all-time high in 1995 when the top 20 percent of the population took home 48.5 percent of the national income (the highest proportion ever recorded), and it has remained unchanged since then (see Figure 4.8). Thus, the distribution of income by population quartiles has not changed significantly since 1995, nor has the GINI index, a standard measure of the extent of income equality.[12] Most of the income and wealth gains from economic growth between 1973 and 1995, then, went mainly to upper-income groups, rather than being evenly distributed across the entire population. Recent economic good times have not managed to redistribute income downward from the top.[13]

It is worth noting that income inequality is greater in the United States than in any other Western democratic nation.[14] Figure 4.9 shows how selected countries compare on the GINI Index of income inequality; in the GINI Index, a score of 0.0 represents perfect equality in income distribution in a population and 1.0 means perfect inequality, where one person has all of the income. We are clearly the leader on this measure.

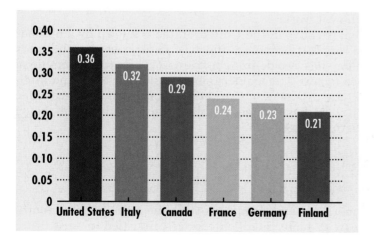

Figure 4.9 ● Comparative Income Distribution, 1999

The GINI Index is a standard measure of income inequality used by economists. A GINI Index of 1.00 is equal to perfect inequality, where a single person has everything and all others have nothing. A score of 0.00 is perfect equality, where the income share of every person is the same. The higher the score, the greater the level of income inequality. Note that the GINI score for the United States is higher than that of other highly developed capitalist societies.

Source: GINI Index at **www.panix.com/~dhenwood/**

Among Americans, wealth (financial assets such as real estate, stocks and bonds, and so on) is even more unequally distributed than income. According to a study by economist Edward Wolff, the top 1 percent of households—with a net worth of at least $2.3 million—owns more than 42 percent of the nation's wealth, up from 21 percent in 1975.[15] Inequality of wealth today seems similar to that of the 1920s and is more unequally distributed here than in any other Western democratic nation.[16]

LongmanParticipate

CourseCompass

visual literacy
**Understanding the
Distribution of
Wealth in America**

Why worry about income and wealth inequality? Inequality is particularly important in determining how well democracy works. Extensive *material inequality,* as we suggested in Chapter 1, may undermine the possibilities for *political equality,* one of the foundations of democracy. People with access to financial resources can use their resources to enhance their political voice and their ease of access to public officials. Poorer Americans are less likely to exercise their right to vote or to participate in other ways in politics. People with little money are unlikely to make contributions to political campaigns or to groups that will fight for their interests. Those with more income are more likely than others to have computers and Internet access in their homes and are more likely, as a result, to be informed, linked with others into political groups, and in touch with government decision makers. That is why, as we pointed out in Chapter 1, Thomas Jefferson feared that democracy would be at risk in a highly unequal society.

The American Economy

Virtually everything we have discussed so far in this chapter is shaped by the American economy. The growth, diversification, and geographic dispersion of the American population, for instance, can be traced to economic changes. Occupations, standards of living, and the distribution of income and wealth are closely connected to the operations of our economic institutions. Even important elements of the American political culture, as we shall soon see, are associated with our economy and how it works.

capitalism

An economic system based on private ownership and the existence of markets to coordinate most economic activities.

The economic system we have in the United States is known by a number of names: **capitalism**, market economy, and free enterprise are the most common. Such an economy has two defining features: (1) private ownership of economic factors such as factories, machinery, office buildings, land, and intellectual property and (2) the existence of markets to coordinate most economic activity. American capitalism has changed a great deal over the years, going through a number of distinct stages.

The Industrial Revolution and the Rise of the Corporation

Until the Civil War, American capitalism (except in the slave-holding South) was highly competitive, with many small enterprises, first tied to agriculture and then increasingly to manufacturing. After the Civil War, and partly as a result of it, the economy became increasingly industrialized and concentrated in giant enterprises.[17] By the turn of the twentieth century, the United States was the world's leading industrial power.

Industrial enterprises grew to unprecedented size in the late nineteenth and early twentieth centuries. Workers were gathered into enormous workplaces that required coordination by an army of managers. Partly, this change in scale was related to technology: the steam engine, electrical power, and the assembly line provided the means of bringing thousands of working people together for industrial production. Partly, this change in scale was tied to cost: most of the new industrial technologies required unheard-of levels of investment capital. Large enterprises were also encouraged by changes in the laws of incorporation, which allowed competing corporations to merge into single, giant enterprises. A wave of mergers between 1896 and 1904 fashioned the corporate-dominated economy familiar to us today.[18]

The Post–World War II Boom

The American economy and American corporations grew impressively during the first two-thirds of the twentieth century. Although thrown off track by the Great Depression for a decade, World War II and the Cold War that followed, with their spurs to government spending, research and development, and technological innovation, pushed the economy forward once again. The enormous growth in the wealth of the American economy after World War II, fueled by the activities of the major corporations, was the foundation of the rapid improvements in the American standard of living and the growth of the middle class.

After World War II, the largest American corporations increasingly looked abroad for sources of raw materials and markets for their finished products. This phenomenon was not entirely new; American oil companies, for instance, had scoured the world for petroleum reserves and markets in the early part of the twentieth century. But in the postwar period, many other corporations joined the game. American corporations dominated world markets during this time. In 1975, 11 of the largest 15 corporations in the world were American; in 1981, 40 percent of the world's total foreign direct investment was still accounted for by the United States.[19] The global reach of corporate activities inevitably affected U.S. foreign policy. With worldwide economic interests at stake, American political leaders came under great pressure to pay attention to developments and events in the far corners of the world.

The Temporary Fall from Grace

Although the U.S. economy continued to grow in the 1970s and 1980s, its rate of growth began to fall behind that of Western Europe and Japan, even as American corporations began to feel the pinch of intense competition from foreign corporations. Between the early 1970s and the late 1980s, the U.S. share of world manufacturing declined. The United States lost ground in steel, autos, machine tools, electronics, computer chips, and finance.

The relative decline in America's manufacturing position had a devastating impact on the wages of blue-collar workers, raised protectionist sentiments, and spurred proposals to shield American industry from foreign competition. The intensity of the fight over the North American Free Trade Agreement (NAFTA) and the General Agreement on Tariffs and Trade (GATT) shows how America's changing economic position in the world generated a set of important issues in American politics.

Globalization and the American Economy

In the 1990s, however, the American economy rebounded, with its corporations once again becoming the key players in the industries that count the most. The economies once seen as the principal threats to America's position—the European Union, Japan, and the so-called Asian tigers—began to lose ground. The reason for the turnaround has been the subject of much debate and disagreement among

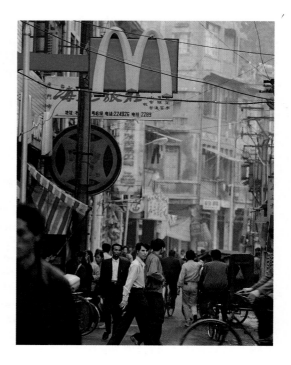

The largest American corporations are also global corporations in the sense that they produce and sell their products all over the world. This McDonald's is in Xiamen, China.

economists and business leaders—some point to the lighter hand of government and labor unions in the United States, some point to stronger entrepreneurial traditions here, and still others credit the existence of freer markets—but all seem to agree that American corporations were better positioned to succeed in the new global economy that blossomed in the 1990s.

The most important characteristic of this new global economy is the integration of much of the world into a single market and production system. Today the largest corporations design, manufacture, market, sell, and finance their products and services across a wide range of countries and are not constrained much by national boundaries. General Motors, for example, produces and sells more cars abroad than it does in the United States. Boeing designs and assembles the 777 near Seattle, but many parts of the plane are manufactured by subcontractors in Japan, China, England, Germany, and Australia.

Corporations are able to operate globally because of three revolutions. First, the revolution in telecommunications and computers enables corporate managers to coordinate the activities of scores of manufacturing plants, subcontractors, shippers, sales representatives, and retail outlets all over the world. Second, the revolution in transportation (air cargo, truck and ship containerization, and package express services) allows corporations to assemble parts for manufacturing from multiple locations and to ship final products from almost anywhere in the world, speedily and at relatively low cost. Third is the revolution in global financial markets, encompassing stocks, bonds, insurance, and a range of credit instruments, where billions of dollars are moved instantaneously to where they are needed, based mainly on decisions made by private and institutional investors, not governments.

U.S. corporations are proving to be the dominant actors in the new global economy. Behind the apparent decline in the competitiveness of the American economy in the 1970s and 1980s, something startling seems to have been going on. Leaving older industries such as mining, steel, and shipbuilding to others, American companies proved to be particularly adept in areas such as computer software, biotechnology, business services (insurance, law, accounting, advertising, and so on), computer chips, Internet services, telecommunications, military and commercial aircraft, and popular entertainment. In the emergent global economy, Microsoft, Intel, Boeing, American Airlines, Disney, Amazon.com, Sun, and Cisco are the companies that draw increasing attention.

U.S. corporations—and foreign ones, as well—are growing larger through mergers and acquisitions. Even the largest companies have learned that size matters in the battle for global market share, whether in banking (note the merger of NationsBank Corp and BankAmerica Corp), media and entertainment (note AOL's purchase of TimeWarner), airlines (note United's bid to purchase USAir), telecommunications (note Deutsche Telekom's purchase of Sprint), and software and the Internet (AOL again).

To many commentators, globalization, with its national-borders-spanning web of interconnected finance, trade, and information, means that national governments have lost or will soon lose a substantial part of their power to control what goes on within their own countries.[20] If, for example, a government puts pressure on investors to behave in a certain way, they may invest their money elsewhere. Try to control the information your citizens have access to, and they will turn to the Web, e-mail, fax transmissions from abroad, pirated videocassettes, and satellite TV. The jury is still out on the degree to which national governments have lost or will lose power to their own citizens, global corporations, and transnational organizations such as the World Trade Organization, but it is something to watch closely. The internal political life of nations, including the United States, it is fair to say, will be affected one way or another.

The dynamism of the American economy in the 1990s had several effects that were politically consequential. On the one hand, the steady economic growth, low inflation, and heady stock market performance of that period (since reversed) helped fuel an impressive rate of job creation, low levels of unemployment, and heightened consumer confidence. On the other hand, the new global economy is one in which certain skills are highly sought after and rewarded—software engineers, portfolio managers, Web site creators, filmmakers, and business strategists, for example—while others are not—low-skill manual and service workers, for example. For the former, work tends to be both exciting and lucrative. For the latter, work is routine, not very well paid, and characterized by frequent layoffs and part-time status. This may be why a booming economy in the 1990s did not diminish income inequality in the United States.

The new global economy also ties the fates of nations together as never before. Witness how the Internet, global telecommunications systems, and media corporations force people in the rich democracies to pay attention to events in distant places such as Bosnia, Kosovo, and Sierra Leone.

The United States in the International System

It is often said that the United States is the world's last remaining superpower. If this is true, then it took awhile to reach this status. For most of the nineteenth century, the attention of most Americans and their leaders was focused on the North American continent. Their energies were devoted primarily to filling in a vast, continental-scale nation-state—which required, of course, moving Native Americans aside, buying territories from France and Spain, and seizing our present Southwest from Mexico—and to building an industrial economy. The great expanse of the Atlantic Ocean allowed our domestic growth and development to move forward, unhindered by the European powers. Our foreign policy was **isolationist**: American policy leaders believed in attending to our own affairs and staying out of world affairs, unless directly threatened. Starting toward the end of the nineteenth century, however, our attentions began to turn abroad, and our growing economic power inevitably provided a seat at the table of the world's most important nations. It was World War II, however, that propelled the United States into its position as the world's most important power.

isolationism

The policy of avoiding involvement in foreign affairs.

The United States as a Superpower I

World War II thrust the United States into the leadership position that its economic position in the world had portended since 1900. The war stimulated a massive expansion of the entire industrial economy. At the same time, the financial and manufacturing infrastructures of our prewar economic rivals—Britain, France, Japan, and Germany—were devastated by the war.

The United States emerged from the war with a large military establishment and military superiority in most important areas. There was also a new belief among both the population and the nation's leaders that isolationism was dangerous and contrary to our long-term national interests.

Within a decade of the end of World War II, the United States stood as the unchallenged economic, political, and military power among the Western nations. For the first time in its history, the United States was willing and able to exercise leadership on the world level. It was the United States that pulled together the major capitalist nations for the first time in their history into a political and economic partnership. It provided funds for rebuilding Europe and for development projects in the Third World. It successfully pushed

WEB EXPLORATION

Post–Cold War Foreign Policy

Issue: In the post–Cold War period, neither American leaders nor the American people are entirely clear about how the United States ought to relate to the rest of the world.

Site: See what the public thinks about specific issues regarding our role in the international community at Public Agenda On-Line. In the "Course Documents" section of your online course, in the "Web Explorations" section for Chapter 4, click on "Post–Cold War Foreign Policy" and then open "world role." Select "America's Global Role," then select "major proposals."

What You've Learned: What do Americans believe to be the best course of action? Should we approach foreign political, military, and economic problems unilaterally, going it alone, as it were? Or should we mainly engage the world through international organizations and in cooperation with our allies? Do you agree or disagree with most Americans on these issues? If you disagree, what would you say to other Americans to change their minds?

HINT: Your answer will probably depend greatly on your own ideas concerning our obligations, the usefulness and risks of U.S. interventions, and how much attention we need to pay to problems at home. There is no wrong answer here.

for free international trade and provided a stable dollar to serve as the basis of the international monetary system. And it organized and largely paid for the joint military defenses of them all. Is it any wonder, then, that *Life* magazine editor Henry Luce was moved to label the period the "American century"?

The fly in the ointment, of course, was the Soviet Union. Although badly crippled by the war (it is said that 20 million of its citizens died in the conflict), the Soviet Union entered the postwar era with the world's largest land army, superpower ambitions of its own, and a strong desire to keep the nations on its periphery in eastern and southern Europe in hands it considered friendly. In the ensuing **Cold War**, which began in the late 1940s and lasted for four decades, the two superpowers faced each other as leaders of conflicting political, economic, and ideological alliances; became engaged in a nuclear arms race; and fought surrogate wars with each other in various locations in the Third World, from the Belgian Congo to Central America to Afghanistan.

America's superpower status had many implications for U.S. politics and government policies. For one thing, superpower status required a large military establishment and tilted government spending priorities toward national defense. For another thing, as we will see in later chapters, it enhanced the role of the president in policymaking and diminished that of Congress.

Cold War

The period of tense relations between the United States and the Soviet Union from the late 1940s to the late 1980s.

The United States as a Superpower II

The 1980s and 1990s saw startling changes in the world's military, political, and economic systems, all of which, at least nominally, heightened U.S. power in the world. Communism collapsed in Eastern Europe. The Soviet Union ceased to exist. China switched to a market economy. Most developing countries rejected the socialist development model, embraced "privatization," and welcomed foreign investment. Moreover, the United States took the lead in the global economy.

Oddly, however, although the last "superpower," the United States does not have its way on all important matters, either with allies or enemies. With the threat of the Soviet Union no longer supplying the glue to hold them together, U.S. allies feel freer to go their own way on a wide range of international issues. The United States struggles with the European Union over trade issues, for example, and could not agree with the Europeans for a very long time on what to do about the ethnic conflicts in Bosnia or about Saddam Hussein and Iraq. Disagreements about nuclear proliferation have strained U.S. relations with Russia, while security issues, human rights violations, and protection of intellectual property have been an irritant in our relations with China. Nor is the United States able single-handedly to bring the Palestinians, Syrians, and Israelis together, or to stop some countries from protecting terrorists.

Americans also seem unsure about what role they want to play in the world. Although a minority of Americans harbor "isolationist" feelings—"let other countries take care of their own problems"—most realize that the United States, for its own good, cannot retreat from the world behind a "fortress America" wall. Most realize that we are simply too connected to the rest of the world, through trade, finance, transportation, and communications, to stay apart. The real disagreement among citizens and leaders alike is over how we should be engaged with the world. One camp believes that we should approach most world problems, whether economic or military, on a multinational, cooperative basis, through international organizations. The other camp believes that the United States is now powerful enough that it can act unilaterally in most cases where our vital national interests are at stake.

With the collapse of communism in the Soviet Union and Eastern Europe—the toppling of the Berlin Wall in 1989 pictured here was one of the most dramatic events in that process—the United States–USSR bipolar world ceased to exist, giving way to a world with multiple centers of power.

The Foundation Beliefs of American Political Culture

The kinds of choices Americans make in meeting the challenges posed by a changing economy, society, and post–Cold War world will depend a great deal on the kinds of values and beliefs Americans have regarding human nature, society, economic relations, and the role of government. Government policies tend to reflect our ideas and beliefs as a people. The fundamental values and beliefs that have political consequences make up the American *political culture*. The general outlines of the American political culture are discussed in this section.

Evidence strongly suggests that Americans share a political culture.[21] To be sure, we are a vast, polyglot mixture of races, religions, ethnicities, occupations, and lifestyles. Nevertheless, one of the things that has always struck observers of the American scene is the degree to which a broad consensus seems to exist on many of the fundamental beliefs that shape our political life. We focus here not on transitory ideas about particular issues that are in the headlines at the moment but on what might be called *foundation beliefs,* beliefs that shape how people classify, think about, and resolve particular issues that arise in the headlines or in their local communities.

Competitive Individualism

Americans tend to believe that an individual's fate is (and ought to be) tied to his or her own efforts. Those with talent, grit, and the willingness to work hard are more likely than not to end up on top, it is believed; those without at least some of these qualities are more likely to wind up on the bottom of the heap. Americans tend to assume that people generally get what they deserve.

Americans also tend to believe that people are naturally competitive, always striving to better themselves in relation to others. Popular literature in America has always conveyed this theme, ranging from the Horatio Alger books of the late nineteenth century to the many contemporary self-help books with keys to "getting ahead," "making it," and "getting rich."

The belief in competitive individualism affects how Americans think about many issues, including inequality. Americans overwhelmingly endorse the idea of "equality of opportunity" (the idea that people ought to have an equal shot in the competitive game of life), for instance, yet they overwhelmingly reject the idea that people should have equal rewards. Not surprisingly, Americans tend to look favorably on government programs that try to equalize opportunity— Head Start, education programs of various kinds, school lunch programs, and the like—but are generally against programs such as welfare, which seem to redistribute income from the hardworking middle class to individuals who are considered "undeserving."

Because it is assumed that people get different rewards based on their own efforts, a belief in equality of opportunity is consistent with highly unequal outcomes; that is, Americans seem to find inequality of income and wealth acceptable, as long as it is the outcome of a process in which individuals compete fairly with one other.[22] In Sweden, by contrast, citizens generally believe that equality of condition is an important value and support government policies that redistribute income.[23]

WEB EXPLORATION

American Ambivalence About the Role of Government

Issue: Americans hold surprisingly ambivalent attitudes on the proper role of government.

Site: Go to the National Public Radio site, and look at the results of the NPR, Kaiser Family Foundation, and Kennedy School of Government poll on American attitudes about the proper role for the federal government. In the "Course Documents" section of your online course, in the "Web Explorations" section for Chapter 4, click on "American Ambivalence About the Role of Government" and then open "government."

What You've Learned: Is there a difference in how Americans respond to questions about the role of government in the abstract and to questions about specific programs? Are Americans in general agreement about the proper role of government, or do they vary in some systematic way? What do you think the role of government should be? Do you tend to agree with most Americans on this issue or not?

HINT: It has often been said that Americans are philosophical conservatives and programmatic liberals.

In Japan, commitment to the work team and the company are more important cultural values than they are in the United States.

Limited Government

Closely associated with the idea of individualism is the belief that government must be limited in its power and responsibilities, for taken too far, a powerful government is likely to threaten individual rights and economic efficiency. This idea—drawn from Adam Smith and John Locke, our early history, and the words of the Declaration of Independence—remains attractive to most Americans even today, when we expect government to do far more than the framers ever imagined. This belief is not universally shared. In countries such as Japan, Sweden, Germany, and France, where governments have always been powerful and have played an important role in directing society and the economy, limited government has little attraction for either the political leaders or the public.

Free Enterprise

Americans tend to support the basic precepts of free enterprise capitalism: the primacy of private property and the efficiencies of the free market. Private property notions, articulated by the philosopher John Locke, have been reinforced by the experience of fairly widespread property ownership in the United States compared with that in many other countries.[24] Locke argued that God gave the earth and its resources in common to human beings and also gave human beings abilities that they have a right and an obligation to use. When they use these abilities, people turn common property into private property. By mixing their labor with the naturally occurring abundance of the earth, Locke argued, people are justified in taking the product of that effort for their own as private property. Because people are different in their abilities and their willingness to work, this process will always result in inequality. Inevitably, some will end up with more property than others.

The basic theory of the free market was worked out by Adam Smith in his classic work, *The Wealth of Nations*. Smith taught that if the market were left alone to operate naturally, following the laws of supply and demand, it would coordinate economic life in a nearly perfect fashion. Because the market is efficient and effective if left alone, government should not interfere with its operations. Although few Americans now accept this "pure" free market ideal, most Americans today, as in the past, believe that the private sector is usually more effective and efficient than the public sector. Given the esteem in which competitive individualism, private property, and the market are held, as well as the historical success of the American economy, it is entirely understandable that Americans tend to hold the business system (though not large corporations) in very high regard.

This set of ideas about individualism, limited government, and the free market (what some people call *classical liberalism*)[25] influences many aspects of public policy in the United States. Eminent economist John Kenneth Galbraith once decried the fact that ours is a society in which great private wealth exists side by side with public squalor. By that, he meant that Americans favor private consumption over public services and amenities and private over public initiatives.[26] In other rich democracies, citizens and political leaders tend to believe that extensive and high-quality public services in mass transit, health care, housing, and education are part and parcel of the good society.

Citizenship and the Nature of the Political Order

Certain beliefs about what kind of political order is most appropriate and what role citizens should play shape the actual daily behavior of citizens and political decision makers alike.

Democracy   At the time of the nation's founding, democracy was not highly regarded in the United States. During our history, however, the practice of democracy has been enriched and expanded, and the term *democracy* has become an honored one.[27] While regard for democracy is one of the bedrocks of the American belief system today, Americans have not necessarily always behaved democratically. After all, African-Americans were denied the vote and other citizenship rights in many parts of the nation until the 1960s. It is fair to say, nevertheless, that most Americans believe in democracy as a general principle and take seriously any claim that their behavior is not consistent with it.

Freedom and Liberty   Foreign visitors have always been fascinated by the American obsession with individual "rights," the belief that in the good society, government leaves people alone in their private pursuits. Studies show that freedom (also called *liberty*) is at the very top of the list of American beliefs and that it is more strongly honored here than elsewhere.[28] From the very beginning, what attracted most people to the United States was the promise of freedom in the New World. Many came for other reasons, to be sure: a great many came for strictly economic reasons, some came as convict labor, and some came in chains as slaves. But many who came to these shores seem to have done so to taste the freedom to speak and think as they chose, to worship as they pleased, to read what they might, and to assemble and petition the government if they had a mind to.

As in many cases, however, to believe in something is not necessarily to act consistently with that belief. There have been many intrusions on basic rights during our history. Later chapters address this issue in more detail.

Populism

The term *populism* refers to the hostility of the common person to power and the powerful. While public policy is not often driven by populist sentiments (for the powerful, by definition, exercise considerable political influence), populism has always been part of the American belief system and has sometimes been expressed in visible ways in American politics.

One of the most common targets of populist sentiment has been concentrated economic power and the people who exercise it. Andrew Jackson mobilized this sentiment in his fight against the Bank of the United States in the 1830s. The Populist movement of the 1890s aimed at taming the new corporations of the day, especially the banks and the railroads. Corporations were the target of popular hostility during the dark days of the Great Depression and also in the 1970s, when agitation by consumer and environmental groups made the lives of some corporate executives extremely uncomfortable.

Populism is also hostile to the concentration of power in government. Alabama's segregationist governor, George Wallace, successfully tapped into this sentiment in his run for the Democratic presidential nomination in 1968, when he complained about the "pointy-headed intellectuals in Washington." The populist sentiment is evident today in efforts to impose term limits on public officials and in the popularity of anti-establishment figures such as Gov. Jesse Ventura of Minnesota.

Structural Influences on American Politics

We have now examined a number of structural factors that influence American politics. In Chapters 2 and 3, we examined the constitutional rules; in this chapter, we considered the main features of American society, economy, political culture, and the international system and how each influences important aspects of politics and government in the United States. These structural factors are interrelated. The kind of constitutional rules we have are, to a substantial degree, shaped by our beliefs about the nature of the individual, society, and government that make up our political culture. The political culture, in turn, with its ideas celebrating the market, competitive individualism, and private property, is perfectly attuned to a free enterprise economy. How the economy operates and develops has a lot to do with the life of the American people (where people live, what kind of work they do, and so on), as does the nation's place in the world. The characteristics of the American population trigger their own effects; the populace's level of education and skill has a lot to do with American economic performance, for instance.

HOW DEMOCRATIC ARE WE?

PROPOSITION: The kind of economy, society, and culture we have in the United States makes it difficult to have a real democracy because the key components of a working democracy—popular sovereignty, political equality, and political liberty—cannot flourish.

AGREE: The free enterprise capitalist system in the United States results in large inequalities in income and wealth that inevitably spill over into political life, making political equality hard to achieve. Moreover, the system's rapid economic and technological changes often contribute to anxiety, fear, and anger among the public, interfering with the compromise and deliberation central to democratic life. Finally, economic and technical change is further fragmenting our highly individualistic culture, making a sense of community and public responsibility even less likely than before.

DISAGREE: American society is open, diverse, and filled with opportunity for those who are ambitious. Economic growth is raising the living standards of the population across the board, which bodes well for democracy; note the evidence that high living standards and democracy are strongly related. Also, economic, technological, and social changes are allowing more and more people to develop their abilities and capacities, to become informed, to link together with others who share their public concerns, to get involved in community and political affairs, and to have their voices heard by public officials.

THE AUTHORS: There is something to be said for each argument. There are some developments and conditions in American society, economy, culture, and world position that are most certainly democracy-enhancing, as the "disagree" position argues. There are other developments and conditions that are worth worrying about, however. First, substantial income and wealth inequality cannot help but undermine political equality. Second, even if popular control over the government in Washington exists (which remains an open question), it may well be the case that this government is not the center of the most important decisions affecting our lives; the rapid globalization of our economy puts important decision-making power into the hands of private investors, currency traders, and the executives of global manufacturing, banking, telecommunications, and transportation corporations.

Summary

How politics and government work is shaped by such structural factors as the nature of society, the economy, the nation's place in the world, and the political culture.

The most important changes in the American population are its growth; its diversification along ethnic, religious, and racial lines; its relocation from rural to urban and suburban areas and to the Sun Belt; and its gradual aging. Americans enjoy a very high standard of living, but inequality is substantial and poverty is surprisingly persistent. These factors affect the agenda of American politics and the distribution of political power.

The American economy is a market economy that has changed over the years from a highly competitive, small-enterprise form to a corporate-dominated one with a global reach. Economic change has had important reverberations in American politics.

The emergence of the United States as a superpower in the twentieth century changed the content of foreign policy, the balance of power between the president and Congress, the size of the federal government, and the priorities of the government's budget. The collapse of socialism in Eastern Europe affirmed the position of the United States as the world's most important military power.

Americans believe strongly in individualism, limited government, and free enterprise. Beliefs about democracy, liberty, and the primacy of the common people also help define the political culture. The political culture shapes American ideas about what the good society should look like, the appropriate role for government, and the possibilities for self-government.

Suggestions for Further Reading

Bellah, Robert N., Richard Madsen, William M. Sullivan, Ann Swidler, and Steven M. Tipton. *Habits of the Heart.* Berkeley, CA: University of California Press, 1985.
    A convincing description of competitive individualism and its effects.

Chafe, William H. *The Unfinished Journey: America Since World War II,* 2nd ed. New York: Oxford University Press, 1995.
    A history of postwar America, with special attention to how structural transformations have shaped American political life.

Dicken, Peter. *Global Shift: The Internationalization of Economic Activity,* 3rd ed. New York: Guilford Press, 1998.
    A comprehensive look at the scope, causes, and consequences of economic globalization.

Friedman, Thomas L. *The Lexus and the Olive Tree.* New York: Farrar, Straus & Giroux, 1999.
    A somewhat breathless yet informative account of globalization and how it is transforming societies around the world, including the United States.

Hochschild, Jennifer L. *Facing Up to the American Dream.* Princeton, NJ: Princeton University Press, 1995.
    A brilliant examination of the ideology of the American dream and how race and social class affect its interpretation and possibilities.

Hughes, James W., and Joseph J. Seneca, eds. *America's Demographic Tapestry.* New Brunswick, NJ: Rutgers University Press, 1999.
    A collection of research essays on the underlying demographic changes that are transforming the United States.

Ohmae, Kenichi. *The End of the Nation State.* New York: Free Press, 1995.
    A provocative essay suggesting that globalization has diminished almost to extinction the role of nation-states and national governments.

Wilson, William Julius. *When Work Disappears: The World of the New Urban Poor.* New York: Knopf, 1996.
    A powerful analysis of how globalization and technological change have adversely affected inner-city poor neighborhoods.

Internet Sources

The Economist   **http://www.economist.com/**
    The home page of one of the world's leading publications on the U.S. and international economies.

Fedstats   **http://www.fedstats.gov/**
    Statistical information on the U.S. economy and society from more than 70 government agencies.

Globalization and Democracy Homepage
http://www.colorado.edu/IBS/GAD/gad.html
   Information on a National Science Foundation–funded graduate training and research program, directed by one of the authors of this textbook.

Statistical Abstract of the United States   **http://www.census.gov/statab/www/**
   A vast compendium of statistical information on the government, the economy, and society.

Statistical Resources on the Web
www.umich.edu/libhome/Documents.center/stats.html
   A vast compendium of statistical information on society, economy, and culture for the United States and other countries, organized by the University of Michigan library in a very user-friendly format.

Yahoo/ Business and Economy   **http://www.yahoo.com/Business_and_Economy/**
   A gateway to a wealth of information about business and the economy.

Yahoo/Society and Culture   **http://www.yahoo.com/Society_and_Culture/**
   A gateway to a wealth of information about social and cultural issues.

Notes

1. Material for this opening story is from the following sources: "Profile: Loretta Sanchez," *Congressional Quarterly Weekly Report* (January 4, 1997), Vol. 51, no. 1, p. 52; Don Terry, "Bitter Rematch Reflects Changes in Orange County," *New York Times,* National Edition (October 28, 1998), p. A24; Francis X. Clines, "An Underdog Savors the Limelight," *New York Times,* National Edition (December 18, 1996), p. B12.

2. Princeton Survey Research Associates and Knight Ridder Survey, May, 1997; Princeton Survey Research Associates and PEW Research Survey, November, 1997, reported at Public Agenda On-Line at **www.publicagenda.org/**.

3. Michael Reich, "The Proletarianization of the Workforce," in Richard Edwards, Michael Reich, and Thomas A. Weisskopf, eds., *The Capitalist System* (Englewood Cliffs, NJ: Prentice Hall, 1966), p. 125.

4. Stanley Lebergott, "The American Labor Force," in Lance E. Davis, ed., *American Economic Growth* (New York: Harper & Row, 1972), p. 187; ibid., p. 124.

5. U.S. Bureau of the Census, news release, November 5, 1997.

6. *Human Development Report, 1999* (New York: The United Nations, 1999).

7. Daniel Weinberg, "Press Briefing," September 30, 1999, U.S. Bureau of the Census, Washington, D.C.

8. Stanley B. Greenberg, *Middle-Class Dreams* (New York: Times Books, 1995); Susan J. Tolchin, *The Angry American* (Boulder, CO: Westview Press, 1999).

9. "Economic Optimism Abounds," *The Public Perspective* (June–July 1999), pp. 38–39.

10. Peter Gottschalk, "Inequality, Income Growth and Mobility," *Journal of Economic Perspectives,* 11, no. 2 (Spring 1997): 13–19.

11. William Julius Wilson, *When Work Disappears: The World of the New Urban Poor* (New York: Knopf, 1996).

12. Weinberg, "Press Briefing"; Daniel Weinberg et. al., "Fifty Years of U.S. Income Data from the Current Population Survey," *American Economic Association Papers and Proceedings* (May 1999): 125–147.

13. Richard Stevenson, "In a Time of Plenty, the Poor Are Still Poor," *New York Times* (January 23, 1999), p. A1.

14. Gottschalk, "Inequality, Income Growth and Mobility."

15. Edward Wolff, "International Comparisons of Wealth Inequality," *Review of Income and Wealth,* 42, no. 4 (December 1996).

16. Ibid.

17. See Edward S. Greenberg, *Capitalism and the American Political Ideal* (Armonk, NY: Sharpe, 1985), ch. 4.

18. On this history, see Thomas C. Cochran and William Miller, *The Age of Enterprise* (New York: Harper & Row, 1961); ibid.; Louis M. Hacker, *American Economic Growth and Development* (New York: Wiley, 1970); Robert Wiebe, *The Search for Order* (New York: Hill & Wang, 1967).

19. U.S. Department of Commerce, *International Direct Investment* (Washington, D.C.: U.S. Government Printing Office, 1984), p. 1.

20. For a flavor of this literature, see Thomas L. Friedman, *The Lexus and the Olive Tree* (New York: Farrar, Straus & Giroux, 1999); Kenichi Ohmae, *The End of the Nation State* (New York: The Free Press, 1995); Saskia Sassen, *Losing Control: Sovereignty in an Age of Globalization* (New York: Columbia University Press, 1996); and Susan Strange, *The Retreat of the State* (Cambridge, U.K.: Cambridge University Press, 1996).

21. Jennifer L. Hochschild, *Facing Up to the American Dream* (Princeton, NJ: Princeton University Press, 1995), ch. 1.

22. See Jennifer L. Hochschild, *What's Fair? American Beliefs about Distributive Justice* (Cambridge, MA: Harvard University Press, 1981); Herbert McClosky and John R. Zaller, *The American Ethos: Public Attitudes Toward Capitalism and Democracy* (Cambridge, MA: Harvard University Press, 1984); Sidney Verba and Gary R. Orren, *Equality in America* (Cambridge, MA: Harvard University Press, 1985).

23. Verba and Orren, *Equality in America,* p. 255.

24. Alexis de Tocqueville, *Democracy in America* (1845).

25. On the domination of classical liberalism in America, see Louis Hartz, *The Liberal Tradition in America* (New York: Harcourt, Brace, 1955). But also see Rogers M. Smith, "Beyond Tocqueville, Myrdal, and Hartz: The Multiple Traditions of America," *American Political Science Review,* 87, No. 3 (September 1993), pp. 549–566.

26. John Kenneth Galbraith, *American Capitalism* (Boston: Houghton Mifflin, 1956); see also McClosky and Zaller, *The American Ethos,* pp. 270–271.

27. Russell Hanson, *The Democratic Imagination in America* (Princeton, NJ: Princeton University Press, 1985).

28. McClosky and Zaller, *The American Ethos,* p. 18.

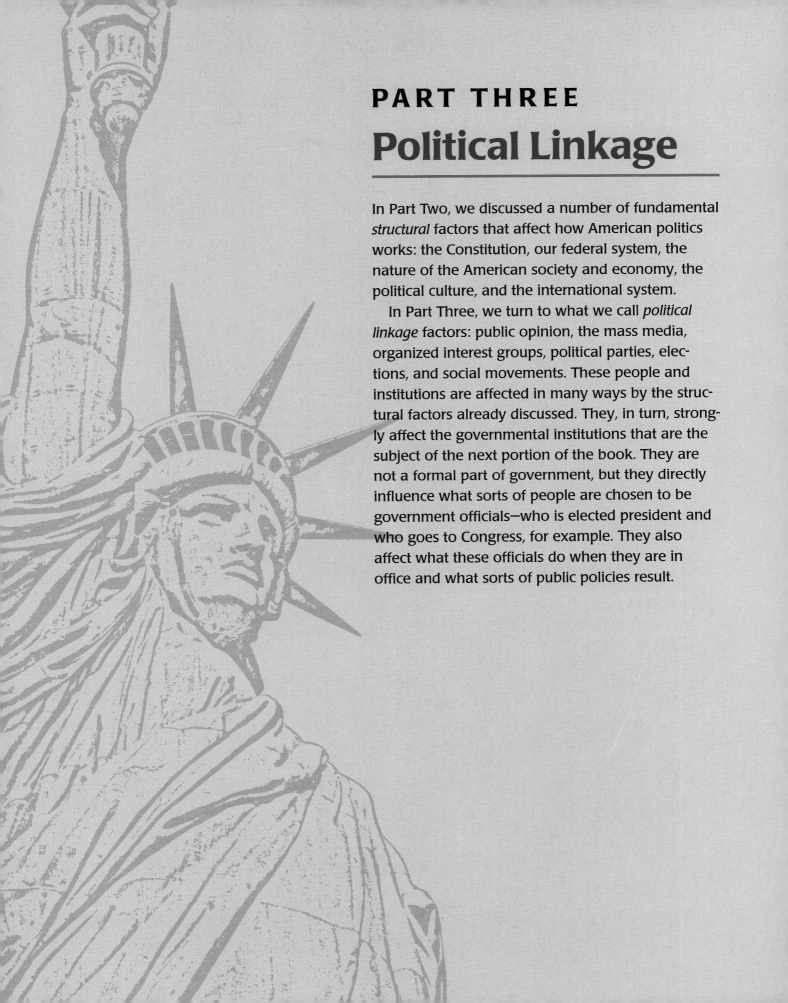

PART THREE
Political Linkage

In Part Two, we discussed a number of fundamental *structural* factors that affect how American politics works: the Constitution, our federal system, the nature of the American society and economy, the political culture, and the international system.

In Part Three, we turn to what we call *political linkage* factors: public opinion, the mass media, organized interest groups, political parties, elections, and social movements. These people and institutions are affected in many ways by the structural factors already discussed. They, in turn, strongly affect the governmental institutions that are the subject of the next portion of the book. They are not a formal part of government, but they directly influence what sorts of people are chosen to be government officials—who is elected president and who goes to Congress, for example. They also affect what these officials do when they are in office and what sorts of public policies result.

Public Opinion

The Vietnam War and the Public

On August 2, 1964, the Pentagon announced that the U.S. destroyer *Maddox,* while on "routine patrol" in international waters in the Gulf of Tonkin near Vietnam, had undergone an "unprovoked attack" by three communist North Vietnamese PT boats. Two days later, the Pentagon reported a "second deliberate attack" on the *Maddox* and its companion destroyer, the *C. Turner Joy.* In a nationwide television broadcast, President Lyndon Johnson referred to "open aggression on the high seas" and declared that these hostile actions required that he retaliate with military force. Air attacks were launched against four North Vietnamese PT boat bases and an oil storage depot.[1]

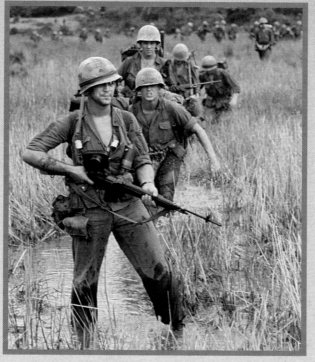

Years later, the *Pentagon Papers,* a secret Defense Department study, revealed that the American people had been deceived. The *Maddox* had not been on an innocent cruise; it had, in fact, been assisting South Vietnamese gunboats make raids on the North Vietnamese coast. The second "attack" apparently never occurred; it was imagined by an inexperienced sonar operator in dark and stormy seas. At the time, however, few skeptics raised questions. On August 7, 1964, by a vote of 88–2, the Senate passed the Tonkin Resolution, which approved the president's taking "all necessary measures," including the use of armed force, to repel any armed attack and to assist any ally in the region. A legal basis for full U.S. involvement in the Vietnam War had been established.

For more than a decade, the United States had been giving large-scale military aid to the French colonialists, and then to the American-installed but authoritarian South Vietnamese government, to fight nationalists and communists in Vietnam. More than 23,000 U.S. military advisers were there by the end of 1964, occasionally engaging in combat. On the other side of the world, the American public knew and cared little about the guerrilla war. In fact, few knew exactly where Vietnam was. Nevertheless, people were willing to go along when their leaders told them that action was essential to resist communist aggression.

After the Tonkin incident, people paid more attention. Public support for the war increased. When asked in August what should be done next in Vietnam, 48 percent said to keep troops there, get tougher, or take definite military action while only 14 percent said negotiate or get out.[2] Through the fall of 1964, more people wanted to step up the war than wanted to pull out, and many endorsed the current policy. In 1965, after the United States had begun the heavy "Rolling Thunder" bombing of North Vietnam, and after large numbers of U.S. troops had gradually engaged in combat in South Vietnam, public support of the war continued. Month after month, pollsters found that only a small minority wanted to withdraw from Vietnam; as many or more wanted to escalate the war further, and the majority favored continuing the current policy.

But the number of U.S. troops in Vietnam rose rapidly, from 184,300 at the end of 1965 to 536,100 at the end of 1968, and casualties increased correspondingly. A total of 1,369 Americans were killed in 1965; 5,008 in 1966; 9,377 in 1967; and 14,589 in 1968. Many thousands more were wounded, and others were captured or missing.[3] Television news began to display weekly casualty counts in the hundreds, with pictures of dead American soldiers going home in body bags. The war became expensive, as politicians put it, in "American blood and treasure." Senate hearings aired antiwar testimony. Peace marches and demonstrations, though resented by much of the public, nonetheless increased pressure to end the war.

By December 1967, about as many people (45 percent) agreed as disagreed with the proposition that it had been a "mistake" to send troops to fight in Vietnam. A large majority said they favored "Vietnamization," bringing U.S. troops home as South Vietnamese replaced them.

Then catastrophe struck. In January 1968, during Vietnam's Tet holidays, the North Vietnamese army launched what became known as the *Tet Offensive:* massive attacks throughout South Vietnam, including an assault on the U.S.

embassy in Saigon. The American public was shocked by televised scenes of urban destruction and bloody corpses, of U.S. soldiers destroying Ben Tre village "in order to save it," of marines bogged down in the rubble of the ancient city of Hue, and of a 77-day siege of Khe Sanh. The chief lesson seemed to be that a U.S. victory in Vietnam, if feasible at all, was going to be very costly.

After Tet, criticism of the war by politicians, newspaper editorials, television commentators such as Walter Cronkite, and others mushroomed, and public support for the war diminished. President Johnson—staggered by a surprisingly strong vote for antiwar candidate Eugene McCarthy in the New Hampshire primary—announced that he would limit the bombing of North Vietnam, seek a negotiated settlement, and withdraw as a candidate for reelection. In March 1968, only 41 percent of Americans described themselves as hawks (supporters of the war), a sharp drop from the 61 percent of early February. Anger over Vietnam contributed to the election defeat of the Democrats the following November.

By January 1969, when the Nixon administration took office, a substantial majority of the public favored monthly reductions in the number of U.S. soldiers in Vietnam: 57 percent approved the idea, while only 28 percent disapproved. In June,

Nixon announced the withdrawal of 25,000 troops, followed by announcements of 35,000 more in September, another 50,000 in December, and 150,000 during the following year. Large majorities of the public approved the withdrawals. Most said they wanted to continue them even if the South Vietnamese government collapsed. There can be little doubt that public opinion influenced U.S. disengagement from the war.

This did not mean that a majority of Americans wanted to get out of Vietnam immediately; most disliked the idea of a communist victory. But antiwar marches and demonstrations continued during 1970 and 1971, and many people wanted a faster pace of withdrawal. Gradually, U.S. troops came out of Vietnam; in January 1973, after the intensive Christmas bombing of North Vietnam, a peace agreement was finally signed. Two years later, the North Vietnamese army took control of Saigon and reunified Vietnam, a nation that had been divided since the end of World War II.

The Vietnam story shows how government officials can sometimes lead or manipulate opinion, especially when it concerns obscure matters in faraway lands, and how opinion is affected by events and their presentation in the mass media. The story also shows that public opinion, even on foreign policy matters, can have a strong effect on policymaking.

▶ Thinking Critically About This Chapter

This chapter is about the content of public opinion, how it is formed, and what effect it has on American politics and government.

Using the Framework. You will learn in this chapter how public opinion is shaped by a wide range of structural level factors, including historical events, the political culture, family and community socialization, and economic and social change. You will also learn how public opinion influences the behavior of political leaders and shapes many of the policies of the federal government.

Using the Democracy Standard. Based on the standard of democracy described in Chapter 1, public opinion should be one of the decisive factors in determining what government does. You will see in this chapter, however, that while the influence of public opinion is important, public officials must pay attention to other political forces as well. They sometimes pay close attention to public opinion; at other times, they pay only slight attention to it. ▶

Democracy and Public Opinion

public opinion

Political attitudes expressed by ordinary citizens.

The political attitudes expressed by ordinary citizens are known collectively as **public opinion**. If democracy is, as Abraham Lincoln put it, "government of the people, by the people, and for the people," public opinion—especially the collective policy preferences of ordinary citizens—plays a crucial part in democratic government. In a perfect democracy, based on popular sovereignty and majority rule, the government would do exactly what its citizens wanted, at least in the long run.

An important test of how well democracy is working, then, is how closely government policy corresponds to the expressed wishes of its citizens. To what extent does the government respond to public opinion, as opposed, say, to the demands of organized interest groups?

Curiously, however, many leading political theorists, including some who say they believe in democracy, have expressed grave doubts about the wisdom of the public. James Madison, Alexander Hamilton, and other Founders of our national government worried that the public's "passions" would infringe on liberty and that public opinion would be susceptible to radical and frequent shifts.[4] Journalist and statesman Walter Lippmann declared that most people do not know what goes on in the world; they have only vague, media-provided pictures in their heads. Lippmann approvingly quoted Sir Robert Peel's reference to "that great compound of folly, weakness, prejudice, wrong feeling, right feeling, obstinacy and newspaper paragraphs which is called public opinion."[5]

Modern survey researchers have not been much kinder. The first voting studies, carried out during the 1940s and 1950s, turned up what scholars considered appalling evidence of public ignorance, lack of interest in politics, and reliance on group or party loyalties rather than judgments about the issues of the day. Repeated surveys of the same individuals found that their responses seemed to change randomly from one interview to another. Philip Converse, a leading student of political behavior, coined the term *nonattitudes:* on many issues of public policy, many or most Americans seemed to have no real views at all but simply offered "doorstep opinions" to satisfy interviewers.[6]

What should we make of this? If ordinary citizens are poorly informed and their views are based on whim, or if they have no real opinions at all, it hardly seems desirable—or even possible—that public opinion should determine what governments do. Both the feasibility and the attractiveness of democracy seem to be thrown into doubt. When we examine exactly what sorts of opinions ordinary Americans have, however, and how those opinions are formed and changed, we will see that such fears about public opinion have been greatly exaggerated.

What People Know About Politics

Years ago, people who wanted to find out anything about public opinion had to guess, based on what their barbers or taxi drivers said, on what appeared in letters to newspaper editors, or on what sorts of one-liners won cheers at political rallies. But the views of personal acquaintances, letter writers, or rally audiences are often quite different from those of the public as a whole. Similarly, the angry people who called in to radio talk shows at the beginning of the Clinton administration tended to be more conservative and anti-Clinton than most Americans.[7] Listeners could easily get a mistaken impression of what was on their fellow citizens' minds. To figure out what the average American thinks, we cannot rely on unrepresentative groups or noisy minorities.

Measuring What People Think

A clever invention, the opinion poll or **sample survey**, now eliminates most of the guesswork in measuring public opinion. A survey consists of systematic interviews conducted by trained professional interviewers, who ask a standardized set

sample survey

An interview study asking questions of a set of people who are chosen as representative of the whole population.

of questions of a rather small number of randomly chosen Americans—usually about 1,000 or 1,500 of them. Such a survey can reveal with remarkable accuracy what all 260 million or so of us are thinking.

The secret of success is to make sure that the sample of people interviewed is representative of the whole population, that is, that the proportions of people in the sample who are young, old, female, college-educated, black, rural, Catholic, southern, western, and so forth are all about the same as in the U.S. population as a whole. This representativeness is achieved best when the people being interviewed are chosen through **random sampling**, which ensures that each member of the population has an equal chance of being chosen. Then survey researchers can add up all the responses to a given question and compute the percentages of people answering one way or another. Statisticians can use probability theory to tell how close the survey's results are likely to be to what the whole population would say if asked the same questions. Findings from a random sample of 1,500 people have a 95 percent chance of accurately reflecting the views of the whole population within about 3 or 4 percentage points.[8]

Perfectly random sampling is not feasible. Personal interviews have to be clustered geographically so that interviewers can easily get from one respondent to another. Telephone interviews—the cheapest and most common kind—are clustered within particular telephone exchanges. Still, the samples that survey organizations use are sufficiently representative so that survey results closely reflect how the whole population would have responded if everyone in the United States had been asked the same questions at the moment the survey was carried out.

When you are interpreting surveys, you need to pay close attention to the precise wording of the questions. It often makes a big difference exactly how questions are asked. In one survey, for example, support for a constitutional amendment requiring a balanced budget dropped from 70 percent to 31 percent when the question specified that Medicare would be cut.[9] Moreover, "closed-ended" or "forced-choice" questions, which ask the respondents to choose among preformulated answers, do not always reveal what people are thinking on their own or what they would come up with after a few minutes of thought or discussion. For that reason, "open-ended" questions are sometimes asked to yield more spontaneous answers, and small discussion groups or "focus groups" are

random sampling

The selection of survey respondents by chance, with equal probability, to ensure their representativeness of the whole population.

LongmanParticipate

CourseCompass

simulation
You Are a Polling Consultant

Exit polls, which survey the opinions of people as they leave the polling place after voting, are a major source of information on who votes and how they make voting decisions. They are also the basis for network election-night reports on "who won" announcements, made well before all the ballots have been counted.

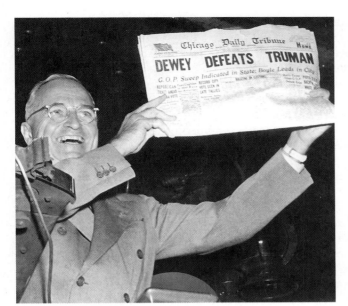

Harry Truman mocks an edition of the *Chicago Tribune* proclaiming his Republican challenger, Thomas Dewey, president. Opinion polls stopped asking questions too early in the 1948 election campaign, missing Truman's last-minute surge.

brought together to show what emerges when people talk among themselves about the topics a moderator introduces.

Individuals' Ignorance

Several decades of polling have shown that most ordinary Americans do not know or care a lot about politics. Nearly everyone knows some basic facts, such as the name of the capital of the United States and the length of the president's term of office. But only about two-thirds of adults know which party has the most members in the House of Representatives. Only about one-half know that

WEB EXPLORATION

Survey Validity

Issue: Seeing the flood of polls about elections and government policies in the news media, many people ask, "How come I've never been asked about my opinions?"

Site: You can take part in a political survey by accessing "Doonesbury On-Line" through the "Course Documents" section of your online course. In the Web Explorations section for Chapter 5, click on "Survey Validity" and then open "poll" and answer the questions posed there. Also, look at "Previous Questions and Results."

What You've Learned: How do your views on the issues compare with others who have taken part? Given what you have learned about surveys and random sampling in this textbook, what would you conclude about the validity of this poll?

HINT: Remember that survey validity depends on the "randomness" of the sample.

there are two U.S. senators from their state, and fewer can name their representative in the House. Only about 30 percent know that the term of a U.S. House member is two years.[10] And barely one in four Americans can explain what is in the First Amendment.[11]

People have particular trouble with technical terms, geography, and abbreviations. In the 1960s, for example, a substantial majority of Americans did not know that the Soviet Union was not a member of NATO (the North Atlantic Treaty Organization), an alliance directed against the Soviet Union. In the 1980s, very few could identify the important SALT negotiations (the Strategic Arms Limitation Talks) between the United States and the Soviet Union. Today, many are fuzzy about the location of such places as Bosnia, Iraq, and Kosovo.

The things that most Americans don't know may not be vital to their role as citizens, however. If citizens are aware that there is a military alliance of Western countries, for example, or that arms control talks went on between the United States and the Soviet Union, is it crucial that they recognize the acronyms *NATO* and *SALT?* How important is it for people to know about the two-year term of office for the U.S. House of Representatives, as long as they are aware of the opportunity to vote each time it comes along? Perhaps most people know as much as they need to know in order to be good citizens, particularly if they can form opinions with the help of better-informed cue givers (experts, political leaders, media sources, informed friends, interest groups, and so on) whom they trust or by means of simple rules of thumb.[12]

In any case, the lack of knowledge does not represent just stupidity or laziness. There are good reasons for it. Most people are busy with their jobs and families. They don't have much time or energy left for politics. Unless following politics happens to give them pleasure, there is little reason for them to invest much effort in it. Scholars remind us that a single citizen has only a minuscule chance of determining the outcome of an election in which thousands or millions vote; from a purely selfish point of view, it is not worth a lot of trouble to decide how to vote. The real surprise may be that people know as much as they do.[13]

We do not mean to minimize the consequences of people's lack of political knowledge. It has some extremely important implications. As we will see in Chapter 7, for example, when policy decisions are made in the dark, out of public view, interest groups may influence policies that an informed public would oppose. Nor do we mean to encourage complacency, fatalism, or ignorance. Individuals should take the personal responsibility to be good citizens, and organized efforts to alert and to educate the public are valuable. But low levels of information are a reality that must be taken into account. It is unrealistic to expect everyone to have a detailed knowledge of a wide range of political matters.

ideology

A system of interrelated attitudes and beliefs.

By the same token, we should not expect the average American to have an elaborately worked out **ideology**, or system of interlocking attitudes and beliefs. You yourself may be a consistent liberal or conservative (or populist, socialist, libertarian, or something else), with many opinions that hang together in a coherent structure. But surveys show that most people's attitudes are only loosely connected to each other. Most people have opinions that vary from one issue to another: conservative on some issues, liberal on others. Surveys and in-depth interviews indicate that these are often linked by underlying themes and values, but not necessarily in the neat ways that the ideologies of leading political thinkers would dictate.[14]

For the same reasons, we should not be surprised that most individuals' expressed opinions on issues tend to be unstable. Many people give different answers when the same survey question is repeated four years or two years or even a few weeks after their first response. Scholars have disagreed about what these unstable responses mean, but uncertainty and lack of information very likely play a part.

Collective Knowledge and Stability

None of this, however, means that the opinions of the public, taken as a whole, are unreal, unstable, or irrelevant. The collective whole is greater than its individual parts.

Even if there is some randomness in the average individual's expressions of political opinions—even if people often say things off the top of their heads to survey interviewers—the responses of thousands or millions of people tend to average out this randomness and reveal a stable **collective public opinion**. Americans' collective policy preferences are actually very stable over time. That is, the percentage of Americans who favor a particular policy usually stays about the same, unless circumstances change in important ways. Year after year, for instance, very high and steady majorities of the public have said that they want to spend more on Social Security, health, aid to education, and protection of the environment. Other examples of stability in collective public opinion will be mentioned later in this chapter.

collective public opinion
The political attitudes of the public as a whole, expressed as averages, percentages, or other summaries of many individuals' opinions.

Moreover, even if most people form many of their specific opinions by deferring to others whom they trust (party leaders, television commentators, and the like) rather than by compiling their own mass of political information, the resulting public opinion need not be ignorant or unwise because the trusted leaders may themselves take account of the best available information. Some recent research has indicated that Americans' collective policy preferences react rather sensibly to events, to changing circumstances, and to new information, so that we can speak of a "rational public."[15]

Not all scholars are convinced that public opinion acts rationally, but the evidence is clear, at least, that the American public as a collective whole has real opinions, not just "nonattitudes," and that many of the Founders' fears of capriciousness or fluctuations in public opinion are no longer justified, if they ever were.

How People Feel About Politics

Americans have opinions about many different political matters, including specific policies, basic values, the Republican and Democratic parties, and government itself.

The System in General

At the most general level, Americans are quite proud of their country and its political system. In 1998, for example, only 4.8 percent of Americans agreed with the statement that "there are some countries better than the United States." Well over three-quarters of Americans agreed with the statement that the "American system of government is the best in the world."[16] At the more specific level, however, the picture does not look as rosy. An especially important aspect of public opinion concerns general confidence or trust in government institutions, which dropped sharply in the late 1960s and early 1970s and has stayed low ever since[17] (see Figure 5.1).

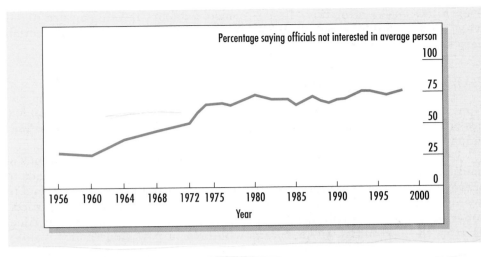

Figure 5.1 ● The Rise in Public Dissatisfaction

In recent years, high and growing numbers of Americans have said that public officials are not interested in the average person.
Sources: National Election Studies, 1956–1972; General Social Survey, 1973–1999.

In 1992, fully 70 percent of Americans said they were "dissatisfied" with the overall performance of the national government, a feeling that contributed to the independent candidacy of Ross Perot and the defeat of President George Bush in that year. This sour mood contributed to the ousting of many Democratic members of Congress in 1994. Confidence and trust in government may have rebounded a bit in recent years, however, no doubt a product of good economic times.[18]

WEB EXPLORATION

Who Do You Trust?

Issue: Americans hold views not only about the content of the policies they want but who they trust to get the job done in various policy areas.

Site: AccessPublic Agenda Online through the "Course Documents" section of your online course. In the "Web Explorations" section for Chapter 5, click on "Who Do You Trust?" and open "trust." Select three major policy areas from the list on the left. For each policy area, select "Who Should Decide?" and examine the poll results on what the public thinks about who it can trust to get the job done.

What You've Learned: Who do the American people trust the most to give them the public policies they want most? Congress or the President? Republicans or Democrats? The public or business leaders?

HINT: Americans clearly want certain things to be done by government and other things left to the private sector. They also make clear distinctions between the parties and the branches of government.

Americans report very high levels of patriotism compared with people in other rich democracies, as well as higher levels of confidence in their fundamental government and economic institutions (although not necessarily confidence in their present leaders).

Similarly, citizens' sense of **political efficacy**—their feeling that they can make a difference and that government will respond to their concerns—has dropped markedly over the past three decades. In 1998, 62 percent said that "the federal government doesn't care what people like me think," up from 36 percent in 1964; 67 percent believe that government "is run for a few big interests."[19] (Interestingly, although disaffected with government and public officials, Americans reported that they were confident about the future of their families and their country, happy with the economy, and satisfied with their private lives and jobs by the end of the 1990s.)[20]

political efficacy

The sense that one can affect what government does.

Government Performance

One important aspect of happiness or unhappiness with government is a judgment about how well the president has been doing his job. For many decades, pollsters have been asking people whether they approve or disapprove of the president's handling of his job. The percentage of people saying that they approve—the **presidential approval rating**—is taken as a crucial indicator of a president's popularity. Trends in presidential popularity are often displayed in a sort of rising and falling "fever chart." Approval tends to fluctuate up and down with particular events—Lyndon Johnson's approval fluctuated with events in Vietnam, and he decided not to run for reelection when his ratings fell to historic lows after the Tet Offensive—but in the current era, most presidents have come on hard times. Richard Nixon, Gerald Ford, and Jimmy Carter all had low approval ratings by the end of their terms. George Bush reached a record 89 percent approval in March 1991 in the aftermath of the Gulf War, but fell below 30 percent by the summer, an unprecedented collapse. Oddly, Bill Clinton enjoyed the highest job approval ratings of any recent president in the two final years of his term (although his job approval rating was not matched by public judgments of his character), in spite of the fact that he was impeached by the House of Representatives.

presidential approval rating

A president's standing with the public, indicated by the percentage of Americans who tell survey interviewers that they approve a president's "handling of his job."

LongmanParticipate

CourseCompass

timeline
Public Opinion and Presidential Approval

Public opinion about the president is influenced heavily by structural factors and events. Here George Bush and General Norman Schwarzkopf exult during a victory parade after the Persian Gulf War. As often happens in times of international crisis, Bush's popularity was boosted by the war. However, soon after the war ended, as people turned their attention to the domestic economy mired in recession, his popularity fell sharply.

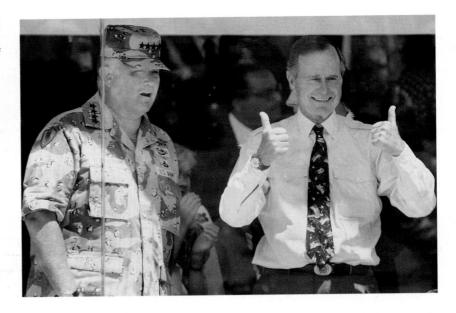

We will see in later chapters that a president's popularity has very important consequences. It is a good predictor of whether he will win reelection (if he is running) and whether his party will win or lose congressional seats. Presidential popularity may also affect how much influence the president has in Congress and how effectively he can persuade the public to agree with his policy stands. A president who is very popular with the public can be a political powerhouse; an unpopular president is in serious trouble.

The public's evaluations of presidents' handling of their jobs depend on how well things are actually going. The state of the economy is especially important: when the country is prosperous and ordinary Americans are doing well and feeling confident about the future, the president tends to be popular; when there is high inflation or unemployment or when general living standards remain stagnant, the president's popularity falls. International crises may lead the public to "rally 'round the flag" and support the president (providing that leaders in both parties are doing so), but that solidarity lasts only a little while unless the crisis works out well. If bad news keeps coming, people begin to disapprove of the president's performance.[21] In 1980, for example, the long drawn-out Iran hostage crisis undermined President Carter's popularity and political influence and cost him the election against Ronald Reagan in November.

Evaluations of Congress have not been surveyed as regularly as those of the president, but it appears that Congress is usually less popular than the president.[22] The Democratic-controlled Congress of the 1980s and early 1990s, for example, was thoroughly disliked by the time the Democrats were ousted from control in 1994. Because the public overwhelmingly disapproved of the way the House and Senate conducted the impeachment and trial of President Clinton, public approval of Congress never got much above 40 percent in 1999.[23]

Party Loyalty

Historically, one of the most important political attitudes in the United States has been identification with a political party. Many Americans still feel such an identification. When survey researchers ask people whether, generally speaking, they consider themselves Republicans, Democrats, independents, or something else, more than 60 percent pick one of the two major parties.[24] That sense of belonging to a party is called **party identification**. Among the remainder, many say they "lean" toward one party or the other and are sometimes included among those who identify with that party.

Many people begin to identify with a party when they are rather young. Usually they adopt the same party as their parents and tend to stick with it through the rest of their lives, although the extent and strength of party identification have slipped in recent years. People use the party label to help organize their thinking about politics: to guide them in voting, in judging new policy proposals, and so on. For example, people who consider themselves Republicans are much more likely than Democrats to vote for Republican candidates and to approve of Republican presidents; they tend to belong to different social and economic groups; and they are somewhat more likely to favor policies associated with the Republican party.

Between Roosevelt's highly popular New Deal of the 1930s and the late 1960s, more Americans identified themselves as Democrats than as Republicans, making the Democrats the majority party. The Democrats' advantage began to shrink, until the parties reached relative parity in the early 1980s during Ronald Reagan's term. Although Democrats have taken a small lead again over Republicans, independents make up the largest group today (see Figure 5.2).

The party balance among voters has important effects on who rules in Washington, D.C., especially on which party controls Congress. Democrats controlled Congress for most of the time from the New Deal until the end of the 1970s. Changing partisanship helped Republicans to win majorities in the Senate from 1981 to 1986, however, and to gain control of both houses of Congress in 1994 and to retain control in 1996 and 1998.

In recent decades, along with a decline in the proportion of people who identify with one of the two parties, there has been a rise in the number of broadly defined independents (including "leaners"), from around 20 percent in the mid-1970s to slightly under 40 percent today. Although some scholars maintain that these figures exaggerate the rise of independents because many "leaners" behave the same way as people who say they consider themselves Republicans or Democrats,[25] there has clearly been a decline in the proportion of Americans who identify strongly with either of the two major parties. Scholars do not agree about why this decline has occurred.[26]

party identification

The sense of belonging to one or another political party.

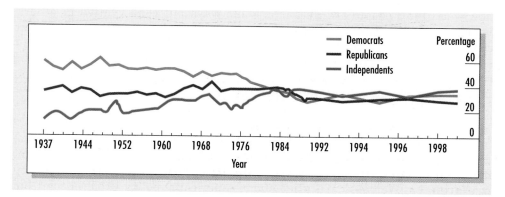

Figure 5.2 ● **Trends in Party Identification**

Over the years, the proportion of people calling themselves Republicans has increased, while the proportion of Democrats has decreased. More and more Americans today call themselves independents.
Source: Gallup surveys.

Government's Role

We saw in Chapter 4 that the foundation beliefs of Americans, which, taken together, make up what we have chosen to call the American political culture, include support for both free enterprise capitalism and democracy. Most Americans, for example, support the idea that, other things being equal, economic growth, efficiency, and opportunity require free markets, competition between firms, protection of private property rights, and limited government interference in economic affairs. Most Americans also support the idea that the best form of government is one in which individual freedoms exist, where citizens enjoy equal rights to participate in the political process, and where government leaders are responsible and responsive to the wishes of the people. Many scholars have pointed out that support for free enterprise capitalism, with its emphasis on freedom and liberty and a small role for government, may sometimes conflict with support for democracy, with its emphasis on government doing what the people want it to do, even if it means regulating the economy (e.g., environment, consumer safety, and the like) or redistributing income (e.g., progressive income tax).[27]

Most Americans, then, believe in both capitalism and democracy (and their respective core values, freedom and equality), but they divide on the relative priority they give to each. Some Americans—those we usually label **economic conservatives**—tend to put more emphasis on economic liberty and freedom from government interference; they believe that a free market offers the best road to economic efficiency and a decent society. Others—whom we usually label **economic liberals**—stress the necessary role of government in ensuring equality of opportunity, regulating potentially damaging business practices, and providing safety nets for individuals unable to compete in the job market. Government regulation of the economy and spending to help the disadvantaged are two of the main sources of political disputes in America; they make up a big part of the difference between the ideologies of liberalism and of conservatism. It is also useful to distinguish between **social liberals** and **social conservatives**, who differ on such social issues as abortion, prayer in the schools, homosexuality, pornography, crime, and political dissent. Those who favor free choices and the rights of the accused are often said to be liberals, while those preferring government enforcement of order and traditional values are called conservatives. It should be apparent that opinions on economic and social issues do not necessarily go together, however. Many people are liberal in some ways but conservative in others. Followers of Ross Perot and Jesse Ventura, for example, tended to be economic conservatives (in favor of less government, balanced budgets, and so on) but social liberals. African-Americans of a religious bent, by contrast, tend to be social conservatives (opposed to abortion and gay rights) but economic liberals (in favor of government help for the poor).

Policy Preferences

According to democratic theory, one of the chief determinants of what governments do should be what the citizens *want* them to do, that is, citizens' **policy preferences**. We can learn a lot about Americans' policy preferences from graphs that show what percentages of the public have favored various government policies at different times. Besides showing which sorts of policies have been favored and which have been opposed, these graphs indicate that collective public opinion is generally stable and that the public often distinguishes sharply among different policy alternatives.

economic conservatives
People who favor private enterprise and oppose government regulations on spending.

economic liberals
People who favor government regulation of business and government spending for social programs.

social liberals
People who favor civil liberties, abortion rights, and alternative lifestyles.

social conservatives
People who favor traditional social values; they tend to support strong law-and-order measures and to oppose abortion and gay rights.

policy preferences
Citizens' preferences concerning what policies they want government to pursue.

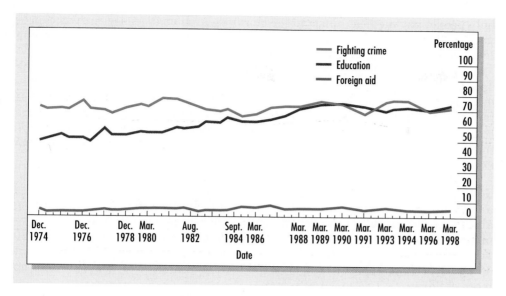

Figure 5.3 ● **Public Support for Spending Programs**

Large, fairly stable majorities of Americans have favored increased spending for fighting crime and aiding education, but very few have favored increased foreign aid.
Source: General Social Survey, 1973–1999.

Spending Programs   As Figure 5.3 indicates, for example, large and rather stable majorities of Americans (around 70 percent in recent years) think that we are spending "too little" on fighting crime and on education. The public also gives high and stable support to Social Security, Medicare, and environmental programs. Substantial majorities, moreover, want the federal government to

WEB EXPLORATION

Race Relations

Issue: Two approaches for improving the situation of racial minorities have been contending for the public's approval: ending discrimination and taking positive steps to rectify past discrimination (busing to aid integration, affirmative action in jobs and education).

Site: You can follow public opinion on race relations at the Gallup Poll through the "Course Documents" section of your online course. In the "Web Explorations" section for Chapter 5, click on "Race Relations" and then open "race." Select "Gallup Poll," then "Social and Economic Indicators," then "Race Relations."

What You've Learned: Where do you stand on race relations? Answer each of the Gallup questions in this section. Do your views converge with or diverge from the majority of your fellow citizens?

HINT: Your views will probably depend on two things: your judgment about how much race relations have already improved in the United States and your ideas about the role of government in society.

help people pay medical bills and for more research on diseases such as cancer and AIDS. And fewer than one in three Americans believe that we are spending too much on national defense.[28]

By contrast, few people—only about 5 percent—think too little is being spent on foreign aid; many more think too much is being spent. Except for disaster relief, foreign aid is generally unpopular. (The reason may be, in part, that few realize how little is spent on foreign aid—only about 1 percent of the budget. When this is made clear, support for economic aid rises sharply.)[29] Large majorities of the public oppose military aid or arms sales abroad. The space program wins only slightly greater support.

Social Issues   As Figure 5.4 shows, Americans make sharp distinctions among different circumstances when deciding whether they favor permitting abortions. For much of the past 25 years, about 90 percent of Americans have favored allowing legal abortion if a woman's health is endangered. About 80 percent would permit abortion in cases of serious birth defects. But only about 40 or 50 percent approve of abortion if a woman is poor or simply wants no more children.

This same graph indicates that approval of abortion under each of the different circumstances rose markedly between 1965 and the early 1970s. Since no surveys were conducted for several years in between, we cannot tell exactly when public opinion changed or how smoothly it did so, but nearly all of the change occurred before the U.S. Supreme Court's *Roe* v. *Wade* decision in January 1973, which declared that the Constitution protects a woman's right to have an abortion. Changing public attitudes may have affected the Court's decision; they did not result from it.

Other surveys have revealed strong liberalizing trends, over many years, concerning civil rights and civil liberties. Beginning in the 1940s or 1950s, more and more Americans have favored having black and white children go to

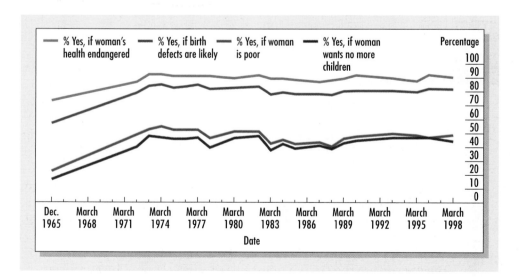

Figure 5.4 ● **Public Approval for Allowing Abortions**

Public opinion about abortion varies greatly with the circumstances. Large majorities favor allowing abortions if the woman's health is endangered or in the case of serious birth defects, but less than half the public would allow abortions in cases of poverty or simply wanting no more children.

Source: General Social Survey, 1965–1999.

Public opinion polls show that Americans strongly support the idea of integrated public schools. They do not support every method that courts and reformers have proposed for achieving integration, however. Integration-related busing schemes, for example, find little support among the public.

the same schools and integrating work, housing, and public accommodations. (At the same time, however, there is considerable opposition to busing and affirmative action.) These issues are explored in depth in Chapter 16. More and more members of the public have also favored letting various dissenting groups (communists, socialists, atheists, and others) teach school, speak in public, and have their books in libraries. These trends are discussed further in Chapter 15.

Attitudes about the rights of gays and lesbians are more complicated. Although a slight majority of Americans agree with the statements that "people living in a homosexual relationship is not acceptable" and that "homosexual behavior is morally wrong,"[30] the opinion climate for gays and lesbians may be improving. For one thing, the percentages agreeing with these statements declined by almost 20 percentage points between 1986 and 1998; for another, strong majorities agree that gays and lesbians should not be discriminated against in jobs, education, and housing. About four in ten Americans would bar gays and lesbians from jobs as schoolteachers or clergy, for example, down from six in ten in the late 1970s.[31] And, 76 percent say they favor federal "hate crime" legislation to protect gays and lesbians.[32] Some scholars speculate that gay and lesbian social movements have been primarily responsible for changing the opinion climate.[33]

On a number of issues, Americans are socially conservative. Large majorities, for example, favor allowing organized prayer in the public schools, banning pornography, preventing flag burning, penalizing drug use, punishing crimes severely, and imposing capital punishment for murder. Yet large majorities favor various types of gun regulations, which are thought of as liberal measures.

Foreign Policy   In the realm of foreign policy, public opinion sometimes changes rapidly. Major international events affect opinions, as we saw in the chapter opening vignette in the case of hawks and doves after the Tet Offensive during the Vietnam War. But often foreign policy opinions are quite stable. Since World War II, for example, two-thirds or more of those giving an opinion have usually said that the United States should take an "active part" in world

Public opinion surveys have consistently indicated high public support for stricter federal gun control laws. At a general level, around two-thirds of Americans say they want stricter laws. Several specific proposals receive even higher levels of support. For example, 80 percent want a nationwide ban on assault weapons, while 70 percent want the government to ban gun sales by mail-order and over the Internet. Although some laws, such as the Brady Bill–which requires background checks of gun buyers and a waiting period–have passed Congress, proposals for stricter control over the sale and distribution of weapons almost never get very far. Taking a broad look at how structural, political linkage, and governmental factors affect gun control legislation will help explain the situation.

Governmental Action

Major gun control bills fail to get legislated.

Governmental Level

- The reelection calculations of members of Congress favor doing nothing: voting for stricter laws invites the opposition of intense minorities, such as the NRA; voting against such laws does not alienate many voters.
- Republican presidents have generally opposed stricter gun control laws.
- Democratic presidents have either had other legislative priorities or have faced daunting GOP opposition in Congress when they have introduced gun control proposals.

Political Linkages Level

- A majority of Americans supports gun control, but don't rank it very high among their priorities for government action.
- Voters rarely take gun control into account when deciding who they will vote for.
- The National Rifle Association funnels substantial amounts of money into congressional, presidential, referenda, and issue campaigns.
- Many candidates are reluctant to attract the negative attention of the National Rifle Association; many others want NRA campaign contributions.

Structural Level

- The Second Amendment to the Constitution guarantees that "the right of the people to keep and bear arms shall not be infringed."
- The gun has long been an important icon of American popular culture.

affairs. The exact percentage favoring an active role has varied somewhat, rising to a peak of about 83 percent in 1965, near the onset of the Vietnam War; dropping to about 62 percent after the failure of that war; and recovering a bit in later years. But the percentage has remained consistently high, not fluctuating much with alleged public moods.[34]

As we have seen, however, general support for internationalism does not imply support for foreign aid (opposition to military aid is especially high), and the public has been quite hesitant to use U.S. troops abroad. Just before U.S. troops were sent as peacekeepers to Bosnia, for example, 78 percent of the public opposed the idea, and only 17 percent were in favor.[35] Opposition faded as the operation began to look less risky, but any substantial casualties abroad arouse large-scale public disapproval. This is probably why President Clinton ruled out the use of ground troops in Kosovo to stop ethnic cleansing by Serb militias and the Yugoslav army.

Although not many Americans embrace pure **isolationism**—the view that the United States should not be involved abroad and should only pay attention to its own affairs—the public (and political and economic leaders as well) is divided over whether its involvement in the world should take a **unilateralist** or a **multilateralist** form. Unilateralists want to go it alone, taking action when it suits our purposes, and not necessarily seeking the approval or help of international organizations such as the United Nations or regional organizations such as NATO. Unilateralists are also uncomfortable with entering into too many international treaties. Multilateralists believe that the protection of American interests requires continuous engagement in the world, but do not think that the United States has the resources or ability to accomplish its ends without cooperating with other nations and with international and regional organizations. According to most surveys, roughly two out of three Americans are in the multilateralist camp, telling pollsters they oppose unilateral U.S. military intervention in most cases and support cooperation with the U.N. and NATO and international treaties on human rights, the environment, and arms control.[36]

isolationism

The policy of avoiding involvement in foreign affairs.

unilateralist

The stance toward foreign policy that suggests that the United States should "go it alone," pursuing its national interests without seeking the cooperation of other nations or multilateral institutions.

multilateralist

The stance toward foreign policy that suggests that the United States should seek the cooperation of other nations and multilateral institutions in pursuing its goals.

How People Differ

In talking about American public opinion as a collective whole, we should not ignore important distinctions among different sorts of people in different circumstances. Black people and white people; Catholics, Jews, and Protestants; southerners and northeasterners; poor people and rich people; women and men—all tend to differ from one another in their political attitudes.

Race and Ethnicity

Among the biggest differences are those between white and black Americans. Hispanics and Asian-Americans also have some distinctive political opinions. Many white ethnic groups, however, are no longer much different from other members of the population.

African-Americans   On many core beliefs about the American system, few differences are discernible between black and white Americans. Similar percentages of each group believe, for example, that people can get ahead by working hard, that providing for equal opportunity is more important than ensuring equal outcomes, and that the federal government should balance its budget. On a range of other political issues, however, the racial divide looms large.

African-Americans have been reliable Democratic Party voters since the Great Depression and the New Deal, a tendency that has become even more pronounced over the past three decades as the Democratic and Republican positions on the federal government's civil rights role have diverged.

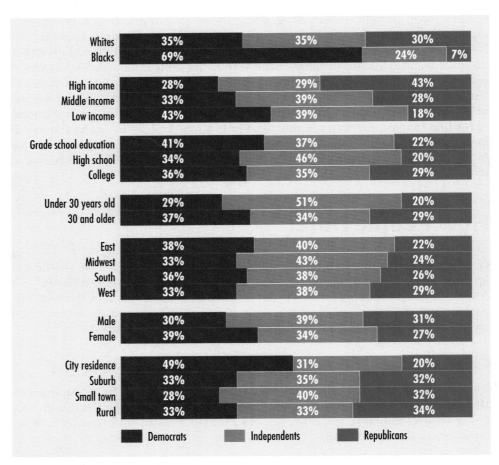

Figure 5.5 ● Party Loyalties Among Various Social Groups

Blacks, city dwellers, women, and people of lower-income and educational levels tend to be Democrats, while whites, suburbanites, men, the college-educated, and people with high incomes tend to be Republicans.

Source: General Social Survey, 1999.

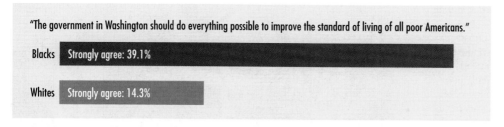

Figure 5.6 ● **Government Help for the Poor**

Many more black than white Americans feel that the government should help improve poor people's standard of living.

Source: General Social Survey, 1999.

Blacks, who stayed loyal to the Republican party (the party of Lincoln) long after the Civil War, became Democrats in large proportions with the New Deal of the 1930s. Most black Americans have remained Democrats, especially since the civil rights struggles of the 1960s. Today African-Americans are the most solidly Democratic of any group in the population: some 69 percent call themselves Democrats, while only about 7 percent call themselves Republicans (see Figure 5.5). In 1996, African-Americans supported Democrat Bill Clinton by a margin of 84 percent to 12 percent; white Americans cast their votes for Robert Dole by a margin of 46 percent to 43 percent.[37]

Black Americans also tend to be much more liberal than whites on economic issues, especially those involving aid to minorities or help with jobs, housing, medical care, education, and so on, as indicated in Figure 5.6. This liberalism reflects African-Americans' economically disadvantaged position in American society and the still-real effects of slavery and discrimination. On some social issues, however, blacks tend to hold strong religious values and to be rather conservative: more are opposed to abortion, for example, than are whites. Overall, more blacks consider themselves "liberal" (37 percent in 1998) than consider themselves "conservative" (31 percent, the rest being "moderate"), while the proportions among white voters are almost exactly reversed.[38] Black and white divisions are most apparent on issues related to affirmative action and the criminal justice system. While 80 percent of African-Americans say they think affirmative action programs should be continued, only 35 percent of whites agree.[39] Similarly, 71 percent of black Americans believe that the criminal justice system is biased against blacks, a position held by only 30 percent of whites.[40]

Hispanics   Hispanics—people of Spanish-speaking background—are the fastest-growing ethnic group in America, now making up slightly more than 11 percent of the population. However, the Hispanic population itself is quite diverse. Cuban-Americans, many of them refugees from the Castro regime, tend to be conservative, Republican, strongly anticommunist (recall the emotional case of the Cuban boat child, Elian Gonzales), and skeptical of government programs. The much more numerous Americans of Mexican or Puerto Rican ancestry, by contrast, are mostly Democrats and quite liberal on economic matters, although rather traditional on social questions—reflecting their predominant Roman Catholicism.

Hispanics have been one of the least politically active groups in the United States, although they have begun to vote in increasing numbers (see the opening story in Chapter 4). Low incomes, suspicion of the authorities, and lack of facility with the English language had long discouraged participation. Now, mobilized by

Cuban-Americans are strongly anti-Communist, with special levels of hostility directed at the Cuban regime and its leader Fidel Castro. Here Cuban-Americans demonstrate in Miami at the home of the relatives of Elian Gonzales, demanding that the young boy be granted political asylum and not be sent back to Cuba. After a series of victories in the courts, the U.S. Immigration and Naturalization Service prevailed, and Elian Gonzales was allowed to leave with his father for Cuba.

social movement groups and worried about anti-immigration and anti-immigrant state and national legislation, this sleeping giant of American politics seems to be awakening.

Asian-Americans   Asian-Americans, a small but growing part of the U.S. population, come from quite diverse backgrounds in Japan, Korea, Vietnam, Thailand, China, and elsewhere. As a group, Asian-Americans have tended to be successful educationally and economically, to participate fairly actively in politics, and to be conservative and Republican.

White Ethnics   Other ethnic groups are not so distinctive in their political opinions. Irish-Americans and people of Italian, Polish, and other southern or eastern European ancestry, for example, became strong Democrats as part of the New Deal coalition. But as they achieved success economically, their economic liberalism faded, and their social conservatism prevailed. By the 1980s, these groups were not much different from the majority of Americans.

Religion

Ethnic differences are often interwoven with differences in religious faith and values.

Catholics   Roman Catholics, who constitute about 31 percent of the U.S. population, were heavily Democratic after the New Deal but now resemble the majority of Americans in their party affiliations. Catholics' economic liberalism has faded somewhat with rises in their income, although this liberalism remains substantial. Catholics have tended to be especially concerned with family issues and to espouse measures to promote morality (e.g., antipornography laws) and law and order. But most American Catholics disagree with many church teachings: they support birth control and the right to have abortions in about the same proportions as do other Americans. Two-thirds favor allowing priests to marry and allowing women to be priests.[41]

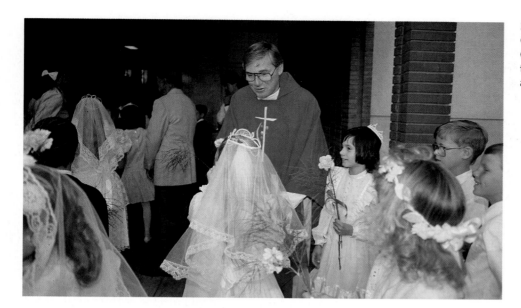

First communion at a Roman Catholic church in Tarzana, California. Practicing Catholics tend to be economically liberal and socially conservative.

Jews   American Jews (only about 2 percent of the U.S. population) began to join the Democratic party in the 1920s and did so overwhelmingly in the 1930s, in response to Franklin D. Roosevelt's New Deal social policies and his foreign policy of resisting Hitler. Most Jews have stayed with the party. Next to African-Americans, they remain the most Democratic group in the United States: about 44 percent identify themselves as Democrats and only 20 percent as Republicans. In the 2000 presidential election, Jews cast 79 percent of their votes for Gore and only 19 percent for Bush.

Jews are exceptionally liberal on such social issues as civil liberties and abortion. They also tend to be staunch supporters of civil rights, despite tensions with blacks over such matters as U.S. policy toward Israel and the Palestinians and anti-Semitic remarks by some black leaders. Rising incomes have somewhat undercut Jews' economic liberalism, but they remain substantially more supportive of social welfare policies than other groups.

Mormons   The 4 million or so Mormons, members of the fast-growing Church of Jesus Christ of Latter-day Saints, are distinguished by being the most staunchly conservative and most solidly Republican of any major religious denomination. According to the General Social Survey, Mormons were 57 percent Republican and only 33 percent Democrat in 1998, whereas Presbyterians were 53 percent Republican (35 percent Democrat), Episcopalians were 41 percent Republican (20 percent Democrat), and Lutherans were 43 percent Republican (26 percent Democrat).

Protestants   Protestants, who constitute a large majority of Americans, do not differ much from the U.S. average in most respects. But Protestants come in many varieties, from the relatively high-income (socially liberal, economically conservative) Episcopalians and Presbyterians to the generally liberal Unitarian-Universalists and middle-class northern Baptists to the lower-income and quite conservative Southern Baptists and evangelicals of various denominations.

In the early 1980s, evangelical Christians played an important part in the "new right" segment of Ronald Reagan's conservative movement, working hard against abortion, against pornography, for law and order, and for their version of family values. Disappointed by failures to achieve their national goals at that time, some turned toward local and state politics and had considerable success in picketing and disrupting abortion clinics, changing public school curricula, and pushing anti-gay-rights referenda. The Christian Coalition provided much energy and activism for the Republicans' 1994 congressional election victory. Fully 76 percent of white born-again Christians voted for Republican House candidates in that year, while only 24 percent voted for Democrats.[42] In 1996, they voted for Dole over Clinton by a 65–26 margin.

Region

It is still true that "the South is different." Regional differences have been reduced because of years of migration by southern blacks to northern cities, the movement of industrial plants and northern whites to the Sun Belt, and economic growth catching up with that of the North. But the legacy of slavery and segregation, a large black population, and late industrialization have made the South a unique region in American politics.

Even now, white southerners tend to be somewhat less enthusiastic about civil rights than northerners; only people from the Mountain West are nearly as conservative on racial issues.[43] Southerners also tend to be conservative on social issues, such as school prayer, crime, women's rights, and abortion, and supportive of military spending and a strong foreign policy (although fairly liberal on economic issues, such as job guarantees and health insurance).

These distinctive policy preferences have undercut southern whites' traditionally strong identification with the Democratic party, especially since the 1960s and 1970s, when the national Democrats became identified with liberal social policies and antiwar foreign policy. The white South's switch to the Republican party in the 1994 elections, in fact, is one of the major reasons

The skyline of New York City, where political attitudes on such issues as the environment differ from those of people living in the Sawtooth Mountains in Stanley, Idaho.

Republicans were able to win control of Congress. Figure 5.5 on page 134 shows differences in party loyalties among regional and other social groups.

On many issues, northeasterners tend to be the most different from southerners, with midwesterners, appropriately, in the middle. Pacific Coast residents resemble northeasterners in many respects, but people from the Rocky Mountain states tend to be quite conservative; between the 1950s and the 1980s, they moved strongly against government job guarantees and health insurance assistance, for example.[44] The mountain states' traditions of game hunting in wide-open spaces have led them, like southerners, to cherish the right to bear firearms and to resist gun controls.

Social Class

Compared with much of the world, the United States has had rather little political conflict among people of different income or occupational groupings; in fact, rather few Americans think of themselves as members of a social "class" at all. When forced to choose, about half say they are "working class" and about half say they are "middle class."[45] In Great Britain, on the other hand, where the real occupational structure is similar to that of the United States, 72 percent of the population calls itself "working class."[46]

Still, since the time of the New Deal, substantially more low-income people—poor people, as well as blue-collar workers and union members—have identified themselves as Democrats rather than as Republicans (see Figure 5.5 on page 134). The opposite is true at the top of the income and occupational scales. More business executives, doctors, lawyers, and other highly paid people identify themselves as Republicans. In 1996, 59 percent of Americans with incomes under $17,000 thought of themselves as Democrats, but only 10 percent of those with incomes over $50,000 did so.[47] This is one of the most enduring differences between the Republican and Democratic parties.

Lower-income people also have some distinctive policy preferences. Not surprisingly, they tend to favor much more government help with jobs, education, housing, medical care, and the like, whereas the highest-income people, who would presumably pay more and benefit less from such programs, tend to oppose them. Although all groups in the population have moved away from wanting to aid the poor, people earning low incomes are somewhat more willing to help (see Figure 5.7). To complicate matters, however, some groups of high-income

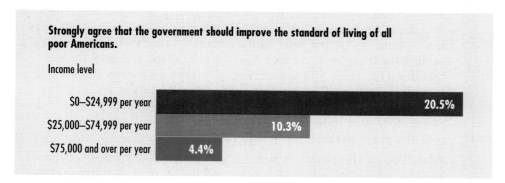

Figure 5.7 ● **Attitudes Toward Government Help for the Poor, by Income Level**

Few Americans are now eager to aid the poor, but low-income people are somewhat more supportive than others.

Source: General Social Survey, 1999.

people—especially highly educated professionals—tend to be very liberal on social issues involving sexual behavior, abortion rights, free speech, and civil rights. They also tend to be especially eager for government action to protect the environment. Once again, no simple "liberal" versus "conservative" distinction can accurately sum up all differences in opinions.

Education

The level of formal education that people reach is closely related to their income level because education helps people earn more and also because the wealthy can pay for more and better schooling for their children. But education has some distinct political effects of its own.

As we will see in Chapter 10, education is generally considered the strongest single predictor of participation in politics. College-educated people are much more likely to say that they vote, talk about politics, go to meetings, sign petitions, and write letters to officials than people who have attained only an elementary or a high school education. The highly educated know more about politics. They know what they want and how to go about getting it, joining groups and writing letters, faxes, and e-mail messages to public officials.

People with more schooling also have some distinctive policy preferences. As we have indicated, they are especially protective of the civil rights, civil liberties, and individual freedom of atheists, homosexuals, protesters, and dissenters. Education may contribute to tolerance by exposing people to diverse ideas or by training them in elite-backed norms of tolerance.

The most highly educated people tend to be the most tuned in to news and commentary in the media, and to change their opinions somewhat more quickly than others do. This is unusual; most of the groups that we have discussed, even those with rather distinctive policy preferences, tend to change opinion together, in the same direction, at about the same times.[48]

WEB EXPLORATION

The Gender Gap

Issue: There has been much talk of a "gender gap" in the United States.

Site: Examine male and female political attitudes and behaviors by accessing the American National Election Study through the "Course Documents" section of your online course. In the "Web Explorations" section for Chapter 5, click on "The Gender Gap" and then open "gender gap." Look at a few survey questions from each category, including partisanship, ideology, and stance on public policies. For each question, select "percent among demographic groups who responded," and you will see how men and women have responded over the years to the same questions.

What You've Learned: Is there a "gender gap"? If there is one, does the gap exist in all areas of politics and policy, or is the gap more pronounced on some issues compared with others?

HINT: As a measuring rod to determine the seriousness of the "gender gap," look at the differences between whites and blacks on the same survey questions.

Gender

Women were prevented from participating in politics for a large part of our history; they got the vote, by constitutional amendment, only in 1920. Not all women immediately took advantage of this new opportunity. For many years, women voted and participated in politics at lower rates than men—about 10 or 15 percent lower in the elections of the 1950s, for example. Only after the women's movement gained force during the 1970s did substantial numbers of female candidates begin to run for high office. Although an office-holding gap remains, the participation gap has virtually disappeared.[49] We will explore this in more depth in Chapter 10.

A partisan "gender gap" first appeared in the 1980s and persists today, with the percentage of women who identify themselves as Democrats about 9 or 10 percentage points higher than men (see Figure 5.5 on page 134). The difference between men and women is primarily a product of declining Democratic Party identification among men, particularly in the South.[50]

Women also differ somewhat from men in certain policy preferences. Women tend to be more opposed to violence, whether by criminals or by the state. More of them oppose capital punishment and the use of military force abroad. More favor arms control and peace agreements. Women also tend to be somewhat more supportive of protective policies for the poor, the elderly, and the disabled.[51]

Contrary to the common impression, as a group, women have not been particularly more supportive than men of women's rights or abortion choice. This is another case, like that of Catholic Americans and the Catholic church, in which the opinions of ordinary members of social groups are not necessarily the same as those of the organizations that claim to represent them. Women do differ among themselves, however; professionals and others working outside the home are much more liberal on these issues than homemakers are.

Age

The young and the old differ on certain matters that touch their particular interests: the draft in wartime, the drinking age, and, to some extent, Social Security and Medicare. Also, people over the age of 60 tend to be more critical of government, perhaps because their expectations about what government can and should deliver are higher.[52] But the chief difference is that young people are more attuned to the particular times in which they are growing up. Those who were young during the 1960s were especially quick to favor civil rights for blacks, for example. In recent years, young people have been especially concerned about environmental issues. Often social change occurs by generational replacement. Old ideas, like the Depression-era notion that women should stay at home and "not take jobs away from men," die off with old people.

Public Opinion and Policy

We have argued that one crucial test of how well democracy is working is how closely a government's policies correspond to the expressed wishes of its citizens. How close, then, is the relationship between what American citizens want—that is, collective public opinion in the whole nation—and what the U.S. government actually does?

LongmanParticipate

visual literacy
Who Are Liberals and Conservatives? What's the Difference?

LongmanParticipate

participation
Which Are You: Liberal or Conservative?

The Effects of Public Opinion on Policy

Our opening vignette about the Vietnam War suggests that at least under some circumstances, public opinion does affect policymaking. Other evidence also indicates that it often does so, though not always.

The Supreme Court, for example, rendered its historic *Roe* v. *Wade* decision in 1973 after a decade-long decline in the public's opposition to abortion. Congress passed the equally historic Civil Rights Act of 1964 after a period of time when public support for racial segregation was declining. On the other hand, high levels of public support for gun control have not led to strong federal gun control laws. And House Republicans studiously ignored strong public sentiments against the impeachment of President Clinton.

Usually, public opinion influences policymaking in less dramatic ways. Looking at many different policy issues—foreign and domestic—one scholar found that about two-thirds of the time, U.S. government policy coincides with what opinion surveys say the public wants. The same two-thirds correspondence has appeared when other scholars investigated how *changes* in public opinion relate to changes in federal, state, and local policy. Moreover, when public opinion changes by a substantial and enduring amount and the issue is prominent, government policy has moved in the same direction 87 percent of the time within a year or so afterward.[53]

Another study shows that substantial swings in the national political mood have occurred over the past half century or so and that public policy follows accordingly. As the American people have moved first in a liberal direction, then a conservative direction, and back again over the years, elected leaders in Washington have shaped their policies to fit the public mood, being more activist in liberal periods and less activist in conservative periods.[54]

According to still another study, the policies enacted in particular *states* correspond rather closely to the opinions of the states' citizens; that is, the states with mostly liberal citizens tend to have mostly liberal policies, and the states with mostly conservative citizens have mostly conservative policies.[55] Using sophisticated research methods, this study largely dismissed the possibility that policy differences cause the opinion differences (i.e., that citizens go along with whatever their government is doing). Public opinion seems to be a significant influence on government policy. Changes in opinion really do bring about changes in policy.

Opinion Manipulation

This evidence does not completely settle the matter. For one thing, even if public opinion is a "proximate" influence on policy—that is, even if opinion "stands next to" policymaking and directly affects it—we still need to know what factors affect public opinion itself. If public opinion can be manufactured by the media or easily manipulated by interest groups or political leaders (as in the Tonkin Gulf example), it would not make much sense to talk about democratic policymaking. It would be the media and political and economic leaders really controlling policy, with public opinion simply acting as a transmission belt.[56]

We have, however, already mentioned reasons for being skeptical of the idea that public opinion can be pushed around at will. Usually, personal experiences, objective events, and structural realities, rather than politicians' rhetoric, have the most to do with the shape of public opinion. Of course, some exceptions, like Tonkin, stand out; they may be most common in foreign affairs, where the government can sometimes control what information is made available. We need to discuss opinion manipulation further in later chapters. For

HOW DEMOCRATIC ARE WE?

PROPOSITION: Public opinion is not very important in determining what the federal government does in the United States.

AGREE: Although the news media publish polls and talk a great deal about their meaning and effect on politics, public opinion is far less important than interest groups, business firms, large contributors, and periodic elections in determining what policies are enacted. There are simply too many examples of government acting contrary to the views of the public—including the disconnect between the expressed views of the public and government action on gun control, the impeachment of Bill Clinton, and health care—to plausibly argue for public opinion as a decisive tool of democracy.

DISAGREE: Political leaders pay very close attention to public opinion when they are in the midst of deciding on alternative courses of action. (Some would argue that they do entirely too much of this, in fact.) It is why congressional incumbents, presidents, and government agencies spend so much time and money polling their relevant constituencies. And it is no mystery why elected officials do this, as do their challengers: public opinion is eventually translated into votes at election time. So, staying on the right side of public opinion, giving people what they want in terms of policies, as it were, is how people gain and keep elected offices. Thus, public opinion strongly influences what government does.

THE AUTHORS: While there have been occasional cases in which political leaders have either ignored or acted contrary to public opinion, the evidence suggests that, for the most part, at least over the long run, the public gets the government policies it prefers. We have seen that the correlation between public preferences and policy outcomes is pretty high. This would suggest that public opinion is a powerful tool of democracy in the United States. However, it is worth noting the degree to which this tool still falls short. For one thing, the federal government takes action in a wide range of areas where the public has no opinion at all. Regulation of financial services and telecommunications comes to mind. It is here that interest groups and large contributors may play particularly important roles. Moreover, although public opinion plays an important role in most government policies, it may itself be a product of incomplete information from the media and political leaders or of manipulation.

now, however, the main point is that public opinion is a substantial and important proximate influence on policymaking.

Summary

Public opinion consists of the political attitudes and beliefs expressed by ordinary citizens; it can be measured rather accurately through polls and surveys. The democratic ideals of popular sovereignty and majority rule imply that government policy should respond to the wishes of the citizens. An important test of how well democracy is working, therefore, is how closely government policy corresponds to public opinion.

Most people do not know a lot of facts about politics and do not have well-worked-out ideologies or highly stable policy preferences. Contrary to the fears of the Founders and others, however, the *collective* public opinion of Americans is real and stable, and it takes account of the available information.

Many Americans feel less trust in government than in the past and disapprove of the performance of political leaders. Party loyalty, although still widespread, has declined in strength. Most Americans strongly believe in freedom, economic liberty, capitalism, equality of opportunity, and democracy. Liberals and conservatives disagree about economic regulation and safety nets for the unfortunate. Majorities of the public favor government action on crime, education, medical care, and the environment. Support is lower for defense and the space program and much lower for foreign aid. Support for civil rights, civil liberties, and the right to have an abortion has increased, but the public is conservative about patriotism, crime, prayer, and obscenity.

People learn their political attitudes and beliefs from their families, peers, schools, and workplaces; they also respond to political events and the mass media. Structural factors in the society, the economy, and the international system strongly affect public opinion. Opinions and party loyalties differ according to race, religion, region, urban or rural residence, social class, education level, gender, and age. Blacks, Jews, city dwellers, women, and low-income people tend to be particularly liberal and Democratic; white Protestants, suburbanites, males, and the wealthy tend to be conservative and Republican.

Public opinion has substantial effects on what federal, state, and local governments do, but responsiveness to public opinion is incomplete.

Suggestions for Further Reading

Glynn, Carroll K., Susan Herbst, Garrett J. O'Keefe, and Robert Y. Shapiro, *Public Opinion.* Boulder, CO: Westview Press, 1999.
> *The most comprehensive overview of what scholars have learned about the formation and effects of public opinion in American politics.*

Hochschild, Jennifer L. *What's Fair? American Beliefs about Distributive Justice.* Cambridge, MA: Harvard University Press, 1986.
> *Public opinion explored through in-depth interviews with a small number of people.*

McClosky, Herbert, and John R. Zaller. *The American Ethos: Public Attitudes Toward Capitalism and Democracy.* Cambridge, MA: Harvard University Press, 1984.
> *A major study of some of Americans' most important beliefs and values.*

Nye, Joseph S., Jr., Philip D. Zelikow, and David C. King, eds. *Why People Don't Trust Government.* Cambridge, MA: Harvard University Press, 1997.
> *A balanced and detailed account by leading scholars of why trust in government in the United States has declined so dramatically over the past three decades.*

Page, Benjamin I., and Robert Y. Shapiro. *The Rational Public: Fifty Years of Trends in Americans' Policy Preferences.* Chicago: University of Chicago Press, 1992.
> *Extensive description of opinion trends, arguing that the public is rational.*

Internet Sources

Doonesbury **www.doonesbury.com/strawpoll/**
> *A daily online poll on current issues.*

Gallup Organization **www.gallup.com/**
> *Access to recent Gallup polls as well as to the Gallup archives.*

General Social Survey **www.icpsr.umich.edu/GSS99/**
> *Online access to the National Opinion Research Center's biennial survey of American attitudes.*

National Election Studies **http://www.umich.edu/~nes**
> *Biennial survey of voters, focusing on electoral issues.*

Polling Report   **www.pollingreport.com**
 A compilation of surveys from a variety of sources on politics and public affairs.

Roper Center   **www.lib.uconn.edu/RoperCenter/**
 Access to the main repository in the United States of public opinion polls on government and politics.

Social Science Data Collection   **http://ssdc.ucsd.edu/**
 Lists of articles and books about polling, published public opinion polls, and raw polling data.

Notes

1. Joseph C. Goulden, *Truth Is the First Casualty: The Gulf of Tonkin Affair—Illusion and Reality* (Chicago: Rand McNally, 1969).

2. All public opinion polls cited in this chapter opening vignette are from John E. Mueller, *War, Presidents and Public Opinion* (New York: Wiley, 1973).

3. U.S. Department of Defense, OASD (Comptroller), *Selected Manpower Statistics* (Washington, D.C.: Government Publications, June 1976), pp. 59–60.

4. Alexander Hamilton, James Madison, and John Jay, *The Federalist Papers,* ed. Clinton Rossiter (New York: New American Library, 1961; originally published 1787–1788). See Benjamin I. Page and Robert Y. Shapiro, *The Rational Public: Fifty Years of Trends in Americans' Policy Preferences* (Chicago: University of Chicago Press, 1992), chs. 1 and 2.

5. Walter Lippmann, *Public Opinion* (New York: Macmillan, 1922), p. 127.

6. Philip E. Converse, "The Nature of Belief Systems in Mass Publics," in David Apter, ed., *Ideology and Discontent* (New York: Free Press, 1964), pp. 206–261; Philip E. Converse, "Attitudes and Non-Attitudes: Continuation of a Dialogue," in Edward R. Tufte, ed., *The Quantitative Analysis of Social Problems* (Reading, MA: Addison-Wesley, 1970), pp. 168–189.

7. Times Mirror Center for the People and the Press, "The Vocal Minority in American Politics," press release, July 16, 1993.

8. Robert S. Erikson, *American Public Opinion: Its Origins, Content, and Impact,* 5th ed. (New York: Macmillan, 1995), tells much more about the techniques and the results of polling. Also see Carroll J. Glynn, Susan Herbst, Garrett J. O'Keefe, and Robert Y. Shapiro, *Public Opinion* (Boulder, CO: Westview Press, 1999), ch. 3.

9. Elizabeth Kolber, "Public Opinion Polls Swerve with the Turns of a Phrase," *New York Times* (June 5, 1995), pp. A1, C11.

10. Erikson, *American Public Opinion;* Page and Shapiro, *The Rational Public,* pp. 9–14. We also calculated some percentages from the National Opinion Research Center's General Social Survey.

11. Glynn et. al., *Public Opinion,* Table 8.1, p. 252.

12. Paul M. Sniderman, Richard A. Brody, and Philip E. Tetlock, *Reasoning and Choice: Explorations in Political Psychology* (New York: Cambridge University Press, 1991); see also Michael X. Delli Carpini and Scott Keeter, *Information and Empowerment: What Americans Know about Politics and Why It Matters* (New Haven, CT: Yale University Press, 1996); Samuel Popkin, *The Reasoning Voter* (Chicago: University of Chicago Press, 1991).

13. See Anthony Downs, *An Economic Theory of Democracy* (New York: Harper, 1957), chs. 11–13.

14. Robert E. Lane, *Political Ideology: Why the American Common Man Believes What He Does* (New York: Free Press, 1962); Jennifer L. Hochschild, *What's Fair? American Beliefs about Distributive Justice* (Cambridge, MA: Harvard University Press, 1986); and Glynn et. al., *Public Opinion,* ch. 8.

15. Page and Shapiro, *The Rational Public.*

16. General Social Survey, 1998.

17. Joseph S. Nye Jr., Philip D. Zelikow, and David C. King, eds., *Why People Don't Trust Government* (Cambridge, MA: Harvard University Press, 1997).

18. *American National Election Studies, 1948–1998* (Ann Arbor: University of Michigan, 1999).

19. Ibid.

20. See the collection of poll results at Polling Report Online.Com at **www.pollingreport.com/national.htm.**

21. Samuel Kernell, "Explaining Presidential Popularity," *American Political Science Review,* 72 (June 1978), pp. 506–522; Richard A. Brody, *Assessing the President: The Media, Elite Opinion, and Public Support* (Stanford, CA: Stanford University Press, 1991).

22. Albert H. Cantril and Susan Davis Cantril, *Reading Mixed Signals* (Washington, D.C.: Woodrow Wilson Center Press, 1999), pp. 30–31.

23. PollingReport.Com.

24. The Gallup Poll, April 9, 1999.

25. Bruce E. Keith, David B. Magleby, Candice J. Nelson, Elizabeth Orr, Mark C. Westlye, and Raymond E. Wolfinger, *The Myth of the Independent Voter* (Berkeley, CA: University of California Press, 1992).

26. Walter Dean Burnham, "The Appearance and Disappearance of the American Voter," in Richard Rose, ed., *Electoral Participation: A Comparative Analysis* (Beverly Hills, CA: Sage, 1980), pp. 35–73; Michael B. MacKuen, Robert S. Erikson, and James A. Stimson, "Macropartisanship," *American Political Science Review,* 83 (1989), pp. 1125–1143.

27. Herbert McClosky and John R. Zaller, *The American Ethos: Public Attitudes Toward Capitalism and Democracy* (Cambridge, MA: Harvard University Press, 1984); and Glynn et. al., *Public Opinion,* ch. 8.

28. Princeton Survey Research Associates/PEW Research Center, May 1997.

29. Steven Kull, *Americans and Foreign Aid: A Study of American Public Attitudes* (Washington, D.C.: Program on International Policy Attitudes, 1995).

30. Survey by Roper Starch Worldwide, July, 1998, reported in Kenneth Sherrill and Alan Yang, "From Outlaws to In-Laws," *Public Perspective* (January/February, 2000), pp. 20–31.

31. Gallup Poll, February 8–9, 1999.

32. *Time*/CNN Survey, October 14–15, 1998.

33. Sherrill and Yang, "From Outlaws to In-Laws."

34. William Caspary, "The 'Mood Theory': A Study of Public Opinion and Foreign Policy," *American Political Science Review,* 64 (1970), pp. 536–547; John E. Rielly, ed., *American Public Opinion and U.S. Foreign Policy, 1995* (Chicago: Chicago Council on Foreign Relations, 1995), p. 13; and Princeton Survey Associates/PEW Research Center, October 1999.

35. *Time*/CNN Survey, December 7, 1994.

36. Summary of polls on American foreign policy reported at *The Public Agenda On-Line* at **www.publicagenda.org/.**

37. *New York Times*/CBS News Poll, November 13, 1996.

38. General Social Survey, 1998.

39. CBS News/*New York Times* Poll, December 1997.

40. CBS News Poll, September 5–6, 1995.

41. Ari L. Goldman, "Catholics Are at Odds with Bishops," *New York Times* (June 19, 1992), p. A8; *Time*/CNN Poll, December 12, 1994.

42. "Portrait of the Electorate," *New York Times* (November 13, 1994), p. 15.

43. Peter F. Galderisi et al., eds., *The Politics of Realignment* (Boulder, CO: Westview Press, 1987), pp. 91–97.

44. Ibid., pp. 94–95.

45. National Election Studies, 1998.

46. Bernadette C. Hayes, "The Impact of Class on Political Attitudes," *European Journal of Political Research* 27 (1995), p. 76.

47. National Election Studies, 1996.

48. John R. Zaller, *The Nature and Origins of Mass Opinion* (New York: Cambridge University Press, 1992); Page and Shapiro, *The Rational Public,* ch. 7.

49. M. Margaret Conway, Gertrude A. Steuernagel, and John R. Terocik, *Women and Political Participation* (Washington, D.C.: Congressional Quarterly Press, 1997).

50. Karen M. Kaufmann and John R. Petrocik, "The Changing Politics of American Men," *The American Journal of Political Science* 43 (July 1999), pp. 864–887.

51. Robert Y. Shapiro and Harpreet Mahajan, "Gender Differences in Policy Preferences: A Summary of Trends from the 1960s to the 1980s," *Public Opinion Quarterly,* 50 (1986), pp. 42–61; and Glynn et. al., *Public Opinion,* pp. 235–238.

52. Cantril and Cantril, *Reading Mixed Signals,* Table 2.4, p. 22.

53. Alan D. Monroe, "Consistency Between Public Preferences and National Policy Decisions," *American Politics Quarterly,* 7 (January 1979), pp. 3–19; Benjamin I. Page and Robert Y. Shapiro, "Effects of Public Opinion on Policy," *American Political Science Review,* 77 (1983), pp. 175–190.

54. James A. Stimson, *Public Opinion in America: Moods, Cycles and Swings* (Boulder, CO: Westview Press, 1991).

55. Gerald C. Wright Jr., Robert S. Erikson, and John P. McIver, "Public Opinion and Policy Liberalism in the American States," *American Journal of Political Science,* 31 (1987), pp. 980–1001. See also Robert S. Erikson, Gerald C. Wright Jr., and John P. McIver, *Statehouse Democracy: Public Opinion and Democracy in the American States* (New York: Cambridge University Press, 1994).

56. Zaller, *Nature and Origins of Mass Opinion.*

CHAPTER 6

The Mass Media

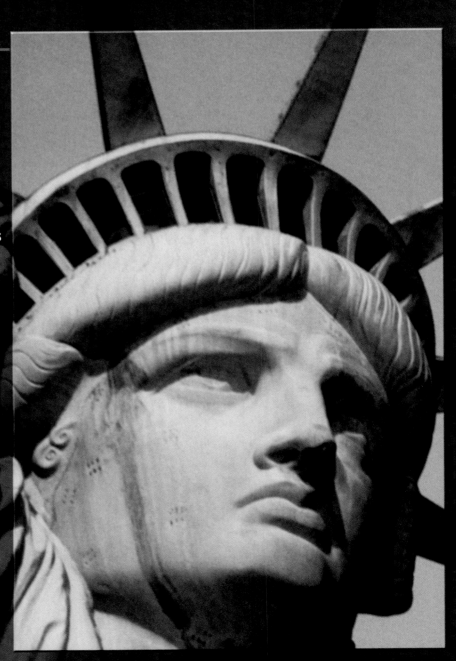

Vernon Jordan Meets the Press

The "buzz" inside the Beltway was that Vernon Jordan, advisor, close confidant, and golfing partner of President Bill Clinton, was being investigated by Special Prosecutor Kenneth Starr for obstruction of justice. Word had it that Vernon Jordan, a prominent Washington attorney and former civil rights leader, had instructed Monica Lewinsky to lie about her sexual relationship with the president before Starr's grand jury. The evidence, it was said, was in one of the taped conversations Lewinsky had been having with disgruntled federal employee Linda Tripp.[1]

As is now widely known, Tripp was taping her conversations with Lewinsky at the suggestion of New York book agent Lucianne Goldberg in an effort to help Tripp put together a book exposing the president. Goldberg and Tripp had carefully scripted the telephone conversations with Lewinsky, leading her into areas they wanted her to talk about, encouraging Lewinsky to elaborate the most telling and titillating details, and cajoling her to continue when her interest flagged. Their plan, it seems, was to use the tapes to tweak the interest of one or more of the major newspapers or newsmagazines as a way to hype interest in a book that had yet to be written. After *Newsweek* turned down the opportunity to run a story based on Goldberg and Tripp's characterizations of what was on the tapes, the story of the "story that did not happen" appeared on gossip-webster Matt Drudge's Web site. From there, the story was picked up by ABC's *This Week with Sam Donaldson and Cokie Roberts,* then by other political talk shows, and then (with the apparent help of Kenneth Starr's staff) the *Washington Post.* The rest, as they say, is history.

The *Washington Post* headlined on January 21, 1998, that "Clinton and Jordon directed her [Lewinsky] to testify falsely." *Good Morning America* said the same day that Lewinsky had claimed on the tape that Jordan had "instructed her to lie." Over the next weeks and months, similar reports kept circulating. Although the various media outlets carried Jordan's denials, reporters implied that he was being less than truthful, equivocating, evading, and, as *Time* magazine put it on February 2, "wrapping himself in a protective layer of syntax." Other media outlets carried stories, none corroborated, about Jordan's womanizing and rich lifestyle. *Meet the Press* passed on the rumor that Starr was granting "limited immunity" for Jordan's testimony before the grand jury, implying that Jordan was about to be charged with a crime. All the major TV networks picked up the story as did all the major newsmagazines. Television, magazine, and newspaper pundits commentated on and argued endlessly about Jordan's misbehavior, what it meant for his future, and what it meant for the Clinton presidency. In all of this media frenzy, not a single reporter or commentator had ever listened to the tape or read the tape transcript.

When Kenneth Starr finally submitted his report to Congress urging the impeachment and removal from office of Bill Clinton, there was nothing in its pages about Vernon Jordan telling Monica Lewinsky to lie. Nor was there any such evidence in Linda Tripp's tape transcripts, which were also submitted to the House of Representatives and subsequently released to the public. Starr reported that Lewinsky had testified to his grand jury that neither the president nor Vernon Jordan had ever told her to lie. She repeated this testimony in the Senate trial of the president. The Vernon Jordan story, in the end, was baseless, a frenzy in which media outlets fed on the material supplied by other media outlets, in the effort to fill space and time in the unending news cycle. Unfortunately, the way the story played in the media—rumor treated as fact, reporting taking a back seat to argument and punditry, infotainment pushing aside serious analysis, speed bumping aside accuracy—has become all too familiar to Americans.

Thinking Critically About This Chapter

In this chapter, we turn our attention to the mass media in the United States to learn how it is organized, how it works, and what effects it has on the quality of our political life.

Using the Framework. In this chapter you will learn about the role the mass media play in influencing significant actors in the political system, including citizens and elected leaders. You also will learn how the mass media can shape what government does. And, you will learn how the mass media are influenced by changes in technology and business organization, and by government regulation and constitutional rules regarding freedom of the press.

Using the Democracy Standard. Using the tools presented in Chapter 1, you will be able to evaluate the degree to which the mass media support or do not support democracy in the United States. You will be able to judge whether the mass media promote popular sovereignty, political equality, and liberty. Finally, you will see how certain changes in the media are cause for concern in terms of the health of democracy. ▶

Roles of the Mass Media in Democracy

Journalist and scholar Walter Lippmann once declared that "a free press is not a privilege but an organic necessity in a great society. Without criticism and reliable and intelligent reporting, the government cannot govern."[2]

The central idea of democracy is that ordinary citizens should control what their government does. However, citizens cannot hope to control officials, to choose candidates, to speak intelligently with others about public affairs, or even to make up their minds about what policies they favor unless they have good information about politics. Most of that information must come through the mass media, whether newspapers, radio, television, or, increasingly, the Internet. How well democracy works, then, depends partly on how good a job the mass media are doing.

Watchdog over Government

watchdog

The role of the media in scrutinizing the actions of government officials.

One role of the media in a democracy is that of **watchdog** over government. The idea is that the press—acting as a better protector than the voyeuristic pet in the cartoon—should dig up facts and warn the public when officials are doing something wrong. Citizens can hold officials accountable for setting things right only if they know about errors and wrongdoing.

The First Amendment to the Constitution ("Congress shall make no law . . . abridging the freedom . . . of the press") helps ensure that the media will be able to expose officials' misbehavior without fear of censorship or prosecution. This is a treasured American right that is not available in many other countries. Under dictatorships and other authoritarian regimes, the media are usually tightly controlled. Even in a democratic country such as Great Britain, strict secrecy laws limit what the press can say about certain government activities. In many countries, including France, Israel, and Sweden, the government owns and operates major television channels and makes sure that the programs are not too critical.[3] Although freedom of the press is not

PUBLIC WATCHDOG

© Reprinted by permission Tribune Media Services.

perfect in the United States, the media enjoy greater freedom than their counterparts in other countries.

But how often do the media in the United States fulfill their watchdog role? Even without formal censorship or government ownership of the media, various factors, including the way in which the mass media are organized and their routines of news gathering, may limit how willing or able the media are to be critical of government policies. In addition, the media may be too quick to blow scandals out of proportion and to destroy political leaders' careers.[4]

Clarifying Electoral Choices

A second role of the mass media in a democracy is to make clear what electoral choices the public has: what the political parties stand for and how the candidates shape up in terms of personal character, knowledge, experience, and positions on the issues. Without such information, it is difficult for voters to make intelligent choices.

How much or how little attention do the media pay to candidates' stands on public policies? Do they devote too much coverage to the horse race aspect of campaigns instead? In scrutinizing the character and personality of candidates, do the media go overboard in digging up dirt and reporting negative material even when it is very minor?

Providing Policy Information

A third role of the mass media is to present a diverse, full, and enlightening set of facts and ideas about public policy. Citizens need to know how well current policies are working, as well as the pros and cons of the alternative policies that might be tried, to formulate sensible preferences. In a democracy, government should respond to public opinion, but that opinion should be well informed.

How much policy information do the U.S. media actually convey, and how accessible is it? How diverse and how accurate is that information? Is it biased— toward liberalism, for example, or toward conservatism? Are some voices heard and others ignored? We will address such questions in this chapter.

Other Roles

Whether or not they fulfill these three ideal roles, the mass media clearly play important parts in the political system. They act as amplifiers for speaking to citizens and trying to persuade them. The media also serve as channels of communication among political and governmental institutions, helping Congress, the president, and members of the executive branch to figure out what the others are doing. Finally, the media may themselves be political actors, with their own goals and interests, trying to influence politics just as other interest groups do. Thus the mass media serve as a critical link among political and governmental institutions, and they also act as political institutions in their own right.

The Media Landscape

LongmanParticipate

CourseCompass

timeline
**300 Years of
U.S. Media**

The media have changed greatly over our history and continue to change ever more rapidly. Taken together, they represent, at least potentially, a multitude of ways for the public to gain access to political news, analysis, and commentary.

Newspapers

The first newspapers in the early Republic were not meant for the mass public. Newspapers were expensive and directed at an elite audience. Newspapers were highly specialized, with the most common being about business affairs or highly partisan organs of political parties, either Federalist or Democratic Republican.

CourseCompass

WEB EXPLORATION

Internet News

Issue: The Internet is becoming an increasingly important source of news for the public.

Site: Go to America Online (if you are a member), Netscape, or Yahoo! and to the *New York Times* or the *Chicago Tribune* through through the "Course Documents" section of your online course. In the "Web Explorations" section for Chapter 6, click on "Internet News" and then open "Internet News." Select one Internet news source and one newspaper.

What You've Learned: Follow the news on the Net and at one of the newspapers for one week. How good is the news about government, politics, and public policies on the Internet site compared with the news provided by the most serious daily newspapers in the United States? Does the Internet site provide enough quality information for citizens of a healthy democracy, or do you think it too skimpy to serve this important democratic function?

HINT: Do an analysis of what kinds of stories are covered, what proportion of news coverage is devoted to public affairs, how fair the coverage is to the various sides of the issues, and how much information is provided to help you understand what is at stake on the most important issues.

Technological changes and the gradual democratization of American life made newspapers into a "mass" phenomenon. By the mid-1830s, "penny papers" such as the *New York Herald* reached mass audiences of ordinary working people by means of low prices and human-interest stories, written in a breezy and often sensational style. The invention of the telegraph allowed news to be gathered and distributed quickly, eventually to millions of people. In the 1840s, several New York newspapers formed the Associated Press (AP) to cooperate in gathering news and distributing it by telegraph. In the late nineteenth century, Joseph Pulitzer of the *New York World* (1883) and William Randolph Hearst of the *New York Journal* invented **yellow journalism,** a new sort of newspaper that combined sensationalism and political crusades with oversized headlines and full-color illustrations and comics. One Hearst crusade in 1898 helped provoke war against Spain over Spanish control of Cuba, a key step in the emergence of the United States as a world power. Today's tabloids, like the *New York Post,* are less likely to start wars, but their journalistic techniques still resemble Hearst's yellow journalism.

yellow journalism
Sensational newspaper stories with large headlines and, in some cases, color cartoons.

The development of wire services such as the AP, the United Press International, and the Scripps-Howard Service (the last two are now defunct) meant that more political news could be spread much more quickly, to much bigger audiences, and, inevitably, in a much more nationally uniform way than ever before. Homogenization was accentuated by the development of large "chains" of newspapers, owned by the same company and pursuing uniform editorial policies. Most major metropolitan newspapers today are parts of such chains (which are themselves often parts of larger multimedia companies). They depend mainly on the AP for national and international news, syndicated columnists for their editorial page, and their own reporters to cover local affairs.

In addition to the chain-associated metropolitan dailies, newspapers come in three rough categories. First, there are newspapers that give serious, in-depth attention to domestic and international political affairs. Most notable is the *New York Times,* which claims to publish "all the news that's fit to print" and aspires to be America's "newspaper of record." It remains the preeminent U.S. newspaper for reporting on international affairs. It is rivaled only by the

William Randolph Hearst's *New York Journal* stirred war fever in 1898 with unsubstantiated charges that the Spanish had destroyed the U.S. battleship *Maine* in Cuba.

Washington Post for the extent of its domestic political reporting and by the *Wall Street Journal* for business and financial news. The *Los Angeles Times,* the *Miami Herald,* and the *Chicago Tribune* also fall on the serious side of the news spectrum. Second, there are newspapers in urban areas that address minority communities of one kind or another and the issues that directly concern them, including gays and lesbians, African-Americans, Hispanics, and Asian-Americans. Finally, there are the sensation-driven supermarket tabloids, such as the *National Inquirer,* the *Globe,* and the *Star,* which also do political stories, many of which eventually end up in the more mainstream press.

Today, despite all of the innovations making newspapers accessible and entertaining, Americans are relying less and less on them for their information about the world in favor of television and radio.[5] This may be a problem for democracy because television and radio have traditionally been less comprehensive and more shallow in their news coverage than the nation's top newspapers. Ironically, as a way to recapture some of their lost readership, many newspapers have followed the lead of *USA Today* and have been remaking themselves in the image of television: more color, short articles, human-interest stories, and tips for living (money, diet, exercise) and less political news and discussion of public policies.

Magazines

Several journals of political opinion and analysis were founded in the nineteenth century. Some of these, such as *The Nation* and the *Atlantic Monthly,* are still published, and a wide range of other journals—liberal, conservative, radical, and reactionary—have entered the political debate.

Beginning in the 1920s, Henry Luce's *Time,* the weekly newsmagazine, brought analysis and interpretation of the week's news, written in a brisk and colorful style, to hundreds of thousands and then millions of readers; it later drew competition from *Newsweek* and *U.S. News & World Report.* Large-circulation magazines such as the *Saturday Evening Post, Life,* and especially *Reader's Digest* gained circulations in the millions. Countless specialized journals appeared, providing information and entertainment of diverse sorts.

Radio

Radio significantly changed the face of the mass media. Commercial radio stations with broad audiences were established during the 1920s and were soon organized into networks that shared news and other programs. In the depths of the Great Depression of the 1930s, millions of Americans could hear the reassuring voice of President Franklin Roosevelt giving "fireside chats." Later, millions could hear the latest news about the battles with Japan and Nazi Germany during World War II.

Radio, once thought vanquished by the television juggernaut, has been reborn, especially for commuters, joggers, and people who work at home. Besides music, AM and FM stations offer frequent news bulletins and call-in talk shows, on which all manner of political opinions, including the cranky and the outrageous, are voiced. Disproportionately male and politically conservative (both callers and listeners),[6] syndicated talk show hosts such as Rush Limbaugh (with an estimated audience of 20 million)[7] have become a political force, able to generate a flood of mail to Congress or the White House and even to force decisions on Washington policymakers.

Radio is not all sound and populist fury, however. Public Broadcasting System (PBS) stations provide extended news analysis and commentary, often

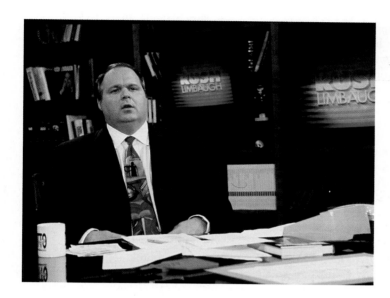

Talk radio has become a very influential—and decidedly conservative—voice in American politics. Right-wing personality Rush Limbaugh, who often criticizes the mass media as being too liberal, draws a large and loyal audience.

thoughtful and occasionally unorthodox, on programs such as *Morning Edition* and *All Things Considered*.

Television

The television revolution transformed American media yet again. Television was invented before World War II; it was developed commercially in the late 1940s and entered American households on a large scale in the 1950s. Scores and then hundreds of television stations were established around the country, most eventually affiliating with one of the three major networks—ABC, CBS, and NBC—which provided the bulk of prime-time programming. The networks also produced and distributed national news programs, which in 1963 were expanded from 15 minutes to 30 minutes of early evening time, and became the main source of national news for most Americans. Today, cable, all-news networks such as CNN and MSNBC have eaten into the network television news

The Vietnam War was the first American war fully covered by television. Footage of American deaths and casualties, as well as visual reminders of the terrible consequences of the conflict on the Vietnamese civilian population, helped turn public opinion in the United States against the war. This still from television footage of children napalmed by an accidental American attack on the village of Trang Bang is a particularly powerful example of the war coming home to American living rooms.

monopoly, while political junkies can turn to C-SPAN for live coverage of Congress and other inside-the-beltway activities. The BET offers news on public affairs that are of particular interest to African-Americans. According to a multitude of polls, Americans name television as their most important source of news, and most say they trust television a great deal.[8]

The Internet

Personal computers and modems, appearing in a rapidly increasing number of homes, schools, and offices, create opportunities to gather political and public policy information from a host of sources on the Internet, including libraries, government agencies, online newspapers and magazines, special interest groups, scholars, and public interest organizations. Among the most informative of these "broadcast" Web sites—in the sense that the information flow is essentially one-way, much as it is with traditional mass media—is Project Vote Smart (at **www.vote-smart.org/**), where citizens can now track legislation as it makes its way through Congress and learn how their representatives voted, and the Public Agenda (**www.publicagenda.org**), where citizens can garner a mountain of information about the leading issues of the day, including the main arguments and supporting evidence for different points of view. This medium has a ways to go to catch up to traditional mass media, however; during the 1996 election season only 5 percent of the public reported visiting a politically oriented Web site.[9] Candidates made a huge investment in campaign Web sites for the 2000 election cycle, so the pace of politically oriented Internet use has probably increased substantially.

The true promise of the Internet, however, is in its capacity to serve as an interactive, two-way communications medium[10] in which citizens can talk back to political leaders and deliberate with one another. Already scores of political chat rooms exist, members of Congress register public opinion coming via e-mail,

WEB EXPLORATION

Online Political Participation

Issue: Get involved! There are a number of virtual political communities on the Internet where you can gain information and interact with other people who share your political views.

Site: Visit the conservative "Town Hall" site and the liberal "Turn Left" site. Visit the "Course Documents" section of your online course, open the "Web Explorations" section for Chapter 6, click on "Online Political Participation," and select "online participation."

What You've Learned: Each site has a bulletin board where you can join others in a discussion of the main issues on today's political agenda. Better yet, open yourself to other viewpoints; if you are liberal, visit the conservative site; if you are conservative, visit the liberal site. Do you see any merit in the views being expressed at these sites? Have you learned anything from them?

HINT: Crossing ideological lines with an open mind is hard to do. Keep trying. It's worth the effort.

citizens communicate and share documents with others in their interest groups, and many online magazines and newspapers encourage reader online feedback and commentary. Information technology keeps advancing, opening up possibilities such as two-way video communication and instant electronic referendum voting.

We are also discovering—whether for better or worse is not yet clear—that almost anyone with an Internet connection can become a combination reporter, editor, and publisher. The most famous of these instant media moguls, if you will, is Matt Drudge, whose "Drudge Report" played such a large role in the news cycle leading to the Clinton impeachment, and the distinction between rumor and fact is very fine indeed in this "report." His Web site is not the only one of its kind, and many more, from diverse political perspectives, are certain to follow.

Commentators disagree about the democratic potential of the Internet. To many, the scarcity of editorial gatekeepers with a strong sense of journalistic integrity on the Internet means that citizens cannot be certain about the reliability of information found at most sites.[11] Also, the Internet makes it easier for fringe groups such as the "militia movement" and hate groups such as the "skinheads" and neo-Nazis to spread their messages and recruit new members. On the other hand, say other commentators, the Internet gives citizens fuller and easier access to information and opinions about government performance, electoral choices, and policy options. And it allows geographically diverse individuals and groups to organize politically and convey their views to policymakers. Some even suggest that the Internet ought to be thought of as a new space for participation in the political process, equal in stature to other participatory spaces in American politics.[12]

How the Media Work

The precise ways in which the media are organized and function affect whether citizens get the kinds of information they need for democracy to work properly.

Organization of the Mass Media

Nearly all media in the United States are privately owned businesses. Most are either very large businesses in their own right or, more typically, part of very large corporate empires.

Corporate Ownership

Some television stations and newspapers—especially the smaller ones—are still owned locally, by families or by groups of investors, although they account for a rapidly declining share of the total. Most of the biggest stations and papers, however, as well as the television and cable networks, are owned by large media corporations, some of which, in turn, are subsidiaries of enormous conglomerates.

Each media sector is dominated by a few firms. Gannett (*USA Today* and 87 other dailies), Knight-Ridder, and Newhouse dominate the newspaper business. Three corporations—Time Warner (with 40 percent of all magazine revenues), Rupert Murdoch's News Corp., and Gannett—control most magazine publishing. And America Online (AOL) is in the process of taking over Time Warner. General Electric, Westinghouse, Disney, and Time Warner dominate network television. Six corporations receive more than half of all book-publishing revenues. And four firms (Warner Communications, Gulf+Western,

Rupert Murdoch has built a global media and entertainment empire. He has combined newspaper, television, radio, movie, and publishing companies, as well as sports teams, under the News Corp umbrella.

Universal-MCA, and Columbia Pictures) get most of the gross box office revenues from movies.[13]

There has been a strong tendency for newspapers to merge. The vast majority of towns and cities that have any newspaper at all have only one. About two dozen cities, including San Francisco, Seattle, Detroit, and Cincinnati still have two newspapers, but they are often owned by the same people and share printing and other facilities.[14] "Alternative" weeklies in major cities, although popular with many younger readers, have a relatively small circulation and do not provide a full range of political news.

Mergers across media lines have accelerated in recent years. In the late 1990s, Disney bought ABC/Cap Cities, Time Warner acquired Turner Broadcasting (and was later bought by AOL), and Westinghouse Electric bought CBS. Then Viacom and CBS merged, bringing together many familiar media and entertainment names: MTV, Nickelodeon, Showtime, Paramount Pictures, Simon and Schuster Publishers, Blockbuster Video, and CBS TV and radio. In a stunning deal in early 2000, AOL acquired Time Warner, merging news, publishing, entertainment, and Internet resources into a single giant company.

Very late to join the merger game, radio is also consolidating at an extraordinarily rapid pace. Given leave by the Telecommunications Act of 1996, which revoked the long-standing rule that no person or corporation could own more than 24 radio stations nationwide and no more than one FM and one AM station in each market, buyouts and mergers proliferated in the late 1990s. The result is that six or seven national conglomerates will soon control radio broadcasting in every medium-sized and large market in the United States.[15]

Scholars disagree about the effect of corporate ownership and increased media concentration. A few see efficiency gains and an increase in the output and availability of information. But some critics maintain that the concentrated corporate control of our mass media adds dangerously to the already strong business presence in American politics (see Chapter 7). Others worry that increased concentration of ownership may lead to less diversity of news and opinion. Others worry that news organizations may pull their punches when reporting about the activities of their corporate parents or partners. Will MSNBC—a joint news venture of Microsoft and NBC—report fairly and accurately about Microsoft activities, for example? Will ABC News go easy on Disney, which owns ABC?[16]

Uniformity and Diversity   Whoever owns them, most newspapers and television stations depend largely on the same sources for news. Political scientist Lance Bennett points out that while there is a growing diversity of news outlets in the United States—more specialized magazines, television channels, and newspaper home pages on the Web—news sources are contracting. That is to say, much of what comes to us over a multitude of media avenues originates in fewer and fewer centralized sources.[17] Almost all major newspapers in the country now subscribe to the AP wire service. The AP supplies most of the main national and international news stories, even those that are rewritten to carry a local reporter's byline. Most of what appears on network and cable television news, too, is inspired by the AP wire. National and local television news organizations depend on centralized news and video suppliers, with fewer of them using their own reporters. This is why viewers are likely to see the same news (and sports) footage on different stations as they switch channels, although each station adds its own "voice-over" from a reporter or news anchor. In most cases, the person doing the voice-over has no direct relationship to the story.

Along with the centralization and homogenization of the mass media, however, there is also quite a lot of diversity, for anyone who makes the effort to seek it out. People who are especially interested in politics can find special publications that look at the world in a way that they find compatible or interesting, whether it is the *Weekly Standard* or *National Review* (conservative), *The Nation* (liberal), *Commentary* (neoconservative), *Mother Jones* (irreverent), the *New York Review of Books* (intellectual and critical), the *New Yorker*, *Rolling Stone*, or dozens of others with small circulations. The World Wide Web also provides a wealth of information uncontrolled by government or corporations. And new Internet political magazines such as *Slate* are beginning to appear. African-American, Spanish-language, and gay and lesbian newspapers, magazines, and Web sites are also increasingly available. The audiences for these news sources, however, represent but a small fraction of the number of people who depend on the mass media for their news.

Profit Motives   Media corporations, like other corporations, are in business primarily to make a profit. This fact has important consequences. It means, for example, that the major mass media must appeal to large audiences and get many people to buy their publications or the products they advertise. If most people are mainly interested in entertainment and want their news short, snappy, and sensational—what has come to be called **infotainment**—that is what they will get on network and cable television news and in *USA Today*. The process is especially well developed in evening local news broadcasts where coverage of politics and government have been "crowded out by coverage of crime, sports, weather, lifestyles and other audience-grabbing topics, . . ."[18]

infotainment
The merging of hard news and entertainment in news presentations.

The profit motive also means that the biggest mass media tend to avoid controversial material that might seem "extreme" or offensive to substantial groups of viewers. Examples are legion. General Motors once canceled its sponsorship of an Easter program on the life of Jesus because evangelical groups objected. A number of public television stations refused to air a program on Palestinian grievances because of strong objections by Jewish groups. When controversial material sells, however, the mass media are willing to risk some criticism. Note, for example, the success of network television programs such as *Law and Order* and *NYPD Blue*.

Political Newsmaking

The kind of news that the media present is affected by the organization and technology of news gathering and news production. Much depends on where reporters are, what sources they talk to, and what sorts of video pictures are available.

The Limited Geography of Political News   For national news, most reporters are located inside the beltway in Washington, D.C., site of the main federal government institutions, or in New York City, the center of most media operations. Thus, the national news has a strong Washington–New York orientation.

The major television networks and most newspapers cannot afford to station many reporters outside Washington or New York. The networks usually add just Chicago, Los Angeles, Miami, and Houston or Dallas. Some significant stories from outside the main media centers simply do not make it into the national news. CNN and other news-only channels have a big advantage on fast-breaking news, which they are ready to cover (through their own reporters or the purchase of local footage) and to use immediately on their continuous newscasts.

While some newspapers have strong regional bureaus, the majority print mostly wire service reports of news from elsewhere around the country. The television networks' assignment editors also rely on the wire services to decide what stories to cover; during one month that was studied, NBC got the idea for 70 percent of its domestic film stories from the wire services.[19]

Because it takes time to shoot pictures, transport them back to the studio, and process and edit them, most television news stories are assigned to predictable events—news conferences and the like—long before they happen, usually in one of the cities with a permanent television crew. For such spontaneous news as riots, accidents, and natural disasters, special video camera crews can be rushed to the location, but they usually arrive after the main events occur and have to rely on "reaction" interviews or aftermath stories.

Dependence on Official Sources   Most political news is based on what public officials say. This fact has important consequences for how well the media serve democracy.

Beats and Routines   A newspaper or television reporter's work is usually organized around a particular **beat**, which he or she checks every day for news stories. Most political beats center on some official government institution that regularly produces news, such as a local police station or city council, the White House, Congress, the Pentagon, an American embassy abroad, or a country's foreign ministry.

In fact, many news reports are created or originated by officials, not by reporters. Investigative reporting of the sort that Bernstein and Woodward did on Watergate is rare (see The Struggle for Democracy box, "Covering the Watergate Scandal") because it is so time-consuming and expensive. Most reporters get most of their stories quickly and efficiently from press conferences and the press releases that officials write, along with comments solicited from other officials.

One pioneering study found that government officials, domestic or foreign, were the sources of nearly three-quarters of all news in the *New York Times* and the *Washington Post*. Moreover, the vast majority, 70 to 90 percent of all news stories, were drawn from situations over which the newsmakers had substantial control: press conferences (24.5 percent), interviews (24.7 percent), press releases (17.5 percent), and official proceedings (13 percent).[20] The same is true of wire service reports and local newspapers.

Military Actions   Dependence on official sources is especially evident in military actions abroad. Because it is wary of the release of information that might help an adversary or undermine public support for U.S. actions—as in Vietnam—the Defense Department carefully restricts the access of reporters to military personnel and the battlefield and provides carefully screened information for use by the mass media. The Pentagon carefully managed the flow of

beat

The assigned location where a reporter regularly gathers news stories.

Journalists and government officials often socialize together, raising questions about the media's ability to serve as honest watchdog. Here reporter Sam Donaldson chats with Secretary of Health and Human Services Donna Shelala at a Washington gala.

information in the invasion of Grenada in 1983, the Gulf War in 1991, and peacekeeping missions in Bosnia and Kosovo. Information management was especially evident during the Gulf War in the lavish praising of the performance of "smart" bombs, carefully targeted at military objectives. Only long after the war ended did the Pentagon admit that most "smart" weapons did not work as touted and that conventional bombs did most of the damage.

Mutual Needs   Reporters and officials work with each other every day. They need each other. Reporters want stories; they have to cultivate access to people who can provide stories with quotes or anonymous leaks. Officials want favorable publicity and want to avoid or counteract unfavorable publicity. Thus, a comfortable relationship tends to develop. Even when reporters put on a show of aggressive questioning at White House press conferences, they usually work hard to stay on good terms with officials and to avoid fundamental challenges of their positions.

The media's heavy reliance on official sources means that government officials are sometimes able to control what journalists report and how they report it. The Reagan administration was particularly successful at picking a "story of the day" and having many officials feed that story to reporters, with a unified interpretation.[21] Reliance on officials also means that when officials of both parties agree, debate tends to be constricted. This was true for the momentous Telecommunications Act of 1996, which helped usher in the current dramatic changes in the business of mass media and telecommunications but which occasioned little public debate.

Newsworthiness   Decisions about what kinds of news to print or to televise depend largely on professional judgments about what is **newsworthy**. Exactly what makes a story newsworthy is difficult to spell out, but experienced editors make quick and confident judgments of what their audiences (and their employers) want. If they were consistently wrong, they would probably not remain in their jobs very long.

In practice, newsworthiness seems to depend on such factors as novelty (man bites dog, not dog bites man), drama and human interest (the fight over custody of Elian Gonzalez), relevance to the lives of Americans, high

newsworthy

Worth printing or broadcasting as news, according to editors' judgments.

THE STRUGGLE FOR DEMOCRACY

Covering the Watergate Scandal

A ringing telephone woke 29-year-old *Washington Post* reporter Bob Woodward on Saturday morning, June 17, 1972. Could he come to the office? Five men had been arrested for burglary at the headquarters of the Democratic National Committee in the opulent Watergate apartment-office complex; they were carrying photographic equipment and electronic gear.

In the *Post*'s newsroom, Woodward learned the details that had been phoned in by a veteran police reporter. The five men, arrested at 2:30 A.M., had been wearing business suits and surgical gloves and carrying a walkie-talkie, 40 rolls of film, cameras, lock picks, pen-size tear gas guns, bugging devices, and many sequentially numbered $100 bills.

The Yale-educated Woodward also learned that hard-driving college dropout Carl Bernstein (only 28 years old but with 12 years of newspaper experience) was working on the same story for the *Post*. The collaboration between Woodward and Bernstein started uneasily but eventually produced one of the most remarkable stories in the history of American journalism.

At the preliminary hearing in court that afternoon, Woodward heard accused burglar James McCord describe his profession as "security consultant," recently retired from government: "CIA," he whispered to the judge. Meanwhile, Bernstein learned from Miami contacts that the four other accused burglars had anti-Castro Cuban backgrounds and possible CIA (Central Intelligence Agency) connections. The *Post*

ran a front-page story on Sunday about the attempt to bug the Democrats, leaving the burglars' motives a mystery.

The Associated Press wire service revealed that McCord was the security coordinator for the Committee to Reelect the President (CREEP), the chief Republican campaign organization in 1972. John Mitchell, President Nixon's campaign manager and former attorney general, denied that the burglars had been acting for the campaign. A police source told the *Post*, however, that the burglars' address books and papers referred to E. Howard Hunt, "W. House," or "W.H." With a few phone calls, Woodward was able to establish that Hunt was a consultant working for Charles W. Colson, special counsel to the president of

stakes (e.g., physical violence or conflict), and celebrity (e.g., the death of John F. Kennedy Jr. in an airplane crash). Some trivial topics are judged newsworthy, such as the hairstyles of Simpson trial stars Marcia Clark and Kato Kaelin. As the term *news story* implies, news works best when it can be framed as a familiar kind of narrative: an exposé of greed, sex, or corruption; conflict between politicians; or a foreign affairs crisis. On television, of course, dramatic or startling film footage helps make a story gripping. Important stories without visuals are often pushed aside for less important stories for which visuals exist.

Episodic Foreign Coverage   Very few newspapers other than the *New York Times* can afford to station reporters abroad. Even the *Times* and the networks and wire services cannot regularly cover most nations of the world. They keep reporters in the countries of greatest interest to Americans—those that have big effects on American interests or enjoy close economic or cultural ties with the United States, such as Great Britain, Germany, Japan, Israel, Russia, and the United States. "White House Consultant Linked to Bugging Suspects," Woodward's story was headlined.

Presidential press secretary Ronald Ziegler described the incident as a "third-rate burglary attempt," not worthy of further White House comment; President Nixon flatly said that "the White House has had no involvement whatever." But *Newsday* and the *New York Times* established that the CREEP office of G. Gordon Liddy, a former White House aide, had received many phone calls from one of the burglars. The *Times* reported that $100,000 in that burglar's bank account had come from a Mexico City lawyer. Bernstein traced $25,000 of the money to the head of Nixon's 1968 Midwest campaign, who told Woodward that it consisted of contributions that he had personally turned over to the finance chairman of CREEP.

Woodward and Bernstein discovered that the Watergate break-in was just the tip of an iceberg. CREEP had kept hundreds of thousands of dollars in a secret fund, controlled by top White House and campaign officials, which they had used to carry out extensive espionage, sabotage, and dirty tricks against Democratic candidates. They had provided psychiatric records that caused Thomas Eagleton to resign as George McGovern's vice-presidential running mate; they had disrupted schedules and harassed candidates' families. The October 10 "Woodstein" story put the picture together: "FBI Finds Nixon Aides Sabotaged Democrats." Over the next few days, the

Post, Time magazine, and the *New York Times* reported several direct links to the White House, including some through Chief of Staff H. R. Haldeman.

A grand jury indicted only Hunt, Liddy, and the five burglars, and Watergate was not much of an issue in the 1972 presidential election, in which Nixon overwhelmingly defeated McGovern. Only later revelations provoked the series of trials, congressional investigations, and impeachment hearings that eventually drove Nixon from office and convicted his attorney general, his chief of staff, and others of crimes.

But Bernstein's and Woodward's tenacious investigative reporting set those events in motion. In May 1973, the *Post* won the Pulitzer Prize for distinguished public service in journalism. Some observers complained that the *Post* had unfairly hounded the Nixon administration, but most concluded that it had shown how a free press can serve democracy well by digging out important facts for the American people. However, many people complain today that the Watergate journalism style has now permeated the media and that reporters have become zealots, savaging politicians and political leaders for wrongdoing large and small. What do you think? Have the media gone too far in their watchdog role?

Source: Based on Carl Bernstein and Bob Woodward, *All the President's Men* (New York: Simon & Schuster, 1974).

China—and they have regional bureaus in Africa and Latin America. In many countries, however, they depend on "stringers" (local journalists who file occasional reports). During major crises or big events, the media send in temporary news teams, such as the armies of reporters that swarmed to Bosnia and Kosovo during the conflicts with the Serbs. The result is that most media devote most of their attention to limited areas of the world, dropping in only occasionally on others.

Foreign news, therefore, tends to be episodic. An unfamiliar country, such as Rwanda or Haiti, suddenly jumps into the headlines with a spectacular story of a coup, an invasion, or a famine, which comes as a surprise to most Americans because they have not been prepared by background reports. For a few days or weeks, the story dominates the news, with intensive coverage through pictures, interviews, and commentaries. Then, if nothing new and exciting happens, the story grows stale and disappears from the media. Most viewers are left with little more understanding of the country than they began with. Thus, they find it difficult to form judgments about U.S. foreign policy.

Local news is increasingly dominated by stories about crime, both petty and not so petty, crowding out a great deal of more important substantive information about government policies and social and economic conditions.

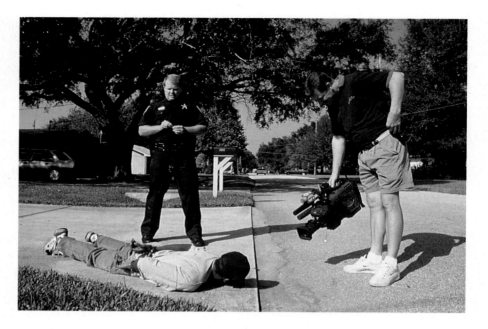

Interpreting

Political news does not make much sense without an interpretation of what it means. Under the informal rules of **objective journalism**, however, explicit interpretations by journalists are avoided, except for commentary or editorials that are labeled as such. Thus, even if a reporter knows that an official is lying, he or she cannot say so directly but must find someone else who will say so for the record. Staged events—such as a news conference held in a national park to announce a bill to protect the environment—cannot be identified by reporters as staged events. In news stories, most interpretations are left implicit (so that they are hard to detect and hard to argue with) or are given by so-called experts who are interviewed for comments. Often, particular experts are selected by print, broadcast, and telecast journalists because the position the experts will take is entirely predictable.

Experts are selected partly for reasons of convenience and audience appeal: scholars and commentators who live close to New York City or Washington, D.C., who like to speak in public, who look good on camera, and who are skillful in coming up with colorful quotations on a variety of subjects are contacted again and again. They often show up on television to comment on the news of the day, even on issues that are far from the area of their special expertise. In many cases, these pundits are simply well known for being on television often, and are not experts on any subject at all.

The experts and commentators featured in the media are often ex-officials. Their views are usually in harmony with the political currents of the day; that is, they tend to reflect a fairly narrow spectrum of opinion close to that of the party in power in Washington, D.C., or to the prevailing "conventional wisdom" inside the beltway. During the 1980s and early 1990s, for example, the experts most frequently quoted on television were a handful of former Reagan or Bush administration officials and others associated with conservative **think tanks**, such as the American Enterprise Institute and the Center for Strategic and International Studies. The commentator "punditocracy" was also quite conservative.[22]

At other times, with different politicians in power, different kinds of experts have been favored. Antipoverty warriors got a lot of media attention during

objective news

News reported with no evaluative language and with any opinions quoted or attributed to a specific source.

think tanks

Nonprofit organizations that do research on public policy issues and distribute their findings through a variety of outlets. Although formally nonpartisan, most have an identifiable ideological stance.

Lyndon Johnson's administration, for example, and some liberal and centrist voices began to reappear in the media when President Clinton replaced Bush. But radical independent thinkers such as I. F. Stone, whose *Weekly* became influential for a time during the Vietnam War, or Noam Chomsky, a fierce critic of media reporting on U.S. foreign policy today, have rarely penetrated the mainstream media at all. There are also strikingly few racial minorities among commentators in the mainstream media.

Is the News Biased?

Few topics arouse more disagreement than the question of whether the mass media in the United States have a liberal or conservative **bias**—or any bias at all. For years, a number of journalists and scholars have maintained that the media tend to be a pro-establishment, conservative force, reflecting their corporate ownership and their dependence on official sources for news. Conservative critics have counterattacked, arguing that liberal media elites regularly publish and broadcast antiestablishment, antiauthority news with a liberal bias. Others suggest that with minorities so underrepresented in the decision-making levels of the news industry—although there has been a significant increase in the number of minority "on-camera" personalities—minority issues are not treated fully or fairly.[23]

bias

Deviation from some ideal standard, such as representativeness or objectivity.

Liberal Reporters   Surveys of reporters' and journalists' opinions suggest that these individuals tend to be somewhat more liberal than the average American—although by no means radical—on certain matters, including the environment and such social issues as civil rights and liberties, abortion, and women's rights.[24] This is especially true of those employed by certain elite media organizations, including the *New York Times,* the *Washington Post,* and PBS. It is likely that reporters' liberalism has been reflected in the treatment of some stories about such issues as nuclear energy, global warming, and toxic waste. In 1990, for example, an exhaustive three-volume government report that found that damage from acid rain had been greatly overestimated was ignored by virtually all the major media, except *60 Minutes* and the *Wall Street Journal.*[25]

But there is little or no systematic evidence that reporters' personal values regularly affect what appears in the media. Journalists' commitment to the idea of objectivity helps them resist temptation, as do critical scrutiny and rewriting by editors. And in any case, the liberalism of journalists may be offset by their need to rely on official sources and by conservatism among media owners and publishers. It is also difficult to sustain the position that reporters slant their stories in a liberal direction after witnessing the pummeling Bill Clinton received in the media throughout his presidency.

Conservative Owners   The owners and top managers of most media corporations tend to be very conservative. The shareholders and executives of multibillion-dollar corporations are not very interested in undermining capitalism or, for that matter, in increasing their own taxes, raising labor costs, or losing income from offended advertisers. These owners and managers ultimately decide which reporters, newscasters, and editors to hire or fire, promote or discourage. Journalists who want to get ahead, therefore, may have to come to terms with the policies of the people who own and run media businesses.

One sign of conservatism in the media is newspapers' endorsements of presidential candidates, which are decided mostly by owners and publishers. In all six presidential elections from 1968 through 1988, more newspapers—usually many more—backed the Republican than the Democratic candidate. In

1988, for example, one week before the election, 195 dailies had endorsed George Bush, whereas just 51 had endorsed Michael Dukakis.[26] Only in 1992 was the picture different: the "new," friendly-to-business Democrat, Bill Clinton, won a majority of endorsements, as he did in 1996.[27]

What Constitutes Bias?   One reason observers keep arguing about the question of bias is that it is not easy to define or measure. Some scholars have simply counted what proportion of references to some political figure or policy (e.g., presidential candidate Richard Nixon or the Vietnam War) seemed to be positive or negative. However, negative coverage may reflect objectively bad news—for example, Vietnam War casualties or the Watergate revelations—rather than bias, or the media may just be quoting what leading news sources are saying, whether the sources are right or wrong.

A more sophisticated concept of bias involves a deviation from some perfect representation of objective reality. Yet there is lots of room for argument about which aspects of reality are worth reporting and about what the facts are—what is true and what is false. Is the truth whatever our best experts say it is? If so, who gets to decide who the best experts are?

Prevailing Themes in Political News

Even if we cannot be sure whether or how the media are biased, it is easy to identify certain tendencies in media coverage, certain beliefs that are assumed, and certain values and points of view that are emphasized.

Nationalism   Most news about foreign affairs takes a definitely pro-American, patriotic point of view, usually putting the United States in a good light and its opponents in a bad light. It is also ethnocentric, focusing on things that interest and concern ordinary Americans. For example, U.S. newspapers and television in 1980 devoted intensive, yearlong coverage to the fate of 49 Americans held hostage in the U.S. embassy in Tehran, Iran; in the early 1990s, they exhaustively covered a U.S. pilot, Scott O'Grady, who had been shot down over Bosnia. But much less attention has been paid to the slaughter of millions of people in Indonesia, Nigeria, East Timor, Cambodia, and Rwanda.

This nationalistic perspective, together with heavy reliance on U.S. government news sources, means that coverage of foreign news generally harmonizes well with official U.S. foreign policy. Thus, the media tend to go along with the U.S. government in assuming the best about our close allies and the worst about official "enemies." When the U.S. was assisting Iraq in its war against Iran, for example, Saddem Hussein was depicted in a positive light; with the coming of the Gulf War, media characterizations of him changed dramatically.

In foreign policy crisis situations, the reliance on official news sources means that the media sometimes propagate government statements that are false or misleading, as in the announcement of unprovoked attacks on U.S. destroyers in the Gulf of Tonkin at the beginning of the Vietnam War (recall the vignette in Chapter 5). Secret information can also be controlled by the government. The widely reported "missile gap" that led to a big arms buildup during the Kennedy years and the "window of vulnerability" that preceded the Reagan defense budget increases both turned out to be illusions.[28]

Approval of the American Economic System   Another tendency of the media is to run stories generally approving of free markets, free international trade, and minimal regulation. Our economic system wins approval, while variant or alternative systems, such as European social democracies with comprehensive social welfare programs, are generally portrayed more negatively. Countries whose economic policies mirror those of the U.S. economy, such as Poland, are praised, while countries trying to preserve a vibrant welfare state, such as France, are criticized. Individual U.S. corporations are criticized for errors and misdeeds—for example, polluters are likely to be hauled before the court of public opinion—but the economic system itself is rarely challenged. This stance is hardly surprising, since most Americans like the U.S. system, but it may discourage the consideration of alternative approaches to enduring problems.

Negativity and Scandal   Increasingly, political candidates and officials are being subjected to a relentless barrage of negative coverage. Some of this coverage starts with negative advertisements by opponents, which are then sometimes echoed in media reporting. At the beginning of the 1996 campaign, for example, Iowa, New Hampshire, and other states were saturated with ads by Steve Forbes, Bob Dole, and Phil Gramm attacking each other as old and tired, lacking ideas, or favoring the rich. Research has shown that negative ads increase citizens' anger and alienation and discourage them from voting.[29] News stories often picked up and amplified these negative themes.

Incumbent officials also get plenty of negative publicity, especially when even the appearance of wrong-doing in their personal lives creates dramatic human-interest stories. "Whitewater" allegations against President Clinton and First Lady Hillary Rodham Clinton—that they had dealt improperly with a real estate investment and a bank's campaign contributions while Clinton was governor of Arkansas and had obstructed justice while in the White House—were doggedly pursued by the *American Spectator,* the *New York Times,* and other media for most of Clinton's first term. Sex scandals dogged Bill Clinton for most of his presidency and contributed to his eventual impeachment hearings. Sex and financial scandals also claimed, among others, Senator Gary Hart, former House Speakers Jim Wright and Newt Gingrich, and House Speaker–elect Bob Livingston.

LongmanParticipate

CourseCompass

visual literacy
What's in an Ad?

In the view of many observers, the mass media in the United States have become increasingly mired in scandal and sensationalism. During the Pope's historic visit to communist Cuba, for example, the breaking Monica Lewinsky "White House intern" sex scandal dominated television news, talk radio, and newspapers. Dan Rather even left Havana in the middle of the Pope's visit in order to be on top of what CBS News producers considered to be the more important story.

Infotainment   One of the most dramatic changes that has occurred in the news is the insertion of entertainment values into political reporting and news presentation. As little as 15 to 20 years ago, news was monopolized by the three major television networks and the big-city daily newspapers, and the audiences for the news were fairly stable. In the intervening years, we have seen, the media have been revolutionized by the growth of cable television and the Internet and the multiplication of news outlets. In this new world, the networks and the big-city dailies have lost audience, leaving each of the fragments of the old and new media to fight for audience share. The best way to do this, media executives have discovered, is to make the news more entertaining, for the worst sin of this brave new media world is to be boring.[30] All too often, "more entertaining" means that sensation and scandal replace serious public policy issues, short and snappy coverage displaces longer, more analytical coverage, dramatic visuals push aside stories that cannot be easily visualized, and stories that feature angry conflict displace stories in which political leaders are trying to make workable compromises.[31] The current "culture wars" over the various legacies of the 1960s—involving abortion, affirmative action, religious values, gay and lesbian rights, and more—between liberals and conservatives and between Democrats and Republicans, is perfect grist for the infotainment mill. Thus, a current staple of cable and broadcast television public affairs programming is the gathering of **pundits** from both side of the cultural and political divide angrily shouting at each other for 30 minutes or 60 minutes: *The Washington Gang, Politically Incorrect,* and *Hard Ball* are examples. It is highly unlikely that this emergent journalism of assertion and attack improves public understanding of the candidates, political leaders, and public policies.

Conflict and contestation are also evident in coverage of campaigns, where the media concentrate on who is winning and who is losing the race and what strategies candidates are using to gain ground or to maintain their lead. When candidates sometimes make a stab at talking seriously about issues, the media almost always treat such talk as a mere stratagem of the long campaign. The perpetual struggle between Congress and the president, built into our constitutional system, is also perfect for the infotainment news industry, especially if the struggle can be personalized, as it was in the years when House Speaker Newt Gingrich was doing battle with President Bill Clinton.

pundits

Somewhat derisive term for print, broadcast, and radio commentators on the political news.

LongmanParticipate

CourseCompass

participation
Where Do You Get Your News, and How Reliable Is It?

Limited, Fragmented, and Incoherent Political Information   Most communications scholars agree that the media coverage of political news has certain distinctive features that result from characteristics of the mass media themselves, including the prevailing technology and organization of news gathering, corporate ownership, and the profit-making drive to appeal to mass audiences. These characteristics of the media mean that news, especially on television, tends to be episodic and fragmented rather than sustained, analytical, or dispassionate.[32] Information comes in bits and pieces, out of context, and without historical background.

Effects of the Media on Politics

The old idea that the mass media have only "minimal effects" on politics is now discredited. The contents of the media do make a difference; they affect public opinion and policymaking in a number of ways, including setting the agenda for public debate and framing how issues are understood.[33]

USING THE FRAMEWORK

Why Was the Monica Lewinsky Story on the TV News for Almost a Year? It Seemed Like Overkill to Me.

President Clinton's sexual liaison with White House intern Monica Lewinsky dominated the nation's political news from the early summer of 1998 through the end of the Senate impeachment trial of the president in early 1999. It was almost as if nothing else of importance was happening in the nation or around the world. Why is that? Taking a look at how structural, political linkage, and governmental factors affected news coverage will help explain the situation.

Governmental Action

Impeachment hearings and vote in the House provided dramatic news material.

Senate deliberations and vote to remove the president from office provided dramatic news material.

Governmental Level

- President Clinton engaged in behavior that was offensive to most Americans.

- Many members of Congress believed that President Clinton had obstructed justice in the Paula Jones and Monica Lewinsky affairs.

- A bitter partisan atmosphere permeated the 105th Congress.

- The Republican Congress and Democratic President Bill Clinton were bitterly deadlocked on a wide range of issues; severe tensions existed between the two branches of government.

Political Linkages Level

- Media television executives used "attack journalism," "infotainment," and scandal as a way to attract viewers from a highly fragmented set of media consumers.

- The media fell into their "one big story at a time" syndrome, also evident in the O. J. Simpson and JonBenet Ramsey cases.

- Web-based and scandal-sheet papers fed leads to major mainstream media.

- The Republican Party used the Lewinsky scandal in advertising for the 1998 congressional elections.

- Conservative interest groups also saw advantages in a weakened President Clinton and ran ad campaigns highlighting the Lewinsky matter.

Structural Level

- Technological innovations multiplied the number of television channels, all of which require content to fill the hours.

- As the Internet developed, it became (among other things) a medium for the distribution of information, opinion, and rumors.

Agenda Setting

agenda setting

Influencing what people consider important.

Several studies have demonstrated the effect known as **agenda setting**. The topics that get the most coverage in the media are the same ones that most people tell pollsters are the most important problems facing the country. This correlation does not result just from the media's printing what people are most interested in; it is a real effect of what appears in the media. In controlled experiments, people who are shown doctored television news broadcasts emphasizing a particular problem (e.g., national defense) mention that problem as being important more often than people who have seen broadcasts that have not been tampered with.[34]

Of course, media managers do not arbitrarily decide what news to emphasize; their decisions reflect what is happening in the world and what American audiences care about. If there is a war or an economic depression, the media report it. But some research has indicated that what the media cover sometimes diverges from actual trends in problems. Publicity about crime, for example, may reflect editors' fears or a few dramatic incidents rather than a rising crime rate. When the two diverge, it seems to be the media's emphasis rather than real trends that affects public opinion.[35]

When the media decide to highlight a human rights tragedy in "real time," such as "ethnic cleansing" in Kosovo, public officials often feel compelled to act. When the media ignore equally troubling human tragedies, such as the genocide in Rwanda, public officials can attend to other matters. One scholarly study shows that in the foreign policy area, media choices about coverage shape what presidents pay attention to.[36]

Framing and Effects on Policy Preferences

framing

Providing a context for interpretation.

Experiments also indicate that the media's **framing**, or interpretation of stories, affects how people think about political problems and how they assign

WEB EXPLORATION

Agenda Setting

Issue: Scholarly research shows that the mass media help set the political agenda for both political leaders and ordinary citizens.

Site: Access the Center for Media and Public Affairs through the "Course Documents" section of your online course. Go to the "Web Explorations" section for Chapter 6, click on "Agenda Setting," and open "agenda setting" so that you can see what kinds of stories have received the most media attention in different years.

What You've Learned: Look at the most recent survey and compare it with a survey from the early 1990s. Has the emphasis in the news changed? Are the same kinds of stories carried year after year or not? Is there more or less substantive news about government and politics? Is there more or less news about scandals and government wrong-doing?

HINT: Even a cynic might be surprised to learn how much news coverage is directed at scandal and sensation.

blame. Whether citizens ascribe poverty to the laziness of the poor or to the nature of the economy, for example, depends partly on whether the media run stories about poor individuals (implying that they are responsible for their own plight) or stories about overall economic trends such as wage stagnation and unemployment.[37]

What appears in the media affects people's policy preferences as well. One study found that changes in the percentages of the public that favored various policies could be predicted rather accurately by what sorts of stories appeared on network television news shows between one opinion survey and the next. News from experts, commentators, and popular presidents had especially strong effects, while news openly attributed to interest groups had no impact or even a negative effect.[38]

Impact on Policymaking

By affecting what ordinary Americans think is important, how they understand problems, and what policies they want, the media indirectly affect what government does, because the government responds to public opinion. Heavy support for the North American Free Trade Agreement (NAFTA) by the *New York Times* and other media, for example, probably helped counteract initial public opposition due to fears of job losses. In addition, the media affect who is elected to office. As we will see in Chapter 10, media stories about the character of presidential and other candidates have enormous effects on fund-raising and on citizens' judgments of who would make a good leader. Thus, early press portrayal of George W. Bush as a "fresh face" in the Republican Party capable of winning the presidential election helped him raise record-setting amounts of money for his campaign.

Moreover, what appears in the media has a direct effect on policymaking. Policymakers learn about the world and about each other's activities from the media. Investigative journalism that exposes problems, for example, often leads local, state, or federal officials to act. Sometimes, journalists and politicians actively work together: the journalists expose problems that the politicians want to solve, and then the politicians' statements, hearings, and bills prolong the story for journalists to continue reporting.[39]

Cynicism

Americans are quite cynical about the political parties, politicians, and incumbent political leaders. To some extent, this has been true since the founding of the nation. Nevertheless, scholars and political commentators have noted a considerable increase in negative feelings about the political system over the past two decades or so (see Chapter 5 for details), and many commentators believe that mass media coverage of American politics has a great deal to do with this attitude change.[40] As the adversarial attack journalism style has taken over political reporting, serious consideration of the issues or of the behavior of institutions has taken a back seat to a steady diet of charges about personal misbehavior. When President George Bush, for example, joined a world leader to describe the nature of the agreement they had reached, reporters asked him instead about rumors of an extramarital affair a few years earlier. With the message being delivered by the mass media that political issues are really about special-interest maneuvering, that political leaders and aspiring political leaders never say what they mean or mean what they say, that all of them have something in their personal lives they want to hide, and that even the most admired of the lot have feet of clay, is it any wonder

© By permission of Mike Luckovich and Creators Syndicate.

that the American people are becoming increasingly disenchanted with the whole business?

Government Regulation of the Media

Our Constitution protects freedom of the press, and the U.S. government has less legal control over the media than the governments of most other countries do. But our government has the authority to make various technical and substantive regulations on the electronic media, if it wishes.

Print Media

Early in American history, government sometimes interfered with the press in a heavy-handed way. Under the Alien and Sedition Acts of 1798, for example, several Anti-Federalist newspaper editors were jailed for criticizing John Adams's administration. In recent years, however, the Constitution has been interpreted as forbidding government from preventing the publication of most kinds of political information or from punishing its publication afterward. The main exceptions involve national security, especially during wartime.

Prior Restraint Several U.S. Supreme Court decisions, beginning in the 1920s and 1930s, have ensured the press a great deal of constitutional protection. The First Amendment provision that Congress shall make no law "abridging freedom of speech, or of the press" has been held by the Supreme Court to prevent the federal censorship of newspapers or magazines. Only under the most pressing circumstances of danger to national security can the government engage in **prior restraint** and prevent the publication of material to which it objects (see Chapter 15).

On June 30, 1971, for example, the Supreme Court denied a request by the Nixon administration to restrain the *New York Times* and the *Washington Post* from publishing excerpts from the *Pentagon Papers,* a secret Defense

prior restraint

The government's power to prevent publication, as opposed to punishment afterward.

Coverage of the Persian Gulf War, even more than that of previous wars, was carefully controlled and censored by the U.S. military.

Department history of the United States's involvement in Vietnam. The Court declared that "the Government 'thus carries a heavy burden of showing justification for the enforcement of such a restraint.' . . . The Government had not met that burden." Justice Hugo Black's concurring opinion has become an important statement on freedom of the press.

Wartime Controls   In a sense, however, *the Pentagon Papers* case was an easy one because it concerned the right to publish a two-year-old history and analysis of past government policy, not information about current military or foreign policy actions that could jeopardize American lives. During wartime, the government has almost always asserted broad powers to control what reporters can see and what they can print. During World War II, for example, the Office of Censorship monitored all news entering and leaving the country, but it focused mainly on news about casualties and troop and ship movements rather than on political matters.

WEB EXPLORATION

Regulating the Internet

Issue: Whether to regulate the Internet, and how to do so, is a hot political topic today.

Site: Access the Public Agenda Online through the "Course Documents" section of your online course. Go to the "Web Explorations" section for Chapter 6, click on "Regulating the Internet," and open "net regulation." Under "issues," select "Internet Speech/Privacy." Read the materials in the following sections: "Overview," "Fact File," and "Framing the Debate."

What You've Learned: After you have read and thought about this material, go to the section entitled "Public Opinion/ Major Proposals." How do you compare with the general public on proposals to regulate the Internet? Are you in the mainstream with respect to the chief proposals, or do you have a different opinion?

HINT: Your views on this matter will probably have a lot to do with how much confidence and trust you have in government compared with your confidence and trust in the private market to manage potentially harmful effects of the Internet.

Relatively free media access to the Vietnam War eventually brought a flood of negative stories.[41] U.S. officials, having learned their lesson, restricted access to the 1991 war with Iraq. During that war, the military imposed an elaborate system of control and censorship, requiring reporters to work only in escorted pools, limiting their access to U.S. troops, and censoring their stories. The media went along with these restrictions at the time, and large majorities of the public approved of it, but the result was incomplete and misleading coverage.[42]

The Electronic Media

The electronic media are more directly regulated by government than the print media, although such regulation has been diminishing.

Government Licensing of the Airwaves

The federal government has broad powers to regulate the use of the airwaves, which are considered public property. Ever since the passage of the Radio Act of 1927 and the Communications Act of 1934, which established the Federal Communications Commission (FCC), the government has licensed radio and television stations and has required them to observe certain rules as a condition for obtaining licenses.

FCC rules specify the frequencies on which stations can broadcast and the amount of power that they can use, in order to prevent interference among broadcasters of the sort that had brought chaos to radio during the 1920s. Government regulations divide the VHF television band into 12 channels and allocate them in such a way that most major cities have three VHF stations—the main reason for the early emergence of just three major networks. The development of cable television greatly expanded variety and competition.

For a long time, to prevent monopolies of scarce channels, federal rules prohibited networks or anyone else from owning more than five VHF stations around the country. Deregulation during the 1990s loosened these rules. Now, one company's stations can cover up to 35 percent of U.S. households.

The Telecommunications Act of 1996, which revolutionized the industry by allowing telephone companies, cable companies, and broadcasters all to compete with one another, also provided that new frequencies, to be used for high-definition TV, should be given to broadcasters free of charge. Critics called this a giveaway of public airwaves worth as much as $70 billion; they wanted government to require new public services or to auction off the frequencies to generate public revenue. The 1996 act also removed most restrictions on the number of radio and television stations that a company could own nationally and locally, encouraging a wave of mergers in the late 1990s and into the new century.

Public Service Broadcasting

The FCC was mandated by Congress to regulate the airwaves for the "public interest, convenience, or necessity." This vague phrase has been interpreted as including "the development of an informed public opinion through the public dissemination of news and ideas concerning the vital public issues of the day," with ideas coming from "diverse and antagonistic sources," and with an emphasis on service to the local community.

In practice, this requirement has mainly meant FCC pressure (backed up by the threat of not renewing stations' licenses) to provide a certain number of hours of news and "public service" broadcasting. Thus, government regulation created an artificial demand for news programming, before it became profitable, and contributed to the rise and expansion of network news and to the development of documentaries and news specials. In that way, government regulation presumably contributed to informed public opinion and to democracy. Recently, however, this public service requirement has been eroded and the amount of this kind of programming has declined.

Fairness   For many years, the **fairness doctrine** of 1949 required that licensees present contrasting viewpoints on any controversial issue of public importance that was discussed. This requirement led to efforts at balance—presenting two sides on any issue that was mentioned—and sometimes to the avoidance of controversial issues altogether. It was left mostly up to broadcasters, however, to decide what was important or controversial and what constituted a fair reply and a fair amount of time to give it.

Fairness is not easy to define: which of the unlimited number of possible opinions deserves a hearing? The FCC itself long ago made clear that it did not intend to make time available to "communist viewpoints," and both of the "two sides" that the media air are usually quite mainstream.

fairness doctrine
The former requirement that television stations present contrasting points of view.

Equal Time   Similarly, the **equal time provision** of the 1934 Communications Act required that except for news programs, stations that granted (or sold) air time to any one candidate for public office had to grant (or sell) other candidates equal time. This requirement threatened to cause the media great expense when minor party candidates insisted on their share of air time or when opponents wanted to reply to political speeches by incumbent presidents in election years. Contrary to its intent, therefore, this requirement led to some curtailment of political programming.

The equal time provision was suspended in 1960 to allow televised debates between candidates John F. Kennedy and Richard M. Nixon, and in 1976 and 1980, the FCC permitted the staging of the Ford–Carter and Carter–Reagan debates as "public meetings," sponsored by the League of Women Voters, to get around the provision. In 1983, the FCC declared that radio and television broadcasters were free to stage debates at all political levels among candidates of their own choosing.[43]

equal time provision
The former requirement that television stations give or sell the same amount of time to all competing candidates.

Rate Regulation   Federal and local regulation of the rates charged by cable TV firms (many of them monopoly providers in local areas) has been imposed, removed, and imposed once again. Most recently, with the Telecommunications Act of 1996, cable rate regulation was scheduled to be ended by 1999, by which

Election year debates, such as this 2000 debate between presidential candidates George W. Bush and Al Gore, have become a regular television feature and may have a profound effect on elections.

As Internet usage has expanded in the United States, various and sundry individuals and groups have called for tighter federal regulation of the new medium, primarily to protect children from material with sexual content and to prevent dissemination of hate material. So far, none of the bills passed by Congress to achieve these regulatory goals has passed constitutional muster with the Supreme Court.

time it was thought, competition from the telephone companies would serve to keep cable rates down. This remains to be seen.

The Internet

When television and radio were introduced, the industries were regulated by the federal government almost immediately. This has not been the case for the Internet, despite its extraordinary growth and social impact. Although initially a product of government encouragement and financial support—it was first created to link together university and government defense researchers[44]—the Internet has been relatively free from regulation, although there have been calls for government to prevent certain content from appearing on it. The few attempts that have been made have not been successful. Congress, for example, tried to ban obscenity on the Net, but the Supreme Court in 1997 declared the statute an unconstitutional restriction of free speech. When the Clinton administration tried to prevent people from posting encryption codes, a federal court declared the effort as unconstitutional on the same grounds. In the view of the federal courts, at this writing, the Internet is an open medium where people are free to express their views, no different from dissemination of ideas by voice from atop a soap-box or by a pamphlet. Statute and case law in this area is sure to grow, however, as the Internet comes to play an ever larger role in our lives, so the story of Internet regulation is not yet finished.[45]

Taken as a whole, then, government regulation of the media does not now amount to much. The trend has been toward a free market system with little government interference.

HOW DEMOCRATIC ARE WE?

PROPOSITION: The mass media are an important ingredient in making American politics democratic.

AGREE: Without the information provided by the media, ordinary citizens would have little hope of learning what is happening abroad; they could not begin to think about what sorts of policies the United States should pursue in foreign affairs. Nor, without media, could most Americans learn what their government is doing domestically or what sorts of candidates are running for office or what kinds of public policies are being considered.

In these respects, the spread of the mass media in the United States, and the penetration of millions of homes by newspapers, radio, television, and computers, has undoubtedly helped democracy. It has made it much easier for ordinary citizens to form policy preferences, to judge the actions of government, and to figure out whom they want to govern them. Mass media thus tend to broaden the scope of conflict and contribute to political equality. When citizens, rather than just political leaders or special-interest groups, know what is going on, they can have a voice in politics. Moreover, interactive media and media-published polls help politicians hear that voice.

DISAGREE: Scholars and media critics who want the media to be highly informative, analytical, and issue-oriented are appalled by the personalized, episodic, dramatic, and fragmented character of most news stories, which do not provide sustained and coherent explanations of what is going on. Others worry about ideological biases they think arise from a leftist media elite or from a corporate-owned media industry. Some criticize the media's patriotic and ethnocentric tendencies to support official U.S. foreign policy and even to pass along deliberate untruths stated by government officials. If the media regularly present one-sided or false pictures of politics, people may form mistaken policy preferences. Government responsiveness to manipulated preferences would not be truly democratic.

Still other critics worry that constant media exposés of alleged official wrongdoing or government inefficiency, and the mocking tone aimed at virtually all political leaders by journalists and talk radio hosts, have fueled the growing political cynicism of the public. If this is true, the media are not serving democracy as well as they might.

THE AUTHORS: It is undeniably the case that the media have not performed their civic responsibilities very well. They do tend to trivialize, focus on scandal and entertainment, and offer fragmented and out-of-context political and governmental information. However, things may not be quite as bad as they first appear. For one thing, for those who are truly interested in public affairs, there is now more readily accessible information than at any time in our history. For those willing to search for it, there is now little information that is relevant to public affairs that can be kept hidden, ranging from official government statistics to academic and other expert studies. Additionally, the American people have demonstrated an admirable ability on many occasions to sift the wheat from the chaff, to glean the information they need from the background noise, as it were.[46]

Summary

The shape of the mass media in the United States has been determined largely by structural factors: technological developments, the growth of the American population and economy, and the development of a privately owned, corporation-dominated media industry.

The profit motive leads the major media to appeal to large audiences by limiting the quantity and depth of political news, by appealing to patriotism and other mainstream political values, and by emphasizing dramatic stories with visual impact and human interest.

News gathering is organized around New York City, Washington, D.C., and a handful of major cities in the United States and abroad. Most foreign countries are ignored unless there are crises or other big stories to communicate. Most news comes from government officials, who cultivate friendly relations with the press and provide accessible press conferences and information handouts.

Observers disagree about whether the media are biased in a liberal or a conservative direction. Reporters tend to be liberal, especially on social issues, but this tendency may be balanced or reversed by conservative owners and editors. The U.S. media tend to reflect ethnocentrism, support U.S. foreign policy, and celebrate American-style capitalism. They also broadcast negative campaign ads, publicize personal scandals, and sharply criticize officials who have lost popularity.

Media stories have substantial effects on the public's perceptions of problems, its interpretations of events, its evaluations of political candidates, and its policy preferences.

The media, especially the print media, are protected from many kinds of government interference by the First Amendment to the Constitution. But censorship occurs during wars and crises, and officials have indirect ways of influencing the news. The electronic media are legally open to direct regulation, but such regulation, including the fairness doctrine and the equal time provision, has mostly lapsed. The Internet remains relatively free from government regulation.

Suggestions for Further Reading

Bagdikian, Ben H. *The Media Monopoly,* 5th ed. Boston: Beacon Press, 1997.
An analysis of the corporate structure of the media and its consequences.

Bennett, W. Lance. *News: Politics of Illusion,* 3rd ed. New York: Longman, 1996.
A critique of the news as trivial and uninformative.

Graber, Doris, Denis McQuail, and Pippa Norris, eds. *The Politics of News; the News of Politics.* Washington, D.C.: Congressional Quarterly Press, 1998.
A collection that reports state-of-the-art scholarship on the subject of the mass media and American politics.

Kovach, Bill, and Tom Rosenstiel. *Warp Speed: America in the Age of Mixed Media.* New York: The Century Foundation Press, 1999.
A sober and sometimes somber description of the effect of the rapidly changing mass media industry on American politics and government.

Page, Benjamin I. *Who Deliberates? Mass Media in Modern Democracy.* Chicago: University of Chicago Press, 1996.
A discussion of how the media do or do not serve democracy well, with illustrative case studies.

Internet Sources

Almost every television news organization has a Web site on the Internet:

ABC News   **http://www.abc.com**

CBS News   **http://www.cbs.com**

CNN Interactive   **http://www.cnn.com/**

NBC News   **http://www.nbc.com**

The same is true of the major national newspapers:

Chicago Tribune **http://www.chicagotribune.com**

Los Angeles Times **http://www.latimes.com**

New York Times **http://www.nytimes.com**

San Jose Mercury News **http://www.sjmercury.com**

USA Today **http://www.usatoday.com**

Washington Post **http://www.washingtonpost.com**

Other sources for studies on media trends and effects on society include:

The Center for Media and Public Affairs **www.cmpa.com**
Studies, commentaries, and forums on media and public affairs.

The Pew Research Center for the People and the Press **www.people-press.org/**
The most complete public opinion surveys on citizen evaluations of the quality of media coverage of public affairs.

Notes

1. The source for this vignette is Bill Dovach and Tom Rosenthal, *Warp Speed: America in the Age of Mass Media* (New York: The Century Fund Press, 1999).

2. Walter Lippmann, address in London, May 27, 1965.

3. Doris Graber, *Mass Media and American Politics,* 4th ed. (Washington, D.C.: Congressional Quarterly Press, 1993), p. 35.

4. See Suzanne Garment, *Scandal: The Crisis of Mistrust in American Politics* (New York: Random House, 1991).

5. Dovach and Rosenthal, *Warp Speed.*

6. Diana Owen, "Talk Radio and Evaluations of President Clinton," *Political Communications,* 14 (1997), pp. 333–353.

7. Richard Davis, "Understanding Broadcast Political Talk," *Political Communications,* 14 (1997), p. 328.

8. Kenneth Dautrich and Thomas H. Hartley, *How the News Media Fail American Voters* (New York: Columbia University Press, 1999).

9. Ibid., p. 33.

10. Regis McKenna, *Real Time* (Cambridge: Harvard University Press, 1997).

11. Dovach and Rosenthal, *Warp Speed,* pp. 52–57.

12. Erik P. Bucy et. al., "The Engaged Electorate: New Media Use as Political Participation," in Lynda Lee Kaid and Dianne G. Bystrom, eds., *The Electronic Election* (Mahwah, NJ: Lawrence Erlbaum and Associates, Publishers, 1997).

13. Ben H. Bagdikian, *The Media Monopoly,* 5th ed. (Boston: Beacon Press, 1997).

14. Ibid., p. 124.

15. Eric Boehler, "The Merger Frenzy," *Rolling Stone* (October 17, 1996), p. 40.

16. Symposium, "The Real Dangers of Conglomerate Control," *Columbia Journalism Review* (March–April 1997), pp. 47–51.

17. W. Lance Bennett, *News: The Politics of Illusion,* 3rd ed. (New York: Longman, 1996), p. 15.

18. Doug Underwood, "Market Research and the Audience for Political News," in Graber, McQuail, and Norris, *The Politics of News* (Washington, D.C.: CQ Press, 1998), p. 171.

19. Edward Jay Epstein, *News from Nowhere: Television and the News* (New York: Vantage, 1973), p. 142.

20. Leon V. Sigal, *Reporters and Officials: The Organization and Politics of News Reporting* (Lexington, MA: Heath, 1973), p. 124.

21. Mark Hertsgaard, *On Bended Knee* (New York: Farrar, Straus & Giroux, 1988), p. 5.

22. Lawrence C. Soley, *The News Shapers: The Sources Who Explain the News* (New York: Praeger, 1992); Eric Alterman, *Sound and Fury: The Washington Punditocracy and the Collapse of American Politics* (New York: HarperCollins, 1992).

23. Robert M. Entman, "Blacks in the News: Television, Modern Racism and Cultural Change," *Journalism Quarterly* 69, no. 2 (Summer, 1992), pp. 341–361; and Clint C. Wilson II, and Felix Gutierrez, *Race, Multiculturalism, and the Media* (Thousand Oaks, CA: Sage Publications, 1995).

24. William Schneider and I. A. Lewis, "Views on the News," *Public Opinion,* 8 (August–September 1985), p. 7; Karlyn Keene et al., "Monitoring Media Attitudes," *American Enterprise* (July–August 1990), p. 95; S. Robert Lichter, Stanley Rothman, and L. S. Lichter, *The Media Elite* (Bethesda, MD: Adler & Adler, 1986).

25. Howard Kurtz, "Acid Rain on the Media Parade: A Big Report Pooh-Poohing the Danger Gets Scant Press," *Washington Post Weekly Edition* (January 21–27, 1991), p. 38.

26. *Editorials on File,* 19 (November 1–15, 1988), p. 1272.

27. *Editor and Publisher* (October 24, 1992), pp. 9–10, 44; *Editor and Publisher* (November 7, 1992), pp. 8–11.

28. Fred Kaplan, *The Wizards of Armageddon* (New York: Simon & Schuster, 1983); Tom Gervasi, *The Myth of Soviet Military Supremacy* (New York: Harper & Row, 1986).

29. Thomas E. Patterson, *Out of Order* (New York: Knopf, 1993); Steven Ansolabehere and Shanto Iyengar, *Going Negative: How Attack Ads Shrink and Polarize the Electorate* (New York: Free Press, 1996).

30. Kovach and Rosenstiel, *Warp Speed,* p. 66.

31. W. Lance Bennett, *News: The Politics of Illusion,* 3rd ed. (New York: Longman, 1996), p. 15; and Kovach and Rosenstiel, *Warp Speed.*

32. Bennett, *News.*

33. David L. Paletz, "The Media and Public Policy," in Graber et. al., *The Politics of News.*

34. Shanto Iyengar and Donald R. Kinder, *News That Matters* (Chicago: University of Chicago Press, 1987).

35. G. Ray Funkhauser, "The Issues of the Sixties: An Exploratory Study in the Dynamics of Public Opinion," *Public Opinion Quarterly,* 37 (Spring 1973), pp. 62–75.

36. George C. Edwards, "Who Influences Whom? The President, Congress and the Media," *The American Political Science Review* 93 (June, 1999), pp. 327–344.

37. Shanto Iyengar, *Is Anyone Responsible? How Television News Frames Political Issues* (Chicago: University of Chicago Press, 1991).

38. Benjamin I. Page, Robert Y. Shapiro, and Glenn R. Dempsey, "What Moves Public Opinion?" *American Political Science Review,* 81 (1987), pp. 23–43.

39. David L. Protess, Fay Lomax Cook, Jack C. Doppelt, James S. Ettema, Margaret T. Gordon, Donna R. Leff, and Peter Miller, *The Journalism of Outrage: Investigative Reporting and Agenda Building in America* (New York: Guilford Press, 1991).

40. Stephen C. Craig, ed., *Broken Contract: Changing Relations Between Americans and Their Government* (Boulder, CO: Westview Press, 1996); Bennett, *News;* Thomas E. Patterson, "Bad News, Period," *PS* (March 1996), pp. 17–20.

41. Daniel C. Hallin, *The "Uncensored War": The Media and Vietnam* (Berkeley, CA: University of California Press, 1989).

42. W. Lance Bennett and David L. Paletz, eds., *Taken by Storm: The Media, Public Opinion, and U.S. Foreign Policy in the Gulf War* (Chicago: University of Chicago Press, 1994).

43. Doris Graber, *Mass Media and American Politics,* 4th ed. (Washington, D.C.: Congressional Quarterly Press, 1993), pp. 67–68.

44. Dan Schiller, *Digital Capitalism: Networking in the New Global Market System* (Cambridge, MA: MIT Press, 1999).

45. Lawrence Lessig, *Code and Other Laws of Cyberspace* (New York: Basic Books, 1999).

46. John A. Ferejohn and James H. Kuklinski, eds., *Information and Democratic Processes* (Urbana: University of Illinois Press, 1990); Benjamin I. Page, *Who Deliberates? Mass Media in Modern Democracy* (Chicago: University of Chicago Press, 1996).

CHAPTER 7

Interest Groups and Corporations

IN THIS CHAPTER

- Interest groups in democratic theory
- Why interest groups have proliferated
- How interest groups lobby the government
- How interest groups try to mobilize the grass roots
- Biases in the interest group system
- Why large corporations hold a privileged position

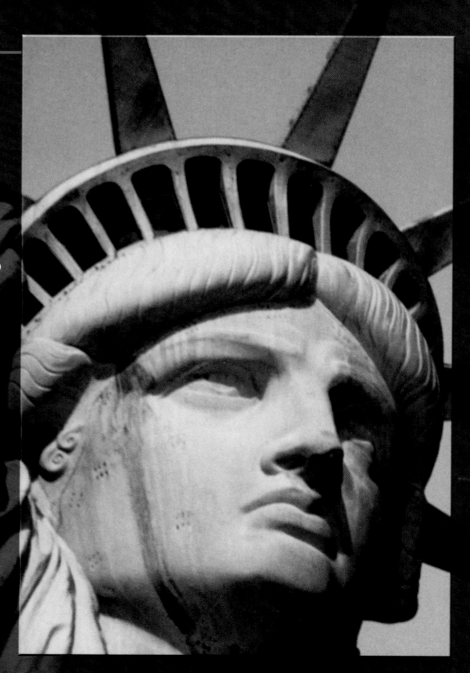

Lobbying for China

In 1997, the annual congressional debate on renewal of China's "most favored nation" (MFN) status reached fever pitch. The requirement that certain nations seek "most favored" status to avoid extremely high tariffs and other restrictions on their products is reserved under American law for communist countries (China, Cuba, North Korea) and a handful of so-called rogue states (Iran, Iraq, Libya) that are not members of the World Trade Organization. Each year, the president makes a determination about these nations, which Congress can override by a two-thirds vote. Presidential determinations about China's trade status had easily prevailed since 1981.

The political coalition that formed in 1997 to oppose granting MFN to China was made up of a surprising assortment of private and public interest groups and human rights organizations. Many human rights groups, such as Amnesty International, joined the battle because of the Chinese government's brutal repression of the pro-democracy movement in Beijing's Tiananmen Square in 1989, its abysmal human rights record in general, and its occupation of Tibet. Christian fundamentalists, through organizations such as the Family Research Council, used the MFN legislation to voice their concerns about the treatment of Christians in China and Chinese government family planning practices. MFN was also opposed by groups and individuals, such as the AFL-CIO and anti–free trade politicians such as Dick Gephardt (D–Mo.), who believe that free trade with low-wage countries depresses the wages of American workers. Finally, a number of software and entertainment companies, including Microsoft, opposed MFN for China because of the Chinese government's toleration of software pirating.

Despite this impressive array of opponents, there were not enough votes in Congress in 1997 to override President Clinton's granting of MFN to China for another year. There are many reasons for this, including the fact that many reasonable people believe that a policy of free trade with a country such as China not only benefits both parties economically but also will, in the long run, undermine the country's autocratic government and improve human rights and the chances for democracy. Equally important, perhaps, was the impressive array of American corporations that wanted open trade with China and were willing to lobby intensively for a favorable decision on MFN. The Boeing Corporation was especially involved in this campaign, primarily because its growth and profitability in the near future depend heavily on the sale of commercial aircraft to China.[1] Locked in an intense global competition with the European Airbus consortium for sales in China and elsewhere and knowing that the Chinese government was happy to play off Boeing and Airbus for favorable policy decisions by their governments, Boeing became a strong advocate for MFN and other policies favorable to China. Boeing lobbied members of Congress directly, contributed to the campaign war chests of candidates from both parties, asked its nearly 200,000 employees to get involved in the political process, and encouraged local political and business leaders in communities where Boeing has major plants (the Puget Sound region; Long Beach, California; St. Louis; and Wichita, Kansas) to talk to members of Congress.

Boeing was not alone; an impressive collection of companies doing business there lobbied Congress to approve MFN status for China. These included some of America's most important companies: the Big Three auto companies, defense high-technology firms such as TRW and United Technologies, Cargill (food products), General Electric, Caterpillar, and Aetna Insurance.[2] Many large and medium-sized export-oriented firms and associations lobbied through the 1,000-member Business Coalition for U.S.–China Trade (members include the National Association of Manufacturers, the National Retail Federation, the Business Roundtable, and the U.S. Chamber of Commerce). This impressive coalition greatly strengthened the hands of President Clinton and the congressional Republican leadership, both of whom were favorably disposed to free trade and renewal of China's MFN status.

The same interest group coalitions surrounded the debate in 2000 when Congress finally approved a bill to grant China permanent trade status, ending the annual battle. But the issue of free trade remains an important part of the American political agenda and will remain so for many years (see Chapter 18 for more about the trade issue).

Thinking Critically About This Chapter

This story about the 1997 battle over MFN certification for China tells us a lot about how many important government policies are made in the United States and the central role that interest groups and corporations play in shaping them.

Using the Framework. You will see in this chapter how interest groups, in combination with other political linkage institutions, help convey the wishes and interests of people and groups to government decision makers. You will also learn how the kind of interest group system we have in the United States is, in large part, a product of structural factors, including our constitutional rules, political culture, social organization, and economy.

Using the Democracy Standard. Interest groups have long held an ambiguous place in American politics. To some, interest groups are "special" interests that act without regard to the public interest and are the instruments of the most privileged parts of American society. To others, interest groups are simply another way by which people and groups in a democratic society get to have their voices heard by government leaders. Using the democracy standard described in Chapter 1, you will be able to choose between these two positions. ▶

Interest Groups in a Democratic Society: Contrasting Views

interest group

Any private organization or association that seeks to influence public policy as a way to protect or advance some interest.

Interest groups are private organizations that try to shape public policy. They are made up of people who share an interest that they are trying to protect or advance with the help of government. To do this, interest groups try to

WEB EXPLORATION

What Are Interest Groups?

Issue: Interest groups are different in important ways from political parties.

Site: Access the Republican National Committee and one of its most closely allied interest groups, the National Right to Life Committee, through the "Course Documents" section of your online course. Go to the "Web Explorations" section for Chapter 7, click on "What Are Interest Groups?," and open "Interest groups." At each site, examine the public policy issues that are addressed. Select "key issues" for the GOP, and "press releases" for the NRLC.

What You've Learned: What differences are there between the two on the range of issues each pays attention to? How would you explain differences (if there are any) in the issue agendas of the political party and the interest group?

HINT: Only one of these two types of institutions is in the business of trying to elect its people to office and gain control of the government.

In the late nineteenth century, most Americans thought of the Senate as the captive of large corporate trusts and other special-interest groups, as depicted in this popular cartoon, "Bosses of the Senate."

influence the behavior of public officials, such as presidents, members of Congress, bureaucrats, or judges. These efforts are often perceived by officials as pressuring them, so interest groups are often called **pressure groups.** The term **lobby** is also commonly used—because of the practice of interest group representatives' talking to representatives and senators in the lobbies outside committee rooms—as in references to the "dairy lobby" or the "gun lobby."

pressure group

An interest group or lobby; a group that brings pressure to bear on government decision makers.

lobby

An interest or pressure group that seeks to convey the group's interest to government decision makers.

The Evils of Factions

The danger to good government and the public interest from interest groups is a familiar theme in American politics. They are usually regarded as narrowly self-interested, out for themselves, and without regard for the public good.

This theme is prominent in *The Federalist,* No. 10, in which James Madison defined **factions** (his term for interest groups and narrow parties, which he thought were dangerous to good government) in the following manner: "a number of citizens, whether amounting to a majority or a minority of the whole, who are united and actuated by some common impulse of passion, or of interest, adverse to the rights of other citizens or to the permanent and aggregate interests of the community."[3] The "evils of factions" theme recurs throughout our history, from the writings of the "muckrakers" at the turn of the twentieth century to the GOP primary campaign of John McCain in 2000.

faction

Madison's term for groups or parties that try to advance their own interests at the expense of the public good.

Interest Group Democracy: The Pluralist Argument

According to many political scientists, however, interest groups do not hurt democracy and the public interest but are an important instrument in attaining both. The argument of these **pluralist** political scientists is shown in Figure 7.1 and goes as follows:[4]

- Free elections, while essential to a democracy, do not adequately communicate the specific wants and interests of the people to political leaders. These are more accurately, consistently, and frequently conveyed to political leaders by the many groups and organizations to which people belong.

- Interest groups are easy to create; people in the United States are free to join or to organize groups that reflect their interests.

pluralist

A political scientist who views American politics as best understood in terms of the interaction, conflict, and bargaining of groups.

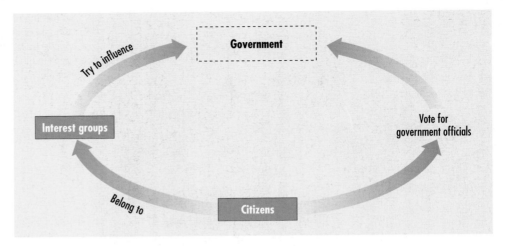

Figure 7.1 ● The Pluralist View of American Politics

In the pluralist understanding of the way American democracy works, citizens have more than one way to influence government leaders. In addition to voting, citizens also have the opportunity to participate in organizations that convey member views to officials. Because of weak political parties, federalism, checks and balances, and the separation of powers, access to such leaders is relatively easy.

- Because of federalism, checks and balances, and the separation of powers, government power in the United States is broadly dispersed, leaving governmental institutions as remarkably porous and open to the entreaties of the many and diverse groups that exist in society.

- Because of the ease of group formation and the accessibility of government, all legitimate interests in society can have their views taken into account by some public official. Thus, the system is highly democratic.

Pluralists see interest groups, then, not as a problem but as an additional tool of democratic representation, similar to other democratic instruments such as public opinion and elections. We shall explore the degree to which this position is valid in this and other chapters.

Interest Group Formation: Structural, Political Linkage, and Governmental Factors

LongmanParticipate

CourseCompass

timeline
Interest Groups in America

Nobody knows exactly how many interest groups exist in the United States, but there is wide agreement that the number began to mushroom in the late 1960s and has grown steadily ever since. We have a more precise count, however, of the number of paid lobbyists who work for interest groups in Washington and try to affect government policies. In 1996, more than 17,500 lobbyists worked there, up from 4,000 in 1977.[5]

Much of the increase in the number of interest groups can be explained by the growing number of public interest or citizen groups organized around some cause or idea, rather than an economic or occupational interest, the traditional basis for forming interest groups. These include environmental, consumer protection, anti-abortion, family values, good government, civil rights, pro-life, and women's organizations. Nevertheless, business, producer, and occupational groups still dominate by their sheer numbers: one study done during the Reagan years showed that corporations made up 52 percent of all organizations with Washington representatives, that trade and other business associations accounted for another 20 percent, and that professional associations accounted for an additional 8 percent, for a total of 80 percent of the organizations.[6] And there is reason to believe that the proportion of the total made up by citizen groups has actually declined since then.[7]

There are a number of reasons so many interest groups exist in the United States.

Diverse Interests

First of all, being a very diverse society, there are simply lots of interests in the United States. Racial, religious, ethnic, and occupational diversity is pronounced. Our economy is also strikingly complex and multifaceted, and becoming more so. In a free society, these diverse interests usually take organizational forms. Thus, the computer revolution has spawned computer chip manufacturers, software companies, software engineers, computer magazines, Internet services, technical information providers, computer component jobbers, Web designers, and countless others. Each has particular interests to defend or advance before government, and each has formed an association to try to do so. Thus, software engineers have an association to look after their interests. So do software and hardware companies, Internet access providers, digital information providers, industry writers, and so on.

Rules of the Game

The rules of the political game in the United States encourage the formation of interest groups. The First Amendment to the Constitution, for instance, guarantees citizens the right to speak freely, to assemble, and to petition the government, all of which are essential to citizens' ability to form organizations to advance their interests before government. Moreover, the government is organized in such a way that officials are relatively accessible to interest groups. Because of federalism, checks and balances, and the separation of powers, there is no dominant center of decision making, as there is in unitary states such as Great Britain and France. In unitary states (see Chapter 3), most important policy decisions are made in parliamentary bodies. In the United States, important decisions are made by many officials, on many matters, in many jurisdictions. Consequently, there are many more places where interest group pressure can be effective. Finally, there are no strong, centralized political parties in the United States, as there are in the European democracies, that might serve to overcome the decentralized, fragmented quality of the policymaking process in the United States. The result is relatively easy access to public officials in the United States.

The Growth in Government

Government does far more today than it did during the early years of the Republic. As government takes on more responsibilities, it quite naturally comes to have a greater effect on virtually all aspects of economic, social, and personal life. People, groups, and organizations are increasingly affected by the actions of government, so the decisions made by presidents, members of Congress, bureaucrats, and judges are increasingly important. It would be surprising indeed if in response, people, groups, and organizations did not try harder to influence the public officials' decisions that affect them.

Government often encourages the formation of groups and associations to help carry out and monitor its policies or to achieve other ends. The War on Poverty during the 1960s, for example, required that programs of poverty relief had to be at least partly administered by organizations of the poor in urban neighborhoods. Where such organizations did not exist, the legislation mandated that they be created. According to political scientist Anne Costain, a commissioner of the Equal Employment Opportunity Commission (EEOC) played an important role in the formation of the National Organization for Women (NOW) because he wanted a counterweight to the overwhelming influence of African-American civil rights groups over the EEOC.[8]

Disturbances

The existence of diverse interests, the rules of the game, and the importance of government decisions and policies enable and encourage the formation of interest groups, but formation seems to happen only when interests are threatened, usually by some change in the social and economic environment or in government policy. This is known as the **disturbance theory** of interest group formation.[9] The Christian Coalition was created at a time when many evangelical Christians felt threatened by family breakdown, an increase in the number of abortions, the sexual revolution, and the growing voice of gays and lesbians.

disturbance theory

A theory that locates the origins of interest groups in changes in the economic, social, or political environment that threaten the well-being of some segment of the population.

Incentives

Some social scientists argue, however, that people are not inclined to form groups, even when their common interests are threatened, unless the group can

WEB EXPLORATION

Internet Lobbying

Issue: Scientific and technological changes create new companies, problems, and opportunities that help propel the formation of new interest groups.

Site: Access the Public Agenda Online through the "Course Documents" section of your online course. Go to the "Web Explorations" section for Chapter 7, click on "Internet Lobbying," and open "Online Lobbying." Select "Internet Speech and Privacy," then select "Sources and Resources."

What You've Learned: Examine the long list of organizations that are concerned about free speech and privacy on the Internet, a medium of communication that hardly existed for most Americans as recently as the mid-1990s. Examine the Web sites of several of these organizations. What are they worried about? What do they want government to do?

HINT: Diverse groups will worry about a wide range of potential problems arising from a new technological development and will disagree about what they want government to do about it.

Discontent among American farmers in the late nineteenth century led to the formation of protest organizations and, eventually, the Populist party. One predecessor of the Populist party was the Grange, which fought for social and cultural benefits for isolated rural communities.

offer a selective, material benefit to them.[10] A selective, material benefit is something tangible that is available to the members of an interest group but not to nonmembers. If someone can get the benefit without joining the group, then joining makes no sense as he or she can obtain the same benefit without contributing. This is known as the **free rider** problem, and it generally comes into play when a group is interested in a collective good, such as a government program or action that will be good for all the members of some category whether they belong to a formal organization or not. All women with young children gain when the National Organization for Women helps influence Congress to pass the Family Leave Act and are not required to join the organization to enjoy the benefit. People join, it is argued, when an association has benefits that are available only to its members—for example, discounted life and health insurance programs for the members of the Wheat Growers Association.

free rider

One who gains a benefit without contributing; explains why it is so difficult to form social movements and noneconomic interest groups.

This theory emphasizes how difficult and unlikely it is that interest groups will form at all. It cannot account very well, therefore, for the upsurge in group formation during the 1960s and 1970s, especially of the public interest and ideological variety.[11] The proliferation of such groups suggests that groups form not only around selective, material incentives but also around "purposive" (ideological, issue-oriented) incentives and around "solidaristic" (in the sense of being part of something that one values) ones. People often join groups, for instance, because they believe in a particular cause (e.g., nuclear disarmament, civil rights, prayer in the public schools, or an end to legal abortion) or because they enjoy the companionship afforded by belonging to a group.

What Interests Are Represented

What kinds of interests find a voice in American politics? A useful place to start is with political scientist E. E. Schattschneider's distinction between "private" and "public" interests. Although the boundaries between the two are sometimes fuzzy, the distinction remains important: public interests are connected in one way or another to the general welfare of the community; private interests, by contrast, are associated with benefits for some fraction of the community.[12] The latter are mainly economic interests, groups with some tangible stake they wish to protect or to advance by means of government action. The former are mainly noneconomic groups motivated by some ideology, by the desire to advance a general cause—civil rights or environmental protection—or by the commitment to some public policy—gun control or an end to abortion. Private interest groups mainly provide selective benefits to their members; public interest groups mainly provide solidaristic and purposive incentives.

Private Interest Groups

Many different kinds of private interest groups are active in American politics.

Producers   Producer groups represent enterprises that produce some good or service. In this category, we would include businesses of various kinds. Because of the vast resources at the disposal of business and because of their strategic role in the health of local, state, and national economies, groups and associations representing producers wield enormous power in Washington. Large corporations are able to mount their own lobbying efforts and join with others in influential associations such as the Business Roundtable. Medium-sized businesses are well represented by organizations such as the National Association of Manufacturers and the U.S. Chamber of Commerce. Even small businesses have proved to be quite influential when joined in associations such as the National Federation of Independent Business, which helped stop the Clinton health plan in 1994. Agriculture has more than held its own over the years through such organizations as the American Farm Bureau Federation and scores of commodity groups, including the American Dairy Association and the American Wheat Growers Association. Business has always been a powerful player in national politics and seems to have become stronger in recent years, especially as large corporations such as Microsoft, Intel, Caterpillar, Archer Daniels Midland, and Chase Bank become more important in the global economy.

Professionals   Professional organizations represent the interests of professionals, such as doctors, lawyers, and dentists. Because of the prominent social position of professionals in local communities and their ability to make substantial campaign contributions, such organizations are very influential in the policymaking process on matters related to their professional expertise and concerns. The American Medical Association (AMA) and the American Dental Association (ADA), for instance, lobbied strongly against the Clinton health care proposal and helped kill it in the 103rd Congress.

Unions   Although labor unions are sometimes involved in what might be called public interest activities (such as supporting civil rights legislation), their main role in the United States has been to protect the jobs of their members and to secure maximum wages and benefits for them. Unlike labor unions in many parts of the world, which are as much political and ideological organizations as economic ones, American labor unions have traditionally focused on so-called bread-and-butter issues. Union lobbying activities are directed at issues that affect the ability of unions to protect the jobs, wages, and benefits of their members and to maintain or increase the size of the union membership rolls. As an important part of the New Deal coalition that dominated American politics well into the late 1960s, labor unions were influential at the federal level during the years when the Democratic party controlled Congress and often won the presidency.

John Sweeney, the president of the AFL-CIO labor federation, has attempted to reinvigorate the organizing efforts and political presence of the labor movement. Here he addresses a crowd on the need to raise the minimum wage.

Although organized labor is still a force to be reckoned with in electoral politics, most observers believe that the political power of labor unions has eroded in dramatic ways over the past several decades.[13] In 1993, for example, organized labor pulled out all the stops in a campaign to kill the North American Free Trade Agreement (NAFTA) but was unsuccessful even though Democrat Bill Clinton was president and a Democratic majority sat in both houses of Congress. Union opposition also failed to stop the China trade bill in 2000. Organized labor's main long-range problem in American politics and its declining power relative to business in the workplace is its small membership base; in 1999, only 13.9 percent of American workers were in labor unions.[14]

Public Interest Groups

Public interest groups, sometimes called *citizens' groups,* try to get government to act in ways that will serve the general public and the public interest—as they define the public interest, of course—rather than the direct economic or occupational interests of their members.[15] People active in such groups tend to be motivated by ideological concerns or a belief in some cause.

Public interest groups of one kind or another have always been around, but a great upsurge in their number and influence has taken place since the late 1960s.[16] Many were spawned by social movements (see Chapter 8). The environmental movement created organizations such as the Environmental Defense Fund, the Nature Conservancy, Clean Water Action, and the Natural Resources Defense Council, for example. The evangelical Christian upsurge led to the creation of such organizations as the Moral Majority, the Christian Coalition, the National Right-to-Life Committee, and the Family Research Council. The gay and lesbian movement eventually led to the creation of organizations such as the Gay and Lesbian Alliance Against Defamation (GLAAD). Some, like the American Civil Liberties Union, committed to the protection of First Amendment freedoms (see Chapter 15), the Children's Defense Fund, an advocate for poor children, and the National Association for the Advancement of Colored People (NAACP), have been around for many years.

Most citizen groups retain a professional, paid administrative staff and are supported by generous donors, membership dues, and/or donations generated by direct-mail campaigns. Most also depend on grassroots volunteers to support their activities.

Pat Robertson, TV evangelist and founder of the politically influential Christian Coalition, addresses members of the organization at its annual meeting. Long-time staff director and political strategist Ralph Reed—no longer with the Christian Coalition—is on the right.

What Interest Groups Do

Interest groups are in the business of conveying the views and defending the interests of individuals and groups to public officials. There are two basic types of interest group activity: the inside game and the outside game.[17] The inside game—the older and more familiar of the two—involves the direct contact of interest group representatives and government officials. The outside game involves interest group mobilization of public opinion, voters, and important contributors in order to bring pressure to bear on elected officials.

The Inside Game

The term *lobbying* conjures up visions of a cigar-chomping interest group representative, his arm around the shoulder of an important senator or representative, advising him on how he ought to vote on some obscure provision of the Tax Code and slipping an envelope, fat with currency, into his jacket pocket. Or it conjures up images of favors given: paid vacations to exotic locations, honorarium payments for brief speeches at association meetings, and other exchanges verging on bribery.

The images both reveal and confuse. These things surely happened in the past, some continue to happen today, and some will surely happen in the future. In general, however, the images do not help us understand the intricacies of the inside game. This game does not involve bribes. Rather, it is more the politics of insiders and the "old boy" network (although, increasingly, women are also part of the network). It is the politics of one-on-one persuasion, in which the skilled lobbyist tries to get a decision maker to understand and sympathize with the interest group's point of view or to see that what the interest group wants is good for his or her constituents. Access is critical if one is to be successful at this game, as is an intimate understanding of the game itself.

Many of the most successful lobbyists are recruited from the ranks of retired members of the House, the Senate, and high levels of the bureaucracy.

The promise of lucrative employment based on their skills—and especially on their many contacts—is what keeps so many of them around Washington after they leave office. The very best of them have been in and out of one office or another in one administration or another for many years, know the D.C. scene as a wine connoisseur knows wine, and are compensated very well for their services. What works at key moments in the policy process may be a phone call to the right person, an important piece of intelligence picked up during a lunch conversation, or an introduction made at a diplomatic reception.

The inside game seems to work best when the issues are narrow and technical, do not command much media attention or public passion, and do not stir up counteractivity by other interest groups. This is not to say that interest groups play a role only on unimportant matters. Great benefit can come to an interest group or a large corporation from a small change in a single provision of the Tax Code or in a slight change in the wording or timing of an administrative ruling.

Lobbyists from citizens groups also play the inside game, often with great skill and effect. Many environmental regulations have been strengthened because of the efforts of skilled lobbyists from the Sierra Club, for example.

Lobbying Congress   The essence of the inside game in Congress is the cultivation of personal relationships with people who matter—Senate and House leaders, other influential and well-placed legislators, chairpersons of important committees or subcommittees, and key staff members. Because much of the action in Congress takes place in the committees and because senators and representatives are busy with a wide range of responsibilities, cultivating relationships with important staff members is especially important for successful

WEB EXPLORATION

Group Rating of Elected Officials

Issue: One of the most familiar activities of interest groups, especially citizens groups, is to rate members of Congress on how they voted on issues important to group members.

Site: Access Project VoteSmart through the "Course Documents" section of your online course. Go to the "Web Explorations" section for Chapter 7, click on "Group Rating of Elected Officials," and open "group ratings." Under "Offices," select "Congress." Next select your state, then choose one of the two senators from your state and the representative for your congressional district (if you don't know who that is, simply enter your ZIP code). At the page on your senator and representative, select "special interest groups."

What You've Learned: Scroll down through the list. Choose four groups you admire and see how they rate your elected members of Congress. Do the groups you admire rate them about the same, or do they vary significantly? Using what you have learned, would you vote for your current senator and member of the House?

HINT: Interest groups generally have a very narrow focus and pick votes on bills in Congress that are of special interest to them in calculating their ratings; even ideologically similar organizations may choose different votes for their rating system.

An important part of the job of the lobbyist is to convey the views and concerns of interest group members to representatives and senators. The ability to hire and deploy lobbyists, however, is not randomly distributed among Americans. Those with the greatest economic resources tend to dominate the "inside game" of interest group politics.

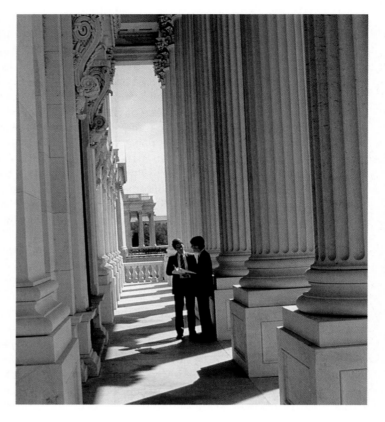

lobbyists. As one lobbyist put it, "If you have a staff member on your side, it might be a hell of a lot better than talking to the member [of Congress]."[18]

Interest group representatives sometimes testify at committee or subcommittee hearings. The hearing is less important in shaping legislation than the direct forms of contact we have described. However, testifying at a committee hearing has its political uses. It can be used by the lobbyist to make a case to the public on a pending piece of legislation, or it can be used to show members of the interest group or the chief executive officer (CEO) of the corporation that the lobbyist is doing a good job. Interest group testimony can be used by the legislator to build public support for something that he or she wants to do. Recent research shows that liberal citizens groups that lobby on environmental, civil rights, consumer, and educational issues have been particularly effective at the committee hearing stage of the legislative process.[19]

Lobbyists are also expected to attend and make contributions at various congressional fundraisers. The *Washington Post* counted 23 such events on a single day, June 24, 1999, a nonelection year.[20]

Lobbying the Executive Branch   Career civil servants and political appointees in the executive branch have a great deal of discretionary authority because Congress often legislates broad policies, leaving it to bureaucratic agencies to fill in the details. Because of this, interest groups try to establish stable and friendly relationships with the agencies of the executive branch that are most relevant to their interests. Pharmaceutical companies, for example, stay in touch with the relevant people at the Food and Drug Administration (FDA).

The key to success in lobbying the executive branch is similar to that in lobbying Congress: personal contact and cooperative long-term relationships.

Interest group representatives can convey technical information, present the results of their research, help a public official deflect criticism, and show that what the group wants is compatible with good public policy and the political needs of the official.

Lobbying the Courts
Interest groups sometimes lobby the courts, although not in the same way as they lobby the other two branches. A group may find that neither Congress nor the White House is favorably disposed to its interests and will bring a test case to the courts. Realizing that the improvement of the lot of African-Americans was very low on the agenda of presidents and members of Congress during the 1940s and 1950s, for example, the NAACP turned to the courts for satisfaction. The effort eventually paid off in 1954 in the landmark *Brown* v. *Board of Education* decision.

Interest groups sometimes lobby the courts by filing *amicus curiae* ("friends of the court") briefs in cases involving other parties. In this kind of brief, a person or an organization that is not a party in the suit may file an argument in support of one side or the other in the hope of swaying the views of the judge or judges. Major controversies before the Supreme Court on such issues as abortion, free speech, or civil rights attract scores of amicus curiae briefs.

Interest groups also get involved in the appointment of federal judges. Particularly controversial appointments, such as the Supreme Court nominations of Robert Bork (whom many women's and civil rights interests considered too conservative) in 1987 and Clarence Thomas (who was opposed by liberal and women's groups) in 1992, drew interest group attention and strenuous efforts for and against the nominee.

LongmanParticipate

CourseCompass

simulation
**You Are
a Lobbyist**

The Outside Game

The outside game is being played when interest groups try to identify and mobilize **grass roots** support for its goals and to bring it to bear on elected officials.

Mobilizing Membership
Interest groups with a large membership base try to persuade their members to send letters and to make telephone calls to senators and representatives when an important issue is before Congress. They sound the alarm, using direct mail and, increasingly, e-mail. They define the

grass roots

The constituents, voters, or rank-and-file of a party.

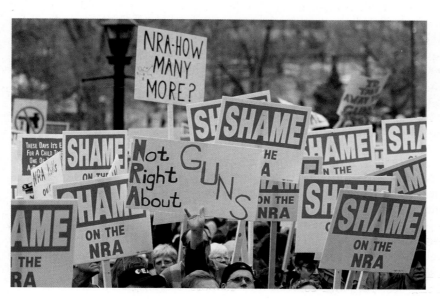

Mass demonstrations, designed to attract public attention through media coverage, are important tools in the arsenals of many interest groups. Here anti-gun groups show their displeasure with the National Rifle Association's opposition to gun control at the NRA's annual meeting in Denver in 1999, only weeks after the massacre at Columbine High School.

threat to members, suggest a way to respond to the threat, and supply the addresses, phone numbers, and e-mail addresses of the people to contact in Washington. Members are grouped by congressional district and state and are given the addresses of their own representatives or senators. The National Rifle Association (NRA) mobilizes its members whenever the threat of federal gun control rears its head. Environmental organizations sound the alarm whenever Congress threatens to loosen environmental protections.

Organizing the District
Members of Congress are especially attuned to the individuals and groups in their states or districts who can affect their reelection prospects. The smart interest group, therefore, not only will convince its own members in the state and district to put pressure on the senator or congressional representative but will also make every effort to be in touch with the most important campaign contributors and opinion leaders there.

Shaping Public Opinion
"Educating" the public on issues that are important to the interest group is one of the central features of new-style lobbying. The idea is to shape opinion in such a way that government officials will be favorably disposed to the views of the interest group. These attempts to shape public and elite opinion come in many forms. One strategy is to produce and distribute research reports that bolster the group's position. Citizen groups such as the Environmental Defense Fund and the Food Research and Action Center have been very adept and effective in this area.[21]

Another strategy is media advertising. Sometimes this takes the form of pressing a position on a particular issue, such as NARAL's advertising against the nomination of Robert Bork to the Supreme Court. Sometimes it is "image" advertising, in which some company or industry portrays its positive contribution to American life.[22]

In the effort to shape public opinion, the well-heeled interest group will also prepare materials that will be of use to radio and television broadcasters and to newspaper and magazine editors. Many produce opinion pieces, magazine articles, television spots and radio "sound bites," and even television documentaries. Others stage events to be covered as news. The environmentalist group Greenpeace puts the news media on full alert, for example, when it tries to disrupt a whaling operation or a nuclear weapons test.

Finally, interest groups, using the latest computer technology, identify target groups to receive information on particular issues. Groups pushing for cuts in the capital gains tax rate, for instance, will direct their mail and telephone banks to holders of the American Express card or to addresses in ZIP code areas identified as upper-income neighborhoods.

Getting Involved in Campaigns and Elections
Interest groups try to increase their influence by getting involved in political campaigns. Many interest groups, for example, rate members of Congress on their support for the interest group's position on a selection of key votes. The ratings are distributed to the members of the interest group and other interested parties in the hope that the ratings will influence their voting behavior.

Interest groups also encourage their members to get involved in the electoral campaigns of candidates who are favorable to their interests. Groups often assist campaigns in more tangible ways—allowing the use of their telephone banks, mailing lists, fax and photocopy machines, computers, and the like. Some interest groups help with fund-raising events or ask members to make financial contributions to candidates.

Interest groups also endorse particular candidates for public office. The strategy may backfire and is somewhat risky, for to endorse a losing candidate is to risk losing access to the winner. Nevertheless, it is fairly common now for labor unions, environmental organizations, religious groups, and ideological groups to make such endorsements.

Interest groups are also an increasingly important part of campaign fund-raising. Many of them channel money directly to candidates, give soft money to political parties to be used in electoral campaigns, and run independent issue campaigns.

Possible Flaws in the Pluralist Heaven

Political scientist E. E. Schattschneider once observed that the flaw in the pluralist (or interest group) heaven is "that the heavenly chorus sings with a strong upper class accent." If his observation is accurate, then political equality is undermined by the interest group system, and democracy is less fully developed than it might be. In this section, we look at possible inequalities introduced by interest groups and evaluate their effects.

Representational Inequalities

Not all segments of society are equally represented in the interest group system. The interest group game in Washington, D.C., is dominated, in sheer numbers and weight of activity, by corporations, industry trade associations, and professional associations, although liberal and conservative citizen groups play an important role. In addition, among citizen groups, those whose members are among the better educated and more affluent tend to be more visible and effective.[23]

Resource Inequalities

Corporations and professionals are the most economically well off parts of American society. It is hardly surprising that interest groups representing them can afford to spend far more than other groups to hire professional lobbying firms, form their own Washington liaison office, place advertising in the media, conduct targeted mailings, mobilize their members to contact government officials, and pursue all of the other activities of old- and new-style lobbying.

Corporate, trade, and professional associations also dominate the world of political action committees, both in sheer numbers (see Figure 7.2) and levels of spending, although labor unions and large and committed citizenship organizations such as the NRA and the Sierra Club are also important. During the 1998 election cycle, for example, **political action committees (PACs)** representing business and the professions accounted for 53 percent of the $503 million spent by all PACs on candidates for federal office, while labor unions accounted for just 24 percent.[24] PACs representing the least-privileged sectors of American society are notable for their absence. As former Senator (R–Kans.) and presidential candidate Robert Dole once put it, "There aren't any poor PACs or food stamp PACs or nutrition PACs or Medicaid PACs."[25]

PACs have become proportionally less important in campaign financing as **soft money** and **independent expenditures** have become more important. Soft money is money given by interest groups and individuals to the political

political action committee (PAC)

A private organization whose purpose is to raise and distribute funds to candidates in political campaigns.

soft money

Expenditures by political parties on general public education, voter registration, and voter mobilization.

independent expenditures

Money spent on behalf of candidates by interest groups and individuals who are not connected to a candidate's campaign organization.

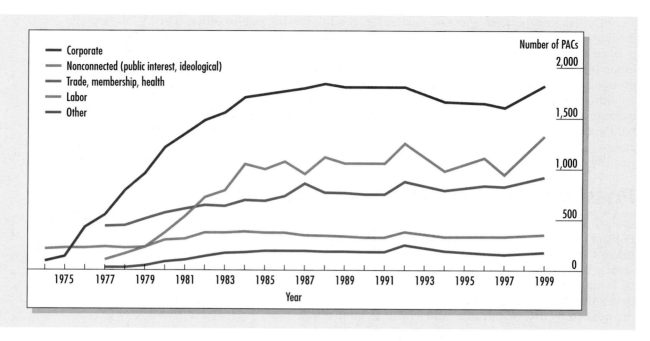

Figure 7.2 ● **PACs in the United States, 1974–1999**

Political action committees play an important role in financing congressional elections. The growth in the share provided by corporate, nonconnected (ideological), and trade groups is particularly striking, as is the relatively small share accounted for by organized labor.

Source: Federal Election Commission.

LongmanParticipate

CourseCompass

visual literacy
PACS and the Money Trail

parties for "party-building" activities but that is increasingly used to supplement the campaigns of candidates for federal office. Such contributions are largely unregulated and growing exponentially, more than doubling between each election cycle from 1995–1996 to 1999–2000. Of this total, about 63 percent came from corporations, trade associations, and professional organizations.[26] AT&T alone gave $1.3 million in 1999, split between the Republican and Democratic parties. Independent expenditures—money spent by interest groups on behalf of candidates—show a similar growth trajectory and pattern of giving by interested groups.

Interest groups don't contribute money to campaigns and to candidates without some expectation of a return on their investment (see the "Using the Framework" box). It has been argued that there are so many interest groups around that they tend to neutralize one another, hence contributions don't really matter. This may, in fact, sometimes be true on high-visibility issues in which the public and an array of interest groups are engaged. Where interest groups seem to matter the most is in the small details of legislation, forged mainly in the committees and subcommittees of Congress: a small subsidy in a defense spending bill or a waiver for a particular industry or company in an environmental bill.

Access Inequality

Inequalities of representation and resources are further exaggerated by the ability of some groups, especially those representing large corporations, to gain a permanent foothold within the government. Although scholars have not

USING THE FRAMEWORK

Whatever Happened to the Airline Passengers Fairness Act?

Senate Bill 383, the Airline Passengers Fairness Act, was introduced in February 1999. Senator John McCain, a long-time critic of the existing campaign financing system and its dependence on corporate and trade association contributions, and an early candidate for the Republican presidential nomination, was one of the Act's most prominent sponsors. Yet, after days of spirited testimony before the Senate Commerce Committee, and within days of a vote on the bill in committee, McCain backed away from the original Act and offered a softer version, which included accepting the proposal of the airlines that they voluntarily improve customer service. Taking a broad look at how structural, political linkage, and governmental factors contributed to the softening of the Airline Passenger Fairness Act will help explain the situation.

Governmental Action

A weakened version of the Airline Passenger Fairness Act is reported to the Senate by the Commerce Committee.

Governmental Level

- Senate Bill 383 is introduced.
- Bill is referred to the Commerce Committee.
- Hearings are held.

- Committee members confer on the bill.
- Senator McCain offers a substitute bill that is approved by the Commerce Committee.

Political Linkages Level

- Constituent complaints about airline service increased.
- Customer satisfaction with airlines fell throughout the 1990s.
- Consumer organizations such as the Aviation Consumer Action Project publicized complaints, offered research findings on airline consumer service, and called for congressional action.
- Airline companies and airline trade associations made $1.3 million in campaign contributions in the first six months of 1999 and spent about $3 million on lobbying activities.

- Airline companies announced a voluntary plan to improve customer service.
- Airline companies made major infusion of "soft" money (about $225,000) to both political parties in the week before the committee vote.

Structural Level

- Economic boom and globalization increased the demand for airline travel.
- A deregulated airline environment allowed airline companies to make the most of their own policies unconnected to safety.
- Airline companies increased their capacity, but in the process, decreased leg room, overbooked flights, experienced increased delays, and lost more passenger luggage.

capture

A situation in which a regulated industry exercises substantial influence on the government agency regulating it.

interest group liberalism

A political regime in which interest groups help formulate and carry out government policies.

iron triangle

An enduring alliance of common interest among an interest group, a congressional committee, and a bureaucratic agency.

reached a consensus on its exact form and extent, they have identified several basic forms of this phenomenon, which they call *subgovernments*.

What some scholars call **capture** is a form of government–business relationship in which an independent regulatory agency acts in partnership with the industry it is supposed to regulate.[27] **Interest group liberalism** is an arrangement in which aspects of federal government policymaking are turned over to interest groups.[28] Many (though not all) of the most important of these arrangements involve business and the professions. Thus the private medical community is involved in deciding local payment guidelines in the Medicare program. An **iron triangle** is an alliance of a private interest group (usually, but not always, a corporation or business trade association), an agency in the executive branch, and committees or subcommittees in Congress. The goal of the iron triangle is to advance and protect government programs that work to the mutual benefit of its members. An example is shown in Figure 7.3.

Many political scientists argue that the capture and iron triangle arrangements are no longer very common.[29] Policy, they suggest, is no longer formed in the dark, out of public sight. Many political scientists today are more apt to talk about "issue networks," in which each major policy arena attracts its own broad and diverse set of actors.[30] A set of corporations, bureaucratic agencies, and congressional committees is still involved, to be sure, but so are a broad range of interest groups (including public interest groups) and policy experts. On narrower and less public issues, however, a good many political scientists and Washington observers still believe that subgovernments are alive and well.[31]

Whether subgovernments are more open than in the past or not, what is clear is that access to government is not equal for all interests. Some are more privileged than others.

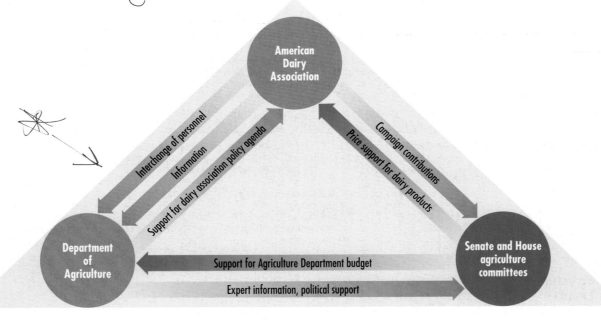

Figure 7.3 ● Iron Triangle

In an iron triangle, an alliance based on common interests is formed among a powerful corporation or interest group, an agency of the executive branch, and congressional committees or subcommittees. In this example from the dairy industry, an alliance is formed among parties that share an interest in the existence and expansion of dairy subsidies. Most scholars think iron triangles are less common today than in the past.

The Special Place of Business Corporations

Economist and political scientist Charles Lindblom argues that corporations wield such disproportionate power in American politics that they undermine democracy. He closes his book *Politics and Markets* with this observation: "The large private corporation fits oddly into democratic theory. Indeed, it does not fit."[32] Let's see why he reached this somber conclusion.

We have already learned about many of the advantages that corporations and business trade associations representing groups of corporations enjoy over others in the political process. The largest corporations are far ahead of their competitors in the number of interest organizations that represent them, the number of lobbyists they employ, the level of resources they can and do use for political purposes, the ease of access they have to government officials, and their ability to shape public perceptions and opinions.

An additional source of corporate power is the general regard in which business is held in American society and the central and honored place of business values in our culture. Faith in free enterprise gives special advantages to the central institution of free enterprise, the corporation (see Chapter 4). Any political leader contemplating hostile action against corporations must contend with business's special place of honor in the United States.

Business corporations are also unusually influential because the health of the American economy—and thus the standard of living of the people—is tied closely to the economic well-being of large corporations. It is widely and not entirely unreasonably believed that what is good for business is good for America. Because of their vital role in the economy, government officials tend to interpret business corporations not as "special interests" but as the voice of the national interest and to listen more attentively to their demands than they do to those of other sectors of American society. In this sense, corporations enjoy a privileged position in American politics.

Corporations are also powerful because their mobility is an important counterweight to any government effort (local, state, or national) to raise taxes or impose regulations that business deems especially onerous. Increasingly, large

WEB EXPLORATION

Corporations and Political Money

Issue: It has been suggested that corporations and business and professional associations dominate the campaign finance system, adding to their political influence.

Site: See who contributed what during the 2000 elections by accessing the Center for Responsive Politics through the "Course Documents" section of your online course. Go to the "Web Explorations" section for Chapter 7, click on "Corporations and Political Money," and open "corporate money." Select "Who's Getting," then select "top contributors" for each presidential candidate.

What You've Learned: Categorize the contributors in this list and the amounts spent. Is the claim of corporate and business dominance supported by the evidence?

HINT: Don't stop at the top 10 or top 20; use the entire list.

Because the well-being of many Americans depends on the well-being of American corporations, political leaders often equate the interests of business with the interests of the nation. Here President George Bush celebrates the opening of a Toys Я Us store during a trip to Japan to promote U.S. exports.

corporations are able to design, produce, and market their goods and services all over the world; they are not irrevocably tied to a single location. If government threatens their interests, large corporations can credibly counter with a threat to move all or part of their operations elsewhere. In this new global economic environment, political leaders are increasingly of a mind to maintain a friendly and supportive business climate.

Large corporations do not, of course, run the show entirely. Although they have the most resources, for instance, these resources do not translate automatically into real political influence. One interest group may have enormous resource advantages over other interest groups, for instance, but may use its resources ineffectively. Or an interest group with great resources may find itself opposed by other interest groups that together are able to mobilize impressive resources of their own. A powerful interest group may also find that an elected politician is not cooperative because the voters in the district are of a different mind from the interest group. So even with this immense set of resources, business power is not automatically and inevitably translated into political power.[33]

Nor does business always get its way in Washington. There are many issues of great importance on which business in general, or one corporation in particular, loses in the give-and-take of politics. There are times when business finds itself squared off against powerful coalitions of other interest groups (labor, consumer, and environmentalist groups, let us say). On occasion, corporations also find themselves at odds with one another on public policy issues. Thus, Microsoft and Sun Microsystems want very different policies regarding federal anti-trust policy.

Most important, corporate political power is not a constant in American politics; it waxes and wanes over time.[34] Corporate political power was most impressive during the 1920s, the Reagan 1980s, and in the 104th Congress after the 1994 elections, for instance. Corporations were less able to get their way during other periods, such as the early 1970s, when the power of corporations was almost matched by that of the consumer and environmental movements.

Corporate power seems to reach its apex under certain conditions.[35] During bad economic times, for instance, Americans are more interested in getting the economy going again than in undertaking reforms that might cut into corporate profits. Politicians in bad times are more solicitous of corporate interests. In good economic times (the late 1960s and the late 1990s, for example), politicians are less worried about corporate profits drying up if tax money is used for social purposes.

Corporations are most powerful when they can build alliances among themselves. Most of the time, corporations are in competition with one another; they do not form a unified political bloc capable of moving government to action on their behalf. On those few occasions when corporations feel that their collective interests are at stake, however, they are capable of coming together to form powerful political coalitions. As political scientist David Vogel put it, "When business is both mobilized and unified, its political power can be formidable."[36] During the mid-1970s, corporations felt that they were under assault, and they responded by building broad political coalitions that proved quite effective. These became the foundation of the movement for deregulation, tax cuts, and curtailment of domestic programs, an important part of the conservative trend in American politics that led to the election of Ronald Reagan in 1980 and the Republican capture of Congress in 1994.

In our view, the best way to think about corporations in American politics is to see their power waxing and waning within their overall privileged position. Corporate power may be greater at certain times and weaker at other times, but always in a game in which corporations enjoy advantages over other groups. If corporations feel that their collective interests are at stake—as when labor unions are particularly aggressive or when government's regulatory burden is perceived to be too heavy—and they are able to present a united front, they are simply unbeatable. This cannot be said about any other sector of American society.[37]

Curing the Mischief of Factions

Americans have been worried about the "mischief of factions" ever since James Madison wrote about them in *The Federalist,* No. 10 (see the Appendix). Over the years, various things have been tried to control the purported negative effects of these special interests. Disclosure has been the principal tool of regulation. In 1946, Congress imposed a requirement (in the Federal Regulation of Lobbying Act) that all lobbyists working in Congress be registered. The Lobby Disclosure Act of 1995 requires a wider range of political actors to register as lobbyists and makes them report every six months on which policies they are trying to influence and how much they are spending to do it. So far, the new law has not been strongly enforced.[38]

Reformers have also tried to regulate some of the most troublesome abuses of the politics of factions. Sections of the Ethics in Government Act (1978) aim at the so-called revolving door in which former government officials become lobbyists for interests with whom they formerly dealt in their official capacity. The act forbids ex-officials from lobbying their former agency for a year or lobbying at all on any issue in which the official was substantially involved. Bill Clinton instituted strong ethics rules, requiring that senior executive branch appointees refrain from lobbying their former agencies for five years after leaving public service and from ever representing foreign governments. Finally, the 1995 Act says that former U.S. Trade Representatives and their deputies are banned for life from lobbying for foreign interests.

While such steps are to be applauded, many observers worry that these reforms have not gone to the heart of the problem. Some political scientists have suggested that we focus our efforts instead on strengthening the institutions of majoritarian democracy. The key institution of majoritarian democracy, at least in theory (as we shall see in Chapter 9), is the political party. Parties can, as political scientist Walter Dean Burnham put it, "generate countervailing collective power on behalf of the many individually powerless against the relatively few who are individually—or organizationally—powerful."[39] Others believe that the narrowness of interest group politics might be tempered by strengthening the presidency, our only nationally elected office.[40]

 ## HOW DEMOCRATIC ARE WE?

PROPOSITION: Because they represent narrow and special interests, the proliferation of interest groups has made American politics less and less democratic.

AGREE: The interest group system is by and for the privileged. The democratic principle of "political equality" is violated because powerful interest groups that play a major role in shaping public policies in the United States represent, by and large, wealthier and better-educated Americans, corporations, and other business interests and professionals such as doctors and lawyers.

DISAGREE: The interest group system enhances democracy because it gives individuals and groups another tool to keep elected and appointed officials responsive and responsible to their needs, wants, and interests. Political parties are important for making popular sovereignty work, to be sure, but being broad and inclusive umbrella organizations, they often ignore the interests of particular groups. And, although elections are essential for keeping public officials on their toes, they happen only every two to four years. The day-to-day work of popular sovereignty is done by interest groups. Additionally, the rise of citizen groups has made the interest group system less unequal; a wider range of groups is now in the game.

THE AUTHORS: The interest group system plays a potentially valuable role in democracy by keeping officials responsive to a wide range of groups and interests among the public, especially in the periods between elections. It is also the case that the rise of citizen groups, including those devoted to civil rights, consumers, the environment, family values, and abortion (both for and against), means that more people participate in the political process than is apparent from election turnout. However, the issue of political inequality remains and cannot be easily ignored by those who would like American politics to be more democratic. Despite the rise of citizen groups, corporations, industry trade associations, and professional association still have a disproportionate share of political resources and influence. And among citizen groups, representation tends to tilt toward the interests of the more affluent and educated.

Summary

Americans have long denigrated special interests as contrary to the public good. Some political scientists, however, see interest groups as an important addition to the representative process in a democracy.

The United States provides a rich environment for interest groups because of our constitutional system, our political culture, and the broad responsibilities of our government.

A number of interests are accommodated in our interest group system. The most important private interests include business, agriculture, labor, and the professions. Public interest or citizens' groups try to advance some issue or ideological interest that is not connected to the direct material benefit of their own members. There has been a significant expansion in the number of such groups since 1968.

Interest groups attempt to influence the shape of public policy in a number of ways. In the inside game, interest group representatives are in direct contact with government officials and try to build influence on the basis of personal relationships. In the outside game, interest groups attempt to apply indirect pressure to officials by mobilizing other groups, the members of their own group, public opinion, elite opinion, and the electorate to support their positions on policy matters.

Business, trade, and professional associations dominate the interest group system, although citizen groups are also influential. They enjoy clear advantages over other groups in terms of resources and access to public officials. The business corporation holds an especially privileged place in the interest group system because of the support of business values in our culture and the perceived importance of the corporation to the economic well-being of Americans.

Efforts to control the "mischief of factions" have mainly been regulatory in nature. Some reformers believe that interest groups will only cease to be a problem if the parties and presidency are strengthened.

Suggestions for Further Reading

Berry, Jeffrey M. *The New Liberalism: The Rising Power of Citizen Groups.* Washington, D.C.: Brookings, 1999.

> *A controversial book that argues that liberal citizen groups representing consumer, civil rights, and environmental interests are more influential in the halls of Congress than either business or conservative citizens groups.*

Clawson, Dan, Alan Neustadt, and Mark Weller. *Dollars and Votes: How Business Campaign Contributions Subvert Democracy.* Philadelphia: Temple University Press, 1998.

> *The best book ever written about the campaign finance system, based on interviews with corporate personnel responsible for making PAC and soft money contributions to candidates and parties.*

Dahl, Robert A. *A Preface to Democratic Theory.* Chicago: University of Chicago Press, 1956.

> *The leading theoretical statement of the pluralist position and the democratic role of the interest group.*

Keck, Margaret, and Kathryn Sikkink. *Activists Beyond Borders.* Ithaca, NY: Cornell University Press, 1998.

> *An examination of how public interest groups are increasingly operating at the global level.*

Kollman, Ken. *Outside Lobbying: Public Opinion and Interest Group Strategies.* Princeton, NJ: Princeton University Press, 1998.
> *The first systematic study of how interest groups try to influence government policies by focusing their efforts on shaping public opinion.*

Lindblom, Charles. *Politics and Markets.* New York: Basic Books, 1977.
> *A controversial and widely commented-on book in which one of the leading pluralist theorists concludes that the modern corporation is incompatible with democracy.*

Olson, Mancur. *The Logic of Collective Action.* Cambridge, MA: Harvard University Press, 1965.
> *A "rational choice" argument on the place of material and selective benefits in the formation and maintenance of groups and on the difficulty of forming groups based on values and ideology.*

Vogel, David. *Fluctuating Fortunes: The Political Power of Business in America.* New York: Basic Books, 1989.
> *A look at the political power of large corporations during the 1970s and 1980s; useful for its wealth of information, even though the author sometimes underestimates the extent of the political power of business.*

Internet Sources

CapWeb Conservative Organizations **www.capweb.net/classic/jefferson/right/orgs**
> *A portal to conservative groups and organizations.*

Center for Responsive Politics **www.opensecrets.org/**
> *Follow the money trail—who gets it? who contributes?—in American politics.*

Justice on Campus **http://joc.mit.edu/**
> *An organization committed to the preservation of free expression and the due process rights of students on college campuses.*

Labor Net **www.labornet.org**
> *Access to labor unions and information on labor issues.*

National Organization for Women **www.now.org**
> *The women's organization that has long been a "player" in Washington politics.*

National Rifle Association **http://www.nra.org/**
> *Home page of one of America's most politically successful interest groups.*

Project VoteSmart **www.vote-smart.org/**
> *Information on interest group campaign contributions to and ratings for all members of Congress.*

Rightgrrl **www.rightgrrl.com/**
> *Conservative women's issues and organizations.*

Student Environmental Action Committee **http://www.seac.org/**
> *A grassroots coalition of student environmental groups.*

Yahoo/Organizations and Interest Groups **http://www.yahoo.com/ Government/Politics/**
> *Direct links to the home pages of scores of public and private interest groups as well as to Washington lobbying firms.*

Notes

1. "China: the Great Brawl," *Business Week* (June 16, 1997), p. 34.
2. Ibid.

3. Alexander Hamilton, James Madison, and John Jay, *The Federalist Papers,* ed. Clinton Rossiter (New York: New American Library, 1961), No. 10. (Originally published 1787–1788.)

4. Arthur F. Bentley, *The Process of Government* (Chicago: University of Chicago Press, 1908); David Truman, *The Governmental Process* (New York: Knopf, 1951); V. O. Key Jr., *Politics, Parties, and Pressure Groups* (New York: A. Crowell, 1952); Robert A. Dahl, *A Preface to Democratic Theory* (Chicago: University of Chicago Press, 1956); Robert A. Dahl, *Who Governs?* (New Haven, CT: Yale University Press, 1961). See also Jeffrey M. Berry, *The New Liberalism: The Rising Power of Citizen Groups* (Washington, D.C.: Brookings, 1999).

5. Arthur C. Close, ed., *Washington Representatives, 1977–1996* (Washington, D.C.: Columbia Books, 1996).

6. Kay Lehman Schlozman and John T. Tierney, *Organized Interests and American Democracy* (New York: Harper & Row, 1986), pp. 77–78.

7. Berry, *The New Liberalism,* pp. 20–21.

8. Anne Costain, *Inviting Women's Rebellion* (Baltimore: Johns Hopkins University Press, 1992).

9. Truman, *The Governmental Process.*

10. Mancur Olson, *The Logic of Collective Action* (Cambridge, MA: Harvard University Press, 1965).

11. On Olson's theory, see Brian Barry and Russell Hardin, eds., *Rational Man and Irrational Society?* (Newbury Park, CA: Sage, 1982); Dennis Chong, *Collective Action and the Civil Rights Movement* (Chicago: University of Chicago Press, 1991); Russell Hardin, *Collective Action* (Baltimore: Johns Hopkins University Press); Terry Moe, *The Organization of Interests* (Chicago: University of Chicago Press, 1980).

12. E. E. Schattschneider, *The Semi-Sovereign People* (New York: Holt, Rinehart & Winston, 1960).

13. Berry, *The New Liberalism;* Thomas Byrne Edsall, *The New Politics of Inequality* (New York: Norton, 1984); Michael Goldfield, *The Decline of Organized Labor in the United States* (Chicago: University of Chicago Press, 1987); Edward S. Greenberg, *Capitalism and the American Political Ideal* (Armonk, NY: Sharpe, 1985); David Vogel, *Fluctuating Fortunes: The Political Power of Business in America* (New York: Basic Books, 1989), ch. 8.

14. U.S. Bureau of Labor Statistics, 2000.

15. Jeffrey M. Berry, *Lobbying for the People* (Princeton, NJ: Princeton University Press, 1977), p. 7; Berry, *The New Liberalism,* p. 2.

16. Berry, *Lobbying for the People;* David Broder, *Changing the Guard* (New York: Simon & Schuster, 1980); Hugh Heclo, "Issue Networks and the Executive Establishment," in Anthony King, ed., *The New American Political System* (Washington, D.C.: American Enterprise Institute, 1978); Schlozman and Tierney, *Organized Interests;* Jack L. Walker Jr., "The Origins and Maintenance of Interest Groups in America," *American Political Science Review,* 77 (1983), pp. 390–406.

17. Jack L. Walker Jr., *Mobilizing Interest Groups in America* (Ann Arbor: University of Michigan Press, 1991).

18. Jeffrey M. Berry, *The Interest Group Society* (Glenview, IL: Scott, Foresman, 1989), p. 141.

19. Berry, *The New Liberalism.*

20. Susan Glasser and Ben White, "The Dashing Life of Washington Lobbyists," *Washington Post National Edition* (July 12, 1999), p. A13.

21. Berry, *The New Liberalism.*

22. Schlozman and Tierney, *Organized Interests,* p. 175.

23. Berry, *The New Liberalism.*

24. Federal Election Commission.

25. "Money Talks, Congress Listens," *Boston Globe* (December 12, 1982), p. A24.

26. Federal Election Commission, *Soft Money Expenditures* (Washington, D.C.: U.S. Government Printing Office, 2000).

27. Marver Bernstein, *Regulating Business by Independent Commission* (Princeton, NJ: Princeton University Press, 1955).

28. Theodore J. Lowi, *The End of Liberalism* (New York: Norton, 1969).

29. Berry, *The New Liberalism;* Allan J. Cigler, "Interest Groups," in William Crotty, ed., *Political Science: Looking to the Future,* vol. 4 (Evanston, IL: Northwestern University Press, 1991); Robert H. Salisbury et al., "Who Works with Whom? Interest Group Alliances and Opposition," *American Political Science Review,* 81 (1987), pp. 1217–1234.

30. Jeffrey M. Berry, "Citizen Groups and the Changing Nature of Interest Group Politics in America," *The Annals,* 528 (1993), pp. 16–23; Heclo, "Issue Networks"; Robert H. Salisbury, John P. Heinz, Edward O. Laumann, and Robert L. Nelson, "Triangles, Networks, and Hollow Cores," and Mark P. Petracca, ed., "The Rediscovery of Interest Group Politics," in Mark P. Petracca, ed., *The Politics of Interests: Interest Groups Transform* (Boulder, CO: Westview Press, 1992).

31. Richard Smith, "Interest Group Influence in Congress," *Legislative Studies Quarterly,* 20 (1995), pp. 89–139.

32. Charles Lindblom, *Politics and Markets* (New York: Basic Books, 1977), p. 356. For criticisms from the left, see John Manley, "Neo-Pluralism: A Class Analysis of Pluralism I and Pluralism II," *American Political Science Review,* 77 (1983), pp. 368–383. For criticisms from the right, see Irving Kristol, *Two Cheers for Capitalism* (New York: Basic Books, 1977); James Q. Wilson, "Democracy and the Corporation," in Robert Sessen, ed., *Does Big Business Rule America?* (Washington, D.C.: Ethics and Public Policy Center, 1987). For a recent dissent see Mark Smith, "Public Opinion, Elections, and Representation Within a Market Economy," *American Journal of Political Science* 43, no. 3 (1999), p. 842.

33. Dan Clawson, Alan Neustadt, and Mark Weller, *Dollars and Votes* (Philadelphia: Temple University Press, 1998), pp. 26–28, 64–71, 97–99.

34. Vogel, *Fluctuating Fortunes.*

35. Ibid.

36. Ibid, p. 291.

37. Jeffrey Berry disagrees in *The New Liberalism.*

38. Roger H. Davidson and Walter J. Oleszek, *Congress and Its Members* (Washington, D.C.: CQ Press, 2000), pp. 351–352.

39. Walter Dean Burnham, *Critical Elections and the Mainsprings of American Politics* (New York: Norton, 1970), p. 133.

40. John E. Chubb and Paul E. Peterson, "American Political Institutions and the Problem of Governance," in John E. Chubb and Paul E. Peterson, eds., *Can the Government Govern?* (Washington, D.C.: Brookings Institution, 1989).

Social Movements

Women Win the Right to Vote

The struggle for women's suffrage (e.g., the right to vote) was long and difficult. The main instrument for winning the struggle to amend the Constitution to admit women to full citizenship was a powerful social movement that dared to challenge the status quo, used unconventional tactics to gain attention and sympathy, and demanded bravery and commitment from many women.[1] One of these women was Angelina Grimké.

Abolitionist Angelina Grimké addressed the Massachusetts legislature in February 1838, presenting a petition against slavery from an estimated 20,000 women of the state. In doing so, she became the first woman to speak before an American legislative body. Because women at this time were legally subordinate to men and shut out of civic life—the life of home and church were considered their proper domains—Grimké felt it necessary to defend women's involvement in the abolitionist movement to end slavery. She said the following to the legislators:

> *Are we aliens because we are women? Are we bereft of citizenship because we are mothers, wives and daughters of a mighty people? Have women no country—no interests staked in public weal—no partnership in a nation's guilt and shame? . . . I hold, Mr. Chairman, that American women have to do this subject [the abolition of slavery], not only because it is moral and religious, but because it is political, inasmuch as we are citizens of the Republic and as such our honor, happiness and well-being are bound up in its politics, government and laws.*

Although this bold claim of citizenship for women did not fall on receptive ears—Grimké was derided as ridiculous and blasphemous by press and pulpit—it helped inspire other women who had entered political life by way of the abolitionist movement to press for women's rights as well. Meeting at Seneca Falls, New York, in 1848, a group of women issued a declaration written by Elizabeth Cady Stanton stating that "all men and women are created equal, endowed with the same inalienable rights." The declaration,

much like the Declaration of Independence on which it was modeled, then presented a long list of violations of rights.

The Seneca Falls Declaration remains one of the most eloquent statements of women's equality ever written, but it failed to have an immediate effect because most politically active women (and men) in the abolitionist movement believed that their first order of business was to end slavery. Women's rights would have to wait.

After the Civil War destroyed the slave system, women's rights leaders such as Stanton, Susan B. Anthony, and Lucy Stone pressed for equal citizenship rights for all, white or black, male or female. They were bitterly disappointed when the Fourteenth Amendment, ratified after the war, declared full citizenship rights for all males born or naturalized in the United States, including those who had been slaves, but failed to include women. Women's rights activists realized that they would have to fight for rights on their own, with their own organizations.

Women's rights organizations were formed soon after the Civil War. For more than two decades, though, the National Woman Suffrage Association (NWSA) and the American Woman Suffrage Association (AWSA) feuded over how to pressure male politicians. Susan B. Anthony (with the NWSA) and Lucy Stone (with the AWSA) were divided by temperament and ideology. Anthony favored pressing for a broad range of rights and organized dramatic actions to expose men's hypocrisy. At an 1876 centennial celebration of the United States in Philadelphia, Anthony and several other women marched onto the platform, where the emperor of Brazil and other dignitaries sat, and handed over a declaration of women's rights. They then marched off the platform and read the declaration aloud. Stone favored gaining the vote as the primary objective of the rights movement and quieter methods of persuasion such as petitions.

In 1890, the two main organizations joined together to form the National American Woman Suffrage Association (NAWSA). They dropped such controversial NWSA demands as divorce reform and legalized prostitution in favor of one order of business: women's suffrage. The movement was now focused, mostly united, and growing more powerful every year. One major boost was the endorsement of women's suffrage by the Women's Christian Temperance Union (WCTU), a vigorous organization whose primary goal was the abolition of the liquor trade. The NAWSA and the WCTU joined other women's groups to form an umbrella group, the General Federation of Women's Clubs (GFWC), which boasted 2 million members by 1910.

In 1912, the NAWSA organized a march to support a constitutional amendment for suffrage. More than 5,000 women dressed in white, some on horseback, paraded through the streets of Washington before Woodrow Wilson's inauguration. The police offered the marchers no protection from antagonistic spectators who pelted the marchers with rotten fruit and vegetables and an occasional rock, despite the legal parade permit they had obtained. This lack of protection outraged the public and attracted media attention to the suffrage movement. The NAWSA took advantage of the favorable publicity, launching a petition drive and sending regular delegations to press President Wilson for a national solution.

Almost immediately after the United States entered World War I in April 1916, with the express purpose of "making the world safe for democracy," women began to picket the White House, demanding that full democracy be instituted in America. One demonstrator's sign quoted directly from President Wilson's war message—"we shall fight . . . for the right of those who submit to authority to have a voice in their own government"—and asked why women were excluded from American democracy. As the picketing at the White House picked up in numbers and in intensity, the police began arresting large groups of women. Other women took their place. The cycle continued until local jails were filled to capacity. When suffragists began a hunger strike in jail, authorities responded with forced feedings and isolation cells. By November, public outrage forced local authorities to relent and free the women. By this time, public opinion had shifted in favor of women's right to vote, the main focus of the women's rights campaign.

In the years surrounding U.S. entry into the war, other women's groups worked state by state, senator by senator, pressuring male politicians to support women's suffrage. After two prominent senators from New England were defeated in 1918 primarily because of the efforts of suffragists and prohibitionists, the political clout of the women's groups became apparent to most elected officials. In June 1919, Congress passed the Nineteenth Amendment, and the necessary 36 states ratified it the following year. By uniting around a common cause, women's organizations gained the right to vote for all women.

Although few social movements have been as effective as the women's suffrage movement in reaching their primary goal, other social movements have also played an important role in American political life. This chapter is about what social movements are, how and why they form, what tactics they use, and how they affect American political life and what government does.

▶Thinking Critically About This Chapter

This chapter is about the important role of social movements in American government and politics.

Using the Framework. You will see in this chapter how social movements are a response to structural changes in the economy, culture, and society and how they affect other political linkage actors and institutions—parties, interest groups, and public opinion, for example—and government. You will learn, most importantly, under what conditions social movements most effectively shape the behavior of elected leaders and the content of government policies.

Using the Democracy Standard. At first glance, because social movements are most often the political instrument of minorities, it may seem that they have little to do with democracy. You will see in this chapter, however, that social movements play an especially important role in our democracy, principally by broadening public debate on important issues and bringing outsiders and nonparticipants into the political arena.   ▶

What Are Social Movements?

Social movements are loosely organized collections of people and groups who act over time, outside established institutions, to promote or resist social change. Today's Christian conservative movement, for example, is a broad collection of people, churches, and other organizations that have come together to resist the **secularization** of American society and to promote religious values in American life.

secularization
The spread of nonreligious values and outlooks.

Although they share some similarities, social movements are different from political parties and interest groups. Unlike political parties, for example, the sole aim of social movements is not to elect their own members to public office, although they may sometimes try to do so. Unlike interest groups, the sole aim of social movements is not to lobby political decision makers about legislative matters, although they may sometimes try to do this as well. What sets social movements apart from parties and interest groups is their focus on broad, societywide issues and their tendency to act outside the normal channels of government and politics, using unconventional and often disruptive tactics.[2] Some scholars call social movement politics "contentious politics."[3] When suffragists disrupted meetings, went on hunger strikes, and marched to demand the right to vote, they were engaged in contentious politics.

This general definition of social movements requires further elaboration if we are to understand their role in American politics. Here we highlight some important things to know about them.

- *Social movements are generally the political instruments of political outsiders.* Social movements often help people who are outside the mainstream gain a hearing from the public and from political decision makers. The women's suffrage movement forced the issue of votes for women onto the public agenda. The civil rights movement did the same for the issue of equal citizenship for African-Americans. Gays and lesbians forced the

WEB EXPLORATION

Change and Grievances

Issue: Social movements tend to be created by groups of people who have grievances about particular changes in their environment.

Site: Access Public Agenda Online through the "Course Documents" section of your online course. Go to the "Web Explorations" section for Chapter 8, click on "Change and Grievances," and open "grievances." Select three policy areas listed on the left. In the Public Opinion Section for each policy area, select "people's chief concerns."

What You've Learned: What aspects of economic, cultural, technological, or political change are Americans most worried about? Do you see any prospect that people will form into social movements around any of these concerns?

HINT: Remember that social movements are very hard to start and maintain, so the grievances must be deeply felt and tied to problems that are not easily solved by mainstream political organizations.

country to pay attention to issues that had long been left "in the closet." Insiders don't need social movements; they can rely instead on interest groups, political action committees (PACs), lobbyists, campaign contributions, and the like to make their voices heard.

● *Social movements are mass grassroots phenomena.* Because outsiders and excluded groups often lack the financial and political resources of insiders, they must take advantage of what they have: numbers, energy, and commitment. To gain attention, moreover, social movements often use unconventional tactics, such as demonstrations and sit-ins. Officials and citizens almost always complain that social movements are ill-mannered and disruptive. For social movements, that is precisely the point.

● *Social movements are populated by individuals with a shared sense of grievance.* People would not take on the considerable risks involved in joining others in a social movement unless they felt a strong, shared sense of grievance against the status quo and a desire to bring about social change. Social movements tend to form when a significant number of people come to define their own troubles and problems not in personal terms but in more general social terms (the belief that there is a common cause for all of their troubles) and when they believe that the government can be moved to take action on their behalf. Because this is a rare combination, social movements are very difficult to organize and sustain.

Major Social Movements in the United States

Many social movements have left their mark on American political life and have shaped what government does in the United States. Here we describe some of the most important.

The *abolitionists* aimed to end slavery in the United States. They were active in the northern states in the three decades before the outbreak of the Civil War. Their harsh condemnation of the slave system helped bring on the war that ended slavery.

The *Populist* movement was made up of disaffected farmers of the American South and West in the 1880s and 1890s who were angry with business practices and developments in the American economy that were adversely affecting them. Their aim was to force public ownership or regulation of banks, grain storage companies, and the railroads. For a short time, they were quite successful, winning control of several state legislatures, sending members to Congress, helping to nominate William Jennings Bryan as the Democratic candidate for president in 1896, and forcing the federal regulation of corporations (e.g., in the Interstate Commerce Commission Act).

The *women's suffrage* movement, active in the late nineteenth and early twentieth centuries, aimed to win the right to vote for women. As we saw in the chapter opening vignette, the movement won its objective when the Nineteenth Amendment to the Constitution was ratified in 1920.

The *labor* movement represents efforts by working people over the years to protect jobs, ensure decent wages and benefits, and guarantee safe workplaces. The periods of greatest militancy—when working people took to the streets and the factory floors to demand recognition of their unions—were in the 1880s, the

1890s, and the 1930s. The labor movement eventually forced the federal government to recognize the right of working people to form labor unions to represent them in negotiations with management.

A *peace* movement in one form or another has been around since the time of World War I, when it tried to encourage resistance to the draft. Its strategy of encouraging Americans to refuse service on religious or moral grounds—known as *conscientious objection*—was carried over to World War II, the Korean War, and the Vietnam War. The movement also focused on the threat of nuclear war, taking shape as "ban the bomb" protests in the 1950s, "nuclear freeze" demonstrations in the 1980s, and attempts in the 1980s to force local governments to declare their localities "nuclear-free zones," where no nuclear weapons could be manufactured or stored.

The *civil rights* movement began in the late 1950s, reached the peak of its activity in the mid-1960s, and gradually lost steam after that. The movement is one of the most influential on record, having pressed successfully for the end of formal segregation in the South and discriminatory practices across the nation (see Chapters 1 and 16). The main weapons of the movement were nonviolent civil disobedience and mass demonstrations.

The *anti–Vietnam War* movement was active in the United States in the late 1960s and early 1970s. Its aim was to end the war in Vietnam. It used a wide variety of tactics in this effort, from mass demonstrations to voting registration and civil disobedience.

The *women's* movement has been important in American life since the late 1960s. Its aim has been to win civil rights protections for women and to broaden the participation of women in all aspects of American society, economy, and politics. Although it did not win one of its main objectives—passage of the **Equal Rights Amendment (ERA)** to the U.S. Constitution—the broad advance of women on virtually all fronts in the United States attests to its overall effectiveness.

Equal Rights Amendment (ERA)

Proposed amendment to the U.S. Constitution stating that equality of rights shall not be abridged or denied on account of a person's sex.

Social movements activists often use dramatic behavior and symbols to gain media and public attention for their cause. Here an antiwar activist in San Francisco protests U.S. actions during the Vietnam War. This particular protest was part of the multicity "moratorium" movement in 1969 that involved hundreds of thousands of people.

The *environmental* movement has been active in the United States since the early 1970s. Its aim has been to encourage government regulation of damaging environmental practices and to raise the environmental sympathies of the public. While the vitality of the movement has waxed and waned over the years, the public's strong support for environmental regulation suggests that it has been unusually successful. Although disruptive tactics have sometimes been used, the movement has depended more on legal challenges to business practices and the creation of lobbying organizations.

The *gay and lesbian* movement began in earnest in the late 1960s. Its aim was to gain the same civil rights protections under the law enjoyed by African-Americans and other minority groups and to gain respect from the public. Ranging from patient lobbying and voting to mass demonstrations and deliberately shocking actions by groups such as ACT-UP, the movement's efforts have been partially successful—antidiscrimination and domestic partner laws have been passed in many communities, for example—but have also sparked strong counterattacks by groups such as the Christian Coalition that are opposed to their objectives.

Religious fundamentalist movements have occurred at several different moments in American history and have been very influential. These movements have brought together strongly religious people trying to infuse American society and public policies with their values. These movements were particularly vital during the decades preceding the American Revolution and the Civil War; in the late nineteenth and early twentieth centuries, when religious revivals swept across the country, and in our own day. The contemporary movement of Christian conservatives falls within this tradition and has become very important in American politics, especially on the issues of abortion, school prayer, educational curriculum, and censorship of the media. The *pro-life (antiabortion)* movement is part of the current larger religious fundamentalist movement. Its main objective is to end the legal availability of abortion in the United States.

An emergent *antiglobalization* movement announced itself to the public with demonstrations against the World Trade Organization in Seattle in late 1999. This movement is extremely diverse and includes people who are worried about the effects of globalization on the environment, income inequality in the United States and Third World countries, food safety, labor rights, unfair trade, and national sovereignty.

Social Movements in a Majoritarian Democracy

At first glance, social movements do not seem to fit very well in a democracy. First, social movements usually start out with only a small minority of people, whereas democracy requires majority rule. Second, social movements often use disruptive tactics, when it seems that many channels already exist (e.g., voting, petitioning and writing to policymakers, writing letters to newspapers) for people to express their grievances. In this section, we talk about how social movements can (and often do) help make American politics more democratic.

Encouraging Participation

Social movements may increase the level of popular involvement and interest in politics. In one sense, this is true simply by definition: social movements are

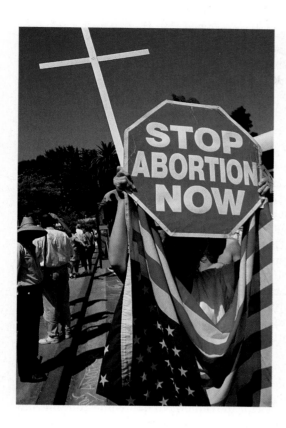

In recent years, many religious Americans have become politically active because of their objection to the general secularization of American life and social trends such as gay rights and abortion, which they consider contrary to traditional family values. Here a group of fundamentalist Christians demonstrates against the legal protection of abortion.

the instruments of outsiders. Thus, the women's suffrage movement showed many middle-class women that their activities need not be confined exclusively to home, family, church, and charity work and encouraged them to venture into political life by gathering petitions or joining demonstrations demanding the vote for women. The civil rights movement in the 1960s encouraged southern African-Americans who had long been barred from the political life of their communities to become active in their own emancipation. The Christian conservative movement spurred the involvement of previously politically apathetic evangelicals.

Social movements also encourage popular participation by dramatizing and bringing to public attention a range of issues that have been ignored or have been dealt with behind closed doors. The reason is that their contentious actions make these movements' members highly visible. They offer irresistible fare for the television camera. This ability to make politics more visible—called broadening the **scope of conflict** by political scientist E. E. Schattschneider[4]—makes politics the province of the many rather than the few.

Overcoming Political Inequality

Social movements also sometimes allow individuals and groups without substantial resources to enter the game of politics. Many social movements are made up of people who do not have access to the money, time, contacts, or organizational resources that fuel normal politics.[5] The ability of those without resources to disrupt the status quo by mobilizing thousands to take to the streets to voice their demands—what sociologists call **mass mobilization**—is a powerful political tool for people on the outside looking in. In the right circumstances, the disruptive politics of social groups can become as politically

scope of conflict

The number of groups involved in a political conflict; few groups mean a narrow scope of conflict, and many groups mean a wide scope of conflict.

mass mobilization

The process of involving large numbers of people in a social movement.

useful as other resources such as money and votes. Seemingly politically powerless women were able to mobilize to win the vote in the early part of the twentieth century; seemingly politically powerless blacks in the Deep South were able to secure full citizenship rights in the 1960s.

Creating New Majorities

Over time, social movements may also help create new majorities in society. Social movements are the province of minorities, of course, and in a majoritarian democracy, minorities should have their way only if they can convince enough of their fellow citizens that what they want is reasonable. Before the 1930s, for instance, only a minority of Americans may have been convinced that labor unions were a good idea. The **Great Depression** and a vigorous, militant labor movement changed the opinion climate in the nation and created the basis for federal laws protecting the right of working people to form labor unions. Such issues as gender-based job discrimination and pay inequity were not important to the general public until they were brought center stage by the women's movement. The anti–Vietnam War movement began with only a few, such as Mary Beth Tinker (see The Struggle for Democracy box, "Mary Beth Tinker Protests the War"), but eventually won over the majority.

Great Depression

The period of economic crisis in the United States that lasted from the stock market crash of 1929 to America's entry into World War II.

Overcoming Gridlock

Sometimes it takes the energy of a social movement to overcome the antimajoritarian aspects of our constitutional system (see Chapter 2) and get anything done at all. As political scientist Theodore Lowi describes the issue:

WEB EXPLORATION

Movements and Political Participation

Issue: A common claim for social movements as a democratic instrument is that they increase political participation by outsiders.

Site: Access the American National Election Study through the "Course Documents" section of your online course. Go to the "Web Explorations" section for Chapter 8, click on "Movements and Political Participation," and open "participation." Select "Political Involvement and Participation in Politics." Choose various questions related to political participation, including voting. At the bottom of the page where you find general results, the results are broken down by racial groups and gender.

What You've Learned: Did the Civil Rights movement and the women's movement increase political participation among African-Americans and women? Did participation increase in the period during and immediately after the social movements were at their height?

HINT: For African-Americans, the relevant dates are the early 1960s to the present; for women, the relevant dates are the early 1970s to the present.

THE STRUGGLE FOR DEMOCRACY

Mary Beth Tinker Protests the War

In 1965, the war in Vietnam was just beginning to escalate, and widespread opposition had not yet appeared. Taking an open antiwar stand against prevailing opinion was not easy at that time, and few people took the risk. One who did was Mary Beth Tinker, a 13-year-old eighth-grader in Des Moines, Iowa, who felt strongly that the war was wrong. To express her feelings, she chose to wear a black armband to school. As she described it:

I went to school and I wore the armband all morning. The kids were kind of talking, but it was all friendly, nothing hostile. Then I got to my algebra class, right after lunch, and sat down. The teacher came in, and everybody was kind of whispering; they didn't know what was going to happen. Then this guy came to the door of the class and he said, Mary Tinker, you're wanted out here in the hall. Then they called me down to the principal's office.

Mary was suspended from school by the principal, a decision that was eventually upheld by the school board. She and her parents insisted that Mary had the right to wear an armband as long as it did not disrupt classes or bother her classmates, but school officials were adamant. Mary held her ground, even in the face of several attempts to intimidate her.

People threw red paint at our house, and we got lots of calls. We got all kinds of threats to our family, even death threats. They even threatened my little brothers and sisters, which was really sick. People called our house on Christmas Eve and said the house would be blown up by morning. There was a radio talk-show host . . . who started in on our family, the Tinker family. . . . One night he said that if anyone wanted to use a shotgun on my father he would pay court costs if anything happened.

Mary's right to wear an armband to protest the war in Vietnam was eventually upheld by the U.S. Supreme Court. By the time the Court ruled on the case, many other Americans had joined Mary in her opposition to the government's Vietnam policy.

Source: Peter Irons, *The Courage of Their Convictions* (New York: Free Press, 1988), pp. 231–253.

Our political system is almost perfectly designed to maintain an existing state of affairs. . . . Our system is so designed that only a determined and undoubted majority could make it move. This is why our history is replete with social movements. It takes that kind of energy to get anything like a majority. . . . Change comes neither from the genius of the system nor from the liberality or wisdom of its supporters and of the organized groups. It comes from new groups or nascent groups—social movements—when the situation is most dramatic.[6]

It is important to note that many of the social reforms of which most Americans are most proud—women's right to vote, equal citizenship rights for African-Americans, Social Security, collective bargaining, and environmental protection—have been less the result of "normal" politics than of social movements started by determined and often disruptive minorities.

Factors That Encourage the Creation of Social Movements

A certain combination of factors, mainly structural, is apparently necessary for a social movement to develop.[7] We review the most important ones here.

Social movements are a response to a real, immediate social distress or injustice. When women began to enter the job market in increasing numbers during the 1960s and 1970s, discriminatory hiring, barriers to career advancement, and unequal pay were unspoken realities of the business world. As more and more women refused to accept these injustices, the women's movement emerged.

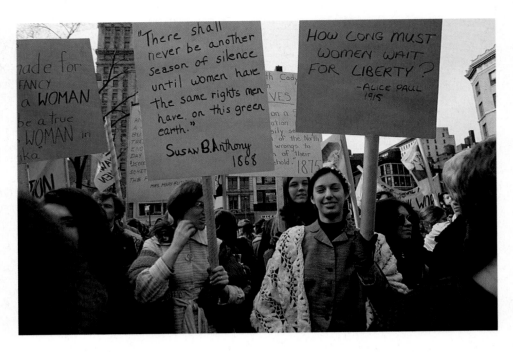

The Existence of Social Distress

People who are safe, prosperous, and respected generally have no need of social movements. By contrast, those whose lives are difficult and unsafe or whose way of life or values are threatened, or whose way of life is disrespected, often find social movements an attractive means of calling attention to their plight and of pressing for changes in the status quo.[8]

Social distress caused by economic, social, and technological change helped create the conditions for the rise of most of the major social movements in American history. For example, the Populist movement occurred after western and southern farmers suffered great economic reverses during the latter part of the nineteenth century. The labor movement during the 1930s was spurred by the Great Depression—the virtual collapse of the industrial sector of the American economy, historically unprecedented levels of unemployment, and widespread destitution. The rise of the Christian conservative movement seems to be associated with the perceived threat of the apparent decline in religious and family values in American life. For many women, distress caused by discriminatory hiring, blocked career advancement—in the form of the "glass ceiling" and the "mommy track"—and unequal pay at a time when they were entering the job market in increasing numbers during the 1960s and 1970s made participation in the women's movement attractive.[9] Discrimination, police harassment, and violence directed against them spurred gays and lesbians to turn to "contentious politics."[10] The AIDS epidemic added to their sense of distress and stimulated further political participation.

Availability of Resources for Mobilization

Social strain and distress are almost always present in society. But social movements occur, it seems, only when the aggrieved group has the resources (including skilled leaders) sufficient to organize those who are suffering strain and distress.[11] The grievances expressed by the labor movement had existed for a long time in the United States, but it was not until a few unions developed—

generating talented leaders, a very active labor press, and widespread media attention—that the movement began to take off. The women's movement's assets included a sizable population of educated and skilled women, a lively women's press, and a broad network of meetings to talk about common problems[12] (generally called *consciousness-raising groups*). The Christian conservative movement could build on a base of skilled clergy (for instance, Jerry Falwell and Pat Robertson), an expanding evangelical church membership, religious television and radio networks, and highly developed fund-raising technologies. Gay and lesbian activists could depend on a rich assortment of organizations, an active press, and the financial support of gay- and lesbian-owned businesses. The antiglobalization movement skillfully used the Internet to organize its protest in Seattle against the WTO.

For its part, the 1960s civil rights movement could count on organizationally skilled clergy and close-knit congregations, black-owned newspapers and radio stations, an expanding pool of college-educated African-American youth, and blocs of African-American voters located in electorally important states. The existence of such experienced, tested, and effective organizations as the Congress of Racial Equality (CORE), the Urban League, and the National Association for the Advancement of Colored People (NAACP) was especially valuable.

A Supportive Environment

The rise of social movements requires more than the existence of resources for mobilization among aggrieved groups. The times must also be right, in the sense that a degree of support and tolerance must exist for the movement among the public and society's leaders.[13] The civil rights movement took place when overt racism among the public was declining (even in the South; see

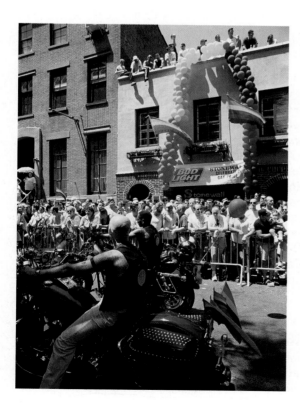

Gays and lesbians have become much more politically visible and assertive since the "Stonewall" incident and riots in 1969. Here, a gay-pride parade in New York calls attention to the gay and lesbian communities and to the issues the members of these communities want placed on the political agenda.

Table 8.1 ● **White Support for Integration, 1942–1963**

	Total	South	North
"Negroes should have as good a chance as white people to get any kind of job"			
1944	42%	—	—
1963	83%	—	—
"White students and Negro students should go to the same schools"			
1942	30%	2%	40%
1956	49%	15%	61%
1963	62%	31%	73%
There should not be "separate sections for Negroes on streetcars and buses"			
1942	44%	4%	57%
1956	60%	27%	73%
1963	79%	52%	89%
Would not make any difference to them if "a Negro with the same income and education as you moved into your block"			
1942	35%	12%	42%
1956	51%	38%	58%
1963	64%	51%	70%

Sources: Stephen Thernstrom and Abigail Thernstrom, *America in Black and White* (New York: Simon & Schuster, 1997), p. 141. Data from William G. Mayer, *The Changing American Mind: How and Why American Public Opinion Changed Between 1960 and 1988* (Ann Arbor: University of Michigan Press, 1993), p. 366; Paul B. Sheatsley, "White Attitudes Toward the Negro," *Daedalus*, 95 (1966) pp. 219, 222.

Table 8.1), and national leaders were worried about the bad effects of segregation in the South on American foreign policy. Christian conservatives mobilized in an environment in which many other Americans were also worried about changes in social values and practices and when the Republican party was looking for a way to detach traditional Democratic voters from their party. The labor movement's upsurge during the 1930s coincided with the electoral needs of the Democratic party.[14] The women's movement surged at a time when public opinion was becoming much more favorable toward women's equality.[15] In 1972, for example, two out of three Americans reported to pollsters that they supported the ERA; the same proportion said they believed that the issues raised by the women's movement were important.[16] Gays and lesbians benefited from the more tolerant attitudes toward minorities generated by other social movements.

A Sense of Efficacy Among Participants

Some scholars believe that to develop an effective social movement, people who are on the outside looking in must come to believe that their actions can make a difference, that other citizens and political leaders will listen and respond to their grievances. A *sense of efficacy* is what political scientists call this "I can make a difference" attitude. Without a sense of **political efficacy**, grievances might explode into brief demonstrations or riots, but they would not support a long-term effort requiring time, commitment, and risk.

political efficacy
The sense that one can affect what government does.

It may well be that the highly decentralized and fragmented nature of our political system helps sustain a sense of efficacy, since movements often find places in the system where they will be heard by officials. Christian conservative social movements have had little effect on school curricula in unitary political systems like that of Great Britain, for instance, where educational policy is made centrally, so few try to do anything about it. In the United States, Christian conservatives know they can gain the ear of local school boards and state officials in regions where religious belief is strong. Gays and lesbians have been able to convince public officials and local voters to pass antidiscrimination ordinances in accepting communities, such as San Francisco, California, and Boulder, Colorado.

A Spark to Set Off the Flames

Social movements require, as we have seen, a set of grievances among a group of people, the resources to form and sustain organization, a supportive environment, and a sense of political efficacy among the potential participants in the movement. But they also seem to require something to set off the mix, some dramatic precipitating event (or series of events), sometimes called a *catalyst,* to set them in motion. Passage of the Fourteenth Amendment, protecting the citizenship rights of males, galvanized the early women's suffrage movement, as we saw in the opening vignette. The gay and lesbian movement seems to have been sparked by the 1969 "Stonewall rebellion," three days of rioting set off by police harassment of the patrons of a popular gay bar in Greenwich Village in New York. The most important catalyst for the civil rights movement was Rosa Parks's simple refusal to give up her seat on a Montgomery, Alabama, bus in 1957.

A number of catalytic events also galvanized the women's movement. There was the 1963 publication of Betty Friedan's *Feminine Mystique,* in which she spoke to women's discontent ("a problem that has no name," as she put it) as no one had done before. The example set by the civil rights movement showed

Social problems often simmer quietly until a catalytic event brings about a social movement. In 1955, Rosa Parks refused to give up her seat to a white person on a Montgomery city bus as required by law. Her arrest sparked a year-long bus boycott that signaled the beginning of the American civil rights movement.

President Clinton awards Rosa Parks a presidential medal to honor her courage 41 years after her simple action on a Montgomery, Alabama, bus helped spark the rise of the Civil Rights movement.

many women that outsiders could gain a hearing in American politics if they were willing to use collective-action tactics. There was also resentment over the failure of the federal government to enforce Title VII of the 1964 Civil Rights Act, which guaranteed women protections in the area of equal employment. Finally, younger women active in the civil rights and anti–Vietnam War movements discovered that they were not well treated within these movements, despite the movements' rhetoric of equality, and concluded that women's problems could be addressed only if women took their own political initiative.

Tactics of Social Movements

Social movements tend to use unconventional tactics to make themselves heard. Such tactics depend on the dramatic gesture and are often disruptive. As you saw in the opening vignette, the women's suffrage movement used mass demonstrations and hunger strikes to great effect. The labor movement invented **sit-down strikes** and plant takeovers as its most effective weapons in the 1930s. Pro-life activists added to the protest repertoire clinic blockades and the harassment of clinic patients, doctors, employees, and their families. More extreme elements within these groups have even added violence against clinics and doctors, including murder.

The most effective tool of the civil rights movement was nonviolent **civil disobedience**, a conscious refusal to obey a law that a group considers unfair, unjust, or unconstitutional. A particularly dramatic and effective use of this tactic took place in Greensboro, North Carolina. Four black students from North Carolina Agricultural and Technical State University sat down at a "whites only" lunch counter in a Woolworth's store on February 1, 1960, and politely asked to be served. When requested to leave, they refused. They stayed put and remained calm even as a mob of young white men screamed at them,

sit-down strike

A form of labor action in which workers stop production but do not leave their job site.

civil disobedience

Intentionally breaking a law and accepting the consequences as a way to publicize the unjustness of the law.

The sit-down strike was invented by labor movement activists in the American auto industry in the 1930s. Here union members strike but stay put on the job site, daring management to use violence to end the work stoppage.

squirted them with ketchup and mustard, and threatened to lynch them. Each day, more students from the college joined them. By the end of the week, more than 1,000 black students had joined the sit-in to demand an end to segregation. These actions ignited the South. Within two months, similar sit-ins had taken place in nearly 60 cities across nine states; almost 4,000 young people had tasted a night in jail for their actions. Their bravery galvanized other blacks across the nation and generated sympathy among many whites. The student sit-in movement also spawned a new and more impatient civil rights organization, the Student Non-Violent Coordinating Committee (SNCC). (See the story of SNCC in Chapter 1.)

Another particularly effective use of nonviolent civil disobedience was organized in Birmingham, Alabama, by the spiritual leader of the civil rights

Nonviolent civil disobedience proved the most effective tool of the civil rights movement. By violating unjust laws quietly and nonviolently, protesters alerted outsiders to the injustice of their situation. The sit-in at a "whites only" lunch counter in Greensboro, North Carolina—shown here—sparked similar protests all over the country, and the arrests of the protesters generated sympathetic interest among previously apathetic whites.

integration

Policies encouraging the interaction of different races, as in schools or public facilities.

movement, Dr. Martin Luther King Jr., who led a series of massive nonviolent demonstrations to demand the **integration** of schools and public transportation. Nonviolent demonstrators, most of them schoolchildren, were assaulted by snarling police dogs, electric cattle prods, and high-pressure fire hoses that sent demonstrators sprawling. Police Commissioner Eugene "Bull" Connor filled his jails to overflowing with hundreds of young marchers, who resisted only passively, alternately praying and singing civil rights songs, including "We Shall Overcome." The quiet bravery of the demonstrators and the palpable sense among public officials and private-sector leaders in the nation that matters were quickly spinning out of control convinced President John Kennedy on June 11, 1963, to introduce his historic civil rights bill for congressional consideration.

Why Social Movements Decline

Even strong and influential social movements are difficult to sustain. There are many factors, both internal to the movements and external to them, that contribute to decline.

- *The unexpected problem of success.* Success may undermine a social movement as surely as failure. Unless it can find other issues around which to organize, a social movement will find that achieving its central goal destroys its very reason for being. The abolitionist movement, for example, became irrelevant with the passage of the Thirteenth Amendment ending slavery.

- *Factionalism.* A social movement must successfully address three different audiences: the movement's activists, the general public, and public officials. More specifically, it must maintain the enthusiasm of activists, attract more activists and support from the aggrieved group, gain sympathy from the general public, and force a positive response from public officials. These often contradictory objectives may lead to internal fragmentation over strategy, tactics, and ideology. Such divisions within social movements may become quite heated, since movements attract people who feel passionately about some problem, who have risked a great deal to get involved, and who are attempting to change an entrenched status quo. In such a context, it is difficult to keep disputes at a low temperature. The civil rights movement was fragmented by the radicalization of portions of the black community and the rise of the ideology of black pride and empowerment (termed *black power*) as the reigning ideology among many blacks, especially the young. Frustrated by the lack of progress on many fronts and taking pride in black identity, many in the movement rejected the gradualist and integrationist orientation for a radical and separatist one. The commitment to nonviolence, while retained by King's Southern Christian Leadership Conference (SCLC) and the NAACP, was renounced by SNCC, by the Black Muslims and their popular spokesman Malcolm X, and by the new Black Panther party, led by Huey Newton and Bobby Seale. The movement never recovered from this split.

- *Erosion of public support.* Social movements also decline when popular support of their goals begins to erode. Less public support usually translates into fund-raising difficulties, less responsiveness on the part of public officials, and greater tolerance of groups that oppose the goals of the social movement. Public support may be eroded for any number of reasons. The public may perceive that enough has been done already to meet the grievances of the members of the movement or that the movement has gone too far, asking too much of other Americans. This happened to the civil rights movement. White Americans overwhelmingly supported an end to segregation and discrimination based on race (see Table 8.1) during the heyday of the movement in the 1960s. And for the most part, these objectives of the movement were met in the United States. But when the civil rights movement shifted its demands from ending discrimination and admitting African-Americans to full citizenship to **affirmative action**—the demand for racial preferences in hiring, college admissions, and government contracts—public support eroded dramatically (see Chapter 16 for more on affirmative action).

affirmative action

Programs of private and public institutions favoring the hiring of certain minorities in an attempt to compensate for past discrimination.

- *Declining commitment among movement activists.* Activists may sometimes simply grow weary of their struggle. Because social movements ask so much of their activists in terms of time, financial sacrifice, and risk (of injury, job loss, jail sentences, etc.) and because they depend on nonmaterial inducements to encourage participation (ideology, an attractive goal, a sense of solidarity, etc.), it is difficult to sustain high levels of active involvement for very long.

- *The rise of opposition.* Finally, successful social movements almost always spark a reaction from groups that oppose their gains.[17] The size, commitment, and resources of opposition groups may match or even exceed those of the protest movement itself.[18] The women's and the gay and lesbian rights movements, for example, sparked a powerful backlash among Christian conservatives. The Moral Majority was formed right after the Supreme Court, buttressed by changing public attitudes about women's issues, ruled abortion to be legal in 1973 (*Roe* v. *Wade*). After gay and lesbian activists succeeded in convincing several local governments to pass antidiscrimination ordinances, Christian conservatives, including the Christian Coalition, organized state-level ballot initiatives to roll back the ordinances.[19]

Successful social movements such as the civil rights movement often generate counter-movements opposed to their main goals and aspirations. Here the Ku Klux Klan marches to protest the Martin Luther King Jr. holiday.

Why Some Social Movements Succeed and Others Do Not

Social movements have had a significant effect on American politics and on what government does. Not all social movements are equally successful, however. What makes some more successful than others seems to be the proximity of the movement's goals to American values, its capacity to win public attention and support, and its ability to affect the political fortunes of elected leaders.

Low-Impact Social Movements

A social movement will have little effect if it has few followers or activists, has little support among the general public, and is unable to disrupt everyday life significantly or to affect the electoral prospects of politicians. The poor people's movement, which tried to convince Americans to enact policies that would end poverty in the United States, failed to make much of a mark in the late 1960s.

A social movement is particularly unlikely to have an effect on policy when it stimulates the formation of a powerful countermovement. The rational politician may find it prudent to take no action at all when he or she has difficulty calculating the relative weight of the two sides in a dispute between movements. This is one of several things that happened to the proposed Equal Rights Amendment banning discrimination on the grounds of sex. The ERA failed to receive the approval of the necessary three-fourths of the states after anti-ERA forces (mainly Christian conservatives) rallied to block action during the 1970s.[20]

WEB EXPLORATION

Movements and Public Support

Issue: The federal government and state and local governments have all passed laws banning racial discrimination. Comparatively few governments, however, have passed laws banning discrimination based on sexual orientation.

Site: Access the Gallup Poll through the "Course Documents" section of your online course. Go to the "Web Explorations" section for Chapter 8, click on "Movements and Public Support," and open "support." Select "Gallup Poll," then "Social and Economic Indicators." Follow the survey results over time under "race relations" and "homosexual relations."

What You've Learned: Are Americans more receptive to the claims of racial minorities than they are to the claims of gays and lesbians? How has the pattern changed over the years? Would you say there is evidence in the polls that the public is more likely to support antigay and antilesbian discrimination in the future?

HINT: Americans seem very conflicted about homosexuality and how governments ought to respond to the claims of gays and lesbians for full civil rights, although the climate for such claims has been improving.

Repressed Social Movements

Social movements committed to a radical change in the society and the economy tend to threaten widely shared values and the interests of powerful individuals, groups, and institutions. As a result, they rarely gain widespread popular support and almost always arouse the hostility of political leaders. Such movements very often face repression of one kind or another.[21] In the late nineteenth and early twentieth centuries, for instance, the labor movement was hindered by court injunctions, laws against the formation of labor unions, violence by employer-hired armed gangs, and strikebreaking by the National Guard and the U.S. armed forces. In 1877, 60,000 National Guardsmen were mobilized in ten states to break the first national railroad strike. The strike against Carnegie Steel in 1892 in Homestead, Pennsylvania, brought the mobilization of 10,000 militiamen, the arrest of 16 strike leaders on conspiracy charges, and the indictment of 27 labor leaders for treason. The Pullman strike of 1894 was abruptly ended by the use of federal troops and by the arrest and indictment of union leaders.

Partially Successful Social Movements

Some social movements have enough power and public support to generate a favorable response from public officials but not enough to force them to go very far. In these situations, government may respond in a partial or half-hearted way. President Franklin D. Roosevelt responded to the social movements pressing for strong antipoverty measures during the Great Depression by proposing the passage of the Social Security Act, which fell far short of movement expectations.[22] The pro-life movement discovered that President Reagan was willing to use movement rhetoric to appoint sympathetic judges but was unwilling to submit antiabortion legislation to Congress. Christian conservatives enjoyed some legislative successes during the height of their power in the 1990s, but failed to achieve their primary objectives: enactment of a law to ban late-term (in their words, "partial birth") abortions and the removal of Bill Clinton from office through the impeachment process.

Gays and lesbians enjoyed some successes, but setbacks as well. The AIDS epidemic helped focus public attention on a range of other issues related to gay and lesbian rights, and several local communities across the nation legislated bans on housing and job discrimination, while still other communities passed same-sex domestic partner ordinances. Same-sex marriage was being considered in a number of states by the mid-1990s. However, the "backlash" created by these successes mobilized opposition groups who were successful winning local and statewide initiatives aimed at ending what its advocates called "special rights" for gays and lesbians, and a number of state legislatures passed bills to prevent same-sex marriages. However, in 1999, the Vermont Supreme Court ruled that the state legislature must either equalize benefits under state programs for same-sex partners and married couples or legalize same-sex marriage. The legislature chose the former in 2000. The mixed picture of success and failure of the gay and lesbian movement may be explained, perhaps, by the overall shape of public opinion in the United States, which is itself mixed. A substantial majority of Americans report, for example, that while they support the general principle of nondiscrimination against gays and lesbians in the areas of jobs and housing, as well as in the provision of education and government benefits,[23] they do not approve of homosexuality and strongly oppose same-sex marriage.

USING THE FRAMEWORK

"Why Didn't Bill Clinton Deliver on His Promise to Drop All Restrictions on Gays and Lesbians in the Military?"

Almost immediately after he was elected to office in 1992, Bill Clinton announced that, in his constitutional capacity as Commander-in-Chief, he intended to lift restrictions on gays and lesbians in the armed forces of the United States. In doing so, he was delivering on a campaign promise he had made to gay and lesbian organizations. After only a few weeks, however, he backed off from his promise and instituted a policy that came to be called "don't ask, don't tell, don't pursue." This policy of "turning a blind eye," as it were, satisfied no one. Taking a broad view at how structural, political linkage, and governmental factors affected Clinton's ultimate policy on gays and lesbians in the military will shed light on this situation.

Governmental Action

Bill Clinton announces that he will institute a "don't ask, don't tell" policy for gays and lesbians in the military.

Governmental Level

- Members of Congress from both parties strongly oppose lifting restrictions on gays and lesbians in the military.

- The Chiefs of each of the branches of the military vehemently and publicly oppose lifting restrictions.

- The president, though committed to lifting restrictions on gays and lesbians, realizes that pushing the policy will lead to tension with Congress and the military services, and get his new administration off to a shaky start, so he retreats.

Political Linkages Level

- Gays and lesbians form and effectively use social protest groups.

- The gay and lesbian movement creates a backlash, particularly among religious conservatives in all denominations.

- Gays and lesbians play an increasingly open role in political campaigns, as candidates, financial contrib-utors, and party activists.

- The Republican Party makes rolling back the so-called gay agenda a major part of their platform.

- The Democratic Party welcomes gay and lesbian support and participation.

- The mass media and entertainment industries become more sympathetic to gays and lesbians.

- Public opinion is conflicted; Americans support nondiscrimination against gays and lesbians in principle, but oppose gays and lesbians on a wide range of specific proposals.

Structural Level

- Higher levels of education among the population increases toleration of alternative lifestyles.

- Urbanization creates enclaves where gays and lesbians build communities, create social networks, and develop economic and political resources.

- The individualistic component of American culture and the Fourteenth Amendment to the Constitution favor a nondiscriminatory environment.

- The strongly religious component of American culture is also the foundation for anti-homosexual attitudes.

Successful Social Movements

Social movements that have many supporters, win wide public sympathy, do not challenge the basics of the economic and social orders, and wield some clout in the electoral arena are likely to achieve a substantial number of their goals. The women's suffrage movement, described in the opening vignette, is one of the best examples. The civil rights movement is another, yielding, after years of struggle, the Civil Rights Act of 1964 and the Voting Rights Act of 1965. These enactments helped sound the death knell of the "separate but equal" doctrine enunciated in the infamous *Plessy* decision (1896), engineered the collapse of legal segregation in the South, and made the guarantee of full citizenship rights for African-Americans a reality. The Voting Rights Act was particularly important in transforming the politics of the South. Black registration and voting turnout increased dramatically all over the region during the late 1960s and the 1970s. Elected black officials filled legislative seats, city council seats, the mayors' offices in large and small cities, and sheriffs' offices. Between 1960 and 1997, the number of elected black officials in the United States increased from a mere 40 to over 8,600 (see Figure 8.1).

Elected white officials, tacking with the new winds of change, soon began to court the black vote. George Wallace, who first became famous by "standing in the schoolhouse door" to prevent the integration of the University of Alabama and who once kicked off a political campaign with the slogan "Segregation Today, Segregation Tomorrow, Segregation Forever," actively pursued the black vote in his last run for public office.

Movements can be successful even if no new laws are passed. Other measures of success include increased respect for members of the movement,

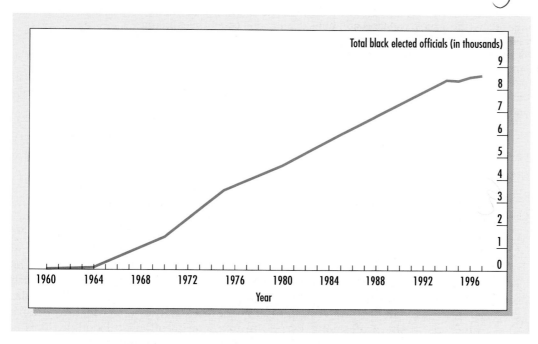

Figure 8.1 ● **Black Elected Officials in the United States, 1960–1997 (all levels of government)**

One of the success stories of the civil rights movement is the growing number of black officials being elected in the United States.

Source: U.S. Bureau of the Census.

HOW DEMOCRATIC ARE WE?

PROPOSITION: Social movements make American politics more democratic.

AGREE: Our constitutional system favors the *status quo*. The system of federalism, separation of powers, and checks and balances makes it extremely difficult to institute fundamentally new policies or to change existing social and economic conditions. The primacy of the status quo is further enhanced by the political power of economically and socially privileged groups and individuals. Social movements represent a way—a difficult way, to be sure—by which political outsiders and the politically powerless can become players in the political game. Movements are a way such groups and individuals can gain a hearing for their grievances, work to win over a majority of their fellow citizens, and force elected leaders to take action.

DISAGREE: Social movements are the tool of small minorities who force elected officials to respond to their demands because of the tangible threat of social disruption. Based on the age-old notion that "the squeaky wheel gets the grease," troublesome and disruptive groups can often get their way, even though the majority does not favor such action. In addition, because social movements often defy the law and social conventions, they tend to tear at the foundations of a stable democracy.

THE AUTHORS: Although social movements can sometimes get their way on public policies without or against the majority of Americans, in the long run, social movements only succeed when they are able to convince a majority of their fellow citizens that what the social movement seeks is legitimate. Strong social movements generate attention to a range of specific issues, widespread public debate, and (sometimes) countersocial movements. The government policies that eventually come out of this complex process sometimes favor the demands of the social movement, sometimes contradict them, and sometimes incorporate them into a broader compromise. Whatever the policy outcome, the social movement element of the American political system adds to the strength of our democracy.

changes in fundamental underlying values, and increased representation of the group in decision-making bodies. The women's movement has had this kind of success. Although the Equal Rights Amendment (the movement's main goal) failed, women's issues came to the forefront during these years, and to a very substantial degree, the demands of the movement for equal treatment and respect made great headway in many areas of American life.[24] Issues such as pay equity, family leave, sexual harassment, and attention to women's health problems in medical research are now a part of the American political agenda. Women have made important gains economically and are becoming more numerous in the professions, corporate managerial offices (although there is some evidence that a glass ceiling remains in place), and political office.

Summary

Social movements emphasize rather dramatically the point that the struggle for democracy is a recurring feature of our political life. They are mainly the instruments of political outsiders who want to gain a hearing in American politics. Social movements often contribute to democracy by increasing the visibility of important issues, by encouraging wider participation in public affairs, and sometimes by providing the energy to overcome the many anti-majoritarian features of our constitutional system.

Social movements try to bring about social change through collective action. Their rise is tied to the availability of organizational and leadership resources to a group of people who have a strong sense of grievance. Successful social movements happen, moreover, only if the political environment is supportive, in the sense that at least portions of the general population and some public officials are sympathetic to the movements' goals. The decline of particular social movements is associated with a number of things, including goal attainment, factional splits, the exhaustion of movement activists, and the replacement of grassroots activity by formal organization.

Social movements have had an important effect on our political life and in determining what our government does. Some of our most important legislative landmarks can be attributed to them. However, social movements do not always get what they want. They seem to be most successful when their goals are consistent with the central values of the society, have wide popular support, and fit the needs of political leaders.

Suggestions for Further Reading

Branch, Taylor. *Parting the Waters: America in the King Years, 1954–1963.* New York: Simon & Schuster, 1988.
> *A detailed and compelling description of the civil rights movement, with a particular focus on Martin Luther King Jr.; winner of the National Book Award and the Pulitzer Prize.*

Bruce, Steve. *The Rise and Fall of the New Christian Right.* New York: Clarendon Press, 1990.
> *The most complete analysis of the Christian conservative movement and its effect on American politics.*

Chafe, William H. *The Unfinished Journey: America Since World War II,* 2nd ed. New York: Oxford University Press, 1995.
> *A justly celebrated history of America since 1945, with a particular focus on the civil rights and women's movements.*

Evans, Sarah M. *Born for Liberty: A History of Women in America.* New York: Free Press, 1997.
> *A compelling and widely used history of women in America, both substantively rich and a joy to read.*

Klein, Ethel. *Gender Politics: From Consciousness to Mass Politics.* Cambridge, MA: Harvard University Press, 1984.
> *An analytically sophisticated and empirically detailed examination of the emergence of the women's movement and feminist politics.*

Martin, Marc, and Paula D. McClain, *The Almanac of Women and Minorities in American Politics.* Boulder, CO: Westview Press, 1999.
> *A detailed, in-depth compendium about every aspect of women's and minorities' places in American political life.*

Miller, James. *Democracy Is in the Streets.* New York: Simon & Schuster, 1987.
> *A sophisticated account of the student antiwar movement and its roots in a particular strand of participatory democratic theory.*

Piven, Frances Fox, and Richard A. Cloward. *Poor People's Movements*. New York: Vintage, 1979.
> *A controversial treatment of poor people's movements that argues that they are successful only as long as and to the extent that they remain grassroots, disruptive insurgencies.*

Riggle, Ellen D. B., and Barry L. Tadlock, eds. *Gays and Lesbians in the Democratic Process*. New York: Columbia University Press, 1999.
> *A collection of essays representing the best in recent scholarship on gays and lesbians in American politics and on public policies that affect them.*

Internet Sources

Afronet **www.afronet.com/**
> *A Web site devoted to materials on African-American political, social, economic, and cultural life.*

Christian Coalition **www.cc.org/**
> *Information and links from the nation's most influential Christian conservative organization.*

Yahoo!Society and Culture **www.yahoo.com/Society_and_Culture/**
> *A gateway with links to a multitude of social movements, issues, and groups.*

Notes

1. James MacGregor Burns and Stewart Burns, *A People's Charter: The Pursuit of Rights in America* (New York: Knopf, 1991), ch. 5; E. McGlen and Karen O'Connor, *Women's Rights* (New York: Praeger, 1983), ch. 3.

2. Joyce Gelb, *Feminism and Politics: A Comparative Perspective* (Berkeley, CA: University of California Press, 1989), pp. 14, 30. See also Doug McAdams, *Political Process and the Development of Black Insurgency* (Chicago: University of Chicago Press, 1982); David Plotke, "Citizenship and Social Movements," paper delivered at the annual meetings of the American Political Science Association, Washington, D.C., September 2–5, 1993.

3. Sidney Tarrow, "Social Movements as Contentious Politics," *American Political Science Review,* 90 (1996), pp. 853–866.

4. E. E. Schattschneider, *The Semi-Sovereign People* (New York: Holt, Rinehart & Winston, 1960), p. 142.

5. Richard Polenberg, *One Nation Divisible* (New York: Penguin, 1980), p. 268.

6. Theodore J. Lowi, *The Politics of Disorder* (New York: Basic Books, 1971), p. 54.

7. Doug McAdams, John D. McCarthy, and Mayer N. Zald, "Social Movements," in Neil J. Smelser, ed., *Handbook of Sociology* (Newbury Park, CA: Sage, 1994); Sidney Tarrow, *Social Movements, Collective Action, and Politics* (New York: Cambridge University Press, 1994).

8. Neil J. Smelser, *Theory of Collective Behavior* (New York: Free Press, 1962).

9. Barbara Sinclair Deckard, *The Women's Movement* (New York: Harper & Row, 1983); Ethel Klein, *Gender Politics: From Consciousness to Mass Politics* (Cambridge, MA: Harvard University Press, 1984), ch. 2.

10. Donald P. Haider-Markel, "Creating Change—Holding the Line," in Ellen D. B. Riggle and Barry L. Tadlock, eds., *Gays and Lesbians in the Political Process* (New York: Columbia University Press, 1999).

11. William Gamson, *The Strategy of Social Protest* (Homewood, IL: Dorsey, 1975); John D. McCarthy and Mayer N. Zald, "Resource Mobilization and Social Movements: A Partial Theory," *American Journal of Sociology,* 82 (1977), pp. 1212–1241.

12. Jo Freeman, *The Politics of Women's Liberation* (New York: McKay, 1975).

13. McAdams, *Political Process;* Peter K. Eisenger, "The Conditions of Protest Behavior in American Cities," *American Political Science Review,* 67 (1973), pp. 11–28.

14. Frances Fox Piven and Richard A. Cloward, *Poor People's Movements* (New York: Vintage, 1979), ch. 3.

15. Klein, *Gender Politics,* pp. 90–91.

16. National Opinion Research Center, General Social Survey, 1972.

17. David S. Meyer and Suzanne Staggenborg, "Movements, Countermovements and the Structure of Political Opportunity," *American Journal of Sociology,* 101 (1996), pp. 1628–1660.

18. L. Marvin Overby and Sarah Ritchie, "Mobilized Masses and Strategic Opponents: A Resource Mobilization Analysis of the Nuclear Freeze and Clean Air Movements," *Western Political Quarterly,* 44 (1991), pp. 329–351.

19. Marieka Klawitter and Brian Hammer, "Spatial and Temporal Diffusion of Local Antidiscrimination Policies for Sexual Orientation," in Riggle and Tadlock, eds., *Gays and Lesbians in the Democratic Process.*

20. Jane Mansbridge, *Why We Lost the ERA* (Chicago: University of Chicago Press, 1986).

21. See David Caute, *The Great Fear* (New York: Simon & Schuster, 1978); Robert Justin Goldstein, *Political Repression in Modern America* (Cambridge, MA: Schenkman, 1978); Alan Wolfe, *The Seamy Side of Democracy* (New York: McKay, 1978).

22. Edward S. Greenberg, *Capitalism and the American Political Ideal* (Armonk, NY: Sharpe, 1985).

23. Gregory B. Lewis and Marc A. Rogers, "Does the Public Support Equal Employment Rights for Gays and Lesbians?" in Riggle and Tadlock, eds., *Gays and Lesbians in the Democratic Process.*

24. William H. Chafe, *The Unfinished Journey: America Since World War II* (New York: Oxford University Press, 1986); Deckard, *The Women's Movement;* Klein, *Gender Politics,* ch. 2; Freeman, *Politics of Women's Liberation.*

CHAPTER 9
Political Parties

The Rise of the Campaign Party Machine

If the status of their national committees is any indicator, the Republican and Democratic parties are healthy, vital, and growing organizations. Each of the national committees has a shiny new office building in Washington, D.C. Out of these buildings come a range of services for party candidates. In-house TV and radio studios provide attack ads aimed against the other party and its candidates, tailored for the particular district or state in which the ads will be used, while other ads extol its own party and achievements. Direct mail campaigns are mounted to disseminate information and party positions on the issues and to make appeals for campaign contributions. News releases are prepared for the media, as are campaign-oriented sound and video bites to be used as news clips on local radio and television. Each of the parties also produces training courses for potential candidates, complete with "how-to" manuals and videos. The Republican National Committee also has an ISP (Internet service provider) for the 2000 campaign and beyond; on its portal, for $19.95 a month, subscribers get access not only to the Internet but also receive information about GOP events and developments and news about the nefarious behavior of Democrats and hear appeals to make monetary contributions to the party (soft money) and to party candidates (hard money).

To carry out these activities, both the Republican and Democratic National Committees have steadily increased the number of employees in their national offices, especially finance, advertising, computer, campaign planning, and video specialists and support personnel, and have expanded their budgets to carry out an ever broader range of campaign activities for party candidates. Each of the national committees,

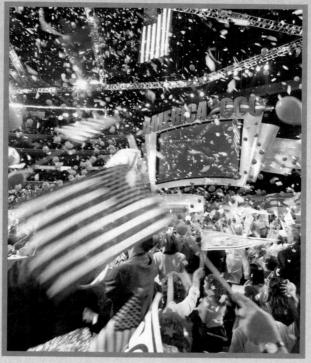

that is to say, has become a highly professionalized campaign organization, filled with highly skilled people, who can provide party candidates with what they need to wage first-rate electoral efforts.

In spite of all of this activity, the public's attachment to and involvement with the parties is becoming weaker and weaker, leading some scholars to talk about the "baseless parties."[1] The evidence is everywhere: scholarly and media polls show that the number of independents compared with party identifiers has increased, as has "split ticket" voting; turnout for elections is at an all-time low; vital grassroots party organizations have withered and disappeared in many areas; fewer people volunteer to work in candidate campaigns; and regard for both parties has declined, as has confidence in the ability of either one to solve pressing national problems.

What seems to be happening, according to several scholars, is that parties have changed from being community-based organizations with close links to voters to being campaign service organizations whose main customers are party candidates. It is almost as if the parties do not require the involvement of the public, except as voters. Parties are apparently happy if their efforts manage to get people to the polls who will vote for their candidates and discourage people who might be inclined to vote for candidates in the other parties. If this description of "baseless" parties is accurate, it would mark an important change in the traditional role of our political parties and have important implications for how well democracy works in the United States. We will examine these issues in this chapter as well as in the next one on elections and political participation.

▶Thinking Critically About This Chapter

This chapter is about American political parties, how they evolved, what they do, and how their actions affect the quality of democracy in the United States.

Using the Framework. You will see in this chapter how parties work as political linkage institutions connecting the public with government leaders and institutions. You will see as well how structural changes in the American economy and society have affected how our political parties function.

Using the Democracy Standard. You will see in this chapter that political parties, at least in theory, are one of the most important instruments for making popular sovereignty and majority rule a reality in a representative democracy, particularly in a system of checks-and-balances and separated powers such as our own. Evaluating how well our parties carry out these democratic responsibilities is one of the main themes of the chapter.   ▶

The Role of Political Parties in a Democracy

Political parties are organizations that try to win control of government by electing people to public office who carry the party label. In representative democracies, parties are the principal organizations that recruit candidates for public office, run their candidates against the candidates of other political parties in competitive elections, and try to organize and coordinate the activities of government officials under party banners and programs.

Many political scientists believe that political parties are essential to democracy.[2] They agree with E. E. Schattschneider that "political parties created democracy and . . . modern democracy is unthinkable save in terms of the parties."[3] What Schattschneider and others see in the political party is the main instrument of popular sovereignty and, especially, majority rule: "The parties are the special form of political organization adapted to the mobilization of majorities. How else can the majority get organized? If democracy means anything at all it means that the majority has the right to organize for the purpose of taking over the government."[4]

In theory, political parties can do a number of things to make popular sovereignty and political equality possible:[5]

- *Keeping elected officials responsive.* Political parties can provide a way for the people to keep elected officials responsive through competitive elections. Competitive party elections help voters choose between alternative policy directions for the future. They also allow voters to make a judgment about the past performance of a governing party and decide whether to allow that party to continue in office. And, a party can adjust its **party platform**—the party's statement of its position on the issues—to reflect the preferences of the public as a way to win elections (these three ways in which elections relate to democracy are discussed in Chapter 10).

- *Including a broad range of groups.* Political parties can enhance political equality in a democracy because they tend to include as many groups as they possibly can. Parties are by nature inclusive, as they must be if they are to create a winning majority coalition in elections. It is customary for parties in the United States to recruit candidates for public office from

party platform
A party's statement of its positions on the issues of the day.

LongmanParticipate

CourseCompass

visual literacy
Comparing Political Party Platforms

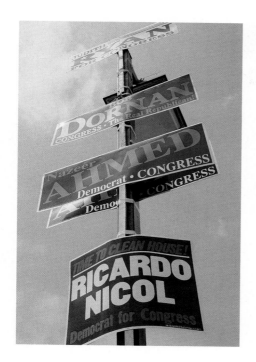

Political parties generally try to broaden their appeal by running candidates from a wide range of ethnic, racial, and religious groups.

many ethnic and racial groups and to include language in their platforms to attract a diversity of groups.

● *Stimulating political interest.* When they are working properly, moreover, political parties stimulate interest in politics and public affairs and increase participation.[6] They do this as a natural by-product of their effort to win or retain power in government; they mobilize voters, bring issues to public attention, and educate on the issues that are of interest to the party. Party competition, by "expanding the scope of conflict," attracts attention and gets people involved.[7]

● *Ensuring accountability.* Finally, parties can help make officeholders more accountable. When things go wrong or promises are not kept, it is important in a democracy for citizens to know who is responsible. Where there are many offices and branches of government, however, it is hard to pinpoint responsibility. Political parties can simplify this difficult task by allowing for collective responsibility. Citizens can pass judgment on the governing ability of a party as a whole and decide whether to retain the incumbent party or to throw it out of office in favor of the other party.

Political parties, then, can be tools of popular sovereignty. Whether our own political parties fulfill these responsibilities to democracy is the question we explore in the remainder of this chapter as well as in Chapter 10.

History of the Two-Party System

The United States comes closer to having a "pure" two-party system than any other nation in the world. Most Western democracies have multiparty systems (see Table 9.1). In the United States, however, two parties have dominated the political scene since 1836, and the Democrats and the Republicans have controlled the presidency and Congress since 1860. Minor or third parties have

Table 9.1 ● Party Systems in Other Democratic Nations, 1999

Parliamentary democracies, where electoral rules and traditions favor the existence of small parties, tend to be multiparty systems, in contrast to the American two-party system. This table shows the many parties that hold seats in the parliaments of other advanced liberal democracies.

Nation	Parties with Seats in Parliament	Nation	Parties with Seats in Parliament
Italy	Democratic Party of the Left	Japan	Liberal Democratic
	Italian Popular		New Frontier
	Italian Republican		Democratic
	Democratic Union		Communist
	Italian Renewal		Social Democratic
	Green		Clean Government
	Forza Italia		New Socialist
	Christian Democratic Center	Germany	Christian Democratic Union
	National Alliance		Christian Social Union
	Communist		Social Democratic
	Northern League		Green
	Italian Social Movement		Free Democratic
	Italian People's Party		Democratic Socialist
Spain	Popular	France	Socialist
	Socialist Workers		Rally for the Republic
	Convergence and Union		Union for French Democracy
	United Left		Communists
	Basque National		Green
	Canarian Coalition		National Front
	Republican Left of Catalonia	Sweden	Social Democratic
	Basque Solidarity		Moderate
			Center
United Kingdom	Labour		Liberal
	Conservative		Christian Democratic
	Liberal Democratic		Green
	Ulster Unionist		
	Scottish Nationalist	Australia	Labor
	Welsh Regionalist		Social-Liberal
	Social Democratic and Labour		National
	Sinn Fein		Democrat
	Democratic Unionist		Green
	Alliance of Northern Ireland		Conservative
		Canada	Liberal
			Canadian Alliance
			Bloc Quebecois
			Progressive Conservative
			New Democratic Party

Sources: Arthur S. Banks, Alan J. Day, and Thomas C. Muller, eds., *Political Handbook of the World* (Binghamton, NY: CSA Publications, 1996); "Parliaments Around the World," **http://www.agora.stm.it/elections/home.htm.**

rarely polled a significant percentage of the popular vote in either presidential or congressional elections (more will be said later about third parties and independent candidates), although they are sometimes successful at the state and local levels. Jesse Ventura, for example, was elected governor of Minnesota in 1998 as the nominee of the Reform Party.

Although the United States has had a two-party system for most of its history, it has not been static. The party system has, in fact, changed a great deal, both mirroring and playing a central role in the dynamic and sometimes chaotic story of the development of the United States, as described in Chapter 4. There have been six relatively stable periods in the history of the two-party system in the United States, each stretching over 30 or 40 years, interspersed with much shorter periods of transformation or **realignment**. Realignment is a transition period, most notable in our history in 1896 and 1932, when a party system dominated by one of the two major parties is replaced by another system dominated by the other party.[8] Figure 9.1 shows this history in graphic form.

LongmanParticipate

CourseCompass

timeline
Parties that Made American History

realignment

The process by which one party supplants another as the dominant party in a political system.

The First Party System: Federalists Versus Democratic Republicans

Although the Founders were hostile to parties in theory, they created them almost immediately. The first was formed in the 1790s by George Washington's energetic secretary of the treasury, Alexander Hamilton. In a successful effort to push through the administration's ambitious legislative program, Hamilton persuaded sympathetic members of Congress to form a loosely organized party that eventually took the name Federalist.

Thomas Jefferson, James Madison, and others formed a party in Congress to oppose the Hamilton domestic program and Federalist foreign policy. They used the label Republican, although the Federalists tried to discredit them by calling them Democratic Republicans (the term *democratic* was a term of derision, not praise, in those days).

CourseCompass

WEB EXPLORATION

Multiparty Systems

Issue: Unlike the United States, most democratic countries have a multiparty system.

Site: Access Political Sources through the "Course Documents" section of your online course so you can examine the multiparty systems in other democracies. Go to the "Web Explorations" section for Chapter 9, click on "Multiparty Systems," and open "multiparty." Select four major democratic countries; then look in the section describing recent parliamentary elections.

What You've Learned: What is the average number of major parties represented in the parliament? How would you characterize the major parties in an ideological or public policy sense? Is the range of political issues covered by their parties greater or lesser than what is covered in our politics?

HINT: Multiparty systems usually encourage the representation of a broader range of ideological positions than in two-party systems.

First Party System
Federalists vs.
Democratic Republicans
(Democratic Republican party
dominates after 1800)

"Era of Good Feelings" (no parties)

Second Party System
Democrats vs. Whigs
(Evenly matched)

Realignment

Third Party System
Democrats vs. Republicans
(Evenly matched)

Realignment

1790   1816   1828   1860   1868   1896

Figure 9.1 ● Party Systems in the United States

American politics has been characterized by a series of stable-political-party eras punctuated by brief periods of transition from one party era to another.

The Federalist party gradually disappeared, tainted by its pro-British sympathies during the War of 1812 and its image as a party of the wealthy and the aristocratic in an increasingly democratic America. By 1816, the first two-party system had evolved into a one-party or no-party system, generally known (because of the absence of party competition) as the Era of Good Feelings.

The Second Party System: Democrats Versus Whigs

The Era of Good Feelings gave way in the late 1820s to a strong two-party system that grew out of the disputed presidential election of 1824. In that election, Andrew Jackson won a plurality of the popular and electoral votes but failed to win a majority of either. The House of Representatives chose John Quincy Adams as president. Supporters of Jackson formed an opposition that soon became the Democratic party, while supporters of Adams and his ally in the House, Speaker

The second party system was characterized by well-organized parties, skilled in the use of methods (such as this parade) to mobilize the "common man" to participate in electoral politics.

| Fourth Party System | | Fifth Party System | | Sixth Party System |
| Democrats vs. Republicans (Republican dominance) | Realignment | Democrats vs. Republicans (Democratic dominance) | Realignment | (Divided government; no dominant party) |

1932 1936   1968

Henry Clay, organized as the Whig party. Starting in 1828, when Jackson defeated Adams for the presidency, the Democrats won six of the next eight presidential elections.

Each of the parties split apart as the nation drifted toward civil war. The Whig party simply disintegrated and disappeared. Several of its fragments came together with *Free-Soilers* (who opposed the expansion of slavery into the western territories) and antislavery Democrats to form a new Republican party—the ancestor of the present-day Republicans—which ran its first presidential candidate, John Frémont, in the election of 1856. The Democrats survived but could not agree on a single candidate to run against Republican Abraham Lincoln in 1860, so each wing of the party nominated its own candidate.

From the Civil War to 1896: Republicans and Democrats in Balance

Once the southern states had reentered the Union after Reconstruction, the Republicans and the Democrats found themselves roughly balanced in national politics. Between 1876 and 1896, the Democrats managed to control the presidency for 8 of 20 years, the Senate for 6 years, and the House of Representatives for 14 years. Each party had a strong regional flavor. The Democratic party was primarily a white southern party, although Catholics and many workers in northern urban areas also supported it. The Republicans (also known as the "Grand Old Party," or GOP) became a party of business, the middle class, and newly enfranchised African-Americans.

The Party System of 1896: Republican Dominance

Beneath the apparent calm of a balanced two-party system, however, a storm was brewing. The late nineteenth century was a time of rapid economic and social change and disruption, one effect of which was to spawn a host of protest movements and third parties. The Populist party, the most important of them, garnered 8.5 percent of the total vote in the 1892 election and won four states in the electoral college, running on the slogan, "Wealth belongs to him who creates it." During the 1890s, Populist party candidates also won governorships in eight states and control of at least as many state legislatures.

In 1896, the Populist party joined with the Democratic party to nominate a single candidate for the presidency, the charismatic orator William Jennings Bryan, who urged "free coinage of silver" to help debtors with cheaper currency. The threat of a radical agrarian party, joining blacks and whites, farmers and labor unionists, proved too much for many Americans and contributed to one of the most bitter electoral campaigns in U.S. history. Conservative Democrats deserted their party to join the Republicans. Businesses warned each other and their workers in no uncertain terms about the dangers of a Populist-Democratic victory. Newly formed business organizations, such as the National Association of Manufacturers, spread the alarm about a possible Democratic victory. In the South, efforts to intimidate potential black voters increased dramatically.[9]

The Republicans won handily and dominated American politics until the Great Depression and the election of 1932. Between 1896 and 1932, the Republicans won control of both houses of Congress in 15 out of 18 elections and of the presidency in seven out of nine.

The New Deal Party System: Democratic Party Dominance

New Deal

The programs of the administration of President Franklin D. Roosevelt.

The Great Depression, the **New Deal**, and the leadership of President Franklin D. Roosevelt ushered in a long period of Democratic party dominance. From 1932 through 1964, the Democrats won seven of nine presidential elections, controlled the Senate and the House of Representatives for all but four years, and prevailed in a substantial majority of governorships and state legislatures across the nation. Democratic dominance was built on an alliance of workers, Catholics, Jews, unionists, small and medium-sized farmers, urban dwellers, white ethnics, southerners, and blacks that came to be known as the **New Deal coalition**.

New Deal coalition

The informal electoral alliance of working-class ethnic groups, Catholics, Jews, urban dwellers, racial minorities, and the South that was the basis of the Democratic party dominance of American politics from the New Deal to the early 1970s.

The Sixth Party System: Dealignment and Divided Government

The New Deal coalition began to disintegrate in the 1968 election (won by Republican Richard Nixon) and finally collapsed in 1994.[10] Although Democrats continued to control Congress for much of the period, they lost the Senate to the Republicans from 1981 to 1986, the presidency for all but six years during this period (Carter, 1977–1980; Clinton, 1993–1994), and both houses of Congress between 1995 and 2001. 1968 began a period of divided government in which one party controlled the executive and the other party controlled all or part of the leg-

Franklin D. Roosevelt, here campaigning for the presidency in 1932, fashioned an electoral coalition, based on the urban working class, racial and ethnic minorities, Catholics and Jews, big cities, and the South, that allowed the Democratic party to dominate American politics for almost four decades.

islative branch. (Republicans won the presidency and Congress in 2000, however.) Also, during this period, the two parties became more closely competitive in elections at all levels across the nation as the Democrats gradually lost their big lead over the Republicans in party identification.

In the transition from the fifth party system to the sixth, a classic party realignment—the replacement of a system dominated by one party by a system dominated by the other party—did not take place as in the elections of 1896 and 1932. Scholars, journalists, and politicians have come to call the process of transition to the sixth party system **dealignment**. Dealignment may be thought of as a transformation in the party system in which a previously dominant party loses preeminence (the Democrats in this case) but no new party takes its place as the dominant party on a long-term basis. This new party system is characterized by the relative parity of the major parties in a context where the population not only identifies less with either party but also becomes increasingly alienated from both parties and less confident that they can solve the nation's problems.[11]

LongmanParticipat

CourseCompass

timeline
**Patterns of
Presidential Elections:
Realignment
and Dealignment**

dealignment
A gradual reduction in the dominance of one political party without another party supplanting it.

Why a Two-Party System?

Most Western democracies have multiparty systems, with more than two major parties. Why are we so different from other countries? There are several possible answers.

Electoral Rules

The kinds of rules that organize elections help determine what kind of party system exists.[12] Which rules are chosen, then, has important consequences for a nation's politics.

Proportional Representation
Most other democratic nations use some form of **proportional representation** (PR) to elect their representatives. In PR systems, each party is represented in the legislature in rough proportion to the percentage of the popular vote it receives in an election. In a perfect PR system, a party winning 40 percent of the vote would get 40 seats in a 100-seat legislative body, a party winning 22 percent of the vote would get 22 seats, and so on. In such a system, even very small parties would have a reason to maintain their separate identities, for no matter how narrow their appeal, they would win seats as long as they could win a proportion of the popular vote. Voters with strong views on an issue or with strong ideological outlooks could vote for a party that closely represented their views. A vote for a small party would not be wasted, for it would ultimately be translated into legislative seats and, perhaps, a place in the governing coalition.

proportional representation
The awarding of legislative seats to political parties to reflect the proportion of the popular vote each party receives.

Israel and the Netherlands come closest to having a pure PR system, organized on a national basis; most Western European nations depart in various ways from the pure form. Most, for instance, vote for slates of party candidates within multimember electoral districts, apportioning seats in each district according to each party's percentage of the vote. Most also have a minimum threshold (often 5 percent) below which no seats are awarded.

Winner-Take-All, Plurality Election, Single-Member Districts
Elections in the United States are organized on a winner-take-all, single-member-district basis. Each electoral district in the United States, whether it is an urban ward,

A presidential election is decided by which candidate has won a majority in the electoral college, *not* by a majority of the total votes cast. That is why on election night every four years the television networks focus on state-by-state victories and defeats.

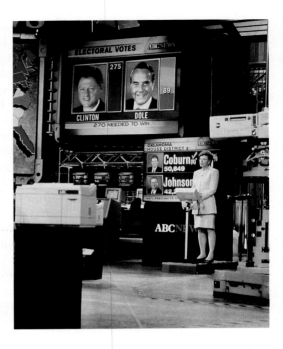

a county, a congressional district, or a state, elects only one person to a given office and does so on the basis of whoever wins the *most* votes (not necessarily a majority). This arrangement creates a powerful incentive for parties to coalesce and for voters to concentrate their attention on big parties. Let's see why.

From the vantage point of party organizations, this type of election discourages minor-party efforts because failure to come in first in the voting leaves a party with no representation at all. Leaders of such parties are tempted to merge with a major party. By the same token, a disaffected faction within a party is unlikely to strike out on its own because the probability of gaining political office is very low.

WEB EXPLORATION

Third Parties in the United States

Issue: We have a two-party system, but many minor parties exist here.

Site: Learn more about these minor, or third, parties at Politics1 through the "Course Documents" section of your online course. Go to the "Web Explorations" section for Chapter 9, click on "Third Parties in the United States," and open "third parties."

What You've Learned: Examine the platforms and activities of several minor parties. Do any of them address issues that neither of the major parties has tackled? Do you find any of them appealing? If you like one of the parties, and that party appears on the ballot, will you vote for that party or not? What are your reasons?

HINT: People with very strong views on a handful of issues are often unhappy with the two main parties.

From the voter's point of view, a single-member, winner-take-all election means that a vote for a minor party is wasted. People who vote for a minor party may feel good, but most voters have few illusions that such votes will translate into representation and so are not inclined to cast them.

Note that the most important office in American government, the presidency, is elected in what is, in effect, a single-district (the nation), winner-take-all election. The candidate who wins a majority of the nation's votes in the electoral college wins the presidency (see Chapter 10). A party cannot win a share of the presidency; it is all or none. In parliamentary systems, the executive power is lodged in a cabinet, however, where several parties may be represented.

Restrictions on Minor Parties

Once a party system is in place, the dominant parties often establish rules that make it difficult for other parties to get on the ballot. A number of formidable legal obstacles stand in the way of third parties and independent candidates in the United States. While many of these restrictions have been eased because of successful court challenges by recent minor-party and independent presidential candidates such as Ross Perot, the path to the ballot remains tortuous in many states, where a considerable number of signatures is required to get on the ballot

The federal government's partial funding of presidential campaigns has made the situation of third parties even more difficult. Major-party candidates automatically qualify for federal funding once they are nominated. Minor-party candidates must attract a minimum of 5 percent of the votes cast in the general election to be eligible for public funding, and they are not reimbursed until after the election. In recent decades, only the Reform Party among the legion of minor parties has managed to cross the threshold to qualify for federal funding.

Popular Attitudes

The attitudes of the American people are also an important factor in maintaining a two-party system. Once a party system is in place, it comes to seem natural, the only possible kind of party system. This attitude is passed on to children by families, schools, and the media. Children learn that there are only Democrats and Republicans and that their family is one or the other. We have discovered, however, that these ties to the two parties have been gradually but steadily eroding. This situation may account for the flurry of independent candidacies and third-party efforts in recent elections.

Absence of a Strong Labor Movement

The relative weakness of the American labor movement has already been noted in several places in this book. In the Western European countries, the organized labor movement was instrumental in the creation of Socialist and Labor political parties that challenged classical Liberal (free enterprise, small government) and traditional Conservative (monarchist, Catholic, and aristocratic) parties. The British Labour party, for instance, was created by trade union officials and Socialists in 1906. Strong Socialist and Labor parties in Europe did not replace traditional Liberal and Conservative parties (except in Great Britain) but spurred them on to more spirited organizing and electioneering of their own. The result has been the creation of a basic three-party system in many European countries—Conservative, Liberal, and Labor or Socialist—

with a number of small satellite parties (encouraged by PR electoral systems) clustered about them.

The Role of Minor Parties in the Two-Party System

Minor parties have played a less important role in the United States than in virtually any other democratic nation.[13] In our entire history, only a single minor party (the Republicans) has managed to replace one of the major parties. Only six (not including the Republicans) have been able to win even 10 percent of the popular vote in a presidential election, and only seven have managed to win a single state in a presidential election. Ross Perot won only 8 percent in 1996 as the candidate of the Reform Party which he founded.

Minor parties have come in a number of forms.

- *Protest parties* sometimes arise as part of a protest movement. The Populist party, for instance, grew out of the western and southern farm protest movements in the late nineteenth century. The Green Party was an off-shoot of the environmental and antiglobalization movements.

- *Ideological parties* are organized around coherent sets of ideas. The several Socialist parties have been of this sort, as has the Libertarian party. The Green Party ran in the 2000 elections on an anticorporate, antiglobalization platform.

- *Single-issue parties* are barely distinguishable from interest groups. What makes them different is their decision to run candidates for office. The Prohibition party and the Free-Soil party fall into this category as does Perot's "balanced budget" Reform Party in 1996.

- *Splinter parties* form when a faction in one of the two major parties bolts to run its own candidate or candidates. An example is the Bull Moose Progressive party of Teddy Roosevelt, formed after Roosevelt split with the Republican party regulars in 1912.

Minor parties do a number of things in American politics. Sometimes they articulate new ideas that are eventually taken over by one or both major parties. The Socialist party under Norman Thomas, for example, advocated public

Candidates such as Ralph Nader and third parties such as the Green Party often bring up issues the main parties are unable or unwilling to address.

works projects as a way to battle unemployment during the Great Depression, an idea that became part of the Democrats' New Deal legislative package.

Sometimes minor parties allow citizens with grievances to express themselves in a way that is not possible within the major parties. More cynical scholars suggest that unhappy groups are thus able to "blow off steam" without seriously disturbing the normal political process or threatening holders of public office. Less cynical scholars believe that expressions of discontent and the threat that major-party voters will defect keep the major parties responsive.

The Parties as Organizations

I don't belong to an organized political party. I'm a Democrat.

—WILL ROGERS

American parties don't look much like the parties in other democratic countries. In most democratic countries, the political parties are fairly well-structured organizations led by party professionals and committed to a set of policies and principles. They also tend to have clearly defined membership requirements, centralized control over party nominations and electoral financing, and disciplinary authority over party members holding political office.

The Ambiguous Nature of American Political Parties

The classic boss-led political machines of American folklore—long identified with such names as Tammany Hall, "Boss Tweed" of New York, Richard Daley of Chicago, and Huey Long of Louisiana—have disappeared from the cities and states where they once existed, mainly because of reforms that ended party control over government contracts and jobs. Political machines run by a "boss" have never existed at the national level. There have been leaders with clout, reputation, and vision, to be sure, but never a boss who could issue commands. Even popular, charismatic, and skillful presidents, including George Washington, Abraham Lincoln, Woodrow Wilson, Franklin Roosevelt, Harry Truman, John Kennedy, and Ronald Reagan, have had nearly as much trouble controlling the many diverse and independent groups and individuals within their own parties as they have had dealing with the opposition.

The vagueness of party membership is a good indicator of the ambiguous nature of our parties. Think about what it means to be a Republican or a Democrat in the United States. Americans do not join parties in the sense of paying dues and receiving a membership card. To Americans, being a member of a party may mean voting most of the time for the candidate of a party or choosing to become a candidate of one of them. Or it may mean voting in a party primary. Or it may mean contributing money to, or otherwise helping in, a local, state, or national campaign of one of the party candidates. Or it may just mean that one generally prefers one party to another most of the time. These are loose criteria for membership, to say the least—looser than for virtually any other organization that one might imagine.

The Organization of American Political Parties

The Republican and Democratic parties are not organizations in the usual sense of the term but rather loose collections of local and state parties, campaign committees, candidates and officeholders, and associated interest groups that get together every four years to nominate a presidential candidate. Unlike a corporation, a bureaucratic agency, a military organization, or even a political party in most other countries, the official leaders of the major American parties cannot issue orders that get passed down a chain of command. The various elements of the party are relatively independent from one another and act in concert not on the basis of orders but on the basis of shared interests, sentiment, and the desire to win elections. Most important, the national party is unable to control its most vital activity—the nomination of candidates running under its party label—or the flow of money that funds electoral campaigns or the behavior of its officeholders.

Party Conventions This is not to suggest that the parties are entirely devoid of tools to encourage coordination and cooperation among their various levels. The national party conventions are the governing bodies of the parties (see Chapter 10). Convention delegates meet every four years not only to nominate presidential and vice-presidential candidates but also to write a party platform and to revise party rules. (The proceedings are sometimes contentious, as The Struggle for Democracy box on page 252, "Fannie Lou Hamer and the Mississippi Freedom Democratic Party," shows.)

Although the national convention is the formal governing body of each of the parties, it cannot dictate to party candidates or party organizations at other levels of jurisdiction. The presidential nominee need not adhere to either the letter or the spirit of the party platform, for instance, although most nominees stay fairly close to the platform most of the time (usually because the winning candidate's supporters control the platform-writing committee). State and local party organizations may nominate whomever they choose to run for public office and may or may not support key planks in the party platform.

National Party Committees The Democrats and Republicans each have a national committee whose responsibility is to conduct the business of the party during the four years between national conventions. Although the national committees have little direct power, they provide valuable services for local

WEB EXPLORATION

State Parties

Issue: In our federal system, state party organizations are relatively independent from the national parties.

Site: Access your state Republican, Democratic, and Reform parties through the "Course Documents" section of your online course. Go to the "Web Explorations" section for Chapter 9, click on "State Parties," and open "state parties."

What You've Learned: How vital and active are the political parties in your state? Evaluate the range of the activities of each of the parties in your state. Which of the parties is most engaged in presenting a coherent party program, making contact with voters, and finding out what voters want?

HINT: Try to look past issues of Web site design ("bells and whistles") and focus instead on substantive party activities.

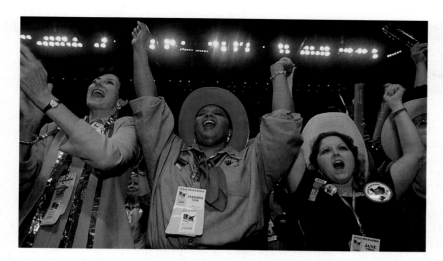

National party conventions serve several purposes for American political parties. Every four years, delegates choose presidential and vice-presidential candidates, settle party rules, write the party platform, repair or build political coalitions, and, as shown here, attempt to whip up enthusiasm for their nominees.

and state parties and for party candidates at all levels. These include campaign training materials, issue and policy research, design and maintenance of Web sites, assistance in creating radio and TV spots and other campaign materials, and research on the opposition.

In recent years, the national committees have become formidable campaign finance machines. Because the campaign finance laws restrict the amount of money that individuals and organizations can give to candidates but allow virtually unlimited contributions to the parties for "party-building" activities (called "soft money"), an ever-increasing proportion of campaign spending is accounted for by the parties. Although the parties are not permitted to use soft money to tell voters to cast their ballot for Candidate X, they can use it to attack the opposing candidate and party, celebrate the program and ideas of their own party, and sing the virtues of Candidate X.

The national committees are made up of elected committeemen and committeewomen from each of the states, a sizable staff, and a chairperson. The national committees rarely meet. The real business of the committee is run by the party chair, assisted by the committee staff. The chair exercises little power when a president from the party is in office because the party chair is compelled to take direction from the White House. When the opposition controls the presidency, the party chair exercises more influence in party affairs, although the extent of that power is still not very great.

Congressional Campaign Committees Almost as old as the national party committees, but entirely independent of them, are the congressional campaign committees that aid members of Congress in their campaigns for reelection. They help raise money, provide media services (making short videotapes of the members of Congress for local television news shows, for instance), conduct research, and do whatever else the party members in Congress deem appropriate. These committees are controlled by the party members in Congress, not the party chair, the national committees, or even the president. Much as with the national committees, the congressional campaign committees have become highly professionalized and well funded.[14]

State Party Organizations As one would expect in a federal system, separate political party organizations exist in each of the states. Although tied together by bonds of ideology, sentiment, and campaign money and constrained in what

THE STRUGGLE FOR DEMOCRACY

Fannie Lou Hamer and the Mississippi Freedom Democratic Party

Fannie Lou Hamer's story electrified the nation and threatened to ruin Lyndon Johnson's party. Testifying in 1964 before the Credentials Committee of the Democratic National Convention and a national television audience, Hamer, a 40-year-old black sharecropper from Mississippi, described what had happened to her when she tried to register to vote: "They beat me and they beat me with a long, flat blackjack. I screamed to God in my mind. My dress worked itself up. I tried to pull it down. They beat my arms until I had no feeling in them."

The 1964 Democratic convention in Atlantic City was meant to be a celebration of President Lyndon Johnson and a launching pad for the fall presidential campaign against Republican Barry Goldwater. The idea was to downplay intraparty conflicts, convey a message of unity and purpose to the country, and focus on defeating the Republicans. The appeal of the Mississippi Freedom Democratic Party (MFDP) to the Credentials Committee to be seated in place of the state's official Democratic party delegation in the racially charged atmosphere of 1964 threatened to throw a monkey wrench into the party works.

The MFDP had been created by black and white Mississippians in 1963 as a vehicle to encourage black political participation in the most segregated state in the Union. Only 5 percent of blacks in the state were registered to vote. Efforts by blacks to register were typically met with firings, threats, mortgage foreclosures, and violence. Hamer and the others who had founded the MFDP thought that they had a good chance to be seated at the convention. The regular Mississippi Democratic party remained lily-white (precinct and county party meetings were closed to blacks) at a time when the national party had embraced the civil rights cause, and it openly supported the Republican candidate Barry Goldwater. The insurgents believed that a new party organization, open to all Mississippians and committed to supporting the Democratic party nominee and platform in Atlantic City, could not fail to win the fight to be seated as the official delegation. Many Mississippians, black and white, put their reputations, fortunes, and lives on the line to change the political climate of their state. Eventually, more than 80,000 citizens of the state participated in MFDP delegate selection meetings—far more than participated in the affairs of the regular party.

Lyndon Johnson would have none of it. He was angry that the credentials fight was detracting from his nomination, and he feared that replacing the official delegation would lead to the wholesale defection of the South in the November elections. He rejected a compromise offer by several leading Democrats to seat both delegations. All he was willing to deliver were two at-large seats to the MFDP and a pledge that no segregated delegations would be seated at future Democratic conventions. The pledge was made official party policy and eventually made American politics more democratic by lowering racial barriers to participation in party affairs in all of the states. It was a bitter pill to swallow, however, for those who had risked so much to be there and who had expected so much. Hamer and the other MFDP delegates left Atlantic City in anger and disgust.

Sources: William H. Chafe, *The Unfinished Journey: America Since World War II* (New York: Oxford University Press, 1986), pp. 311–314; Godfrey Hodgson, *America in Our Time* (New York: Vintage, 1978), pp. 213–215; Taylor Branch, *Parting the Waters: America in the King Years, 1954–1963* (New York: Simon & Schuster, 1988), pp. 819–820.

they can do by rules set by the national party committees and conventions—rules on how to choose delegates to the national convention, for example—the state party organizations are relatively independent of one another and of the national party. Each state party chooses its own officials, for instance, writes its own party platform setting out its stands on the issues, and decides how much and in what forms to be involved in the fall electoral campaigns for local, state, and national offices.

Associated Interest Groups Although not technically part of the formal party organizations, some groups are so closely involved in the affairs of the parties that it is hard to draw a line between them and the political parties. The Christian Coalition, for example, is barely distinguishable from the Republican party; it contributes campaign money almost exclusively to GOP candidates, gives soft money only to the Republican party, runs its own candidates in the Republican primaries, and counts many of its members among the delegates to the Republican National Convention. Organized labor has had a similar relationship with the Democratic party since the Great Depression and the New Deal.

The Primacy of Candidates

American politics is candidate-centered, meaning that candidates are primary in our political system and parties are secondary.[15] In the United States, not only are candidates relatively immune from party pressure, but their electoral needs also shape what parties are and what they do.[16] Candidates have independent sources of campaign financing, their own campaign organizations, and their own campaign themes and priorities. And party organizations are becoming but another part, an important part to be sure, of candidates' campaign armament.

In the past party candidates were usually nominated in district, state, and national conventions, where party regulars played a major role. They are now almost exclusively nominated in primaries or grassroots caucuses, where the party organizations are almost invisible. Nomination comes to those who are

In candidate-centered politics, office seekers typically run as individuals without visible reminders of their party affiliation. Parties are not absent, however; they are usually there to help with fund raising, fashioning attack ads against the opposition, and getting out the party faithful to vote on election day.

In most European countries, people vote for parties rather than individual candidates. These party activists are urging British voters to cast their ballots for the Labour party, for example, rather than for the rival Conservative party.

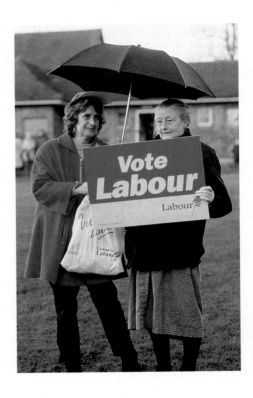

best able to raise money, gain access to the media, form their own electoral organizations, and win the support of powerful interest groups (such as the National Rifle Association or the National Education Association).

Nominees are so independent they sometimes oppose party leaders and reject traditional party policies. Republicans were embarrassed when David Duke, former Grand Wizard of the Ku Klux Klan, was elected to the Louisiana state legislature in 1988 under the Republican banner and ran for the governorship as a Republican in 1990, despite the opposition of state and national Republican officials.

In Germany, by way of contrast, individual candidates for the Bundestag (the equivalent of the House of Representatives) are less important than the political parties. Candidates are nominated by local party committees dominated by party regulars. Party lists for the general election are drawn up by state party organizations. Money for conducting electoral campaigns, moreover, is mostly raised and spent by the party organizations, not individual candidates. Finally, the campaign is waged between the parties and their alternative programs, not between individual candidates, and the electorate tends to make its choices based on feelings about the parties rather than about the candidates. Most of the Western European democracies have similar party systems.

Ideology and Program

Because the Republican and Democratic parties are both broad coalitions, seeking to attract as many voters as possible in order to prevail in winner-take-all, single-member-district elections, there are strong pressures on them to be ideologically ambiguous. But each party has a core of supporters, such as delegates to the party convention and caucus attendees, who are more ideologically oriented than the general public. The result is a party system composed of parties less ideologically focused and identifiable than the parties in other democratic countries, but with significant ideological and policy differences between them nevertheless. In addition, the parties seem to be getting much more ideologically distinct.[17]

Ideology may be understood as an organized set of beliefs about the fundamental nature of the good society and the role government ought to play in achieving it. In other Western democracies, it is common for the major parties to be quite closely connected with an ideology, in the sense that their activists, members, and officeholders identify with it; campaign with themes based on its ideas; and are guided by it in their governmental actions. Socialist and Labor parties often line up in elections against Liberal and Conservative or Catholic parties, with Marxist, Christian Socialist, Monarchist, Neo-Fascist, Nationalist, and other parties entering into the contest as well.

Ideological contests in the European manner are not the norm in U.S. elections because both American parties share many of the same fundamental beliefs: free enterprise, individualism, the Constitution, the Bill of Rights, and so on. Nevertheless, the differences between Democrats and Republicans on many issues, especially on affirmative action, abortion, and the role of government in the economy are real, important, and enduring and are becoming more distinctive.

Public Perceptions of Party Ideologies

For one thing, the Democratic and Republican parties differ in the electorate's perceptions of them. According to studies by the Center for Political Studies of the University of Michigan, 58 percent of the American people report that they see the parties as different on a whole range of issues.[18] Most see the Democrats as the more **liberal** party (in the sense of favoring an active federal government, helping citizens with jobs, education, medical care, and the like) and the Republicans as the more **conservative** (opposing such government activism). The parties also differ in terms of who supports them. Americans who classify themselves as liberals overwhelmingly support Democratic candidates; self-described conservatives overwhelmingly support Republicans. This alignment is not surprising.

liberal

The political position that holds that the federal government has a substantial role to play in economic regulation, social welfare, and overcoming racial inequality.

conservative

The political position that holds that the federal government ought to play a very small role in economic regulation, social welfare, and overcoming racial inequality.

Ideology in Party Platforms

Our parties also tend to write different political platforms at their conventions. Scholars have discovered persistent differences in the platforms of the two parties in terms of rhetoric (Republicans tend to talk more about opportunity and freedom), issues (Democrats worry more about poverty and social welfare), and the public policies advocated.[19] The House Republicans' Contract with America, formulated for the 1994 congressional elections under the leadership of Newt Gingrich, was a particularly clear and coherent conservative ideological statement. It was used as a blueprint for action by the House Republican majority in the 104th Congress.

The Ideologies of Party Activists

The activists of one party are quite different in their views from activists and voters in the other party, as well as the general public. Republican delegates to the 2000 Republican National Convention, for example, as in all recent conventions, were more conservative than Republican voters and much more conservative than the average registered voter. They were also much more hostile to affirmative action, social spending programs, and gun control than Republican voters and registered voters in general. Analogously, delegates to the Democratic National Convention in 2000 were more liberal than Democratic voters and registered voters (though not by much) and much more favorable to gun control, affirmative action, and a woman's right to an abortion than the other two groups.[20]

Party Ideologies in Action   Finally, the parties differ in what they do when they win. Republican members of Congress tend to vote differently from Democrats, the former being considerably more conservative on domestic issues. This difference translates into public policy. Republicans and Democrats produce different policies on taxes, corporate regulation, and welfare when they are in power.[21] This became especially clear in the 104th Congress, where the Republicans waged a unified campaign against spending, taxing, regulatory, and entitlement programs.

Growing Ideological Differences Between the Parties   The Republican party has become much more conservative since the mid-1970s, advocating free markets and less regulation, low taxes, a halt to most abortions, diminished social spending, opposition to affirmative action, and a hard line on "law and order." The party seems to have settled on a vision in which government helps create a society where individuals are free to pursue their own happiness and to take the consequences if they fail, without government providing a minimum standard of living below which people cannot fall. This growing conservatism is a product of the increasing influence in the party of the business community, anti-tax and anti-big government groups, the white South and suburbs, and Christian fundamentalists. It is also a product of the declining influence in party affairs of the Northeastern states, the home of GOP moderates (represented in the past by such figures as Nelson Rockefeller of New York and John Chafee of Rhode Island).[22]

It is worth pointing out that not all Republicans support a consistently conservative agenda. Many candidates and party activists support abortion rights, are willing to maintain the current level of immigration, and believe government has a role to play in protecting the environment. Many Republican governors, including John Engler of Michigan and Christine Whitman of New

WEB EXPLORATION

Public Evaluations of the Parties

Issue: In the eyes of the public, each of the major parties has different strengths when it comes to conducting the people's business.

Site: Examine public evaluations of the parties by accessing Public Agenda Online through the "Course Documents" section of your online course. Go to the "Web Explorations" section for Chapter 9, click on "Public Evaluations of the Parties," and open "evaluations." From the list of policy areas on the left, look in turn at "America's global role," "crime," the "economy," and "Social Security." For each, examine the "Who Should Decide?" section.

What You've Learned: Which of our two major parties do you trust to best manage government policies related to America's global role, crime, the economy, and Social Security? Compare your own views with those of other Americans. Are your views similar to those of other Americans or are they significantly different?

HINT: It has often been pointed out that, while Americans say they are "moderates" or "conservatives," they very often take liberal positions on specific issues. Where you fit may depend on whether you fall into the same pattern.

The overwhelming support for Newt Gingrich's Contract with America by Republican candidates for the House of Representatives in 1994 shows how strongly conservative the party became in the mid-1990s.

Jersey (now head of the EPA), depart from their party's conservative mainstream on social issues, for example. George W. Bush straddled the ideological fence during the 2000 campaign by stressing "compassionate conservatism," though he pushed firmly conservative programs and appointees during his first months in office. Still other GOP leaders, seeing the growing influence of Hispanic voters in large states such as Florida, Texas, and California, have urged their co-partisans to cut their "English-only" and "cuts in government benefits" immigrants to rhetoric.

The Democratic party is split between a very liberal congressional wing—made much more liberal over the past two decades by the declining influence of Southern conservatives in the party (their House and Senate seats became mostly Republican)—and a more "centrist" wing, represented by the Democratic Leadership Council, Bill Clinton, and Al Gore. The former supports traditional Democratic party programs in which government plays a central role in societal improvement, leveling the playing field for all Americans regardless of race or gender, encouraging economic growth, providing substantial social safety nets, and protecting civil liberties. The latter wing of the party opposes racial quotas and set-asides and supports lower taxes, deregulation, and a crackdown on crime. During the Clinton years, the president and congressional Democrats, not surprisingly, often found themselves at loggerheads, especially over the budget, welfare reform, and trade. The trade issue has been particularly divisive for Democrats, with free-traders Clinton and Gore and their allies facing off against organized labor and environments, important parts of the party base.

The Parties in Government and in the Electorate

Fearful of the tyrannical possibilities of a vigorous government, the framers designed a system of government in which power is so fragmented and competitive that effectiveness is unlikely. One of the roles that political parties can play in a democracy such as ours is to overcome this deadlock by persuading officials of the same party in the different branches of government to cooperate with one another on the basis of party loyalty.[23] The constitutionally designed conflict between president and Congress can be bridged, it has been argued, when a single party controls both houses of Congress and the presidency.

The problem of governing presented by fragmented and separated powers in the United States is almost unique among the rich democracies. In parliamentary systems such as those of Great Britain, Germany, and Japan, there is no separation of powers between the branches of the national government. The executive and the legislative branches are combined; the prime minister is the leader of the majority party in the parliament and is elected by and from that body. Members of the cabinet, the heads of the executive departments of government, are themselves members of the parliament.

We will learn in considerable detail what parties do in government in later chapters on Congress (Chapter 11), the president (Chapter 12), the executive branch (Chapter 13), and the courts (Chapter 14). In general, we will see that the parties only partially improve the coherence and responsiveness of our government. The parties seem to be the best institutions we have for making government work in a cohesive and responsive fashion—when the same party controls the legislative and executive branches—but they do not consistently do the job very well. Because they are unable to command the complete loyalty and attention of their adherents or to direct the behavior of their officeholders much, American parties are tremendously handicapped in playing this important role.

The Problem of Divided Government

For most of the past three decades, Republicans controlled the presidency, while Democrats controlled one or both houses of Congress. After the 1994 election, the situation reversed, with Republicans gaining control of Congress and Democrats retaining the presidency (see Figure 9.2). After the 2000 elections, unified government returned for a few months until moderate Republican Senator James Jeffords quit his party, giving the Democrats control of the Senate. (Republicans retained control of the House and the presidency.)

Divided party control of the federal government has worried scholars and journalists for many years and has produced a substantial amount of literature that examines its causes and assesses its effects.[24] Many scholars and journalists believe the effects to be unfortunate. At best, they suggest, divided party control adds to the gridlock and paralysis that are built into the constitutional design of our system of government.[25] At worst, they suggest, divided party control gives rise to a state of near civil war between the two branches, in which each tries to damage the other in the interests of advancing the fortunes of its party.[26]

Some scholars have begun to argue, however, that divided party control may not be very important. They point to cases in which unified party control did not have good results and cases in which divided control did not prevent the fashioning of coherent policy. Unified party control of government under the Democrats after the 1936 election did not guarantee a vigorous and effective federal government in the last years of Roosevelt's New Deal. Democratic presidents Carter and Clinton did not produce impressive periods of government performance even when both enjoyed Democratic majorities in Congress. There

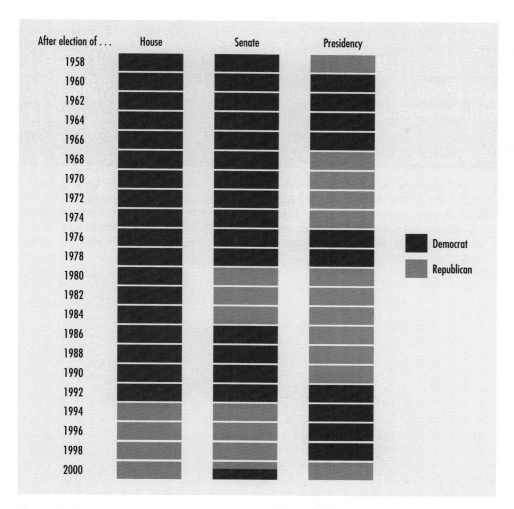

Figure 9.2 ● **Party Control of Congress and the Presidency**

One of the most striking things about our recent political history is the persistence of split party control of the presidency and Congress. Scholars disagree about the effects of this development: some believe it has crippled the government; others say split party control makes no difference.

is some evidence, moreover, that gridlock is no more prominent in periods of divided party control than in periods of unified control.[27] Having completed their studies before the appearance of intense partisan gridlock in the middle and late 1990s, these scholars have no doubt underestimated the detrimental effects of divided government. Anyone witnessing the closing of the federal government during the presidential–congressional budget battles and the intensely partisan impeachment process cannot feel sanguine about divided government.

Parties in the Electorate

Parties are not only organizations and officeholders but also images in the minds of voters and potential voters, mental cues that affect the behavior of the electorate. This aspect of the parties was discussed in Chapter 5 and will be

USING THE FRAMEWORK

Why Are Things So Gridlocked in Washington? Why Can't the President and Congress Seem to Get Anything Done?

In the 1990s, official Washington not only seemed to come to a screeching halt, but there was a dramatic decline in the atmosphere of civility in Congress and in the relations between Congress and the president. Fierce partisan warfare broke out over President Clinton's health care proposal, the federal budget (which led to the closure of the federal government at one point), foreign policy issues (Haiti, Bosnia, Kosovo, and the Test Ban Treaty), abortion and, of course, the impeachment of the president. Taking a look at how structural, political linkage, and governmental factors affect party politics and policymaking in Washington will help explain the situation.

Governmental Action

Government inaction on the nation's agenda in the late 1990s.

Governmental Level

- Democratic President Bill Clinton and the Republican-controlled 104th, 105th, and 106th Congresses battled over most important issues, reaching agreement on only a few of them.

Political Linkages Level

- Neither party has a commanding lead in party identification nationally.

- Congressional elections have become very close and hotly contested, with control of Congress hanging in the balance every two years.

- The political parties have each become more ideological, with the virtual disappearance of conservative Democrats in the South and Mountain West and liberal Republicans in New England.

- Partisan warfare and scandals have become standard fare in the mass media, making cooperation and civility in public affairs, in general, and between the parties, in particular, less likely.

Structural Level

- The Constitution created a system in which tension always exists between the president and Congress.

- Immigration to the United States and migration flows within the United States have changed the balance of power between the parties and the regional power bases of the parties; California, the coastal West, and New England have become strongly Democratic, and the South and the Mountain West have become strongly Republican.

- The end of the Cold War ended the semi-crisis atmosphere that encouraged the political parties in Congress, and the Congress and the president, to cooperate with one another on a wide range of issues.

HOW DEMOCRATIC ARE WE?

PROPOSITION: American political parties don't ensure that government is responsive and responsible to the people.

AGREE: Our parties are so loose and fragmented in an organizational sense, and often so mushy in an ideological sense, that voters do not know what they are getting when they put a party in office and cannot be assured that the majority party will be able to carry out its program, even if it wanted to do so. Matters are made worse by our constitutional system of separation-of-powers and checks-and-balances that undermines coherent government even when the presidency and Congress are held by the same party and that lead to gridlock when the two branches are controlled by different parties.

DISAGREE: Our parties are the only mechanism we have for allowing voters to decide on a program for the government and to hold elected officials responsible in a collective sense. Interest groups and social movements are much too narrow; only parties seek to be inclusive and present broad programs for public approval. Moreover, the parties are becoming better organized and more ideologically distinctive, so voters increasingly know what they are getting when they put a party in office.

THE AUTHORS: It is sad but true that our present parties are the only institution we have for ensuring responsiveness and responsibility. The rise of well-financed, professionally managed, state, national, and congressional campaign organizations, which focus on television and direct mail contact with voters, has impoverished the party "grass roots," made the parties seem distant to citizens, and contributed to the decline of party identification and regard among the public. Finally, the rise in the ideological coherence of the parties, potentially a boon to responsiveness and responsibility in government when a single party controls the presidency and Congress, adds to the possibilities of gridlock in periods of divided government.

considered in greater detail in Chapter 10. We will simply reiterate the points that Americans are less inclined than in the past to identify with or to have confidence in a party and are less willing to vote a straight party ticket. Each of these factors suggests that the two major parties are no longer as central as they once were in tying people's everyday concerns to their choices in the political system. We must also note a growing distaste among the public for the parties as professional campaign organizations, with their stables of consultants and relentless advertising campaigns.

Summary

The American party system is unique among the Western democracies in several respects. First, ours is a relatively pure two-party system and has been so since the 1830s. Second, our major parties are candidate-centered, having very little power in their national party organizations to affect the behavior of individual candidates, officeholders, or state and local party organizations. American parties are less ideological than parties in other democracies, but the enduring and important differences between Democrats and Republicans are becoming more evident.

Although made up of the same two parties for well over a century, the two-party system has not been stagnant. It has undergone a series of realignments, spurred by structural changes in society and the economy, in which the relative power of the parties has shifted, as have the voting alignments of the public, the dominant political coalitions, and public policy.

The parties play an important role in government, sometimes contributing to governmental effectiveness and policy coherence. In the era of divided government, however, parties often contribute to gridlock.

Suggestions for Further Reading

Aldrich, John. *Why Parties?* Chicago: University of Chicago Press, 1995.
Uses a rational-choice perspective from economics to show that the parties we have are the product of the rational pursuit of the goals of office seekers and officeholders.

Burnham, Walter Dean. *Critical Elections and the Mainsprings of American Politics.* New York: Norton, 1970.
The classic analysis of the realignment process in the American party system.

Key, V. O., Jr. *Southern Politics.* New York: Knopf, 1949.
A penetrating and entertaining look at politics in the South in the 1940s and 1950s, when real political parties did not exist there. As such, it shows what politics might look like in the United States if party decline continues.

Mayhew, David R. *Divided We Govern: Party Control, Lawmaking, and Investigations, 1946–1990.* New Haven, CT: Yale University Press, 1991.
A sophisticated attempt to assess the effect of divided government. Argues that the alarm about divided government has been overstated.

Mennefee-Libey, David. *The Triumph of Campaign-Centered Politics.* New York: Chatham House, 2000.
A vivid description of how the requirements of modern campaign politics have changed the political parties.

Reichley, A. James. *The Life of the Parties: A History of American Political Parties.* New York: Free Press, 1992.
The leading history of the American party system, with special attention paid to the question of party decline in the modern era and what might be done about it.

Rosenstone, Steven J., Ray L. Behr, and Edward T. Lazarus. *Third Parties in America: Citizen Response to Major Party Failure.* Princeton, NJ: Princeton University Press, 1996.
A rigorous analysis of the conditions under which third parties and independent candidates emerge in American politics.

Internet Sources

Democratic National Committee   **www.democrats.org/**
Information about Democratic party candidates, party history, convention and national committees, state parties, stands on the issues, affiliated groups, upcoming events, and more.

National Political Index   **http://www.politicalindex.com/**
Links to state and local parties and affiliated organizations and interest groups.

Political Resources on the Web   **www.politicalresources.net/**
Information about political parties in all democratic countries.

Republican National Committee   **http://www.rnc.org/**
Information about Republican party candidates, party history, convention and national committees, state parties, stands on the issues, affiliated groups, upcoming events, and more.

The Reform Party   **www.reformparty.org/**
Learn about Reform Party candidates, proposals, and issue positions.

Notes

1. David Menefee-Libey, *The Triumph of Campaign-Centered Politics* (New York: Chatham House Publishers, 2000); and Daniel M. Shea, "The Passing of Realignment and the Advent of the 'Baseless' Party System," *American Politics Quarterly* 27 (January 1997), pp. 33–57.

2. Robert A. Dahl, *On Democracy* (New Haven, CT: Yale University Press, 1998).

3. E. E. Schattschneider, *Party Government* (New York: Holt, Rinehart & Winston, 1942), p. 208.

4. Ibid.

5. See A. James Reichley, *The Life of the Parties: A History of American Political Parties* (New York: Free Press, 1992), ch. 1.

6. Steven J. Rosenstone and John Mark Hansen, *Mobilization, Participation, and Democracy in America* (New York: Macmillan, 1993).

7. E. E. Schattschneider, *The Semi-Sovereign People* (New York: Holt, Rinehart & Winston, 1960).

8. On realignment, see Walter Dean Burnham, *Critical Elections and the Mainsprings of American Politics* (New York: Norton, 1970); Walter Dean Burnham, "Critical Realignment Lives: The 1994 Earthquake," in Colin Campbell and Bert A. Rockman, eds., *The Clinton Presidency* (Chatham, NJ: Chatham House, 1996); William Nisbet Chambers and Walter Dean Burnham, eds., *The American Party Systems* (New York: Oxford University Press, 1967); Jerome Clubb, William H. Flanigan, and Nancy H. Zingale, *Partisan Realignment* (Newbury Park, CA: Sage, 1980); V. O. Key Jr., "A Theory of Critical Elections," *Journal of Politics* 17 (1955), pp. 3–18; James L. Sundquist, *Dynamics of the Party System* (Washington, D.C.: Brookings Institution, 1973).

9. C. Vann Woodward, *The Strange Career of Jim Crow* (New York: Oxford University Press, 1966).

10. John Aldrich and Richard Niemi, "The Sixth American Party System," in Stephen C. Craig, *Broken Contract: Changing Relationships between Americans and Their Government* (Boulder, CO: Westview Press, 1996).

11. Helmut Norpoth and Jerrold Rusk, "Partisan Dealignment in the American Electorate," *American Political Science Review* 76 (September 1982), pp. 719–736. Also see Larry Sabato, *The Party's Just Begun* (Glenview, IL: Scott, Foresman, 1988); Sundquist, *Dynamics of the Party System;* Martin P. Wattenberg, *The Decline of American Political Parties* (Cambridge, MA: Harvard University Press, 1994); Stanley B. Greenberg, *Middle-Class Dreams* (New York: Times Books, 1995); Everett C. Ladd, "The 1994 Congressional Elections," *Political Science Quarterly* 110, pp. 1–23.

12. The classic statement on electoral rules is Maurice Duverger, *Political Parties* (New York: Wiley, 1954).

13. Much of this discussion is drawn from Steven J. Rosenstone, Roy L. Behr, and Edward H. Lazarus, *Third Parties in America* (Princeton, NJ: Princeton University Press, 1984).

14. Shea, "The Passing of Realignment and the Advent of the 'Baseless' Party System."

15. Menefee-Libey, *The Triumph of Candidate-Centered Politics.*

16. J. A. Schlesinger, "The New American Political Party," *American Political Science Review* 79 (1985), pp. 1152–1169; and John Aldrich, *Why Parties?* (Chicago: University of Chicago Press, 1995).

17. J. L. Jackson, N. Clayton, and J. C. Green, "Issue Networks and Party Elites in 1996," in J. C. Green and D. M. Shea, eds., *The State of the Parties* (Lanham, MD: Rowman and Littlefield, 1999); and Gerald Pomper, "Parliamentary Government in the United States," in Green and Shea, eds., *The State of the Parties*.

18. *National Election Studies* (Ann Arbor: University of Michigan, 1999).

19. Alan D. Monroe, "American Party Platforms and Public Opinion," *American Journal of Political Science* 27 (February 1983), p. 35; Gerald M. Pomper, *Elections in America* (New York: Longman, 1980), p. 169.

20. "Convention Delegates: Who They Are and How They Compare on Issues," *The New York Times* (August 14, 2000), p. A17.

21. Douglas Hibbs, *The American Political Economy* (Cambridge, MA: Harvard University Press, 1987); Dennis P. Quinn and Robert Shapiro, "Business Political Power: The Case of Taxation," *American Political Science Review* 85 (1991), pp. 851–874.

22. Thomas Byrne Edsall, *The New Politics of Inequality* (New York: Norton, 1984); Kevin P. Phillips, *Boiling Point: Democrats, Republicans, and the Decline of Middle-Class Prosperity* (New York: Random House, 1993); David Vogel, *Fluctuating Fortunes: The Political Power of Business in America* (New York: Basic Books, 1989); Roger Davidson and Walter Oleszek, *Congress and Its Members* (Washington, D.C.: CQ Press, 2000), pp. 190–192.

23. James MacGregor Burns, *Deadlock of Democracy* (Englewood Cliffs, NJ: Prentice Hall, 1967).

24. Morris P. Fiorina, *Divided Government* (New York: Macmillan, 1992); Gary Jacobson, *The Electoral Origins of Divided Government: Competition in U.S. House Elections* (Boulder, CO: Westview Press, 1990); David R. Mayhew, *Divided We Govern: Party Control, Lawmaking, and Investigations, 1946–1990* (New Haven, CT: Yale University Press, 1991).

25. Hedrick Smith, *The Power Game* (New York: Random House, 1988), p. 652.

26. Benjamin Ginsberg and Martin Shefter, *Politics by Other Means: The Declining Significance of Elections in America* (New York: Basic Books, 1990).

27. Mayhew, *Divided We Govern*.

CHAPTER 10

Participation, Voting, and Elections

IN THIS CHAPTER

- The role of elections in a democracy

- How African-Americans, women, and young people won the right to vote

- Why many Americans don't vote

- How to run for the presidency

- What part money plays in presidential elections

- How voters decide to vote

- Why elections matter

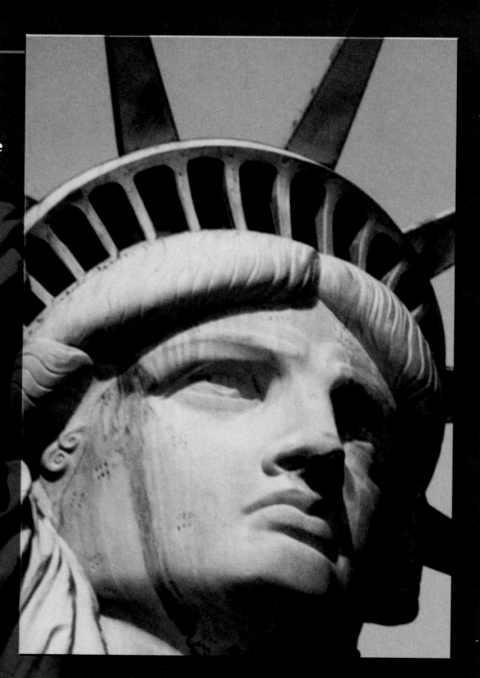

The 2000 Presidential Contest

After an extraordinarily long, expensive, and, to many Americans, exhausting campaign that had sparked little interest and enthusiasm among the public, the finale of the 2000 presidential election campaign could not have been more exciting or historically significant: a near dead-heat between Republican George W. Bush and Democrat Al Gore (the closest popular vote split, in fact, since the 1960 election between John F. Kennedy and Richard Nixon, and the smallest electoral vote margin since 1916); excruciatingly close races in New Hampshire, New Mexico, Wisconsin, Iowa, and Oregon; and the drama of Florida—where election officials, faced with a legally mandated recount, demands for hand recounts in selected counties, loads of absentee ballots mailed from abroad, multiple charges of ballot confusion and irregularities, and voter lawsuits—could not certify a winner until well after election day.

The Florida certification for George W. Bush brought his total electoral vote to 271 and decided the outcome of the national election. The deadlock in Florida was broken only after the controversial intervention by the U.S. Supreme Court. In a 5-4 decision, it overturned a Florida Supreme Court ruling and stopped the ballot count then underway. This had the effect of ratifying the earlier certification of Bush's victory by Florida Secretary of State Katherine Harris. George W. Bush took office on January 20, 2001 as the first president since Benjamin Harrison in 1889 to have won the Electrol College vote but to have lost the national popular vote (see our website at www.ablongman.com/greenberg for more detailed information and commentary on the election).

The 2000 presidential election nicely highlights the fact that we choose our presidents not by direct popular vote but by the vote of the Electoral College. (You may want to read again about the Electoral College in Chapter 2 on the Constitution. We also examine the Electoral College in more detail later in this chapter and provide a rich Web Exploration on the topic as well.) It is the case, of course, that the winner of the popular vote and the winner of the electoral vote are the same almost all the time, but not always. Twice before, in 1876 and in 1888, the candidate with fewer national popular votes was elected to the presidency by virtue of a majority in the Electoral College.

It is important to know that the electoral vote is what really counts because it shapes the strategy and tactics of the presidential campaigns. It helps explain why the campaign for the presidency is about candidates attempting to put together a package of states whose electoral votes come to a total of 270 or more. In the 2000 election each party started with a solid base of states with a known number of electoral votes. Bush's electoral vote base was in Texas, most of the South, and the Mountain West; Gore's electoral vote base was in New York, much of New England, and California. The battle for an electoral vote majority was joined in what came to be called the "battleground" states of Florida, Pennsylvania, Ohio, Illinois, Michigan, Wisconsin, Missouri, and Iowa, where the contest could go either way and electoral votes were abundant. It was in these states that the campaigns focused most of the visits of their candidates and spent most of their television, radio, and print advertising dollars.

The long campaign for the presidency, which started in earnest for George W. Bush and Al Gore at least a full year before the actual vote, evoked none of the passion, acrimony, and ideological conflict that would eventually surround the tallying of the vote. From the beginning, despite occasional forays to shore up their support on the Left (Gore) and on the Right (Bush), both candidates clung to predominantly centrist and nonideological themes. Debates between the candidates and parties were mostly about alternative approaches to Social Security, education, and prescription drug benefits. Gore tried to link himself to the economic successes of the Clinton years, while also desperately trying to distance himself from the Clinton scandals, stressing that he was his own man, willing to fight every day for ordinary, hard-working Americans. Bush tried to portray himself as a "compassionate conservative," a different and less strident sort of Republican—he even chided congressional Republicans for caring too little about the poor—committed to cutting taxes and reducing the size of the federal government, yet supportive of efforts to help those who genuinely needed help. Although Green Party candidate Ralph Nader tried to push Gore from the Left and Reform Party candidate Pat Buchanan tried to pressure Bush from the Right, neither was successful in changing the main thrust of the campaign. Nader ultimately played a decisive role in the election outcome; his 90,000-plus votes in Florida, an overwhelming majority of whom would otherwise have gone to Gore, according to the polls, cost Gore Florida and an Electoral College majority in the country.

The presidential contest, more substantive and less heated than recent ones, failed to truly engage the public. No galvanizing issues divided the country; traditional campaign organizing themes such as the Cold War or the New Deal or the Great Society seemed beside the point in a period of American economic boom and prosperity and military and diplomatic preeminence in the world; and many important and potentially divisive issues such as race, income inequality, and American foreign policy in a post–Cold War world were hardly on the radar screen of the candidates.

The 2000 presidential election falls into the general category of elections that political scientists call the "electoral competition" model in which each party attempts to capture the voters in the middle of the political spectrum, while trying to hold on to as much of its base as possible. Such elections tend to be low-intensity affairs in which the sharp edges of party disagreement are softened in order to attract as many voters from the broad, nonideological, and politically unengaged middle as possible. Although there were some elements of what political scientists call "retrospective" voting in the 2000 election (many voters, for example, chose Al Gore on the grounds that he would continue the economic good times of the Clinton years; many other voters chose Bush because they wished to reject other aspects of the Clinton legacy, particularly the moral aspect), and some elements of what scholars call "prospective" voting (for example, choosing one candidate over another on the basis of the coherent programmatic or ideological direction being offered for the future), both campaigns recognized that the electorate was in a nonideological mood, tired of intense partisanship and government gridlock, and not inclined to favor harsh attacks or elaborate visions of the future, and responded accordingly. Gore's effort to paint Bush as not quite smart enough for the job, and Bush's effort to remind the public of Gore's exaggerations and questionable fundraising activities, which took up much of the campaign, were hardly the stuff of high political drama.

It is ironic, then, that the vote tallying process in Florida and the closeness of the presidential and congressional contests in the nation led to such fierce partisan acrimony in the end. What it portends for the future is not yet clear, although it has surely not made the leadership job of the newly elected president any easier. To many Americans, the president is neither the choice of a substantial majority of American voters nor the carrier of a mandate to carry forward a set of domestic and foreign policy programs. To complicate matters further, President Bush faces a sharply and evenly divided House and Senate, where ambitious presidential programs are almost certain to have tough sledding.

Thinking Critically About This Chapter

The story of the 2000 presidential election focuses our attention on the issue of democratic control of the national government through the electoral process and on the degree to which the public participates in this key activity of the representative democratic process.

Using the Framework. You will see in this chapter that elections are affected by the different rates of participation of groups in American society and how structural factors such as constitutional rules, unequal access to resources, and cultural ideas help determine why some groups participate more than others. You will also learn how elections affect the behavior of public officials.

Using the Democracy Standard. We suggest in this chapter that elections are the lynchpin of any discussion about the democratic quality of any system of government because they are, in theory, the main way that popular sovereignty and political equality are possible. You will see in this chapter that while elections in the United States do much to make our system democratic, they fall short of their democratic promise. ▶

Elections and Democracy

Elections are fundamental to democratic politics, the chief means by which citizens control what their government does. Many important struggles for democracy in the United States have involved conflicts over the right to vote. But can elections actually ensure that governments will do what their people want? How? In a small, participatory democracy such as a town meeting, the answer is easy: people simply vote directly on what to do. In a large, complicated society such as the entire United States, however, where only representative democracy is possible, it is not obvious how the people might control their representatives. How can ordinary citizens make certain that elected officials will respond to them, that these officials will work for what the people want rather than pursue their own ends or cater to special interests?

Democratic theorists have suggested several processes by which two-party elections of representatives, like those we have in the United States, can bring about the democratic control of government. We will briefly discuss three of these processes, indicating how they might work in theory and what could go wrong in practice.[1] The rest of this chapter is concerned with what actually happens in American national elections and whether elections really bring about democratic control.

Responsible Party Government

The idea of **responsible party** government is based on the old commonsense notion that elections should present a "real choice": political parties should stand for different policies, the voters should choose between them, and the winning party should carry out its mandate.

Theory For this system to work perfectly, each of the two parties must be cohesive and unified; each must take clear policy positions that differ significantly from the other party's positions; the citizens must accurately perceive these positions and vote on the basis of them; and the winning party, when it

responsible party

A political party that takes clear, distinct stands on the issues and enacts them as policy.

takes office, must do exactly what it said it would do. If all these conditions are met, then obviously the party with the more popular policy positions will win and enact its program. Government will do what the majority of the voters want.[2]

Problems Even if an election were to work exactly as the responsible party ideal dictates, however, a serious problem arises. There is no actual guarantee that either party would take policy positions that pleased the voters, only that the winning party's stand is less *unpopular* than the loser's. Also, crucial decisions about what the parties stand for and what choices they present to the voters would be made by someone other than ordinary citizens—by party leaders or perhaps by interest groups.

Moreover, the conditions under which responsible party government is supposed to work are not fully met—and are not ever likely to be met—in the United States. As we saw in Chapter 9, the Republican and Democratic parties are *not* very unified or ideologically cohesive, for reasons deeply rooted in our Constitution and our political structure. The parties are sometimes deliberately ambiguous on where they stand and are not always distinctly different from each other. Furthermore, the voters do not vote solely on the issues. And the parties do not always keep their promises once in office.

Clearly, then, the responsible party idea does not correspond exactly to what happens in American elections. But we will see that it comes close enough to the truth to describe at least a part of reality. Also, theories about responsible parties provide some useful standards for judging what may be wrong with U.S. elections and how they might be improved, particularly with respect to the clarity of stands on issues.

Electoral Competition

electoral competition

The process by which parties seeking votes move toward the center of the political spectrum.

A very different, and less obvious, sort of democratic control might come about through a process of **electoral competition** over issues. Here unified parties compete for votes by taking the *most popular* positions they can. Both parties are therefore likely to end up standing for the *same* policies: those favored by the most voters.

Theory Scholars have proved mathematically that if citizens' preferences are organized along a single dimension (such as the liberal–conservative continuum shown in Figure 10.1), and if parties purely seek votes, both parties will take positions exactly at the *median* of public opinion, that is, at the point where exactly one-half the voters are more liberal and one-half are more conservative. If either party took a position even a bit away from the median, the other party could easily win more votes by taking a position closer to the median.[3]

If electoral competition drives parties together in this way, and if they keep their promises, then, in theory, it should not matter which party wins; the winner enacts the policies that the most voters want. Democracy is ensured by the hidden hand of competition. According to this economic style of thinking, selfish, vote-seeking parties do what the voters want, in just the same way that selfish, money-seeking firms are forced to produce what consumers want.

To be sure, electoral competition processes cannot ensure that the parties will educate or mobilize voters, as in a responsible party process. However, they hold out the promise that popular sovereignty and a perfectly democratic outcome—rather than just the lesser of two evils—may result from elections.

Problems Again, however, the conditions needed for electoral competition to work perfectly are not likely to be met in the real world. Electoral competition

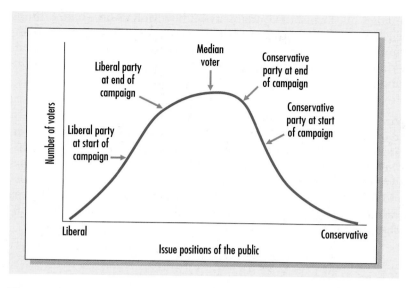

Figure 10.1 ● **Electoral Competition Model**

This model suggests that in the interest of winning the election, parties will move toward the median voter (where most votes are to be had) as the campaign progresses.

ensures democratic control only if the parties are unified and take clear stands, for pure and direct vote-seeking reasons; it can break down if the parties are fragmented or ambiguous, care about policies, or seek contributors' dollars rather than citizens' votes. In order for democratic control to be complete, everyone has to vote. Moreover, the voters must consider nothing but the issues (e.g., not being distracted by candidates' personalities or images) and must know exactly where the parties stand. And the parties have to keep their promises. There are reasons to doubt that any of these things will happen flawlessly.

Still, we will see that these conditions are close enough to the truth so that electoral competition does work, to a significant extent, in real elections. Indeed, electoral competition is probably one of the main reasons that government policy is significantly influenced by public opinion. Also, by looking at how actual elections deviate from the theoretical ideal of electoral competition (e.g., how money and campaign contributions sometimes push parties away from popular policies), we can see specific ways in which American elections might be improved as instruments of democracy.

Electoral Reward and Punishment

A third process by which elections might bring about democratic control of government is **electoral reward and punishment**.

Theory   Here the idea is that the voters simply make retrospective, backward-looking judgments about how well incumbent officials have done in the past, rewarding success with reelection and punishing failure by throwing the incumbents out. The result, in theory, is that politicians who want to stay in office have strong incentives to bring about peace and prosperity and to solve problems that the American people want solved. Politicians' ambitions force them to anticipate what the public wants and to accomplish it.[4]

The reward-and-punishment process of democratic control has the advantage of simplicity. It requires very little of voters: no elaborate policy preferences,

electoral reward and punishment

The tendency to vote for the incumbents when times are good and against them when times are bad.

no study of campaign platforms, just judgments of how well or how badly things have been going. Also, like electoral competition, it relies on politicians' selfishness rather than their altruism. It allows time for deliberation, and it lets leaders try out experimental or temporarily unpopular policies, as long as the results work out well and please the public in time for the next election.

Problems   However, reward and punishment may be a rather blunt instrument. It gets rid of bad political leaders only after (not before) disasters happen, without guaranteeing that the next leaders will be any better. It relies on politicians *anticipating* the effects of future policies, which they cannot always do successfully. Moreover, the reward-and-punishment process focuses only on the most crucial issues and may leave room for unpopular policies on matters that are less visible. It may also encourage politicians to produce deceptively happy but temporary results that arrive just in time for Election Day and then fade away.

Imperfect Electoral Democracy

We will see that each of the three processes of democratic control we have discussed works, to some extent, in American elections. On occasion, even, the three processes converge and help produce an election that is enormously consequential for the direction of the nation. The 1932 election was one of these occasions, and is described in the "Using the Framework" feature.

WEB EXPLORATION

Party Platforms and Electoral Theory

Issue: According to democratic theorists, elections can ensure popular accountability in representative democracies in three ways: by allowing the public to choose between future courses of action (responsible party government), by allowing voters to render judgments about a party's performance in office (electoral reward and punishment), and by forcing parties and candidates to offer platforms that conform to what the public wants (electoral competition).

Site: Access the Democratic and Republican National Committees through the "Course Documents" section of your online course. Go to the "Web Explorations" section for Chapter 10, click on "Party Platforms and Electoral Theory," and open "national committees." Look at the official platforms passed at their respective conventions aimed at the 2000 elections.

What You've Learned: How did each party present itself during the 2000 national election cycle in terms of the models of electoral democracy described in this chapter? Did Republicans and Democrats ask voters to choose a future direction for government or ask them to simply make a judgment about the party's past performance? Or did the parties simply try to position themselves in terms of where they judged the voters to be?

HINT: You will probably discover that each of the parties shows signs of trying to do all three, although the emphasis will probably be on one.

USING THE FRAMEWORK

When Have the American People Used Their Vote in a National Election to Significantly Change the Course of Government?

Occasionally in American history, a national election is so consequential that it alters the overall direction of government policy and the role of government in the United States. The election of Franklin Delano Roosevelt and an overwhelmingly Democratic Congress in the 1932 elections was just such a moment. In the first 100 days of his administration, Roosevelt launched his New Deal, convincing Congress to pass bills to regulate the banking and securities industries, to bail out failing banks and protect the deposits of the public, to launch public works and relief efforts, and to provide price supports for farmers. This revolution in the role of the federal government was made possible by the 1932 elections, but to fully understand what happened, structural, political linkage, and governmental factors have to be taken into account.

Governmental Action

The New Deal is launched.

Governmental Level

- Franklin Roosevelt interpreted the 1932 election as a mandate for immediate and far-reaching actions by the federal government to meet the crisis of the Great Depression.

- Roosevelt mobilized business and labor leaders, as well as the public, behind his emergency program.

- The Democratic-controlled Congress, aware of Roosevelt's enormous popularity, and concerned about the national crisis, pass all of the president's emergency measures.

Political Linkages Level

- Public opinion strongly supported a greater role for the federal government in fighting the depression, as did many business leaders.

- Social disorder was widespread, leading to concerns that the country was near the point of collapse.

- Social movements that demanded government action were growing and making their presence felt.

- Democrats won big majorities in the House (313 out of 435 total seats) and the Senate (59 of 96 seats).

- Roosevelt won an overwhelming victory in the 1932 presidential election, tallying 472 electoral votes to Hoover's 59.

Structural Level

- The 1932 election was held in the midst of the Great Depression, with unemployment reaching 33 percent, bank failures at an all-time high, and industrial and farm production at 50 percent of their levels in the mid-1920s.

- The preamble to the Constitution says that the Constitution was intended to create a government that would "…insure Domestic tranquility…[and]…promote the general Welfare."

But none of the three processes works well enough to guarantee perfectly democratic outcomes most of the time. In certain respects, they conflict: responsible parties and electoral competition, for example, tend to push in opposite directions. In other respects, all three processes require similar conditions that are not met in reality.

To pin down politicians' responsibility, all three require more unified political parties than we actually have. Similarly, they cannot ensure government responsiveness to all citizens unless *all* citizens have the right to vote and exercise that right. Unfortunately, millions of Americans cannot or do not go to the polls. Their voices are not heard; political equality is not achieved.

Another problem for all three processes is that money, organizational resources, and active campaigning—not just citizens' policy preferences and votes—may influence the stands that parties take and the outcomes of elections. Thus, money givers, activists, and the leaders of organized groups have more influence than ordinary citizens do; again, political equality is not realized.

Political Participation

participation

Political activity, including voting, campaign activity, contacting officials, and demonstrating.

unconventional participation

Political activity in the form of demonstrations or protests.

conventional participation

Political activity related to elections (voting, persuading, and campaigning) or to contacting public officials.

franchise

The right to vote.

Political **participation** is political activity by individual citizens. It includes **unconventional participation**, in demonstrations, boycotts, and the like, of the sort we discussed in Chapter 8, and also **conventional participation**, such as writing letters to the editor on political issues, contacting officials, going to public meetings, working in campaigns, and giving money, which we focus on here. The most basic form of conventional political participation, the one that plays the most central part in theories of democratic control through elections, is the act of voting.

Expansion of the Franchise

Until passage of the Fourteenth and Fifteenth Amendments after the Civil War, it was up to each state to determine who within its borders was eligible to vote. In the early years of the United States, many of the states limited the legal right to vote—called the **franchise**—quite severely. In fact, a majority of people could not vote at all. Slaves, Native Americans, and women were excluded altogether. In most states, white men without a substantial amount of property were not allowed to vote. In some states, white men with certain religious beliefs were excluded.

One of the most important developments in the political history of the United States, an essential part of the struggle for democracy, has been the expansion of the right to vote. The extension of the franchise has been a lengthy and uneven process, spanning 200 years.

suffrage

The right to vote.

White Male Suffrage   The first barriers to fall were those concerning property and religion. So strong were the democratic currents during Thomas Jefferson's presidency (1801–1809) and in the years leading up to the election of Andrew Jackson in 1828 that by 1829, property and religious requirements had been dropped in all states except North Carolina and Virginia. That left universal **suffrage**, or the ability to vote, firmly in place for most adult white males in the United States.[5] Most of Europe, including Britain, did not achieve that degree of democracy until after World War I.

Early U.S. elections were poorly organized and hard to get to. In addition, only a small proportion of the population was eligible to vote.

Blacks, Women, and Young People   Despite this head start for the United States compared with the rest of the world, however, the struggle to expand the suffrage to include African-Americans, women, and young people proved difficult and painful. Ironically, universal white male suffrage was often accompanied by the withdrawal of voting rights from black freedmen, even in states that did not permit slavery.[6] It took the bloody Civil War to free the slaves and the Fifteenth Amendment to the U.S. Constitution (1870) to extend the right to vote to all black males, in both North and South. Even so, most blacks were effectively disfranchised in the South by the end of the nineteenth century and remained so until the 1960s civil rights movement and the Voting Rights Act of 1965 (see Chapter 1).

Women won the right to vote with the Nineteenth Amendment to the Constitution (1920), after a long political battle (see the opening vignette in Chapter 8 for details of this struggle). Residents of the District of Columbia were allowed to vote in presidential—but not congressional—elections after 1961, and 18- to 20-year-olds gained the franchise only in 1971 (see The Struggle for Democracy box, "Young People Win the Right to Vote").

The result of these changes at the state and national levels was an enormous increase in the proportion of Americans who were legally eligible to vote: from about 23 percent of the adult population in 1788–1789 to nearly 100 percent—practically all citizens except convicted felons and people in mental institutions—by the beginning of the 1970s.

Direct Partisan Elections   A related trend has involved the more direct election of government officials, replacing the old indirect methods that insulated officials from the public. At the same time, the development of a two-party system has clarified choices by focusing citizens' attention on just two alternatives for each office.

By the time of the Jefferson-Adams presidential campaign of 1800, which pitted the new Republican and Federalist parties against each other, most

THE STRUGGLE FOR DEMOCRACY

Young People Win the Right to Vote

On June 19, 1968, students at University of the Pacific in Stockton, California, formed a group called Let Us Vote (LUV) and began a national campaign to lower the voting age from 21 to 18.[a] In 1971, LUV won: the Twenty-Sixth Amendment to the U.S. Constitution established the right of 18- to 20-year-olds to vote in all federal, state, and local elections, overriding contrary state laws and adding about 11 million young people to the electorate. How this important expansion of democracy came about illustrates certain complexities of our federal system.

At the structural level, international events—especially the Vietnam War—and changing demographics helped fuel the drive for the new amendment. That thousands of young men were mature enough to fight and die for their country provided an overwhelming moral argument in favor of letting them vote. Getting young people to "work within the system," rather than protesting outside it (as thousands of antiwar demonstrators were then doing), provided a strong practical argument. Moreover, evidence that young people were better educated than their elders—more of them were completing high school and going on to college—undermined the old argument that youths were incapable of making intelligent political decisions.

Political support was widespread. Student groups such as LUV and public interest lobbies such as Common Cause put their energy into the amendment and won support from such diverse groups as the American Legion, the Junior Chamber of Commerce, and the American Federation of Labor and Congress of Industrial Organizations (AFL-CIO). Democrats saw the registration of millions of young voters as an opportunity to move the electorate in their own liberal direction. When surveys showed young people to be little different in their political affiliations from anyone else, however, and when it became clear that radical student protesters were a small minority, Republicans jumped on the bandwagon and supported the amendment as well.

The Twenty-Sixth Amendment also gained impetus from the need to cure a peculiar new problem of American federalism: dual systems of voter registration. Beginning in 1970, by congressional legislation,

national elections for Congress and the presidency included 18- to 20-year-old participants, but many state and local elections did not. The U.S. Supreme Court had upheld the constitutional power of the states to set the voting age for their own elections. The result was a mess. Different groups of voters had to be registered separately for the two kinds of elections, even when both were held at the same time and in the same place.

After Congress overwhelmingly voted for the Twenty-Sixth Amendment in March 1971, it took only two months and seven days—the shortest time ever for a constitutional amendment to be ratified—for it to be approved by the required 38 states. (One 64-year-old state representative in Alabama, trying to stop it with a filibuster, despaired: "I'm physically unable to stand here any longer.") After Ohio became the thirty-eighth and decisive state to ratify the amendment, President Nixon said, "Some 11 million young men and women who have participated in the life of our nation through their work, their studies, and their sacrifices for its defense now are to be fully included in the electoral process of our country. I urge them to honor this right by exercising it, by registering and voting in each election."[b]

[a] "Collegians Open Voting-Age Drive," *New York Times* (December 20, 1968), p. 51.

[b] "States Ratify Full 18-Year-Old Vote," *New York Times* (July 1, 1971), p. 1.

state legislatures had stopped picking the presidential electors themselves (as the Constitution permits). Instead, the legislatures allowed a popular vote for electors, most of whom were pledged to support the presidential candidate of one party or the other.

This is the same system we use today: in practically every state, there is a winner-take-all popular vote for a slate of electors, who are pledged ahead of time to a particular candidate. In fact, only the name of the candidate and the party to whom the electors are pledged, not the names of the electors we are actually voting for, appears on the ballot. Thus, when the winning electors meet as the **electoral college** in their respective states and cast ballots to elect the president, their actions are generally controlled by the popular vote that chose them. This system, odd and cumbersome as it is, ensures that American citizens choose their president more or less directly.

By 1840, the parties had started nominating presidential candidates in national conventions instead of congressional caucuses. Later still, the parties began letting voters elect many convention delegates directly, in primaries, instead of having party activists choose them through state caucuses or state conventions. These innovations have probably increased the democratic control of government, although we will see that each of them has antidemocratic features, too.

The direct popular election of U.S. senators did not replace their being chosen by state legislatures until 1913, with the Seventeenth Amendment to the Constitution. Since 1913, all members of the Senate have been subject to direct choice by the voters.

Taken together, the expansion of the franchise and the development of direct, two-party elections have represented major successes in the struggle for democracy. But victory is not yet complete.

electoral college

Representatives of the states who formally elect the president; the number of electors in each state is equal to the total number of its senators and congressional representatives.

The Vanishing Electorate

During the first 100 years or so of the United States's existence, not only did more and more people gain the right to vote but higher and higher proportions of eligible voters actually turned out on Election Day and voted. It is not easy to be sure of the exact **turnout** percentages because of data inaccuracies and voting fraud, but in presidential elections, the figure of roughly 11 percent of eligible voters who turned out in 1788–1789 jumped to about 31 percent in 1800 (when Thomas Jefferson was first elected) and to about 57 percent in 1828 (Andrew Jackson's first victory). By 1840, the figure had reached 80 percent, and it stayed at about that level until 1896.[7]

The disturbing fact is that today, a much smaller proportion of people participate in politics than did during most of the nineteenth century. Since 1912, only about 55 to 65 percent of eligible Americans have voted in presidential elections (see Figure 10.2) and still fewer in other elections: 40 to 50 percent in off-year (non-presidential-year) congressional elections and as few as 10 to 20 percent in primaries and minor local elections. In recent years, the turnout rate has dropped to the low end of those ranges.

In 1996, 51 percent of eligible voters did not vote in the presidential election; in 2000, 49 percent failed to vote. Americans who take part in the full range of elections—off-year congressional elections, primaries, local and state elections—are but a small minority of the population. Our voting turnout rate is also exceptionally low compared with that of the other rich democracies (turnout rates regularly top 75 percent in Belgium, Sweden, Denmark, and Italy). Most observers consider this a serious problem for democracy in America, particularly because (as we will see) people who vote tend to be different from those who do not. Nonvoters do not get an equal voice in political choices. Political equality, one of the key elements of democracy, is violated.

turnout

The proportion of eligible voters who actually vote in a given election.

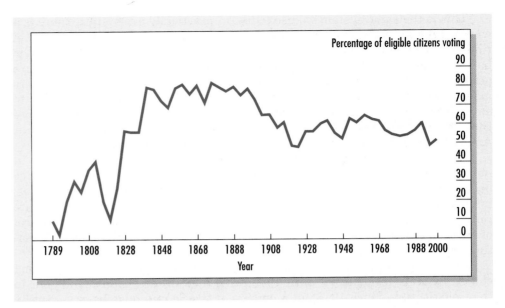

Figure 10.2 ● **The Rise and Fall of Turnout in Presidential Elections, 1789–2000**

Turnout in presidential elections rose sharply during the nineteenth century but declined in the twentieth century.

Sources: U.S. Bureau of the Census; and "Election Summary," *New York Times* (November 9, 2000), p.A1.

Causes of Low Turnout   Why do so few Americans participate in elections? Scholars have identified several possible factors.

Barriers to Voting   In the United States, only citizens who take the initiative to register before an election are permitted to vote. People who move from one community to another, for example, must register to vote in their new location. In one presidential election, about 35 percent of the nonvoters, but only 16 percent of voters, said that they had moved in the past two years.[8]

In most European countries with high turnout rates, the government, rather than individual citizens, is responsible for deciding who is listed as eligible to vote. In some countries, such as Belgium and Italy, moreover, citizens are *required* to vote and may be fined if they don't. Moreover, in most countries, all election days are holidays on which people don't have to go to work.

The United States could certainly increase political equality and popular sovereignty by making voting easier. One way to do so would be to ease registration requirements,[9] perhaps allowing registration by postcard or same-day registration at polling places. The federal "motor voter" law passed in 1993, providing for registration in motor vehicle bureaus and other government offices, was a step in this direction. Another way would be to ease the voting act itself, by making every election day a holiday or by allowing an extended voting period such as the two-and-a-half weeks tried in Texas or by broadening the right of absentee voting as in California or by allowing voting by mail over an extended period as in Oregon.

Lack of Attractive Choices   Some scholars believe that the nature of the political parties and the choices that they offer also affect turnout. Countries with proportional representation and multiparty systems—that is, with diverse and competitive parties from which to choose—have averaged an 83 percent

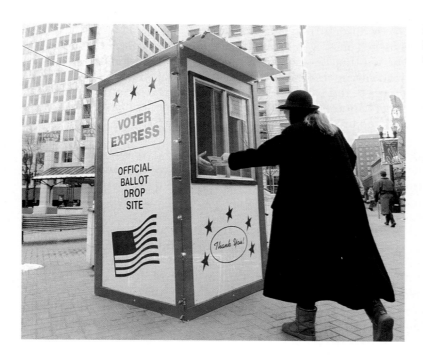

In Oregon, voting entirely by mail (or by dropping off ballots in convenient collection boxes) has saved the state money and increased turnout.

turnout rate, whereas single-district, plurality-vote countries (which usually have just two parties) have had a voter turnout rate that is closer to 70 percent. Many American citizens may not like the candidates of either of the major parties well enough to bother voting for them and see no reason to vote for a third-party or independent candidate who has no chance of winning.

Changes in Eligibility Rules   Changes in eligibility rules have also affected turnout rates, at least temporarily. As Figure 10.2 indicates, turnout as a proportion of eligible voters dropped just after women were enfranchised in 1920 because at first, women were less likely to vote than men. But that difference gradually disappeared. In fact, in recent elections, women voted at rates slightly higher than men. Similarly, turnout percentages dropped a bit after 18-year-olds won the vote in 1971 because young people do not participate as much, probably because they are less firmly established in their local communities.

Alienation   That many Americans feel apathetic toward or alienated from politics has undoubtedly contributed to declines in turnout.[10] Much of this can be traced back as far as the 1960s, to the assassination of popular leaders (John F. Kennedy, Robert Kennedy, Martin Luther King Jr.) and to the Vietnam War, urban unrest, and the Watergate and Iran-Contra scandals.[11] More recently, the turn of the mass media to "infotainment" and scandals as staples of what they do (see Chapter 6), has probably discouraged potential voters. Some scholars blame the increase in negative campaign advertising as a leading culprit, although other scholars disagree, saying that such ads sometimes even spur people to vote.[12]

Lack of Voter Mobilization by the Parties   A related factor may be the failure of the political parties to rouse low-income citizens, especially African-Americans and Latinos. In recent years, neither the Republican nor the Democratic party has seemed very eager to increase the number of voters among the poor.[13]

Republicans have traditionally avoided mobilizing low-income Americans in favor of more privileged ones. Democrats have made occasional forays but have probably been worried that low-income people might support candidates such as Jesse Jackson who are more liberal than most party officials. Increasingly, as suggested in Chapter 9, the parties also seem less interested in involving the grass roots and more interested in raising soft money for big donors to run highly professionalized but distant campaigns.[14]

Campaigning Involvement and Contacting Public Officials   Despite the low voter turnout levels in the United States, however, Americans are actually more likely than people in other countries to participate actively in campaigns.[15] During the 1996 presidential campaign, some 7 percent of adults said they gave money to a party or candidate, 9 percent said they had attended political meetings, 10 percent had attended a political rally, and 4 percent had worked actively in a campaign organization.[16] Much the same thing is true of contacting public officials; about one-third (34 percent) of Americans say they have done so during the past year, most often with local elected officials.[17] Americans are also far more likely than citizens in other democracies to be involved in organizations, of both the private and public variety (see Chapter 7), that play such an important role in our electoral politics.[18]

Who Participates?

Not all Americans participate equally in politics; the evidence shows that political participation varies a great deal according to people's income, education, age, and ethnicity. This means that some kinds of people have more representation and influence with elected officials than others and that, other things being equal, are more likely to get their preferences and interests reflected in what government does. This unequal representation, which violates the fundamental democratic norm of political equality (see the discussion of this point in Chapter 1), suggests that American politics is not as democratic as it might be.

Income and Education

For the most part, politically active people tend to be those with higher-than-average incomes and more formal education.[19] These people are also more likely to vote. In 1996, 79 percent of those with incomes of $90,000 or above said they had voted, but only 51 percent of those with incomes under $20,000 said they had done so. Only 34 percent of the unemployed said they had voted.[20] In 1996, 73 percent of adults with four or more years of college reported that they had voted, but only 49 percent of high school graduates and 30 percent of those who had not graduated from high school had done so (see Figure 10.3).

Some statistical analyses have indicated that the crucial factor in voter turnout is level of formal education. When other factors are controlled, college-educated people are much more likely to tell interviewers that they have voted than the less educated. There are several possible reasons: people with more education learn more about politics, are less troubled by registration requirements, and are more confident in their ability to affect political life.

At the same time, citizens with lower incomes also tend to participate less by working in campaigns, giving money, contacting officials, and the like. Wealthier Americans, who have more time, more money, and more knowledge of how to get things done, tend to be much more active politically. As a result, they may have

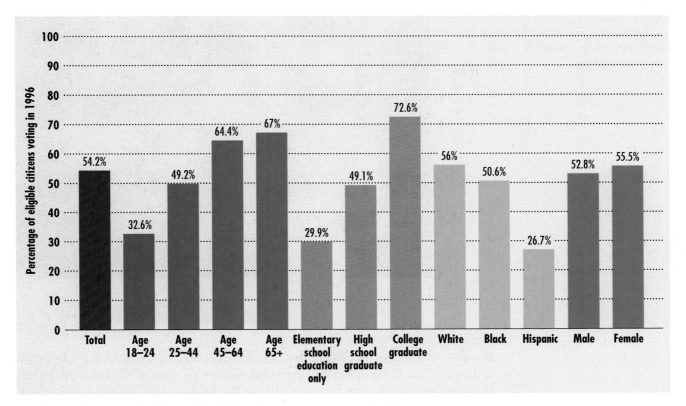

Figure 10.3 ● **1996 Presidential Election Turnout by Social Group**

Age, education, race, ethnicity, and gender all affect voting habits. Members of certain social groups are more likely to vote in elections than others.

Source: U.S. Bureau of the Census.

more political clout than their fellow citizens. This class bias in political participation is much greater in the United States than in most other advanced countries because none of our political parties explicitly represent and try to mobilize the working and lower classes, as parties in parliamentary democracies do.

Race and Ethnicity

In the past, fewer black people than whites voted, but now the proportions are more nearly equal: 56 percent of whites and 51 percent of blacks voted in 1996 (see Figure 10.3). The remaining differences result from blacks' lower average levels of income and education. Blacks are at least equally likely to vote, and sometimes more likely, than whites of similar educational and income backgrounds.

Hispanics, however, have historically had very low participation rates; only 27 percent voted in 1996. Many Hispanics are discouraged from participating by low incomes, language problems, or suspicion of government authorities. But, in the 1998 elections, the turnout rate for Hispanics jumped to 50 percent and made a difference in states where Hispanic voters are concentrated and where several anti-immigrant measures were on the ballot: California, Texas, and Florida. It will be interesting to see if Hispanic voting rates hold firm at this level or move back toward more traditional levels. For their part, Asian-Americans show growing levels of participation, especially in giving money to candidates and parties.

Hispanics have the potential to be an important force in American politics, but low registration and voting rates have limited their influence until quite recently.

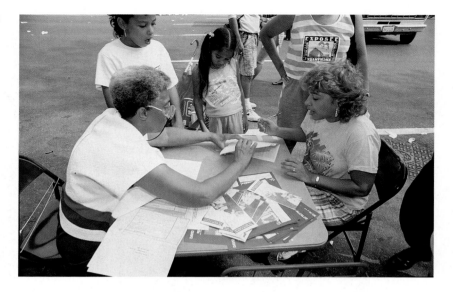

Age

The very young are less likely than their elders to vote: Only 33 percent of 18- to 24-year-olds did so in 1996, compared with 81 percent of 65- to 74-year-olds. Young people tend to be less rooted in communities, less familiar with registration and voting procedures, and less clear about what stake they have in elections.[21]

CourseCompass

WEB EXPLORATION

Young People and the Vote

Issue:　Only a minority of Americans regularly vote, with the lowest rates found among those in the 18- to 29-year-old category.

Site:　Access the Gallup Poll through the "Course Documents" section of your online course. Go to the "Web Explorations" section for Chapter 10, click on "Young People and the Vote," and open "vote." Select the special report dated November 2, 1999, and read about who votes regularly and why.

What You've Learned:　Do you vote regularly? Do your friends and acquaintances vote regularly? If not, do your reasons and those of your friends and acquaintances match the reasons given in the Gallup report? Does the report ring true? Do Gallup's findings trouble you in any way, or do you think that nonvoting is not much of an issue?

HINT:　Politicians generally respond not to the public in the abstract but to voters who have a say in whether they win or hold their offices. Low voter turnout among young Americans may be one reason government leaders seem to pay more attention to issues that matter for older Americans.

Gender

The gender gap in voting participation (but not in other forms of campaign activity)[22] has disappeared entirely. Indeed, in 1996, women voted at slightly higher rates than men (again, see Figure 10.3). This was not always the case. This has changed over the past two decades because the educational attainments of women have improved; more women than ever are in the paid workforce; and women's issues, such as pay equity and abortion, have become prominent parts of the political agenda.

Does It Matter Who Votes?

Some observers have argued that it doesn't matter if many people don't vote because their preferences aren't much different from those who do; the results would be about the same if everyone voted. In some elections, nonvoters have shown support for the same candidate who won, so their votes would apparently have changed nothing,[23] and some surveys have indicated that nonvoters' policy preferences are little different from those of voters. A few scholars have even claimed that low voter turnout is a positive benefit, on the supposition that less educated people are uninformed on the issues anyway and that nonvoting increases the stability of the system and discourages demagoguery.[24]

However, we should not be too quick to accept these arguments, just as few now accept the nineteenth-century view that there was no need for women to vote because their husbands could protect their interests. Even when the expressed preferences of nonvoters or nonparticipators do not look very distinctive, their objective circumstances, and therefore their needs for government services, may differ markedly.[25] Latinos, the young, and citizens with low incomes might benefit from government programs that are of less interest to other citizens. A political system that included and mobilized these people vigorously might produce quite different policies. Of course, we cannot be sure that they would do so, but one sign of what a difference participation can make is that when black Americans won effective voting rights, the number of elected black officials rose sharply and non-black politicians and officials paid more attention to black constituents (see Chapters 1 and 8).

In any case, broader participation in U.S. elections would increase popular sovereignty and political equality and would thus contribute to democracy. The limited number of Americans who vote is one major respect in which the struggle for democracy has not fully succeeded.

LongmanParticipate

CourseCompass

visual literacy

Voter Turnout: Who Votes? Do Americans Vote as Much as Other Citizens?

Campaigning for Office

The ideas we discussed about how elections might ensure democratic policy-making all depend in various ways on what sorts of choices are presented to the voters. It makes a difference what kind of people run for office, whether they take clear policy stands, whether those stands differ from each other, and whether they stand for what the average voter wants. In evaluating how democratic our elections are, therefore, we need to examine what kinds of alternatives are put before the voters in campaigns. In this chapter, we focus on presidential campaigns. Congressional campaigns are addressed in Chapter 11.

Contending for the Party Presidential Nomination

The major party candidates for president of the United States are formally chosen well before the November election, and are effectively chosen even before the parties hold nominating conventions. In 2000, it was evident by mid-March that George W. Bush and Al Gore would be the presidential candidates of their respective parties, for example. Candidates are drawn from a rather small pool. Despite what some parents tell their children, not every American has a significant chance of becoming president or of being nominated for president by a major party.

Who Has a Chance In any given presidential election, only a handful of candidates are serious possibilities. So far in American history, these have virtually always been middle-aged or elderly white men with extensive formal educations, fairly high incomes, members of a Protestant denomination, and substantial experience as public figures—usually as government officials (especially governors or senators) or military heroes. Movie stars, media commentators, business executives, and others who would be president almost always have to perform lesser government service before they are seriously considered for the presidency. Ronald Reagan, for example, most of whose career was spent acting in motion pictures and on television, served as governor of California before being elected president.

In recent years, the presidency has been practically monopolized by former governors (who have demonstrated executive ability), vice-presidents (who have had a close look at how the job is done), and U.S. senators (who have been exposed to a wide range of U.S. foreign and domestic policies). The best single stepping-stone to become president is clearly the vice-presidency, itself usually filled by former senators or governors. Since 1900, 5 of the 18 presidents have succeeded from the vice-presidency after the president's death or resignation, and two others, Nixon and Bush (the elder), were former vice-presidents elected in their own right.

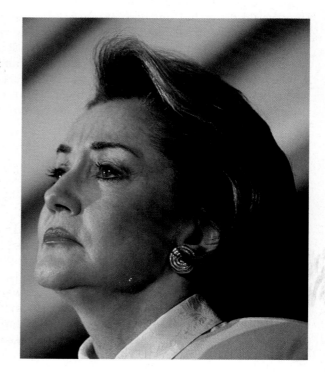

Elizabeth Dole's bid to become the first woman presidential nominee of one of the two major parties ended early when she was unable to attract much financial support or support among Republican voters. She was forced to withdraw from the race before the first GOP nomination contest in the 2000 campaign, the Iowa caucuses.

Serious candidates for president almost invariably represent mainstream American values and policy preferences. Seldom does an "extreme" candidate get very far. Serious candidates are also generally acceptable to the business community and have enthusiastic support from at least some sectors of industry or finance. And they must be considered "presidential" by the mass media.

Getting Started   A person who wants to run for the presidency usually begins at least two or three years before the election by testing the waters, asking friends and financial backers if they will support a run, and observing how people react to the mythical "Great Mentioner." A friendly journalist may write that Senator Blathers "has been mentioned" as a smart, attractive, strong candidate; Blathers waits to see whether anyone agrees. The would-be candidate may commission a national survey to check for name recognition and a positive image. He or she may put together an exploratory committee to round up private endorsements, commitments, and financial contributions, perhaps setting up private political action committees to gather money.

Many potential candidates, even prominent ones, drop out before getting started. Thus, Lamar Alexander, Dan Quayle, and Elizabeth Dole dropped out of the 2000 Republican nomination fight well before the first major hurdle, the Iowa caucuses, citing their failure to raise enough money as the deciding factor.

If all goes well in the early stages, the presidential aspirant becomes more serious, assembling a group of close advisers, formulating strategy, officially announcing his or her candidacy, forming a fund-raising operation, and putting together organizations ("Draft Blathers" or "Citizens for Blathers" committees) in key states. Early money is crucial to finance organization and advertising and to qualify for federal matching funds later.[26] Those who fail to raise early money almost always fail in the first primaries and eventually drop out. By October 1999, months before the first primary, George W. Bush had already gathered $57 million, discouraging several potential rivals; Steve Forbes had set aside almost as much from his personal fortune.

One important early decision concerns how to pitch the campaign: as an outsider getting rid of the mess in Washington, D.C. (Steve Forbes)? As the most competent and most centrist standard-bearer for the party (Bob Dole or Al Gore)? As the voice for a particular program (the focused anti-abortion approach of Gary Bauer and Alan Keyes) or for a vague but inclusive philosophy (the "compassionate conservatism" of George W. Bush)? Or, as a person with particular character traits, tested under extreme conditions (John McCain)? Another major decision involves which state primaries, caucuses, and straw votes to enter. Each entry takes a lot of money, energy, and organization, and any loss is damaging; many candidates drop out after just a few early defeats, as Steve Forbes and Gary Bauer did in 2000. To win the nomination, it is generally necessary to put together a string of primary victories.

Deciding on the theme of the campaign and the strategy to deliver the message is increasingly in the hands of hired pollsters and campaign consultants.[27] Alternative approaches to themes, messages, and issues are proposed; tested with the public in focus groups and surveys; and then crafted into stump speeches, television and radio spots, and Web pages.

Primaries and Caucuses   Party nominees for president are chosen every four years at national party **conventions**, made up of state delegations from around the country. Since the 1970s, most of the delegates to the conventions have been chosen in state **primary elections**, with direct voting by citizens. (Some primaries are open to all voters, as in the 2000 GOP primaries in South Carolina and Michigan; others are closed, reserved for those who register with

LongmanParticipate

CourseCompass

simulation
**You Are a
Presidential
Campaign
Consultant**

convention

A gathering of delegates who nominate a party's presidential candidate.

primary elections

State elections in which delegates to national presidential nominating conventions are chosen.

Senator John McCain acknowledges his supporters after his upset of front-runner George W. Bush in the 2000 GOP New Hampshire primary. Although McCain won a handful of additional primaries, he was unable to hold off the Bush onslaught and lost his nomination bid.

caucus

A meeting of party activists to choose delegates to a national presidential nominating convention.

the party whose primary election it is.) The Democrats' popularly elected delegates are supplemented by "superdelegates," usually members of Congress or local officials. A few states use **caucuses**, where active party members and officials choose delegates to state conventions, which in turn select the delegates to the national convention.

Because the states and the parties—not the federal government—control this nominating process, the system is a disorganized, even chaotic one, and it changes from one election to the next. Some states have primaries for both parties on the same day (including the all-important New Hampshire primaries); others hold primaries for the parties on separate dates. States are particularly anxious that they are not ignored, so an increasing number of them have moved their primary dates forward in the calendar. States with late primaries, even very large ones such as California, have discovered in recent elections that the winners of early primaries had, for all intents and purposes, sewed up the party nominations, discounting the importance of their own primaries. As a result, the primary season was "front-loaded" in 2000, with the bulk of delegates selected for both parties between the New Hampshire primaries on February 1 and the Illinois primaries on March 21.

It is especially important for a candidate to establish momentum by winning early primaries and caucuses. Early winners get press attention, financial contributions, and better standings in the polls as voters and contributors decide they are viable candidates and must have some merit if people in other states have supported them. All these factors—attention from the media, money, and increased popular support—help the candidates who win early contests go on to win more and more contests.[28]

Since 1952, no national party convention has taken more than one ballot to nominate its candidate for the presidency, and the preconvention front-runner has always been the nominee. Now the trick is to win delegates in primaries and caucuses, which, in reality, decide the nomination.[29]

How to Win   Four main factors affect candidates' success in gathering delegates.

1. *General attractiveness,* especially the personal image conveyed by television, but also the candidate's stands on issues and his or her connections in the public mind with the good or bad times that the country is enjoying.

2. *Viability,* as judged by the media and as reflected in the polls. Citizens are reluctant to nominate or vote for someone who has no chance of winning.

3. *Organizational strength,* particularly the number of hardworking activists who will pack the caucuses, stuff envelopes, go door to door, and get voters to the polls.

4. *Money* to pay for the television ads, organization, and travel that a campaign requires. Money can help make candidates look more attractive, win votes, seem more viable, and build strong organizations.

The Convention   Because the front-runner now comes to the national convention with enough delegates to win on the first ballot, the gathering has become a coronation ceremony in which prepledged delegates ratify the selection of the leading candidate, accept that candidate's choice for the vice-presidency, and put on a colorful show for the media and the country. Enthusiasm and unity are staged for the national television audience; it is a disaster if serious conflicts break out or the timing goes wrong.

Rarely nowadays is there a real contest at the national convention, in which delegates actually require repeated balloting to make a choice. Rarely, for example, do they have to decide between their "professional" heads and their "purist" hearts—whether to nominate a likely winner or someone who stands for ideas that they hold dear (as when the Republicans renominated President Ford rather than their favorite, Ronald Reagan, in 1976).

The impression conveyed by political conventions can have an important impact on elections. Violent confrontations between police and demonstrators opposed to the Vietnam War during the 1968 Democratic convention in Chicago hurt nominee Hubert Humphrey's chances. In contrast, the 1996 Democratic convention (also in Chicago) more nearly resembled a coronation ceremony.

The evidence from polls indicates that at virtually all recent national conventions, the party nominee has been the surviving candidate who has had the most support from rank-and-file party identifiers in the nation as a whole. The candidates who have survived the hurdles of raising money, mobilizing activists, and winning primary votes do not, of course, necessarily include the most popular potential presidents in the country; if they did, Colin Powell would probably have won the Republican presidential nomination in 1996. And the big differences between the delegates of the two parties tend to push the two parties' nominees and issue positions away from each other, in a responsible party rather than a purely electoral competition process. Still, the parties do try to appeal to the voters.

Nomination Politics and Democracy   What does all this have to do with democratic control of government? Several things. On the one hand, as we have indicated, the nomination process has some success in coming up with candidates who take stands with wide popular appeal, much as electoral competition theories dictate. On the other hand, as the sharp differences between Republican and Democratic convention delegates suggest, Republican and Democratic nominees tend to differ in certain systematic ways, in responsible party fashion. Party platforms—the parties' official statements of their stand on issues—tend to include appeals to average voters but also distinctive appeals to each party's constituencies.

Both these tendencies might be considered good for democracy. However, the crucial role of party activists and money givers in selecting candidates means that nominees and their policy stands are chosen partly to appeal to party elites and financial contributors, rather than to ordinary voters. Thus, neither party's nominee may stand for what ordinary citizens want, the result being voter dissatisfaction and no ideal democratic outcome.

Incumbents   We have been focusing on how outsiders and political challengers try to win party nominations. Things are very different for incumbent presidents seeking reelection, like Bill Clinton in 1996 or George Bush in 1992. These candidates must also enter and win primaries, but they have the machinery of government working for them and, if times are reasonably good, a unified party behind them. They campaign on the job, taking credit for policy successes while discounting or blaming others such as Congress for failures. Winning renomination as president is usually easy, except in cases of disaster such as the 1968 Vietnam War debacle for Lyndon Johnson (see Chapter 5).

The Autumn Campaign

Incumbents and challengers alike, having won a party nomination, must face the autumn campaign, which traditionally began in early September (on Labor Day) but now tends to start right after the conventions or even earlier. In 2000, for example, George W. Bush and Al Gore were aiming fire at each other by March and April.

For the general election, if not before, the candidates set up a campaign organization in each state, sending aides to coordinate backers and local party leaders. Intense money raising continues, and a new round of public financing kicks in. Candidates plan itineraries to make three or four speeches in different media markets each day, concentrating on big states but also touching the whole

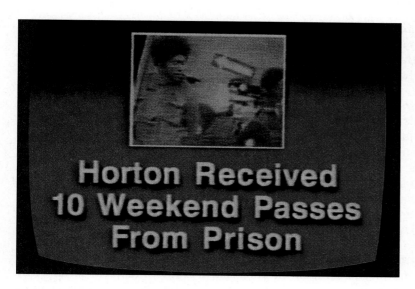

In 1988, a Republican group used the case of Willie Horton, a convicted murderer who raped a woman while on furlough from a Massachusetts prison, to imply that Democratic presidential candidate Michael Dukakis, Massachusett's governor at the time, was soft on crime.

country. In all of this, hired pollsters and campaign consultants are deeply involved, playing a role in virtually all tactical and strategic decision making.[30]

A new media blitz begins, with many brief spot commercials on television, including "attack" ads such as Clinton's in 1992 mocking George Bush's "read my lips, no new taxes" pledge (which he did not keep) and Dole's in 1996 pointing to Clinton's flawed character. Political consultants use voter focus groups to identify hot-button emotional appeals. Negative advertising has been heavily criticized as simplistic and misleading, but it has often proved effective and is difficult to control or counteract.

Another element of strategy is to get potential supporters registered and to the polls. Organized labor often energizes turnout campaigns for the Democrats, and conservative Christian groups do so for the Republicans. As we have noted, low-income and minority citizens have sometimes been ignored by both major parties; the Nation of Islam and various Hispanic groups now show signs of trying to mobilize them. Asian-Americans are also becoming more active.

Informing Voters   What kinds of information do voters get in presidential campaigns?

Issues   Some of this information concerns issues. In accord with electoral competition theories, both the Republican and the Democratic candidates usually try to appeal to the average voter by taking similar, popular stands on policy, especially foreign policy. Gore and Bush both stayed close to the center in 2000, as did Clinton and Dole in 1996. But as responsible party theories suggest, Republican and Democratic candidates usually do differ somewhat on a number of issues, such as medical care, federal aid to education, social welfare, civil rights, the environment, and abortion. On these issues, the Democratic candidate tends to take a more liberal stand than the Republican, just as Democratic party identifiers, activists, money givers, and convention delegates tend to be more liberal than their Republican counterparts.

Presidential candidates usually do not say a great deal about specific policies; they tend to be vague and ambiguous to avoid offending voters who disagree with them. No one could object to George Bush's 1988 promises to be an "education president" and an "environmental president" or to Clinton's 1996 promise to "build a bridge to the twenty-first century." Candidates often emphasize symbolic matters that appeal to virtually everyone, such as George Bush's invocation of the American flag and the Pledge of Allegiance. In 2000, however, Gore and Bush talked a great deal about issues and policies.

Past Performance   Often candidates talk about past performance and future goals. The "outs" blame the "ins" for wars, recessions, and other calamities. The "ins" brag about how they have brought peace and prosperity and paint a warm picture of a glorious future, without saying exactly how it will come about.

Incumbent presidents, of course, can do things that accurately or inaccurately suggest successful performance. They can try to schedule recessions for off years, pumping up the economy in time for reelection. Or they can make dramatic foreign policy moves just before Election Day, like Nixon's 1972 trips to the Soviet Union and China.

Personal Characteristics   Most of all, however, voters get a chance to learn about the real or alleged personal characteristics of the candidates. Even when the candidates are talking about something else, they give an impression of either competence or incompetence. Jimmy Carter, for example, emphasized his expertise as a "nuclear engineer," whereas Gerald Ford was haunted by films of him stumbling on airplane ramps.

Candidates also come across as warm or cold. Dwight D. Eisenhower's radiant grin appeared everywhere in 1952 and 1956, as Reagan's did in 1984, but Richard Nixon was perceived as cold and aloof in 1968, despite clever efforts at selling his personality.

Still another dimension of candidates' personalities is strength or weakness. George Bush overcame the so-called wimp factor in 1988 with his tough talk about crime and the flag. Merely by surviving many personal attacks in 1992 and 1996, Clinton appeared strong and resilient.

The sparse and ambiguous treatment of policy issues in campaigns, as well as the emphasis on past performance and personal competence, fits better with ideas about electoral reward and punishment than with responsible parties or issue-oriented electoral competition. Candidate personalities are not irrelevant to the democratic control of government. Obviously, it is useful for voters to pick presidents who possess competence, warmth, and strength. And citizens may be more skillful in judging people than in figuring out complicated policy issues.

Voters can be fooled, however, by dirty tricks or slick advertising that sells presidential candidates' personalities and tears down the opponent. Moreover, the focus on personal imagery may distract attention from policy stands. If candidates who favor unpopular policies are elected on the basis of attractive personal images, democratic control of policymaking is weakened. By the purchase of advertising and the hiring of smart consultants, money may, in effect, overcome the popular will.

Money and Elections

Most observers agree that money creates problems in U.S. presidential elections. The main problem is probably not that too much money is spent but that the money comes from private sources that may influence government policymaking after the election is over.

The Cost of Presidential Campaigns   Presidential campaigns cost a great deal of money. In 1996, for example, *prenomination* spending by all candidates totaled $237.2 million, up from $153.2 million in 1992.[31] The Clinton and Dole

© 1997 Dayton Daily News/Tribune Media Services

campaigns, taking into account Democratic and Republican National Committee expenditures for them, spent another $328.1 million. In 2000, contenders had raised more than $210 million before the first primary in New Hampshire. In the general election, the Gore and Bush campaigns spent at record levels. In addition, the political parties spent a lot of unregulated **soft money**, some of which helps presidential candidates as well as candidates for the House and the Senate. Interest groups also run parallel campaigns on the issues, which are often thinly veiled additions to the campaigns of the candidates and the parties, as we reported in Chapter 7.

Looked at from another angle, however, total presidential campaign spending may not be so big, even if it has topped $1 billion, as some have suggested. The advertising budgets of Procter & Gamble and Philip Morris, by way of comparison, are each more than $2 billion per year. Far more problematic than the cost of presidential elections for democracy, we would argue, is the source of campaign money.

soft money

Expenditures by political parties on general public education, voter registration, and voter mobilization.

Where Does the Money Come From?   Since 1971, part of the money for presidential election campaigns has come from the federal treasury, paid by the taxpayers. Taxpayers can check off a box on their tax returns to authorize a $3 contribution from public funds. The government matches small contributions to candidates during the primaries and finances the party nominees who agree to spending limits. In 2000, the Gore and Bush campaigns each received $68 million. Public financing, although not popular with all citizens, has the advantage of eliminating any question of bribery or buying of favors from private interests. In 1996, however, public money accounted for only about 20 percent of Clinton's and Dole's total expenditures. The remainder came from contributions by individuals, businesses, labor unions, and special-interest groups. Similar pattern of money giving held for the 2000 presidential contest. The same "reforms" of 1974 and later that required candidates to report the sources of their funds and that prohibited any individual from contributing more than $1,000 directly to a candidate also left large loopholes. For example, political action committees (PACs) were legalized, even for businesses and unions, that had previously been prohibited from making political contributions. PACs are now allowed to contribute up to

$5,000 per candidate per election; furthermore, people are permitted to contribute $5,000 to each of as many PACs as they like, so that big interests (e.g., major corporations and large membership organizations) simply create multiple PACs or bundle contributions from individual members and employees.

Most important, people and organizations can contribute unlimited amounts of soft money to national, state, and local political parties, as reported in Chapter 7. And people and organizations can spend unlimited amounts of money in support of any candidate so long as the ad or appeal does not specifically ask people to vote for or against a particular candidate. The "fat cats" are back, if they ever left; anyone who wants to invest a lot of money in politics can figure out a way to do it under the present rules.

Does Money Talk?   Does money determine the outcome of the presidential elections in November? Scholars are generally agreed that it does not.[32] Once a presidential campaign is under way, each of the major party candidates has at his disposal all of the organizational resources of the party organization and money from traditional party contributors and allied interest groups; each candidate generally has enough money to run a credible campaign. Where money seems to count the most is in the campaigns within each of the parties for the nomination. In the general election, one cannot safely predict the outcome based on who has spent the most money.

Money may talk at a later stage, however. It is widely believed, although difficult to prove, that contributors of money often get something back. The point is not that presidential candidates take outright bribes in exchange for policy favors. Indeed, exchanges between politicians and money givers are complex and varied, sometimes yielding little benefit to contributors. Undeniably, however, cozy relationships do tend to develop between politicians and major money givers. Contributors gain access to, and a friendly hearing from, those whom they help to win office.

WEB EXPLORATION

Money and Presidential Campaigns

Issue: Money is the "mother's milk" of politics, as the saying goes, and presidential campaigns require lots of milk.

Site: Follow the money trail to the presidential candidates and the political parties at the Center for Public Integrity site through the "Course Documents" section of your online course. Go to the "Web Explorations" section for Chapter 10, click on "Money and Presidential Campaigns," and open "money." Select "Campaign 2000," then "The Buying of the President 2000." Select "The Money Trail." Next select the "Top 25 Career Patron List," and see who supported George W. Bush, John McCain, Al Gore, and Bill Bradley.

What You've Learned: Do you discern any pattern in the profile of contributors to the major party presidential candidates? By region? By industry? By interest group? Are there any surprises in the list of contributors?

HINT: Note that contributions from big business are not confined to Republican presidential candidates.

It is clear that money givers are different from average citizens. They have special interests of their own. As we have indicated, a large amount of campaign money comes from large corporations, investment banking firms, wealthy families, labor unions, professional associations (e.g., doctors, lawyers, or realtors), and issue-oriented groups such as the National Rifle Association, the Christian Coalition, and the National Abortion Rights League. The big contributors generally do not represent ordinary workers, consumers, or taxpayers, let alone minorities or the poor. Surveys show that the individuals who give money tend to have much higher incomes and more conservative views on economic issues than the average American.[33]

The result is political inequality. Those who are well organized or have a lot of money to spend on politics have a better chance of influencing policy than ordinary citizens do, and they tend to influence it in directions different from those the general public would want. This is one way in which the interest groups described in Chapter 7 can turn their economic power into political power, overcoming the legal equality embodied in the idea of one person, one vote. The role of money in presidential nomination and election campaigns (and in congressional campaigns, as we show in Chapter 11) is a major problem for the working of democracy in the United States.

Election Outcomes

After the parties and candidates have presented their campaigns, the voters decide. Exactly how people make their voting decisions affects how well or how poorly elections contribute to the democratic control of government.

How Voters Decide

Years of scholarly research have made it clear that feelings about the parties, the candidates, and the issues have substantial effects on how people vote.[34]

Social Characteristics   People's socioeconomic status, religion, and ethnic background are significantly related to how they vote. Since the 1930s, for example, African-Americans, Jews, and lower-income citizens have tended to vote heavily for Democrats, while white Protestants and upper-income Americans have voted mostly for Republicans: in 2000, 90 percent of blacks, but only 42 percent of whites, voted for Al Gore against George W. Bush; 57 percent of people with family incomes under $15,000, but only 44 percent of those with incomes over $75,000, voted for Gore; and 79 percent of Jews, but only 18 percent of white born-again Christians, voted for Gore. Recently, women have voted for Democrats in greater number than have men; they cast 54 percent of their vote for Gore in 2000. Older people have traditionally supported Democratic candidates more often, although this has begun to change. In 2000, they gave 50 percent of their vote to Bush. (see Figure 10.4).

Party Loyalties   To some extent, these social patterns work through long-term attachments to, or identification with, political parties. As indicated earlier, a majority of Americans still say they consider themselves Republicans or Democrats. Party loyalties vary among different groups of the population, often because of past or present differences between the parties on policy issues, especially economic and social issues.[35] For this reason, party cues help many people vote for candidates who are close to them on the issues.

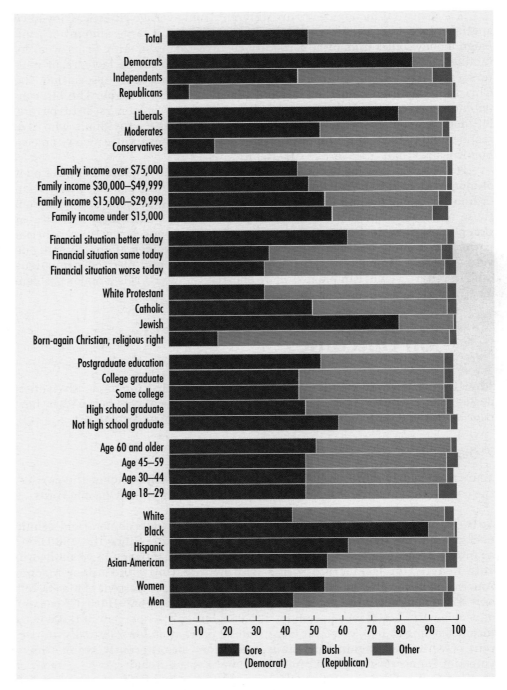

Figure 10.4 ● **Presidential Vote in 2000, by Social Group**

Minorities, lower-income voters, and women tended to vote for Al Gore in the 2000 election, while white Protestants, higher-income people, and men tended to favor George W. Bush.

Source: *Voter News Service,* November 8, 2000.

Party loyalties are very good predictors of how people will vote.[36] Those who say they consider themselves Republicans tend to vote for Republican candidates in one election after another, and those who consider themselves

Ronald Reagan's warmth, charm, and sincerity contributed to his enormous appeal not only among Republican voters but among Democrats as well. His personal attractiveness helped overcome the slight lead held by Democrats in voter party identification and contributed to Republican victories in the 1980 and 1984 presidential elections.

Democrats vote for Democratic candidates. This is especially true in congressional elections and in state and local races, where most voters know little more about the candidates than their party labels, but the party loyalty factor is extremely important in presidential elections as well. Thus, in 2000, 86 percent of Democratic identifiers voted for Gore, and 91 percent of Republican identifiers voted for Bush.

Candidates   Another reason presidential election outcomes have not simply reflected the party balance and the Democrats have lost so often is that voters pay a lot of attention to their perceptions of the personal characteristics of candidates. They vote heavily for candidates who have experience, appear strong and decisive, and convey personal warmth. The Republican candidate in 1952 and 1956, Dwight D. Eisenhower, had a tremendous advantage in these respects over his Democratic opponent, Adlai Stevenson;[37] so did Republicans Richard Nixon over George McGovern in 1972, Ronald Reagan over Walter Mondale in 1984, and George Bush over Michael Dukakis in 1988. Only in 1964 did the Democratic candidate (Lyndon Johnson) appeal to voters substantially more than the Republican candidate (Barry Goldwater). In elections between 1952 and 1972, the contrast between Republican and Democratic candidates typically gained the Republicans 4 or 5 percentage points—just enough to overcome the Democrats' advantage in the **normal vote.**

Issues   Voters also pay attention to issues. Sometimes this means choosing between different policy proposals for the future (as in the responsible party voting model), such as Reagan's 1980 promises to cut back federal government activity or Clinton's 1992 pledges of jobs and a middle-class tax cut. More often, however, issue voting has meant **retrospective voting** (the electoral reward and punishment model), making judgments about the past, especially on major questions about war or peace and the state of the economy. The voters tend to reward the incumbent party for what they see as good times and to punish it for what they see as bad times, though this did not occur in 2000 for reasons that are still being debated by political observors.[38]

normal vote

The proportion of the votes that each party would win if party identification alone affected voting decisions.

retrospective voting

Voting on the basis of past government performance.

Foreign Policy   Foreign policy can be important. Bitter disillusionment over the Korean War hurt the Democrats in 1952, just as the Vietnam War cost them in 1968, and unhappiness about American hostages in Iran and the Soviet intervention in Afghanistan hurt Jimmy Carter in 1980. During nearly all of the past half-century, in fact, Republican candidates have been seen as better at providing foreign policy strength and at keeping us out of war.

The Economy   The economy also matters a great deal. After severe economic downturns, Americans tend to vote the incumbent party out of office, as they did the Republicans during the Great Depression in 1932. Since that time, the Democrats have generally been seen as the party of prosperity. This advantage disappeared for a while, after a combined onslaught of inflation and recession hurt Democrat Jimmy Carter in the 1980 election. But in 1992, the electorate punished Republican George Bush for the poor state of the economy and in 1996 rewarded Bill Clinton for being president during good economic times.

New Issues   In recent years, new issues have also become important to voters. These include deficit cutting, law and order, the environment, affirmative action, and abortion. Becoming increasingly important are issues related to globalization, including free trade.

The Electoral College

As many Americans may have learned for the first time in 2000, the outcome of presidential elections is determined not by the number of popular votes cast for each candidate; it depends on the votes in the electoral college.

When American voters think they are voting for a presidential candidate whose name appears on the ballot, they are actually voting for a slate of **electors**—equal to the number of U.S. senators and representatives from their state—who have promised to support the candidate. (Very rarely have electors reneged on their promises and cast ballots for someone else.) Nearly all states now have winner-take-all systems, which select the entire slate of electors for the candidate who won the most popular votes; Maine and Nebraska, in slight variations, choose electors by congressional district rather than statewide.

The "college" of electors from the different states never actually meets; instead, the electors meet in their respective states and send to Washington, D.C., lists of how they have voted (see the Twelfth Amendment to the Constitution). If a candidate receives a majority of all the electoral votes in the country, he is elected president. Not since 1824 has it been necessary to resort to the odd constitutional provisions that apply when no one gets a majority of electoral votes: the House of Representatives chooses among the top three candidates, by majority vote of state delegations.

Most of the time, this peculiar electoral college system works about the same way as if Americans chose their presidents by direct popular vote, though this was not true in 2000 when Bush won the electoral vote while losing the popular vote. The old idea that electors would exercise their independent judgments is long gone. But the system does have certain consequences:

●   *It magnifies the popular support of winners.* A candidate who wins in many states, by a narrow margin in each, can win a "landslide" in the electoral college. In 1996, for example, Bill Clinton's 49 percent of the popular vote translated into 379 electoral votes, or 70 percent of the total. Ordinarily, this magnification just adds legitimacy to the democratic

electors

Representatives who are elected in the states to formally choose the U.S. president.

choice, especially when the winner has only a **plurality** of the popular vote, that is, more than anybody else but less than a majority of all votes. Many of our presidents have been elected with less than 50 percent of the popular vote—most recently, Clinton (1992 and 1996), Richard Nixon (1968), John Kennedy (1960), and Harry Truman (1948).

- *It may let the less popular candidate win.* A president can be elected who had *fewer* votes than an opponent, if those votes happened to produce narrow margins in many states. Such a result has occurred three times—in 1876, when Rutherford Hayes defeated Samuel Tilden, in 1888, when Benjamin Harrison beat the more popular Grover Cleveland, and in 2000, when George W. Bush defeated Al Gore. (Gore beat Bush by over one-half a million votes nationally). Several early-nineteenth-century presidents were probably chosen with only small fractions of the popular vote, although we cannot be sure because some of the statistics are unreliable. Most notably, in 1824, John Quincy Adams defeated the very popular Andrew Jackson in the House of Representatives.

- *It discourages third parties.* Our constitutional arrangements for a single president and single-member congressional districts (rather than proportional representation) already discourage third parties; if candidates cannot win a plurality, they get nothing. The electoral college adds symbolically to this discouragement: a third party with substantial support may get no electoral votes at all, if its support is scattered among many states. In 1992, for example, Ross Perot's impressive 19 percent of the popular vote translated into zero electoral votes because he failed to win a plurality in any single state.

plurality

More votes than any other candidate but less than a majority of all votes cast.

WEB EXPLORATION

The Electoral College

Issue: Although it had been until 2000 a very long time since a presidential candidate had won the popular vote but lost the electoral college vote (which determines who will be president), it remains the case that the margin of the electoral vote victory of a candidate always looks very different from the popular vote victory.

Site: Compare the popular vote and the electoral college vote through the "Course Documents" section of your online course. Go to the "Web Explorations" section for Chapter 10, click on "The Electoral College," and open "college." Select "Electoral College Boxscores," then look at the period 1944–1996.

What You've Learned: Calculate the winner's percentage of the popular vote and the electoral vote for each election. What is the main effect of the Electoral College? Is the effect you found good or bad for American democracy? Would you support a proposal to change our present system into a direct popular voting system? Why?

HINT: Some scholars believe that the magnification of the winning candidate's margin of victory adds to the winner's mandate and legitimacy among the people, making for more effective government.

HOW DEMOCRATIC ARE WE?

PROPOSITION: Elections don't matter much in determining what government leaders do. It's probably the reason so many Americans don't bother to vote.

AGREE: The people are not able to control the government by means of elections. For one thing, our political parties are such that they undermine the ability of elections to play the democratic role reserved for them in responsible party government, electoral competition, and electoral reward-and-punishment theories of democratic elections. The kinds of parties we have do not allow voters to choose future policy directions or hold elected officials responsible for their actions, or allow parties to conform to the wishes of the median voter. For another thing, the political equality norm of democracy is violated by the role of interest groups and money in elections. Fully aware of this, and unhappy about it, potential voters stay away from the polls.

DISAGREE: Scholars have shown that government officials, in the long run, do what the American people want them to do about two-thirds of the time. Although a variety of instruments help convey what the people want to officials—public opinion polls, interest groups, and social movements—it is ultimately the fact that officials must face the voters that keeps them in line. Although nonvoting is a problem, it is not entirely clear why so many people stay away from the polls.

THE AUTHORS: In terms of the responsible party idea, the fact that Republicans tend to be more conservative than Democrats on a number of economic and social issues provides voters with a measure of democratic control by enabling them to detect differences and make choices about the future. Alternatively, through electoral punishment, voters can exercise control by reelecting successful incumbents and throwing failures out of office, thus making incumbents think ahead. Finally, electoral competition forces the parties to compete by nominating centrist candidates and by taking similar issue stands close to what most Americans want. This, in fact, may be the chief way in which citizens' policy preferences affect what their government does.

Clearly, then, U.S. elections help make the public's voice heard, but they do not bring about perfect democracy. Two key reasons are the limited and biased participation of citizens and the effects of money and activists on election outcomes. Uneven participation and the role of money and activists both impair political equality by giving some people more political influence than others.

Although elections provide a strong measure of democratic control, low voter turnout remains a problem. The causes of low turnout are varied and not strictly related to the inability of elections to provide perfect popular control of government. Low voter turnout is also explained by registration requirements, inequality of resources among citizens, tepid mobilization actions by the parties, and the "infotainment" orientation of the mass media.

People who would like to abolish the electoral college point to its narrowing of choices and the possibility of undemocratic outcomes. Those who like it claim that it discourages fraud by limiting the votes that any one state can cast, that the two-party system it encourages is good, and that the added legitimacy of electoral college "landslides" is helpful—or at least harmless.

Summary

Elections are the most important means by which citizens can exert democratic control over their government. Voters can choose *responsible parties* to carry out their distinctive programs. *Electoral competition* forces vote-seeking parties and candidates to appeal to the center of public opinion. *Electoral reward and punishment* gives officials incentives to carry out policies that will win public approval. However, none of these processes guarantees a perfectly democratic outcome.

Political participation can be conventional (voting, helping in campaigns, and contacting officials) or unconventional (protesting or demonstrating). The right to vote, originally quite limited, was expanded in various historical surges to include nearly all adults and to apply to most major offices. Turnout has declined, however, and in recent years, only about half the eligible voters have cast ballots for the presidency.

Candidates for president start by testing the waters, raising money, and forming campaign organizations; in a series of state primaries and caucuses, they seek delegates to the national nominating conventions, which generally choose a clear front-runner or the incumbent president. During the campaign, the candidates are generally vague about issues; they concentrate on building personal images and emphasizing past performance.

About one-third of the cost of presidential campaigns is paid from public funds; the rest of the money comes from individuals and organizations, many of which seek self-benefiting policies. Contributions probably hurt democracy by leading to a degree of political inequality.

Voters' decisions depend heavily on party loyalties, the personal characteristics of the candidates, and the issues, especially the state of the economy and of U.S. foreign policy. After recessions and unsuccessful wars, the incumbent party generally loses. The electoral college does not always accurately reflect popular votes. Elections matter not only when there is a clear choice but also when electoral reward or punishment occurs or when electoral competition forces both parties to take similar popular stands.

Suggestions for Further Reading

"Anonymous." *Primary Colors: A Novel of Politics.* New York: Random House, 1996.
Journalist Joe Klein's lively and sometimes ribald account of Bill Clinton's campaign for the 1992 Democratic presidential nomination, thinly disguised as fiction.

Ferguson, Thomas. *Golden Rule.* Chicago: University of Chicago Press, 1995.
A highly critical account of the role of money in recent elections.

Fiorina, Morris P. *Retrospective Voting in American National Elections.* Cambridge, MA: Harvard University Press, 1981.
A sophisticated statistical analysis of voting on the basis of party loyalty and past- and future-oriented issues.

Greenberg, Stanley, and Theda Skocpol. *The New Majority: Toward a Popular Progressive Politics.* New Haven, CT: Yale University Press, 1997.
A bold argument on how the Democratic party might forge a new and enduring majority in American politics.

Polsby, Nelson W., and Aaron Wildavsky. *Presidential Elections,* 10th ed. New York: Free Press, 2000.
A thorough textbook on the presidential nominating process, campaigning, and voting.

Verba, Sidney, Kay Lehman Schlozman, and Henry E. Brady. *Voice and Equality: Civic Volunteerism in American Politics.* Cambridge, MA: Harvard University Press, 1995.
A comprehensive analysis of inequalities in political participation and their meaning for the quality of democracy in the United States.

Internet Sources

The Center for Public Integrity   **www.publicintegrity.org/**
An especially good site for following the money trail—how campaign money is gathered and spent.

Democratic National Committee   **www.democrats.org/**
Official site of the Democratic Party with information on party positions and candidates, how to work as a volunteer or contribute money, and more.

E-Vote   **www.evote.com/**
Up-to-the-minute news and commentary on national campaigns.

The National Archives Electoral College Site
www.nara.gov/fedreg/elctcoll/index.html top
Everything there is to know about the law and practices of the Electoral College and the process by which it elects the president.

Project Votesmart   **www.vote-smart.org/**
A political portal loaded with links to information about candidates, parties, and issues.

Republican National Committee   **www.rnc.org/**
Official site of the Republican Party with information on party positions and candidates, how to work as a volunteer or contribute money, and more.

Notes

1. For further discussion, see Benjamin I. Page, *Choices and Echoes in Presidential Elections: Rational Man and Electoral Democracy* (Chicago: University of Chicago Press, 1978), ch. 2; Robert A. Dahl, *Democracy and Its Critics* (New Haven, CT: Yale University Press, 1989).

2. See Austin Ranney, *The Doctrine of Responsible Party Government: Its Origins and Present State* (Urbana: University of Illinois Press, 1962); E. E. Schattschneider, *Party Government* (New York: Holt, Rinehart & Winston, 1942).

3. Anthony Downs, *An Economic Theory of Democracy* (New York: Harper & Row, 1957); Otto Davis, Melvin Hinich, and Peter Ordeshook, "An Expository Development of a Mathematical Model of the Electoral Process," *American Political Science Review* 64 (1970), pp. 426–448.

4. See V. O. Key Jr., *Public Opinion and American Democracy* (New York: Knopf, 1961); Morris P. Fiorina, *Retrospective Voting in American National Elections* (Cambridge, MA: Harvard University Press, 1981).

5. Chilton Williamson, *American Suffrage* (Princeton, NJ: Princeton University Press, 1960), pp. 223, 241, 260. More precisely, there was universal suffrage for white male taxpayers.

6. See John Hope Franklin, *From Slavery to Freedom* (New York: Knopf, 1967); Leon Litwack, *North of Slavery* (Chicago: University of Chicago Press, 1961).

7. Walter Dean Burnham, "The Turnout Problem," in A. James Reichley, ed., *Elections, American Style* (Washington, D.C.: Brookings Institution, 1987), pp. 113–114.

8. *New York Times* (November 21, 1988), p. B16.

9. Nelson W. Polsby and Aaron Wildavsky, *Presidential Elections,* 10th ed. (New York: Chatham House/Seven Bridges Press, 2000), p. 6.

10. Polsby and Wildavsky believe that barriers to registration are more important than alienation in explaining nonvoting. See Ibid., pp. 5–7.

11. Joseph S. Nye Jr., Philip D. Zelikow, and David C. King, eds., *Why People Don't Trust Government* (Cambridge, MA: Harvard University Press, 1997).

12. See "Forum" in *The American Political Science Review* 93 (December 1999), pp. 851–910.

13. Walter Dean Burnham, "The Class Gap," *New Republic* (May 9, 1988), pp. 30–34; Steven J. Rosenstone and John Mark Hansen, *Mobilization, Participation, and Democracy in America* (New York: Macmillan, 1993); Michael Martinez and David Hill, "Did Motor Voter Work?" *American Politics Quarterly* 27 (1999), pp. 308–309.

14. David Meneffee-Libey, *The Triumph of Campaign-Centered Politics* (New York: Chatham House/Seven Bridges Press, 2000).

15. Russell Dalton, *Citizen Politics in Western Democracies* (Chatham, NJ: Chatham House, 1988), p. 42.

16. National Opinion Research Center, *The General Social Survey, 1999.*

17. Sidney Verba, Kay Lehman Schlozman, and Henry E. Brady, *Voice and Equality: Civic Volunteerism in American Politics* (Cambridge, MA: Harvard University Press, 1995), pp. 51, 56.

18. Jack C. Doppelt and Ellen Shearer, *Non-Voters: America's No-Shows* (New York: Sage, 1999); Jeffrey Berry, *The New Liberalism* (Washington, D.C.: Brookings, 1999), pp. 39–40.

19. Verba, Schlozman, and Brady, *Voice and Equality,* ch. 7; Sidney Verba and Norman H. Nie, *Participation in America* (New York: Harper & Row, 1972).

20. 1996 American National Election Study.

21. Susan A. MacManus, *Young v. Old* (Boulder, CO: Westview Press, 1996), ch. 2.

22. M. Margaret Conway, Gertrude A Steuernagel, and David W. Ahern, *Women and Political Participation* (Washington, D.C.: CQ Press, 1997), ch. 5.

23. E. J. Dionne, "If Nonvoters Had Voted: Same Winner, but Bigger," *New York Times* (November 21, 1988), p. B16.

24. Bernard R. Berelson, Paul F. Lazarsfeld, and William N. McPhee, *Voting* (Chicago: University of Chicago Press, 1954).

25. Sidney Verba, Kay Lehman Schlozman, Henry E. Brady, and Norman H. Nie, "Citizen Activity: Who Participates? What Do They Say?" *American Political Science Review* 87 (1993), pp. 303–318.

26. Polsby and Wildavsky, *Presidential Elections,* pp. 67, 99–101.

27. Ibid., pp. 65–66.

28. Larry Bartels, *Presidential Primaries and the Dynamics of Public Choice* (Princeton, NJ: Princeton University Press, 1988); John H. Aldrich, *Before the Convention* (Chicago: University of Chicago Press, 1980).

29. Stephen J. Wayne, *The Road to the White House, 1992* (New York: Worth, 2000).

30. Polsby and Wildavsky, *Presidential Elections,* pp. 157, 173, 182.

31. These and the following figures are from the Federal Election Commission's final report on the 1995–1996 election cycle.

32. Polsby and Wildavsky, *Presidential Elections,* p. 151.

33. See Verba, Schlozman, and Brady, *Voice and Equality.*

34. Efforts to sort out their relative contributions include Benjamin I. Page and Calvin Jones, "Reciprocal Effects of Policy Preferences, Party Loyalties, and the Vote," *American Political Science Review* 73 (1979), pp. 1071–1089; Gregory B. Markus and Philip E. Converse, "A Dynamic Simultaneous Equation Model of Public Choice," *American Political Science Review* 73 (1979), pp. 1066–1070.

35. Carlos Elordi, "Ideology: Assessing Its Impact on Political Choices," *Public Perspective* (March/April 2000), pp. 34–35.

36. Larry M. Bartels, "Partisanship and Voting Behavior, 1952–1996," *American Journal of Political Science* 44 (January 2000), pp. 35–50.

37. Donald E. Stokes, "Some Dynamic Elements of Contests for the Presidency," *American Political Science Review* 60 (1966), pp. 19–28.

38. Fiorina, *Retrospective Voting.*

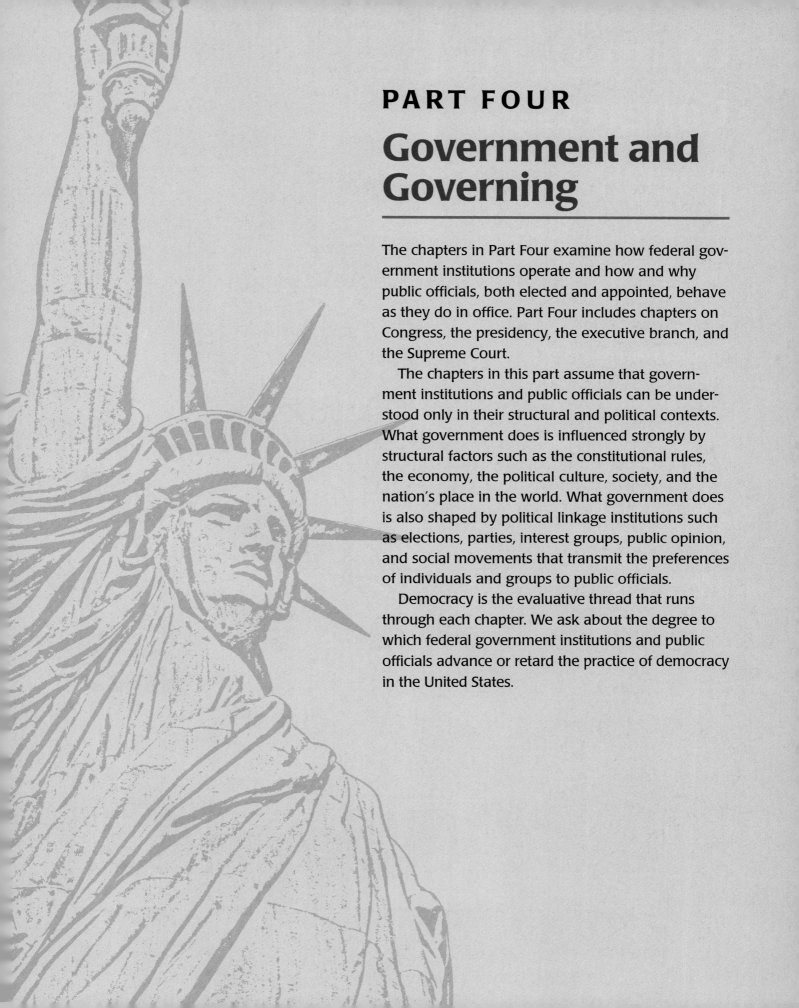

PART FOUR

Government and Governing

The chapters in Part Four examine how federal government institutions operate and how and why public officials, both elected and appointed, behave as they do in office. Part Four includes chapters on Congress, the presidency, the executive branch, and the Supreme Court.

The chapters in this part assume that government institutions and public officials can be understood only in their structural and political contexts. What government does is influenced strongly by structural factors such as the constitutional rules, the economy, the political culture, society, and the nation's place in the world. What government does is also shaped by political linkage institutions such as elections, parties, interest groups, public opinion, and social movements that transmit the preferences of individuals and groups to public officials.

Democracy is the evaluative thread that runs through each chapter. We ask about the degree to which federal government institutions and public officials advance or retard the practice of democracy in the United States.

CHAPTER 11
Congress

As Close as It Gets

Midway through 1999, House Minority Leader Dick Gephardt decided against trying to wrest the Democratic presidential nomination from Al Gore. His decision turned largely on his calculation that Democrats were poised to wrest control of the House of Representatives from Republicans, an eventuality that would make him the Speaker of the House, arguably one of the most powerful offices in the national government.

To Gephardt and most other political observers, a Democratic majority was within reach; Republican vulnerability seemed palpable at the beginning of the campaign season. For one thing, the Republican majority in the House in the 106th Congress was only 13—a mere seven-seat Democratic gain would switch party control of the House—down from its recent high-water mark of 95 in the 104th Congress that resulted from the GOP's landslide victory in the 1994 elections. Moreover, of the 435 House seats up for election in 2000, fully 26 of the 35 or so House districts considered to be "in play" were currently held by Republicans, and only 9 were currently held by Democrats; the remainder of the 435 districts were considered safe seats where little discernible inter-party competition existed, and where incumbents were almost certain to win reelection. Additionally, most political observers believed the Democrats had a clear lead on the issues that were of most interest to the American people, with Democratic-sponsored bills before the House on prescription drug coverage under Social Security and on campaign finance reform. Moreover, Democratic candidates had the advantage of having a Democratic president in office during a period of extraordinarily good economic times, and most observers assumed that this good fortune would spill over into favorable votes for House candidates of the president's party. Gephardt and others also believed that several Republican House incumbents were vulnerable to defeat on the issue of the impeachment and trial of Bill Clinton, considered by a vast majority of Americans, according to the polls, to have been highly unfair, unnecessary, and overly partisan. Democratic party operatives could hardly wait to use the daily pictures of the House impeachment managers marching off to the Senate to act as prosecutors of the president in their House election campaign advertising. And last, but certainly not least, the Democratic congressional party's 2000 campaign chest was brimming with dollars, larger by a factor of 10 than what had been available for the 1998 campaign. All signs pointed, then, to a Democratic Party takeover of the House of Representatives.

In an outcome that surprised most observers, and despite a record infusion of cash and a much-better-than-anticipated turnout among both African-Americans and voters from union households (traditionally Democratic in their voting behavior; see Chapters 5 and 10), the Democrats hardly made any gains at all in the House, increasing their advantage by only two to three seats. (At this writing, the outcomes of two races have not been decided. See the most current numbers at our web site at **www.ablongman.com/greenberg**.) The Republicans thus retained control of the House in the 107th Congress—the first time they had won control of the House of Representatives for four successive terms since 1922—and Dennis Hastert (R–IL) remained Speaker of the House while Dick Gebhardt remained Minority Leader.

To many observers, the Democrats may have missed their best chance to win control of the House of Representatives for some time to come, given both the close partisan division among voters in the country and the Republican control of many governorships and statehouses in the critical period of reapportionment of congressional seats following the 2000 census. The latter is particularly important, with Republicans likely to pick up additional seats in a reapportioned House of Representatives from Republican states in the South and Mountain West and in the Republican-friendly suburbs across the nation. National Republican Congressional Committee Chairman Thomas M. Davis boasted after the elections that "Democrats have lost their once-in-a-generation chance to win back control of the House."[1]

The 2000 election left Republicans in control of the Senate, as well, but only by a razor-thin margin of 50–49, with one race not settled at this writing (please refer to our web site at **www.ablongman.com/greenberg** for the most current information), the closest division between the parties since 1954. Democrats defeated four incumbent Republicans and lost only one of their own, Charles Robb of Virginia. Three of the Democratic victories were particularly noteworthy. In New York, Hillary Rodham Clinton defeated former Congressman Rick Lazio by a double-digit margin in one of the best-funded, most contentious, and most closely watched campaigns in the nation (Lazio was a late replacement for New York City Mayor Rudolf Guilliani, who dropped out of the race because of health and marital problems). Winning after a 16-month marathon effort to win over New Yorkers to her candidacy—after all, she had never been a citizen of New York State prior to her run for office, and she had been a highly controversial figure in national politics—Hillary Clinton became the only First Lady in our history to have won elective office, and the first woman Senator from New York. (Her election also guaranteed the highest number of women in the Senate in American history, a total of 12 or 13, depending on the final outcome of a very close election in the state of Washington that has not been decided as we go to press with this book. Check the latest figures on Senate composition at our web site). In New Jersey, John S. Corzine, former cochairman of the investment firm of Goldman, Sachs & Company, spent $62 million of his own money—roughly double the previous record set in the 1994 election by Michael Huffington in California—to defeat Representative Bob Franks by a narrow margin in an open-seat election to succeed the retiring Frank Lautenberg. And, perhaps most surprising of all, voters in Missouri voted late Gov. Mel Carnahan into office over incumbent Senator John Ashcroft even though he had died in an airplane crash three weeks earlier. His wife Jean, after some hesitation, said she would serve if her husband won election and if she were appointed by Governor Roger Wilson to take his place. Senator Ashcroft graciously conceded after his defeat and told his many angry Republican supporters that he would not be a party to any effort to refuse her a seat in the Senate.

After a long and often bitter campaign, Hillary Rodham Clinton won the Senate contest in New York and became the only First Lady in American history to be elected to public office.

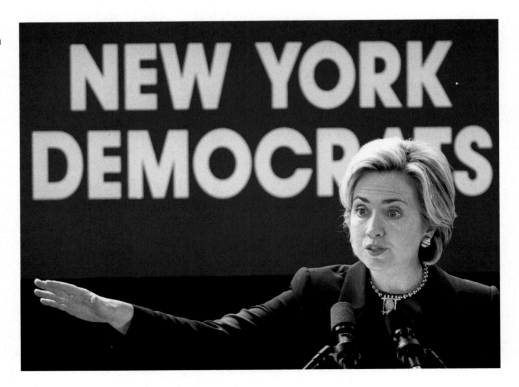

So, in the end, after a long and expensive campaign season in which congressional candidates spent a record amount of money (almost $700 million, with another $400 million spent on these campaigns by Democratic and Republican party committees), the close division that had existed between Democrats and Republicans in the 106th Congress became even tighter. With exit polls reporting no great issues defining the national campaigns for the public and voter interest fairly low, neither party was able to win a significant mandate for its program in the 2000 elections. In the worst-case scenario, this exceedingly close division between the parties, a closer division than at any time in recent American history, could lead to even greater gridlock in Washington, as each congressional party maneuvers to position itself for the 2002 congressional elections. The acrimony and partisan bickering surrounding the Florida presidential recount and the closeness of the presidential election (in terms of both the popular vote and the electoral vote) may poison the well even more, accentuating the possibilities for gridlock in Congress. On the other hand, it is at least conceivable that a substantial number of legislators from each side of the aisle may choose bipartisanship, recognizing, perhaps, that the general public is growing weary of partisan acrimony and that passage of even a minimum legislative program will require working across party lines. Only time will tell which of these scenarios will describe the legacy of the 107th Congress.

▶Thinking Critically About This Chapter

In this chapter, we turn our attention to the Congress of the United States, examining how Congress works as both a representative and governing institution.

Using the Framework. In this chapter you will learn how the way in which Congress works is affected by other government actors and institutions; political linkage level factors such as interest groups, public opinion, the media, and elections; and structural factors, such as constitutional rules and economic and social change.

Using the Democracy Standard. Using the concept of democracy developed in Chapter 1, you will be able to evaluate how well Congress acts as a democratic institution. You will see that the story of Congress and democracy is a mixed one: Congress is, at times and under certain circumstances, highly responsive to the American public; at other times and under other circumstances, it is most responsive to special interest groups and large contributors. ▶

Structural Foundations of the Modern Congress

A number of structural factors have strongly shaped how the modern Congress works. The most important of these factors are reviewed in this section.

As we saw in Chapter 2, the framers of the Constitution were concerned about the possibility of government tyranny. Yet they also wanted an energetic government capable of accomplishing its assigned tasks. These multiple objectives and concerns are reflected in the constitutional design of Congress.

Empowering Congress

enumerated powers

Powers of the federal government specifically mentioned in the Constitution.

The framers began by empowering Congress, making the legislative branch the center of lawmaking in the federal government. In Article I, Section 1, of the Constitution, they gave Congress the power to make the laws: "All legislative power herein granted shall be vested in a Congress of the United States." For the framers, Congress was the main bearer of federal governmental powers. In listing its powers and responsibilities in Article I, Section 8—the **enumerated powers**—they were largely defining the powers and responsibilities of the national government itself.[2] The framers enhanced the enumerated powers by adding the **elastic clause**, granting broad power to Congress to pass whatever legislation was necessary to carry out its enumerated powers

elastic clause

Article I, Section 8, of the Constitution, also called *the necessary and proper clause;* gives Congress the authority to make whatever laws are necessary and proper to carry out its enumerated responsibilities.

Constraining Congress

bicameral

As applied to a legislative body, consisting of two houses or chambers.

Worried that too strong a legislative branch would lead to tyranny, the framers also limited congressional power. As we learned in Chapter 2, they made Congress a **bicameral** body—divided into two chambers—so that legislation could occur only after patient deliberation. Single-house legislative bodies, they believed, would be prone to rash action. They then added provisions—Article I, Section 9—specifically to prohibit certain kinds of actions: **bills of attainder**, **ex post facto laws**, the granting of titles of nobility, and the suspension of the right of **habeas corpus**. In the 1st Congress, additional constraints on congressional action were added in the form of the Bill of Rights. Note that the First Amendment, perhaps the most important constitutional provision protecting political liberty, begins with the words "Congress shall make no law. . . ."

bill of attainder

A governmental decree that a person is guilty of a crime that carries the death penalty, rendered without benefit of a trial.

ex post facto law

A law that retroactively declares some action illegal.

We also learned in Chapter 2 that the national government was organized on the basis of a "separation of powers" and "checks and balances" so that "ambition might check ambition" and protect the country from tyranny (see *The Federalist,* No. 51, in the Appendix). This means that although the framers envisioned the legislative branch as the vital center of a vigorous national government, they wanted to make sure that Congress would be surrounded by competing centers of government power. We will see that this fragmentation of

habeas corpus

The legal doctrine that a person who is arrested must have a timely hearing before a judge.

WEB EXPLORATION

Historical Development

Issue: Although rooted in the Constitution, Congress has also changed a great deal over the years.

Site: Learn more about the development of the Senate through the "Course Documents" section of your online course. Go to the "Web Explorations" section for Chapter 11, click on "Historical Development," and open "history." Select "Senate History," then "Institutional Development," then "Origins and Development." Read the essay.

What You've Learned: What changes in the Senate over the years have been most significant? What about the Senate has changed the least, that is to say, what is most enduring?

HINT: Political parties, the admission of new states, and a constitutional amendment have played important roles in changing the Senate.

governmental power in the United States affects how Congress works and often makes it difficult for it to fashion coherent and effective public policies.

Bicameralism and Representation

Congress is organized into two legislative chambers with different principles of representation as well as different constitutional responsibilities. While we often use the word "Congress" and think of it as a single institution, it is worth remembering that the House and Senate are very different from one another and are "virtually autonomous chambers."[3] In what came to be known as the Great Compromise, the framers decided to apportion the House of Representatives on the basis of population and the Senate on the basis of equal representation of the states (see Chapter 2 for details). The terms of office of the members of the House of Representatives were set at two years. The terms of the members of the Senate were set at six years, with only one-third of the seats up for election in each two-year election cycle. We learn in this chapter how these differences affect the legislative process.

The Constitution called for the election of senators by state legislatures, not by the people. Again, the objective seems to have been to insulate one house of Congress from popular pressures and to make it a seat of deliberation and reflection. As James Madison put it, "The use of the Senate is to consist in its proceeding with more coolness . . . and with more wisdom than the popular branch."[4] The election of senators by the state legislatures could not survive the democratizing tendencies in the country, however. The Seventeenth Amendment, passed in 1913, gave the people the power to elect senators directly (see The Struggle for Democracy box, "The Direct Election of Senators").

In addition to its general grants of power to Congress, the Constitution assigns particular responsibilities to each of the legislative chambers (see Table 11.1). For example, the House of Representatives has the power to impeach the president for "high crimes and misdemeanors," which it did in the case of Bill Clinton; the Senate has the power to conduct the trial of the president and

Table 11.1	**Constitutional Differences Between the House and the Senate**	
	Senate	**House of Representatives**
Term	6 years (one-third elected in November of even-numbered years)	2 years (entire membership elected in November of even-numbered years)
Representatives	2 per state	Varies with population size (minimum of 1 per state)
Total membership	100	435 (determined by Congress)
Minimum age for membership	30 years	25 years
Powers	Advice and consent for judicial and upper-level executives branch appointments	Origination of revenue bills
	Trial of impeachment cases	Bringing of impeachment charges
	Advice and consent for treaties	

THE STRUGGLE FOR DEMOCRACY

The Direct Election of Senators

By the end of the nineteenth century, the selection of senators by state legislatures, in addition to being out of step with the strong democratic sentiments of the time, had become riddled with corruption and inefficiency. Outright bribery of state legislators by prospective senatorial candidates had become widespread. To be successful at bribery required, of course, access to funds that allowed one to outspend rivals. This, in turn, required that prospective senators be personally wealthy—hence, the popular designation of the Senate in the late nineteenth century as the "millionaires' club"—or tied to powerful economic interests. In one notorious case, William Lorimer of Illinois was elected to the Senate in 1909, despite widely publicized evidence that he was being paid by several large corporations (yet had no apparent duties) and had paid off key Illinois legislators to secure his election.

Another problem was that party competition in the states made it difficult for state legislatures to agree easily on a selection. Things became especially difficult when one party controlled the state house of representatives and the other party controlled the state senate or when party competition was close and each took turns in power. In the first type of situation, deadlocks would develop that would deprive states of representation in the Senate. During the 1890s, several states were without one of their senators for more than two years. In 1895, the Delaware legislature took 217 ballots over a period of three months without being able to make a decision. In the second type of situation, winning parties in the legislature would throw out the other party's senators, substituting their own people as quickly as possible. Sometimes the U.S. Senate would refuse to seat these new people, further confusing the situation and diminishing the representation of the state in Washington, D.C.

The call for the direct election of senators was first made by labor and farmers' groups in the last third of

the nineteenth century, mainly on the grounds of democracy and the need to separate the U.S. Senate from the "grip of the plutocrats." Progressive reformers added their own voices, mainly on the grounds of efficiency and good government. By the turn of the twentieth century, as far as we are able to tell in the absence of polling, most Americans favored the direct election of senators. Both parties endorsed the idea. The House of Representatives passed resolutions in favor of a constitutional amendment changing the Senate selection process in every Congress after 1900. But the constitutional proposal, not surprisingly, died in the Senate each time.

Frustrated in the Senate, reformers did an end run, concentrating on the states. They enacted laws mandating popular referendums on potential Senate candidates and compelling state legislatures to follow the referendum results when choosing senators. By 1912, 29 states had instituted these electoral reforms, effectively placing the selection of senators in the hands of the people in a majority of the states. The method passed an important test in 1910 in Nevada, when a Democrat-controlled state legislature elected Republican George Nixon to the Senate because he had won a popular referendum over his Democratic rival.

The U.S. Senate, seeing the handwriting on the wall, finally gave in and approved a proposal for a constitutional amendment for the direct election of senators in 1912. The requisite number of states had approved the Seventeenth Amendment by 1913.

Sources: Bob Dole, *Historical Almanac of the United States Senate* (Washington, D.C.: U.S. Government Printing Office, 1989), pp. 180–184; J. W. Peltason, *Understanding the Constitution* (New York: Holt, Rinehart & Winston, 1988), p. 254.

remove him from office, if the impeachment charges are proved to its satisfaction (which they were not for Clinton).

Federalism

Congress is also greatly affected by the federal design of the Constitution. As we learned in Chapter 3, in our federal system, some powers and responsibilities are granted to the national government, some are shared between the national government and the states, and some are reserved for the states. It is inevitable in such a system that conflicts will occur between state governments and the national government and its legislative branch. Such conflicts some-times reach the Supreme Court for resolution. In *United States* v. *Lopez* (1995), for instance, the Court ruled that Congress had gone too far in the use of its commerce clause powers when it passed a law banning firearms in and around public schools. Although the goal of the law might be worthy, such a matter, in the opinion of the Court, was the business of the states, not Congress.

Federalism also infuses "localism" into congressional affairs.[5] Although Congress is charged with making national policies, we should remember that the members of the Senate and the House come to Washington as the repre-sentatives of states and districts. They are elected by and are beholden to the voters at home and have voters' interests and opinions in mind even as they struggle with weighty issues of national importance. They inevitably bring local and state concerns to bear when making national policies.

LongmanParticipate

CourseCompass

comparative
**Comparing
Legislatures**

Representation and Democracy

Members of Congress serve as our legislative representatives. But do they carry out this representative responsibility in a way that can be considered democratic? To answer this question, we need to look at several aspects of rep-resentation.

Styles of Representation

In a letter to his constituents written in 1774, English politician and philosopher Edmund Burke described two principal styles of representation. As a **delegate**, the representative tries to mirror perfectly the views of his or her constituents. As a **trustee**, the representative acts independently, trusting to his or her own judg-ment of how to best serve the public interest. Burke preferred the trustee

delegate

According to the doctrine articu-lated by Edmund Burke, an elect-ed representative who acts in perfect accord with the wishes of his or her constituents.

trustee

According to Edmund Burke, a representative who believes that his or her own best judgment, rather than instructions from con-stituents, should be used in making legislative decisions.

CourseCompass

WEB EXPLORATION

Demographic Representation

Issue: Some people believe that groups are best represented in Congress when members of the group hold office in the House and Senate.

Site: Access the U.S. Senate through the "Course Documents" sec-tion of your online course. Go to the "Web Explorations" section for Chapter 11, click on "Demographic Representation," and open "demographics." Select "Senate History," then "Statistics," then examine "women in the Senate" and "minorities" in the Senate.

What You've Learned: Calculate the numbers of women and minori-ties that have served in the Senate. Has the number increased over the years, stayed the same, or decreased? How would you go about explaining the patterns you have uncovered?

HINT: Because senators, unlike representatives, are elected from a statewide con-stituency, rather than from relatively homogeneous and smaller House districts, minorities have had a hard time getting elected.

approach: "Your representative owes you, not his industry only, but his judgment; and he betrays you, instead of serving you, if he sacrifices it to your opinion."[6]

Campaigning for Congress in Illinois several decades later, Abraham Lincoln argued otherwise: "While acting as [your] representative, I shall be governed by [your] will, on all subjects upon which I have the means of knowing what [your] will is."[7] (If only he had had access to public opinion polls!)

The members of Congress choose between these two styles of representation probably less according to their personal tastes than according to judgments about the relative safety of their seats. Representatives and senators without real electoral competition can better afford to choose the trustee style. Senators with six-year terms face the electorate less often than members of the House, so they are freer than representatives to assume the trustee style.

Members of Congress: Race, Gender, and Occupation

One way to represent is to be demographically similar to the people one is representing. If we want a political system in which the views of women are taken into account, for instance, we might want a significant number of women in Congress. From this perspective, a perfectly representative legislative body would be similar to the general population in race, sex, ethnicity, occupation, religion, age, and the like. In this sense, the U.S. Congress is highly *unrepresentative*.

Gender and Race Both women and racial minorities are significantly underrepresented in Congress, particularly in the Senate, despite recent gains. We can see this in Figure 11.1, which compares the distribution of women and minorities in the 106th Congress (1999–2000) with their distribution in the country as a whole.

Black representation reached its peak during the post–Civil War Reconstruction period, when blacks played an important political role in several southern states. They disappeared from Congress for many years after the reimposition of white supremacy in the South at the end of the nineteenth century. Although a handful of black representatives from northern cities served during the first half of the twentieth century—Oscar De Priest from Chicago's predominantly black South Side and Adam Clayton Powell from New York City's Harlem, for instance—no significant numbers of black legislators entered Congress until the late 1960s. Even though their number increased from 26 to 37 between the 102nd (1991–1992) and 106th Congresses (1999–2000), their numbers are still well below what one might expect, given the proportion of blacks in the American population. All but four twentieth-century African-American representatives were Democrats. In the 106th Congress, there was only one black Republican representative, J. C. Watts of Oklahoma.

Hispanics are even more poorly represented than African-Americans relative to their proportion of the population, but the increase in their number in recent years has given the Hispanic caucus a greater voice in legislative affairs than in the past. Only six served in the House and Senate in the 106th Congress. One Native American, Ben Nighthorse Campbell (R–Colo.), holds a seat in the U.S. Senate.

The first woman to sit in Congress was Jeannette Rankin of Montana, a suffragist and pacifist, elected in 1916. The number of women in Congress increased during the 1990s, with the big gain coming in the 1992 elections (often called the "year of the woman"), which sent 48 women to the House and 7 to the Senate in the 103rd Congress (compared with 29 and 2 in the 102nd). Proportionally, however, female representation in Congress is quite low, given

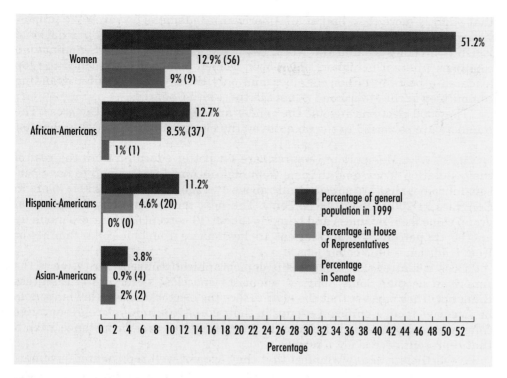

Figure 11.1 ● Women and Minorities in Congress

Although their numbers in Congress have increased in recent years, women and racial minorities are still substantially underrepresented compared with their proportion in the American population. This graph compares the percentage of women and racial minorities in each house of the 106th Congress with their percentages in the population in 1999. (Refer to the chapter opening vignette for information on the 107th Congress elected in 2000.)

Source: U.S. Bureau of the Census, *Statistical Abstract of the United States.*

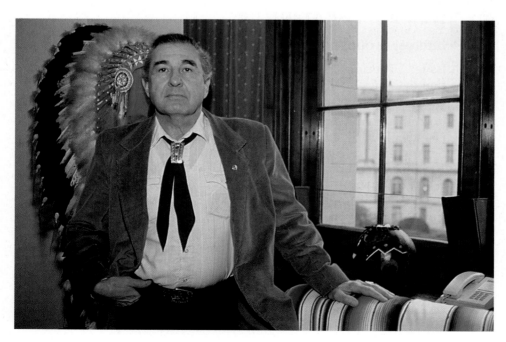

Ben Nighthorse Campbell of Colorado is the first and only Native American to be elected to the U.S. Senate. He surprised both his constituents and colleagues when he switched his party affiliation from Democratic to Republican after he was elected to office.

that slightly more than half of all Americans are female; however, the proportion of women in the House of Representatives is about average for national legislative bodies around the world (with the exception of the Scandinavian countries where it is higher).[8] Moreover, women have not yet reached the top leadership posts in either chamber, and only three women chaired standing committees in the House and Senate in the 106th Congress.

The 2000 elections affected the gender and racial makeup of Congress. The numbers are reviewed in the vignette on the elections that opens this chapter.

Occupation   Members of Congress are far better educated than the rest of the population. They tend to come from high-income families and to have personal incomes that are substantially above average. There were 230 lawyers in Congress in 2000 (about 43 percent). The next most numerous occupational group came from business and banking (about 30 percent). Educators made up another 18 percent.[9] Notably absent are lawmakers from blue-collar families or from traditional blue-collar jobs.

Does it matter that Congress is demographically unrepresentative of the American people? Some political scientists and close observers of Congress think not. They suggest that the need to face the electorate forces lawmakers to be attentive to all significant groups in their **constituencies**. A representative from a farm district tends to listen to farm **constituents**, for instance, even if that representative is not a farmer.

Nevertheless, many who feel that they are not well represented—women, African-Americans, Asian-Americans, Hispanics, blue-collar workers, gays and lesbians, those with disabilities, and the poor—often believe that their interests would get a much better hearing if their numbers were substantially increased in Congress. The demographic disparity between the American population and the makeup of Congress suggests a violation of the norm of political equality, an important element of democracy.

constituency

The district of a legislator.

constituent

A citizen who lives in the district of an elected official.

WEB EXPLORATION

Interest Groups and Campaigns

Issue: The support of interest groups is important for winning election to Congress.

Site: Access Project Vote Smart through the "Course Documents" section of your online course. Go to the "Web Explorations" section for Chapter 11, click on "Internet Groups and Campaigns," and open "scores." Select "Special Interest Groups," then enter your ZIP code. Examine how various interest groups have "scored" your senators and representative.

What You've Learned: Which interest groups believe your representative and senators have performed well? Which interest groups believe they have not done a good job? How would you judge the performance of your senators and representative based on the evidence from interest group evaluations?

HINT: These scores can be quite helpful if you are clear about what each of the interest groups stands for.

The Electoral Connection

The election is the principal instrument in a democracy for linking citizens to government officials. Let's see how congressional elections affect the quality of representation in the United States.

Electoral Districts   Each state is entitled to two senators. Equal representation gives extraordinary power in the Senate to states with small populations. Alaska, for instance, has exactly the same number of senators as California, but it has only one-fiftieth of California's population. This arrangement can substantially distort popular sentiment and thus diminish democracy.

Representation in the House of Representatives is determined by a state's population. **Reapportionment**, or redistribution of the 435 House seats among the states, occurs every ten years, after the national census (see Figure 11.2 for the most recent changes). After the census, some states keep the same number of seats; others gain or lose them. States gaining or losing seats must then redraw the boundary lines of their congressional districts. In the past, this reapportionment was left entirely to the state legislatures. Very often, the result was congressional districts of vastly different population size—in New York in the 1930s,

> **reapportionment**
>
> The redrawing of congressional district boundaries to account for changes in population.

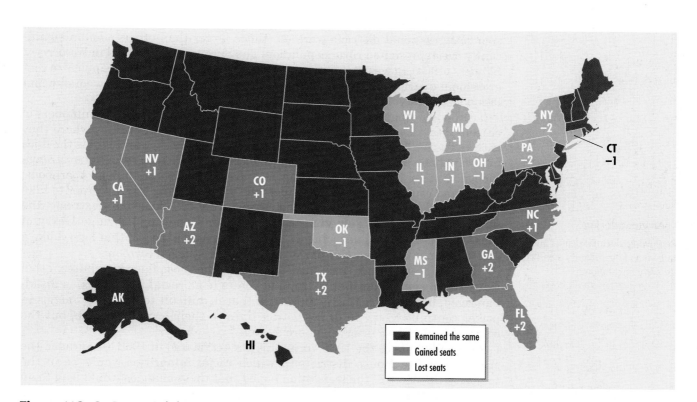

Figure 11.2 ● **States Gaining and Losing Congressional Seats Following the 2000 Census**

The number of representatives for each state in the House of Representatives is based on the size of its population. Because the relative sizes of the states' populations change over time, the number of representatives from each state is recalculated after each census. This map shows which states gained and lost representatives after the 2000 census.

Source: Estimates from Election Data Services, Washington, D.C., reported in D'Vera Cohn, "South, West to Pick Up 10 Seats in House," *Washington Post* (December 30, 1999), p. A4.

The term *gerrymander* is derived from this 1812 Elkanah Tinsdale cartoon, which lampoons a Massachusetts district drawn to ensure the election of a Republican candidate. The "Gerry-mander" was named after Massachusetts Governor Elbridge Gerry, who signed the bill that created the salamander-shaped district.

some congressional districts were ten times larger than others—and a significantly overrepresented rural population. The Supreme Court ruled in *Wesberry* v. *Sanders* (1964), however, that the principle of one person, one vote applies to congressional districts. Today, all congressional districts are of roughly equal population size.

Although congressional districts must hold approximately equal numbers of citizens, state legislatures are relatively free to draw district lines where they choose. The party that controls the state legislature usually tries to draw the lines in a way that will help its candidates win elections.[10] The results are often strange indeed. Rather than creating compact and coherent districts, neighborhoods, towns, and counties can be strung together in odd-looking ways in order to take full partisan advantage of the redistricting process. Taken to an extreme, the process is known as **gerrymandering**, after Governor Elbridge Gerry of Massachusetts, who signed a bill in 1811 that created a district that looked like a salamander. It made wonderful raw material for editorial cartoonists.

The Supreme Court has tried to prevent the most flagrant abuses, especially when some identifiable group of voters (e.g., racial minorities) is disadvantaged, but redistricting is a practice that is difficult to regulate. Parties in power continue to try to draw district lines to their own advantage, but the courts may begin to intervene here as well.

Amendments to the 1965 Voting Rights Act passed in 1982 encouraged the states to create House districts in which racial minorities would be in the majority. Sponsors of the legislation hoped that these changes would lead to an increase in the number of members of racial minority groups elected to the House. The result was the formation of 24 new **majority-minority districts**, 15 with African-American majorities and 9 with Hispanic-American majorities.[11] Each of these districts did, in fact, elect a member of a racial minority group to office, accounting for most of the increase in minority representation after the 1992 congressional elections. The creation of such districts tended to undermine Democratic party strength in other districts, however, because it took away traditionally Democratic-oriented minority group voters from them. Naturally, the Republicans were happy to support minority group efforts to

gerrymandering
Redrawing electoral district lines to give an advantage to a particular party or candidate.

majority-minority districts
Districts drawn to ensure that a racial minority makes up the majority of voters.

form their own districts. Concentrating black voters in homogeneous districts has tipped the balance to Republicans in many other districts, especially in the South. One unhappy result is that policies favored by a majority of African-American citizens are less likely to be enacted because of the decreased strength of the Democrats in the House, despite an increase in the number of African-American representatives.[12]

The creation of some of these districts took great imagination. North Carolina's Twelfth District, for instance, created after the 1990 census, linked a narrow strip of predominantly African-American communities along 160 miles of Interstate 85 connecting Durham and Charlotte. After first encouraging the creation of majority-minority districts, the Supreme Court has had second thoughts about districts that are highly irregular in form, noncontiguous, unconnected to traditional political jurisdictions (*Shaw* v. *Reno,* 1993), or drawn solely to aid one race (*Miller* v. *Johnson,* 1995). The issue of majority-minority districts is not settled, however; the courts, state legislatures and Congress are still trying to figure out what to do.

Money and Congressional Elections   Running for the House or the Senate is a very expensive proposition, and it keeps getting more expensive. In the 1999–2000 election cycle, candidates spent almost $1 billion. The average Senate race now costs about $3.5 million, while the price tag for a House race in a competitive district is about $1 million.[13] This spending by the candidate's campaign is but the tip of the iceberg. To the grand total, we must add the dollars raised and spent by parties on soft money party-building activities and money raised and spent by private groups on issue advertising to get the full picture. Such interest group parallel campaigns, many of which involve attack ads on candidates the groups do not want to see elected, are essentially unregulated, with no limits on spending.

Incumbents, especially in the House, have an easier time raising money than their challengers and spend more. **Open-seat election** races in which no incumbent is involved also attract and use lots of money (see Figure 11.3). Being a member of the majority party in Congress also serves as a magnet for money because contributors generally want to be able to have access to those in power.[14]

There is nothing particularly surprising about the increased costs of political campaigns, given the ever-greater reliance on expensive campaign technologies such as mass and targeted mailings; polling; focus groups; television, radio, and print advertising; Web sites; and phone banks. Also important is the decline of party loyalty in the electorate, which compels candidates to try to reach potential voters on their own.

Congressional campaign money comes from four main sources: individuals, political action committees (PACs), political parties, and the candidates themselves (see Figure 11.4). The largest share comes from individual contributors, 53 percent in 1998. PACs are the next largest, contributing 32 percent of all campaign money in that election cycle.

PACs are allowed to contribute up to $5,000 per candidate per election, and they can give to as many candidates as they wish. The private groups that sponsor PACs are also free to spend without limit when publicizing their positions on public issues, as you have seen. Such issue campaigns are often thinly veiled efforts to help a particular candidate or party.

Many especially wealthy candidates support their election campaigns out of their own pockets. Michael Huffington spent $28 million of his own money in an attempt to win a Senate seat from California in 1994, but he lost to Dianne Feinstein anyway.

LongmanParticipate

simulation
You Are Redrawing District Lines After the Census

open-seat election
An election in which there is no incumbent officeholder.

LongmanParticipate

participation
The Prepared Voter Kit

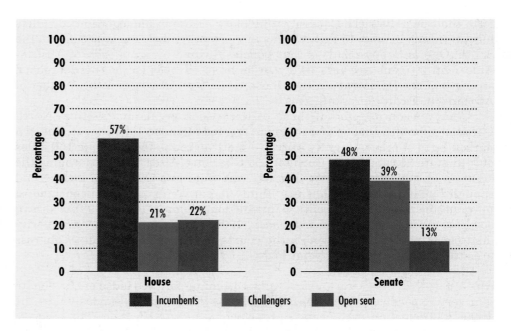

Figure 11.3 ● **Campaign Money Spent by Incumbents, Challengers, and Open-Seat Candidates, 1998**

Because campaign contributors want to have access to important decision makers in Congress, they tend to give a disproportionate share to incumbents rather than to challengers, especially in the House. This is one of the most important electoral advantages of incumbents.

Source: Federal Election Commission.

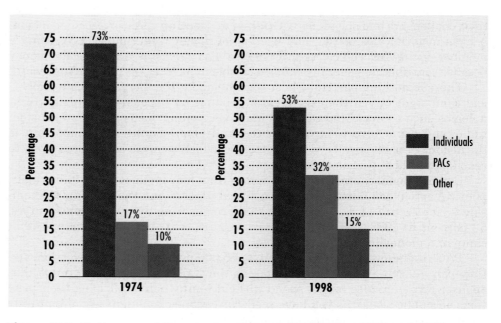

Figure 11.4 ● **Sources of Congressional Campaign Money, 1974 and 1998**

Although the largest share of campaign contributions still comes from individuals, the share contributed by political action committees (PACs) has grown significantly, as shown by a comparison of the sources of campaign giving in 1974 and 1998.

Source: Federal Election Commission.

Congressional candidates also receive campaign money from national, congressional, and state party committees. Party committees are allowed to make a $5,000 contribution per campaign to each House candidate. National and senatorial party committees are allowed to give $17,000 to each candidate for each stage of the electoral process. And as you learned in Chapter 9, there are no limits to soft-money party expenditures that indirectly help party candidates. The role of the party committees will become ever more important in the aftermath of a recent Supreme Court decision (*Colorado Republican Federal Campaign Committee* v. *Federal Election Committee*) affirming the right of party organizations to make unlimited independent expenditures on behalf of candidates.

Many Americans say they want to change the system of funding campaigns. Why it is so hard to do is examined in the "Using the Framework" feature.

The Incumbency Factor   Incumbents—current officeholders—win at much higher rates in the House today than ever before. The ability of House incumbents to get reelected improved especially from the late 1940s into the early 1990s (see Figure 11.5), allowing the Democratic party to maintain control over the House of Representatives for four decades (from 1955 to 1994), even as Republicans such as Dwight Eisenhower, Richard Nixon, Ronald Reagan, and George Bush were winning presidential elections. In spite of mounting discontent with Congress and the anti-incumbent talk of recent years, members of the House of Representatives who choose to run for reelection are still almost always successful. Recently, incumbent senators have been doing almost as well. In the 1992 and 1994 elections, when anti-incumbent feelings seemed to be running extraordinarily high, 88 percent and then 92 percent of current members were nevertheless reelected to the House. In 1998, incumbents were even more successful, with a 98 percent success rate in the House and 90 percent in the Senate. In 2000, 98 percent of incumbents returned to the House and 79 percent returned to the Senate.

High incumbent success rates in elections do not necessarily translate into stagnation, however. There is still a great deal of membership turnover in Congress because of voluntary retirements or the defeat of incumbents at the

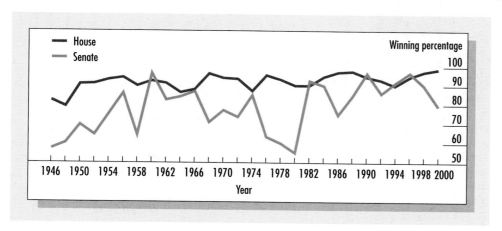

Figure 11.5 ● Rates of Incumbent Reelection in Congress

The probability that incumbents will be reelected remains at historic highs. This does not mean, however, that the membership of Congress is stagnant. Turnover in membership is substantial because of retirements and the defeat of incumbents in primary elections.

Source: Calculations by the authors from various issues of the *Congressional Quarterly Weekly Report.*

USING THE FRAMEWORK

Why Can't We Seem to Do Anything About Getting Big Money Out of Politics?

Americans have been hearing about campaign finance reform for a long time now, yet nothing seems to ever get accomplished. Many citizens seem frustrated by the delays; many experts are alarmed by the growing infusion of "special interest" money into elections. Why is it so hard to make progress on this front? Here we take a broader view of the question, considering how structural, political linkage, and governmental factors help us understand why change has not occurred.

Governmental Action

Campaign finance reform bills die in the House and Senate.

Governmental Level

- The Supreme Court has ruled that government cannot limit the amount of money spent during campaigns by candidates, individuals, and organizations (although it can limit hard-money contributions to candidates).

- Incumbent representatives, senators, and presidents have been very successful under the existing system of campaign finance; it is not necessarily in their interest to reform the system.

Political Linkages Level

- Private groups of all political persuasions have worked in Congress and in the states to block campaign finance reform in order to preserve their influence in electoral campaigns.

- Voters have not shown much interest in demanding that local, state, or national candidates support campaign finance reform.

- Public opinion surveys show that Americans want campaign finance reform but care more about other things, including the state of the economy, crime, and education.

- Political party committees at all levels find the existing system to be compatible with their interests.

Structural Level

- Income and wealth inequality give some Americans but not others the means to contribute to candidate and issue campaigns.

- The Bill of Rights protects free expression by all citizens, as well as freedom of association; individuals can support who they want in the political arena and can form groups to advance their political causes.

Members of Congress must spend a considerable amount of their time staying in touch with their constituents. Here Representative Rosa DeLauro (D–CT) visits a school in her district.

nomination stage of the electoral process. Retirement is especially important. For example, senators Bob Kerry (D–Neb.), Daniel Patrick Moynihan (D–NY), Frank Lautenberg (D–NJ), Connie Mack (R–FL), and Robert Bryan (D–NV) all chose not to seek reelection in 2000.

Why Incumbents Have the Advantage   Incumbency continues to be a valuable resource. For one thing, as you have seen, incumbents attract and spend more money than their rivals. Many contributors look at campaign contributions as an "investment" in access to key members of Congress.[15] To contribute to a challenger is to jeopardize access if the challenger loses, which is most often the case.

Incumbents also use the congressional machinery to help their reelection chances.[16] Already well known to voters because they garner so much free media coverage, members of Congress have many ways to advertise their accomplishments and keep their names before the public. For instance, the **franking privilege** allows them to mail newsletters, legislative updates, surveys, and other self-promoting literature free of charge. The House and the Senate also provide travel budgets for lawmakers to make periodic visits to their states or districts. Because members believe that time spent in their districts helps their electoral chances—a belief supported by a great deal of research[17]—they spend lots of time back home.[18] Some manage to spend three or four days a week in their districts or states, meeting constituents, giving speeches, raising money, and keeping in the public eye. The congressional leadership helps by trying to schedule important legislative business for the Tuesday-to-Thursday period.

Incumbents also use their offices to "service the district." One way is through **casework**, helping constituents cut through the red tape of the federal bureaucracy, whether it be by speeding up the arrival of a late Social Security check or expediting the issuance of a permit for grazing on public land.[19] Generous budgets for establishing and staffing offices in the constituency help representatives and senators do casework. Another way to service the district is to provide **pork**—federal dollars for various projects in the district or state. In 1998, with the federal

LongmanParticipate

CourseCompass

visual literacy
Why Is It So Hard to Defeat an Incumbent?

franking privilege

Public subsidization of mail from the members of Congress to their constituents.

casework

Services performed by members of Congress for constituents.

pork

Also called *pork barrel;* projects designed to bring to the constituency jobs and public money for which the members of Congress can claim credit.

Federal projects awarded to districts are part of what is commonly called the legislative *pork barrel*. Pork has long been an important reelection resource for congressional incumbents because they can claim credit for having obtained it for their constituents.

budget in surplus, members of Congress heightened their prospects in the coming congressional elections by passing a massive highway spending bill that included more than 1,400 "demonstration projects" targeted for specific roads and bridges in 400 congressional districts.

LongmanParticipate

CourseCompass

participation
Write to Your Congressperson

LongmanParticipate

CourseCompass

simulation
You Are a Professional Campaign Consultant

How Representative? Representatives and senators pay a great deal of attention to the interests and the preferences of people in their districts and states. Because they are worried about being reelected, they try to see as many people as they can during their frequent visits home, and they pay attention to their mail and the public opinion polls. Moreover, they vote on and pass laws in rough approximation to public opinion. Members of Congress vote in a manner that is consistent with public opinion in their districts about two-thirds of the time[20] (although House Republicans acted in marked contrast to public opinion on the Clinton impeachment), and Congress produces laws that are consistent with national public opinion at about the same rate.[21]

In a substantial number of cases, however, Congress does *not* follow public opinion. Moreover, on many issues of high complexity or low visibility, such as securities regulation, the public may have no opinions. It is in these areas that one can most fully see the influence of money and interest groups at work. The lobbying community, as we have learned, overwhelmingly represents business and the professions. Moreover, legislators, who are almost entirely on their own in organizing and financing their reelection campaigns, are tempting targets for interest groups. To the degree that these influences distort popular sovereignty and undermine political equality, democracy is impaired.

How Congress Works

Congress is a vital center of decision making and policymaking in our national government. It is not a place where the executive's bills are simply rubber-stamped, as legislative bodies do in many parliamentary systems. By all accounts, Congress is the most influential and independent legislative body among the Western democratic nations. In this section, we turn our attention to how Congress is organized and how it functions as a working legislative body.

The majority party organizes the House at the beginning of each session of Congress and generally has its way if its members remain disciplined. Here the leadership of the minority Democrats in the 104th Congress protest their exclusion from House deliberations by holding mock sessions outside on the Capitol lawn.

Political Parties in Congress

Political parties have a very strong presence in Congress. Its members come to Washington, D.C., as elected candidates of a political party. At the start of each session, they organize their legislative business along political party lines. At the start of each new Congress, each **party caucus** meets to select party committees and leaders. The majority party in the House selects the Speaker of the House, while the majority party in the Senate selects the president pro tempore (usually its most senior member) and the majority leader. The majority party in each house also selects the chairs of the committees and subcommittees and determines the party ratios for each.

party caucus

An organization of the members of a political party in the House or Senate.

The Party Composition of Congress   The Democratic party dominated the modern Congress until the 1994 elections (see Figure 11.6). The Democratic domination of House elections remained solid even in the face of GOP landslide wins in the presidential elections of 1980 (Reagan), 1984 (Reagan), and 1988 (Bush). In the Senate, Republicans were in the majority for only ten years during this same period. Democratic party domination ended with the 1994 elections, however, when Republicans won the control of both houses of Congress for the first time in 40 years. The Republicans repeated their feat in 1996 and 1998. In 2000, Republicans retained control of both houses of Congress once again, but with razor-thin margins (see the chapter opening vignette).

Party Voting in Congress   The political parties provide important glue for the decentralized fragments of Congress and the legislative process. Party labels are important cues for members of Congress as they decide how to vote on issues before the committees and on the floor of the House and the Senate. We know this from a long tradition of research on party divisions in roll call voting. This research tells us that party affiliation is the best predictor of the voting behavior of members of the Congress and that it is becoming ever more important.[22] That is to say, both houses of Congress are becoming more **partisan**.

partisan

A committed member of a party; seeing issues from the point of view of the interests of a single party.

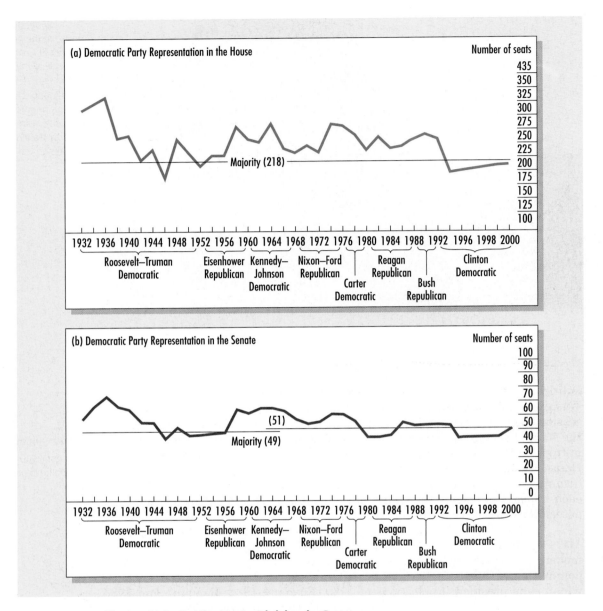

Figure 11.6 ● **The Party Division in Congress**

Democrats were in the majority in both houses of Congress for most of the years between the early 1930s and 1994. Democratic dominance ended with the 1994 elections, when the Republicans won majority control of both houses for the first time in 40 years. They repeated their victories in 1996 and 1998 and barely held on in 2000.

Sources: Harold W. Stanley and Richard G. Niemi, *Vital Statistics on American Politics,* 1999–2000 (Washington, D.C.: Congressional Quarterly Press, 2000) and additional calculations by the authors.

Figure 11.7 shows how often the average Democrat and the average Republican voted with his or her party in partisan votes in Congress.[23] You can see that partisanship is very high—now members vote along party lines in four out of every five votes—and has been steadily increasing. Partisanship was particularly high among Republicans in the 104th Congress, especially in the House, where Newt Gingrich led a party effort to legislate the provisions of the

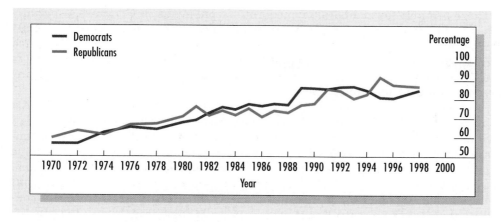

Figure 11.7 ● **Partisan Roll Call Votes in Congress**

Partisanship has been growing in Congress. One indicator is the increase in the percentage of times the average Democrat and Republican in the House and Senate sided with his/her party on partisan votes—those votes when a majority of Democrats voted against a majority of Republicans.

Source: Calculations by the authors from various issues of the *Congressional Quarterly Weekly Report.*

House GOP's congressional campaign platform, the Contract with America. Extraordinary levels of partisanship were also evident in the House on votes to impeach President Clinton in December 1999, and in the votes associated with his trial in the Senate in early 1999. The ill-will between the parties carried over into the 106th Congress. The *New York Times,* in apparent frustration at the persistent partisan gridlock in Congress (and between Congress and the president), titled a major article on the mood inside the beltway, "Compromise Takes a Holiday."[24]

There are a number of reasons within-party unity is increasing. For one thing, southern conservative Democrats—frequent allies of Republicans in Congress in the past—are fast disappearing, as many politicians and voters have switched over to the Republican party in the rapidly realigning South.

One of the most important and wide-ranging activities of Congress is oversight of federal government activities. Here Senator Fred Thompson (R–TN) presides over hearings of his Government Affairs Committee, investigating campaign finance irregularities in the 1996 election.

There are also fewer liberal or moderate Republicans in Congress, especially since the tidal wave of conservative Republicans that were elected in 1994 entered Congress. The strong ideological leadership of Speaker Newt Gingrich from 1995 through 1998 made Republicans in the House even more united. On bills derived from the Contract with America, for example, House Republicans voted as a near-unanimous bloc.

It's not entirely clear whether party voting differences are caused directly by party affiliation or indirectly by the character of constituencies or ideology. Some scholars have found strong independent party effects regardless of constituency or ideology. Others argue that the tendency of people in the same party to vote together is a reflection of the fact that Democratic lawmakers tend to come from districts and states that are similar to each other and that Republican lawmakers come from places that are different from the constituencies of Democrats. Republicans generally come from higher-income districts than Democrats. Democratic districts, in turn, tend to contain more union members and racial minorities. The strongest tie, in this line of argument, is between the member of Congress and the constituency, not between the member and the party.[25]

Increasingly, internal party unity and conflict between the parties seem attributable to ideology. Both in the electorate and among the members of Congress, Democrats are becoming more consistently liberal, while Republicans are becoming more consistently conservative. People who see the world in liberal terms tend to drift toward the Democratic party, while those who see the world in conservative terms find their way to the Republican party. Ideology thus strengthens the glue of party unity and increases partisanship.

Congressional Leadership

The political parties work through the leadership structure of Congress because the leaders of the majority political party are, at the same time, the leaders of the House and the Senate.[26]

Leadership in the House   The leader in the House of Representatives is the Speaker of the House. This position is recognized in the Constitution and stands in the line of succession to the presidency, immediately after the vice-presidency. The Speaker is treated by his colleagues, the president, and the media as the spokesperson for the House in general and for the majority party in Congress in particular, especially if the Speaker has broad public policy aims and is able to maintain control of the majority on important legislative matters.

Until 1910, the Speaker exercised great power over the House legislative process. The bases of his power were his right to appoint committees and their chairs and his position as chair of the powerful Rules Committee. The revolt of the rank and file against Speaker "Uncle Joe" Cannon in 1910 resulted in the Speaker's removal from the Rules Committee and the elimination of the Speaker's power to appoint committees and their chairs.

From 1910 until the early 1970s, the weakened Speaker competed with a handful of powerful committee chairs for leadership of the House. A few Speakers, such as Sam Rayburn of Texas, were able to lead by sheer dint of their personalities and legislative skills, but power tilted toward the committee chairs most of the time.

The Democratic Caucus staged a revolt against the committee system after 1974 and restored some of the powers of the Speaker, especially in making committee assignments. The Democratic Caucus also gave the Speaker more power to refer bills to committee, control the House agenda, appoint members to select committees, and direct floor debate. This change gave Speakers Tip O'Neill, Jim Wright, and Tom Foley considerable leadership resources. The Republican Caucus gave even more power to control the House legislative process to their first Speaker since 1954, Newt Gingrich. Some scholars suggest that Gingrich's speakership was the most powerful one since Cannon's.[27] Ironically, his power and visibility led to a precipitous decline in his public standing in 1996 when Americans turned against most elements of the Gingrich agenda. Because many Republicans also believed that Gingrich's unpopularity helped reelect Bill Clinton to the presidency and made Gingrich a weak negotiator with the president after the 1996 election, some House members tried unsuccessfully to depose him in 1997. Unexpected losses of Republican House seats in the 1998 elections, after a campaign featuring a Gingrich-designed advertising blitz to impeach the president, led to his resignation of the Speakership and from the House. He was succeeded eventually as Speaker by Dennis Hastert of Illinois, a person much less charismatic than Gingrich, less skillful in marshalling his small majority, and more tied to the traditional way of doing things in the House. In returning more power to the committee chairs, honoring the seniority principle, and operating behind the scenes, Hastert refashioned the Speakership into something resembling what the office looked like prior to Gingrich's tumultuous tenure.

The majority party in the House also selects a majority leader to help the Speaker plan strategy and manage the legislative business of the House. Neither House nor party rules spell out the responsibilities of this office. The nature of the job depends very much on what the Speaker wants and on the majority leader's talents and energy. In the 106th Congress, partly because of Hastert's understated style and his apparent aversion to the media spotlight, it appeared to many observers that majority leader Tom DeLay of Texas was the real leader of the House of Representatives.[28]

LongmanParticipate

CourseCompass

timeline
The Speaker of the House

CourseCompass

WEB EXPLORATION

Parties and Leaders in Congress

Issue: Much of what Congress does is determined by the parties and the leadership in the House and Senate.

Site: Access the home pages of the Speaker of the House and of the Senate Majority Leader through the "Course Documents" section of your online course. Go to the "Web Explorations" section for Chapter 11, click on "Parties and Leaders in Congress," and open "leaders." For the House, select "leadership offices" then "Office of the Speaker." For the Senate, select "Senators" then "Senate Leadership."

What You've Learned: At these sites, you will be able to examine not only the biographies of the present leaders, but also the party legislative programs each has fashioned for his institution. What do you think of these programs? Would they be good for America if they were successfully legislated?

HINT: Your answer will probably depend a great deal on whether you identify with one of the parties and its agenda.

whip

A political party member in Congress charged with keeping members informed of the plans of the party leadership, counting votes before action on important issues, and rounding up party members for votes on bills.

The Speaker is also assisted by a party **whip**, who acts as a liaison between the leaders and the rank and file. The whip (helped by deputy whips) counts heads on important bills, explains leadership positions, tries to persuade, gathers legislative intelligence, and makes sure that the faithful get to the floor to cast their votes.

The minority party elects a minority floor leader, who acts as the chief spokesperson and legislative strategist for the opposition. The minority leader not only tries to keep the forces together but also seeks out members of the majority party who might be won over against the House leadership on key issues. Minority leader styles differ greatly. Republican Robert Michel of Illinois tried to cooperate with the Democratic party majority, believing that this was the only way to win approval for portions of the GOP agenda. Dick Gephardt of Missouri, like Gingrich, used the minority leader position to vigorously attack the majority Republicans.

Leadership in the Senate   Leadership in the Senate is less visible. Senators with formal leadership titles exercise little influence. The presiding officer of the Senate is the vice-president of the United States, but he is rarely in evidence and has no power other than the right to break tie votes. The majority party elects a president pro tempore (always the member with the most seniority) to preside in the absence of the vice-president.

The Senate majority leader is as close as one comes to a leader in this body, but the powers of the office pale before those of the Speaker of the House. The Senate majority leader has some influence in committee assignments, office space designation, and control of access to the floor of the Senate. The majority leader is also important in the scheduling of the business of the Senate. The degree of actual influence is based less on formal powers, however, than on skills of personal persuasion, the respect of colleagues, visibility in the media as majority party spokesperson, and a role at the center of many of the various communication networks.

The power of the position is thus personal and not institutional; it cannot be passed on to the next leader. The Senate remains a body of independent,

Later president of the United States, Lyndon B. Johnson of Texas was one of the most effective majority leaders in the history of the United States. Here he urges Senators Kennedy, Symington, Humphrey, and Proxmire to vote for an important civil rights bill.

relatively equal members loosely tied together by the thin threads of party loyalty, ideology, and mutual concern about the next election. It is not an environment conducive to decisive leadership.

The Senate minority leader exercises even less power than the majority leader. A skilled politician can use the position, however, to articulate the minority legislative program, to rally the troops for partisan battle when necessary, and to force concessions from the majority. Robert Dole of Kansas (majority leader in the 104th Congress and Republican presidential candidate in 1996) was extremely effective, as was Everett Dirksen of Illinois in the early 1960s.

Congressional Committees

Most of the work of Congress takes place in its many committees and subcommittees. Committees are where many of the details of legislation are hammered out and where much of the oversight of executive branch agencies takes place.

Why Congress Has Committees
Committees serve several useful purposes. For one thing, they allow Congress to process the huge flow of business that comes before it. The committees serve as screening devices, allowing only a small percentage of the bills put forward to take up the time of the House and the Senate.

Committees are also islands of specialization, where members and staff develop the expertise to handle complex issues and to meet executive branch experts on equal terms. The Ways and Means Committee of the House can go toe to toe with the Treasury Department, for instance. Committee expertise is one of the reasons Congress remains a vital lawmaking body.

Members of Congress also use their committee positions to enhance their chances for reelection. Rational lawmakers usually try to secure committee assignments that will allow them to channel benefits to their constituents or to advance an ideological agenda popular in their district or state.

Types of Committees in Congress
There are several kinds of committees, each of which serves a special function in the legislative process.

Standing committees are set up permanently, as specified in the House and Senate rules. These committees are the first stop for potential new laws. The ratio of Democrats to Republicans on each committee is set for each house through a process of negotiation between the majority and minority party leaders. The majority party naturally enjoys a majority on each of the committees and controls the chair, as well as a substantial majority on the most important committees, such as the Budget and Finance Committee in the Senate and the Rules Committee and the Ways and Means Committee in the House. The ratio of Democrats and Republicans on committees is a point of considerable contention between the two parties.

The avalanche of legislative business cannot be managed and given the necessary specialized attention in the full House and Senate standing committees. For most bills, **hearings**, negotiations, and **markup** take place in subcommittees. It is in the subcommittees, moreover, that most oversight of the executive branch takes place. The number of subcommittees multiplied in the House under Democratic party leadership in the 1970s, and their powers relative to the full committees were enhanced. These changes substantially decentralized power in the House, giving rise to what some congressional scholars have called "subcommittee government."

The tide turned in the early 1990s after party leaders and many in Congress came to realize that congressional effectiveness was being undermined by radical

standing committees
Relatively permanent congressional committees that address specific areas of legislation.

hearings
The taking of testimony by a congressional committee or subcommittee.

markup
The process of revising a bill in committee.

decentralization. Although Democrats made the first moves (when they were in the majority) in cutting the number of subcommittees and giving more power to the party leadership, the most dramatic changes came after the Republican capture of both houses of Congress in 1994. In control of the House machinery for the first time in 40 years, Republicans cut the number of committees and subcommittees from 146 to 116, slashed the number of committee staff by almost a third, gave more power over existing subcommittees to committee chairs, and granted more power over legislative business to Speaker of the House Newt Gingrich. The Senate pared its total number of committees and subcommittees from 111 to 99.

select committees

Temporary committees in Congress created to conduct studies or investigations. They have no power to report bills.

Select committees are temporary committees created to conduct studies or investigations. They have no power to send bills to the House or Senate floor. They exist to resolve matters that standing committees cannot or do not wish to handle. Often the issues before select committees are highly visible and gain a great deal of public attention for their members. Select committees investigated the Watergate scandal, the Iran-Contra affair, and the purported Chinese nuclear spying effort at the Los Alamos federal laboratories.

joint committees

Congressional committees with members from both the House and the Senate.

Joint committees, with members from both houses, are organized to facilitate the flow of legislation. The Joint Budget Committee, for instance, helps speed up the normally slow legislative process of considering the annual federal budget.

conference committees

Ad hoc committees, made up of members of both the Senate and the House of Representatives, set up to reconcile differences in the provisions of bills.

Before a bill can go to the president for signature, it must pass in identical form in each chamber. The committee that irons out the differences between House and Senate versions is called a **conference committee**, and one is created anew for each piece of major legislation. While it is probably an exaggeration to call conference committees the "third house of Congress," as some political observers do, there is no denying their central role in the march of bills through the legislative labyrinth. Although they are supposed to reconcile versions of bills coming out of the House and the Senate, conference committees sometimes add, subtract, or amend provisions that are of great consequence. Much of the power of conference committees comes from the fact that bills reported by them to the House and Senate must be voted up or down; no new amendments are allowed.

How Members of Congress Get on Committees Because committees are so central to the legislative process, getting on the right one is important for reelection and for achieving policy goals. Committee assignments are determined by the political parties, guided by the members' **seniority** and preferences. Each party in each chamber goes about the assignment process in a slightly different way. House Democrats use their Steering Committee, chaired by their floor leader, to make assignments. House Republicans have their own Steering Committee on which the Speaker (when Republicans are in the majority) has direct control of one-fourth of the votes. The Speaker also appoints Republican members to the Rules and Ways and Means Committees. In the Senate, both parties use small steering committees made up of party veterans and leaders to make assignments. For Republicans, the key player in the appointment of this committee is the chair of the Republican Conference (all Republican senators); for Democrats, the key player is the Floor Leader.

seniority

Length of service.

Lawmakers generally try to land positions on committees that will help them serve their constituents and better their prospects for reelection. Thus, they will try to join a committee that directly serves their constituency— Agriculture if the member is from a farm district or state or Interior if the member is from a mining or oil district—or one of the elite committees, such as Rules, Ways and Means, Finance, or Appropriations. Appointment to an elite

The U.S. Navy discharged Keith Meinhold after he challenged President Clinton's "don't ask, don't tell" policy on homosexuals in the military by announcing that he was gay on a network television program. A federal district court judge ordered him reinstated. Clinton's "don't ask, don't tell" policy was itself the result of a compromise with the powerful chairs of the congressional armed forces committees in Congress who opposed his intention to allow gays and lesbians to serve in the military.

committee gives a lawmaker not only high visibility and a central role in policymaking but also a strategic vantage point from which to help the constituency and his or her own reelection prospects. There is a long waiting list for assignments to the most powerful committees, so new members are unlikely to be appointed to them. For assignments to nonelite standing committees, congressional leaders try to accommodate the wishes of their members, within the constraints of the seniority system.[29]

The seniority principle usually prevails in the appointment of committee and subcommittee chairs. For most of the twentieth century before the 1970s, appointment by seniority was an unbreakable rule. The most senior committee member of the majority party automatically became chair of the committee; the most senior member of the minority party automatically became the **ranking minority member**. Both Republicans and Democrats in the House instituted the secret ballot among party members for the election of chairs after 1974, however, and seniority was occasionally ignored. Once again, Speaker Gingrich broke long traditions when, in the 104th and 105th Congresses, he sometimes bypassed the most senior committee members in favor of members who would support his conservative legislative program.

ranking minority member
The minority party member with the greatest seniority on a committee.

The Role of Committee Chairs

Not long ago, chairs of committees were the absolute masters of all they surveyed. From 1910, when substantial power was stripped from the Speaker of the House and distributed to committee chairs, until the early 1970s, when the Democrats reined in the autocratic chairs they had created, the heads of congressional committees went unchallenged. Committee chairs hired and assigned staff, controlled the budget, created or abolished subcommittees at will, controlled the agenda, scheduled meetings, and reported (or refused to report) bills to the floor.

Things are different today. Committee chairs now exercise more power over subcommittees and their resources than they did in the 1970s and 1980s, but they have seen much of their power migrate to the party leadership in each house.[30] Republicans in the House and Senate even imposed term limits of six years on committee chairs. The upshot is that decisions that were entirely the province of the chair in the past are now shared with others.

Still, committee chairs remain the most influential and active members of their committees. They cannot command obedience, but they are at the center of all of the lines of communication, retain the power to schedule meetings and control the agenda, control the committee staff, manage committee funds, appoint members to conference committees, and are usually the most senior and experienced members of their committees, to whom some deference is owed.

Rules and Norms in the House and Senate

Like all organizations, Congress is guided by both formal rules and informal norms of behavior.[31] Rules specify precisely how things should be done and what is not allowed. Norms are generally accepted expectations about how people ought to behave and how business ought to proceed. Although the Constitution mandates each chamber to create its own rules, and hence, their formal rules differ considerably, some norms of behavior are common to both houses of Congress.

Members of the House are expected to become specialists in some area or areas of policy and to defer to the judgment of the specialists on most bills. This mutual deference is known as **reciprocity**. The norm of reciprocity is much less evident in the Senate. Because there are fewer members, because they are elected on a statewide basis, and because the Senate has been the breeding ground for many presidential candidacies, a senator has more prestige and power than a representative. As a result, senators are generally unwilling to sit quietly for a term or two, waiting their turn. It is not unusual for a first-term senator to introduce major bills and make important speeches. In the House, such a thing was very unusual in the past. There, the old rule held sway: "To get along, go along."

It is expected in both chambers that lawmakers will respect, or at least tolerate, the reelection motivations of their colleagues. They are expected, for instance, to support a legislative schedule that allows for abundant visits back to the constituency and to vote funding for campaign-related activities such as the right to send mail to constituents free of charge and budgets for district offices. They must learn, moreover, to put up with activities that have no specific legislative purpose but allow their fellow lawmakers to advertise, take credit, and take positions—good examples are the insertion of materials into the *Congressional Record* and speeches on the floor tailored to the evening news back home.

At one time, senators and representatives were expected to act with courtesy and civility toward one another, even if they detested one another—hence the informal prohibition against the use of names and the elaborate references to the "honorable gentleman from Wisconsin" or the "senior senator from California." This expectation of civility has largely disappeared in recent years, especially in the House, as Congress has become a more partisan and ideological place. The nastiness surrounding the Senate hearings on the nominations of Robert Bork and Clarence Thomas for the Supreme Court evinced this mood change; so did the successful effort, led by then–minority whip Newt Gingrich, to topple Speaker Jim Wright in the House.[32] Partisan warfare over the financing of the Clinton presidential campaign, the issue of late-term abortions, the Lewinsky affair, and the impeachment and trial of President Clinton reached white-hot intensity in the late 1990s.

reciprocity

Deferral by members of Congress to the judgment of subject-matter specialists, mainly on minor technical bills.

Legislative life is much more rule-bound in the House of Representatives, because of its large size, than in the Senate; it tends to be more organized and hierarchical (see Table 11.2). Leaders in the House have more power, the majority party exercises more control over legislative affairs, the procedures are more structured, and the individual members have a harder time making their mark. It is geared toward majority rule, with the minority playing a lesser role. The Senate tends to be a more open and fluid place, and it lodges less power in its leaders than the House does. Each senator is more of an independent operator than his or her House colleagues. The Senate is a much more relaxed place, one that accommodates mavericks, tolerates the foibles of its members, and pays more attention to members of the minority party. It is a place where the minority and individual senators play important roles in the legislative process.

Differences between the House and the Senate are especially apparent in floor debate. Bills are scheduled for floor debate in the Senate, for instance, not by a powerful committee but by **unanimous consent**, meaning that business can be blocked by a single dissenter. In the Senate, in a growing practice that is beginning to draw criticism, each senator has the power to place a hold on a bill or nomination to delay consideration by the whole body. Unlike the House, where debate on a bill is strictly regulated as to amendments and time limit, the Senate's tradition allows for unlimited numbers of amendments and unlimited debate. Senators in the minority have periodically used this tolerance of unlimited amendments and debate to good effect. Because limiting debate is so difficult in the Senate, the opponents of a bill can tie up legislative business by refusing to stop debating its merits. This practice is known as the **filibuster**. During a filibuster, senators opposing a bill have been known to talk for hour upon hour, often working in shifts. The only requirement is that they say something; they cannot

unanimous consent

Legislative action taken "without objection" as a way to expedite business; used to conduct much of the business of the Senate.

filibuster

A parliamentary device used in the Senate to prevent a bill from coming to a vote by "talking it to death," made possible by the norm of unlimited debate.

Table 11.2	Differences Between House and Senate Rules and Norms
Senate	**House**
Informal, open, nonhierarchical	Rule-bound, hierarchical
Leaders have few formal powers	Leaders have many formal powers
Members may serve on two or more major committees	Members restricted to one major committee
Less specialized	More specialized
Unrestricted floor debate	Restricted floor debate
Unlimited amendments possible	Limited amendments
Amendments need not be germane	Amendments must be germane
Unlimited time for debate unless shortened by unanimous consent or halted by invocation of cloture	Limited time for debate
More prestige	Less prestige
More reliance on staff	Less reliance on staff
Minority party plays a larger role	Minority party plays a smaller role
Less partisan	More partisan

hold the floor without speaking. During a filibuster, senators need not even talk about the bill itself; Senate rules do not require remarks to be germane. Senators have read from novels or quoted verse, have told stories about their children, and have quoted long lists of sports statistics. The purpose is to force the majority to give up the fight and move on to other business. The filibuster record for a single senator belongs to Strom Thurmond of South Carolina, who held the floor for more than 24 hours opposing a 1957 civil rights bill.

When a very strong majority favors a bill or when a bill that has great national import and visibility is before the body, the Senate can close debate by invoking **cloture**. Cloture requires support by three-fifths of those present and voting. It is very rarely tried; it very rarely succeeds. A Republican filibuster in 1993 forced President Clinton to abandon his economic stimulus plan after Democrats failed to convince any Republicans to join them in a vote to invoke cloture. Republican filibusters in 1994 and 1997 blocked consideration of campaign finance reform. Cloture is so difficult to invoke that the mere threat of a filibuster by a determined minority party, a growing trend in the Senate, often forces the majority to comply with the wishes of the minority. Many observers believe that the increasing use of the filibuster threat circumvents majority rule and therefore undermines democracy.

cloture

A vote to end a filibuster or a debate; requires the votes of three-fifths of the membership of the Senate.

Legislative Responsibilities: How a Bill Becomes a Law

We can put much of what we have learned to work by seeing how a bill moves through the legislative labyrinth to become a law. The path by which a bill becomes a law is so strewn with obstacles that few bills survive; in fact, only about 6 percent of all bills that are introduced are enacted. To make law is exceedingly difficult; to block bills from becoming laws is relatively easy. At each step along the way (see Figure 11.8), a "no" decision can stop the passage of a bill in its tracks. As one account points out, members of the House or the Senate have "two principal functions: to make laws and to keep laws from being made. The first of these [they] perform only with sweat, patience, and a remarkable skill in the handling of creaking machinery; but the second they perform daily, with ease and infinite variety."[33]

What follows describes how a bill becomes a law most of the time. Minor bills are often considered in each house under special rules that allow shortcuts. Thus, in the House, the "suspension calendar" and the "corrections calendar" set aside certain times for consideration of minor matters. It is also worth noting that bills involving the federal budget—authorization and appropriations bills—have several unique aspects to them, several of which are described in the chapter on domestic policy.

Introducing a Bill   A bill can be introduced only by a member of Congress. In reality, bills are often written in the executive branch. The initial draft of the bill that became the Tax Reform Act of 1986, for instance, was fashioned in the Treasury Department by a committee headed by the department's secretary, James Baker. After their 1994 electoral landslide victory, however, congressional Republicans largely ignored legislative proposals from the Clinton administration, focusing instead on the promises in their Contract with America. Bills are often written by interest groups. Industry trade groups, for example, wrote substantial parts of bills designed to roll back timber and mining regulations in 1995.

With the exception of tax bills (which must originate in the House), a bill may be introduced in either the House or the Senate. In the House, a member

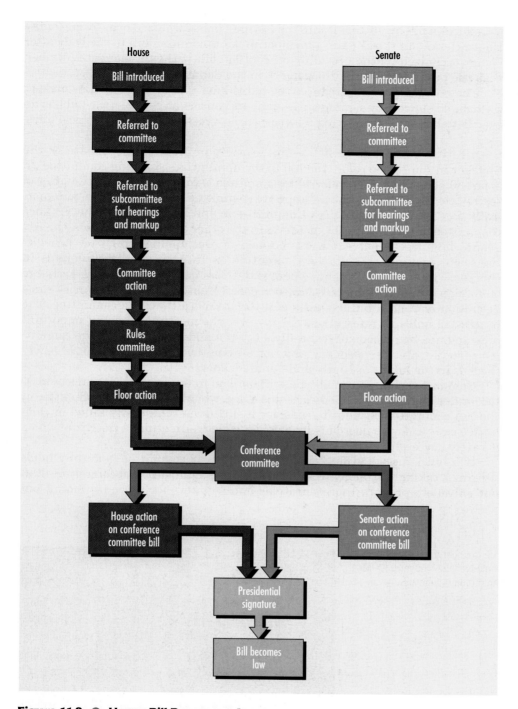

House

Bill introduced

Referred to committee

Referred to subcommittee for hearings and markup

Committee action

Rules committee

Floor action

Senate

Bill introduced

Referred to committee

Referred to subcommittee for hearings and markup

Committee action

Floor action

Conference committee

House action on conference committee bill

Senate action on conference committee bill

Presidential signature

Bill becomes law

Figure 11.8 ● **How a Bill Becomes a Law**

This diagram shows the path by which most bills introduced in Congress become law. As explained in the text, the road that bills must travel is complex and difficult, and few bills survive it. A bill can be derailed at any stop in its passage. A subcommittee can refuse to report a bill; a bill may be defeated on the floor of each chamber; a conference committee may fail to reach an agreement on a compromise; the conference bill may be defeated in either chamber; or the president may veto the bill.

hopper

The box in the House of Representatives in which proposed bills are placed.

introduces a bill by putting it into the **hopper** (a box watched over by one of the House clerks). In the Senate, a member must announce a bill to the body after being recognized by the presiding officer. The bill is then assigned a number, with the prefix *H.R.* in the House or *S.* in the Senate.

The lawmaker who introduces the bill is known as its *sponsor*. Lawmakers try to build support by signing on as many cosponsors as possible; the bill has an even better chance of surviving if its cosponsors cross party and ideological lines.

Committee Action on a Bill   The presiding officer in the Senate or the Speaker in the House refers the bill to the appropriate standing committee. In about 80 percent of cases, referral to committee is routine; the subject matter of the bill clearly indicates the appropriate committee. Revenue bills go automatically to the Ways and Means Committee in the House and to the Finance Committee in the Senate, for instance. In the other 20 percent of cases, the relevant committee is not so obvious because of overlapping committee jurisdictions. For instance, the House Committee on International Relations is in charge of "international policy," whereas the Commerce Committee is in charge of "foreign commerce generally." In such cases, House leaders can exercise some discretion or send a bill (or parts of a bill) to more than one committee. The practice of multiple referral usually involves the most complex and important bills and has increased substantially since the mid-1970s.[34] The more committee referrals are discretionary and not automatic, of course, the more power there is in the hands of House and Senate leaders.

Committee chairs normally pass the bill on to the appropriate subcommittee for hearings. Many a bill dies at this stage, when either the subcommittee or the full committee declines to consider it further. A bill quietly killed in committee can reach the floor only by a device called a **discharge petition**, which is rarely successful.

discharge petition

A petition signed by 218 House members to force a bill that has been before a committee for at least 30 days while the House is in session out of the committee and onto the floor for consideration.

If a bill is accepted for consideration, the subcommittee generally holds hearings, taking testimony from people for and against it. Subcommittee staff not only help prepare representatives and senators for the questioning but

Congressional staff help members of Congress carry out their many legislative responsibilities. Here Representative Dick Gephardt (D–MO) meets with a member of his staff to plan the day's activities.

also often take part in the questioning themselves. The subcommittee may then forward the bill as rewritten by the staff and subcommittee members to the full committee, or it can decide to allow the bill to go no further.

Rewriting the bill in committee is called the *markup* (discussed earlier), which usually occurs amid very intense bargaining and deal making, with an eye toward fashioning a bill that will muster majority support in the full committee and on the floors of the House and the Senate and that will gain the support of the president. The staff plays a central role in the markup. Lawmakers and staff are also usually in contact with relevant interest groups and executive branch policymakers during this rewrite stage.

The subcommittee reports its action to the full committee. The committee chair, in consultation with other important members of his or her committee, may opt for the committee to hold its own hearings and markup sessions, may decide to kill the bill outright, or may simply accept the action of the subcommittee. If the subcommittee has done its job well and has consulted with the most important players on the full committee (especially the chair), the committee will simply rubber-stamp the bill and move it along for floor action.

Floor Action on a Bill   If a bill is favorably reported from committee, congressional leaders schedule it for floor debate. In the House, a bill must first go to the Rules Committee, which must issue a rule under whose terms the bill will be considered. A rule specifies such things as the amount of time for debate and the number (if any) and nature of amendments allowed. The Rules Committee may choose not to issue a rule at all or to drag its feet, as it did with civil rights bills until the mid-1960s. This has happened less often in recent years because both Democratic and Republican Speakers have had more power over Rules Committee appointments. The committee can also grant a "closed rule," allowing only a yes or no vote without amendments, as it generally does with tax bills.

Floor debate in the Senate, where rules do not limit debate as in the House, is much more freewheeling. Floor debate is also more important in the Senate in determining the final form a bill will take because Senate committees are less influential than House committees. Senators are also less likely to defer to committee judgments.

After floor debate, the entire membership of the chamber votes on the bill, either as reported by the committee or (more often) after amendments have been added. If the bill receives a favorable vote, it then goes through the same obstacle course in the other chamber or awaits action by the other house if the bill was introduced there at the same time.

Conference Committee   Even if the bill makes it through both houses, its journey is not yet over. Bills passed by the House and the Senate almost always differ from one another, sometimes in minor ways and sometimes in quite substantial ways. Before the bill goes to the president, its conflicting versions must be rewritten so that a single bill gains the approval of both chambers of Congress. This compromise bill is fashioned in a conference committee made up of members from both the House and the Senate, customarily from the relevant committees.

There are ways to avoid "going to conference," and each is used frequently:

1. One house may simply adopt the bill from the other house, word for word.
2. Members of the two houses may confer throughout, sending bills back and forth, so that the differences are ironed out before final passage.[35]

A bill from a conference committee must be voted yes or no on the floors of the House and the Senate; no amendments or further changes are allowed. If, and only if, both houses approve it, the bill is forwarded to the president for consideration.

Presidential Action   Because the president plays an important constitutional role in turning a bill into a law, he or his assistants and advisers are usually consulted throughout the legislative process. If the president approves the bill, he signs it and it becomes law. If he is not particularly favorable but does not want to block the bill, it becomes law after ten days if he takes no action. He can also **veto** the bill and return it to Congress. A bill can still become law by a two-thirds vote of each house, which will override the president's veto. A president can also kill a bill at the end of a congressional session if he takes no action and Congress adjourns before ten days pass. This is known as a **pocket veto**.

Legislative Oversight of the Executive Branch

Oversight is another important responsibility of Congress. Oversight involves keeping an eye on how the executive branch carries out the provisions of the laws that Congress has passed and on possible abuses of power by executive branch officials, including the president.

Oversight is primarily the province of the committees and subcommittees of Congress, and it is among Congress's most visible and dramatic roles. High-profile examples of legislative probes of alleged administrative misconduct include Watergate, the Iran-Contra affair, Whitewater, the savings-and-loan collapse and bailout, purported Chinese nuclear spying, and the Branch Davidian tragedy at Waco.

Hearings are an important part of the oversight process. Testimony is taken from agency officials, outside experts, and such congressional investigatory institutions as the Government Accounting Office and the Office of Technology Assessment. The hearings are not simply information-gathering exercises, however. As often as not, they are designed to send signals from committee members to the relevant part of the bureaucracy. Hearings that focus on the overly aggressive efforts of Internal Revenue Service agents to collect taxes, for instance, are a clear signal to IRS officials that they had better rein in their agents before the next round of hearings on the budget.

Congress spends an increasing amount of its time on oversight. Given the scale of federal government activities, however, it can pay attention to only the small tip of the iceberg that is the executive branch. For the most part, members of Congress pay attention to matters brought to them by others, mainly by constituents, the media, and interest groups.[36] This ensures not only that important problems will be attended to but also that the representatives and senators who are involved can claim credit and stockpile goodwill (and contributions) for the next election cycle. One problem with this "fire alarm" model of oversight, however, is the favored attention it gives to the concerns of organized interest groups.

Congress's most powerful instrument of oversight of the Executive Branch is impeachment. This is a blunt tool, rarely used, except in the most partisan atmosphere or in cases involving truly egregious executive behavior. Only seven executives have ever been removed from office by the Senate. No president has ever been convicted, but the impeachment processes in the House of presidents Johnson, Nixon, and Clinton were so divisive that Congress treads very cautiously in this area.

veto

Presidential disapproval of a bill that has been passed by both houses of Congress. The president's veto can be overridden by a two-thirds vote in each house.

pocket veto

Rejection of a bill if the president takes no action on it for ten days and Congress has adjourned during that period.

LongmanParticipate

CourseCompass

simulation
You Are a Member of Congress

Congress, Public Policy, and the American People

The way Congress is organized and operates greatly influences the kinds of public policies we have, how people feel about government, and the quality of democracy in the United States.

Congress as Policymaker

A frequently heard criticism of Congress is that it is so parochial and fragmented that it cannot fashion coherent national policy.[37] The argument goes this way. First, Congress is filled with members who are judged by the voters on the basis of their individual attributes and service to the district and to interest groups, not on the basis of the performance of Congress as a whole. One result is that lawmakers worry more about themselves than about the standing and effectiveness of their institution or its collective national policymaking responsibilities.[38]

Second, because lawmakers are responsive to organized interests, serve the constituency as their first order of business, and try to avoid difficult decisions that might put their reelection at risk (or so it is claimed), Congress cannot easily tackle the nation's most difficult problems or think about solutions in general terms. Congress would rather practice "distributive" politics, in which benefits are parceled out to a wide range of constituency and interest group claimants. While this pattern conforms to the self-interested electoral calculations of the individual member, it is, according to many observers, the basis for the overall ineffectiveness and decline of Congress as a national policy-making institution.

It is hard to assess the validity of these criticisms. The evidence is mixed. Congress has, at times, fashioned broad and coherent national policies in response to tangible problems and strong majority opinions. We have also seen that Congress retains a far greater policymaking role than legislative bodies in parliamentary systems and that on domestic issues, it is becoming ever more forceful. Nevertheless, historically, Congress has functioned best as a policy-maker when the president, supported by the existence of a national majority in favor of a particular course of action, is able to provide strong leadership. Franklin Roosevelt's New Deal legislative program, Lyndon Johnson's Great Society, and Ronald Reagan's conservative triumphs in 1981 come to mind. For a time, during Newt Gingrich's leadership of the conservative revolution in the House of Representatives in the 104th Congress, it appeared that a major legislative program could be passed without (or against) presidential leadership. Once most bills from the Contract with America failed to become law, however, it became apparent again that the creation of broad and coherent national policies requires presidential leadership.

Congress and the American People

Although Americans tend to approve of their own representatives and senators, they have low regard for Congress as an institution. Except in rare instances, fewer Americans say they believe Congress is "doing a good job" than believe that the president is doing a good job. Fewer report having "a great deal of confidence" in Congress as an institution than for the Supreme Court or the president. This pattern has endured for a long time and shows no sign of abating.[39] Approval and confidence ratings, much as those for the president, tend to track the economy and confidence about the future among Americans, being higher in good times and lower in bad times. But it is inescapable that when it comes to national institutions, Congress does not fare well.

Scholars and journalists have advanced a number of reasons for this state of affairs, including rising partisanship, gridlock in Congress and between Congress and the president, and the apparent influence in Congress of special interests. Two scholars have a unique and intriguing alternative explanation: the American people, they suggest, often do not really like the messiness of the democratic process itself, so evident in the give-and-take of the legislative process. As they put it,

> *People do not wish to see uncertainty, conflicting opinions, long debate, competing interests, confusion, bargaining, and compromised, imperfect solutions. They want government to do its job quietly and efficiently, sans conflict and sans fuss. In short . . . they often seek a patently unrealistic form of democracy.*[40]

HOW DEMOCRATIC ARE WE?

PROPOSITION: Congress is out of touch with the American people and doesn't do what the people want it to do.

AGREE: Although representatives and senators must ultimately face the voters, their reelection prospects are strongly related to how much money they can raise for their campaigns. With a healthy campaign war chest, as well as the advantages they have as incumbents, representatives and senators can get their message to voters and make the case that they should remain in office. Building a healthy campaign war chest also depends heavily on money from special interests and wealthy individuals. It is not surprising, then, that they pay particular attention to what these contributors want. Additionally, as we have demonstrated in this chapter, the way Congress is set up makes it very difficult to turn the wishes of the majority into concrete laws, even if members of Congress are inclined to be responsive.

DISAGREE: Although they have to attend to the interests of big contributors, representatives and senators are ultimately accountable to the voters. It is for this reason that they pay a great deal of attention to their constituent mail, spend substantial time in the home district and state talking to the voters, and invest heavily in polling to stay in touch. And, in the end, on most major issues, Congress legislates in ways that match what the American people want.

THE AUTHORS: If you believe, as the framers did, that Congress ought to be a deliberative body, free from popular pressures, acting in the public interest as representatives and senators define it, then the failure to legislate exactly as the public would want will cause you no great anxiety. If you believe that Congress ought to be democratically responsive, then you might take solace in the evidence that shows that Congress follows public opinion to a substantial degree in the long run. However, whatever you believe about the nature of the relationship between the public and Congress, you ought to be discomforted by the disproportionate role of special interests and large contributors on a wide range of important issues, particularly those that are out of public view.

Summary

The framers of the Constitution wanted to fashion a legislative branch that was both energetic and limited. They granted Congress legislative power, gave it an existence independent of the executive branch, and enumerated an impressive range of powers. They also gave the other branches powers to check legislative excesses, created a bicameral body, and strictly denied certain powers to Congress.

Structural change in the nation has shaped Congress, influencing it to increase in size, expand the volume and complexity of its business, and become more institutionalized and professional.

Congress is a representative institution. Its members are constantly balancing the preferences of the people in their constituencies and important interest groups and contributors. Because elections are the most important mechanism for representation, and because they are the way in which members attain office, elections dominate the time and energy of lawmakers and shape how Congress organizes itself and goes about its business.

To conduct its business, Congress depends on an elaborate set of norms and rules and a web of committees and subcommittees, political parties, legislative leaders, and an extensive staff. Several of these elements encourage fragmentation, decentralization, and occasional gridlock but also allow the development of the specialized expertise that enables Congress to meet the executive branch on equal terms. Other tools help the members coordinate and expedite legislative business.

Suggestions for Further Reading

Caro, Robert. *The Years of Lyndon Johnson.* New York: Knopf, 1982.
This classic and award-winning biography of Lyndon Baines Johnson of Texas reveals more about how Congress worked in the "old days" than virtually any academic treatise.

Davidson, Roger H., and Walter J. Oleszek. *Congress and Its Members,* 7th ed. Washington, D.C.: Congressional Quarterly Press, 2000.
The classic textbook on Congress, now in its seventh edition.

Fenno, Richard F., Jr. *Home Style: House Members in Their Districts.* Boston: Little, Brown, 1978.
A modern classic that examines what members do in their districts and why.

McLoughlin, Merrill, ed. *The Impeachment and Trial of President Clinton.* New York: Times Books, 1999.
The complete transcripts of Congress's attempt to remove the president from office; a fascinating window on how Congress works.

Oleszek, Walter J. *Congressional Procedures and the Policy Process.* Washington, D.C.: Congressional Quarterly Press, 1996.
The most comprehensive compilation yet published of the rules and operations of the legislative process in Congress, written by a scholar who served as the policy director of the Joint Committee on the Organization of Congress.

Sinclair, Barbara. *Unorthodox Lawmaking: New Legislative Processes in the U.S. Congress.* Washington, D.C.: Congressional Quarterly Press, 1997.
Argues that the traditional textbook rendition of "how a bill becomes a law" has dramatically changed over the past two decades.

Specialized newspapers and journals: *The Hill, Roll Call, Congressional Quarterly, National Journal.*
Valuable sources for up-to-the-minute, in-depth coverage of what is happening in Congress.

Internet Sources

Capweb **www.capweb.net**
An extremely rich site for information on Congress. Features include commentary on the issues before Congress, access to information on pending legislation, legislative schedules and ways to contact members of Congress, caucuses, committees, rules, histories of the House and Senate, and much more. Links, as well, to Congressional Quarterly *(journal) and* The Hill *(weekly newspaper), the House and Senate, and the other two federal branches.*

Federal Election Commission **http://www.fec.gov/**
Information on campaign finance for presidential and congressional elections.

Thomas **http://thomas.loc.gov/**
Expansive repository of information on the House of Representatives, including the full text and progress of bills, the Congressional Record, *legislative procedures and rules, committee actions, and more.*

U.S. House of Representatives Home Page **http://www.house.gov/**
House schedule, House organization and procedures, links to House committees, information on contacting representatives, and historical documents on the House of Representatives.

U.S. Senate Home Page **http://www.senate.gov/**
Similar to the House of Representatives Home Page, focused on the Senate. One exciting new feature is a virtual tour of the Capitol.

Notes

1. Juliet Eilperin and Matthew Vita, "Elections Narrow GOP Advantage in the House," *The Washington Post,* November 8, 2000, p. A1. Additional source materials for this story of the 2000 elections are from Mark Preston, "A House and Senate Divided," *Rollcall,* November 9, 2000, p. 1; John Mercurio, Rachel Van Dongen, and Paul Kane, "Democrats Fall Short in the House," *Rollcall,* November 9, 2000, p. 1; and "Party Fundraising Escalates," *The Federal Election Commission,* November 3, 2000.

2. Roger H. Davidson and Walter J. Oleszek, *Congress and Its Members,* 7th ed. (Washington, D.C.: Congressional Quarterly Press, 2000), pp. 17–18.

3. Davidson and Oleszek, *Congress and Its Members,* p. 25.

4. Quoted in Charles Warren, *The Supreme Court in U.S. History* (Boston: Little, Brown, 1919), p. 195.

5. Walter J. Oleszek, *Congressional Procedures and the Policy Process,* 4th ed. (Washington, D.C.: Congressional Quarterly Press, 1996), p. 4.

6. Quoted in Charles Henning, *The Wit and Wisdom of Politics* (Golden, CO: Fulcrum, 1989), p. 235.

7. Abraham Lincoln, announcement in the *Sagamo Journal,* New Salem, Illinois (June 13, 1836).

8. Paul Lewis, "In the World's Parliaments, Women Are Still a Small Minority," *New York Times* (March 16, 1997), p. 7.

9. Davidson and Oleszek, *Congress and Its Members,* pp. 128–129.

10. Gary W. Cox and Jonathan Katz, "The Reapportionment Revolution and Bias in U.S. Congressional Elections," *American Journal of Political Science* 43 (1999), pp. 812–840.

11. Davidson and Oleszek, *Congress and Its Members,* pp. 53–55.

12. Charles Cameron, David Epstein, and Sharon O'Halloran, "Do Majority-Minority Districts Maximize Black Representation in Congress?" *American Political Science*

Review 90 (1996), pp. 794–812; David Epstein and Sharon O'Halloran, "A Social Science Approach to Race, Districting and Representation," *American Political Science Review* 93 (1999), pp.187–191; and David Lublin, *The Paradox of Representation: Racial Gerrymandering and Minority Interests* (Princeton: Princeton University Press, 1997).

13. Davidson and Oleszek, *Congress and Its Members,* p. 74.

14. Gary W. Cox and Eric Magar, "How Much Is Majority Status in the U.S. Congress Worth?" *American Political Science Review* 93 (1999), pp. 299–309.

15. Richard Hall and Frank W. Wayman, "Buying Time: Moneyed Interests and the Mobilization of Bias in Congressional Committees," *American Political Science Review* 84 (1990), pp. 797–820.

16. David R. Mayhew, *Congress: The Electoral Connection* (New Haven, CT: Yale University Press, 1974).

17. Malcolm Jewell, "Legislators and Their Districts," *Legislative Studies Quarterly* 13 (1988), pp. 403–412.

18. Richard F. Fenno Jr., *Senators on the Home Trail* (Norman, OK: University of Oklahoma Press, 1996).

19. Bruce Cain, John A. Ferejohn, and Morris P. Fiorina, *The Personal Vote: Constituency Service and Electoral Independence* (Cambridge, MA: Harvard University Press, 1987); Glenn Parker, *Homeward Bound: Explaining Change in Congressional Behavior* (Pittsburgh: University of Pittsburgh Press, 1986).

20. Robert S. Erikson, "Constituency Opinion and Congressional Behavior," *American Journal of Political Science* 22 (1978), pp. 511–535; Robert S. Erikson and Gerald C. Wright, "Voters, Candidates, and Issues in Congressional Elections," in Lawrence C. Dodd and Bruce I. Oppenheimer, eds., *Congress Reconsidered,* 4th ed. (Washington, D.C.: Congressional Quarterly Press, 1989), pp. 91–116.

21. Alan Monroe, "Consistency Between Public Preferences and National Policy Decisions," *American Politics Quarterly* 7 (1979), pp. 3–19; Benjamin I. Page and Robert Y. Shapiro, "Effects of Public Opinion on Policy," *American Political Science Review* 77 (1983), pp. 175–190.

22. Davidson and Oleszek, *Congress and Its Members,* p. 267.

23. Ibid., p. 268.

24. Alison Mitchell, "Compromise Takes a Holiday," *New York Times* (August 8, 1999), Section 4, p. 1.

25. Davidson and Oleszek, *Congress and Its Members,* p. 269–270.

26. See John J. Kornacki, ed., *Leading Congress: New Styles, New Strategies* (Washington, D.C.: Congressional Quarterly Press, 1990); David W. Rohde, *Parties and Leaders in the Postreform Congress* (Chicago: University of Chicago Press, 1991).

27. Oleszek, *Congressional Procedures and the Policy Process,* p. 33.

28. Melinda Henneberger, "Delay Holds No Gavel, But Firm Grip on Reins," *New York Times* (June 21, 1999), p. 1.

29. David A. Rohde and Kenneth A. Shepsle, "Democratic Committee Assignments in the House of Representatives: Strategic Aspects of a Social Choice Process," in Matthew D. McCubbins and Terry Sullivan, eds., *Congress: Structure and Policy* (New York: Cambridge University Press, 1987).

30. Lawrence C. Dodd and Bruce I. Oppenheimer, "Revolution in the House: Testing the Limits of Party Government," in Lawrence C. Dodd and Bruce I. Oppenheimer, eds., *Congress Reconsidered,* 4th ed. (Washington, D.C.: Congressional Quarterly Press, 1989).

31. Davidson and Oleszek, *Congress and Its Members,* ch. 8; Donald R. Mathews, *U.S. Senators and Their World* (Chapel Hill, NC: University of North Carolina Press, 1960).

32. Eric M. Uslaner, *The Decline of Comity in Congress* (Ann Arbor, MI: University of Michigan Press, 1996).

33. Robert Bendiner, *Obstacle Course on Capitol Hill* (New York: McGraw-Hill, 1964), p. 15.

34. Garry Young and Joseph Cooper, "Multiple Referral and the Transformation of House Decision Making," in Lawrence C. Dodd and Bruce I. Oppenheimer, eds., *Congress Reconsidered,* 5th ed. (Washington, D.C.: Congressional Quarterly Press, 1993).

35. Oleszek, *Congressional Procedures and the Policy Process,* pp. 253–254.

36. Matthew D. McCubbins and John Schwartz, "Congressional Oversight Overlooked: Police Patrols and Fire Alarms," in Matthew D. McCubbins and Terry Sullivan, eds., *Congress: Structure and Policy* (New York: Cambridge University Press, 1987).

37. Morris P. Fiorina, *Congress: Keystone of the Washington Establishment,* 2nd ed. (New Haven, CT: Yale University Press, 1989); Mayhew, *Congress;* Gary C. Jacobson, *Politics of Congressional Elections,* 2nd ed. (Boston: Little, Brown, 1987).

38. Morris P. Fiorina, "The Decline of Collective Responsibility," *Daedalus* (Summer 1980), pp. 24–37; Cain et al., *The Personal Vote.*

39. Davidson and Oleszek, *Congress and Its Members,* pp. 413–417; and John R. Hibbing and Elizabeth Theiss-Morse, *Congress as Public Enemy: Public Attitudes Toward American Political Institutions* (New York: Cambridge University Press, 1995).

40. Hibbing and Theiss-Morse, *Congress as Public Enemy,* p. 147.

CHAPTER 12
The President

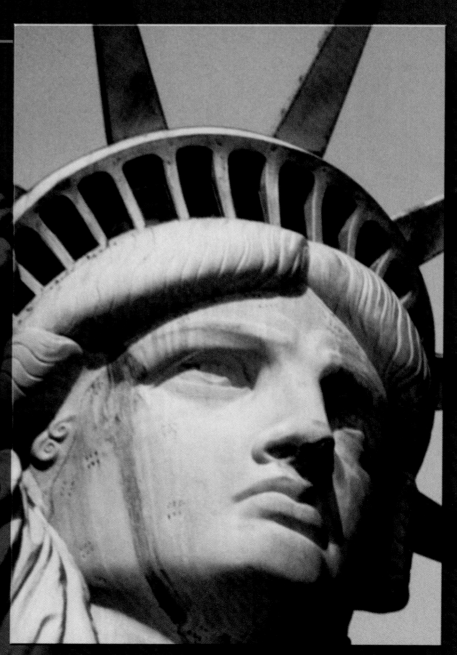

The Reagan Revolution

Ronald Reagan took office in 1981 after a landslide election victory, promising a "new American revolution" that would change the size, reach, and responsibilities of the federal government. To "get government off the backs of the people," he proposed the largest tax cut in American history (directed mainly at upper-income groups and corporations), sharp cutbacks in regulations, and major reductions in domestic social programs. Promising to regain respect and influence for the United States around the world, he also proposed the steepest rise in defense spending in peacetime American history.

The Reagan program was breathtaking in scope. Most observers were skeptical about its chances in Congress, because the Republicans had only a slim majority in the Senate and the Democrats still controlled the House of Representatives, with 243 seats to the Republicans' 192. Surely, the Reagan Revolution would be buried in committees, or compromised, and business would go on as usual.

President Reagan thought otherwise. He brought all his formidable personal skills, energy, and resources to bear on the task of passing his program. Reagan cultivated friendly relations with members of Congress, inviting them to White House breakfasts and passing out tickets for the presidential box at the Kennedy Center for the Performing Arts. He offered shrewd deals to those who would back his tax and budget package: sugar price supports for representatives from Louisiana; Amtrak and Conrail funding increases for moderate Republicans from the Northeast; natural gas deregulation for representatives from the energy states.

Besides carrots, Reagan also used the stick. Democrats from conservative areas in the South, where a majority of voters had supported Reagan, found the White House turning up the heat in their own districts, mobilizing influential groups such as the National Conservative Political Action Committee and the Moral Majority, sending in Vice-President Bush and Representative Jack Kemp, and getting major campaign contributors to urge cooperation with Reagan.[1]

Aiming to put further pressure on Congress, Reagan worked to build up his popularity with the general public. Like most new presidents, Reagan began with a fairly high level of popular approval. He sustained and increased it with his genial and winning public personality, the emotional patriotism that swelled among Americans on the return of U.S. hostages from Iran in January 1981, and the successful launch of the space shuttle *Columbia*. In April, Reagan turned his survival of an assassination attempt into a public relations triumph, displaying courage and humor. While still recovering, he made a dramatic televised appearance before Congress to plead for his programs.

Although polls showed continuing public support for many domestic social programs that Reagan opposed, the politicians were awed by the scale of Reagan's electoral victory and by the height of his popularity. The administration's budget sailed through the Senate by a vote of 72 to 20. Even in the Democrat-controlled House of Representatives, Reagan got his way at every critical juncture, mainly because of support from southern conservative Democrats. Budget aide David Stockman later gloated, "The politicians had flinched. They had rubber-stamped the Reagan Revolution."[2]

The president also worked tirelessly for his tax cut bill. Using the same mix of personal charm and popularity, judicious compromises, winning rhetoric, and hints of retribution for anyone who failed to cooperate, he had his way here as well. The Economic Recovery Tax Act was passed on July 29, 1981.

The Reagan Revolution would prove to have profound effects that lasted on into the 1990s and beyond. The military buildup may have contributed to the collapse of the Soviet Union, which squandered vast resources trying to catch up. Social programs, although not cut as drastically as Reagan wanted, remained under severe pressure in later years because less tax revenue was available. The tax cuts probably contributed to the substantial economic growth of the 1980s but also to a massive increase in the size of the national debt (which *tripled* in the Reagan years) and to dramatic increases in income and wealth inequality. Nevertheless, the Reagan Revolution was a huge political success and played a role in the resurgence of the Republican Party and its eventual capture of Congress in 1994.

What accounts for Reagan's victory? If we take things at face value, it appears that Ronald Reagan was a heroic figure, able single-handedly to shake America from its lethargy and reinvigorate the presidential office.

Without doubt, Reagan's personal skills and energy played an important part. We will see in this chapter, however, that presidential will, determination, and personality are only part of the story. The president always acts in a context defined by the Constitution and the evolution of the office; a particular governmental and political environment; and a larger economic, social, cultural, and international structure. Moreover, what sort of president we have, and what he wants and tries to accomplish, is itself influenced by political and structural factors.

In Reagan's case, the time was ripe for his brand of leadership. The nation had experienced dramatic drops in its international economic and military standing, in its confi-

dence, and in corporate profits and people's standards of living. People were ready, even desperate, for change. Media, business, and academic leaders began calling for a reorientation of public policy. Conservative political action committees, think tanks, and interest groups, fueled by massive corporate funding, mounted a campaign for a conservative policy renewal in Washington and for the election of Reagan and other Republicans.[3] Congress, itself under pressure from financial contributors and unsure how to escape the downward spiral, looked for presidential leadership and ultimately responded when Reagan provided it.

The Reagan Revolution, from this viewpoint, involved much more than Ronald Reagan; to understand it fully requires that we understand not just the personality, style, and effectiveness of Reagan as president but also the governmental, political, and structural contexts within which he operated. The same is true of other presidents.

▶ Thinking Critically About This Chapter

This chapter is about the American presidency, how it has evolved, and what role it plays in American politics and government.

Using the Framework. You will see in this chapter how the presidential office has changed substantially from how the framers envisioned it, primarily because of changes in America's international situation, the nature of its economy, and popular expectations. You will also see how presidents interact with other governmental institutions, such as Congress and the Court, and with political linkage level actors, such as political parties, public opinion, the mass media and interest groups, and how these interactions influence what government does.

Using the Democracy Standard. You will see in this chapter how the presidential office, although not envisioned by the framers to be a democratic one, has become more directly connected to and responsive to the American people. On the other hand, you will be asked to think about whether presidents' growing ability to influence the thinking of the public and shape their perceptions of public events undermines democracy. ▶

The Expanding Presidency

The American presidency has grown considerably since our nation's beginning. The increase has occurred in presidential responsibilities, burdens, power, and impact.

The Earliest and Latest Presidencies Compared

When George W. Bush was sworn into office in January 2001, he presided over a federal budget with more than $1.8 trillion in annual expenditures and a federal establishment with approximately 2.4 million civilian employees. He was

The presidency has grown in scale and responsibility. As commander in chief of the armed forces, President George Washington commanded an army of just over 700 soldiers and had little to do with affairs outside the United States. Today, the president commands a force of about 1.4 million stationed all over the world.

Source: © Gift of Edgar William, Chrysler & Bernice Garbish/The Metropolitan Museum of Art

commander in chief of the armed forces, with about 1.4 million men and women in uniform; hundreds of military bases at home and scattered throughout the world; and perhaps 20,000 deliverable nuclear warheads, enough to obliterate every medium-sized or large city in the world many times over. The United States in 2001 had a population of almost 278 million diverse people; a Gross Domestic Product of more than $9.5 trillion; and a land area of some 3.8 million square miles, stretching from Alaska to Florida and from Hawaii to Maine.[4]

By contrast, when George Washington took office as the first president, he had a total budget (for 1789–1791) of just over $4 million. Washington had only a handful of federal employees. Even by 1801, there were only about 300 federal officeholders in the capital. Washington's cabinet consisted of just five officials: the secretaries of state, war, and the treasury; a postmaster general; and an attorney general (who acted as the president's personal attorney, rather than as head of a full-fledged Justice Department). The entire Department of State consisted of just one secretary, one chief clerk, six minor clerks, and one messenger.

In 1790, only about 700 Americans were in uniform, and they had no way to project force around the world. Federal government functions were few. The entire United States consisted of the 13 original eastern and southeastern states, with only 864,746 square miles of land area; the population was only about 4 million persons, most living on small farms.[5]

The Founders' Conception of the Presidency

The Founders certainly had in mind a presidency more like Washington's than Bush's. As discussed in Chapter 2, Article II of the Constitution provided for a single executive who would be strong, compared with his role under the Congress-dominated Articles of Confederation, but the Constitution's sparse language barely hinted at the range of things twentieth-century presidents would do. The Constitution made the president "commander in chief" of the armed forces, for example, without any suggestion that there would be a vast standing army that presidents could send abroad to fight, without a declaration of war. It empowered presidents to appoint and to "require the opinion in writing" of executive department heads without indicating that a huge federal bureaucracy would evolve. The Constitution provided that presidents could from time to time "recommend . . . measures" to Congress without specifying that these proposals would very often (especially in the twentieth century) come to dominate the legislative agenda. Still, the vague language of the

Constitution proved flexible enough to encompass the great expansion of the presidency.

The Dormant Presidency

In Chapter 4, we described some of the great structural changes in the economy, society, and territory of the United States that led to an enormous expansion of the federal government. Certain presidents played important parts in these trends, and the office of the presidency changed along with the country.

From the time of George Washington's inauguration at Federal Hall in New York City to the end of the nineteenth century, the presidency, for the most part, conformed to the designs of the Founders. The presidency did not, by and large, dominate the political life of the nation. Presidents saw their responsibility as primarily involving the execution of policies decided by Congress. Congress was a fully equal branch of government, or perhaps more than equal.

Structural Factors   Why does the early presidency seem so weak in comparison with the contemporary presidency? Surely, it is not because early presidents were less intelligent, vigorous, or ambitious; some were and some were not. A more reasonable answer is that the nation did not often require a very strong presidency before the twentieth century, particularly in the key areas of foreign policy and military leadership. Only in the twentieth century did the United States become a world power, involved in military, diplomatic, and economic activities around the globe. With that *structural* development came a simultaneous increase in the power and responsibility of the president.

It was not until the late nineteenth century, moreover, that the economy of the United States was transformed from a simple free market economy of farmers and small firms to a corporate-dominated economy, with units so large and interconnected that their every action had social consequences. This transformation eventually led to demands for more government supervision of the American economic system. As this role of government grew, so did that of the president.

Although the presidency was largely dormant until the end of the nineteenth century, events and the actions of several presidents during the early period anticipated what was to happen to the office in our own time. Precedents were set; expectations were formed; rules were changed.

Andrew Jackson was hailed as a hero for opposing the "monster" Bank of the United States.

Source: © Collection of The New York Historical Society

Important Early Presidents   The war hero George Washington solidified the prestige of the presidency at a time when executive leadership was mistrusted. Washington also affirmed the primacy of the president in foreign affairs and set a precedent for fashioning a domestic legislative program. Thomas Jefferson, although initially hostile to the idea of a vigorous central government, boldly made the Louisiana Purchase from France, which roughly doubled the size of the United States and opened the continent for Americans all the way to the Pacific Ocean. Rough-hewn frontiersman Andrew Jackson, elected with broader popular participation than ever before, helped transform the presidency into a popular institution, as symbolized by his vigorous opposition to the Bank of the United States (which was seen by many ordinary Americans as a tool of the wealthy).

James Polk, although often ignored in textbook accounts of "great" presidents, energetically exercised his powers as commander in chief of the armed forces; he provoked a war with Mexico and acquired most of what is now the southwestern United States and California. Abraham Lincoln, in order to win the Civil War, invoked emergency powers based on his broad reading of the Constitution: he raised and spent money and deployed troops on his own initiative, with Congress acquiescing only afterward; he temporarily suspended the right of **habeas corpus** and allowed civilians to be tried in military courts; he unilaterally freed the slaves in the Confederate states by issuing the Emancipation Proclamation.

habeas corpus
The legal doctrine that a person who is arrested must have a timely hearing before a judge.

The Twentieth-Century Transformation

More enduring changes in the presidency came only in the twentieth century, when new structural conditions made an expanded presidency both possible and necessary.

Theodore Roosevelt   Theodore Roosevelt vigorously pushed the prerogatives and enhanced the powers of the office as no president had done since Lincoln. Roosevelt was happiest when he was deploying the troops as commander in chief or serving as the nation's chief diplomat to protect American economic and political interests. On the domestic front, Roosevelt pushed for regulation of the new and frightening business corporations, especially by breaking up **trusts**, and he established many national parks. In Teddy Roosevelt, we see the coming together of an energetic and ambitious political leader and a new set of structural factors in the United States, particularly the nation's emergence as a world power and an industrialized economy.

trusts
Large combinations of business corporations.

Woodrow Wilson   Woodrow Wilson's presidency marked further important steps in the expansion of the federal government and the presidency. Wilson's "New Freedom" domestic program built on the Progressive Era measures of Teddy Roosevelt, including further regulation of the economy by establishment of the Federal Reserve Board (1913) and the Federal Trade Commission (1914). Under Wilson, World War I brought an enormous increase in activity: a huge mobilization of military personnel and a large, new civilian bureaucracy to oversee the production and distribution of food, fuel, and armaments by the American "arsenal of democracy."

Franklin Roosevelt   It was Franklin D. Roosevelt, however, who presided over the most significant expansion of presidential functions and activities in American history. In a very real sense, the founding of the modern American

By staying in touch with and responding to the people during the crisis of the Great Depression, Franklin Delano Roosevelt helped define the modern presidency.

presidency occurred during Roosevelt's administration, in response to the Great Depression and World War II.

In response to the Great Depression, Roosevelt and the Democratic majority in Congress pushed into law a series of measures for economic relief that grew into vast programs of conservation and public works, farm credit, business loans, and relief payments to the destitute. Roosevelt's New Deal also established a number of independent commissions to regulate aspects of business (the stock market, telephones, utilities, airlines) and enacted programs such as Social Security, which provided income support for retired Americans, and the Wagner Act, which helped workers join unions and bargain collectively with their employers.

Even bigger changes, however, resulted from World War II when the government mobilized the entire population and the whole economy for the war effort. With the end of World War II, the United States was established as a military superpower. Since the time of Franklin Roosevelt, all U.S. presidents have administered a huge national security state with large standing armed forces, nuclear weapons, and bases all around the world.

Similarly, World War II brought substantial governmental involvement in the economy, with temporary war agencies regulating prices, rationing necessities, monitoring and stimulating industrial output, and helping develop human resources for domestic production. These agencies were dismantled after the war, but they trained a large cadre of officials in an activist view of what the federal government could and should do, and they set precedents for presidential and governmental actions that continue to the present day. All presidents since Roosevelt have presided over a huge government apparatus that has been active in domestic policy as well as in foreign policy.

John F. Kennedy   Although he accomplished little on the legislative front during his brief time in office—he did introduce the 1964 Civil Rights Act, passed after his death—John F. Kennedy was the first president to appreciate the importance of television as both a campaign tool and as an instrument for influencing the public and political actors in Washington, the states, and other countries. His

John F. Kennedy's charm, wit, good looks, and ease in the public limelight helped make him a master of the then-emergent television medium. Ever since his presidency, all incumbents of the office have tried to use television as an instrument of their office, with some, such as Reagan and Clinton, more successful than others.

televised speeches and press conferences, where his charm, intelligence, and sense of humor were clearly evident, became one of his most effective governing tools. Presidents after him tried to follow his lead, but only Ronald Reagan and Bill Clinton came close to Kennedy's mastery of the medium.

How Important Are Individual Presidents?

We cannot be sure to what extent presidents themselves caused this great expansion of the scope of their office. Clearly, they played a part. Lincoln, Wilson, and Franklin Roosevelt, for example, not only reacted vigorously to events but also helped create events; each had something to do with the coming of the wars that were so crucial in adding to their activities and powers. Yet these great presidents were also the product of great times; they stepped into situations that had deep historical roots and dynamics of their own.

Lincoln found a nation in bitter conflict over the relative economic and political power of North and South and focused on the question of slavery in the western territories; war was a likely, if not inevitable, outcome. Wilson and Franklin Roosevelt each faced a world in which German expansion threatened the perceived economic and cultural interests of the United States and in which U.S. industrial power permitted a strong response. The Great Depression fairly cried out for a new kind of presidential activism. Kennedy faced an international system in which the Soviet Union had become especially strident and menacing. Thus, the great upsurges in presidential power and activity were, at least in part, a result of forces at the *structural* level and the result of developments in the economy, American society, and the international system.

We see, then, that it is this mixture of a president's personal qualities (personality and character) and deeper structural factors (such as the existence of military, foreign policy, or economic crises) that determines which presidents leave a positive historical mark and transform their office. This is reflected in Table 12.1 in which presidential scholars rank the presidents. You will see that in virtually all cases, great presidents were in office during times that demanded and allowed them to be great.

Table 12.1 ● The Public and the Experts on Presidential Greatness

The Public's Top Ten	The Experts' Top Nine
Abraham Lincoln	Abraham Lincoln
John F. Kennedy	Franklin D. Roosevelt
Franklin D. Roosevelt	George Washington
George Washington	Thomas Jefferson
Ronald Reagan	Andrew Jackson
George Bush	Woodrow Wilson
Dwight D. Eisenhower	Theodore Roosevelt
Harry S Truman	Harry S Truman
Richard M. Nixon	James K. Polk
Jimmy Carter	

Sources: The public's list is from the Gallup Poll, 1991. The experts' list is from a poll conducted by the *New York Times* and reported in Arthur M. Schlesinger Jr., "The Ultimate Approval Rating," *New York Times Magazine* (December 15, 1996), pp. 48–49.

WEB EXPLORATION

The Effect of Individual Presidents

Issue: Public conceptions of presidential greatness compared with those of the experts show some similarities and some differences. You can see this in Table 12.1 on public and expert ratings of American presidents.

Site: Access the White House Web site through the "Course Documents" section of your online course. Go to the "Web Explorations" section of Chapter 12, click on "The Effect of Individual Presidents," and open "greatness." Select "White House" history then "United States Presidents." Read the biographies of those presidents from the lists in Table 12.1 of your textbook that you don't know much about but who are listed as great.

What You've Learned: Having read the biographies, do you tend to agree or disagree with the experts? Have you changed your mind about where certain presidents ought to be ranked? Why do you think the public and the experts have dissimilar views about certain presidents?

HINT: Look with extra care at the biography of James K. Polk. Historians tend to admire assertive presidents, those who have expanded the powers of the presidential office. Also, the public pays most attention to recent presidents and to those who are the stuff of American myth and legend.

The Many Roles of the President

Since Franklin Roosevelt's day, the American presidency has assumed powers and duties, unimaginable to the Founders, that touch the daily lives of everyone in the United States and indeed everyone in the world. Political scientist Clinton Rossiter's writings introduced generations of students to the many different hats that presidents wear: chief of state, commander in chief, legislator, manager of the economy, chief diplomat, and party leader.[6]

Chief of State

The president is a symbol of national authority and unity. In contrast to European parliamentary nations such as Britain or Norway, where a monarch acts as chief of state while a prime minister serves as head of the government, in the United States the two functions are combined. It is the president who performs many ceremonial duties (attending funerals, proclaiming official days, honoring heroes, celebrating anniversaries) that are carried out by members of royal families in other nations. Jimmy Breslin, an irreverent New York newspaper columnist, once wrote, "The office of President is such a bastardized thing, half royalty and half democracy, that nobody knows whether to genuflect or spit."[7]

Commander in Chief

The Constitution explicitly lodges command over the American armed forces in the office of president. The development of so-called war powers has grown enormously over the years, to the point where President Bush, in 1990, was quickly able to put more than 500,000 U.S. troops in the Persian Gulf area, poised to strike against Iraq. Despite substantial congressional opposition, President Clinton claimed the power to send several thousand American troops as peacekeepers to Bosnia in 1995, Haiti in 1996, and Kosovo in 1999, and to wage an air war against Serbia to try to prevent "ethnic cleansing."

Legislator

While constitutional responsibility for the legislative agenda seems to rest with Congress, the initiative for public policy has partly shifted to the president and the executive branch over the years, although Republican-controlled Congresses during the 1990s tried with some success to turn the tide. It has become customary for Congress to wait for and respond to presidential State of the Union addresses, budgets, and legislative proposals. The twentieth century is dotted with presidential labels on legislation: Wilson's New Freedom, Roosevelt's New Deal, Truman's Fair Deal, Kennedy's New Frontier, and Johnson's Great Society. Ronald Reagan pushed through major changes in 1981 and remained an important legislative force during much of the 1980s.

Divided party control of government can make a difference, however: Bill Clinton took the initiative during his first two years—on taxes and spending, national service, the North American Free Trade Agreement (NAFTA), health care, crime, and other matters—but then Clinton found himself reacting to proposals from the Republican-controlled 104th Congress. And, for the remainder of the Clinton years, the president and Congress found themselves in an evenly balanced tug-of-war.

Richard Nixon scored a number of foreign policy successes during his presidency, including reestablishing friendly U.S. relations with mainland China after a 23-year break.

Manager of the Economy

We now expect presidents to "do something" about the economy when things are going badly. The Great Depression taught most Americans that the federal government has a role to play in fighting economic downturns, and the example of Franklin Roosevelt convinced many that the main actor in this drama ought to be the president. The role is now so well established that even conservative presidents, such as Ronald Reagan and George Bush, felt compelled to involve

CourseCompass

WEB EXPLORATION

Comparing Democratic Leaders

Issue: The roles and responsibilities of the American president are often quite different from those of the head of the government in other democratic countries, particularly those that are parliamentary in form.

Site: Access the Web page of the Prime Minister of Canada through the "Course Documents" section of your online course. Go to the "Web Explorations" section for Chapter 12, click on "Comparing Democratic Leaders," and open "Prime Minister." Select "The Prime Minister" then "The Role of the Prime Minister." Read about the role of the Prime Minister.

What You've Learned: Compare the description of the role of the Prime Minister of Canada with the various roles played by the President of the United States described in this section of the textbook. In what areas of responsibility are the two offices similar? How are they different?

HINT: Remember that in parliamentary systems, the prime minister attends more to governing and less to ceremonial roles than do American presidents, who combine both.

Bill Clinton encourages the famous handshake between the late Israeli prime minister Yitzhak Rabin and Palestine Liberation Organization chairman Yasser Arafat. The president is the chief diplomat of the United States.

the federal government in the prevention of bank failures, the stimulation of economic growth, and the promotion of exports abroad.

In the rapidly expanding global economy, moreover, presidents have become increasingly engaged in the effort to open world markets on equitable terms to American goods and services. President Reagan pressured Japan into import quotas on automobiles, and President Bush helped push through an agreement with Japan on semiconductors. President Clinton was especially active as a spokesperson for the benefits of the American way of doing business and pushed hard to expand a global free trade regime, negotiating and gaining congressional approval for the NAFTA treaty and the creation of the World Trade Organization under GATT.

Chief Diplomat

The Constitution, by specifying that the president "shall have the power . . . to make Treaties" and to appoint and receive ambassadors, assigns the main diplomatic responsibility of the United States to the presidency. It is in this role, perhaps, that American presidents are most visible: traveling abroad, meeting with foreign leaders, and negotiating and signing treaties. President Bush's successful arms control negotiations with Soviet leaders and his extraordinary efforts to assemble and hold together the multinational coalition against Iraq made the diplomatic function especially prominent in his presidency.

Head of the Political Party

One of the great difficulties all presidents face is the seeming contradiction between their role as president of all the people—as commander in chief and chief diplomat, for example—and their role as leader of their political party, seeking partisan advantage as well as the public good. Much of the apparent contradiction has been eased by the fact that presidents (and other political leaders) generally see the public good and commitment to party principles as one and the same. Thus, Ronald Reagan, as the leader of the Republican party and as president, believed that the public good was served by increasing

LongmanParticipate

CourseCompass

comparative
**Comparing
Chief Executives**

defense spending, deregulating the economy, and decreasing domestic spending. For his part, Lyndon Johnson, as the leader of the Democratic party and as president, believed that the federal government ought to play a leading role in ending racial discrimination and poverty in American life. Often, however, the public has reacted very negatively when presidents play their party leadership role too vigorously, seeing it as perhaps unpresidential.

The President's Staff and Cabinet

Each of the president's functions is demanding; together, they are overwhelming. "Passive" presidents may well be a vanishing breed. Of course, presidents do not face their burdens alone; they have gradually acquired many advisers and helpers. The number and responsibilities of these advisers and helpers have become so extensive, and the functions they perform so essential, that they have come to form what some call the **institutional presidency**.[8]

The White House Staff

The White House staff, for example, which is specially shaped to fit the particular needs of each president, includes a number of close advisers.

Chief of Staff   One top adviser, usually designated **chief of staff**, tends to serve as the president's right hand, supervising other staff members and organizing much of what the president does. Presidents use their chiefs of staff in different ways. Franklin Roosevelt kept a tight rein on things himself, granting equal but limited power and access to several close advisers in a *competitive* system. Dwight Eisenhower, used to the *hierarchical* army staff system, gave overall responsibility to his chief of staff, Sherman Adams. In the early Reagan White House, James Baker shared power *collegially* with Assistant to the President Michael Deaver and Counselor to the President Edwin Meese.

National Security Adviser   Another important staff member in most presidencies is the **national security adviser**, who is also head of the president's National Security Council, operating out of the White House. The national security adviser generally meets with the president every day to brief him on the latest events and to offer advice on what to do. Several national security advisers, including Henry Kissinger (under Nixon) and Zbigniew Brzezinski (under Carter), have been strong foreign policy managers and active, world-hopping diplomats who sometimes clashed with the secretaries of state and defense. Most recent presidents, however, have appointed team players who have closely reflected the president's wishes and quietly coordinated policy among the various executive departments. Condoleezza Rice has followed this pattern in the Bush administration.

Other Advisers   Most presidents also have a top domestic policy adviser who coordinates plans for new domestic laws, regulations, and spending, although this role is often subordinate to that of the chief of staff and is not usually very visible. Close political advisers, often old comrades of the president from past campaigns, may be found in a number of White House or other government posts (James Baker served as Bush's secretary of state, for example) or may have no official position at all, such as Republican consultant Dick Morris, who crafted Clinton's 1996 reelection strategy.

institutional presidency
The permanent bureaucracy associated with the presidency, designed to help the incumbent of the office carry out his responsibilities.

chief of staff
A top adviser to the president who also manages the White House staff.

national security adviser
A top foreign policy and defense adviser to the president who heads the National Security Council.

Prominent in every administration is the press secretary, who holds press conferences, briefs the media, and serves as the voice of the administration. This may or may not be the same person who is director of communications, who generally manages how the president and his activities are presented to the public. These communications and media positions, along with that of an in-house pollster or public opinion surveyor, have become increasingly important as the president's connections with the public have grown closer.

Nearly all presidents have a legal counsel (a hot seat for Bill Clinton's counsel given the Whitewater, campaign finance, and Monica Lewinsky inquiries and his impeachment and trial in Congress), a special assistant to act as a liaison with Congress, another to deal with interest groups, another for political matters, and still another for intergovernmental relations. However, the exact shape of the White House staff changes greatly from one presidency to another, depending on the preferences and style of the president.

For several presidents, their wives became informal yet influential advisers on a wide range of affairs. Eleanor Roosevelt was instrumental in shaping several New Deal programs affecting African-Americans and the poor. Nancy Reagan was not only the protector of the reputation of her husband, Ronald, but also had an important voice in appointments and inner-circle firings. Hillary Clinton was a close policy and political adviser to her husband, Bill.

Power and Accountability   White House staff members are people the president talks to every day; they are the ones who do their best to see that he gets his way. They and their deputies leave "The White House wants . . . " messages all around Washington and are treated with deference, if not affection. Staff members have to speak accurately for the president. They must do what the president wants, or what he *would* want if he knew the details. The ideal staffer knows exactly what the boss wants and does it, with or without being told. Of course, it can be useful for a president to create the *impression* that staff members are acting on their own, particularly when they are doing something unpopular or even illegal. One of Eisenhower's favorite hidden-hand techniques was to have Sherman Adams take the heat for tough decisions.

The Executive Office of the President

One step removed from the White House staff, mostly housed in its own building nearby, is a set of organizations that forms the **Executive Office of the President (EOP)**.

Most important of these organizations is the **Office of Management and Budget (OMB)**. The OMB advises the president on how much the administration should propose to spend for each government program and where the money will come from. The OMB also exercises legislative clearance; that is, it examines the budgetary implications of any proposed legislation and sometimes kills proposals it deems too expensive or inconsistent with the president's philosophy or goals.

The **Council of Economic Advisers (CEA)** advises the president on economic policy. Occasionally, the head of the council exercises great influence, as Walter Heller did during the Kennedy administration. More often, the head of the CEA is inconspicuous.

The Executive Office of the President also includes the **National Security Council (NSC)**, a body of leading officials from the State and Defense Departments, the Central Intelligence Agency (CIA), the military, and elsewhere who advise the president on foreign affairs. The NSC has been particularly

Executive Office of the President (EOP)

A group of organizations that advise the president on a wide range of issues; includes the Office of Management and Budget, the National Security Council, and the Council of Economic Advisers.

Office of Management and Budget (OMB)

An organization within the Executive Office of the President that advises on the federal budget, domestic legislation, and regulations.

Council of Economic Advisers (CEA)

An organization in the Executive Office of the President made up of a small group of economists who advise on economic policy.

National Security Council (NSC)

An organization in the Executive Office of the President made up of officials from the State and Defense Departments, the CIA, and the military, who advise on foreign and security affairs.

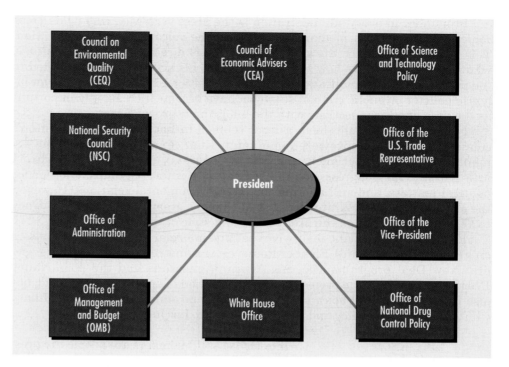

Figure 12.1 ● Executive Office of the President in the Clinton Administration

The Executive Office of the President assists the president's attempt to establish central authority over the wider bureaucracy of the executive branch.

active in crisis situations and covert operations. The NSC staff, charged with various analytical and coordinating tasks, is headed by the president's national security adviser. At times, the NSC staff has gone beyond analysis to conduct actual operations, the most famous of which was the Iran-Contra affair, under the direction of Lieutenant Colonel Oliver North, when weapons were secretly sold to Iran in the hope of freeing U.S. hostages and some of the proceeds were illegally diverted to the Nicaraguan Contra rebels.

In recent years, the Executive Office of the President has also included the Office of Science and Technology Policy, the Council on Environmental Quality, and the Office of the U.S. Trade Representative. Again, however, the makeup of the EOP changes from one administration to another, depending on which national problems seem most pressing and on the preferences and operating styles of individual presidents. One recent arrangement of the EOP is shown in Figure 12.1.

The Vice-Presidency

Vice-presidents find themselves in an awkward position because their main job is simply to be available in case something happens to the president. This happened several times in the twentieth century; Theodore Roosevelt, Calvin Coolidge, Harry Truman, Lyndon Johnson, and Gerald Ford each stepped up from the vice-presidency after the death or resignation of the president.

A Once-Insignificant Office The vice-presidency itself, however, has not always been highly regarded. John Nance Garner, Franklin Roosevelt's first vice-president, has been quoted as saying in his earthy Texan way that the office was

Richard Cheney plays a more important role in fashioning administration policy and strategy than any other vice president in American history. Here Cheney confirms with then-Senate majority leader Trent Lott on George W. Bush's 2002 budget proposal.

"not worth a pitcher of warm piss."[9] Within administrations, vice-presidents used to be fifth wheels, not fully trusted (since they could not be fired) and not personally or politically close to the president. Vice-presidents used to spend much of their time running minor errands of state, attending funerals of foreign leaders not important enough to demand presidential attention, or carrying out limited diplomatic missions. Some vice-presidents were virtually frozen out of the policy-making process. Harry Truman was never informed of the existence of the Manhattan Project, which built the atomic bomb.

Increasing Importance of the Vice-Presidency   Recent presidents, however, have involved their vice-presidents more.[10] Ronald Reagan included George Bush in major policy meetings and put him in charge of antidrug efforts. Bill Clinton gave Al Gore important responsibilities, including the formulation of environmental policy, coping with Ross Perot's opposition to NAFTA, and the ambitious effort to "reinvent government." More than any vice President in recent memory, Dick Cheney is at the center of the policy making process in the Bush White House, serving as one of the presiden't principal advisors on both domestic and foreign policy.

Presidential Succession   In 1804, the Twelfth Amendment fixed the flaw in the original Constitution under which Aaron Burr, Thomas Jefferson's running mate in 1800, had tied Jefferson in electoral votes and tried, in the House of Representatives, to grab the presidency for himself. Since then, vice-presidents have been elected specifically to that office on a party ticket with their presidents. But now there is also another way to become vice-president. The Twenty-Fifth Amendment (ratified in 1967) provides for the succession in case of the temporary or permanent inability of a president to discharge his office. It also states that if the vice-presidency becomes vacant, the president can nominate a new vice-president, who takes office on confirmation by both houses of Congress. This is how Gerald Ford became vice-president in 1973, when Spiro

Agnew was forced to resign because of a scandal, and how Nelson Rockefeller became vice-president in 1974, when Ford replaced Richard Nixon as president.

The Cabinet

The president's cabinet is not mentioned in the Constitution. No legislation designates the composition of the cabinet, its duties, or its rules of operation. Nevertheless, all presidents since George Washington have had one. It was Washington who established the practice of meeting with his top executive officials as a group to discuss policy matters. Later presidents continued the practice, some meeting with the cabinet as often as twice a week, and others paying it less attention or none at all.

Today, the cabinet usually consists of the heads of the major executive departments, plus the vice-president, the director of the CIA, and whichever other officials the president deems appropriate. Often these have included the ambassador to the United Nations.

Limited Role   Rarely, if ever, though, have presidents actually relied on the cabinet as a decision-making body. Presidents know that they alone will be held responsible for decisions, and they alone keep the power to make them. According to legend, when Abraham Lincoln once disagreed with the entire cabinet, he declared, "Eight votes for and one against; the nays have it!"

Most recent presidents have convened the cabinet infrequently and have done serious business with it rarely. Ronald Reagan held only a few cabinet meetings each year, and those were so dull and unimportant that Reagan was said to doze off from time to time. Bill Clinton, with his "policy wonk" mastery of details, thoroughly dominated cabinet discussions.

Why the Weak Cabinet?   One reason for the weakness of the cabinet, especially in recent years, is simply that government has grown large and specialized. Most department heads are experts in their own areas, with little to contribute elsewhere. It could be a waste of everyone's time to engage the secretary of housing and urban development in discussions of military strategy.

President George Bush makes a point to members of his cabinet. Although the cabinet occasionally meets as a body, most presidents do not rely on it very much for making important decisions.

Another reason is that cabinet members occupy an ambiguous position: they are advisers to the president but also represent their own constituencies, including the permanent civil servants in their departments and the organized interests that their departments serve. They may have substantial political stature of their own, somewhat independent of the president's.

Most presidents deliberately appoint some department heads with independent power bases in order to reward parts of their electoral coalitions and to sell their programs to particular interest groups. The secretary of agriculture generally has links with farm organizations, and Treasury secretaries tend to get on well with bankers. These relationships sometimes lead to tension between the president and the department heads, and they make the cabinet an awkward body for doing business.

Close Confidants   Most presidents also try to include in the cabinet some people with whom they have close personal and political ties. Thus, John Kennedy appointed his brother Robert attorney general. When criticized, Kennedy replied (tongue in cheek): "I can't see that it's wrong to give him a little legal experience before he goes out to practice law."[11] Likewise, Richard Nixon appointed his campaign manager and former law partner John Mitchell to that same post, as Ronald Reagan did with Edwin Meese.

The President and the Bureaucracy

Many people assume that the president has firm control over the executive branch, that he can simply order departments and agencies to do something and they will do it. But Richard Neustadt, in his important book *Presidential Power and the Modern Presidents,* showed that that is far from the whole truth.[12]

Giving Orders

In the day-to-day operation of government, direct command is seldom feasible. Too much is going on. Presidents cannot keep personal track of each one

Harry Truman reminded General Douglas MacArthur that the president is the commander in chief of America's armed forces when he fired the general for disobeying presidential orders during the Korean War.

LongmanParticipate

CourseCompass

timeline
**The Executive
Order over Time**

of the millions of government officials and employees. The president can only issue general guidelines and pass them down the chain of subordinates, hoping that his wishes will be followed faithfully. But lower-level officials, protected by civil service status from being fired, may have their own interests, their own institutional norms and practices, that lead them to do something different. President Kennedy was painfully reminded of this during the Cuban Missile Crisis of 1962, when Soviet Premier Khrushchev demanded that U.S. missiles be removed from Turkey in return for the removal of Soviet missiles from Cuba: Kennedy was surprised to learn that the missiles had not already been taken out of Turkey, for he had ordered them removed a year earlier. The people responsible for carrying out this directive had not followed through.[13]

Persuasion

To a large extent, a president must *persuade* other executive branch officials to do things. He must bargain, compromise, and convince others that what he wants is in the country's best interest and in their own interest as well. Neustadt put it strongly: "Presidential power is the power to persuade."[14]

Of course, presidents can do many things besides persuade: appoint top officials who share the president's goals; put White House observers in second-level department positions; reshuffle, reorganize, or even—with the consent of Congress—abolish agencies that are not responsive; influence agency budgets and programs through OMB review; and stimulate pressure on departments by Congress and the public.

Still, the president's ability to gain bureaucratic acquiescence is limited. The federal bureaucracy is not merely a creature of the president but is itself a partly independent governmental actor. It is also subject to influences from the political linkage level—especially by public opinion and organized interests, often working through Congress. Congress, after all, appropriates the money. This constrains what presidents can do and helps ensure that the executive branch will respond to broad forces in society rather than simply to the wishes of one leader.

It's never too late for presidential persuasion. Here Ronald Reagan tries to win one more vote for a bill in the Senate before heading off to a White House reception.

The President and Congress: Perpetual Tug-of-War

The president and Congress are often at odds. This is a *structural* fact of American politics, deliberately intended by the authors of the Constitution.[15]

Conflict by Constitutional Design

The Founders created a system of checks and balances between Congress and the president, setting "ambition to counter ambition" in order to prevent tyranny. Because virtually all constitutional powers are shared, there is a potential for conflict over virtually all aspects of government policy.

Shared Powers   Under the Constitution, presidents may propose legislation and can sign or veto bills passed by Congress, but both houses of Congress must pass any laws and can override presidential vetoes. Presidents can appoint ambassadors and high officials and make treaties with foreign countries, but the Senate must approve them. Presidents nominate federal judges, including U.S. Supreme Court justices, but the Senate must approve the nominations. Presidents administer the executive branch, but Congress appropriates funds for it to operate, writes the legislation that defines what it is to do, and oversees its activities.

Presidents cannot always count on the members of Congress—even members of their own political party—to agree with them. The potential conflict written into the Constitution becomes real because the president and Congress often disagree about national goals, especially when there is **divided government,** that is, when the president and the majority in Congress belong to different parties.

divided government

Control of the executive and the legislative branches by different political parties.

Separate Elections   In other countries' parliamentary systems, the national legislatures choose the chief executives so that unified party control is ensured. But in the United States, there are separate elections for the president and the members of Congress. Moreover, our elections do not all come at the same time. In presidential election years, two-thirds of the senators do not have to run and are insulated from new political forces that may affect the choice of a president. In nonpresidential, "off" years, all members of the House and one-third of the senators face the voters, who sometimes elect a Congress with views quite different from those of the president chosen two years earlier. In 1986, for example, halfway through Reagan's second term, the Democrats recaptured control of the Senate and caused Reagan great difficulty with Supreme Court appointments and other matters. The Republicans did the same thing to Clinton in 1994 after they gained control of Congress.

Outcomes   In all these ways, our constitutional structure ensures that what the president can do is limited and influenced by Congress, which in turn reflects various political forces that may differ from those that affect the president. At its most extreme, Congress may even be controlled by the opposing party. This divided government situation always constrains what presidents can do and may sometimes lead to a condition called "gridlock"[16] in which a president and Congress are locked in battle, neither able to make much headway.

Presidents must cultivate good working relationships with Congress if they are to have any success with their legislative program. Here, President George W. Bush consults with congressional leaders about a pending bill.

What Makes a President Successful with Congress?

A number of political scientists have studied presidents' successes and failures in getting measures that they favor enacted into law by Congress and have suggested reasons some presidents on some issues do much better than others.

Party and Ideology   The most important factor is a simple one: the number of people in Congress who agree with the president in ideology and party affiliation. When the same political party controls both the presidency and Congress, presidents are more likely to get their way. When the opposite party controls Congress, presidents tend to be frustrated. The bigger the majority a president's party has, the better the president does (see Figure 12.2).[17]

This success does not necessarily mean that presidents actively whip their fellow partisans into line. As we have seen, the parties are rather weakly organized in Congress and do not often enforce discipline. But party members do tend to be like-minded; they tend to vote together because they share the same values, and for the same reason, they tend to go along with a president of their own party.[18]

Foreign Policy Issues   Presidents tend to do better on foreign policy issues than on domestic ones. Political scientist Aaron Wildavsky went so far as to refer to "two presidencies," domestic and foreign, with the latter president much more dominant. Wildavsky found that during the 1948–1964 period, 59 percent of presidents' proposals on foreign policy were passed, but only 40 percent of their domestic proposals.[19] The reason is that political leaders generally want to show a unified face to a potentially hostile world.

This difference between domestic and foreign policy success by the president has decreased since the Vietnam War, but it remains significant. Although there was significant dissent, Congress (barely) voted in January 1991 to authorize President Bush to use force against Iraq, once again illustrating presidential primacy in foreign affairs. Congress eventually supported Clinton's decision to send U.S. forces to Haiti, Bosnia, and Kosovo as part of multinational peacekeeping operations. The generalization does not hold, however, when foreign policy concerns trade and other global economic issues.

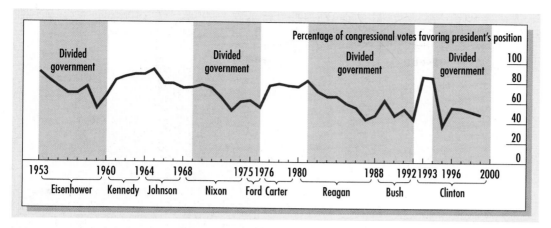

Figure 12.2 ● **Presidential Success in Congress**

The party in control of Congress can have a strong effect on a president's success. In periods of divided government (see shaded areas), when the opposing party has a majority in Congress, policies favoring the president's position receive fewer votes.

Source: Calculated by the authors from various issues of the *Congressional Quarterly Weekly Report.*

Vetoes When the issue is a presidential veto of legislation, the president is again very likely to prevail. Vetoes have not been used often, except by certain "veto-happy" presidents, such as Franklin Roosevelt, Truman, and Ford. But when vetoes have been used, they have seldom been overridden—only 5 percent of the time for Truman and only 1.5 percent for Roosevelt. Bill Clinton did not use the veto at all during his first two years in office, when he had a Democratic majority in Congress, but then used it 11 times in 1995 alone during his budget battles with the Republican-controlled 104th Congress.

WEB EXPLORATION

Impeachment

Issue: Although rarely used, Congress's ultimate weapon in its perpetual struggle with the president is its power to impeach the president and remove him from office.

Site: Access the Jurist Web site at the University of Pittsburgh Law School through the "Course Documents" section of your online course. Go to the "Web Explorations" section for Chapter 12, click on "Impeachment," and open "impeachment." Scroll down to "Texts of Articles of Impeachment" then select and read the Articles of Impeachment as voted by the House against Richard M. Nixon and William J. Clinton.

What You've Learned: Compare the articles of impeachment brought against each president. How serious do you judge the accusations to be against each president? Did Nixon and/or Clinton, in your view, violate their oaths of office? Had you been a senator at the time, would you have voted for removal of the president from office? Why?

HINT: Pay special attention to the "obstruction of justice" charges against the two presidents, and judge their relative seriousness.

As Senate Majority Leader, Lyndon Johnson was famous for exerting strong personal pressure on legislators, a skill he carried with him to the presidency.

The percentage of veto success may be misleadingly high, because presidents like to preserve an image of invulnerability; they generally avoid casting vetoes that might be overridden. Conversely, the mere *threat* of a veto—without any need to carry it out—is often enough to discourage Congress from passing laws that the president will not approve. Clinton was quite successful using this approach with the 105th and 106th Congresses.

Popularity   Although political scientists have had little luck confirming it statistically,[20] most scholars and observers of Washington politics agree that presidential effectiveness with Congress is significantly affected by how popular a president is with the American people. This is probably because of fear among many members of Congress that opposing a highly visible proposal from a popular president might jeopardize their electoral future.

Legislative Skills   Again, although statistical studies of roll call votes reveal little effect of presidents' legislative skills (this may be the result of poor measures of legislative skills), most longtime observers of Washington politics believe that such skills make a difference. Lyndon Johnson's famous wheeling and dealing surely picked up votes for his favored legislation, as did Ronald Reagan's efforts on the 1981 tax and budget measures.

The President and the People: An Evolving Relationship

The complicated relationships among the president, the executive branch as a whole, and Congress have a lot to do with the different political forces that act on them at different times, that is, with the different effects of public opinion, the political parties, and organized interests. Particularly important is the special relationship between the president and the general public, which has evolved over many years

Getting Closer to the People

The Founders thought of the president as an elite leader, relatively distant from the people, interacting with Congress often but with the people only rarely. Most nineteenth-century presidents and presidential candidates thought the same. They seldom made speeches directly to the public, for example, generally averaging no more than ten such speeches per year.[21]

In the earliest years of the American Republic, presidents were not even chosen directly by the voters but by electors chosen by state legislators or, in case no one got an electoral college majority, by the House of Representatives. The Constitution thus envisioned very indirect democratic control of the presidency.

More Democratic Elections   As we have also seen, however, this system quickly evolved into one in which the people played a more direct part. The two-party system developed, with parties nominating candidates and running pledged electors and the state legislators allowing ordinary citizens to vote on the electors. Presidential candidates began to win clear-cut victories in the electoral college, taking the House of Representatives out of the process. Voting rights were broadened as well. Property and religious qualifications were dropped early in the nineteenth century. Later, slaves were freed and given the right to vote; still later, women, Native Americans, and 18-year-olds won the franchise.

Going Public   By the beginning of the twentieth century, presidents began to speak directly to the public. Theodore Roosevelt embarked on a series of

WEB EXPLORATION

The President and Public Opinion

Issue: Effective presidents try to stay attuned to public opinion and have created tools to enhance their ability to track what the public wants.

Site: Access Public Agenda Online through the "Course Documents" section of your online course. Go to the "Web Explorations" section for Chapter 12, click on "The President and Public Opinion," and open "contact the president." Select an issue you care about from the list on the left-hand side of the page. Read background materials on the issue, then examine the competing proposals for addressing the problem you care about in the section "major proposals."

What You've Learned: Decide what you want the federal government to do about the problem you care about. Formulate a policy that you believe would be both achievable and effective. Let the president (or at least one of his staff members) know what action you want taken. Send an e-mail to **President@whitehouse.gov.**

HINT: The more thoughtful your e-mail, the more likely it is to reach the ears of people who matter in the White House.

speech-making tours in order to win passage of legislation to regulate the railroads. Woodrow Wilson made appeals to the public a central part of his presidency and created an entirely new constitutional theory advocating close connections between the president and the public. Wilson saw the desires of the public as the wellspring of democratic government: "As is the majority, so ought the government to be."[22] He argued that presidents are unique because only they are chosen by the entire nation. Presidents, he said, should help educate the citizens about government, interpret their true will, and faithfully respond to it.

Wilson's theory of the presidency has been followed more and more fully in twentieth-century thought and practice. All presidents, especially since Franklin Roosevelt, have attempted to both shape and respond to public opinion; all, to one degree or another, have attempted to speak directly to the people about policy.[23]

Using the Media More and more frequently, presidents go public, using television to bypass the print media and speak to the public directly about policy. They have held fewer news conferences with White House correspondents (where awkward questions cannot be excluded).[24] Richard Nixon pioneered prime-time television addresses, at which Ronald Reagan later excelled. George Bush displayed less rhetorical polish but spoke often to national TV audiences. Bill Clinton was more interactive with citizens, appearing on radio and TV talk shows and holding informal but televised "town hall meetings."

More and more, presidents have traveled outside the White House to make public appearances. Often the settings convey a visual message: Most spectacular is travel abroad, which portrays the chief executive as *presidential,* a head of state, and highlights his foreign policy achievements: Kennedy speaking at the Berlin Wall in 1963; Nixon raising his glass in toast at the Great Hall of the People in Beijing in 1972; Reagan strolling through Red Square in Moscow with Mikhail Gorbachev in 1988.

Leading Public Opinion

Especially since the rise of television, modern presidents have enhanced their power to shape public opinion. Some studies have indicated that when a popular

John F. Kennedy, protesting the wall that divided East and West Berlin, delivers his famous "Ich bin ein Berliner" speech before a crowd of over 250,000 people. Travel abroad, like Kennedy's 1963 visit to West Berlin, is often a spectacular way for the chief executive to display his "presidential" stature.

president takes a stand in favor of a particular policy, the public's support for that policy tends to rise. A determined president, delivering many speeches and messages over a period of several weeks or months, may be able to gain 5 to 10 percentage points in support of that policy in the polls.[25] This is not an enormous effect, but it tends to confirm Theodore Roosevelt's claim that the presidency is a "bully pulpit."

The power to lead the public also implies a power to *manipulate* public opinion, if a president is so inclined—that is, to deceive or mislead the public so that it will approve policies that it might oppose if it were fully informed. Especially in foreign affairs, presidents can sometimes control what information the public gets, in least in the short run. Lyndon Johnson, for example, purposely misstated the facts about the Gulf of Tonkin incident at the beginning of the Vietnam War (recall the story in Chapter 5).

Champions of energetic presidential leadership must face the possibility that that leadership will go wrong and result in demagoguery or manipulation. The dilemma cannot be resolved. The power to do good is the power to do evil as well. But some safeguards may exist, including the capacity of the public to judge character when it is choosing a president, as well as the ability of other national leaders to counteract a deceitful president. Johnson and Nixon learned this bitter lesson—the former declined to run for a second term; the latter resigned.

Responding to the Public

In any case, the relationship between presidents and the public is very much a two-way street. Besides trying to lead the people, presidents definitely tend to respond to public opinion. Electoral competition produces presidents who tend to share the public's policy preferences. Moreover, most presidents want to be reelected or to win a favorable place in history, and they know that they are unlikely to do so if they defy public opinion on many major issues. Usually, they try to anticipate what the public will want in order to win electoral reward and avoid electoral punishment.

Quiet Influence   What presidents *want* to do closely resembles what the public wants—that is one reason they were elected—so often there is no conflict

Modern presidents make concerted efforts to stay in touch with public opinion. Pollster Stanley Greenberg played this role during the first years of the Clinton administration.

to observe. Only occasionally does a modern president get so badly out of touch with the public that the full power of public opinion is revealed.

More often, in day-to-day politics, it simply turns out that what the president does is largely in harmony with what the general public wants. When public opinion moved toward favoring a buildup of defense during the late 1970s, Carter and Reagan followed suit. When the public wanted something done about the welfare problem, Clinton acted in concert with Congress. As a general matter, when polls show that public opinion has changed, presidents have tended to shift policy in the same direction: this has been true about 84 percent of the time.[26]

Listening to the Public   There is plenty of evidence that presidents pay attention to what the public is thinking. At least since the Kennedy administration, presidents and their staffs have carefully read the available public opinion surveys and now have full-blown polling operations of their own.[27] President Clinton employed several of the best pollsters in the business—including Stanley Greenberg (the author's brother)—to chart his electoral campaigns and legislative agenda. Although such polling is often deplored, it helps presidents choose policies that the American public favors and change or discard those that are unpopular.

The Role of Presidential Popularity

presidential popularity

The percentage of Americans who approve a president's handling of his job.

The public also influences presidents through its judgments about presidential performance: that is, through **presidential popularity** or unpopularity. Since the 1930s, Gallup and other poll takers have regularly asked Americans whether they approve or disapprove of "the president's handling of the job." The percentage of people who approve varies from month to month and year to year,

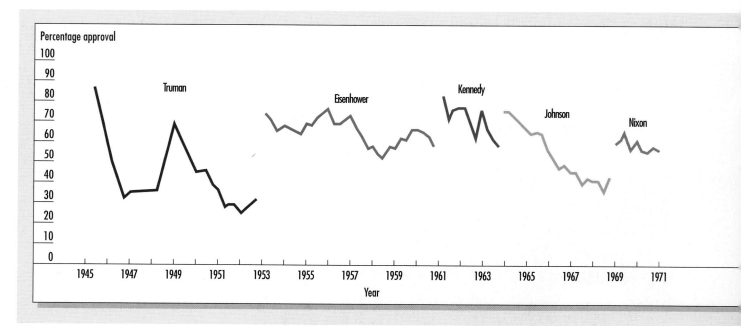

Figure 12.3 ● **Trends in Presidential Popularity, 1945–2000**

Popularity ratings of presidents rise and fall in response to political, social, and economic events.
Source: Gallup surveys.

George Bush's popularity fell dramatically during the 1991–1992 recession; his only hope for reelection was that the economy would recover in time, but it did not.

© By permission of Mike Luckovich and Creators Syndicate.

and as time passes, these varying percentages can be graphed in a sort of fever chart of how the public has thought the president was doing (see Figure 12.3).

A number of factors seem to be especially important in determining presidential popularity, including time, the state of the economy, and foreign policy crises.

Time   Historically, most presidents have begun their terms of office with a majority of Americans—usually 60 percent or more—approving of how they are

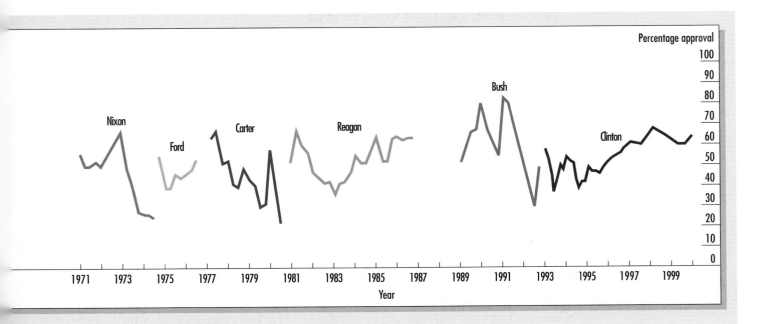

handling their job. Most presidents have tended to lose popularity as time passed. But this loss of popularity does not represent an inexorable working of time; Eisenhower, Reagan, and Clinton actually gained popularity during their second terms. Those who lose popularity do so in response to bad news. Good news generally makes presidents more popular.[28]

The Economy   One of the most serious kinds of bad news involves economic recession. When the economy goes sour, fewer Americans approve of the president. This happened to George Bush in mid-1991, as the economy faltered. On the other hand, the spectacular performance of the American economy in the mid- and late 1990s greatly benefited Bill Clinton, whose historically high approval numbers were sustained even as Congress was attempting to remove him from office.

War   Successful military actions tend to add to presidential popularity, as Ronald Reagan happily discovered after the U.S. invasion of Grenada in 1982. Bush's approval rating soared on the successful conclusion of the war with Iraq. Conversely, an unsuccessful war is bad news for a president, especially a limited war that drags on with high casualty rates, such as the Korean War (which detracted from Truman's already low popularity in 1950 and 1951) or the Vietnam War.

Presidents are generally aware of what helps or hurts them with the public; they know that they will win electoral rewards if things go well but will face electoral punishment if things go badly. They have strong incentives, therefore, to anticipate public reaction and to do things that will please the public.

LongmanParticipate

CourseCompass

participation
Rate the Presidents

Interest Groups, Political Parties, and Social Movements

Presidents are also influenced by organized interest groups, by political parties, and, sometimes, by social movements.

Interest Groups

As we saw in Chapters 7 and 10, interest groups' relationships with presidents, like other aspects of interest group politics, are a sort of unexplored continent. Much of what goes on is probably kept hidden from scholars and observers. But we can be reasonably sure, from various hints and fragments of evidence, that organized groups exert important kinds of influence.[29]

Interest group and other special-interest money helps candidates win presidential nominations and elections, so those who take office do not simply reflect the preferences of ordinary citizens; they tend to share, or at least sympathize with, the goals of their benefactors. At the least, presidents give special access to those who helped get them into office.

Presidents must deal with interest groups, moreover, because in some policy areas it is impossible for the president to govern without their cooperation; this is especially true of businesspeople and the heads of large corporations, who occupy privileged positions as spokespersons for what economic and foreign policies must be carried out if a free enterprise economy is to flourish.[30] When large software firms and film companies complain about copyright infringement in places such as China, presidents listen and fashion policy accordingly.

Precisely which interest groups have the most influence on policy depends partly on which party controls the presidency, because some groups are much more closely allied with one party than with the other. Since the 1930s, for example, organized labor and certain businesses have been closely tied to the Democratic party; more recently, civil rights, women's, trial lawyers, teachers union, and environmental groups have joined this alliance. The Republican party, for its part, has had much closer ties to most manufacturing corporations, small businesses, agribusiness, and organizations of well-to-do professionals, such as doctors and lawyers.[31] The policies of the parties in office tend to reflect these differences.

Political Parties

Republican presidents tend to do different things from Democratic presidents. Changes in party control of the presidency produce significant changes in policy.

Despite the pressure that electoral competition puts on political parties to win votes by moving to the center, the parties also maintain some real differences, as the responsible party model indicates. As we saw in Chapters 9 and 10, the parties consist of activists and financiers with distinctive policy goals and of ordinary voters who differ, although less sharply, in the same sorts of ways.

As a result of party influence, there tend to be partisan cycles of presidential action, with different policies, depending on which party holds office. Democratic presidents tend to fight unemployment,[32] to favor civil rights and environmental measures, and to promote domestic social welfare programs; Republicans tend to worry about inflation, to cut taxes and domestic expenditures, and to take conservative stands on social issues such as abortion.

Social Movements

Social movements occasionally provide yet another political-level influence on presidents. They do so in at least two different ways. Mass demonstrations and protests cause disruptions that are inconvenient or dangerous to ignore, forcing presidents to take action to defuse them. Or mass movements may produce changes in general public opinion that in turn affect presidents. Either way, presidents and other political leaders have to pay attention. The anti–World Trade Organization (WTO) demonstrations in Seattle in late 1999, for example, helped convince Bill Clinton to push the organization to include environmental and labor protections in its rules (see the "Using the Framework" feature).

Structural Influences on the Presidency

Some of the political linkage influences on presidents that we have discussed—especially public opinion—provide substantial continuity from one president to the next. So do a range of governmental factors, including Congress and the courts. Continuity is also provided by the Constitution, which sets the rules of the political game, and the American political culture, which shapes the outlooks of presidents, other political leaders, and the people. Thus, we can speak of an *enduring* presidency, a presidency that does not merely fluctuate with the whims of whoever holds office but that also reflects the goals and preferences of the people, groups, and institutions that make up American society. The enduring presidency is also a product of two structural factors: the international system and the economy.

USING THE FRAMEWORK

How Could President Clinton Support the World Trade Organization, yet Say He Also Sided with the Anti-WTO Protesters in Seattle?

In late November 1999, the Seattle meetings of the World Trade Organization were disrupted by large anti-WTO street demonstrations. The labor, human rights, and environmental organization demonstrators were demanding that the WTO be more open to public scrutiny and accountability and that it write into trade rules protections against child and slave labor and standards for work and environmental protections. President Clinton, one of the nation's leading free traders and a strong proponent of the WTO (he believed the world trading system needed a set of agreed-upon rules to make it safe and fair), nevertheless sided with most of the arguments pushed by the demonstrators (but he deplored the violent tactics of a handful of them). How could he be for both sides in this dispute? Taking a broader look at how structural, political linkage, and governmental factors affected President Clinton's views on global trade issues will help explain this situation.

Governmental Action

The president proposes in his speech to WTO delegates that the organization be more accountable and pay attention to demands for labor and environmental protections in its rules.

Governmental Level

- President Clinton was a strong believer in both free trade and labor and environmental protections.

- The president also felt pressure from interest groups on both sides of the issue; these political pressures accentuated the conflict between his own beliefs.

- President Clinton wanted Al Gore to follow him as president and did not want to alienate the Democratic Party base (which includes labor and environmentalists).

Political Linkages Level

- Many business firms involved in the global economy have lobbied Congress and the President for a world trade regime that emphasizes free and open trade, protection of intellectual property rights, and access to markets.

- Labor and environmental organizations are against a free-trade system without protections for labor and environmental protections in less developed nations; these groups are very important parts of President Clinton's Democratic Party.

- Social movement demonstrators in the streets of Seattle brought the issues of labor and the environment, and the nature of the WTO, to public attention.

- The mass media, although mainly attending to the conflict in the streets of Seattle, also covered the issues raised by the protesters.

Structural Level

- Since the end of World War II, the United States has been the leading proponent among nations for global free trade.

- Globalization of the world economy, pushed by technological revolutions in telecommunications, computers, and transportation, was and is advancing at a rapid rate.

- The United States is the leading nation in the globalizing economy and, overall, has been benefiting from it.

- Some groups in the population are hurt by globalization and rapid technological change, however, or at least perceive they are being hurt.

- The United States has in place a strong set of environmental, labor, and consumer protection laws that some believe will be threatened if the WTO gains too much authority.

The International System

From the end of World War II to the end of the Cold War, all presidents, Republicans and Democrats alike, pursued a broadly similar set of foreign policies. Although postwar presidents differed in their means, they fundamentally agreed on the ends: containment of the influence of the Soviet Union, solidification of the Western alliance, encouragement of open economies in which American business might compete, and opposition to leftist or nationalist movements in the developing world. The reason for this continuity is that U.S. foreign policies reflected the basic features of the international system (particularly its bipolarity, with two superpowers), the U.S. position in that system as the dominant superpower, and the nature of U.S. economic interests in markets, raw materials, and investment opportunities.

When the international system changes, presidential policy tends to change, no matter who is president. Thus, when it became painfully evident by the 1970s that the United States had declined in international economic competitiveness

HOW DEMOCRATIC ARE WE?

PROPOSITION: The presidency has evolved into a highly democratic institution that is responsive to the American people.

AGREE: The framers did not conceive of the office in very democratic terms, but it has become the most democratic institution in the American federal system. It is, after all, the only office directly elected by the American people as a whole. Members of the Supreme Court are not elected by the people, and members of the House and Senate, although elected by the people, represent only congressional districts and states. Being elected by the whole people, it is only the president who can claim a national mandate for his programs and actions. Thus, it is only the president who can overcome the inherent stasis of the constitutional system and move the government to action in the interests of and in response to the American people.

DISAGREE: Although presidents often claim mandates from the people, they are more likely to lead and shape public opinion than to respond to it, especially in the area of foreign and military affairs, so the institution cannot be said to be democratic. Presidents can pretty much go their own way, knowing that the people will eventually follow their lead. Because elections happen only every four years, moreover, and assuming that the public has a short memory, presidents have plenty of time to follow their own agendas early in their term without regard to the public. Because presidents can only serve two terms, then, there is no compelling reason they need to pay close attention to the public during their second term.

THE AUTHORS: It is abundantly clear that the presidency is far more democratic than the framers had intended: presidents are directly elected by the people (although the Electoral College is still in place); their actions are open to intense public scrutiny by the media, interest groups, the courts, and Congress; and they pay close attention to what the public wants, following public opinion polls closely and commissioning their own. They pay close attention to what the people want for a variety of reasons, including their desire to put in place policies that they favor, to leave a legacy, and to attain a honored place in the history books. It is true that presidents can sometimes manipulate the public, especially in foreign and military affairs where presidential constitutional powers are considerable and public scrutiny is lower, but in the end, presidents cannot be successful unless they enjoy strong public support.

and relative economic strength, Presidents Carter and Reagan introduced measures to reduce taxes, to lighten the burden of regulation, to subsidize high-technology industries, and to encourage exports. When the Soviet Union began to move in conciliatory directions and then collapsed, Reagan and Bush responded in friendly fashion, despite their history of fierce anticommunism.

The Economy

Similarly, all presidents, Republican or Democratic, must work to help the economy grow and flourish while keeping unemployment and inflation low. A healthy economy is essential to a president's popularity and continuation in office, to tax receipts that fund government programs, and to the maintenance of social peace and stability. A healthy economy in turn requires that investors continue to have confidence in the future. This has tended to create a set of presidential policies that favor such investors no matter whether a Democrat or a Republican is in the White House.

Summary

The American presidency began small; only a few nineteenth-century presidents (among them Jefferson, Jackson, Polk, and Lincoln) made much of a mark. In the twentieth century, however, as a result of industrialization, two world wars and the Cold War, and the Great Depression, presidential powers and resources expanded greatly. The presidency attained much of its modern shape under Franklin Roosevelt.

Presidents have varied in personality and style, with significant consequences. Despite the enormous resources and large staffs available to presidents, they are constrained in what they can do, especially concerning domestic policy. Presidents cannot always control their own executive branch. They engage in tugs-of-war with Congress, pushing their programs with varying success, depending on their party's strength in the legislature and the nature of the issue.

The presidency has become a far more democratic office than the Founders envisioned. Presidents listen to public opinion and respond to it, in addition to leading (and sometimes manipulating) the public. But presidents are also influenced by interest groups, party activists, and financial contributors in ways that may diverge from what the public wants. Further, presidents are affected by such structural factors as the nature of the American economic and social systems and the U.S. position in the world.

Suggestions for Further Reading

Barber, James David. *The Presidential Character: Predicting Performance in the White House,* 4th ed. Englewood Cliffs, NJ: Prentice Hall, 1992.
> *A fascinating, but controversial, analysis of the nature and effect of presidential personalities.*

Brody, Richard A. *Assessing the President.* Stanford, CA: Stanford University Press, 1991.
> *A thorough analysis of what affects presidents' popularity.*

Cronin, Thomas E., and Michael A. Genovese. *The Paradoxes of the American Presidency.* New York: Oxford University Press, 1998.
> *Examines the implications of our often conflicting and unrealistic expectations about the office of president.*

Eksterowicz, Anthony J., and Glenn P. Hastedt, eds. *The Post-Cold War Presidency.* Boulder, CO: Rowan and Littlefield, 1999.
   A collection of essays by leading scholars on the effect of the end of the Cold War on the American presidency.

Neustadt, Richard E. *Presidential Power and the Modern Presidents: The Politics of Leadership from Roosevelt to Reagan.* New York: Free Press, 1991.
   The classic study of how presidents do or do not get their way, updated to include recent presidencies.

Skowronek, Stephen. *The Politics Presidents Make.* Cambridge, MA: Harvard University Press, 1993.
   An in-depth historical look at the ways in which the political context of the times shapes the nature of the presidency.

Tulis, Jeffrey K. *The Rhetorical Presidency.* Princeton, NJ: Princeton University Press, 1987.
   Traces how presidents have moved from the Founders' conception of a distant relationship with the public to the modern closeness.

Internet Sources

Potus   **www.ipl.org/ref/POTUS**
   Biographies and other information about American presidents.

Presidential Library Consortium   **http://metalab.unc.edu/lia/president/**
   Links to all existing presidential libraries and their vast repositories of information.

Roper Center   **http://www.lib.uconn.edu/RoperCenter/**
   Reports on all major presidential performances and popularity polls.

Watergate Site   **www.washingtonpost.com/wp-srv/national/longterm/ watergate/front.htm**
   Complete information on the Watergate affair: background, congressional testimony, official statements, press coverage, speeches, court rulings, biographies of the leading players, and more.

White House Home Page   **http://www.whitehouse.gov/**
   Information on the first family, recent presidential addresses and orders, text from news conferences, official presidential documents, and ways to contact the White House.

Notes

1. Hedrick Smith, "The President as Coalition Builder: Reagan's First Year," in Thomas E. Cronin, ed., *Rethinking the Presidency* (Boston: Little, Brown, 1982), pp. 277–281.

2. David A. Stockman, *The Triumph of Politics: How the Reagan Revolution Failed* (New York: Harper & Row, 1986), p. 169.

3. Thomas Byrne Edsall, *The New Politics of Inequality* (New York: Norton, 1984); Thomas Ferguson and Joel Rogers, *Right Turn: The Decline of the Democrats and the Future of American Politics* (New York: Farrar, Straus & Giroux, 1986).

4. U.S. Bureau of the Census.

5. U.S. Department of Commerce, *Historical Statistics of the United States, Colonial Times to 1970* (Washington, D.C.: U.S. Government Printing Office, 1971), pp. 8, 1143.

6. Clinton Rossiter, *The American Presidency,* rev. ed. (New York: Harcourt, Brace, 1960).

7. Quoted in Laurence J. Peter, *Peter's Quotations* (New York: Morrow, 1977), p. 405.

8. James P. Pfiffner, *The Modern Presidency* (New York: St. Martin's Press, 1998), ch. 4.

9. Nathan Miller, *FDR: An Intimate History* (Lanham, MD: Madison Books, 1983), p. 276.

10. Thomas E. Cronin and Michael A. Genovese, *The Paradoxes of the American Presidency* (New York: Oxford University Press, 1998), ch. 10; and Joseph A. Pika, "The Vice-Presidency: New Opportunities, Old Constraints," in Michael Nelson, ed., *The Presidency and the Political System,* 4th ed. (Washington, D.C.: Congressional Quarterly Press, 1995), pp. 496–528.

11. Benjamin Bradlee, *Conversations with Kennedy* (New York: Norton, 1975), p. 38.

12. Richard E. Neustadt, *Presidential Power and the Modern Presidents: The Politics of Leadership from Roosevelt to Reagan* (New York: Free Press, 1990).

13. Graham T. Allison, *Essence of Decision: Explaining the Cuban Missile Crisis* (Boston: Little, Brown, 1971), pp. 141–142.

14. Neustadt, *Presidential Power and the Modern Presidents,* ch. 2.

15. Charles O. Jones, *Separate but Equal: Congress and the Presidency* (New York: Chatham House, 1999).

16. For the view that divided government affects the content of public policy, see James L. Sundquist, "Needed: A Political Theory for the New Era of Coalition Government in the U.S.," *Political Science Quarterly* 103 (1988), pp. 613–635; L. Mezey, "The Legislature, the Executive and Public Policy," and N. Pfiffner, "Divided Government and the Problems of Governance," in James Thurber, ed., *Divided Democracy* (Washington, D.C.: Congressional Quarterly Press, 1991). For the view that divided government doesn't matter much, see David R. Mayhew, *Divided We Govern: Party Control, Lawmaking, and Investigations, 1946–1990* (New Haven, CT: Yale University Press, 1991); Charles Jones, *The Presidency in a Separated System* (Washington, D.C.: Brookings Institution, 1994). It may be that divided government matters for some issue areas and not others; for this view, see Martha Gibson, "Issues, Coalitions, and Divided Government," *Congress and the Presidency* 22 (1995), pp. 155–165.

17. George C. Edwards III, *Presidential Influence in Congress* (San Francisco: Freeman, 1980); Jon R. Bond and Richard Fleischer, *The President in the Legislative Arena* (Chicago: University of Chicago Press, 1990); Mark A. Peterson, *Legislating Together* (Cambridge, MA: Harvard University Press, 1990).

18. Terry Sullivan, "Headcounts, Expectations and Presidential Coalitions in Congress," *American Journal of Political Science* 32 (1988), pp. 657–689.

19. Aaron Wildavsky, "The Two Presidencies," in Aaron Wildavsky, ed., *Perspectives on the Presidency* (Boston: Little, Brown, 1975), pp. 448–461.

20. Edwards, *Presidential Influence in Congress,* pp. 90–100; Jon R. Bond and Richard Fleischer, *The President in the Legislative Arena* (Chicago: University of Chicago Press, 1990).

21. Jeffrey K. Tulis, *The Rhetorical Presidency* (Princeton, NJ: Princeton University Press, 1987), chs. 2–3, esp. p. 64.

22. Woodrow Wilson, *Leaders of Men,* ed. T. H. Vail Motter (Princeton, NJ: Princeton University Press, 1952), p. 39; quoted in Tulis, *The Rhetorical Presidency,* ch. 4, which analyzes Wilson's theory at length and expresses some skepticism about it.

23. Tulis, *The Rhetorical Presidency,* pp. 138, 140.

24. Samuel Kernell, *Going Public: Strategies of Presidential Leadership,* 2nd ed. (Washington, D.C.: Congressional Quarterly Press, 1993), p. 92 and ch. 4.

25. Benjamin I. Page and Robert Y. Shapiro, "Presidents as Opinion Leaders: Some New Evidence," *Policy Studies Journal* 12 (1984), pp. 649–661; Benjamin I. Page, Robert Y. Shapiro, and Glenn R. Dempsey, "What Moves Public Opinion," *American Political Science Review* 81 (1987), pp. 23–43; but see Donald L. Jordan, "Newspaper Effects on Policy Preferences," *Public Opinion Quarterly* 57 (1993), pp. 191–204.

26. Benjamin I. Page and Mark P. Petracca, *The American Presidency* (New York: McGraw-Hill, 1983), p. 122. See Benjamin I. Page and Robert Y. Shapiro, "Effects of Public Opinion on Policy," *American Political Science Review* 77 (1983), pp. 175–190.

27. Lawrence Jacobs and Robert Y. Shapiro, "The Rise of Presidential Polling: The Nixon White House in Historical Perspective," *Public Opinion Quarterly* 59, (1995), pp. 163–195.

28. Richard A. Brody, *Assessing the President* (Stanford, CA: Stanford University Press, 1991). See also John E. Mueller, "Presidential Popularity from Truman to Johnson," *American Political Science Review* 64 (1970), pp. 18–34; Samuel Kernell, "Explaining Presidential Popularity," *American Political Science Review* 72 (1978), pp. 506–522.

29. See Mark P. Petracca, ed., *The Politics of Interests* (Boulder, CO: Westview Press, 1992).

30. Charles E. Lindblom, *Politics and Markets* (New York: Basic Books, 1977).

31. Alexander Heard, *The Costs of Democracy* (Chapel Hill, NC: University of North Carolina Press, 1960); Ferguson and Rogers, *Right Turn;* Thomas Ferguson, *Golden Rule* (Chicago: University of Chicago Press, 1995).

32. Douglas A. Hibbs Jr., "Partisan Theory After Fifteen Years," *European Journal of Political Economy* 8 (1992), pp. 361–373.

The Federal Bureaucracy

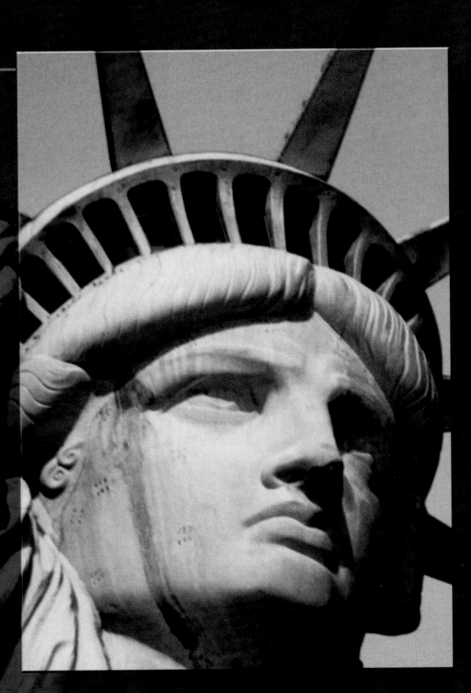

The Federal Bureaucracy Under Siege

When news of the terrorist bombing of the Frederick P. Murrah Federal Building in Oklahoma City hit the airwaves on April 19, 1995, retired sheriff Howard Stewart of Meadville, Pennsylvania, immediately dismissed the speculation of the experts that it was somehow connected to the troubled politics of the Middle East: "When I realized the date [the anniversary of the FBI raid on the Branch Davidians in Waco, Texas], and I thought about all the anger and fear that's out there," Stewart says, "I said to my wife, 'I don't think it was Arabs that did this.'"[1]

Stewart had reason to suspect a homegrown origin for the attack on a government center; he had been hearing some strange antigovernment rumblings in his quiet, conservative rural community, coming not from extremists but from many of its leading citizens. In the coffee shops on Main Street, talk was of a government conspiracy to enslave Americans to the United Nations. Color-coded highway signs, it was being said, were guideposts for foreign invaders. Meadville citizens were particularly upset by federal gun control laws, the 1993 siege in Waco of the Branch Davidians, and restrictive environmental regulations.

Several Meadville residents dismissed the Oklahoma City bombing as the act of a madman, but said they understood how anger against the federal government might trigger something like it:

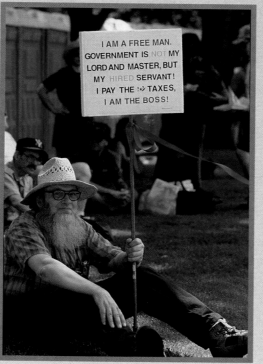

I AM A FREE MAN. GOVERNMENT IS NOT MY LORD AND MASTER, BUT MY HIRED SERVANT! I PAY THE ∷ TAXES, I AM THE BOSS!

"I don't want anything to do with them, but I think I understand their attitude," says Daniel J. Leech, president of Leech Carbide, a local manufacturer. "If you ran a small business, you'd understand, too. People are being squeezed more and more all the time. The government makes it almost impossible for small business to stay in business. Pressure just builds over time."

Leech's remark unleashed a torrent of anger at government among his companions. Doug Lodge, a roofer who lives in farm country, says farmers around him can't drain land because "if a cattail grows, it's wetland; if a beaver moves, it's a habitat."

Anti-federal-government anger is a staple of American political history. In the early days of the nation, many Anti-Federalists believed that the Constitution gave undue power to the central government. Buttressed by the theories of John C. Calhoun, the state of South Carolina passed a resolution in 1830 suggesting that the states had the right to nullify federal laws. Several of the New England states thought about seceding from the union in 1812 to remove themselves from federal authority, and the South did so in 1860, bringing on the Civil War. Many conservatives, including a majority on the Supreme Court for a few years, believed that the expansion of federal authority during the Great Depression in the 1930s was unconstitutional. Many whites in the South grew angry with the federal government in the 1960s and 1970s because of federal championing of civil rights. Antiwar activists during the years of the Vietnam War were unhappy with the Defense Department for waging the war and with the CIA and the FBI for interfering with legitimate protest activities. Much of the corporate community turned against the federal government in the 1980s and 1990s for what seemed like undue zeal on the part of government officials for environmental and consumer protection. Western ranchers opposed to extensive government ownership of land sparked what came to be call the "sagebrush rebellion" in the 1990s. The chorus of anti-federal-government complaints has ebbed and flowed throughout our history.

The anti-federal-government mood that crested in the mid-1990s had a profound effect on public policy, with many historically federal responsibilities transferred to the states. The mood also helped focus critical attention on the federal bureaucracy, that part of the government that carries out federal policy. Complaints about the size, cost, inefficiency, and excessive interference of the "bureaucracy in Washington" are common, as is unhappiness about particular agencies in the executive branch, such as the Internal Revenue Service, the Postal Service, the Bureau of Land Management, and the Bureau of Alcohol, Tobacco, and

Firearms. Members of the U.S. Forest Service report that they hesitate to wear their uniforms in town in several western communities because of the negative reactions the uniform provokes.

One result of the anti-federal-government mood in the country, according to some scholars, is that the bureaucracy is becoming increasingly crippled in its ability to carry out its responsibilities. American citizens and businesses are less cooperative, the morale of federal government workers is falling, talented people are leaving the federal government, and fewer talented people are looking to careers in the public service.[2]

▶ Thinking Critically About This Chapter

This chapter is about the federal bureaucracy, how it is organized, what it does, and what effects its actions have on public policies and American democracy.

Using the Framework. You will see in this chapter how the federal bureaucracy has grown over the years, primarily as a result of structural transformations in the economy and international position of the United States, but also because of the influence of political linkage level actors and institutions, including voters, public opinion, and interest groups. Primary responsibility for many of the enduring features of the federal bureaucracy will be shown to be associated with our political culture and the Constitution.

Using the Democracy Standard. You will see in this chapter that the federal bureaucracy in general, despite much speculation to the contrary, is fairly responsive to the American people, reacting in the long run to pressures brought to bear on it by the elected branches, the president, and Congress. On the other hand, bureaucrats in specific agencies, in specific circumstances, can be relatively immune from public opinion, at least in the short and medium run. You will be asked to think about what this means in terms of our democratic evaluative standard. ▶

A Comparative View of the American Bureaucracy

The American bureaucracy is different from bureaucracies in other democratic nations. Structural influences such as the American political culture and the constitutional rules of the game have a great deal to do with these differences.

Hostile Political Culture

Americans do not trust government; nor do they think it can accomplish most of the tasks assigned to it. They believe, on the whole, that the private sector can usually do a better job. In 1998, according to the American National Election Study, only 34 percent reported that they trusted the government.[3]

This hostile environment influences the bureaucracy in several ways. For one thing, our public bureaucracy is surrounded by more legal restrictions and is subject to more intense legislative oversight than bureaucracies in other countries. Because **civil servants** have so little prestige, moreover, many of the most talented people in our society tend to stay away; they do not aspire to work in government. This is not true in many other democratic countries. In France, Britain, and Germany, for instance, the higher **civil service** positions are filled by the best graduates of the countries' elite universities and

civil servants

Government workers employed under the merit system; not political appointees.

civil service

Federal government civilian employees, excluding political appointees.

are accorded enormous prestige. Finally, the highest policymaking positions in the U.S. executive branch are closed to civil servants; they are reserved for presidential political appointees. This is not true in other democracies.

Incoherent Organization

Our bureaucracy is an organizational hodgepodge. It does not take the standard pyramidal form, as bureaucracies elsewhere do. There are few clear lines of control, responsibility, or accountability. Some executive branch units have no relationship at all to other agencies and departments. As one of the leading students of the federal bureaucracy once put it, other societies have "a more orderly and symmetrical, a more prudent, a more cohesive and more powerful bureaucracy," whereas we have "a more internally competitive, a more experimental, a noisier and less coherent, a less powerful bureaucracy."[4] Our bureaucracy was built piece by piece over the years in a political system without a strong central government. Bureaucracies in other democratic nations were often created at a single point in time, by powerful political leaders, such as Frederick the Great in Prussia and Napoleon in France.[5]

Divided Control

Adding to the organizational incoherence of our federal bureaucracy is the fact that it has two bosses—the president and Congress—who are constantly vying with one another for control. In addition, the federal courts keep an eye on it. This situation is created by the separation of powers and checks and balances in our Constitution, which give each branch a role in the principal activities and responsibilities of the other branches. No other democratic nation has

WEB EXPLORATION

Comparing Bureaucracies as Information Providers

Issue: The bureaucracies of the United States and other democratic governments around the world have been racing to put information about their activities, policies, and services online. Some do it better than others.

Site: Access the Executive Branch Web site at the Library of Congress and the official site of the government of Canada through the "Course Documents" section of your online course. Go to the "Web Explorations" section for Chapter 13, click on "Comparing Bureaucracies as Information Providers," and open "information." Browse each of the sites; examine a number of their most important departments, ministries, agencies, and bureaus.

What You've Learned: Which national government does a better job of serving its constituency on the Web? How informative are the sites? How easy or difficult are they to navigate? Which are more graphically interesting?

HINT: To a large extent, your response to this query is strictly a matter of personal preference. However, one thing to be alert to is whether or not the government sites are simply conveying "good news."

opted for this arrangement. Civil servants in parliamentary democracies are accountable to a single boss, a minister appointed by the prime minister.

Accessibility

Because of incoherent organization, the lack of a chain of command with clear lines of authority and accountability, and divided control at the top, ours is an extremely open and porous bureaucracy. Individuals and groups can get a hearing and a response from bureaucrats at various levels, which is not the case in more hierarchically organized bureaucracies such as in France, Japan, or Germany. In one sense, this is potentially a very democratic arrangement, encouraging citizen participation in bureaucratic affairs. In practice, however, it provides a fertile environment for interest groups that know exactly where to go to get what they want, while the general public is generally unaware.

Transformation of the Bureaucracy

The Structural Context

Executive branch departments and officers are mentioned in the Constitution only in an indirect, offhand way. The Constitution neither specifies the number and kinds of departments to be established nor describes other bureaucratic agencies. The framers apparently wanted to leave these questions to the wisdom of Congress and the president.

We saw in Chapter 12 that the executive branch bureaucracy grew from very modest beginnings in President Washington's administration—with only four executive departments and fewer than 200 employees—to a very large bureaucracy in our own day of about 2.4 million civilian employees working in 14 departments; a White House minibureaucracy; and literally hundreds of bureaus, agencies, commissions, services, and boards. Figure 13.1 depicts the overall organization of the federal government and suggests the extraordinarily wide range of its responsibilities.

A Brief Administrative History of the United States

The most immediate causes for the transformation of the role of the federal government and the scale of the bureaucracy are political linkage sector pressures—from public opinion, voters, parties, interest groups, and social movements—on government decision makers. The more fundamental causes are changes in such structural level factors as the U.S. economy, the nation's population, and the role of the United States in the world.

Nineteenth-Century Changes Until the Civil War, the federal government had few responsibilities, and the administrative apparatus of the executive branch was relatively undeveloped. Rapid population growth, westward expansion, the Industrial Revolution, and economic uncertainty in the last quarter of the nineteenth century gradually changed people's thinking about the appropriate responsibilities of government and the size of the bureaucracy.[6] The Department of the Interior, created in 1849, was given responsibility for Indian affairs, the census, and the regulation of public lands and mining. The Department of Justice was created in 1870 to handle the federal government's growing legal burden in the fields of civil and criminal, antitrust, tax,

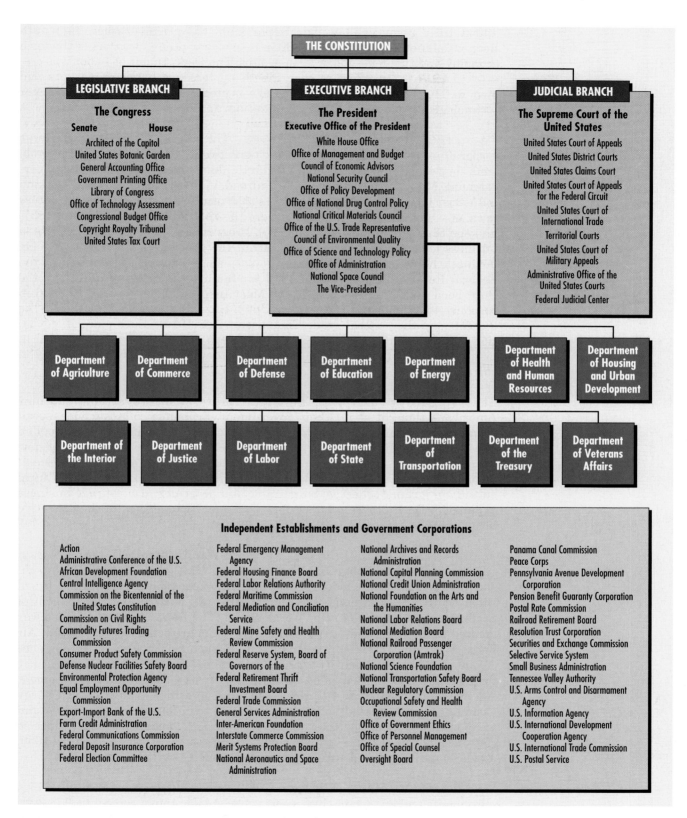

Figure 13.1 ● The Government of the United States

Source: *U.S. Government Organization Manual,* 1999.

and natural resources law. The Department of Agriculture became a full-fledged cabinet department in 1889 in response to economic crisis in the farm economy and the demands of farm groups. The Department of Labor was created in 1913 in an effort to ease the rising tensions between workers and owners. The Department of Commerce was created in the same year to foster technological development, standardization, and business cooperation.

The Corporation and the Progressives   The rise to prominence of the large corporations in the late nineteenth and early twentieth centuries, and the problems they caused, also contributed to a rethinking of the role of the federal government. Monopoly practices in the railroad, manufacturing, oil, and banking industries triggered reform movements that resulted in new federal regulatory laws, of which the most important were the Interstate Commerce Act (1887) and the Sherman Antitrust Act (1890). Progressive reformers and farsighted business leaders, who were worried about the growing public hostility to big business, helped convince Congress to pass such landmark legislation as the Federal Reserve Act (passed in 1914 to stabilize the banking industry), the Pure Food and Drug Act (1906), the Meat Inspection Act (passed in 1906 in response to the horrors reported in Upton Sinclair's "muckraking" book, *The Jungle*), and the Federal Trade Commission Act (1914).[7] Each piece of legislation was a response to a set of problems, each expanded the federal government's responsibilities, and each created a new executive branch agency to carry out the law.

The Great Depression   The Great Depression forever changed how Americans thought about their government. Economic collapse, widespread social distress, and serious threats of violence and social unrest impelled President Franklin Roosevelt and Congress to respond with a range of new programs: work programs for the unemployed, relief for the poor, Social Security, regulation of the banking and the securities industries, agricultural subsidy programs, collective bargaining, and programs to encourage business expansion. Each program added new bureaucratic agencies to the executive branch.

World War II and Its Aftermath   World War II, America's new role as a superpower, and the long Cold War with the Soviet Union also brought a substantial increase in the federal government's responsibilities and in the size of the executive branch. Some old-line departments, such as the Department of State, grew substantially after World War II. The Department of Defense was created by merging the old Army and Navy departments and adding an Air Force component. New administrative units such as the Central Intelligence Agency, the National Security Agency, the National Security Council, the Agency for International Development, and the U.S. Arms Control and Disarmament Agency were created to fill new needs and missions. The Atomic Energy Commission was created both to regulate and to encourage atomic power and weapons production. The Internal Revenue Service expanded its operations so that it could collect the revenues to pay for these new responsibilities. By 1950, a federal bureaucracy of substantial size and effect was firmly in place.[8]

The Regulatory State   During the 1960s and 1970s, successful social reform movements and important changes in public opinion convinced political leaders to take on new responsibilities in the areas of civil rights, urban affairs, environmental and consumer protection, workplace safety, and education. Important among these initiatives was the formation of the Department of

During World War II and the Cold War that followed, the increased responsibilities of a superpower were thrust on the U.S. federal government. The executive branch grew so rapidly during World War II that temporary buildings were constructed along the mall in Washington, D.C., to house such new bureaucratic entities as the Atomic Energy Commission.

Health, Education, and Welfare (now split into the Department of Health and Human Services and the Department of Education). The Environmental Protection Agency was created to monitor compliance with federal environmental laws and to regulate business activities that might pollute the nation's air and water. The Occupational Safety and Health Administration keeps its regulatory eye on potentially dangerous workplace practices. Each expansion of responsibility, as in the past, brought an expansion in the size of the bureaucracy. Although the Reagan Revolution slowed the growth in the federal government's responsibilities, it was unable to roll back most of the programs and agencies created since the Great Depression.

Devolution and Rollback On taking control of Congress after their 1994 landslide electoral victory, Republicans began to pare down the size of the federal government, roll back many of its regulatory responsibilities, and shift a number of functions to the states. For instance, Congress made it more difficult to identify and protect wetlands. It also shifted much of the responsibility for providing public assistance to the states (see Chapter 3). Finally, Congress made deep slashes in the federal budget, which forced substantial "downsizing" in a broad range of executive branch agencies. Increasingly, Republicans especially, but many Democrats as well, are asking what essential services the federal government should provide. This "devolution and rollback" theme was echoed by Bill Clinton in his 1996 State of the Union address, in which he announced the "end of big government." Nevertheless, the federal government's size and reach remain quite substantial in historical terms.

Devolution and rollback may be related to changes in the global economy, where success seems to go to business enterprises that are lean and mean, nimble and entrepreneurial, and to countries that allow their major companies to succeed by lowering regulatory and tax burdens. Whether this is cause or excuse is too early to tell. It may well be that globalization forces are not the cause of these changes, as some analysts suggest, but merely a rhetorical device used by the business community to lighten the burden of government regulation on corporations. Whether cause or rhetorical weapon, political leaders in the United States have been paying attention recently to globalization processes and have acted to diminish the role and size of the federal government and its bureaucracy.

LongmanParticipate

CourseCompass

timeline
Evolution of the Federal Bureaucracy

How the Executive Branch Is Organized

The executive branch is made up of several different kinds of administrative units, which make the federal bureaucracy a very complicated entity.

1. The most familiar are *departments*, which are headed by cabinet-level secretaries, appointed by the president and approved by the Senate (see Table 13.1). Departments are meant to carry out the most essential government functions. The first three ever established were War, State, and Treasury. Departments vary greatly in size and internal organization. The Department of Agriculture, for example, has almost 50 offices and bureaus, whereas the Department of Housing and Urban Development has only a few operating agencies.[9] Over the years, departments (and employees) were added as the need arose, as powerful groups demanded them, or as presidents and members of Congress wished to signal a new national need or to cement political alliances with important constituencies.

2. Subdivisions within cabinet departments are known as *bureaus* and *agencies.* In some departments, such as the Department of Defense, these subdivisions are closely controlled by the department leadership, and the entire department works very much like a textbook hierarchical model. In other cases, where the bureaus or agencies have fashioned their own relationships with interest groups and powerful congressional committees, the departments are little more than holding companies for powerful bureaucratic subunits.[10] During the long reign of J. Edgar Hoover, for instance, the FBI did virtually as it pleased, even though it was (and remains) a unit within the Justice Department.

Table 13.1 ● Employees of Executive Branch Departments, 1999		
Department	Number of Civilian Employees (in thousands)	Change Since 1990 (in thousands)
Agriculture	106	−16
Commerce	50	−20
Defense	718	−316
Education	5	0
Energy	16	−2
Health and Human Services	60	−64
Housing and Urban Development	10	−4
Interior	72	−6
Justice	123	+39
Labor	16	−2
State	25	0
Transportation	65	−2
Treasury	141	−17
Veterans Affairs	240	−8

Source: *The Budget of the United States Government, Fiscal 1999,* tab. 10-1 (estimated figures).

3. _Independent executive agencies_ report directly to the president rather than to a department- or cabinet-level secretary. They are usually created to give greater control to the president in carrying out some executive function or to highlight some particular public problem or issue that policymakers wish to address. The Environmental Protection Agency was given independent status to focus government and public attention on environmental issues and to give the federal government more flexibility in solving environmental problems.

4. _Government corporations_ are agencies that operate very much like private companies. They can sell stock, retain and reinvest earnings, and borrow money, for instance. They are usually created to perform some crucial economic activity that private investors are unwilling or unable to perform. The Tennessee Valley Authority, for example, was created during the Great Depression to bring electricity to most of the upper South; today it provides about 6 percent of all U.S. electrical power. The U.S. Postal Service was transformed from an executive department to a government corporation in 1970 to increase efficiency.

5. _Quasi-governmental organizations_ are hybrids of public and private organizations. They allow the federal government to be involved in a particular area of activity without directly controlling it. They are distinguished from government corporations by the fact that a portion of the boards of directors are appointed by the private sector. The Corporation for Public Broadcasting fits into this category, as does the Federal Reserve Board, responsible for setting the nation's monetary policy.

6. _Independent regulatory commissions_, such as the Securities and Exchange Commission and the Consumer Product Safety Commission, are responsible for regulating sectors of the economy in which it is judged that the free market does not work properly to protect the public interest. The commissions are "independent" in the sense that they stand outside the departmental structure and are protected against direct presidential or congressional control. A commission is run by commissioners with long, overlapping terms, and many require a balance between Republicans and Democrats.

7. _Foundations_ are units that are separated from the rest of government to protect them from political interference with science and the arts. Most prominent are the foundations for the Arts and for the Humanities and the National Science Foundation.

The Immigration and Naturalization Service is now being called on to do more about slowing the flow of illegal immigration, but it must operate within guidelines and budgets determined by Congress.

What Do Bureaucrats Do?

Bureaucrats engage in a wide range of activities that are relevant to the quality of democracy in the United States and affect how laws and regulations work.

Executing the Law

The term *executive branch* suggests the branch of the federal government that executes or carries out the law. The framers of the Constitution assumed that Congress would be the principal national policymaker and stipulated that the president and his appointees to administrative positions in the executive branch "shall take care that the laws be faithfully executed" (Article II, Section 2). For the most part, this responsibility is carried out routinely; mail is delivered, troops are trained, and Social Security checks are mailed on time.

Sometimes, executing the law is not so easy, however, because it is not always clear what the law means. Often (all too often, according to some critics[11]), Congress passes laws that are vague about goals and short on procedural guidelines. It may do so because its members believe that something should be done about a particular social problem but are unclear on specifics about how to solve it or disagree among themselves. The Office of Economic Opportunity, for example, was created in 1965 as part of Lyndon Johnson's War on Poverty, with a mandate to "eliminate poverty," but it received virtually no guidance about what time frame was contemplated or what specific things it ought to do. Vaguely written statutes and directives, then, leave a great deal of discretion to bureaucrats.

Regulating (Rule Making)

Congress often gives bureaucratic agencies the power to write specific rules. Because of the complexity of the problems that government must face, Congress tends to create agencies and to specify the job or mission that it wants done and then charges the agency with using its expertise to do the job. Congress created the Environmental Protection Agency (EPA), for instance, and gave it a mission—to help coordinate the cleanup of the nation's air and water—but it left to the EPA the power to set the specific standards that communities and businesses must meet. The standards set by the EPA have the force of law unless they are rescinded by Congress or overruled by the courts. The Food and Drug Administration (FDA) writes rules about the introduction of new drugs that researchers and pharmaceutical companies are obliged to follow. (See the "Using the Framework" feature for more on the FDA.)

Some critics believe that Congress delegates entirely too much lawmaking to the executive branch, but it is difficult to see what alternative Congress has. It cannot micromanage every issue. And in the end, Congress retains control; it can change the rules written by bureaucrats if they drift too far from congressional intent or constituent desires.

Other critics simply believe that there are too many rules and regulations. When candidates promise to "get government off our backs," the reference is to the purported burdens of regulation. Several attempts have been made to roll back executive branch rule making. Under Ronald Reagan, required **cost-benefit analysis** was introduced as a way to slow the rule-making process, for example. And all recent presidents have used the Office of Management and Budget (OMB) to review "excessive" rule making.

LongmanParticipate

CourseCompass

simulation
You Are the Administrator

cost-benefit analysis

A method of evaluating rules and regulations by weighing their potential costs against their potential benefits to society.

Congress identifies tasks and creates agencies to complete them using their own expertise. For example, the Environmental Protection Agency was created by Congress to clean up and prevent pollution in the nation's air and water; the EPA creates and implements environmental standards without much direct congressional involvement.

Adjudicating

Congress has given some executive branch agencies the power to conduct quasi-judicial proceedings in which disputes are resolved. Much as in a court of law, the decisions of an administrative law judge have the force of law, unless appealed to a higher panel. The National Labor Relations Board, for instance, adjudicates disputes between labor and management on matters concerning federal labor laws. Disputes may involve claims of unfair labor practices, for example—firing a labor organizer falls into this category—or disagreements about whether proper procedures were followed in filing for a union certification election.

It is quite clear that bureaucrats exercise a great deal of discretion. They do not simply follow a set of orders from Congress or the president but find many opportunities to exercise their own judgment. Because bureaucrats make important decisions that have consequences for many other people, groups, and organizations, we can say that they are policymakers. They are *unelected* policymakers, however, and this fact should immediately alert us to some potential problems with regard to the practice of democracy.

Who Are the Bureaucrats?

Because bureaucrats exercise substantial discretion as policymakers, we want to know who they are. How representative are they of the American people? In a democracy, we would probably want to see a pretty close correspondence between the people and bureaucrats. There are several different personnel systems in the executive branch: career civil service, separate merit services in specific agencies, and political appointees.

USING THE FRAMEWORK

How Can a Bureaucratic Agency such as the Food and Drug Administration (FDA) Make Rules on Important Things Like Genetically Engineered Food? The Members of the FDA Aren't Even Elected by the People!

One of the emerging conflicts that will be playing itself out over the next few years, both in the United States and in the global economy, concerns the safety of genetically engineered food and the rules that will apply for protecting the public from its possible harmful effects. In the United States, unless Congress chooses to act in its own right, the rules will be made by the Food and Drug Administration. We can better understand why the FDA can make rules on genetically engineered foods by using a broad perspective that takes into account structural, political linkage, and governmental level factors.

Governmental Action

The FDA issues rules on genetically engineered food products.

Governmental Level

- Congress created the Food and Drug Administration, defined its overall mission, but left room for the FDA to make rules in its areas of responsibility.

- The Court has allowed bureaucratic agencies to make rules within the boundaries set by Congress.

- No laws specifically addressing genetically engineered food have been enacted, leaving rulemaking in this area to the FDA.

- The FDA scientific staff pressed the FDA's leadership to become active in this area of rulemaking.

- The FDA leadership, attentive to the growing interest in rules to regulate in the area of genetically engineered food, held a series of hearings on the subject in 1999.

- The FDA issued rules in 2000 specifying how genetically engineered food is to be tested for safety and wholesomeness and requiring packaging to carry a warning label for consumers.

Political Linkages Level

- Public opinion polls show that some Americans are beginning to worry about genetically engineered food and want some action.

- Interest groups, for and against genetically engineered food, have pressed their positions on public officials, using both "inside" and "outside" forms of lobbying.

- Demonstrators at the WTO protests in Seattle targeted genetically engineered food, putting further pressure on public officials to take action.

Structural Level

- The Constitution says little about the organization and operations of the Executive Branch and leaves the details to be filled in by Congress.

- Scientific researchers have made dramatic breakthroughs in plant and animal genetics, causing some segments of society to call for regulations.

- Global agribusiness corporations are always looking for the most efficient forms of production, and genetically engineered products help them do this.

The Merit Services

Merit services choose employees on the basis of examinations and educational credentials.

Career Civil Service   From the election of Andrew Jackson in 1828 until the late nineteenth century, the executive branch was staffed through what is commonly called the **spoils system**. It was generally accepted that the "spoils of victory" belonged to the winning party. Winners were expected to clear out people who were loyal to the previous administration and to replace them with their own people. Also known as *patronage,* this system of appointment caused no great alarm in the beginning because of the small and relatively unimportant role of the federal government in American society. The shortcomings of the War Department and other bureaucratic agencies during the Civil War, however, convinced many people that reform of the federal personnel system was required. Rampant corruption and favoritism in the government service during the years after the Civil War gave an additional boost to the reform effort, as did the realization that the growing role of the federal government required more skilled and less partisan personnel. The final catalyst for change was the assassination in 1881 of President James Garfield by a person who, it is said, badly wanted a government job but could not get one.

> **spoils system**
> The practice of distributing government offices and contracts to the supporters of the winning party; also called patronage.

The Civil Service Act of 1883, also known as the Pendleton Act, created a bipartisan Civil Service Commission to oversee a system of appointments to certain executive branch posts on the basis of merit. Competitive examinations were to be used to determine merit. In the beginning, the competitive civil service system included only about 10 percent of federal positions. Congress has gradually extended the reach of the career civil service; today, it covers about 60 percent of federal employees. In 1978, Congress abolished the Civil Service Commission and replaced it with two separate agencies, the Office of Personnel Management and the Merit Systems Protection Board. The former administers the civil service laws, advertises positions, writes examinations, and acts as a clearinghouse for agencies that are looking for workers. The latter settles disputes concerning employee rights and obligations, hears employee grievances, and orders corrective action when needed.

Agency Merit Services   Many federal agencies require personnel with particular kinds of training and experience appropriate to their special missions. For such agencies, Congress has established separate merit systems administered by each agency itself. The Public Health Service, for instance, recruits its own doctors. The State Department has its own examinations and procedures for recruiting foreign service officers. The National Aeronautics and Space Administration (NASA) recruits scientists and engineers without the help of the Office of Personnel Management. About 35 percent of all federal civilian employees fall under these agency-specific merit systems.

How Different Are Civil Servants?   Civil servants are very much like other Americans.[12] Their educational levels, regional origins, average incomes, and age distribution match almost exactly those of the general population. Civil servants' political beliefs and opinions also match almost exactly those of the general American public, although they tend to favor the Democrats a bit more than the general public and are slightly more liberal on social issues than the national average.[13] Women and minorities are very well represented (the latter are actually overrepresented), with women holding 43 percent of all nonpostal jobs and African-Americans 17 percent. In addition, the demographic representativeness of the bureaucracy is far greater in the United States than in virtually any other democratic nation.[14]

It is worth noting, however, that women and minorities are overrepresented in the very lowest civil service grades and are underrepresented in the highest. They also are far less evident in the special-agency merit systems (such as the Foreign Service and the FBI) and in the professional categories (scientists at the National Institutes of Health; doctors in the Public Health Service). In Britain and France, for example, people of aristocratic background have long dominated the upper levels of the civil service in the former; graduates of the elite *grandes écoles,* like the École Nationale d'Administration, dominate in the latter.

Political Appointees

The highest policymaking positions in the federal bureaucracy (e.g., department secretaries, assistants to the president, leading officials in the agencies) enter government service not by way of competitive merit examinations but by presidential appointment. About 1,200 of these top appointments require Senate confirmation, and about 2,000 more do not. These patronage positions, in theory at least, allow the president to translate his electoral mandate into public policy by permitting him to put his people in place in key policymaking jobs.

Most presidents use patronage not only to build support for their programs but also to firm up their political coalition by being sensitive to the needs of important party factions and interest groups. Ronald Reagan used his appointments to advance a conservative agenda for America and made conservative beliefs a prerequisite for high bureaucratic appointments.[15] President Clinton, by contrast, promised to make government "look more like America," and he did

WEB EXPLORATION

Who Are the Bureaucrats?

Issue: Although women are well represented in the federal bureaucracy, their presence in the upper-most, politically appointed, decision-making positions in the Executive Branch may be less. Or, they may be well represented in decision-making positions in some agencies and not others.

Site: Access the Plumbook, which lists all federal politically appointed offices, through the "Course Documents" section of your online course. Go to the "Web Explorations" section for Chapter 13, click on "Who Are the Bureaucrats?," and open "how representative?" Select three Executive Branch Departments, and review the names of the people who hold offices in the Departments.

What You've Learned: How well are women represented in the Executive Branch departments you selected? If women are better represented in some as compared with others, why do you think that is the case?

HINT: Because women professionals in American society are most heavily represented in education, welfare, and the health professions, and in the law, the Departments with their principal missions in these areas are likely to have the most women available for appointment.

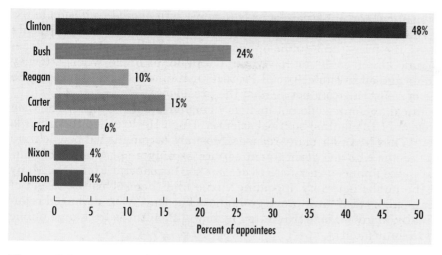

Figure 13.2 ● **Percentage of Women and Minorities Appointed by Presidents to the Executive Branch**

Presidents have appointed women and minorities to top posts in the federal government with increasing frequency. President Clinton had a particularly notable record in this regard.

Source: Calculations by the authors from data in the *Congressional Quarterly Weekly Editions* through 1999 and from the Office of Presidential Personnel.

so by appointing many women and minorities to top posts in his administration. (see Figure 13.2). George W. Bush combined the Reagan and Clinton approaches by making conservative but racially and ethnically diverse appointments.

Top political appointees are not very representative of the American people. They tend to be much better educated and wealthier than other Americans. They also tend to be professionals, independent businesspeople, or executives from large corporations and financial institutions. This narrow and privileged pool of appointees has important ramifications for the practice of democracy, because it is these officials who exercise the most discretion and make the most important policy decisions. To be sure, background is not everything in the determination of the outlook and behavior of political appointees, but it cannot be discounted either.

Despite having been appointed to their posts by the president, political appointees cannot automatically be assumed to do the president's bidding.

Presidents cannot be certain that their appointees will act as members of the presidential team. Attorney General Janet Reno, here testifying before a House committee, made a number of decisions regarding investigations of White House scandals that caused considerable pain for President Clinton.

High-level political appointees are subject to many influences in addition to the president, including Congress, the courts, personnel in their own departments and agencies, the press, and public opinion. The result is sometimes unpleasant. President Clinton could not have been happy, for example, when Attorney General Reno agreed to allow Special Prosecutor Kenneth Starr to investigate allegations of sexual misconduct against the president.

Top political appointees do not last very long on the job. On average, they stay in office only 22 months; political scientist Hugh Heclo called them "birds of passage."[16] They leave for many reasons. Most are accomplished people from the private sector who see government service as only a short-term commitment. Most make financial sacrifices to become top bureaucratic officials. Many don't find the public notoriety appealing. Some find themselves the target of partisan campaigns that later prove groundless but leave with damaged reputations. Finally, many become frustrated by how difficult it is to change public policy and to implement it.

Political and Governmental Influences on Bureaucratic Behavior

Rather than there being a single chain of command, with clear lines of authority, the bureaucracy in general and bureaucrats in particular, must heed several important voices, among the most important of them, the public, the president, Congress, and the courts.

The Public

Most Americans pay little attention to bureaucratic agencies as such. The public focuses mainly on the *content* of public policies rather than on the bureaucratic agencies or the bureaucrats who carry them out. Americans have opinions about Social Security—level of benefits, eligibility, taxes, and so on—but do not concern themselves much with the Social Security Administration per se. In general, then, the public does not directly know or think much about bureaucratic agencies.

There are many exceptions to this generalization, however. Some bureaucratic agencies are constantly in the public eye and occasion the development of opinions. So many businesses are affected by environmental regulations, for instance, that the Environmental Protection Agency finds itself under constant scrutiny. Because taxes are a constant irritant for most people, Americans tend to have opinions—not very favorable, to be sure—about the Internal Revenue Service and its agents.

A disaster can focus public attention on an agency, as NASA discovered to its discomfort with the *Challenger* explosion and the failed Mars missions in 1999. The Branch Davidian tragedy in Waco, Texas, focused a harsh light on the Bureau of Alcohol, Tobacco, and Firearms, the FBI, and Attorney General Janet Reno.

Sometimes an agency will find itself caught in the middle of intense political conflicts where it may be criticized whether it acts or fails to act. The Immigration and Naturalization Service found itself caught in such a place in the fight over custody of the Cuban boat boy Elian Gonzalez, especially after its raid to take him from the home of his Miami relatives.

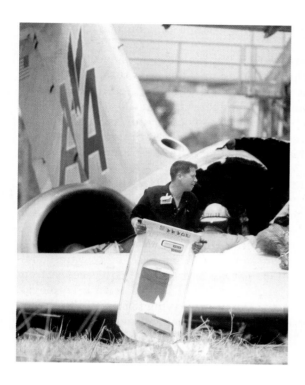

Executive branch agencies such as the Federal Aviation Administration often come to public attention only after a highly visible event such as the crash of this American Airlines passenger plane in Little Rock, Arkansas, in 1999.

The President

The president, as the nation's chief executive, is the formal head of the executive branch. But as we saw in Chapter 12, the president's ability to control the executive branch is limited. Virtually every modern president has been

WEB EXPLORATION

The Presidential Bureaucracy

Issue: As the responsibilities of and the public expectations for the presidency have expanded since the New Deal and the World War II, the president's staff has grown to help handle the workload.

Site: Access the White House Office through the "Course Documents" section of your online course. Go to the "Web Explorations" section for Chapter 13, click on "The Presidential Bureaucracy," and open "White House Office." Under the Executive Branch, select "White House Office." Before doing so, however, try to guess how many people help the president.

What You've Learned: How close did you come to guessing the number of people who work for the president? What functions and responsibilities did you expect to find; were they there? Which functions and responsibilities were there that you did not expect to find?

HINT: Presidents have always needed help in writing their speeches, preparing documents, communicating with the public, and working with Congress. But the staff now also includes people who help on health, economic, national security, and education policies and with relations with interest groups and state and local governments.

perplexed by the discovery that he cannot assume that bureaucrats will do what he wants them to do.[17]

Richard Nixon was so frustrated by his inability to move the federal bureaucracy that he came to think of it as an alien institution filled with Democratic party enemies. His strategy was to intimidate bureaucrats or bypass them. He created the notorious "plumbers" unit in the White House to act as his personal domestic surveillance and espionage unit. Revelation of its activities was one of the factors leading the House Judiciary Committee to recommend approval of three articles of impeachment in the Watergate scandal.

Why Presidents Are Often Stymied by the Bureaucracy   The sheer size and complexity of the executive branch is one reason why presidents are frustrated by it. There is so much going on, in so many agencies, involving the activity of tens of thousands of people, that simply keeping abreast of it all is no easy task. Moreover, because of civil service regulations, presidents have no say about the tenure or salary of most bureaucrats. When presidents want something to happen, they are unlikely to get instantaneous acquiescence from bureaucrats who do not fear them as they would fear a private employer. Presidents also find that they are not the only ones trying to control the actions of bureaucrats; they must always share executive functions with Congress and sometimes with the courts. Finally, bureaucratic agencies are heavily insulated against presidential efforts to control them because of agency alliances with powerful interest groups.

Tools of Presidential Leadership   Presidents are not entirely helpless, of course. They have a number of ways to encourage bureaucratic compliance.[18] Occasionally, because of a crisis or a widely shared national commitment, decisive bureaucratic action is possible, as during Roosevelt's New Deal era, Lyndon Johnson's first years as president, and Ronald Reagan's first administration.

Even during ordinary times, however, the president is not helpless. First, although it is difficult to measure precisely, the president's prestige as our only nationally elected political leader makes his wishes hard to ignore. When Teddy Roosevelt called the presidency a "bully pulpit," he meant that only the president can speak for the nation, set the tone for the government, and call the American people to some great national purpose. A popular president, willing and able to play this role, is hard to resist. Bureaucrats are citizens and respond like other Americans to presidential leadership. When a president chooses to become directly involved in some bureaucratic matter—for example, with a phone call to a reluctant agency head or a comment about some bureaucratic shortcoming during a press conference—most bureaucrats respond.

The power of appointment is also an important tool of presidential leadership. If a president is very careful to fill the top administrative posts with people who support him and his programs, he greatly increases his ability to have his way. Although the Senate must advise on and consent to many of his choices, it rarely interferes, recognizing, perhaps, that a coherent administration requires that a president have his own people in place.

The president's power as chief budget officer of the federal government is also a formidable tool of administration. No agency of the federal bureaucracy, for instance, can make its own budget request directly to Congress. The president's main budgetary instrument, the Office of Management and Budget, also has the statutory authority to block proposed legislation coming from any executive branch agency if it deems it contrary to the president's budget or program.

Congress

Congress also exercises considerable influence over the federal bureaucracy.

Legislating Agency Organization and Mission The president and Congress share control over the executive branch. The congressional tools of control, in fact, are at least as formidable as those of the president.[19] Congress legislates the mission of bureaucratic agencies and the details of their organization and can change either one. Congress can also alter agency policy or behavior.

Confirming Presidential Appointments Although the Senate almost always approves presidential appointments to top positions in the executive branch, it will sometimes use the "advice and consent" process to shape policies in bureaucratic departments and agencies. It occasionally turns down presidential nominations, as it did in the case of George Bush's nominee for the post of defense secretary, John Tower. At other times, it can simply draw out and delay the process in a bid to gain concessions from the president and the nominee on future policies. Senate Foreign Relations Committee Chairman Jesse Helms was a master at this, gaining concessions on policies concerning Cuba, foreign aid, and funding for international population control agencies. Defeat of nominees and long delays are most likely to happen during periods of divided government, when the atmosphere in the Senate is highly partisan.[20]

Controlling the Agency Budget Congress can also use its control over agency budgets to influence agency behavior. In theory, Congress uses the budget process to assess the performance of each agency each year, closely scrutinizing its activities before determining its next **appropriation**, the legal authority for the agency to spend money. Congress has neither the time nor the resources actually to do such a thing and usually gives each agency some small increment over what it had in the previous year.[21] Of course, if a particular agency displeases Congress, its budget may be cut; if a new set of responsibilities is given to an agency, its budget is usually increased. Sometimes these agency budget actions are taken with the full concurrence of the president; often they are not. Congress sometimes lends a sympathetic ear and increases the budgets of agencies that are not favored by the president. In the 1980s, Congress consistently gave more money than President Reagan wanted given to the EPA, the National Institutes of Health, and the National Science Foundation.

appropriation
Legal authority for a federal agency to spend money from the U.S. Treasury.

Oversight Hearings Oversight hearings are an important instrument for conveying the views of the members of Congress to bureaucrats. There is a great deal of evidence that agency heads listen when the message is delivered clearly.[22] The head of the Internal Revenue Service, for example, recently responded to Senate Finance Committee hearings on the agency's harassment of taxpayers by apologizing to taxpayers and promising changes in IRS behavior and policies.

Congress does not always speak with a single voice, however. Congress is a highly fragmented and decentralized institution, and its power is dispersed among scores of subcommittees. Often the activities of a particular bureaucratic agency are the province of more than a single committee or subcommittee, and the probability of receiving mixed signals from them is very high. A skilled administrator can often play these competing forces off of each other and gain a degree of autonomy for his or her agency.

Interest Groups

As we saw in Chapter 7, the federal bureaucracy is permeated by networks of government interest group alliances. Bureaucratic agencies often act as the supporters and protectors of these interest groups against other government bodies, other interests, and the public. Sometimes the symbiotic relationship becomes so pronounced that the private interest group comes to make its own public policies and regulations, with the federal agency serving to legitimize its actions.[23]

Interest groups are able to penetrate the federal bureaucracy and play an important role in its activities partly because of the absence of central administrative direction. With no clear leadership at the top, each agency must fashion its own political alliances to protect itself. Agencies fashion their alliances where they can: with other executive branch agencies when there are common interests, with congressional committees and subcommittees, and with interest groups. When the Reagan administration wanted to cut the annual appropriation for the National Science Foundation in the early 1980s, for instance, the foundation's leaders mobilized friendly members of Congress and university and scientific associations in its defense.

Another reason that agencies welcome interest group alliances is to help in their skirmishes with other federal agencies. The Defense Department and NASA annually disagree about how much of the space program ought to be devoted to military projects. In their struggle before the White House staff, the OMB, and Congress, each throws allied interest groups—defense contractors, scientific organizations, patriotic groups, and so on—into the breach.

Common Criticisms of the Federal Bureaucracy

Bureaucrats are often portrayed in popular culture as lazy paper shufflers or as indifferent, unresponsive, inhumane clerks denying us the benefits or services to which we are entitled. Politicians feed on this popular culture when they "run against Washington," promising to pare the bureaucracy down to size and to get it off the backs of the American people. (Interestingly enough, however, the first-ever "customer satisfaction" survey of federal government services, done in 1999, shows that Americans are only slightly less satisfied with government agencies than with private businesses.[24])

Let's look at the four most common criticisms of the federal bureaucracy and see how much merit they have.

"The Federal Bureaucracy Is Always Expanding"

Surprisingly, this complaint has no basis in fact. Although the number of federal civilian employees expanded dramatically in the first half of the twentieth century, it remained relatively stable at about 3 million from the mid-1960s to the early 1990s and has since dropped to less than 2.4 million, although federal regulations and mandates have required states and localities to hire more people. Government does more and spends more money today than it did in 1950, but it does so with fewer employees. Nor is it the case that all bureaucratic agencies grow without stopping. Even important ones decrease in size, as the Departments of Defense, Agriculture, and State have done since 1970.

"The Federal Bureaucracy Is Ineffective"

The record of the federal bureaucracy with respect to effectiveness—the ability to carry out its missions and reach its goals—is mixed. NASA landed a man on the moon in less than a decade, fulfilling President Kennedy's promise to the American people. But by the same token, NASA has suffered some problems in its shuttle and Mars programs over the years.

People who worry about government effectiveness must contend with the fact that the framers did not necessarily want government to be effective because they were worried first and foremost about tyranny. They created a system in which power would be fragmented. They were willing to trade some efficiency for inoculation against an overbearing and threatening government. Remember also that the federal bureaucracy was not designed as a rational machine with a clear chain of command, as in most democratic nations.

Finally, one must ask, "Compared to what?" Although most of us feel absolutely certain that the federal bureaucracy cannot be as effective in meeting its goals as private organizations, evidence to support such a belief is not overwhelming. Many studies on productivity, costs, and innovation show no public-private differences.[25] Large organizations, public or private, may be quite similar. It took private American automakers at least two decades to formulate an effective response to the challenge of foreign imports, for example. More research needs to be done on this issue, to be sure, but it is prudent to be skeptical of the conventional wisdom about government bureaucratic ineptitude.

"The Federal Bureaucracy Is Wasteful and Inefficient"

Waste in government is such an enduring theme in American politics that it is hard to imagine a political campaign without it. Once again, however, the matter is more complex than it may seem.

In actuality, the opportunity for agencies to waste money is quite limited, because the bureaucracy has discretionary control over only about 5 percent of the total federal budget. Ninety-five percent is earmarked for specific purposes or is distributed to beneficiaries by formula, or **entitlements**. Almost all of the federal budget goes to pay the interest on the national debt, to direct payments to individuals (e.g., military pensions and Social Security benefits), and to grants-in-aid and block grants to states and localities. The small discretionary pot that remains is closely monitored and encumbered with strict rules on its use. None of this suggests that there isn't waste or inefficient use of taxpayers' money in bureaucratic agencies. It is to say, however, that the charges are probably exaggerated. Of course, if what we mean by "waste of taxpayers' money" is spending on programs that we don't like (for some, it may be bilingual education; for others, it may be a new strategic bomber), then our complaint is not with the bureaucracy but with the policymaking branches of the federal government: the president and Congress. Government can seldom please everyone.

Perhaps more important, there are certain things we want government to do that the private sector cannot or will not provide because they are hard to assess in terms of economic costs and benefits. Economists call such products and services—things that society needs but the private sector does not provide—**public goods**. Most Americans want things such as pollution control, first-class airports and harbors, national defense, and basic scientific research, even though private companies are unlikely to provide them. Where there is inefficiency and waste, of course, the president and Congress should insist that the bureaucracy do better.

entitlements
Government benefits that are distributed automatically to citizens who qualify on the basis of a set of guidelines set by law; for example, Americans over the age of 65 are entitled to Medicare coverage.

public goods
Products and services that citizens want but the private sector does not provide, such as national defense and pollution control.

"The Federal Bureaucracy Is Mired in Red Tape"

red tape

Overbearing bureaucratic rules and procedures.

Americans complain incessantly about bureaucratic rules, regulations, formal procedures, and forms—in short, about **red tape**. At one time or another, we have all felt stymied by rules and procedures, irritated by delays, and frustrated by forms. But how valid is the complaint that we are bound up in red tape?

Again, we run into the problem of measurement. Is there more red tape in the federal bureaucracy than in other large institutions such as HMOs, universities, and private corporations? Red tape, moreover, is often in the eye of the beholder. What is a waste of time and an inconvenience to one person may represent good public policy to another. Complaints about red tape are almost always directed at agencies that are carrying out policies we don't like. For example, following federal procedures for the disposal of dangerous chemicals may not be what chemical companies would want to do on their own, but Americans have shown that they want strong environmental protection laws. Monitoring disposal is part of what protects us.

All in all, there is some truth to the stereotypes about the federal bureaucracy: it is large; there are programs that do not work; there is waste and inefficiency; there is a great deal of red tape. We would suggest, however, that the stereotypes greatly exaggerate the extent of the problem because our measuring instruments are very imprecise. Nor do we have reason to believe that the pathologies are unique to the federal bureaucracy. Finally, we must recognize that many of the pathologies, to the extent that they do exist, do not necessarily originate in the bureaucracy but are imposed by the Constitution.

Reforming the Federal Bureaucracy

How should we fix what's wrong with the federal bureaucracy? It depends on what we think is wrong.

Scaling Back the Size of the Bureaucracy

Government activities can be trimmed in two ways: by slimming down and by transferring control.

Cutting the Fat   For observers who worry that the federal bureaucracy is simply too big and costly, what might be called the "meat ax" approach is the preferred strategy. Virtually every candidate worth his or her salt promises to "cut the fat" if elected. Bill Clinton made such a promise during the 1992 presidential campaign, and he carried through after his election. In the early weeks of his administration, he ordered that 100,000 federal jobs be eliminated within four years, that freezes be placed on the salaries of government workers, that cost-of-living pay adjustments be reduced, and that the use of government vehicles and planes be sharply restricted.[26]

privatization

The process of turning over certain government functions to the private sector.

Privatizing   An increasingly popular strategy for scaling back the federal bureaucracy is to turn over some of its functions and responsibilities to the private sector.[27] The **privatization** approach is based on two beliefs:

1. Private business can almost always do things better than the government.

One strong argument against the privatization of government agencies is that private corporations might discontinue or increase the price of services that are costly or marginally profitable. For example, the U.S. Postal Service provides mail delivery to remote and less populous areas, such as the Alaskan outback, for the same cost as it does for the rest of the country. A private, profit-motivated company might be less inclined to do so.

   2. Competitive pressure from the private sector will force government
   agencies to be more efficient.

Many states and local communities have "contracted out" to private companies public services such as trash collecting, the management of jails and prisons, and even the schools. For many years, the federal government has contracted out some activities; the defense contracting system by which the Department of Defense buys fighter planes, submarines, and missiles from private corporations is a good example. Advocates of privatizing simply want the process to go further, turning over to private companies things such as the postal system, the federal prisons, and air traffic control.

   Critics worry that privatizing government carries two significant costs.[28] First, private business might not provide services that do not turn a profit. Delivery of mail to remote locations is something that the Postal Service does, for instance, but that a private company might decide not to do. Second, a private business under government contract is several steps removed from political control, and the normal instruments of democratic accountability, however imperfect, might not be as effective as they are in controlling government agencies. The voice of the public, expressed in public opinion polls or elections, might not be heard with much clarity by private companies, particularly if they are the only supplier of some essential service. Cable TV customers have an inkling, perhaps, of the meaning of "nonaccountability."

LongmanParticipate

CourseCompass

visual literacy
**The Changing Face
of the Federal
Bureaucracy**

Reinventing Government

President Clinton turned over the responsibility for "reinventing government" to Vice-President Al Gore at the beginning of his administration. The expression comes from a popular and influential book by that name written by David Osborne and Ted Gaebler.[29] Their proposal for transforming the federal government involves not only cutting the fat and privatizing (as discussed in the preceding section) but also introducing business principles into the executive branch. Their idea is that government agencies will provide better public services if they are run like private businesses. Forcing agencies to compete for

President Clinton and Vice-President Al Gore cut "red tape" as a dramatic way to introduce Gore's plan to reinvent government by introducing business principles into the operations of the executive branch. Congress approved only a few of the plan's provisions.

WEB EXPLORATION

Improving Bureaucratic Performance

Issue: Although most Americans and politicians think that the way to cut down on supposed government inefficiencies is to cut the size and reach of the federal bureaucracy, there are some who believe that the bureaucracy can be made better by improved customer service and doing a better job of fulfilling legislatively mandated missions.

Site: Access the National Partnership for Reinventing Government through the "Course Documents" section of your online course. Go to the "Web Explorations" section for Chapter 13, click on "Improving Bureaucratic Performance," and open "reinventing government." Select the "Hammer Awards." These are descriptions of award-winning initiatives by government employees to make their agencies work better.

What You've Learned: Are you convinced after reading about these initiatives that the federal bureaucracy can be made to operate better? Or do you think that these are minor improvements, not likely to make much difference in the long run?

HINT: Whatever your views on this issue might be, it is worth noting that continued improvement in bureaucratic performance, whether we are talking about significant or small improvements, will depend on the willingness of future presidents to support something like the "reinventing government" initiative started by President Clinton and Vice-President Gore.

customers, for instance, would motivate government employees to be more attentive to their customers (citizens). Paying employees on the basis of their performance rather than by pay grade (the present system) would make them work harder and better. Allowing agency heads more freedom to experiment—allowing them to be more entrepreneurial, if you will—might lead to innovative solutions to pressing social problems.

Gore's report closely followed the proposals made by Osborne and Gaebler.[30] Although Congress was unwilling to cooperate, many changes were made in the agencies by executive order. The most notable change was the dramatic streamlining of the drug approval process at the FDA.[31]

Protecting Against Bureaucratic Abuses of Power

Many people believe that a bureaucracy of the size and shape of our present one, albeit necessary in a modern society, is potentially dangerous. Closer control over the bureaucracy by elected political bodies and by clear legislative constraints has been the preferred solution. There are many legislative enactments that try to keep bureaucratic activity within narrow boundaries. The Freedom of Information Act of 1966 was designed to enhance the ability of the press and private citizens to obtain information about bureaucratic policies and activities. The Ethics in Government Act of 1978 strengthened requirements of financial disclosure by officials and prohibitions against conflicts of interest.

Some reformers would like to see greater protection provided for **whistle-blowers**—bureaucrats who report corruption, financial mismanagement, abuses of power, or other official malfeasance. All too often, these courageous people, acting in the public interest, are fired or harassed on the job. This happened to Ernest Fitzgerald, a civilian cost accountant at the Pentagon, who lost his job after he revealed $2 billion cost overruns on the C5A military transport plane (he eventually won reinstatement through the courts, but it took 14 years to do so).

whistle-blowers

People who bring official misconduct in their agencies to public attention.

Increasing Popular Participation

Many people worry that federal bureaucrats go about their business without the public's having much say in what they do. Without citizen input, it is argued, bureaucrats lose touch with the people they are supposed to serve—a situation that leads to irrational policies and citizen alienation from the bureaucracy. Citizen participation in agency affairs has been pushed by some reformers as a solution.[32] The antipoverty program of Lyndon Johnson's Great Society required the "maximum feasible participation" of the poor in its design and implementation. President Bush's housing secretary, Jack Kemp, introduced tenant councils to help administer federal housing programs at the neighborhood level.

Increasing Presidential Control

Popular sovereignty requires that the elected representatives of the people closely control the bureaucracy. Popular sovereignty implies that administrative discretion should be narrowed as much as possible and that clear directions and unambiguous policies should be communicated by elected officials to bureaucratic agencies. (Note that this is a very different goal from the one envisioned by the advocates of privatization and reinventing government.) Some have argued that the only public official who has an interest in seeing that the bureaucracy *as a whole* is well run and coherently organized is the president. Accordingly, one suggestion for reform is to increase the powers of the president so that he can be the chief executive, in fact and not just in name.[33]

HOW DEMOCRATIC ARE WE?

PROPOSITION: The federal bureaucracy is inherently undemocratic because it is filled with people, none of whom are elected, who make important government decisions that affect the lives of Americans.

AGREE: The bureaucracy is out of control. Although the number of federal civil servants has stabilized and even declined in the last few years, the federal government and its unelected bureaucrats seem to intrude further and further into our lives. Career civil servants at the Environmental Protection Agency issue rules on how farmers can use wetlands and on which animal species are endangered and protected from hunters. Employees of the Bureau of Land Management make rules for grazing on public lands that ranchers must follow.

DISAGREE: Civil servants are merely carrying out the missions defined for them by elected public officials, namely, Congress and the president. And, because they are especially sensitive to the wishes of the public because of their desire to be effective and to be reelected, the president and members of Congress pay close attention to what civil servants in the bureaucratic agencies are doing and intervene to force changes when civil servants go astray and act contrary to the public interest and the wishes of the public.

THE AUTHORS: While there are very powerful constraints on the actions of civil servants in the federal bureaucracy, they nevertheless enjoy substantial discretion in carrying out their missions. Most of what the bureaucracy does on a day-to-day basis goes unnoticed and unchallenged for a number of reasons. First, there are simply so many decisions being made and rules issued, that no one could possibly keep track of them all. Second, many of the rules and decisions are highly technical in nature, with only specialists and experts paying very close attention. Having said that, however, the bureaucratic system in the United States retains important democratic dimensions. For one thing, civil servants are very much like other Americans, both in their demographic makeup and in what they think the government should be doing. For another thing, interest groups concerned with a particular area of bureaucratic activity do pay close attention, even if the public in general does not, and they do not hesitate to bring their concerns to the attention of elected officials. Finally, when bureaucratic misconduct or mismanagement come to light, elected officials tend to intervene. Knowing this, civil servants try not to stray too far from the mainstream of public and governmental opinion. (See Figure 13.3.)

Summary

The executive branch has grown in size and responsibility. This growth is a consequence of a transformation in the conception of the proper role of government because of structural changes in the economy and the society. Although *bureaucracy* is not a popular concept in the American political tradition, we have created a sizable one. The reason is partly that bureaucratic organizations have certain strengths that make them attractive for accomplishing large-scale tasks.

Bureaucrats are involved in three major kinds of activities: executing the law, regulating, and adjudicating disputes. In each of these, they exercise a great deal of discretion. Because they are unelected policymakers, democratic theory demands that we be concerned about who the bureaucrats are. In the merit services, they are very much like other Americans in terms of background and attitudes. Political appointees, however, the most important bureaucratic decision makers, are very different from their fellow citizens.

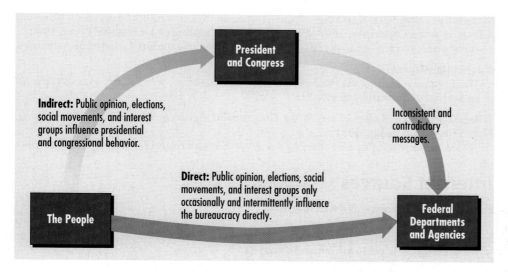

**Figure 13.3 ● Popular Control of the Bureaucracy:
Imperfect Popular Sovereignty**

Popular control of the federal bureaucracy is complex, indirect, and only partially effective. The public does not elect government bureaucrats, and public opinion has little direct effect on their behavior. However, the members of Congress and the president, all of whom are answerable to the electorate and attentive to public opinion, exercise an important influence on bureaucratic behavior. Because elected officials often send mixed signals, however, some of the effectiveness of such controls is diminished.

Several political and governmental actors and institutions affect bureaucratic behavior, including the president, Congress, the courts, as well as public opinion and interest groups. Bureaucratic pathologies, while real, are either exaggerated or the result of forces outside the bureaucracy itself: the constitutional rules and the struggle between the president and Congress. Proposals to reform the executive branch are related to what reformers believe is wrong with the federal bureaucracy. Those who worry most about size and inefficiency propose budget and personnel cuts, privatization, and the introduction of business principles into government. Those who want to make democracy more of a reality propose giving more control over the bureaucracy to the president and diminishing the role of interest groups.

Suggestions for Further Reading

Donahue, John. *Making Washington Work: Tales of Innovation in the Federal Government.* Washington, D.C.: Brookings, 1999.
> *Description of 14 winners of the Ford Foundation's Innovation in Government award; demonstrates that innovation is possible (although difficult) to achieve in the bureaucracy.*

Goodsell, Charles T. *The Case for Bureaucracy,* 3rd ed. Chatham, NJ: Chatham House, 1994.
> *A well-written polemic that gives the other side of the bureaucratic story.*

Osborne, David, and Ted Gaebler. *Reinventing Government.* Reading, MA: Addison-Wesley, 1992.
> *The bible for "reinventing government" advocates.*

Peters, B. Guy. *American Public Policy: Promise and Performance,* 5th ed. New York: Chatham House, 1999.
> *A review of American public policies with a particularly informative discussion of the role of the federal bureaucracy in policy implementation.*

Skowronek, Stephen. *Building a New American State: The Expansion of National Administrative Capacities, 1877–1920.* New York: Cambridge University Press, 1982.
  A careful historical analysis of the first budding of an expanded federal bureaucracy.

Washington Monthly.
  Washington's leading journal of "bureaucracy bashing"; filled with outrageous and (sometimes) illuminating stories.

Wilson, James Q. *Bureaucracy: What Government Agencies Do and Why They Do It.* New York: Basic Books, 1991.
  A look at the federal bureaucracy by one of the nation's leading conservative academics.

Internet Sources

Fedworld **http://www.fedworld.gov/**
  The gateway to the federal government's numerous Web sites and Gophers; connections to virtually every federal department, bureau, commission, and foundation, as well as access to government statistics and reports.

Yahoo: Executive Branch
http://www.yahoo.com/Government/U_S_Government/Executive_Branch/
  Similar to Fedworld; which to use depends on personal taste.

Notes

1. All quotes in this section are from Dale Russakoff, "Panic in Middle America," *Washington Post Weekly Edition* (May 15, 1995), p. 10.

2. Charles T. Goodsell, *The Case for Bureaucracy,* 3rd ed. (Chatham, NJ: Chatham House, 1994); B. Guy Peters, *American Public Policy: Promise and Performance,* 4th ed. (Chatham, NJ: Chatham House, 1996).

3. National Election Study, University of Michigan, 1999.

4. Wallace Sayre, "Bureaucracies: Some Contrasts in Systems," *Indian Journal of Public Administration* 10 (1964), p. 223.

5. Richard J. Stillman II, *The American Bureaucracy* (Chicago: Nelson-Hall, 1987), p. 18.

6. Stephen Skowronek, *Building a New American State: The Expansion of National Administrative Capacities, 1877–1920* (New York: Cambridge University Press, 1982), pp. 19–46.

7. See Edward S. Greenberg, *Capitalism and the American Political Ideal* (Armonk, NY: Sharpe, 1985); Samuel P. Hays, *The Response to Industrialization* (Chicago: University of Chicago Press, 1957); Gabriel Kolko, *The Triumph of Conservatism* (Chicago: Quadrangle, 1967); Robert Wiebe, *The Search for Order, 1877–1920* (New York: Hill & Wang, 1967); James Weinstein, *The Corporate Ideal in the Liberal State* (Boston: Beacon Press, 1968).

8. Matthew A. Crenson and Francis E. Rourke, "American Bureaucracy Since World War II," in Louis Galambos, ed., *The New American State* (Baltimore: Johns Hopkins University Press, 1987).

9. B. Guy Peters, *American Public Policy: Policy and Performance,* 5th ed. (New York: Chatham House Publishers, 1999), p. 95.

10. Ibid., p. 97.

11. Theodore J. Lowi, *The End of Liberalism,* 2nd ed. (New York: Norton, 1979).

12. See Samuel Krislov and David H. Rosenbloom, *Representative Bureaucracy and the American Political System* (New York: Praeger, 1981); Goodsell, *The Case for Bureaucracy.*

13. Stanley Rothman and S. Robert Lichter, "How Liberal Are Bureaucrats?" *Regulation* (November–December 1983), pp. 35–47.

14. See Goodsell, *The Case for Bureaucracy,* ch. 5; Kenneth J. Meier, "Representative Bureaucracy: An Empirical Analysis," *American Political Science Review* 69 (June 1975), pp. 537–539.

15. Richard P. Nathan, *The Administrative Presidency* (New York: Wiley, 1983).

16. Hugh Heclo, *A Government of Strangers* (Washington, D.C.: Brookings Institution, 1977), p. 103.

17. Richard E. Neustadt, *Presidential Power* (New York: Wiley, 1960).

18. Terry M. Moe, "Control and Feedback in Economic Regulation," *American Political Science Review* 79 (1985), pp. 1094–1116; Richard W. Waterman, *Presidential Influence and the Administrative State* (Knoxville, TN: University of Tennessee Press, 1989).

19. Roger H. Davidson and Walter J. Oleszek, *Congress and Its Members,* 5th ed. (Washington, D.C.: CQ Press, 2000), p. 312; and Matthew D. McCubbins, "The Legislative Design of Regulatory Structure," *American Journal of Political Science* 29 (1985), pp. 421–438.

20. Nolan McCarty and Rose Razahgian, "Advice and Consent: Senate Responses to Executive Branch Nominations, 1885–1996," *American Journal of Political Science* 43 (October 1999), pp. 1122–1143.

21. Richard Fenno, *The Power of the Purse* (Boston: Little, Brown, 1966); Aaron Wildavsky, *The Politics of the Budgetary Process* (Boston: Little, Brown, 1964).

22. John A. Ferejohn and Charles R. Shipan, "Congressional Influence on Administrative Agencies: A Case Study of Telecommunications Policy," in Lawrence C. Dodd and Bruce I. Oppenheimer, eds., *Congress Reconsidered,* 4th ed. (Washington, D.C.: Congressional Quarterly Press, 1989).

23. Grant McConnell, *Private Power and American Democracy* (New York: Knopf, 1967), p. 339.

24. "Government Satisfaction Scores" (Ann Arbor, MI: University of Michigan Business School, Dec. 13, 1999).

25. See Goodsell, *The Case for Bureaucracy,* pp. 61–69.

26. Ibid., p. 177.

27. See Emanuel S. Savas, *Privatization: The Key to Better Government* (Chatham, NJ: Chatham House, 1987); Sheila B. Kamerman and Alfred J. Kahn, eds., *Privatization and the Welfare State* (Princeton, NJ: Princeton University Press, 1989).

28. Roberta Lynch and Ann Markusen, "Can Markets Govern?" *American Prospect* (Winter 1994), pp. 125–134.

29. David Osborne and Ted Gaebler, *Reinventing Government* (Reading, MA: Addison-Wesley, 1992).

30. Al Gore Jr., *From Red Tape to Results: Creating a Government That Works Better and Costs Less* (Washington, D.C.: U.S. Government Printing Office, 1993).

31. Jim Collins, "Turning Goals Into Results: The Power of Catalytic Mechanisms," *Harvard Business Review* (July–August 1999), pp. 13–17.

32. Milton Kotler, *Neighborhood Government* (Indianapolis: Bobbs-Merrill, 1969); Marilyn Gittell, *Participants and Participation* (New York: Praeger, 1967).

33. Terry M. Moe, "The Politics of Bureaucratic Structure," in John E. Chubb and Paul E. Peterson, eds., *Can the Government Govern?* (Washington, D.C.: Brookings Institution, 1989), p. 280; John E. Chubb and Paul E. Peterson, "American Political Institutions and the Problem of Governance," in Chubb and Peterson, eds., *Can the Government Govern?* p. 41; James L. Sundquist, *Constitutional Reform and Effective Government* (Washington, D.C.: Brookings Institution, 1986).

CHAPTER 14

The Courts

The Court Changes Course on *Roe* v. *Wade*

On January 22, 1973, the U.S. Supreme Court made abortion legal in the United States. Writing for a 7–2 majority in the case of *Roe* v. *Wade,* Justice Harry Blackmun argued that a state's interest in regulating abortion to protect the life of a fetus can override a woman's fundamental right to privacy only after the second trimester of pregnancy, when the fetus becomes viable. Before *Roe,* the availability of abortion was entirely up to state legislatures, and few were willing to allow the practice.

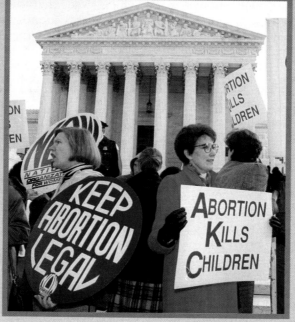

Sixteen years later, in the case of *Webster* v. *Reproductive Health Services* (1989), the Supreme Court retreated from *Roe*'s prohibition against government interference with a woman's right to choose in the first six months of her pregnancy. Speaking for a 5–4 majority, Chief Justice William Rehnquist upheld a Missouri law that barred the use of public money and facilities to perform abortions at any time and required physicians to test for fetal viability at 20 weeks. Significantly, the language in the Court's written opinion invited other states to legislate various limits on abortions, which several have done.

Why did the Supreme Court change its mind? The Constitution had not been amended in the years between *Roe* and *Webster,* yet the Court's interpretation of the constitutional standing of privacy and the right of the states to regulate abortions had changed substantially. To understand this transformation, it is important to understand that judicial decisions are influenced by changes in the political and governmental environment within which the Supreme Court operates. There is no doubt that major transformations had occurred in American politics in the decade and a half following *Roe.* Most important was the rising tide of conservatism in American politics, accompanied by a resurgence in the fortunes of the Republican party, and the near simultaneous decline of liberalism and the fortunes of the Democratic party. This transformation affected all branches of the federal government, including the Supreme Court.

The *Roe* decision was a product of its time. It was decided by a Court in 1973 that could sometimes still muster a liberal majority. Moreover, public opinion had become more supportive of abortion. In addition, the decision was rendered at a time when the women's movement, then at the height of its political influence (see Chapter 8), was pushing unrestricted access to abortion as a major objective.

However, the *Roe* decision also was a catalyst for the growth of the pro-life movement, which is committed to ending legal abortion in the United States. This movement would become an important part of the conservative Republican coalition that dominated American politics in the 1980s.

The conservative movement contributed mightily to the election of Ronald Reagan and a Republican Senate in 1980 and to Reagan's reelection in 1984, and helped refashion the nation's political agenda.

A string of retirements from the Supreme Court gave President Reagan the opportunity to refashion the Court in his own conservative image. Although he lost in his attempt to appoint ultraconservative Robert Bork to the Court, Reagan gained Senate approval for the appointment of other conservatives: Sandra Day O'Connor, Antonin Scalia, and Anthony Kennedy. He also succeeded in elevating Justice William Rehnquist to the position of chief justice. The shift in the nation's politics and the appointive powers of a popular president led to the formation of a new and formidable conservative Supreme Court majority that was willing to reconsider its earlier abortion decision.

This story tells us many things about the Supreme Court that will be elaborated on in this chapter. Like the president and Congress, the Court makes decisions that have important consequences for the American people. Unlike the president and Congress, it does not pass new laws; it merely interprets the meaning of laws and, especially, the Constitution. In doing so, however, the Court cannot help but make law. In this sense, the Court is a national policymaker.

Thinking Critically About This Chapter

Using the Framework. You will see in this chapter that the Court is embedded in a rich governmental, political linkage, and structural environment that shapes its behavior. The other branches of government impinge on its deliberations; political linkage institutions such as elections, interest groups, and social movements matter; and structural factors such as economic and social change influence its agenda and decisions.

Using the Democracy Standard. You will see in this chapter that an unelected Court makes important decisions about public policies, raising fundamental questions about the degree to which popular sovereignty and majority rule prevails in our system. You will also see that the Court often turns its attention to cases that involve issues of political equality and liberty, so essential to the existence of a healthy representative democracy.   ▶

The Structural Context of Court Behavior

The judicial Power of the United States shall be vested in one supreme Court, and in such inferior Courts as the Congress may from time to time ordain and establish.
—U.S. Constitution, Article III, Section 1

We are under a Constitution, but the Constitution is what the judges say it is, and the judiciary is the safeguard of our liberty and our property under the Constitution.
—Chief Justice Charles Evans Hughes (1907)

Constitutional Powers

The Constitution speaks only briefly about the judicial branch and doesn't provide much guidance about what it is supposed to do or how it is supposed to go about its job. The document says little about the powers of the judicial branch in relationship to the other two federal branches or about its responsibilities in the area of constitutional interpretation. Article III is considerably shorter than Articles I and II on Congress and the president. It creates a federal judicial branch; it creates the office of "chief justice of the United States"; it states that judges shall serve life terms; it specifies the categories of cases the Court may or must hear (to be explained later); and it grants Congress the power to create additional federal courts as needed. Article III of the Constitution is virtually devoid of detail.

The Concept of Judicial Review

judicial review

The power of the Supreme Court to declare actions of the other branches and levels of government unconstitutional.

Extremely interesting is the Constitution's silence about **judicial review**, the power of the Supreme Court to declare state and federal laws and actions null and void when they conflict with the Constitution. Debate has raged for many years over the question of whether the framers intended that the Court should have this power.[1]

The framers surely believed that the Constitution ought to prevail when other laws were in conflict with it. But did they expect the Supreme Court to make the decisions in this matter? Jefferson and Madison thought that Congress and the president were capable of rendering their own judgments about the constitutionality of their actions. Alexander Hamilton, however, believed that the power of judicial review was inherent in the notion of the separation of powers

Although the Constitution is silent on the issue of judicial review, most of the Founders probably agreed with Alexander Hamilton (left), who argued that the Supreme Court's power to interpret the Constitution and declare state and federal laws and actions unconstitutional is inherent in the notion of the separation of powers. However, it was not until the Supreme Court's 1803 *Marbury* v. *Madison* decision that Chief Justice John Marshall (right) affirmed the Court's power of judicial review.

and was essential to balanced government. As he put it in *The Federalist,* No. 78 (see Appendix), the very purpose of constitutions is to place limitations on the powers of government, and it is only the Court that can ensure such limits in the United States. The legislative branch, in particular, is unlikely to restrain itself without the helping hand of the judiciary.

Hamilton's view was undoubtedly the prevailing one among the framers. They were firm believers, for instance, in the idea that there was a "higher law" to which governments and nations must conform. Their enthusiasm for written constitutions was based on their belief that governments must be limited in what they could do in the service of some higher or more fundamental law, such as that pertaining to individual rights. The attitudes of the time strongly supported the idea that judges, conversant with the legal tradition and free from popular pressures, were best able to decide when statutory and administrative law were in conflict with fundamental law.[2] (See Table 14.1 on the varieties of law.)

Marbury v. Madison   Chief Justice John Marshall boldly claimed the power of judicial review for the U.S. Supreme Court in the case of *Marbury* v. *Madison* in 1803.[3] The case began with a flurry of judicial appointments by President John Adams in the final days of his presidency, after his Federalist party had suffered a resounding defeat in the election of 1800. The apparent aim of these so-called midnight appointments was to establish the federal courts as an outpost of Federalist party power (federal judges are appointed for life) in the midst of Jeffersonian control of the presidency and the Congress.

William Marbury was one of the midnight appointments, but he was less lucky than most. His commission was signed and sealed, but it had not been delivered to him before the new administration took office. Jefferson, knowing what Adams and the Federalists were up to, ordered Secretary of State James Madison not to deliver the commission. Marbury sued Madison, claiming that the secretary of state was obligated to deliver the commission, and asked the Supreme Court to issue a **writ of mandamus** to force Madison to do so.

Marshall faced a quandary. If the Court decided in favor of Marbury, Madison would almost surely refuse to obey, opening the Court to ridicule for its weakness. The fact that Marshall was a prominent Federalist political figure might even provoke the Jeffersonians to take more extreme measures against the Court. But if the Court ruled in favor of Madison, it would suggest that an executive official could defy without penalty the clear provisions of the law.

writ of mandamus

A court order that forces an official to act.

Table 14.1 ● The Varieties of Law

Law in the United States has four possible sources: a constitution, a legislature, an administrative agency, or a court.

Constitution *Constitutional law* is the most basic form of law in that it sets the rules for the entire governing process and stipulates that no other law or regulation may violate it.

Legislature *Statutes* are the laws made by legislative bodies, including the Congress of the United States.

Administrative agencies *Administrative rules and regulations* are issued by officials of the executive branch when authorized to do so by Congress.

Courts *Court-made law* is fashioned in the course of deciding cases that come before the courts. The interpretations that courts make of all other kinds of law—constitutional, statute, and administrative—are binding on every person and institution that falls within the jurisdiction of the particular court.

Marshall's solution was worthy of Solomon. The Court ruled that William Marbury was entitled to his commission and that James Madison had broken the law in failing to deliver it. By this ruling, the Court rebuked Madison. However, the Court said it could not compel Madison to comply with the law because the part of the Judiciary Act of 1789 that granted the Court the power to issue writs of mandamus was unconstitutional. It was unconstitutional because it expanded the **original jurisdiction** of the Supreme Court as defined in Article III, which could not be done except by constitutional amendment.

original jurisdiction
The authority of a court to be the first to hear a particular kind of case.

WEB EXPLORATION

Origins of Law

Issue: The Supreme Court's power of judicial review—its ability to declare unconstitutional any action by other branches of the national and state governments (thereby rendering them null and void)—presupposes the existence of a fundamental law laid out in the Constitution. The source of the fundamental laws is not the same in all democratic countries, however.

Site: Examine the foundations of law in Great Britain by accessing through the "Course Documents" section of your online course. Go to the "Web Explorations" section for Chapter 14, click on "Origins of Law," and open "sources of law." Enter the site at the bottom of the page where it says "Enter Here." Then, under the Table of Contents, select "The Sources of the Legal System." Compare what you see here to Table 14.1 in the textbook.

What You've Learned: How are the sources of law in Great Britain different from the sources of law in the United States? In what ways are they the same?

HINT: Not all democracies have written constitutions. In Great Britain, parliamentary action serves as the fundamental, living law.

On the surface, the decision was an act of great modesty. It suggested that the Court could not force the action of an executive branch official. It suggested that Congress had erred in the Judiciary Act of 1789 by trying to give the Supreme Court too much power. Beneath the surface, however, was a less modest act: the claim that judicial review was the province of the judicial branch alone. In Marshall's words, in his written opinion, "It is emphatically the province and duty of the judicial department to say what the law is." In making this claim, he was following closely Hamilton's argument in *The Federalist,* No. 78.

Until quite recently, the Supreme Court used the power of judicial review with great restraint, perhaps recognizing that its regular use would invite retaliation by the other branches. Judicial review of a congressional act was not exercised again until 54 years after *Marbury* and was used to declare acts of Congress unconstitutional only about 150 times since then until the late 1990s. In the last few years, however, it has been less reluctant to review and overturn congressional actions. The Court has been much less constrained about over-ruling the laws of the states and localities; it has done so more than 1,000 times.

Judicial Review and Democracy   Judicial review involves the right of a body shielded from direct accountability to the people—federal judges are appointed, not elected, and serve for life (barring unseemly behavior)—to set aside the actions of government bodies whose members are directly elected. Some observers believe that this is the only way to protect the rights of political and racial minorities, to check the potential excesses of the other two government branches and the states, and to preserve the rules of the democratic process. Others believe that judicial review has no place in a democratic society. We come back to this issue later in this chapter.

LongmanParticipate

CourseCompass

comparative

Comparing Judiciaries

The U.S. Court System: Organization and Jurisdiction

Ours is a federal court system. There is one system for the national government (the federal courts) and another in each of the states. Each state has its own system of courts that adjudicate cases on the basis of its own constitution, statutes, and administrative rules. In total, the great bulk of laws, legal disputes, and court decisions (roughly 99 percent) are located in the states. Most important political and constitutional issues, however, eventually reach the national courts. In this chapter, our focus is on the national courts.

Constitutional Provisions

The only court specifically mentioned in the Constitution's Article III is the U.S. Supreme Court. The framers left to Congress the tasks of designing the details of the Supreme Court and establishing "such inferior courts as the Congress may from time to time ordain and establish." Beginning with the Judiciary Act of 1789, Congress has periodically reorganized the federal court system. The end result is a three-tiered pyramidal system (see Figure 14.1), with a handful of offshoots. At the bottom are 94 U.S. federal district courts, with at least one district in each state. In the middle are 13 courts of appeal. At the top of the pyramid is the Supreme Court. These courts are called **constitutional courts** because they were created by Congress under Article III, which discusses the judicial branch. Congress has also created a number of courts to adjudicate cases in highly specialized areas of concern, such as taxes and maritime law. These were

constitutional courts

Federal courts created by Congress under the authority of Article III of the Constitution.

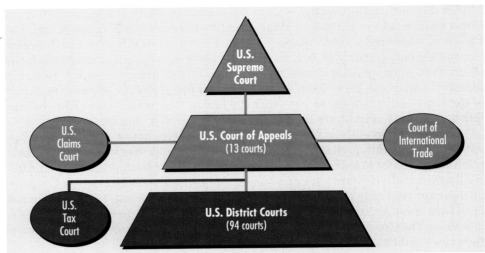

Figure 14.1 ● **The U.S. Federal Court System**

The federal court system is a three-tiered pyramidal system, with the Supreme Court at the top. Below it are 13 federal courts of appeal and 94 district courts, with at least one district in each state. Additional courts exist to hear cases in highly specialized areas, such as taxes, international trade, and financial claims against the U.S. government.

Source: Administrative Office of the U.S. Courts.

established under Article I, which specifies the duties and powers of Congress, and are called **legislative courts**.

Article III does not offer many guidelines for the federal court system, but the few requirements that are stated are very important. The Constitution requires, for instance, that federal judges serve "during good behavior," which, in practice, means for life. Because impeachment by Congress is the only way to remove federal judges, the decision about who will be a judge is an important one. Article III also states that Congress cannot reduce the salaries of judges once they are in office. This provision was designed to maintain the independence of the judiciary by protecting it from legislative intimidation.

Article III also specifies the kinds of cases that are solely the province of the federal courts:

- The Constitution (disputes involving the First Amendment or the commerce clause, for example).
- Federal statutes and treaties (including disputes involving ambassadors and other diplomats).
- Admiralty and maritime issues.
- Controversies in which the U.S. government is a party.
- Disputes between the states.
- Disputes between a state and a citizen of another state.
- Disputes between a state (or citizen of a state) and foreign states or citizens.

legislative courts

Highly specialized federal courts created by Congress under the authority of Article I of the Constitution.

Federal District Courts

Most cases in the federal court system are first heard in one of the 94 district courts. District courts are courts of original jurisdiction, that is, courts where cases are first heard; they do not hear appeals from other courts. They are also trial courts; some use juries—either **grand juries**, which bring indictments, or **petit (trial) juries**, which decide cases—and in some, cases are heard only by a judge.

Most of the business of the federal courts takes place at this level. Almost 300,000 cases are filed annually; roughly 80 percent of them are civil cases, and 20 percent are criminal cases. Civil cases include everything from antitrust cases brought by the federal government (as in the recent Justice Department action against Microsoft) to commercial and contract disputes between citizens (or businesses) of two or more states. Criminal cases include violations of federal criminal laws, such as bank robbery, interstate drug trafficking, and kidnapping.

Most civil and criminal cases are concluded at this level. In a relatively small number of disputes, however, one of the parties to the case may feel that a mistake has been made in trial procedure or in the law that was brought to bear in the trial, or one of the parties may feel that a legal or constitutional issue is at stake that was not taken into account at the trial stage or was wrongly interpreted. In such cases, one of the parties may appeal to a higher court.

U.S. Courts of Appeal

The United States is divided into 12 geographic **circuits** (see the map in Figure 14.2) to hear appeals from the district courts. There is also a thirteenth appeals court, called the U.S. Court of Appeals for the Federal Circuit, located in Washington, D.C., which hears cases on patents and government contracts. More than 50,000 cases are filed annually in the federal appeals courts, although only about 5,000 reach the formal hearing stage (most of these end in negotiated settlements without going to trial). Cases cannot originate in these courts but must come to them from other courts. Because they exist only to hear appeals, they are referred to as **appellate courts**. New factual evidence cannot be introduced before such courts; no witnesses are called or cross-examined. Lawyers for each side argue with one other and make their cases for the judges not by the examination of witnesses or documents but by the submission of **briefs** that set out the legal issues at stake. Judges usually convene as panels of three (on important cases, there are more—sometimes seven members) to hear oral arguments from the lawyers on each side of the case and to cross-examine them on points of law. Weeks or even months later, after considerable study, writing, and discussion among the judges, the panel issues a ruling. In important cases, the ruling is usually accompanied by an **opinion** that sets forth the majority side's reasoning for the decision.

Once appellate decisions are published, they become **precedents** that guide the decisions of other judges in the same circuit. Although judges do not slavishly follow precedents, they tend to move away from them only when necessary and only in very small steps. This doctrine of closely following precedents as the basis for legal reasoning is known as **stare decisis**.

Sometimes, particular circuits play a particularly important role in changing constitutional interpretation. Currently, the Fourth Circuit Court, based in Richmond, Virginia, has been a leader in the trend toward reasserting the power of the states in the federal system.[4]

The Supreme Court

Congress decides how many judges sit on the Supreme Court. The first Court had six members. The Federalists reduced the number to five in 1801 to prevent

grand juries

Groups of citizens who decide whether there is sufficient evidence to bring an indictment against accused persons.

petit (trial) juries

Juries that hear evidence and sit in judgment on charges brought in civil or criminal cases.

circuits

The 12 geographical jurisdictions and 1 special court that hear appeals from the federal district courts.

appellate courts

Courts that hear cases on appeal from other courts.

briefs

Documents setting out the arguments in legal cases, prepared by attorneys and presented to courts.

opinion

The explanation of the majority's reasoning that accompanies a Supreme Court decision.

precedents

Rulings by courts that guide judicial reasoning in subsequent cases.

stare decisis

The legal doctrine that says precedent should guide judicial decision making.

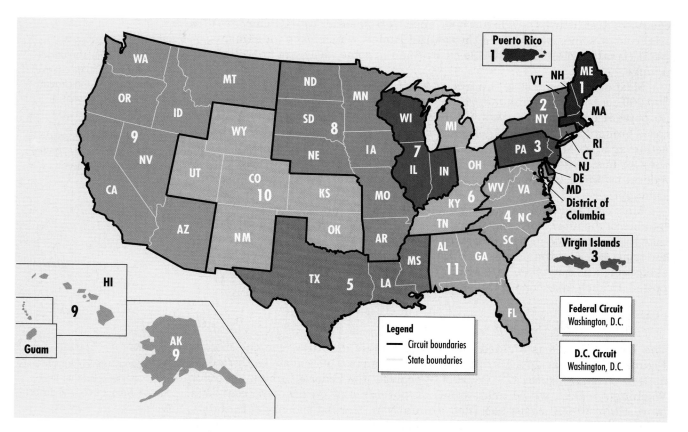

Figure 14.2 ● U.S. Federal Circuit Courts

The United States is divided into 12 geographic regions (including the D.C. Circuit Court), each housing a federal circuit court of appeals; there are also 94 U.S. district courts, where most cases originate. One additional circuit court of appeal, the Federal Circuit Court, is located in Washington, D.C.

Source: Administrative Office of the U.S. Courts.

newly elected president Thomas Jefferson from filling a vacancy. In 1869, Congress set the number at its present nine members (eight associate justices and the chief justice). It has remained this way ever since, weathering the failed effort by President Franklin Roosevelt to "pack" the Court with more politically congenial justices by expanding its size to 15.

The Supreme Court is both a court of original jurisdiction and an appellate court. That is, some cases must first be heard in the Supreme Court. Disputes involving ambassadors and other diplomatic personnel, two or more states, the federal government and a state, or a state and a citizen from another state start in the Supreme Court rather than in some other court.

The Supreme Court also, in its most important role, serves as an appellate court for the federal appeals courts and for the highest courts of each of the states. Cases in which a state or a federal law has been declared unconstitutional or in which the highest state court has denied the claim of one of the parties that a state law violates federal law or the Constitution (see Figure 14.3) are eligible to be heard by the Supreme Court.

Congress determines much of the appellate jurisdiction of the Court. In 1869, a Congress controlled by radical Republicans removed the Court's power to review cases falling under the Reconstruction program for the South. Responding to a plea from Chief Justice Rehnquist to lighten the Court's caseload, Congress

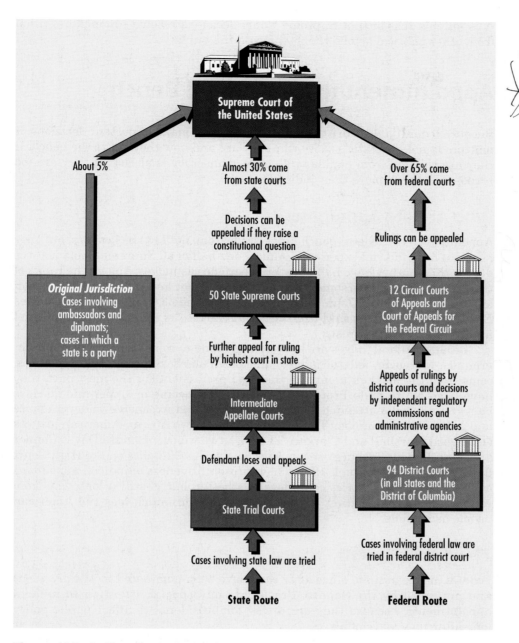

Figure 14.3 ● How Cases Get to the Supreme Court

The vast majority of cases that reach the Supreme Court come to it from the federal court system. Most of the others come on appeal from the highest state courts. A handful originate in the Supreme Court itself.

Source: Adapted from David O'Brien, *Storm Center: The Supreme Court in American Politics,* 3rd ed. (New York: Norton, 1993).

dropped the requirement that the Supreme Court *must* hear cases in which a state court declares a federal statute unconstitutional. It can choose, but is not obligated, to do so.

Because it is the highest appellate court in the federal court system, the decisions and opinions of the Supreme Court become the main precedents on federal and constitutional questions for courts at all other levels of jurisdiction.

It is for this reason that Supreme Court decisions receive so much attention from other political actors, the media, and the public.

Appointment to the Federal Bench

Because federal judges are appointed for life and make important decisions, it matters in a democratic society who they are and how they get to the bench. If they are isolated from popular influence, democracy is at risk. If they are too responsive, they ignore their judicial role.

Who Are the Appointees?

Appointees to the federal bench must (by custom, not law) be lawyers, but they need not have judicial experience. Almost one-half of all Supreme Court justices during this century have had no prior experience as judges. Among the ranks of the "inexperienced" are some of the most prominent and influential justices in our history, including John Marshall, Louis Brandeis, Harlan Stone, Charles Evans Hughes, Felix Frankfurter, and Earl Warren, as well as the present chief justice, William Rehnquist.[5]

Because federal judges are lawyers, they tend to come from privileged backgrounds. Moreover, federal judges, and particularly Supreme Court justices, come from the most elite parts of the legal profession. For the most part, they have been white male Protestants from upper-income or upper-middle-class backgrounds, who attended the most selective and expensive undergraduate and graduate institutions.[6] There have been only two African-American justices (Thurgood Marshall and Clarence Thomas), two women (Sandra Day O'Connor and Ruth Bader Ginsburg), seven Jews, and seven Catholics on the High Court during its history, through 1999. The representativeness of judicial appointees at the circuit and district court levels is better, but is still a long way from reflecting the composition of the legal profession, much less the American people as a whole.

The Appointment Process

Federal judges assume office after they have been nominated by the president and approved by the Senate. Presidents pay special attention to judicial appointments, because they are a way for presidents to affect public policy long after they leave office.

Presidents take many things into consideration besides merit. No president wants a nomination rejected by the Senate, so he and his advisers consult with key senators, especially those on the Judiciary Committee, before nominations are forwarded. Nominations for district court judgeships are subject to what is called **senatorial courtesy**, the right of the senior senator from the president's party in the state where the district court is located to approve the nominee. Senatorial courtesy does not operate, however, in appointments to the circuit courts, whose jurisdictions span more than a single state, or to the Supreme Court, whose jurisdiction is the entire nation. Nevertheless, presidents must be extremely attentive to the views of key senators.

On occasion, despite presidential efforts to placate it, the Senate has refused to give its "consent." Of the 143 nominees for the Supreme Court since the founding of the Republic, the Senate has refused to approve 28 of them, although only 5 in the twentieth century. Rejection of nominees has usually

senatorial courtesy

The tradition that judicial nominations for federal district court appointments be cleared by the senior senator of the president's party from the relevant state.

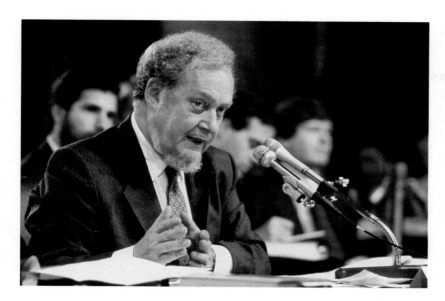

Robert Bork, one of Ronald Reagan's nominees for the Supreme Court, was turned down by a historic margin after lengthy committee hearings and a bruising debate on the floor of the Senate. Many Americans and a majority of senators considered his views too extreme.

happened when the president was weak or when the other party was in control of the Senate. The defeat of Ronald Reagan's nominee, Robert Bork, was the product of deep ideological differences between a Republican president and a Democratic-controlled Senate. There have also been several near defeats. Bush's nominee, Clarence Thomas, was confirmed by a margin of only four votes after questions were raised about his legal qualifications and about sexual harassment charges brought by law professor Anita Hill.

Although presidents must be concerned about the merit of their candidates and their acceptability to the Senate, they also try by their appointments to make their mark on the future. Presidents go about this in different ways.

Many presidents have been interested in nominating judges who shared their ideological and program commitments. John Adams nominated John

WEB EXPLORATION

Who Is Appointed to the Supreme Court?

Issue: Appointees to the Supreme Court come from a very select group of Americans, not at all representative of the general population either in terms of demographic background or achievement and training.

Site: Access the Cornell Law School home page through the "Course Documents" section of your online course. Go to the "Web Explorations" section for Chapter 14, click on "Who Is Appointed to the Supreme Court?," and open "biographies." Read the short biographies of each of the present members of the Supreme Court.

What You've Learned: What kinds of people become justices? What can you say about their occupational and educational backgrounds and their other experiences?

HINT: While they are all lawyers, not all have served as judges. And politics and public service have been part of the equation as well.

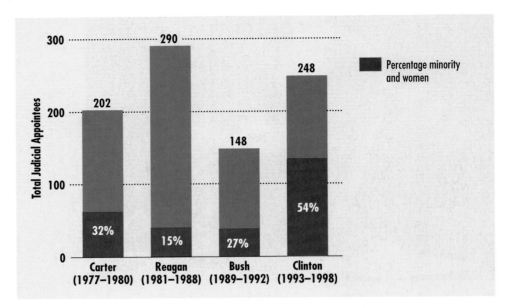

Figure 14.4 ● **Presidential Appointments of Female and Minority Judges, 1977–1998**

President Clinton fashioned a particularly impressive record of nominating women and minorities to the U.S. federal courts.

Source: Sheldon Goldman and Elliot Slotnick, "Clinton's Second-Term Judiciary," *Judicature* 82 (May–June 1999).

Marshall and a number of other judges to protect Federalist principles during the ascendancy of the Jeffersonians. Franklin Roosevelt tried to fill the courts with judges who favored the New Deal. Ronald Reagan favored conservatives who were committed to rolling back affirmative action and other civil rights claims, abortion rights, protections for criminal defendants, and broad claims of **standing** in environmental cases. George Bush continued this conservative drift with his nomination of Clarence Thomas.

Bill Clinton, eager to avoid a bitter ideological fight in the Senate, where he was trying to forge a bipartisan coalition to support the North American Free Trade Agreement and a national crime bill, nominated two moderates for the High Court—Ruth Bader Ginsburg and Stephen Breyer—in the first years of his administration. The Ginsburg nomination was also indicative of Clinton's apparent commitment to diversifying the federal court system. More than one-half of federal court nominees during the first two years of his administration were women and minorities (see Figure 14.4).

Presidents are often disappointed in how their nominees behave once they reach the Court. Dwight Eisenhower was dumbfounded when his friend and nominee, Earl Warren, led the Court to transform constitutional law with regard to civil rights and criminal procedure. Nixon was stunned when Chief Justice Warren Burger voted with a unanimous Court to override the president's claim of **executive privilege** and forced him to give up the documents that would seal his fate in the Watergate affair. George Bush was surprised when his nominee, David Souter, refused to vote for the overturn of *Roe* in *Planned Parenthood* v. *Casey* (1992). Despite these dramatic examples, the past political and ideological positions of federal court nominees are a fairly reliable guide to their later behavior on the bench.[7]

standing

Authority to bring legal action because one is directly affected by the issues at hand.

executive privilege

A presidential claim that certain communications with subordinates may be withheld from Congress and the courts.

The Supreme Court in Action

The Supreme Court meets from the first Monday in October until late June or early July, depending on the press of business. Let's see how it goes about deciding cases.

Norms of Operation

A set of unwritten but clearly understood rules of behavior—called *norms*—shapes how the Court does things. One norm is *secrecy,* which keeps the conflicts between justices out of the public eye and elevates the stature of the Court as an institution. Justices do not grant interviews very often. Reporters are not allowed to stalk the corridors for a story. Law clerks are expected to keep all memos, draft opinions, and conversations with the justices they work for confidential. Justices are not commonly seen on the frantic Washington, D.C., cocktail party circuit. When meeting in conference to argue and decide cases, the justices meet alone, without secretaries or clerks. Breaches of secrecy have occurred only occasionally. As a result, we know less about the inner workings of the Court than about any other branch of government.

Seniority is another important norm. Seniority determines the assignment of office space, the seating arrangements in open court (the most junior are at the ends), and the order of speaking in conference (the chief justice, then the most senior, and so on down the line). Speaking first allows the senior members to set the tone for discussion.

Finally, the justices are expected to stick closely to *precedent* when they decide cases. When the Court departs from a precedent, it is essentially over-ruling its own past actions, exercising judicial review of itself. In most cases, departures from precedent come in only very small steps over many years. For example, several decisions chipped away at the **separate but equal doctrine** of *Plessy* v. *Ferguson* (1896) before it was decisively reversed in *Brown* v. *Board of Education of Topeka* (1954).

Controlling the Agenda

The Court has a number of screening mechanisms to control what cases it will hear so that it can focus on cases that involve important federal or constitutional questions.

Several technical rules help keep the numbers down. Cases must be *real* and *adverse;* that is, they must involve a real dispute between two parties. The disputants in a case must have *standing;* that is, they must have a real and direct interest in the issues that are raised. The Court sometimes changes the definition of *standing* to make access for **plaintiffs** easier or more difficult. The Warren Court favored an expansive definition; the Rehnquist Court, a restricted one. Cases must also be *ripe;* that is, all other avenues of appeal must have been exhausted, and the injury must already have taken place (the Court will not accept hypothetical cases). Appeals must also be filed within a specified time limit, the paperwork must be correct and complete, and a filing fee of $200 must be paid. The fee may be waived if a petitioner is poor and files an affidavit **in forma pauperis** ("in the manner of a pauper"). One of the most famous cases in American history, *Gideon* v. *Wainwright* (1963), which established the right of all defendants to have lawyers in criminal cases, was submitted in forma pauperis on a few pieces of lined paper by a Florida State Penitentiary inmate named Clarence Earl Gideon. The Rehnquist Court has been less friendly to indigent

separate but equal doctrine

The principle articulated in *Plessy* v. *Ferguson* (1896) that laws prescribing *separate* public facilities and services for nonwhite Americans are permissible if the facilities and services are *equal* to those provided for whites.

plaintiff

One who brings suit in a court.

in forma pauperis

Describing a process by which indigents may file a suit with the Supreme Court free of charge.

Most major policy and political disputes in the United States eventually make their way to the Supreme Court, so demonstrations at the Court are common. Here demonstrators for Al Gore and George W. Bush make their feelings known about *Bush* v. *Gore*, then being considered by the justices, which would determine the election outcome in Florida and settle the disputed 2000 presidential election.

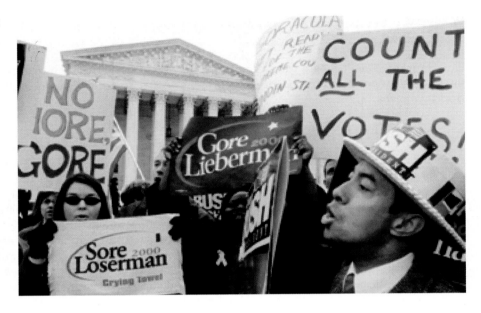

petitions than previous Courts and has taken several steps to cut down what the chief justice calls "frivolous" suits by "jailhouse lawyers."

The most powerful tool that the Court has for controlling its own agenda is the power to grant or not to grant a **writ of certiorari**. A grant of "cert" is a decision of the Court that an appellate case raises an important federal or constitutional issue that it is prepared to consider.[8] Under the **rule of four**, petitions are granted cert if at least four justices vote in favor. There are several reasons a petition may not command four votes, even if the case involves important constitutional issues: It may involve a particularly controversial issue that the Court would like to avoid, or the Court may not yet have developed a solid majority and may wish to avoid a split decision. Few petitions survive all of these hurdles. Of the almost 8,000 cases that are filed in each session, the Court grants cert for only about 140 (this number varies a bit year to year). In cases denied cert, the decision of the lower court stands.

Deciding how freely to grant cert is a tricky business for the Court. Used too often, it threatens to inundate the Court with cases. Used too sparingly, it leaves in place the decisions of 13 different federal appeals courts on substantial federal and constitutional questions, as well as the decisions of state supreme courts.

Deciding Cases

Cases granted cert are scheduled for oral argument. Lawyers on each side are alerted to the key issues that the justices wish to consider, and new briefs are invited. Briefs are also submitted on most important cases by other parties who may be interested in the disputes. These "friend of the court," or **amicus curiae**, briefs may be submitted by individuals, interest groups, or some agency of the federal government, including the Justice Department or even the president.

Each case is argued for one hour, with 30 minutes given to each side in the dispute. Oral argument is not so much a presentation of arguments, however, as it is a give-and-take between the lawyers and the justices and among the justices themselves. When the federal government is a party to the case, the solicitor general or one of his or her deputies presents the oral arguments. Some

writ of certiorari

An announcement that the Supreme Court will hear a case on appeal from a lower court; its issuance requires the vote of four of the nine justices.

rule of four

An *unwritten* practice that requires at least four justices of the Supreme Court to agree that a case warrants review by the Court before it will hear the case.

amicus curiae

Latin for "a friend of the court"; describes a brief in which individuals not party to a suit may have their views heard.

justices—Antonin Scalia, for instance—are famous for their close grilling of lawyers. Ruth Bader Ginsburg often asks that lawyers skip abstract legal fine points and put the issues in terms of their effect on ordinary people.

After hearing oral arguments and reading the briefs in the case, the justices meet in conference to reach a decision. The custom is for each justice to state his or her position, starting with the chief justice and moving through the ranks in order of seniority. Chief justices of great stature and intellect, such as John Marshall and Charles Evans Hughes, used the opportunity to speak first as a way of structuring the case and of swaying votes. Those who did not command much respect from the other justices (for example, Warren Burger) were less able to shape the decision process. (For a listing of chief justices, see Table 14.2.)

Political scientists have tried to determine what factors are most important in predicting how the justices will vote. One approach looks at the ideological predilections of the justices and manages to explain a great deal about their voting behavior.[9] Another approach focuses on the diaries and personal papers of retired justices and shows that a great deal of negotiating and "horse trading" goes on, with justices trading votes on different cases and joining opinions they do not like so that they can have a hand in modifying them.[10] Another approach tries to link voting behavior to social background, types of previous judicial experience, and the political environment of family upbringing.[11] None of these approaches has been totally successful because much of what the Court does in conference is secret and can be only imperfectly reconstructed. About all that one can say is that the justices tend to form relatively stable voting blocs over time. Many scholars attribute the change of direction of the Court on civil rights, church-state issues, and state-federal government relations in the 1995 session and after, for example, to the emergence of a strong conservative bloc (Scalia, Thomas, Rehnquist, Kennedy, and O'Connor). This bloc formed the majority in *Gore* v. *Bush (2000),* which effectively determined the outcome of the presidential election.

The vote in conference is not final. As Justice John Harlan once explained it, "The books on voting are never closed until the decision finally comes down."[12] The justices have an opportunity to change their votes in response to the opinion supporting the majority decision. An opinion is a statement of the

Supreme Court justices here take turns signing opinions that will be published with the Court's decision on a case. Few cases before the Court result in unanimous decisions, so virtually all decisions are announced with attached majority and minority opinions.

Table 14.2 ● **Chief Justices of the Supreme Court**

Chief Justice	Appointing President	Dates of Service
John Jay	Washington	1789–1795
John Rutledge	Washington	1795–1795
Oliver Ellsworth	Washington	1796–1800
John Marshall	J. Adams	1801–1835
Roger Brooke Taney	Jackson	1836–1864
Salmon Portland Chase	Lincoln	1864–1873
Morrison Remick Waite	Grant	1874–1888
Melville Weston Fuller	Cleveland	1888–1910
Edward Douglass White	Taft	1910–1921
William Howard Taft	Harding	1921–1930
Charles Evans Hughes	Hoover	1930–1941
Harlan Fiske Stone	F. Roosevelt	1941–1946
Frederick Moore Vinson	Truman	1946–1953
Earl Warren	Eisenhower	1953–1969
Warren Earl Burger	Nixon	1969–1986
William Hubbs Rehnquist	Reagan	1986–

opinion of the Court

The majority opinion that accompanies a Supreme Court decision.

concurring opinion

The opinion of one or more judges who vote with the majority on a case but wish to set out different reasons for their decision.

dissenting opinion

The opinion of the judge or judges who are in the minority on a particular case before the Supreme Court.

legal reasoning that supports the decision of the Court. There are three kinds of opinions. The **opinion of the Court** is the written opinion of the majority. A **concurring opinion** is the opinion of a justice who supports the majority decision but has different legal reasons for doing so. A **dissenting opinion** presents the reasoning of the minority. Dissenting opinions sometimes become the basis for future Court majorities.

If he or she votes with the majority in conference, the chief justice assigns the opinion. He or she can assign it to any justice in the majority, often to him- or herself. Some jurists and scholars believe that this power to assign is the most important role of the chief justice, and it is guarded jealously. Warren Burger was so eager to play a role in opinion assignments that, much to the distress of his colleagues, he would often delay announcing his vote so that he could place himself with the majority. Justice William Douglas angrily charged that Burger voted with the majority in *Roe* only so that he could assign the case to a justice who was closer to the minority view.[13] If the chief justice's opinion is with the minority, the opinion is assigned by the most senior member of the majority.

The justice assigned to write the opinion does not work in isolation. He or she is assisted not only by law clerks but also by other justices, who helpfully provide memoranda suggesting wording and reasoning. Justices also consider the legal reasoning presented to the Court in amicus curiae briefs.[14] Most opinions go through numerous revisions and are subject to a considerable amount of bargaining among the justices.

Only when an opinion is completed is a final vote taken in conference. The justices are free to change their earlier votes: they may join the majority if they are now persuaded by its reasoning, or a concurring opinion may be so compelling that the majority may decide to replace the original majority opinion with it.

Law Clerks

A word is in order about the important role played by Supreme Court law clerks. Clerks are a very select group of young lawyers recruited from among recent graduates of the most prestigious law schools in the United States. Most of them go on to distinguished legal careers; many become law school professors; a few—William Rehnquist, for instance—become Supreme Court justices. The clerks' main role is to assist the justices to whom they are assigned in the preparation of cases. Clerks prepare memoranda on cases being considered for certiorari, screen petitions for in forma pauperis filings, do legal research, and increasingly write initial drafts of opinions for their justices. Their particular duties and the time they spend on each duty vary widely because each justice decides how to use his or her clerks. Some justices are close to their clerks, treat them very much as colleagues, and give them important responsibilities in writing opinions and in negotiating revisions with the clerks of the other justices. Other justices like to keep their clerks on a shorter lead, giving them less independence. The trend over recent decades has been for clerks to assume more and more responsibility for drafting and revising opinions, although each justice has the final word. This trend represents a dramatic change from the early twentieth century, when justices such as Oliver Wendell Holmes and Louis Brandeis used their clerks mainly as research assistants.[15]

WEB EXPLORATION

Voting Blocs

Issue: The Supreme Court seems at the present time to be split into a semipermanent majority and minority.

Site: Access Cornell Law School's Supreme Court site through the "Course Documents" section of your online course. Go to the "Web Explorations" section for Chapter 14, click on "Voting Blocs," and open "voting blocs." Go to each justice, and select "recent decisions." For each justice, calculate the total number of times he or she has written an opinion on the winning or losing side in a case.

What You've Learned: Based on this set of calculations, would you agree or disagree that fairly stable majority and minority coalitions exist on the present Court?

HINT: "Opinions for the Court" and "concurrences" may be defined as "winning;" "dissenting opinions" and "concurrences in dissent" may be defined as losing.

Under the leadership of Chief Justice John Marshall, the Supreme Court weakened the power of the states to regulate and interfere with interstate commerce, encouraging the emergence of a vital national economy.

The Supreme Court as a National Policymaker

People often say that the Court should settle disputes and not make policy. But because the disputes it settles involve contentious public issues (such as abortion rights and affirmative action) and fundamental questions about the meaning of our constitutional rules, the Court cannot help but make public policy.

It seems likely that the Court recognizes and cultivates its policymaking role. In the main, the Court does not see itself as a court of last resort, simply righting routine errors in the lower courts or settling minor private disputes. It sees itself, instead, as the "highest judicial tribunal for settling policy conflicts" and constitutional issues and chooses its cases accordingly.[16] The fact that decisions are not simply handed down but come with an opinion attached for the purpose of guiding the actions of other courts, litigants, and public officials is another demonstration that the Court recognizes its policymaking role.

Structural Change and Constitutional Interpretation

Scholars generally identify three periods in the history of constitutional interpretation by the Supreme Court in the United States, one stretching from the founding to the Civil War, the next from the end of the Civil War to the Great Depression, and the last from World War II to the present.[17] We will see how changes in constitutional law have been influenced by structural factors, particularly economic change.

Period 1: National Power and Property Rights   We saw in Chapter 4 that the United States experienced significant growth and change during the first 75 years of its existence. This growth was accompanied by changes in constitutional law. Chief Justice John Marshall, who presided over the Supreme Court from 1801 to 1835, was the key judicial figure during this important period in our history.[18] Marshall was a follower of the doctrines of Alexander Hamilton, who believed that American greatness depended on a strong national government, a partnership between government and business in which industry and commerce were encouraged, and a national market economy free of the regulatory restraints of state and local governments. In a string of opinions that have shaped the fundamentals of American constitutional law—especially important are *Fletcher* v. *Peck* (1810), *Dartmouth College* v. *Woodward* (1819), *McCulloch* v. *Maryland* (1819), and *Gibbons* v. *Ogden* (1824), discussed elsewhere in this text— Marshall interpreted the Constitution to mean "maximum protection to property rights and maximum support for the idea of nationalism."[19]

Period 2: Government and the Economy   The Civil War and the Industrial Revolution triggered the development of a mass-production industrial economy dominated by the business corporation. Determining the role to be played by government in such an economy was a central theme of late-nineteenth- and early-twentieth-century American political life. The courts were involved deeply in this rethinking. At the beginning of this period, the Supreme Court took the position that the corporation was to be protected against regulation by both the state and federal governments; by the end, it was more sympathetic to the desire of the people and the political branches for the expansion of government regulation and management of the economy during the crisis of the Great Depression.

The main protection for the corporation against regulation was the Fourteenth Amendment. This amendment was passed in the wake of the Civil War to guarantee the citizenship rights of freed slaves. In one of the great ironies of American history, this expansion of federal power over the states to protect rights—the operative phrase was from Section 1: "nor shall any state deprive any person of life, liberty, or property without due process of law"—was gradually translated by the Court to mean the protection of corporations (which were considered "persons" under the law) and other forms of business from state regulation.

This reading of **laissez-faire** economic theory into constitutional law made the Supreme Court the principal ally of business in the late nineteenth and early twentieth centuries. The Court overturned efforts by both the state and federal governments to provide welfare for the poor; to regulate manufacturing monopolies; to initiate an income tax; to regulate interstate railroad rates; to provide scholarships to students; to regulate wages, hours, and working conditions; and to protect consumers against unsafe or unhealthy products. The Court also supported the use of judicial injunctions to halt strikes by labor unions.

> **laissez-faire**
> The political-economic doctrine that holds that government ought not interfere with the operations of the free market.

The business–Supreme Court alliance lasted until the Great Depression. Roosevelt's New Deal reflected a new national consensus on the need for a greatly expanded federal government with a new set of responsibilities: to manage the economy; to provide a safety net for the poor, the unemployed, and the elderly; to protect workers' rights to form labor unions; and to regulate business in the public interest. The Supreme Court, however, filled with justices born in the nineteenth century and committed to the unshakable link between the Constitution and laissez-faire economic doctrine, was opposed to the national consensus and in 1935 and 1936 declared unconstitutional several laws that were part of the foundation of the New Deal. In an extraordinary turn of events, however, the Supreme Court reversed itself in 1937, finding the Social Security Act, the Labor Relations Act, and state minimum wage laws acceptable. It is not entirely clear why the so-called switch-in-time-that-saved-nine occurred, but surely Roosevelt's landslide reelection in 1936, the heightening of

During the crisis of the Great Depression, the federal government took on greater responsibilities for protecting the welfare of the American people. The Supreme Court was slow to endorse the changes but eventually did so under intense political pressure.

public hostility toward the Court, and Roosevelt's plan to "pack the Court," all played a role. Whatever the reason, the Court abandoned its effort to prevent the government from playing a central role in the management of the economy and the regulation of business, and it came to defer to the political linkage branches of government on such issues by the end of the 1930s. In doing so, it brought another constitutional era to a close.

WEB EXPLORATION

FDR and the Court

Issue: Franklin Roosevelt, frustrated by a Court that, in his view, failed to appreciate the importance of New Deal programs for fighting the Great Depression, tried to expand the Court so that he could appoint new and more sympathetic justices.

Site: Access information about FDR's Court-packing scheme through the "Course Documents" section of your online course. Go to the "Web Explorations" section for Chapter 14, click on "FDR and the Court," and open "court packing."

What You've Learned: What do you think of his plan? Should a group of unelected judges be allowed to overturn programs that the public clearly wants? Would you have voted for or against the proposal?

HINT: The Constitution says nothing about the size of the Supreme Court; Congress can change the number of justices whenever it wishes, but it has not done so for a very long time. Your view on Court packing will probably depend on what you think about how responsive government should be to the majority.

Period 3: Individual Rights and Liberties   Three fundamental issues of American constitutional law—the relationship of the states to the nation, the nature of private property and the national economy, and the role of government in the management of the economy—were essentially settled by the time World War II broke out. Since then, the Court has turned its main attention to the relationship between the individual and government.[20]

Most of this story is told in the chapters on civil rights and civil liberties. For now, it is sufficient to point out that the Court, especially during the tenure of Chief Justice Earl Warren, decided cases that expanded protections for free expression and association, religious expression, fair trials, and civil rights for minorities. In another series of cases dealing with the apportionment of electoral districts, the Court declared for political equality, based on the principle of "one person, one vote." In many of its landmark decisions, the Court applied the Bill of Rights to the states. Although the Court's record was not without blemishes during and after World War II—see the "Using the Framework" feature on *Korematsu* v. *United States* (1944)—it made significant strides in expanding the realm of individual freedom.

Constitutional law and the Court do not stand still, however; both are responsive to changes in the world around them. A new conservative majority has emerged on the Supreme Court, fashioned by the judicial nominations of Presidents Reagan and Bush. This new majority has moved the Court to reconsider many of its earlier decisions on rights and liberties (see Chapters 15 and 16) and on the relationship between the national and state governments (see Chapter 3). Recently, it ruled that Congress had violated areas of state sovereignty when it passed the Americans with Disabilities Act and the Violence Against Women Act. If these trends continue, scholars may soon begin talking about a fourth constitutional period.

The Debate Over Judicial Activism

Has the Court become too involved in national policymaking? Many people think so; others think not. Let us examine several of the ways in which what is called **judicial activism** is expressed.

Judicial Review   We have already seen how the Court, under John Marshall's leadership, claimed the right of judicial review in the case of *Marbury* v. *Madison* (1803). The power was not exercised by the Court to any great extent until the late nineteenth century. The rate of judicial review has picked up during the twentieth century, however, with most of the Court's adverse attention being paid to the states, though it has begun to pay more attention to the national government recently. The trend suggests that the Court has become more willing in modern times to monitor the activities of other governmental entities.

Reversing the Decisions of Past Supreme Courts   We have seen that adherence to precedent is one of the traditional norms that guides judicial decision making. The Warren, Burger, and Rehnquist Courts, however, have not been reluctant to overturn previous Court decisions. The most dramatic instance was the reversal of *Plessy* by *Brown,* although there have been many others, including the *Roe*-to-*Webster* change reviewed in the opening vignette of this chapter, as well as the relatively rapid overturns of precedents involving the rights of criminal defendants.

Deciding "Political" Issues   Critics claim that the Court is taking on too many matters that are best left to the elected branches of government (*Baker* v.

LongmanParticipate

CourseCompass

timeline
Umpiring the Government

---

judicial activism

Actions by the courts that go beyond the strict role of the judiciary as interpreter of the law and adjudicator of disputes.

USING THE FRAMEWORK

If the Supreme Court Exists to Protect Individual Rights, Why Did It Allow the Military to Keep Japanese Americans in Internment Camps During World War II?

On the advice of the U.S. military, President Franklin Roosevelt signed a series of executive orders in early 1942 authorizing the relocation of 112,000 Japanese-Americans living on the West Coast, 70,000 of whom were citizens, into internment camps. In 1944, the Supreme Court in *Korematsu* v. *United States* upheld the legality of the exclusion and confinement orders.

Constitutional scholar Edward Corwin described the internment and the Court's action as "the most drastic invasion of the rights of citizens of the United States by their own government" in modern American history. Taking a broad overview of structural, political linkage, and governmental factors that influenced the Supreme Court's decision will help explain this situation.

Governmental Action

The Supreme Court announces its decision allowing the internment of Japanese Americans in *Korematsu* v. *United States* (1944).

Governmental Level

- Military authorities believed that Japanese-Americans living on the West Coast posed a national security threat to the United States; asked the President to authorize curfews, relocation, and confinement.

- President Franklin Roosevelt, troubled by the action, but fully aware of the feelings of the public and the wishes of military leaders in wartime, signed the necessary executive orders.

- Congress passed supporting legislation making relocation and internment possible.

- The Supreme Court, unwilling to act against opinion of military leaders that Japanese-Americans living on the West Coast posed a national security threat, supported the exclusion order in a case brought by Fred Korematsu.

Political Linkages Level

- Anti-Japanese attitudes were widespread among the public, particularly in the West Coast states.

- Public opinion strongly supported the war against Japan and whatever military policies were necessary to win it.

- The media whipped up hysteria about a possible Japanese invasion.

Structural Level

- Japanese immigrants to the United States in the late nineteenth and early twentieth centuries settled mainly in the West Coast states.

- The Japanese attack on Pearl Harbor on December 7, 1941, plunged the United States into World War II and helped trigger negative attitudes toward Americans of Japanese descent.

- The Constitution vests enormous powers in the president as commander-in-chief during wartime.

THE STRUGGLE FOR DEMOCRACY

One Person, One Vote

Political equality is one of the defining characteristics of democracy (see Chapter 1), yet the principle of *one person, one vote,* meaning that the vote of each citizen carries the same weight as the vote of every other citizen, was not guaranteed by the Supreme Court until the 1960s. The case that opened the door to the transformation of constitutional law in this area was *Baker* v. *Carr* (1962). The Court decided in this case that the federal courts could hear challenges to legislative malapportionment under the equal protection clause of the Fourteenth Amendment. In rendering this decision, the Court reversed long-settled constitutional doctrine and encouraged challenges to malapportionment in the states. By doing so, the Court enriched democracy in the United States.

Malapportionment means drawing legislative district lines in such a way that the resulting districts (state legislative or congressional districts) vary substantially in population. Legislative district lines are generally redrawn after each census to take account of shifts in population in the states. In many cases, however, state legislatures had failed for a very long time to redraw district lines even as the populations of their states were becoming more urban and suburban. The result was that rural legislative districts, with sparse populations, had the same number of representatives as urban and suburban districts with dense populations. In other words, rural populations had more representation than they deserved, based on a one-person, one-vote standard, and urban and suburban populations had less. This arrangement was especially disadvantageous to racial minorities and the poor living in central cities.

In Tennessee, the state constitution required that the legislature reapportion legislative districts after each census, but the legislature had not redrawn legislative district lines since 1901 and showed no signs of doing so after the 1960 census. One legislative district in Memphis had a population 19 times the size of one of the state's rural districts, so that the citizens of the Memphis district enjoyed only one-nineteenth the representation of the rural district in the state legislature. Finding no redress in the Tennessee legislature or the state courts, a group of plaintiffs from Memphis requested that the federal district court put a halt to legislative elections in the state until the situation was rectified. The district court turned down their request, saying that apportionment cases were not the province of the federal courts. The plaintiffs then appealed to the Supreme Court. Much to the surprise of longtime observers of the Court, it accepted the case and eventually ruled in favor of a reexamination of constitutional doctrine on apportionment.

The Supreme Court had long avoided involvement in apportionment controversies, defining them as "political," meaning that they involved issues that the judges thought best left to the political branches (executive and legislative). The doctrine distinguishing "political" matters from "judicial" matters was first articulated by Chief Justice John Marshall in *Marbury* v. *Madison* (1803) and had been refined by Chief Justice Roger Taney in *Luther* v. *Borden* (1849). It was applied to the legislative apportionment issue in *Colegrove* v. *Green* (1946), in which Justice Felix Frankfurter (still on the Court for the *Baker* case) wrote that the "Court ought not to enter this political thicket."

Frankfurter remained strongly opposed on doctrinal grounds to Supreme Court involvement in apportionment cases, so he opposed the Tennessee plaintiffs, but he was also worried that a ruling on the issue would bring a storm of criticism from elected state officials. Fortunately for the principle of political equality, most of the other justices were willing to take the risk; only Justice John Harlan sided with Frankfurter. This willingness can be attributed in large part to the formidable negotiating and opinion-drafting skills of Justice William Brennan, who fashioned the majority coalition. To gain as strong a majority as he could (the vote was 6 to 2, with one justice not voting), Brennan insisted that the decision focus solely on the jurisdictional question—that is, on whether the federal courts could hear malapportionment cases—rather than on the specific merits of the complaints of the Tennessee plaintiffs. He was after bigger fish. Brennan and his brethren knew that a jurisdictional decision would open the door to cases challenging states' failure to provide equal protection for their citizens.

The challenges did indeed flood in (36 in the year after *Baker*), and the Court moved quickly to construct the doctrine of one person, one vote as the basis for political representation in the United States. *Baker* was the opening salvo of a constitutional revolution that eventually transformed American politics and made it more democratic. Chief Justice Earl Warren later said that the decision was the most vital one made during his long tenure on the Supreme Court.

Carr was an important case addressing this issue; see The Struggle for Democracy box, "One Person, One Vote"). An often cited example is the Court's willingness to become increasingly involved in the process of drawing congressional electoral district boundaries in the states. Defenders of the Court argue that when such basic constitutional rights as equality of citizenship are at peril, the Court is obligated to protect these rights, no matter what other government bodies may choose to do.

remedy

An action that a court determines must be taken to rectify a wrong.

Remedies   The most criticized aspect of judicial activism is the tendency for federal judges to impose broad remedies on states and localities. A **remedy** is what a court determines must be done to rectify a wrong. Since the 1960s, the Court has been more willing than in the past to impose remedies that require other governmental bodies to take action. Some of the most controversial of these remedies include court orders requiring states to build more prison space and mandating that school districts bus students to achieve racial balance. Such remedies often require that governments spend public funds for things they do not necessarily want to do. Critics claim that the Court's legitimate role is to prevent government actions that threaten rights and liberties, not to compel government to take action to meet some policy goal.

original intention

The doctrine that the courts must interpret the Constitution in ways consistent with the intentions of the framers rather than in light of contemporary conditions and needs.

strict construction

The doctrine that the provisions of the Constitution have a clear meaning and that judges must stick closely to this meaning when rendering decisions.

Original Intention   Much of the debate about the role of the Court centers on the issue of **original intention**. Advocates of original intention and its twin, **strict construction**, believe that the Court must be guided by the original intentions of the framers and the words found in the Constitution. They believe that the expansion of rights that has occurred since the mid-1960s—such as the new right to privacy that formed the basis of the *Roe* v. *Wade* decision and rights for criminal defendants—is illegitimate, having no foundation in the framers' intentions or the text of the Constitution. Justices Antonin Scalia and Clarence Thomas are the strongest "originalists" on today's Court.

Opponents of original intention believe that the intentions of the Founders are not only impossible to determine but also unduly constricting. In this view, jurists must try to reconcile the fundamental principles of the Constitution with changing conditions in the United States.

When all is said and done, however, it is apparent that the modern Supreme Court is more activist than it was in the past; most justices today hold a more expansive view of the role of the Court in forging national policy than did their predecessors. Because the Court is likely to remain activist–note the present Court's vigorous reinterpretation of the meaning of federalism– the debate about judicial activism is not likely to disappear from American politics.

Outside Influences on the Court

The courts make public policy and will continue to do so, but they do not do so in splendid isolation; many other governmental and political linkage actors and institutions influence what they do. Recall that the influence of structural factors has already been examined at several places in this chapter.

Governmental Factors

The Supreme Court must coexist with other governmental bodies that have their own powers, interests, constituencies, and visions of the public good. Recognizing this, the Court usually tries to stay somewhere near the boundaries of what is acceptable to other political actors. Being without "purse or sword," as Hamilton put it in *The Federalist,* No. 78, the Court cannot force others to obey its decisions. It can only hope that respect for the law and the Court will cause government officials to do what it has mandated in a decision. If the Court fails to gain voluntary compliance, it risks a serious erosion of its influence, for it then appears weak and ineffectual.

Presidential Influence   The president, as chief executive, is supposed to carry out the Court's decrees. However, presidents who have opposed or have been lukewarm to particular decisions have been known to drag their feet as President Eisenhower did on school desegregation after the Court's *Brown* decision.

The president has certain constitutional powers that give him some degree of influence over the Court. In addition to the Court's dependence on the president to carry out its decisions (when the parties to a dispute do not do it voluntarily), the president influences the direction of the Court by his power of appointment. He can also file suits through the Justice Department, try to move public opinion against the Court (as Richard Nixon tried to do), and threaten to introduce legislation to alter the Court's organization or jurisdiction (as Franklin Roosevelt did with his Court-packing proposal).

Congressional Influences   Congress retains the power to change the size, organization, and appellate jurisdiction of the federal courts. During the Civil War, Congress removed the Court's jurisdiction over habeas corpus cases so that civilians could be tried in military courts. Conservative Republicans in Congress have been trying for years to remove the power of federal courts to issue rulings requiring an increase in taxes and to decrease their ability to review the deportation and asylum decisions of the Immigration and Naturalization Service. Congress can also bring pressure to bear by being unsympathetic to pleas from the justices for pay increases or for a suitable budget for clerks or office space. The Senate also plays a role in the appointment process, as we have learned, and can convey its views to the Court during the course of confirmation hearings. Finally, Congress can change statutes or pass new laws that specifically challenge Supreme Court decisions, as it did when it legislated the Civil Rights Act of 1991 to make it easier for people to file employment discrimination suits.

Political Linkage Factors

The Supreme Court is influenced not only by other government officials and institutions but also by what we have termed political linkage factors such as social movements, interest groups, and elections.

Groups and Movements   Interest groups, social movements, and the public not only influence the Court indirectly through the president and Congress but often do so directly. An important political tactic of interest groups and social movements is the **test case**. A test case is an action brought by a group that is designed to challenge the constitutionality of a law or an action by government. Groups wishing to force a court determination on an issue that is important to them will try to find a plaintiff on whose behalf they can bring a suit. When Thurgood Marshall was chief counsel for the NAACP in the 1950s, he spent a long time searching for the right plaintiff to bring a suit that would drive the last nail into the coffin of the *Plessy* separate-but-equal doctrine that was the legal basis for southern segregation. He settled on a fifth-grade girl named Linda Brown who was attending a segregated school in Topeka, Kansas. Several years later, he won the landmark case *Brown* v. *Board of Education of Topeka.*

test case

A case brought to force a ruling on the constitutionality of some law or executive action.

Social movements use test cases to challenge the constitutionality of laws and government actions. After a long search, NAACP attorney Thurgood Marshall selected Linda Brown, a fifth-grader from Topeka, Kansas, as the principal plaintiff in *Brown v. Board of Education of Topeka,* the historic case that successfully challenged school segregation.

class action suit

A suit brought on behalf of a group of people who are in a situation similar to that of the plaintiffs.

Many test cases take the form of **class action suits**. These are suits brought by an individual on behalf of a class of people who are in a similar situation. A suit to prevent the dumping of toxic wastes in public waterways, for example, may be brought by an individual in the name of all the people living in the area who are adversely affected by the resulting pollution. Class action suits were invited by the Warren Court's expansion of the definition of standing in the 1960s. The Rehnquist Court later narrowed the definition of standing, making it harder to bring class action suits.

Interest groups often get involved in suits brought by others by filing amicus curiae briefs. Pro-abortion groups submitted 32 in the *Webster* case; anti-abortion groups added.[21] Such briefs set out the group's position on the constitutional issues or talk about some of the most important consequences of deciding the case one way or the other. In a sense, this activity is a form of lobbying. Some scholars believe that the Court finds such briefs to be a way to keep track of public and group opinion on the issues before it, and helpful to its work.[22]

Leaders The Supreme Court does not usually stray very far from the opinions of public and private sector leaders.[23] Social and economic leaders use their influence in a number of ways. As we learned in earlier chapters, their influence is substantial in the media, the interest group system, party politics, and elections at all levels. It follows, then, that elites play a substantial role in the thinking of presidents and the members of Congress as they, in turn, deal with the Court. In addition to this powerful but indirect influence, the Court is also shaped by developments on issues and doctrine within the legal profession as these are expressed by bar associations, law journals, and law schools.

Although the Court has become an important bulwark of rights and liberties, it has occasionally felt it prudent to go along with the political branches when they have tried to silence dissident voices and keep racial minorities from enjoying the full protection of the law. For instance, it went along with local, state, and federal actions to punish dissident voices during the McCarthy era's anti-Communist hysteria of the 1950s. It also approved the forced relocation and internment of Japanese-Americans during World War II, as shown in the "Using the Framework" feature earlier. Whereas the Warren Court changed much of this, the Rehnquist Court is more inclined to favor the authorities.[24]

Public Opinion   We might think that the Supreme Court is immune from public opinion, since the justices are appointed for life and do not need to face the electorate. There is a great deal of evidence, however, that the Court pays attention to public opinion. Some research shows that the Court conforms to public opinion about as much as the president and Congress do (about three-fifths of the time). Other research shows public support for the Court's actions only about one-third of the time.[25] It is also the case that the Court sometimes takes a very long time to move closer to public and elite opinions. For example, during the Great Depression, the Court's strong commitment to laissez-faire economics in the midst of a national economic emergency almost led to a constitutional crisis.

HOW DEMOCRATIC ARE WE?

PROPOSITION: The Supreme Court was designed to be a non-democratic institution, and it ought to stay that way. It has served us well throughout our history.

AGREE: For a representative democracy to function at all, there must be a referee who stands above the fray, preserving the rules, overseeing the orderly changing of some rules when the situation demands it, protecting minorities against the potentially tyrannical behavior of the majority, and protecting individuals in the exercise of the constitutionally guaranteed rights. The Supreme Court has done a pretty good job carrying out these responsibilities throughout our history.

DISAGREE: A representative democracy cannot remain democratic if one of its core government institutions, with the power to make binding decisions for the nation as a whole, is neither responsible nor responsive to the people. At some point, it cannot avoid going its own way, sometimes legitimately so (e.g., when it has occasionally protected the constitutional rights of unpopular individuals and minority groups) and sometimes illegitimately (e.g., when it has acted to protect the interests of powerful economic interests).

THE AUTHORS: In the conception of democracy used throughout this book, the appropriate role of the Court is to encourage the play of popular sovereignty, political equality, and liberty in American politics. In the game of American politics, the role of the Court ought to be that of a referee ensuring that the rules of democracy will be followed. The rules of the game of democracy involve assurances that the majority will prevail in the determination of public policy, that all members of the society will be allowed to enter on an equal basis into the public dialogue about the public business, and that each individual will be allowed all of the rights of conscience and expression connected with human dignity. We have learned at various places in this book that the Court does not always live up to these standards, but that it must do so for the health of our democracy goes without saying. We have learned that the Court, although sometimes slow in doing so, acts consistently with public opinion about as often as Congress and the president do. We will see in Chapters 15 and 16 on civil rights and civil liberties, moreover, that the Court, although often inconsistent and slow in doing so, has come to play an important and positive role in the protection of rights and liberties in the United States.

Summary

Article III of the Constitution is vague about the powers and responsibilities of the U.S. Supreme Court. Especially noteworthy is the Constitution's silence on the Court's most important power, judicial review. Nevertheless, the Court has fashioned a powerful position for itself in American politics, coequal with the executive and legislative branches.

The federal court system is made up of three parts. At the bottom are 94 federal district courts, in which most cases originate. In the middle are 13 appeals courts. At the top is the Supreme Court, with both original and appellate jurisdiction.

The Supreme Court operates on the basis of several widely shared norms: secrecy, seniority, and adherence to precedent. The Court controls its agenda by granting or not granting certiorari. Cases before the Court wend their way through the process in the following way: submission of briefs, oral argument, initial consideration in conference, opinion writing, and final conference consideration by the justices. Published opinions serve as precedents for other federal courts and future Supreme Court decisions.

The Supreme Court is a national policymaker of considerable importance. Its unelected, life-tenured justices cannot, however, do anything they please, because the Court is significantly influenced by other political linkage and governmental factors. As a result, Court decisions rarely drift very far from public and elite opinion.

Constitutional interpretation by the Supreme Court, heavily influenced by structural changes in American history, has progressed through three stages. In the first, the Court helped settle the question of the nature of the federal union. In the second, it helped define the role of the government in a free enterprise economy. In the third, the Court focused on issues of civil liberties and civil rights.

The decisions of the Court are influenced by structural, political linkage, and governmental factors. The president and Congress are especially important in this regard, but so too are interest groups and public and elite opinion.

Suggestions for Further Reading

Ackerman, Bruce. *We the People: Foundations.* Cambridge, MA: Harvard University Press, 1991.
> *A compelling interpretation of American constitutional history in which popular pressures are the prime cause for major transformations in the U.S. Supreme Court's approach to major issues.*

Barber, Sotirios A. *The Constitution of Judicial Power.* Baltimore: Johns Hopkins University Press, 1997.
> *A compelling defense of an activist Court.*

Clayton, Cornell W., and Howard Gillman, eds. *Supreme Court Decision Making: New Institutionalist Approaches.* Chicago: University of Chicago Press, 1999.
> *An argument by a collection of leading scholars that the most important factor in Supreme Court decision making is neither ideology nor political pressures, but the nature of the law and judicial institutions.*

Lewis, Anthony. *Gideon's Trumpet.* New York: Random House, 1964.
> *The moving story of Clarence Earl Gideon's successful campaign from a Florida prison cell to persuade the Supreme Court that defendants have a right to a lawyer.*

O'Brien, David M. *Storm Center: The Supreme Court in American Politics.* New York: W. W. Norton, 2000.
> *The leading textbook on the Court and how it operates.*

Schwartz, Bernard. *Decision: How the Supreme Court Decides Cases.* New York: Oxford University Press, 1997.

> *A revealing behind-the-scenes look at how the Supreme Court considers and decides the cases before it.*

Sunstein, Cass R. *One Case at a Time.* Cambridge, MA: Harvard University Press, 1999.

> *A defense of the present Supreme Court's tendency to render narrow decisions and avoid breaking ground for grand new constitutional theories; argues that this leaves room for the play of democracy.*

Internet Sources

Federal Courts Home Page   **www.uscourts.gov**

> *Information and statistics about the activities of U.S. District Courts, Circuit Courts of Appeal, and the Supreme Court.*

Legal Information Institute, Cornell University Law School
http://www.law.cornell.edu

> *The gateway to a world of information and links to associated law and court sites on the Web. Among its sections you will find the following: the Supreme Court Calendar; Biographies and Opinions of the Justices; Directories of law firms, law schools, and legal associations; Constitutions and Codes, including U.S. statutes, regulations, and judicial rules of procedure; and Court opinions, including those of state supreme courts.*

The New York Times Supreme Court Guide
www.nytimes.com/library/politics/scotus/index-scotus.html

> *Recently published articles about the Supreme Court and its decisions, biographies of the justices, the Court's current docket, and much more.*

Notes

1. J. M. Sosin, *The Aristocracy of the Long Robe: The Origins of Judicial Review in America* (Westport, CT: Greenwood Press, 1989).

2. Robert G. McCloskey, *The American Supreme Court* (Chicago: University of Chicago Press, 1960), pp. 12–13.

3. On *Marbury,* see Sylvia Snowmiss, *Judicial Review and the Law of the Constitution* (New Haven, CT: Yale University Press, 1990).

4. Neil Lewis, "An Appeals Court That Always Veers to the Right," *New York Times* (May 24, 1999), p. A.1.

5. David M. O'Brien, *Storm Center: The Supreme Court in American Politics,* 3rd ed. (New York: Norton, 1993), p. 68.

6. Robert A. Carp and Ronald Stidham, *Judicial Process in America,* 3rd ed. (Washington, D.C.: Congressional Quarterly Press, 1996), ch. 8; Sheldon Goldman, "Federal Judicial Recruitment," in John B. Gates and Charles Johnson, eds., *The American Courts: A Critical Assessment* (Washington, D.C.: Congressional Quarterly Press, 1991), pp. 195, 199.

7. Ronald Stidham and Robert A. Carp, "Judges, Presidents, and Policy Choices," *Social Science Quarterly* 68 (1987), pp. 395–404; Carp and Stidham, *Judicial Process in America,* ch. 9.

8. For details, see H. W. Perry Jr., *Deciding to Decide: Agenda Setting in the United States Supreme Court* (Cambridge, MA: Harvard University Press, 1991).

9. David Adamany, "The Supreme Court," in Gates and Johnson, *The American Courts,* pp. 111–112; Glendon Schubert, *The Judicial Mind* (Evanston, IL: Northwestern University Press, 1965); Jeffrey A. Segal and Harold J. Spaeth, *The Supreme Court and the Attitudinal Model* (New York: Cambridge University Press, 1993); John D. Sprague, *Voting Patterns of the United States Supreme Court* (Indianapolis: Bobbs-Merrill, 1968).

10. Walter Murphy, *Elements of Judicial Strategy* (Princeton, NJ: Princeton University Press, 1964).

11. Joel B. Grossman, "Social Backgrounds and Judicial Decision-Making," *Harvard Law Review* 79 (1966), pp. 1551–1564; S. Sidney Ulmer, "Dissent Behavior and the Social Background of Supreme Court Justices," *Journal of Politics* 32 (1970), pp. 580–589.

12. John Harlan, "A Glimpse of the Supreme Court at Work," *University of Chicago Law School Record* 1, no. 7 (1963), pp. 35–52.

13. Bob Woodward and Scott Armstrong, *The Brethren: Inside the Supreme Court* (New York: Simon & Schuster, 1979).

14. Lee Epstein and Jack Knight, "Mapping Out the Strategic Terrain: The Informational Role of Amici Curiae," in Cornell Clayton and Howard Gillman, eds., *Supreme Court Decision-Making* (Chicago: University of Chicago Press, 1999).

15. Bernard Schwartz, *A History of the Supreme Court* (New York: Oxford University Press, 1993), p. 369.

16. Herbert Jacob, *Justice in America,* 3rd ed. (Boston: Little, Brown, 1978), p. 245.

17. McCloskey, *The American Supreme Court.*

18. Carp and Stidham, *Judicial Process in America,* p. 28.

19. McCloskey, *The American Supreme Court,* p. 57.

20. Ibid. Also see H. W. Perry Jr., *The Transformation of the Supreme Court's Agenda: From the New Deal to the Reagan Administration* (Boulder, CO: Westview Press, 1991).

21. Edward Lazurus, *Closed Chambers* (New York: Penguin, 1999), pp. 373–374.

22. Epstein and Knight, "Mapping Out the Strategic Terrain."

23. Robert A. Dahl, "Decision Making in a Democracy: The Supreme Court as a National Decision Maker," *Journal of Public Law* 6 (1957), pp. 279–295; Thomas R. Marshall, "Public Opinion, Representation, and the Modern Supreme Court," *American Politics Quarterly* 16 (1988), pp. 296–316; McCloskey, *The American Supreme Court,* p. 22; O'Brien, *Storm Center,* p. 325.

24. Adamany, "The Supreme Court," pp. 15–18; Lincoln Caplan, "The Reagan Challenge to the Rule of Law," in Sidney Blumenthal and Thomas Byrne Edsall, eds., *The Reagan Legacy* (New York: Pantheon Books, 1988); Linda Greenhouse, "The Court's Counterrevolution Comes in Fits and Starts," *New York Times* (July 4, 1993), sec. 4, p. 1.

25. G. Caldeira, "Courts and Public Opinion," in Gates and Johnson, *The American Courts;* Jay Casper, "The Supreme Court and National Policy Making," *American Political Science Review* 70 (1976), pp. 50–63; Marshall, "Public Opinion, Representation, and the Modern Supreme Court"; William Mishler and Reginald S. Sheehan, "The Supreme Court as Counter-Majoritarian Institution: The Impact of Public Opinion on Supreme Court Decisions," *American Political Science Review* 87 (1993), pp. 87–101; Benjamin I. Page and Robert Y. Shapiro, "Effects of Public Opinion on Policy," *American Political Science Review* 77 (1983), p. 183.

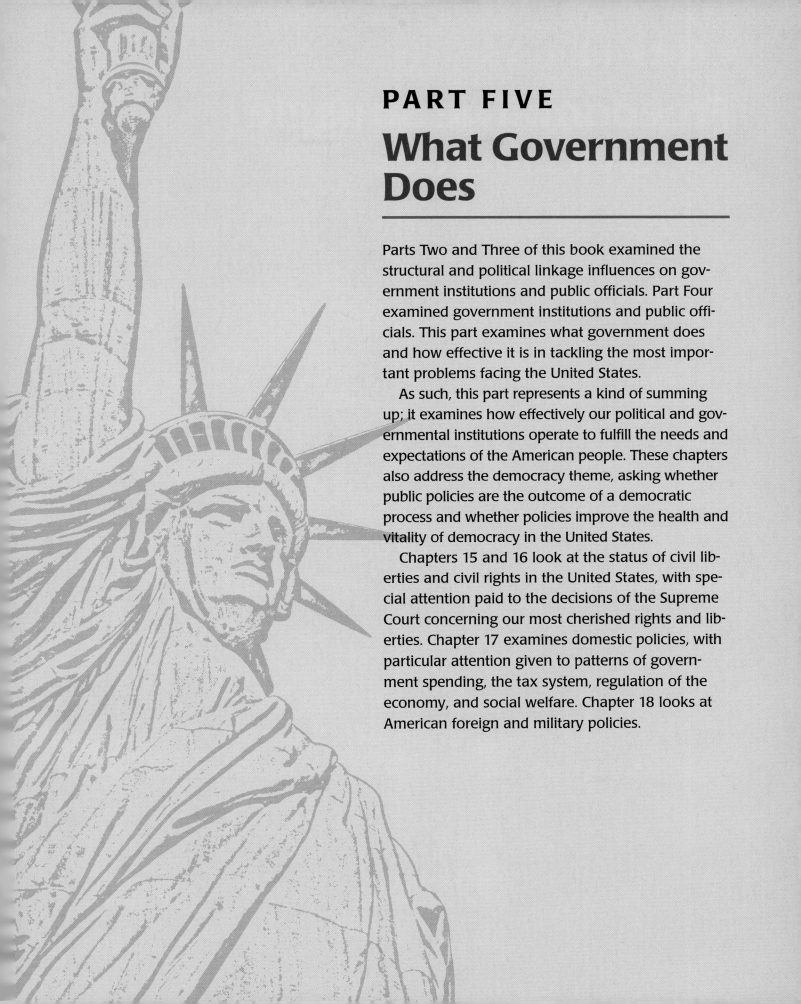

PART FIVE

What Government Does

Parts Two and Three of this book examined the structural and political linkage influences on government institutions and public officials. Part Four examined government institutions and public officials. This part examines what government does and how effective it is in tackling the most important problems facing the United States.

As such, this part represents a kind of summing up; it examines how effectively our political and governmental institutions operate to fulfill the needs and expectations of the American people. These chapters also address the democracy theme, asking whether public policies are the outcome of a democratic process and whether policies improve the health and vitality of democracy in the United States.

Chapters 15 and 16 look at the status of civil liberties and civil rights in the United States, with special attention paid to the decisions of the Supreme Court concerning our most cherished rights and liberties. Chapter 17 examines domestic policies, with particular attention given to patterns of government spending, the tax system, regulation of the economy, and social welfare. Chapter 18 looks at American foreign and military policies.

CHAPTER 15

Freedom: The Struggle for Civil Liberties

IN THIS CHAPTER

- Why liberty is so important in a democracy

- How liberties were gradually applied to the states by the Supreme Court

- How the Supreme Court's interpretation of the meaning of liberties has changed

- How the struggle for democracy has increased the enjoyment of liberties in the United States

Campus Speech Codes and Free Speech

- Khalid Abdul Muhammad, at the time an aide to the Nation of Islam leader Louis Farrakhan, ignites controversy at several universities with a series of fiery appearances. Frequently voicing anti-Semitic themes, Muhammad's speeches polarize campuses: some people defend his First Amendment right to free speech; others denounce his inflammatory tone.

- During a class at the University of Michigan, a student argues that homosexuality could be treated with psychotherapy. He is accused of violating a campus rule against victimizing people on the basis of their sexual orientation.

- At Southern Methodist University, a student is sentenced to work with minority organizations for 30 hours because, among other things, he sang "We Shall Overcome" in a sarcastic manner.[1]

- At the University of Minnesota, four women students brought sexual harassment charges against faculty members in the Scandinavian Studies Department for disagreeing with students about the role of a female character in a story and for greeting a female student in a "nonsupportive" way.[2]

- The University of Montana's harassment policy says that if a woman "feels" she has been mistreated, that alone proves mistreatment.

- Top officials at the University of Texas, Austin, denounce as abhorrent the statement of law school professor Lino Graglia that black and Hispanic students are not competitive with whites in law school because most of them come from cultures that do not encourage academic achievement or look upon academic failure as a disgrace. Although Rev. Jesse Jackson joins hundreds of students and faculty members calling for his dismissal, civil libertarians come to his

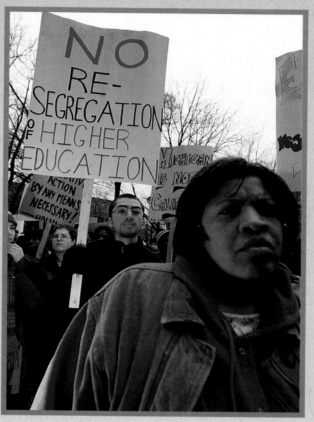

defense on the grounds of the professor's free speech rights under the Constitution.

- Stanford University enacts a speech code in 1990 that prohibits "personal vilification of students on the basis of their sex, race, color, handicap, religion, sexual orientation, or national and ethnic origin." The code is pressed by, among others, the African-American Law Students Association, the Asian-American Law Students Association, and the Jewish Law Students Association. It is strongly opposed by Stanford's eminent constitutional scholar Gerald Gunther, who claims that hate speech should not be banned but vigorously rejected "with more speech, with better speech, with repudiation and contempt." The California Supreme Court in 1995 agrees with the Gunther position, saying that the Stanford code unconstitutionally restricts free speech rights under the First Amendment to the Constitution.[3]

The college campus has become one of the most visible battlegrounds in the continuing struggle over the meaning of free speech in the United States. Campus speech codes have been instituted at many colleges and universities across the country in an effort to rid campuses of speech that may offend women and members of minority groups. Many civil libertarians, like Gerald Gunther, though protective of the rights of minority students to have a supportive learning environment, have fought hard against such codes in the service of free speech and a free society. By and large, the courts have sided with the civil libertarians, as in the Stanford case.

This chapter examines civil liberties in the United States. It shows that the meaning of each of our freedoms—whether of speech, of the press, of association, or of religion—is never settled but is the subject of continuing disagreement and even, on occasion, of contentious political struggle.

Thinking Critically About This Chapter

Using the Framework. You will see in this chapter how structural, political, linkage, and governmental factors influence the meaning and practice of civic freedoms. Although the decisions of the Supreme Court are particularly important in determining the status of civil liberties at any particular moment in American history, you will learn how they are also the product of influences from a wide range of actors, institutions, and social processes.

Using the Democracy Standard. You will see in this chapter how the expansion of the enjoyment of civil liberties in the United States has been a product of the struggle for democracy and how civil liberties are fundamental to the democratic process itself.   ▶

Civil Liberties in the Constitution

civil liberties

Freedoms protected from government interference.

We saw in Chapter 2 that the framers were particularly concerned about establishing a society in which liberty might flourish. While government was necessary to protect liberty from the threat of anarchy, the framers believed that government might threaten liberty if it became too powerful. **Civil liberties** are freedoms protected by constitutional provisions, laws, and practices from certain types of government interference. As embodied in the Bill of Rights, civil liberties are protected by prohibitions against government actions that threaten the enjoyment of freedom.

In the Preamble to the Constitution, the framers wrote that they aimed to "secure the Blessings of Liberty to ourselves and our Posterity." But in the original Constitution, they protected few liberties from the national government they were creating and almost none from state governments. The safeguard against tyranny that the framers preferred was to give the national government little power with which to attack individual liberties. Rather than listing specific prohibitions against certain kinds of actions, they believed that liberty was best protected by a constitutional design that fragmented government power, a design that included separation of powers, checks and balances, and federalism. Still, the framers singled out certain freedoms as too crucial to be left unmentioned. The Constitution prohibits Congress and the states from suspending the writ of **habeas corpus**, except when public safety demands it because of rebellion or invasion, and from passing **bills of attainder** or **ex post facto laws** (see Table 15.1 for an enumeration).

habeas corpus

The legal doctrine that a person who is arrested must have a timely hearing before a judge.

bill of attainder

A governmental decree that a person is guilty of a crime that carries the death penalty, rendered without benefit of a trial.

ex post facto law

A law that retroactively declares some action illegal.

As we saw in Chapter 2, many citizens found the proposed Constitution too stingy in its listing of liberties, so that the Federalists were led to promise a "bill of rights" as a condition for passing the Constitution. The Bill of Rights was passed by the 1st Congress in 1789 and was ratified by the required number of states by 1791. Passage of the Bill of Rights made the constitution more democratic by specifying protections of political liberty and by guaranteeing a context of free political expression that makes popular sovereignty possible.

Looking at the liberties specified by the text of the constitution and its amendments, however, emphasizes how few of our most cherished liberties are to be found in a reading of the bare words of the Constitution. Decisions by government officials and changes brought about by political leaders, interest groups, social movements, and individuals remade the Constitution in the long run; hence many of the freedoms we expect today are not specifically mentioned

Table 15.1 ● Civil Liberties in the U.S. Constitution

The exact meaning and extent of civil liberties in the Constitution are matters of debate, but here are some freedoms spelled out in the text of the Constitution and its amendments or clarified by early court decisions.

CONSTITUTION

Article I, Section 9
Congress may not suspend a writ of habeas corpus.
Congress may not pass bills of attainder or ex post facto laws.

Article I, Section 10
States may not pass bills of attainder or ex post facto laws.
States may not impair obligation of contracts.

Article III, Section 2
Criminal trials in national courts must be jury trials in the state in which the defendant is alleged to have committed the crime.

Article III, Section 3
No one may be convicted of treason unless there is a confession in open court or testimony of two witnesses to the same overt act.

Article IV, Section 2
Citizens of each state are entitled to all privileges and immunities of citizens in the several states.

THE BILL OF RIGHTS

First Amendment
Congress may not make any law with respect to the establishment of religion.
Congress may not abridge the free exercise of religion.
Congress may not abridge freedom of speech or of the press.
Congress may not abridge the right to assemble or to petition the government.

Second Amendment
Congress may not infringe the right to keep and bear arms.

Third Amendment
Congress may not station soldiers in houses against the owner's will, except in times of war.

Fourth Amendment
Citizens are to be free from unreasonable searches and seizures.
Federal courts may issue search warrants based only on probable cause and specifically describing the objects of search.

Fifth Amendment
Citizens are protected against double jeopardy (being prosecuted more than once for the same crime) and self-incrimination.
Citizens are guaranteed against deprivation of life, liberty, or property without due process of law.
Citizens are guaranteed just compensation for public use of their private property.

Sixth Amendment
Citizens have the right to a speedy and public trial before an impartial jury.
Citizens have the right to face their accuser and to cross-examine witnesses.

Eighth Amendment
Excessive bail and fines are prohibited.
Cruel and unusual punishments are prohibited.

there. Some extensions of protected liberties were introduced by judges and other officials. Others have evolved as the culture has grown to accept novel and even once-threatening ideas. Still other liberties have secured a place in the Republic through partisan and ideological combat. The key to understanding civil liberties in the United States is to follow their evolution during the course of our history.

Rights and Liberties in the Nineteenth Century

During the nineteenth century, the range of protected civil liberties in the United States was somewhat different from their range today. Especially noteworthy were the special place of property rights as a freedom to be protected and the understanding that the Bill of Rights did not apply to state governments.

Property Rights in the Early Republic

Liberty may be understood as protection against government interference in certain kinds of activities. Among the few such protections mentioned in the original Constitution was one that concerned the use and enjoyment of private property: "No State shall . . . pass any . . . Law impairing the Obligation of Contracts" (Article I, Section 10). The importance of property rights as a fundamental liberty in the body of the Constitution was reinforced by more than a century of judicial interpretation.

contract clause

The portion of Article I, Section 10, of the Constitution that prohibits states from passing any law "impairing the obligation of contracts."

The Marshall Court (1801–1835)   Although the Supreme Court ruled (in *Barron* v. *Baltimore,* 1833) that the Bill of Rights did not apply to the states, it ruled on several occasions that the **contract clause** in the Constitution directly applied against unwarranted state action. In the hands of Chief Justice John Marshall, the clause became an important defense of property rights against interference by the states. In *Fletcher* v. *Peck* (1810), for example, the Marshall Court upheld a sale of public land, even though almost all of the legislators who had voted for the land sale had been bribed by the prospective purchasers. Chief Justice Marshall argued that even a fraudulent sale created a contract that the state could not void. In *Dartmouth College* v. *Woodward* (1819), Marshall argued that New Hampshire could not modify the charter of Dartmouth College because the original charter constituted a contract, the terms of which could not be changed without impairing the obligations in the original contract. The Founders' attempt to protect the contractual agreements of private parties ballooned in the hands of the Marshall Court to bar virtually any and all changes by the states of established property relations.[4] This expansion of property rights protections made it very difficult for states to regulate business activities.

The Taney Court (1836–1864)   Under the leadership of Chief Justice Roger Taney, the Court began to make a distinction between private property used in ways that encouraged economic growth and private property used for simple enjoyment. In landmark cases, the Taney Court issued rulings favoring the former when the two concepts of property conflicted.[5] In his opinion in *Charles River Bridge* v. *Warren Bridge* (1837), Chief Justice Taney said that Massachusetts, in chartering the Charles River Bridge, had not agreed to create a monopoly that closed off competitors. He ruled that Massachusetts could charter the rival Warren River Bridge because the states should encourage economic competition and technological advances. It did not matter that as a result the stockholders in the Charles River Bridge would lose money. Taney argued that the "creative destruction" of established but idle property in a dynamic market economy is the price of economic and social progress.

Human Property   The defense of property rights was especially and tragically strong when it came to slavery. Until the Civil War, courts in the North and the South consistently upheld the right of slaveholders to recapture fugitive slaves. In his opinion in *Dred Scott* v. *Sandford* (1857)—a case that helped bring on the Civil War—Chief Justice Taney claimed that slaves were not citizens who possessed rights but simply private property belonging to their owners, no different from land or tools.

Property Rights After the Civil War

The Fourteenth Amendment, passed after the Civil War, was designed to guarantee the citizenship rights of the newly freed slaves. It included a clause—the **due process clause**—stating that no state "may deprive a person of life, liberty, or property, without due process of law." Strangely, the Supreme Court in the late nineteenth century interpreted this clause as a protection for businesses against the regulatory efforts of the states.

The Court's most famous decision in this regard was *Lochner* v. *New York* (1905). Lochner ran a bakery in Utica, New York. He was convicted of requiring an employee to work more than 60 hours per week, contrary to a New York state maximum-hours statute. But Justice Rufus Peckham wrote for a 5–4 Supreme Court majority that the right of employer and employee to negotiate hours of work was part of the "liberty" of which, under the Fourteenth Amendment, no person could be deprived without due process of law. In other words, New York State had no right to regulate the hours of labor.

The nineteenth century was an era in which the rights of property were expanded, refined, and altered to become consistent with an emerging, dynamic industrial economy. The twentieth century would bring new approaches to property rights and to political liberties in general. These new approaches would be triggered by structural transformations in the economy and culture, the efforts of new political groups and movements, and the actions of government officials.

> **due process clause**
>
> The section of the Fourteenth Amendment that prohibits states from depriving anyone of life, liberty, or property "without due process of law," a guarantee against arbitrary or unfair government action.

Nationalization of the Bill of Rights

Americans rightly understand the Bill of Rights to be a foundation of American liberties. Until the twentieth century, however, the Bill of Rights did not apply to the states, only to the national government. The Supreme Court only gradually applied the Bill of Rights to the states through a process known as *selective incorporation*.

Selective Incorporation

The framers were worried more about national government intrusion on freedom than about state government intrusion. Most of the states, after all, had bills of rights in their own constitutions, and being closer to the people, state governments would be less likely to intrude on the people's freedom, or so the framers believed. This reading of the Bill of Rights as a prohibition of certain

Whereas the Second Amendment makes it difficult for Congress to pass laws restricting the sale and use of firearms, states can do so more easily because the Second Amendment has not yet been incorporated by the Supreme Court.

actions by the national government seems explicit in the language of many of the first ten amendments. The first, for instance, starts with the words "Congress shall make no law. . . ." This understanding of the Bill of Rights was confirmed by John Marshall in *Barron* v. *Baltimore* (1833). It is apparent that the majority in Congress wanted to change the reach of the Bill of Rights, extending it to the states, however, when it approved the Fourteenth Amendment after the Civil War. Three clauses in this amendment specify that the states cannot violate the rights and liberties of the people living in them:

- The first specifies that all persons born or naturalized in the United States are citizens of both the United States and the states in which they reside.

- The **privileges and immunities clause** specifies that no *state* "shall make or enforce any law which shall abridge the privileges or immunities of citizens of the United States."

- The due process clause specifies that no *state* shall "deprive any person of life, liberty, or property, without due process of law."

Although Congress wrote the Fourteenth Amendment to guarantee that the states would protect all of U.S. citizens' rights and liberties, including those found in the Bill of Rights, the Supreme Court was very slow in **nationalizing** or **incorporating** the Bill of Rights, making it binding on the state governments. Indeed, the Supreme Court has not yet fully incorporated or nationalized the Bill of Rights. Rather, it has practiced what constitutional scholars term **selective incorporation**, only slowly adding, step-by-step, even traditional civil liberties to the constitutional obligations of the states.

Standards for Incorporation

How does the Supreme Court decide whether to incorporate some portion of the Bill of Rights? That is, what standard does the Court use to protect a liberty specified in the Bill of Rights from violation by a state government? The answer is quite simple and is spelled out, strange as it may seem, in footnote 4 of the opinion of the Court in *United States* v. *Carolene Products Company* (1938), written by Justice Harlan Fiske Stone. Stone suggested that most legislative enactments by states would be considered constitutional and subject only to

privileges and immunities clause

The portion of Article IV, Section 2, of the Constitution that states that citizens from out of state have the same legal rights as local citizens in any state.

nationalizing

The process by which provisions of the Bill of Rights become incorporated. See *incorporation*.

incorporation

The gradual use of the Fourteenth Amendment by the Supreme Court to make the Bill of Rights and other constitutional protections binding on the states.

selective incorporation

The U.S. Supreme Court's gradual and piecemeal making of the protections of the Bill of Rights binding on the states.

ordinary scrutiny by the Court. However, the footnote declares, three classes of state actions would automatically be presumed unconstitutional, the burden being on the states to prove otherwise. When state actions are presumed to be unconstitutional, the Court is said to be exercising **strict scrutiny**. The three classes of suspect state actions that bring strict scrutiny are those that seem to

- Contradict specific prohibitions in the Constitution, including those of the Bill of Rights.
- Restrict the democratic process.
- Discriminate against racial, ethnic, or religious minorities.

The first of these is the subject matter of this chapter. The second has been addressed at several points in the text. The third is the subject of Chapter 16.

In the remainder of this chapter, we focus on specific civil liberties, clarifying their present status in both constitutional law and political practice.

> **ordinary scrutiny**
> The assumption that the actions of elected bodies and officials are legal under the Constitution.
>
> **strict scrutiny**
> The assumption that actions by elected bodies or officials violate constitutional rights.

Freedom of Speech

Congress shall make no Law . . . abridging the freedom of speech.
—FIRST AMENDMENT TO THE U.S. CONSTITUTION

Speech can take many forms. The Court has had to consider which forms of speech are protected under the Constitution.

Political Speech   For many people, the right to speak one's mind is the first principle of a free and democratic society. Yet the right to free speech was not incorporated (made applicable to state governments) by the Supreme Court until 1925 in *Gitlow* v. *New York* (1925). Benjamin Gitlow had published *The*

WEB EXPLORATION

Does Your Representative Support First Amendment Freedoms?

Issue: The enjoyment of First Amendment freedoms depends, in part, on how fully they are supported by elected representatives.

Site: Access the ACLU online through the "Course Documents" section of your online course. Go to the "Web Explorations" section for Chapter 15, click on "Does Your Representative Support First Amendment Freedoms?," and open "ACLU." Select "Freedom Scorecard." Enter your ZIP code to see how the ACLU scored your representative and senators.

What You've Learned: Do your representative and senators score well or badly on the ACLU freedom index? Do your representative and senators reflect your own views on civil liberties issues? How would you score on the ACLU index if you represented your district in the House or your state in the Senate?

HINT: Look at the legislation that the ACLU uses to compose their index. You may or may not agree that these votes are important. Depending on your political point of view, you may not agree that a high score on the ACLU index is the best indicator of support for freedom.

Once "free speech" was incorporated by the Supreme Court, states were no longer at liberty to suppress unpopular speech, as many of them had done with some frequency. This radical political rally in Gary, Indiana, in 1919 was broken up by the police soon after this photo was taken.

Left Wing Manifesto, which embraced a militant, revolutionary socialism to mobilize the proletariat to destroy the existing order in favor of communism. Gitlow did not advocate specific action to break the law, but he was nonetheless convicted of a felony under the New York Criminal Anarchy Law (1902).

The Supreme Court majority held that New York State was bound by the First Amendment but then argued that even the First Amendment did not prohibit New York from incarcerating Gitlow for his pamphlet. Said Justice Edward Sanford, "A single revolutionary spark may kindle a fire that, smoldering for a time, may burst into a sweeping and destructive conflagration. It cannot be said that the State is acting . . . unreasonably when . . . it seeks to extinguish the spark without waiting until it has enkindled the flame or blazed into the conflagration." In his famous dissent, Justice Oliver Wendell Holmes said, "Every idea is an incitement. . . . Eloquence may set fire to reason. But whatever may be thought of the redundant discourse before us, it had no chance of starting a present conflagration."

Although the *Gitlow* precedent proved to be an important advance for civil liberties in the United States, the Court was still willing to leave Gitlow in jail and allow the states wide latitude in controlling what they considered dangerous speech. For many years, especially during the 1940s and 1950s anti-Communist "Red scare," the Court deferred to political hysteria and allowed the widespread suppression of what we now consider acceptable speech and publication. The Court seldom moved far ahead of the political branches on free speech issues during this period or later.[6]

This early stage of the nationalization of the Bill of Rights by the Court was helped along by a new force, the American Civil Liberties Union (ACLU), which brought the *Gitlow* appeal. Less than ten years old, the ACLU had little to show for its legal challenges to the suppression of free speech until 1925, when *Gitlow* provided a spark of hope for civil libertarians. The Court's application of the First Amendment to the states provided the ACLU with opportunities to resist censorship and the strangulation of dissent by the states as well as by the national government. Victories remained rare, but the Court's willingness to incorporate free speech encouraged and energized the ACLU.[7]

Freedom of speech has grown in the ensuing years so that far more speech is protected than is not. In general, no U.S. government today may regulate or interfere with the content of speech without a compelling reason. For a reason to be compelling, a government must show that the speech poses a "clear and present danger"—the standard formulated by Holmes in *Schenck* v. *United States* (1919)—that it has a duty to prevent. The danger must be very substantial, and the relationship between the speech and the danger must be direct, such as falsely yelling "Fire!" in a crowded theater. The danger must also be so immediate that the people responsible for maintaining order cannot afford to tolerate the speech. Abstract advocacy of ideas, even ideas considered dangerous by police, politicians, or popular majorities, is protected unless it meets both conditions. Pitcher John Rocker of the Atlanta Braves learned, however, that a private organization can still censor speech. Major League Baseball fined and suspended him and then required him to undergo therapy for making racist remarks in *Sports Illustrated*. Nevertheless, freedom of speech has grown, and with it, an important part of democracy in the United States.

Actions and Symbolic Speech   Difficult questions about free expression persist, of course. Speech mixed with *conduct* may be restricted if the restrictions are narrowly and carefully tailored to curb the conduct while leaving the speech unmolested. Symbolic expressions (such as wearing armbands or picketing) may also receive less protection from the Court. The use of profanity or words that are likely to cause violence ("fighting words") may be regulated in some cases, as may symbolic actions that prevent others from carrying out legitimate activities. Still, freedom of speech throughout the United States has grown to the point at which contenders wrestle with relatively peripheral issues, leaving a large sphere of expressive freedom. *Texas* v. *Johnson* (1989) shows just how far the protection of free speech has expanded. In this case, Gregory Johnson challenged a Texas state law against flag desecration under which he had been convicted for burning an American flag as part of a demonstration at the 1984 Republican convention. Although dominated by a conservative majority, the Rehnquist Court overturned the Texas law, saying that flag burning falls under the free expression protections of the Constitution unless imminent incitement or violence is likely.

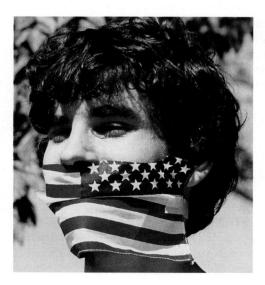

Can state legislatures pass laws prohibiting flag burning? The Supreme Court agreed with this demonstrator that such laws violate the freedom of expression.

Senator Joseph McCarthy issues a warning about the "Red tide" of communism sweeping the nation. McCarthy discovered few communists but managed to wreck the lives of many innocent people and created an atmosphere that threatened liberty in the United States for many years in the 1950s.

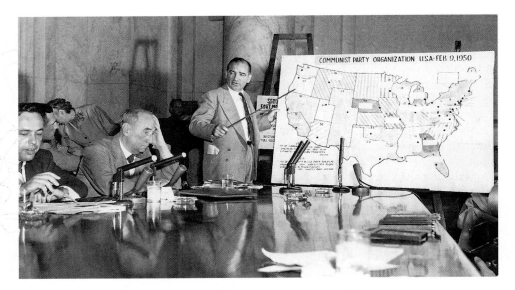

Suppression of Free Expression   A major exception to the expansion of freedom of expression has been the periodic concern about "internal security." The past century has witnessed several periods when dissenters and radicals were persecuted for their political speech and writings. Censorship of dissent and protests during World War I proved to be a portent of abuses after the war. At least 32 states enacted laws to suppress dangerous ideas and talk, and the Lusk Committee in New York State raided the offices of "radicals." Hoping to become president, New York State Attorney General A. Mitchell Palmer conducted raids on the headquarters of suspect organizations in 1919 and 1920, sending the young J. Edgar Hoover out to collect information on radicals and nonconformists.

A similar period of hysteria followed World War II. Its foundations were laid when the Democrat-controlled House of Representatives created the House Committee on Un-American Affairs (generally referred to as the HUAC). When the Republicans won control of the Congress, they professed to see security risks in the Truman administration and Hollywood. HUAC found no spies and contributed little to security, but it managed to ravage lives and reputations (see The Struggle for Democracy box, "Saying No to HUAC"). Soon Democrats and Republicans alike were exploiting the "Red scare" for political gain. The greatest gain (and, subsequently, the hardest fall) was for Senator Joseph McCarthy (R–Wisc.). McCarthy brandished lists of purported communists and denounced all who opposed him as traitors. McCarthy and "McCarthyism" eventually fell victims, however, to the newest force in U.S. politics: television. Once ordinary Americans saw McCarthy and his tactics in their living rooms, support for him declined rapidly. McCarthy's downfall led to a slow retreat from this period of utter disregard for liberty.[8]

Freedom of the Press

Congress shall make no law . . . abridging the freedom . . . of the press.
—FIRST AMENDMENT TO THE U.S. CONSTITUTION

In an aside in the opinion of the Court in *Gitlow* v. *New York* (1925), the Supreme Court included freedom of the press as a freedom guaranteed against state interference by the Fourteenth Amendment. Incorporation of this aspect of the Bill of Rights seems reasonable in light of the importance of the free flow of

THE STRUGGLE FOR DEMOCRACY

Saying No to HUAC

The patience of Representative Harold Velde, current chairman of the House Committee on Un-American Activities, was at an end: "This is not a court of law. We make the rules." Lloyd Barenblatt, a psychology instructor recently fired from Vassar College, would not be allowed to read his opening statement questioning HUAC's right to inquire into the nature of his political beliefs and associations. All HUAC wanted to know of Mr. Barenblatt was "Are you now or have you ever been a member of the Communist Party?"

HUAC was first created in 1938 by House leadership trying to appease conservative Democrats who were worried about purported communist influence in the New Deal. It held few hearings and was not responsible for a single piece of legislation from 1938 to the end of World War II. HUAC became a standing committee of the House of Representatives in the increasingly anti-Soviet climate of 1945, under the chairmanship of John Rankin of Mississippi, one of the House's most openly anti-black, anti-Jewish, and anti–New Deal members. Its charter was broad: "To investigate the extent, character, and objects of un-American propaganda activities in the United States."

For the next 12 years, until 1957, HUAC hauled more than 3,000 witnesses before it, focusing not on pending or proposed legislation or on the behavior of executive branch agencies—the only function of standing committees under the rules of the House—but on rooting out people with suspect ideas from the fields of education, religion, and entertainment. Its preferred mode of operation was to press for public recantations of past political beliefs and memberships and for the naming of past associates. People named by witnesses almost always became the object of public scorn and lost their jobs. People who did not cooperate with HUAC, by refusing to name names (so-called unfriendly witnesses), were subject to contempt of Congress citations, with attendant jail terms.

Despite HUAC's formidable weapons, Lloyd Barenblatt was saying that his beliefs and associations were none of the committee's business: "I object," under the terms of the First Amendment, "to the power and jurisdiction of this committee to inquire into my political beliefs, my religious beliefs, and any other personal and private affairs." At the time, Barenblatt could have avoided a contempt citation had he rested his refusal to cooperate on Fifth Amendment protections against self-incrimination (later HUAC would close this loophole). He was an extremely idealistic young man, however, who believed not only that he had done nothing wrong but also that First Amendment freedoms had to be protected against government intrusions. The members of HUAC and the House were unimpressed and voted a contempt citation for Barenblatt in July 1954. After a series of failed court appeals, including two before the Supreme Court, Barenblatt entered Danbury Federal Penitentiary in 1959.

Barenblatt later reflected on his experience:

Would I do it over again? Yes . . . the experience was one that caused some damage and some enhancement to my life. I lost a lot of friends, and it cost me money and jobs. But I stood up at a time when many people kept quiet, or became informers, or left the country. I am still an American. I am glad I took my stand. I don't regret it.

During the late 1950s, the Supreme Court began a slow process of reining in the HUAC. Much later, the House, finally embarrassed by HUAC's roughshod tactics and the increasing willingness of witnesses (this time, anti–Vietnam War protesters) to defy it, abolished the committee in 1975. The bravery of Lloyd Barenblatt and others in resisting the committee on principled constitutional grounds contributed to the excising of what Representative Robert Drinan called "that self-inflicted wound called HUAC from the body politic."

Source: Peter Irons, *The Courage of Their Convictions* (New York: Free Press, 1988), pp.81–104.

information in a society that aspires to freedom and democracy. In *Near* v. *Minnesota* (1931), the Court made good on the promise of *Gitlow* by invalidating the Minnesota Public Nuisance Law as a violation of freedom of the press.[9] Jay Near published the *Saturday Press,* a scandal sheet that attacked local crime, public officials, and a few other groups that he disliked: Jews, Catholics, blacks,

prior restraint

The government's power to prevent publication, as opposed to punishment afterward.

and unions, for example. Near and his associates were ordered by a state court not to publish, sell, or possess the *Saturday Press*. This sort of state action is called **prior restraint**, because it prevents publication before it has occurred. Freedom of the press is not necessarily infringed if publishers are sued or punished for harming others after they have published, but Minnesota was trying to keep Near and his associates from publishing in the future.

Prior Restraint   The prohibition of prior restraint on publication remains the core of freedom of the press. Freedom of the press and freedom of speech tend to be considered together as freedom of expression, so the general principles applicable to free speech apply to freedom of the press as well. Thus, the Court will allow the repression of publication only if the state can show some "clear and present danger" that publication poses, similar to its position on free speech. In *New York Times* v. *United States* (1971), the Court ruled that the U.S. government could not prevent newspapers from publishing portions of the Pentagon Papers, secret government documents revealing the sordid story of how the United States had become involved in the Vietnam War. A major expansion of freedom of the press in *New York Times* v. *Sullivan* (1964) protects newspapers against punishment for trivial or incidental errors when they are reporting on public persons. This limits the use or threat of libel prosecutions by officials because officials can recover damages only by showing that the medium has purposely reported untruths or has made no effort to find out if what is being reported is true.

Offensive Mass Media   The limits of freedom of expression are often tested by media publications that offend many Americans. Pornography, for example, has challenged the ability of citizens, legislatures, and courts to distinguish art from trash that degrades human beings. Typically, communities and legislatures have tried to regulate or eliminate pornography, while civil liberties lawyers and courts have tried to leave choices up to consumers and the market.

WEB EXPLORATION

"Outrages"

Issue: One of the marks of freedom in the United States is the degree to which First Amendment "watchdogs" are on the alert for violations of civil liberties.

Site: Access the Freedom Forum's "Outrage of the Week" online through the "Course Documents" section of your online course. Go to the "Web Explorations" section for Chapter 15, click on "Outrages," and open "outrages." Look at the "Outrage of the Week" and the section "and Still Outraged by . . ."

What You've Learned: Do you agree that the postings at this site are worthy of the term *outrage*? How serious are the purported violations of liberty reported here? Do the descriptions strike you as factual and informative? Or lurid and inflammatory? Are you outraged or simply annoyed?

HINT: Your degree of outrage may depend on whether you believe the case under review belongs in a court or whether it might be settled by neighbors, relatives, or friends of the disputants.

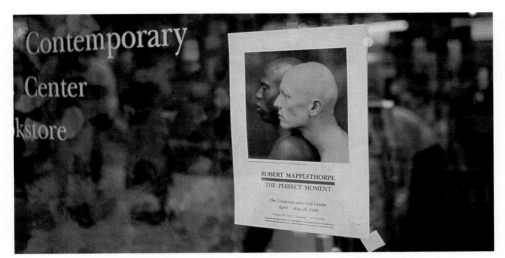

The distinction between art and obscenity can be very difficult to establish, and battles over the banning of controversial works, such as Robert Mapplethorpe's homoerotic photographs, are quite common in American communities.

Pornography is a nonlegal term for sexual materials: the legal term is **obscenity**. Although the courts have held that *obscenity* is unprotected by the First Amendment, the definition of obscenity has provoked constitutional struggles for half a century. Early disputes concerned the importation and mailing of works that we regard today as classics: James Joyce's *Ulysses* and D. H. Lawrence's *Lady Chatterley's Lover,* for example.[10] Although the justices admitted that principled distinctions sometimes eluded them (Justice Potter Stewart once said that he did not know how to define hard-core pornography but that he knew it when he saw it), a reasonably clear three-part test emerged from *Miller* v. *California* (1973):

obscenity

As defined by the Supreme Court, the representation of sexually explicit material in a manner that violates community standards and is without redeeming social importance or value.

1. The average person, applying contemporary community standards, must find that the work as a whole appeals to the prurient interest (lust).

2. The state law must specifically define what sexual conduct is obscene.

3. The work as a whole must lack serious literary, artistic, political, or scientific value.

If the work survives even one part of this test, it is not legally obscene and cannot be regulated under the First Amendment. Community standards, applied by juries, are used to judge whether the work appeals to lust and whether the work is clearly offensive. However, literary, artistic, political, and scientific value (called the *LAPS test,* after the first letter of each of the four values) is *not* judged by community standards but by the jury's assessment of the testimony of expert witnesses. If, and only if, all three standards are met, the Supreme Court will allow local committees to regulate the sale of pornographic materials.

Some feminist activists have attempted to broaden the term *obscenity* to include any communication that degrades women. Activists Andrea Dworkin and Catherine MacKinnon, for example, composed feminist antipornography ordinances that were enacted in Minneapolis and Indianapolis. Such ordinances define pornography as a denial of women's equality, creating a clash between the civil rights of women and the freedom of sellers to sell and buyers to buy pornography. In *American Booksellers Association* v. *Hudnut* (1985), U.S. Judge Sarah Evans Barker found the Indianapolis ordinance a clear violation of freedom of expression. Since the definition of *pornography* in the ordinance went far beyond the constitutional definition of *obscenity* in the *Miller* test, Judge Barker ruled that the ordinance was unconstitutional.

Recently, many Americans have begun to worry about the availability to minors of sexually offensive material on the Internet. Responding to this concern, Congress and President Clinton cooperated in 1996 to pass the Communications Decency Act, which made it a crime to transmit over the Internet or to allow the transmission of indecent materials to which minors might have access. The Supreme Court, in *Reno, Attorney General of the United States* v. *American Civil Liberties Union* (1997), ruled unanimously that the legislation was an unconstitutional violation of the First Amendment, being overly broad and vague and violative of the free speech rights of adults to receive and send information. The strong and unambiguous words of the opinion of the Court make it clear that government efforts to regulate the content of the Internet will not get very far. It may well be the case, however, that Internet-filtering software that allows parents to keep objectionable material from their children will accomplish the same end as government regulation without danger of violating the Constitution.

Free Exercise of Religion

Congress shall make no law . . . prohibiting the free exercise [of religion].
—FIRST AMENDMENT TO THE U.S. CONSTITUTION

For much of our history, Congress did not impede the exercise of religion because it did not legislate much on the subject. Since the states were not covered by the First Amendment, the free exercise of religion was protected by state constitutions or not at all. The Supreme Court was content to defer to the states on issues of religious freedom.

As late as 1940, in *Minersville School District* v. *Gobitis,* the Supreme Court upheld the expulsion of two schoolchildren who refused to salute the flag

---

WEB EXPLORATION

Disputes About Religious Freedom

Issue: Americans continue to disagree with one another about the meaning of religious freedom.

Site: Access the Christian Coalition and Americans United for the Separation of Church and State online through the "Course Documents" section of your online course. Go to the "Web Explorations" section for Chapter 15, click on "Disputes About Religious Freedom," and open "religious freedom." Examine the Coalition's "news releases" section and Americans United's "press releases."

What You've Learned: Compare which issues each organization focuses upon and how the issues are treated by each. Which site is closer to your own understanding of religious freedom? Do you believe there is common ground upon which the two groups might meet, or do you believe that the differences in view are irreconcilable?

HINT: Your views on religious freedom probably depend not only on your specific religious views but upon your support for the doctrine of "separation of church and state."

because it violated their faith as Jehovah's Witnesses. Justice Harlan Stone wrote a stinging dissent:

> The Constitution expresses more than the conviction of the people that democratic processes must be preserved at all costs. It is also an expression of faith and a command that freedom of mind and spirit must be preserved, which government must obey, if it is to adhere to that justice and moderation without which no free government can exist.

Stone's dissent, as well as a series of decisions deferring to state restrictions on Jehovah's Witnesses in 1941 and 1942, eventually moved other justices to Stone's side. In *West Virginia* v. *Barnette* (1943), the Court reversed *Gobitis* and firmly established free exercise of religion as protected against the states.

The core of the nationalized **free exercise clause** today is that government may not interfere with religious *beliefs*. This is one of the few absolutes in U.S. constitutional law. Religious *actions,* however, are not absolutely protected. The Court has upheld state laws, for instance, outlawing the use of peyote (an illegal hallucinogen) in Native American religious ceremonies (*Employment Division* v. *Smith,* 1990). Congress and President Clinton tried to overturn this decision with the Religious Freedom Restoration Act in 1993, but the Act was declared unconstitutional in *City of Boerne* v. *Flores* (1997) because the Act, in view of the Court majority, unduly extended national government power over the states.

free exercise clause

That portion of the First Amendment to the Constitution that prohibits Congress from impeding religious observance or impinging upon religious beliefs.

Establishment of Religion

Congress shall make no law respecting an establishment of religion.
—FIRST AMENDMENT TO THE U.S. CONSTITUTION

Freedom of conscience requires that government not favor one religion over another by granting it special favors, privileges, or status. It requires, in Jefferson's famous terms, "a wall of separation between church and state." Nevertheless, incorporation of the **establishment clause** proved to be a particularly messy matter. In *Everson* v. *Board of Education* (1947), Justice Hugo Black for the Supreme Court determined that no state could use revenues to support an institution that taught religion, thus incorporating the First Amendment ban into the Fourteenth Amendment. But the majority in that case upheld the New Jersey program that reimbursed parents for bus transportation to parochial schools. A year later, Justice Black wrote another opinion incorporating the establishment clause in *McCollum* v. *Board of Education* (1948). This time, a program for teaching religion in public schools was found unconstitutional. In *Zorach* v. *Clauson* (1952), however, the Court upheld a similar program in New York State that let students leave school premises early for religious instruction. The establishment clause had been incorporated, but the justices were having a difficult time determining what "separation of church and state" meant in practice.

establishment clause

The part of the First Amendment to the Constitution that prohibits Congress from establishing an official religion; the basis for the doctrine of the separation of church and state.

The *Lemon* Test   The Warren Court (1953–1969) brought together a solid church-state separationist contingent whose decisions the early Burger Court (1969–1973) distilled into the major doctrine of the establishment clause: the "*Lemon* test." In *Lemon* v. *Kurtzman* (1971), Chief Justice Warren Burger specified three conditions that every law must meet to avoid "establishing" religion:

1. The law must have a secular *purpose*. That secular purpose need not be the only or primary purpose behind the law. The Court requires merely some plausible nonreligious reason for the law.

2. The *primary effect* of the law must be neither to advance nor to retard religion. The Court will assess the probable effect of a governmental action for religious neutrality.

3. Government must never foster *excessive entanglements* between the state and religion.

While lawyers and judges frequently disagree about each of the three "prongs" of the *Lemon* test, the test has erected substantial walls that bar mixing church and state. The Rehnquist Court has been taking some of the bricks out of the walls, however. In *Rosenberger* v. *University of Virginia* (1995), it ruled that the university (a state-supported institution) must provide the same financial subsidy to a student religious publication that it provides to other student publications.

School Prayer and Creation Science   One of the most controversial aspects of constitutional law regarding the establishment of religion concerns school prayer. Although a majority of Americans supports allowing a nondenominational prayer or a period of silent prayer in the schools, the Court has consistently ruled against such practices since the early 1960s. In *Engel* v. *Vitale* (1962), the Court ordered the state of New York to suspend its requirement that all students in public schools recite a nondenominational prayer at the start of each school day. Writing for the majority, Justice Hugo Black found the prayer requirement to be a state-sponsored religious activity "wholly inconsistent with the establishment clause." In *Stone* v. *Graham* (1980), the Court ruled against posting the Ten Commandments in public school classrooms. In *Lee* v. *Weisman* (1992), it ruled against allowing school-sponsored prayer at graduation ceremonies. In *Santa Fe Independent School District* v. *Doe* (2000), the Court ruled that student-led prayers at school-sponsored events such as football games are not constitutionally permissible because they have the "improper effect of coercing those present to participate in an act of religious worship." In these and other cases the Court has consistently ruled against officially sponsored prayer in public schools as a violation of the separation of church and state. The Court has been willing, however, to allow religious groups to meet in public schools

Many school districts still allow religious observations in classrooms, despite a long string of Supreme Court decisions defining such practices as a violation of the doctrine of the separation of church and state.

and to allow students to pray on their own or in unofficial study groups while on public school premises.

Returning prayer to the public schools and making them less secular are very high on the agenda of Christian conservatives. Bills supporting voluntary classroom prayer (such as a moment of silent contemplation) are constantly being introduced into Congress and state legislatures, with little success so far. Christian conservatives have also tried without success to pass a school prayer constitutional amendment. In several very religious communities, school officials have simply ignored the Supreme Court and continue to allow prayer in public classrooms. Giving creation science equal footing with scientific theories of evolution is high on the agenda of many religious groups. In 1999, the school board of the state of Kansas, for example, decided to deemphasize evolution in the curriculum and testing in its high schools. The policy was overturned, however, when voters in 2000 removed "creationists" from the State Board of Education.

With no sign that the tide of religious feeling is about to recede in the United States, school prayer and creation science, and the question of where to draw the line between church and state in general, are likely to be with us for some time to come.

Unstated Rights

The freedoms addressed so far—speech, press, and religion—are explicitly mentioned in the Bill of Rights. The freedom to be left alone in our private lives—what is usually referred to as the *right to privacy*—is nowhere mentioned. Nevertheless, most Americans consider the right to privacy one of our most precious freedoms; most believe we ought to be spared wiretapping, e-mail snooping, and the regulation of consensual sexual activities in our own homes, for instance. Many (though not all) constitutional scholars believe, moreover, that a right to privacy is *inherent* (not explicitly stated) in the Bill of Rights; note the prohibitions against illegal searches and seizures and against quartering of troops in our

LongmanParticipate

CourseCompass

participation
**The Court and
School Prayer**

LongmanParticipate

CourseCompass

participation
**Protect Your
Online Privacy**

WEB EXPLORATION

Privacy and the Internet

Issue: The spread of the Internet raises new privacy issues.

Site: Access the Electronic Frontier Foundation through the "Course Documents" section of your online course. Go to the "Web Explorations" section for Chapter 15, click on "Privacy and the Internet," and open "privacy." Select the section "Top 12 ways to protect your on-line privacy."

What You've Learned: From this listing, figure out what the Electronic Frontier Foundation believes to be the major sources of snooping. Are the perceived threats mainly from government or from the private sector, whether organizations or businesses? Do you agree with the Electronic Frontier Foundation about where threats to privacy might come from? Do you believe that the Constitution protects you from such invasions?

HINT: Privacy is not explicitly mentioned in the Bill of Rights, although many legal scholars and jurists believe that it is implicit. Regardless, the Bill of Rights is aimed at intrusions on freedom by government.

homes, as well as the right to free expression and conscience. Such scholars also point to the Ninth Amendment as evidence that the framers believed in the existence of liberties not specifically mentioned in the Bill of Rights: "The enumeration in the Constitution of certain rights, shall not be construed to deny or disparage others retained by the people." The Supreme Court agreed with this position in *Griswold* v. *Connecticut* (1965), in which it ruled that a constitutional right to privacy exists when it struck down laws making birth control illegal.

Some advocates of the right to privacy see a growing peril in the ability of the new information technology to collect and make accessible a vast amount of data about each and every American. Under a new law designed to root out "deadbeat" dads—fathers who owe child support payments—the federal government, for example, has begun to operate a computerized directory showing every person newly hired by every employer in the country. Federal officials say it will be one of the largest, most up-to-date, and most detailed files of personal information kept by the government.[11]

It is relatively unclear yet whether the courts will support a privacy-based "right to die." So far the Supreme Court has refused to endorse the existence of such a right. Indeed, in *Vacco* v. *Quill* (1997), it threw out two federal circuit court decisions that had overturned state laws in Washington and New York banning doctor-assisted suicide as unconstitutional. The Court majority ruled that states were free to ban doctor-assisted suicide because there is no constitutionally protected right to die. Their ruling did not prohibit states from passing laws establishing such a right, however. Indeed, five of the justices suggested in their written opinions that they might support a claim for the existence of such a right in the future. Justice Sandra Day O'Connor suggested in her written opinion that she would support assisted suicide for dying persons in great pain, and she was joined by Justices Ruth Bader Ginsburg and Stephen G. Breyer. Justices John Paul Stevens and David Souter wrote separate opinions saying they could imagine certain circumstances where "hastening death . . . might be entitled to constitutional protection."

LongmanParticipate

CourseCompass

timeline
**The History
of the
Right to Privacy**

LongmanParticipate

CourseCompass

simulation
**You Are a
Young Lawyer**

Rights of the Accused

Most Americans treasure the constitutional rights and liberties that protect innocent individuals from wrongful prosecution and imprisonment. But most Americans also want to control crime as much as possible. Balancing the two sentiments is not easy. Those alarmed by lawlessness—actual or imagined—tend to support "whatever it takes" to reduce that lawlessness, even if the rights or liberties of others must be restricted. Others are more alarmed by the lawlessness—real or imagined—of police and prosecutors. These advocates of due process values see violations of rights and liberties as unnecessary and dangerous in a free society.

During the 1950s and 1960s, the Warren Court favored the due process approach and subjected the states' criminal procedures to rigorous interpretations of constitutional guarantees. Increased protections for criminal defendants, however, gave many political candidates an electorally useful explanation for rising crime: too much regard for "legal technicalities" was "coddling" the guilty and "handcuffing" the police. Republican presidential candidates Nixon, Ford, Reagan, and Bush all promised to appoint federal court judges who would be more sympathetic to crime control and less insistent on protecting the rights of suspects and defendants. One result of Republican domination of the White House between 1968 and 1993 is that a majority of federal judges have been appointed by presidents who "ran against the courts" on the issue of criminal procedure. A gradual but important shift to a higher regard for crime control than for due process has followed from electoral politics and has reshaped constitutional interpretation.

The shift is obvious in the decisions of the Supreme Court. The Warren Court (1953–1969) expanded due process, preferring constitutional guarantees to efficient law enforcement. The Burger Court (1969–1986) preserved most of the basic due process decisions that the Warren Court had crafted but limited the further growth of protections and introduced many exceptions. The Rehnquist Court (1986–present) has reversed some due process protections.

Unreasonable Searches and Seizures   Consider, for example, the Fourth Amendment, which secures the right of all persons against unreasonable searches and seizures and allows the granting of search warrants only if the police can specify evidence of serious lawbreaking that they reasonably expect to find. Until the Warren Court compelled the states to abide by the Fourth Amendment in 1961, they had frequently used searches and seizures that the federal courts would consider "unreasonable" in an effort to control crime.

In *Mapp* v. *Ohio* (1961), the Supreme Court enunciated the **exclusionary rule** to prevent the police and prosecutors from using evidence that had been gained through warrantless and unreasonable searches to convict people. In this case, the police forcibly entered the apartment of Dollree Mapp looking for a fugitive. They found no fugitive but decided to search Mapp's apartment anyway, even though they had no search warrant. Finding what they considered obscene photos and books, they arrested Mapp under Ohio's law covering the possession of obscene materials. She was convicted, an action later supported by the Ohio Supreme Court. The conviction was overturned by the U.S. Supreme Court. A majority of the justices believed that the threat of perpetrators' being

exclusionary rule
A standard promulgated by the Supreme Court that prevents police and prosecutors from using evidence against a defendant that was obtained in an illegal search.

The right to due process was incorporated into the Constitution from the outset, but it was the Supreme Court's *Miranda* decision in 1966 that required law enforcement officials to inform the accused of their rights at the time of arrest.

freed in cases like this would force the police to play by the constitutional rules. The justices did not believe that due process threatened crime control because police lawlessness was not the only way to deal with crime.

The Warren Court demanded that the police get warrants whenever the person to be subjected to a search had a "reasonable expectation of privacy."[12] The Burger Court limited the places in which privacy could be reasonably expected, allowing searches of moving cars stopped even for routine traffic infractions and of garbage cans set out for collection. The Burger Court authorized a "good faith" exception to the exclusionary rule, under which prosecutors may introduce evidence obtained illegally if they can show that the police had relied on a warrant that appeared valid but later proved to be invalid.[13] The Court allowed another exception for illegally gathered evidence that would have been discovered eventually without the illegal search.[14] The Rehnquist Court has gone well beyond these exceptions. In *Murray* v. *United States* (1988), it allowed prosecutors to use products of illegal searches if other evidence unrelated to the illegal evidence would have justified a search warrant. The combination of "good faith," "inevitable discovery," and "retroactive probable cause" has considerably narrowed the exclusionary rule.

The Rehnquist Court continued to narrow the exclusionary rule when it held in *Minnesota* v. *Carter* (1998) that an officer acting on a drug tip could peer through the gap in Venetian blinds to observe illegal activity without violating the Fourth Amendment. When the Court announced in *Wyoming* v. *Houghton* (1999) that police who have probable cause to search an automobile for illegal substances may also search personal possessions (in this case, a purse) of passengers in the car, the War on Drugs seemed to be trumping privacy. However, the Court also ruled that police could not search every driver or car involved in petty traffic offenses. Thus, a bag of marijuana discovered in a search incident to a speeding ticket in *Knowles* v. *Iowa* (1998) was excluded as the product of an illegal search. These three cases show that the fine-tuning of the "exclusionary rule" continues.

Self-Incrimination   Concerning the Fifth Amendment protection against self-incrimination, the Warren Court similarly waxed, the Burger Court waffled, and the Rehnquist Court waned. The Warren Court determined that the privilege not to be forced to incriminate oneself was useless at trial if the police coerced confessions long before the trial took place. To forestall "third-degree" tactics in the station house, the Court detailed a stringent set of procedural guarantees: the famous rights established in *Miranda* v. *Arizona* (1966). Once detained by authorities, all persons had to be informed of their rights to remain silent and to consult with an attorney. Although the Burger Court upheld *Miranda,* it allowed exceptions: it allowed the use of information obtained without "Mirandizing" suspects if the suspects took the stand in their own defense. It also allowed the use of information obtained without *Miranda* warnings if some immediate threat to public safety had justified immediate questioning and postponing warnings.[15] The Rehnquist Court has gone beyond these exceptions in holding that a coerced confession may be "harmless error" that does not constitute self-incrimination.[16] The main principle of the Miranda decision was upheld by the Rehnquist Court, however, in *Dickerson* v. *United States* (2000).

The Right to Counsel   The Sixth Amendment's right to counsel was nationalized—made binding on the states—in two landmark cases. In *Powell* v. *Alabama* (1932)—the famed Scottsboro Boys prosecution—the Court ruled that legal counsel must be supplied to all indigent defendants accused of a **capital**

LongmanParticipate

CourseCompass

simulation
**You Are
the Police Officer**

capital crime

Any crime for which death is a possible penalty.

crime (any crime in which the death penalty can be imposed). Before this decision, many poor people in the southern states, especially African-Americans, had been tried for and convicted of capital crimes without the benefit of an attorney. Thirty-one years later, in *Gideon* v. *Wainwright* (1963), the Court ruled that defendants accused of any felony in state jurisdictions are entitled to a lawyer and that the states must supply a lawyer when a defendant cannot afford to do so. In this case, Clarence Earl Gideon asked for but was denied a lawyer in a Florida court where he was being tried for having broken into a poolhall. He conducted his own defense and lost. After years of study in his Florida prison's law library and the submission of numerous handwritten appeals to the courts to overturn his conviction, the Supreme Court finally agreed to hear his case, assigning the prominent attorney Abe Fortas (later a Supreme Court justice) to argue for Gideon. Justice Black wrote the following for a unanimous Court:

> Not only . . . precedents but also reason and reflection require us to recognize that in our adversary system of criminal justice, any person hauled into court, who is too poor to hire a lawyer, cannot be assured of a fair trial unless counsel is provided for him. This seems to be an obvious truth.

The Court ordered a new trial. This time, assisted by a public defender supplied by the state of Florida, Gideon was acquitted. By incorporating the Sixth Amendment's guarantee of legal counsel, the Court has ensured that every criminal defendant in the United States can mount a defense regardless of socioeconomic status.

Capital Punishment   The Burger Court examined capital punishment under the Eighth Amendment's prohibition of "cruel and unusual punishment." In *Furman* v. *Georgia* (1972), a split Court found that the death penalty, as used, constituted "cruel and unusual punishment." Congress and 70 percent of the states passed new authorizations of the death penalty, most of which met the Court's objections with procedures to make the infliction of capital punishment less capricious. The Burger Court held that capital punishment was not inherently cruel or unusual in *Gregg* v. *Georgia* (1976). However, the Court tended to create an "obstacle course" of standards that the states had to meet if they wanted to use the death penalty. Basically, the Court insisted that defendants be given every opportunity to show mitigating circumstances so that as few convicts as possible would be killed.

LongmanParticipate

CourseCompass

comparative
**Comparing
Civil Liberties**

The Rehnquist Court has tried to expedite the use of the death penalty. (Some of the reasons are examined in the "Using the Framework" feature.) In *McCleskey* v. *Kemp* (1987), the Court chose to ignore statistical evidence that blacks who kill whites are four times more likely to be sentenced to death than whites who kill blacks. The Court insisted that individual defendants must show that racism played a role in their specific cases. In *Penry* v. *Lynaugh* (1989), the Court allowed the execution of a convicted murderer who had the intelligence of a 7-year-old. In *Stanford* v. *Kentucky* (1989), the Court allowed the execution of a minor who had been convicted of murder.

Chief Justice Rehnquist and some of his colleagues have also worked hard to expedite executions by limiting avenues of appeal and delay. In *McCleskey* v. *Zant* (1991), the Court made delays much less likely by eliminating many means of challenging capital convictions. In its 6–3 decision, the majority reached out to eliminate delays even though no party to the case had requested the Court to do so. In *Keeney* v. *Tamayo-Reyes* (1992), the Court limited the right of "death row" inmates convicted in state courts to appeal to the Supreme

USING THE FRAMEWORK

Why Has There Been a Dramatic Increase in the Number of Death Sentences Carried Out in the United States?

Between the reinstatement of the death penalty by the Supreme Court in 1976 and the end of 1999, 596 inmates were executed in the United States. Of that total, 478 (80 percent) took place in the 1990s. In 1999, 98 executions were carried out, the highest total since 1951, with Texas, Virginia, and Florida leading the way. Although a range of individuals and organizations have been fighting to end the use of the death penalty in the United States, their efforts have been strikingly unsuccessful. We can understand better why this is so by looking broadly at how structural, political linkage, and governmental factors have influenced the death penalty issue.

Governmental Action

38 states allow use of the death penalty; of these, 30 have used it since 1976.

The pace of executions increased steadily during the 1990s.

Governmental Level

- Since 1976, the Supreme Court has supported most state efforts to reinstate the death penalty and to limit the time and number of appeals for death-row inmates.

- The Anti-Terrorism and Effective Death Penalty Act of 1996, passed by a Republican Congress and signed by Democratic president Bill Clinton, placed limits on the appeals process and hastened the execution of many inmates.

- Elected on "get tough on crime" platforms, few governors responded favorably to requests for clemency in death penalty cases.

Political Linkages Level

- Public opinion strongly supports the principle of capital punishment.

- Fear of crime among the public rose throughout the 1980s and 1990s, contributing to the supportive public climate for use of the death penalty; rising fear was a response to both a real increase in violent crime and to mass media sensationalism.

- In response to the public mood during this period, most candidates for elected office took a strong "tough on crime" approach.

- Opponents of capital punishment were not successful in changing public or leadership attitudes.

Structural Level

- The Constitution leaves most of the responsibilty for criminal statute writing, prosecution, and punishment to the states.

- The Constitution prohibits "cruel and unusual punishment," but there is little evidence that the framers considered the death penalty, as such, "cruel and unusual."

- The popular culture has long supported the death penalty.

- Violent crime, much of it drug-related, increased during the 1970s, 1980s, and early part of the 1990s.

The execution by the state of Texas of born-again Christian and convicted murderer Karla Faye Tucker in February 1998 brought the issue of capital punishment to the forefront of network news, news magazines, radio talk shows, and newspapers across America. Tucker was the first woman executed in Texas since the Civil War.

Court. The Court is never entirely predictable, however. In *Wright* v. *West* (1992), it rejected Bush administration efforts to sharply restrict appeals by state prisoners to the federal courts.

The environment for the use of the death penalty has become steadily more favorable in recent decades. The Court has removed most of the obstacles to its use, and public opinion is solidly in favor, though there has been some erosion in the last few years (see Figure 15.1). It is hardly surprising, then, that the number of people executed in the United States in 1999 reached its highest level since 1976 when the Court reinstated the death penalty, with Texas accounting for more than one-third of the total.[17]

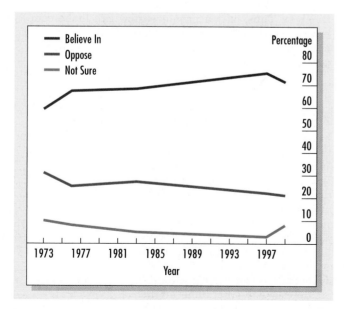

Figure 15.1 ● American Public Opinion on the Death Penalty

Question: Do you believe in capital punishment, that is the death penalty, or are you opposed to it?
Source: Louis Harris and Associates, as reported in *Public Perspective* (October/November 1999), p. 42.

Despite such momentum to expedite executions, the public and many state officials, while still in favor of capital punishment in principle, are having second thoughts about the fairness of its application in practice (a Columbia University study reports that two of every three capital convictions have been overturned on appeal since 1976). At least a dozen state legislatures are considering bills to eliminate or restrict capital punishment. On January 31, 2000, Gov. George Ryan of Illinois stopped all executions in his state system because at least 13 men on death row in Illinois had been shown to have not committed the crimes for which they were sentenced to death. Governor Ryan claimed that he would maintain his moratorium until he could be certain that everyone on death row was truly guilty. Many commentators saluted the moderate Republican's courage, but it remains to be seen how many officials and politicians will follow his example. Interestingly, Texas Gov. (and GOP presidential candidate) George W. Bush stayed an execution in 2000 to allow more time to gather and consider new DNA evidence.

HOW DEMOCRATIC ARE WE?

PROPOSITION: One reason that democracy is alive and well in the United States is that civil liberties are so well developed and protected.

AGREE: Citizens of the United States live in the freest political society in the world. Powerful constraints prevent government from intruding upon people's ability to believe what they want and to exercise their rights of free expression, association, and petition. Although government has violated several of these rights in the past, political practices and Supreme Court decisions have greatly expanded the domain of political freedom in the current era and made violation of basic civil liberties unlikely in the future.

DISAGREE: Although civil liberties today are fairly well protected against intrusions by government, not all people have the capacities and resources to use their liberties effectively. All Americans may enjoy freedom of expression as a formal right, for example, but only a handful can make their voices heard in an effective way. Thus, only a privileged few can make campaign contributions; form political lobbying organizations; and run ads for their favorite candidates, parties, and issues.

THE AUTHORS: It is important to recognize that the freedoms of speech, association, press, conscience, and religion are far more extensively developed and protected in the United States today than they were in the past. There has, in fact, been an enormous expansion of freedom in the United States. However, we must also recognize two "flies in the ointment," as it were. First, the "disagree" position cannot be easily evaded. While formal freedom is available to virtually all Americans, the actual use of several of our civil liberties requires resources that are not available to all. Thus, substantial income and wealth inequality in the United States often creates political inequality. Second, we cannot say with total confidence that freedom cannot and will not be violated by government in the future. Waves of hysteria in the past among political leaders and citizens have led to the violation of civil liberties; given the right conditions—say, war, civil unrest, economic depression—the same might happen again. We can only hope that such a thing will not happen and that people will struggle for democracy if it does.

Summary

The formal foundation of American liberties is found in the Constitution and its amendments, particularly the Bill of Rights and the Fourteenth Amendment, but their actual enjoyment depends on the actions of courts, the behavior of government officials, and the struggle for democracy. American history has witnessed an expansion of the boundaries of liberties, especially during the twentieth century, although much remains to be done.

During the nineteenth century, the Supreme Court concerned itself mainly with rights to property. Somewhat belatedly, it nationalized the constitutional protection of civil liberties (that is, made them applicable to the states) by using the Fourteenth Amendment as its main instrument. The familiar liberties of expression, association, press, and religion, as well as certain due process protections for the accused, were gradually incorporated and guaranteed throughout the nation. The expansion of the rights of the accused was always a hotly disputed political issue, and the conservative orientation of the present Court has resulted in the reversal of many of the due process innovations of the Warren and Burger Courts.

Suggestions for Further Reading

Abraham, Henry J., and Barbara A. Perry. *Freedom and the Court,* 7th ed. New York: Oxford University Press, 1998.
   A trusted introduction to the study of civil rights and liberties for 25 years.

Hentoff, Nat. *Free Speech for Me . . . but Not for Thee: How the American Left and Right Relentlessly Censor Each Other.* New York: HarperPerennial, 1992.
   A disturbing survey of efforts across the nation by both the right and left to censor speech and publications they do not like.

Holmes, Stephen, and Cass R. Sunstein. *The Cost of Rights: Why Liberty Depends on Taxes.* New York: W. W. Norton & Company, 1999.
   An intriguing, novel argument about why rights and liberties are expensive and thus why more rights mean more taxation.

Irons, Peter. *The Courage of Their Convictions.* New York: Free Press, 1988.
   Brief histories of U.S. Supreme Court cases involved in the struggle for civil rights and civil liberties sine 1940.

Lane, Rovet Wheeler. *Beyond the Schoolhouse Gate: Free Speech and the Inculcation of Values.* Philadelphia: Temple University Press, 1995.
   A response, based on educational and constitutional grounds, to those who would censor students in public schools.

Walker, Samuel. *In Defense of American Liberties: A History of the ACLU.* New York: Oxford University Press, 1990.
   A comprehensive review of the American Civil Liberties Union, highlighting most major battles for civil liberties in the twentieth century.

Internet Sources

First Amendment Cyber-Tribune   **http://w3.trib.com/FACT/index.html**
   This site is so complete and well organized that it is the only one recommended in this chapter. This gateway is concerned with each of the First Amendment freedoms discussed in this chapter and provides links for each freedom to background documents, court cases, breaking news, op-ed pieces, bibliographies, First Amendment Web sites, civil liberties organizations, and even an online question-and-answer section.

Notes

1. The first four examples were cited in George F. Will, "Compassion on Campus," *Newsweek* (May 31, 1993), p. 66.

2. Kenneth Lasson, "Political Correctness," *Tennessee Law Review* 63 (Spring, 1996), p. 32.

3. Nat Hentoff, "Chilling Codes," *Washington Post,* Nexis: LEGI-SLATE Article No. 225/226.

4. Laurence H. Tribe, *American Constitutional Law,* 2nd ed. (Mineola, NY: Cornell Law Foundation, 1988), ch. 9.

5. Morton J. Horwitz, *The Transformation of American Law, 1780–1860* (Cambridge, MA: Harvard University Press, 1977); J. Willard Hurst, *Law and the Conditions of Freedom in the Nineteenth-Century United States* (Madison, WI: University of Wisconsin Press, 1956).

6. Robert A. Dahl, "Decision-Making in a Democracy: The Supreme Court as National Policy-Maker," *Journal of Public Law* 6 (1967), pp. 279–295.

7. Samuel Walker, *In Defense of American Liberties: A History of the ACLU* (New York: Oxford University Press, 1990).

8. See Stanley I. Kutler, *The American Inquisition: Justice and Injustice in the Cold War* (New York: Hill & Wang, 1982).

9. See Fred W. Friendly, *Minnesota Rag* (New York: Vintage, 1981).

10. See Charles Rembar, *The End of Obscenity* (New York: Harper & Row, 1968).

11. Robert Pear, "U.S. Inaugurating a Vast Database of All New Hires," *New York Times* (September 20, 1997), p. A1.

12. *Katz* v. *United States* (1967).

13. *United States* v. *Leon* (1984); *Massachusetts* v. *Sheppard* (1984).

14. *Nix* v. *Williams* (1984).

15. *Harris* v. *New York* (1971); *New York* v. *Quarles* (1984).

16. *Arizona* v. *Fulminate* (1991).

17. Jim Yardley, "A Role Model for Executions," *New York Times* (January 9, 2000), p. A1, IV-5.

CHAPTER 16

Civil Rights: The Struggle for Political Equality

IN THIS CHAPTER

- Why civil rights are important in a democracy
- Civil rights in the Constitution
- How civil rights protections expanded
- The present status of civil rights protections for racial minorities, women, and gays and lesbians

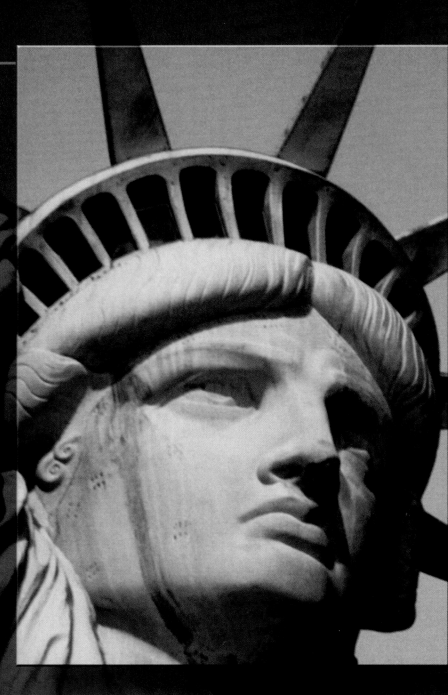

From Martin Luther King to Louis Farrakhan

On August 28, 1963, approximately half a million people converged on the Lincoln Memorial in Washington, D.C., to urge passage of the civil rights bill then being considered by Congress. The gathering was predominantly African-American, but a substantial number of whites were there as well to lend support. The crowd was festive and optimistic. Most who were there believed that Congress had no choice but to pass the civil rights bill because Americans were now ready to accept a fully integrated society without significant barriers to black and white cooperation or to black advancement and equality. The mood of the historic "March on Washington" was perfectly captured by Dr. Martin Luther King Jr. in his memorable "I Have a Dream" speech.

Three decades later, approximately 600,000 African-American men gathered in front of the U.S. Capitol building on a beautiful October day in 1995 in response to a call from Louis Farrakhan, the leader of the Nation of Islam. His "Million Man March" was designed, he said, to encourage self-reliance and responsibility among African-American men. Although few of the attendees said they supported Farrakhan's overall program of racial separatism, anti-Semitism, and hostility to gays and lesbians, three aspects of the event were striking: that so many people responded to the call of a man long regarded as being on the extreme "black nationalist" fringe of American politics, that traditional civil rights organizations had not displayed for many years an equivalent ability to mobilize the African-American population, and that women and white men were conspicuously absent on the speakers' platform and in the crowd.

The Million Man March, with its sometimes harsh separatist temper, reflected the uncertain climate for civil rights in the nation as a whole in the mid-1990s compared with the headier times of the mid-1960s. Long gone was the biracial political coalition that had achieved passage of the 1964 Civil Rights Act and the 1965 Voting Rights Act. Also gone was the optimism about the future of race relations and the

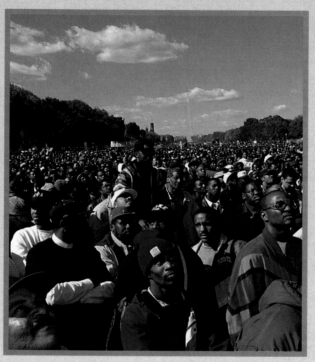

possibilities for an integrated society that had propelled the civil rights movement. In its place stood racial polarization and isolation and competing visions of what civil rights policies might be most appropriate for the future.

That the racial climate had changed was not in question. In 1994, Republicans swept to a stunning victory in congressional elections, running on a "Contract with America" platform that was silent on the need to make further advances in the area of racial justice and filled with promises that most observers believed would adversely affect African-Americans: cuts in a wide range of social programs, punitive anticrime measures, and termination of federal entitlement programs such as Aid to Families with Dependent Children. In 1995, Gov. Pete Wilson convinced the Regents of the University of California to end all affirmative action programs in the statewide university system. In 1996, President Clinton ordered a broad review of federal affirmative action programs after the Supreme Court ruled in *Adarand Construction* v. *Peña* (1995) that it would subject affirmative action to strict scrutiny (i.e., presume such programs to be unconstitutional unless a compelling government interest could be demonstrated). Also in 1996, California voters approved Proposition 209 to end all government affirmative action programs in the state (which the Supreme Court later approved). Voters in the state of Washington followed suit in 1998.

Civil rights are government guarantees of political equality—the promise of equal treatment by government of all citizens and equal citizenship for all Americans. Civil rights became a more prominent part of the American agenda as democracy itself became more widely accepted in the United States. Because most formal barriers to equal participation in political life have been used to exclude groups of people (women, various ethnic groups, and racial minorities), civil rights initiatives over the years have been directed at removing group barriers and at helping groups overcome the disadvantages created by past discrimination.

The expansion of civil rights protections for African-Americans, as well as for other racial, ethnic, and religious minorities, and for women is one of the great achievements of American history. This expansion did not come easily or quickly; it took the struggle of millions of Americans to force change from political leaders and government institutions. But change happened, and the result has been the enrichment of American democracy. As this opening vignette suggests, however, the expansion of civil rights protection in the United States is neither complete nor free of problems.

▶Thinking Critically About This Chapter

Using the Framework. In this chapter, you will see that the meaning of civil rights has changed over the course of American history and learn how structural, political linkage, and governmental factors, taken together, explain that change.

Using the Democracy Standard. In this chapter, you will learn how civil rights is at the very center of our understanding of democracy in the United States. You will see, on the one hand, how the struggle for democracy helped expand civil rights protections. You will see, on the other hand, how the expansion of civil rights has enhanced formal political equality in the United States, one of the basic foundations of a democratic political order. ▶

Civil Rights Before the Twentieth Century

Concern about civil rights protections for women and racial minorities was a comparatively late development in the United States, and most major advances were not evident until well into the twentieth century.

An Initial Absence of Civil Rights

Neither the original Constitution nor the Bill of Rights said anything about political equality beyond insisting that all Americans are equally entitled to due process in the courts. Indeed, the word *equality* does not appear in the Constitution at all. Nor did state constitutions offer much in the way of guaranteeing citizenship equality other than equality before the law. Americans in

Many African-Americans took an active role in fighting for their civil rights before emancipation. Free blacks helped organize the Underground Railroad to smuggle slaves out of the South.

In 1848, Elizabeth Cady Stanton helped organize the Seneca Falls Convention on women's rights. The resulting Declaration of Sentiments and Resolutions was patterned after the Declaration of Independence, stating that "all men and women are created equal," and included a list of the injustice of men against women.

the late eighteenth and early nineteenth centuries seemed more interested in protecting individuals against government (see Chapter 15) than in guaranteeing certain political rights through government.[1] For most racial or ethnic minorities and women, political equality eluded constitutional protection until the twentieth century, although the groundwork was laid earlier.

The political inequality of African-Americans and women before the Civil War is apparent. In the South, African-Americans lived in slavery, with no rights at all. Outside the South, although a few states allowed African-Americans to vote, the number of states doing so actually declined as the Civil

WEB EXPLORATION

The Foundations of Unequal Citizenship

Issue: The Supreme Court was not a friend to equal citizenship claims of African-Americans for much of our history.

Site: You can read about two famous Court decisions regarding the rights of African-Americans at the Oyez Project site at Northwestern University. Access it through the "Course Documents" section of your online course. Go to the "Web Explorations" section for Chapter 16, click on "The Foundations of Unequal Citizenship," and open "court decisions." Select "cases," the "search by subject," then "Discrimination: Race." From the list of cases, select *Dred Scott* v. *Sanford* (1857) and *Plessy* v. *Ferguson* (1896).

What You've Learned: After reading the Abstract of each case, what do you think of the argument that the Supreme Court is the main protector of civil rights in the American system? Can we rely on the Court to do what is right?

HINT: *Dred Scott* affirmed the institution of slavery, and *Plessy* affirmed government-sponsored segregation earlier in our history, but the Court has also changed with the times and with American society.

War approached, even as universal white male suffrage was spreading. In many places outside the slave South, African-Americans were denied entry into certain occupations, required to post bonds guaranteeing their good behavior, denied the right to sit on juries, and occasionally threatened and harassed by mobs when they tried to vote or to petition the government. Chief Justice Roger Taney, in *Dred Scott* v. *Sandford* (1857), went so far as to claim that the Founders believed that blacks had no rights that whites or government were bound to honor or respect. As for women, no state allowed them to vote, few allowed them to sit on juries, and a handful even denied them the right to own property or enter into contracts.

Many African-Americans and women refused to play a passive political role, however, even though the pre–Civil War period was not conducive to their participation in politics. African-Americans, for instance, voted in elections where they were allowed, helped organize the Underground Railroad to smuggle slaves out of the South, and were prominent in the abolitionist movement against slavery. Both black and white women played an important role in the abolitionist movement—the antislavery speaking tours of Angelina and Sarah Grimké caused something of a scandal in the 1840s when women's participation in public affairs was considered improper—and a few began to write extensively on the need for women's emancipation and legal and political equality. In 1848, Elizabeth Cady Stanton issued her call for a convention on women's rights to be held at the village of Seneca Falls, New York. The Declaration of Sentiments and Resolutions issued by the delegates to the convention stands as one of the landmarks in women's struggle for political equality in the United States:

> *All men and women are created equal . . . but the history of mankind is a history of repeated injuries and usurpations on the part of man toward woman, having in direct object the establishment of a direct tyranny over her. . . . [We demand] that women have immediate admission to all the rights and privileges which belong to them as citizens of the United States.*

LongmanParticipate

CourseCompass

timeline
The Fourteenth Amendment

The Civil War Amendments

After the Civil War, the Thirteenth Amendment to the Constitution outlawed slavery throughout the United States, settling the most divisive issue of the nineteenth century. The Fourteenth Amendment reversed *Dred Scott* by making all people who are born or naturalized in the United States, black or white, citizens both of the United States and of the states in which they reside. To secure the rights and liberties of recently freed slaves, Article I of the amendment further provided that "no State shall make or enforce any law which shall abridge the privileges or immunities of citizens of the United States" (the *privileges and immunities clause*); "nor shall any State deprive any person of life, liberty, or property, without due process of law" (the *due process clause*); "nor deny to any person within its jurisdiction the equal protection of the laws" (the *equal protection clause*). The Fifteenth Amendment guaranteed African-American men the right to vote. Imposing as this constitutional language sounds, the Supreme Court would soon transform it into a protection for property rights (as we saw in Chapter 15), but not for African-Americans or women.

Undermining the Civil War Amendments   The privileges and immunities clause was rendered virtually meaningless by the *Slaughterhouse Cases* (1873). Writing for the Court, Justice Samuel Miller found that the clause protected only the rights of citizens of the United States as citizens and not rights that were the responsibility of states. In these cases, the Court denied citizens protection against abuses by state governments, including African-Americans disfranchised by state actions. Within five years of its passage, then, the Fourteenth Amendment had been seriously compromised by the Court, which foiled an attempt by the post–Civil War Radical Republican Congress to amend the Constitution in favor of equality.

The equal protection clause survived the *Slaughterhouse Cases* but soon lost all practical meaning. First, the Court said that the Fourteenth Amendment gave Congress no power to prohibit discrimination unless it was practiced by state government. "Equal protection of the laws" did not, therefore, preclude race discrimination by private owners or managers of restaurants, theaters, hotels, and other public accommodations, the Court said in the *Civil Rights Cases* (1883). Then the Court made even state-sponsored discrimination constitutional in *Plessy* v. *Ferguson* (1896). The Court said that the states could separate the races in intrastate railways if they provided "equal" facilities for the races. This doctrine of "separate but equal" would provide the legal foundation for **Jim Crow** segregation in the South and would remain in force until it was overturned in *Brown* v. *Board of Education of Topeka* more than half a century later.

The Fifteenth Amendment's voting guarantees were rendered ineffectual by a variety of devices invented to prevent African-Americans from voting in the former states of the Confederacy. The **poll tax** was a tax required of all voters in many states, and it kept many African-Americans away from the polls. Even a small tax was a heavy burden for many to bear, given the desperate economic situation of African-Americans in the South in the late nineteenth and early twentieth centuries. Several states required voters to pass a **literacy test** devised and administered by local officials. The evaluation of test results was entirely up to local officials, who rarely passed blacks, even those with a college education or even a Ph.D. degree. If white voters failed the literacy test, many states allowed them to vote anyway under the **grandfather clause**, which provided that anyone whose grandfather had been a voter could vote as well. Since the grandfathers of African-Americans in the South had been slaves, the grandfather clause was no help to them at all. Several states instituted **white primaries** that excluded African-Americans from the process of nominating candidates for local, state, and national offices. The states based these primaries on the argument that political parties were private clubs that could define their own membership requirements, including skin color. For those African-Americans who might try to vote anyway in the face of the poll tax, the literacy test, and the white primary, there was always the use of terror as a deterrent: night riding, bombings, and lynchings were used with regularity, especially during times when blacks showed signs of assertiveness.

The statutory devices for keeping African-Americans away from the polls were consistently supported by state and federal courts until well into the twentieth century. Terror remained a factor until the 1960s, when the civil rights movement (described in detail in Chapter 8) and federal intervention finally put an end to it.

Women and the Fifteenth Amendment   Stung by the exclusion of women from the Fifteenth Amendment's extension of the right to vote to African-Americans—the amendment said only that no state could exclude people on the grounds of "race, color, or previous condition of servitude"—politically active women turned their attention to winning the vote for women. Once the Supreme Court had decided, in *Minor* v. *Happersett* (1874), that women's suffrage was not

Jim Crow

Popular term for the system of legal racial segregation that existed in the American South until the middle of the twentieth century.

poll tax

A tax to be paid as a condition of voting.

literacy test

A device used by the southern states to prevent African-Americans from voting before the passage of the Voting Rights Act of 1965, which banned its use; usually involved interpretation of a section of a state's constitution.

grandfather clause

A device that allowed whites who had failed the literacy test to vote anyway by extending the franchise to anyone whose grandfather had voted.

white primaries

Primary elections open only to whites.

a right inherent in the national citizenship guarantees of the Fourteenth Amendment, women abandoned legal challenges based on their inferior political position and turned to more direct forms of political agitation: petitions, marches, and protests. After many years of struggle, the efforts of the women's suffrage movement bore fruit in the Nineteenth Amendment, ratified in 1920: "The right of citizens of the United States to vote shall not be denied or abridged by the United States or by any State on account of sex." (For more detail on the women's suffrage movement, see the vignette that opens Chapter 8.)

The Contemporary Status of Civil Rights

strict scrutiny

The assumption that actions by elected bodies or officials violate constitutional rights.

We saw in Chapter 15 how the Supreme Court, using the guidelines written by Justice Harlan Fiske Stone in *United States* v. *Carolene Products Company* (1938), gradually extended the protections of the Bill of Rights to the states, based on the Fourteenth Amendment. Recall that among the actions by the states that would trigger **strict scrutiny** were those that either "restricted the democratic process" or "discriminated against racial, ethnic, or religious minorities." This reading of the Fourteenth Amendment, particularly the equal protection clause, lent judicial support to the gradual advance of civil rights guarantees for African-Americans and other minorities and eventually (though less so) for women. In the following sections, we look at the extension of the civil rights of racial minorities, women, and other groups. Here we concentrate mainly (although not exclusively) on Supreme Court decisions (see Chapter 8 for more information on the civil rights, women's, and other movements).

Civil Rights for Racial Minorities

Two basic issues have dominated the story of the extension of civil rights since the mid-1960s:

1. The ending of legal discrimination, separation, and exclusion.
2. The debate over actions to rectify past wrongs.

We examine both in this section.

The End of "Separate but Equal"   We reviewed earlier how the Constitution was long interpreted to condone slavery and segregation. In the twentieth century, however, the legal and political battles waged by the civil rights movement eventually pushed the Supreme Court, the president, and Congress to take seriously the equal protection clause of the Fourteenth Amendment.

In 1944, amid World War II (a war aimed in great part at bringing down the racist regime of Adolf Hitler) and the NAACP's campaign to rid the nation of segregation, the Supreme Court finally declared that race was a **suspect classification** that demanded strict judicial scrutiny. This meant that any state or national enactment using racial criteria was presumed to be unconstitutional. Having declared racial laws suspect, the Court nevertheless decided that the internment of more than 100,000 Japanese-Americans without any due process whatsoever survived strict scrutiny. In *Korematsu* v. *United States* (1944), Justice Hugo Black and the majority deferred to Executive Order 9066 on the basis of the war powers of Congress and the president's prerogative as commander in chief. Because the Supreme Court has often accepted military judgments uncritically, such extreme deference during wartime should perhaps not be very surprising.

suspect classification

The invidious, arbitrary, or irrational designation of a group for special treatment by government.

The erosion of official segregation in education came slowly and reluctantly in many parts of the nation. When ordered by a federal court in 1948 to admit a qualified black applicant, the University of Oklahoma law school did so but forced the lone student to sit separated from other students.

Pressed by the legal efforts of the NAACP, the Court gradually chipped away at *Plessy* and the edifice of segregation (see The Struggle for Democracy box, "The Young Thurgood Marshall," for the story of the NAACP's most important attorney). In *Smith* v. *Allwright* (1944), the Court declared that the practice of excluding nonwhites from political-party primary elections was unconstitutional. Then the Court ruled that the states' practice of providing separate all-white and all-black law schools was unacceptable.

WEB EXPLORATION

The Civil Rights Movement

Issue: The civil rights movement was one of the main forces that changed the citizenship status of African-Americans in the United States.

Site: Access the time line of the modern civil rights movement through the "Course Documents" section of your online course. Go to the "Web Explorations" section for Chapter 16, click on "The Civil Rights Movement," and open "civil rights timeline."

What You've Learned: Taking advantage of the hyperlinks embedded in the time line, examine the profiles of the leading figures in the civil rights movement. In what ways were the leaders of the movement similar to one another? In what ways were they different? What contribution did each make in advancing civil rights?

HINT: Every successful movement has both moderates and radicals who play important, though different, roles.

THE STRUGGLE FOR DEMOCRACY

The Young Thurgood Marshall

*T*hurgood Marshall became one of the nation's most prominent civil rights attorneys, representing Linda Brown and other plaintiffs in Brown v. Board of Education of Topeka, and later a distinguished member of the U.S. Supreme Court. In the following selection, historian William Chafe tells the story of Marshall's early days as a civil rights lawyer in the South, during which he repeatedly risked his life in the struggle for democracy.

During the 1940s Marshall traveled throughout the South, organizing teachers to fight for equal pay, mobilizing parents to insist on equal bus transportation, and enlisting lawyers to risk their practices by standing up for equality. He lived with the people, rarely spending more than a dollar for a meal, never more than two dollars for a room. Wherever he went he built alliances, showing the people he worked with that here was someone they could "travel the river" with. "Everybody loved Thurgood," one NAACP staff officer said, "[he] had the common touch." While previous NAACP leaders had spoken down to the people, another black observed, "Thurgood Marshall was of the people. He knew how to get through to them. Out in Texas or Oklahoma or down the street here in Washington at the Baptist Church, he would make these rousing speeches that would have them all jumping out of their seats."

Marshall's own courage in the face of constant danger became legendary, inspiring others to follow his example. In Tennessee, in the aftermath of the Columbia riot, his car was stopped three times by

police harassing him, trying to scare him away. But Marshall never wavered. As Herbert Hill of the NAACP observed, "He was a very courageous figure. He would travel to the court houses of the South, and folks would come from miles, some of them on muleback or horseback, to see the 'nigger lawyer' who stood up in white men's courtrooms." More to the point, when he got to those courtrooms he often won, demonstrating to local residents that a black man could stand up in the face of white intimidation and prevail.

Source: From William H. Chafe, *The Unfinished Journey: America Since World War II* (New York: Oxford University Press, 1986), p. 149.

The great breakthrough for racial equality came in *Brown* v. *Board of Education of Topeka* (1954), in which a unanimous Court declared that "separate but equal" was inherently contradictory and that segregation was constitutionally unacceptable in public schools. *Brown* was a constitutional revolution, destined to transform racial relations law and practices in the United States.

The white South did not react violently at first, but it did not desegregate either. Once recognition spread that the Court was going to enforce civil rights, however, massive resistance to racial integration gripped the South. This resistance was what Dr. Martin Luther King Jr. and others had to work (and die) to overcome. The Court—even with many follow-up cases—was able to accomplish little before the president and Congress backed up the justices with the 1964 Civil Rights Act and the 1965 Voting Rights Act. These legislative actions were forced by the civil rights movement.

The drive to protect the rights of racial minorities has occupied the nation ever since. The main doctrine on racial discrimination is straightforward: any use of race in law or government regulations will trigger strict scrutiny (a presumption of unconstitutionality) by the courts. Recall from our earlier discussion that a state or the federal government can defend its acts under strict scrutiny only if it can produce a *compelling* government interest for which the act in question is a *necessary* means. Almost no law survives this challenge; laws that discriminate on the basis of race are dead from the moment of passage. Needless to say, other racial minority groups in addition to African-Americans—Hispanics, Asian-Americans, and Native Americans—have benefited from the constitutional revolution that has occurred.

Affirmative Action   Constitutional interpretation now protects racial minorities against discrimination that is sanctioned or protected by law or government action. The issues are not as clear-cut, however, in the area of government actions that *favor* racial minorities (and women) in **affirmative action** programs designed to rectify past wrongs.[2]

> **affirmative action**
>
> Programs of private and public institutions favoring the hiring of certain minorities in an attempt to compensate for past discrimination.

Origins   The main goal of the civil rights movement of the 1950s and 1960s was to remove barriers to equal citizenship for black Americans. President Lyndon Johnson, Robert Kennedy, and Martin Luther King Jr., among others, eventually came to believe that the advancement of black Americans would require more, namely, a broad societal effort to eradicate poverty by equipping the poor, black and white, with the tools for success. This led to the founding of the Johnson administration's Great Society and War on Poverty and programs such as Head Start. After King's assassination, however, many people in government, the media, higher education, and the major foundations began to support the notion that racial progress would happen only if government encouraged racial preferences in hiring, contracts, and college admissions.

Somewhat surprisingly, it was Richard Nixon, not generally thought of as a booster of civil rights, who took the most important step, requiring in his 1969 Philadelphia Plan that construction companies with federal contracts and the associated construction trade unions hire enough blacks and other minorities to achieve "racial balance" (a proportion roughly equal to the racial balance in the community). Most civil rights organizations opposed the plan, believing that it violated basic civil rights principles and would drive a wedge

Dr. Martin Luther King Jr. waves to the March on Washington crowd at the Lincoln Memorial after delivering his "I Have a Dream" speech. This event, one of the high points of the civil rights movement, helped convince Congress to pass the Civil Rights Act of 1964.

between African-Americans and whites in the labor unions (which it eventually did). When the Philadelphia Plan reached the House of Representatives in 1970, Republicans supported it by a margin of 124–41, while Democrats opposed it, 115–84. The two parties soon switched positions on the issue, however. Nixon himself disavowed it in 1972 when he ordered federal agencies to avoid the use of quotas; meanwhile, the Democrats embraced the principle of racial preferences in their platform at the 1972 party convention.

Although initially skeptical of racial preferences, Justices William Brennan, Byron White, Thurgood Marshall, and Harry Blackmun supported temporary programs to remedy the effects of past discrimination. Joined by Justice Lewis Powell, they formed the majority in *Regents* v. *Bakke* (1978), in which the Court authorized a compromise on affirmative action programs. The Constitution and federal law prohibited employers and admissions committees from using strictly racial quotas, the Court said, but it saw no problem with the use of race as one factor among several in hiring or admissions.

Since *Bakke,* government and higher education racial preference programs have become relatively permanent rather than temporary, and their aim has shifted from providing remedies for past discrimination to enhancing diversity. The proliferation of diversity programs, diversity training, and diversity offices has become commonplace in colleges and universities, in government, and in the corporate world.

Why Affirmative Action? According to proponents, affirmative action programs in government and education that promote diversity are needed for the following reasons:

- The effects of past discrimination disadvantage, to one degree or another, all members of discriminated-against groups, so simply removing barriers to advancement is insufficient. The proper remedy is to prefer members of such groups in hiring, contracts, and education until such time as they reach parity with the majority.

- In a diverse society such as the United States, tolerance and a sense of community can develop only if we work together in educational, workplace, and government institutions that are diverse.

- People from disadvantaged and discriminated-against groups will improve themselves only if they have experience with successful role models in important institutions.

Critics of affirmative action are not convinced by these arguments. They believe the following to be true:

- Affirmative action violates one of the most basic American principles: that people be judged, rewarded, and punished as individuals, not because they are members of one group or another.

- Affirmative action benefits those within each preferred group who are already advantaged and need little help. Thus, the main beneficiaries of affirmative action in higher education have been middle-class African-Americans, not the poor.

- Affirmative action seeks to remedy the effects of past discrimination by discriminating against others today simply because they belong to non-preferred groups.

- Affirmative action increases intergroup and interracial tension by heightening the saliency of group membership. That is, social friction is increased by encouraging people to think of themselves and others as members of groups and to seek group advantages in a zero-sum game in which one group's gain is another group's loss.

Public Opinion   In the court of public opinion, the critics of affirmative action as presently practiced have won the day. In survey after survey, a vast majority of Americans approve of the diversity goals of affirmative action—special programs to help those who have been discriminated against get ahead; outreach programs to hire minority workers and find minority students—but disapprove of racial preferences in hiring, awarding of government contracts, and admission to colleges.[3] The 1996 General Social Survey, for example, reports that more than 80 percent of Americans either oppose or strongly oppose preferential hiring of blacks. When asked whether they generally support affirmative action programs involving preferential treatment of particular groups, every major polling organization reports a majority of Americans opposed to them. For example, a *New York Times*/CBS News poll in late 1997 reported that 68 percent of Americans wanted affirmative action programs either fundamentally changed or eliminated.[4]

To many proponents of affirmative action, this is simply a reflection of the enduring racism of Americans. People oppose affirmative action, in this view, because they are hostile to racial minorities. Political scientists Paul Sniderman and Edward Carmines suggest otherwise. In a series of ingenious studies reported in their book *Beyond Race,* they set out to unravel the roots of opposition to affirmative action. Their conclusion is that while some people oppose these programs because of their racist attitudes, most do so because they believe that affirmative action is fundamentally unfair and contrary to American values.[5] Judging, rewarding, and punishing people not as individuals but as members of groups does not seem right to many Americans. We can see this in the fact, as sociologist Seymour Martin Lipset reported after examining a wide range of surveys on the issue, that a majority of women and Hispanic-Americans, not just white males, oppose affirmative action programs as presently constituted.[6] Surprising as it may seem, there is evidence that a majority of African-Americans feel the same way. Figure 16.1 shows that strong

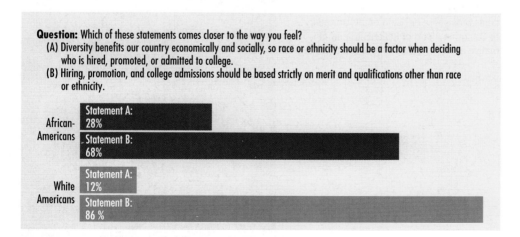

Question: Which of these statements comes closer to the way you feel?
  (A) Diversity benefits our country economically and socially, so race or ethnicity should be a factor when deciding who is hired, promoted, or admitted to college.
  (B) Hiring, promotion, and college admissions should be based strictly on merit and qualifications other than race or ethnicity.

African-Americans	Statement A: 28%
	Statement B: 68%
White Americans	Statement A: 12%
	Statement B: 86 %

Figure 16.1 ● **Attitudes on Affirmative Action**

African-Americans are far more likely than whites, according to a multitude of polls, to support affirmative action programs. However, when African-Americans are asked about specific aspects of these programs, their responses are not much different from whites.
Source: Lou Harris and Associates, 1998.

majorities of both African-Americans and whites believe that hiring, firing, and admission to college should be based on individual qualifications rather than on the need to serve diversity goals.

The position of the public on affirmative action, expressed in surveys and in elections, has obviously affected public policies with affirmative action in retreat in most states and in Washington, D.C. The Supreme Court has been especially notable in this regard.

The Supreme Court's Turnabout on Affirmative Action   Recently, the Court has been taking the position that laws that are not color-blind be subject to strict scrutiny. In *Wygant* v. *Jackson Board of Education* (1986) and *Richmond* v. *Croson Co.* (1989), the Court said that programs that narrowly redress specific violations will be upheld but that broader affirmative action programs that address society's racism will be struck down. In *Adarand Constructors* v. *Peña* (1995), the Court ruled by a 5–4 majority that the federal government must abide by the strict standards for affirmative action programs imposed on the states in the *Richmond* case and could not award contracts using race as the main criterion. In *Miller* v. *Johnson* (1995), the Court ruled, again by a 5–4 majority, that race could not be used as the basis for drawing House district lines in an effort to increase the number of racial minority members in Congress. The Court also refused to overturn a Fifth Circuit Court ruling that race cannot be considered at all in admissions decisions at the University of Texas Law School, putting the *Bakke* principle in jeopardy. And in 1997, the Court refused to overturn a ruling of the Ninth Circuit Court that California's anti–affirmative action Proposition 209 was constitutionally permissible. (See the "Using the Framework" feature.) In several of these decisions, the opinion of the court was written by Justice Sandra Day O'Connor, who, despite having suffered discrimination in law school and in her early law career, believes that affirmative action should be used as a modest, temporary response to past discrimination.

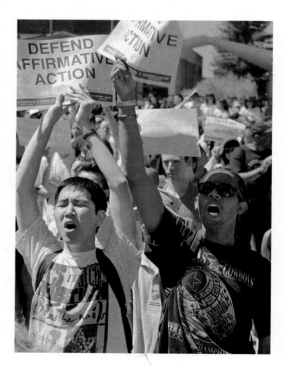

Affirmative action programs are increasingly in jeopardy in the United States. Here students protest the decision of the University of California Board of Regents to end affirmative action in admissions to the university.

USING THE FRAMEWORK

Affirmative Action

In 1997, the Supreme Court refused to overturn the ruling of the Ninth Circuit Court of Appeals that upheld the constitutionality of California's Proposition 209 ending affirmative action programs in the state. The behavior of the Court can be better understood by examining how structural, political linkage, and governmental factors interacted to influence this outcome.

Governmental Action

The Supreme Court turns down the appeal of opponents of California Proposition 209.

Governmental Level

- Republican presidents Reagan and Bush nominated conservatives to the Court.
- The Senate approved the nominees.
- A narrow but firm conservative majority under the leadership of Chief Justice William Rehnquist controls the Court on many issues.

Political Linkages Level

- The majority white population reports in polls that they believe the goals of the civil rights movement have been met.
- Republicans, whose platform rejects affirmative action, reached parity with Democrats in national elections.

- A substantial majority of Americans report support for nondiscrimination laws but distaste for laws that give minorities and women special advantages in college admissions, jobs, and government contracts.

- The Christian conservative movement and other conservative organizations—who are against affirmative action—gained political influence in the 1980s.

- The political influence of civil rights organizations declined in the 1980s and 1990s.
- Republicans won control of the Senate from 1981–1986 and from 1995 to 2000.

Structural Level

- The Fourteenth Amendment's promise of "equal protection of the laws" clearly bars government discrimination against groups of citizens but is unclear about the need for remedies for past discrimination.

- The political culture honors individual rather than group rights and responsibilities.

- The white middle and working classes suffered economic reverses during the 1980s and early 1990s, creating a climate that was generally hostile to affirmative action programs.

LongmanParticipate

CourseCompass

comparative
**Comparing
Civil Rights**

The majority on the Court has apparently reached the conclusion that government programs designed simply to increase racial diversity are no longer acceptable. To be acceptable, affirmative action programs must be confined to redressing past discrimination in a particular occupation, business sector, or institution and must not serve vague societywide goals such as enhancing minority representation. Such programs must also be temporary efforts to transcend past practices and not a permanent feature of hiring, contracting, or admissions. This may put in jeopardy a wide range of diversity initiatives in local school districts, for example, that reserve places for minorities in special magnet schools and in gifted programs. Several cases involving these issues are now working their way up to the Supreme Court.

Civil Rights for Women

The expansion of civil rights protections for women has taken a decidedly different path from that of African-Americans.

Intermediate Scrutiny   For all its egalitarian reputation, the Warren Court did not significantly advance the cause of women's rights. Once the Burger Court seriously looked at sex discrimination laws, it had to decide whether to apply ordinary scrutiny (the presumption of constitutionality that almost all laws survive) or strict scrutiny (the presumption of unconstitutionality that dooms almost all laws). The Burger Court opted for a new position, called **intermediate scrutiny,** but not before coming to the very brink of declaring gender a suspect classification demanding strict scrutiny.

By 1976 the proposed **Equal Rights Amendment** to the Constitution to guarantee full legal equality for women had stalled, falling short of the required three-fourths of the states. Moreover, the Supreme Court did not have the necessary votes for a strict scrutiny interpretation of gender classification. There was support, however, for the new doctrine that came to be called intermediate scrutiny. In *Craig* v. *Boren* (1976), six justices supported Justice William

intermediate scrutiny

A legal test falling between ordinary and strict scrutiny relevant to issues of gender; under this test, the Supreme Court will allow gender classifications in laws if they are *substantially* related to an *important* government objective.

Equal Rights Amendment (ERA)

Proposed amendment to the U.S. Constitution stating that equality of rights shall not be abridged or denied on account of a person's sex.

The women's movement helped raise Americans' awareness of the issue of "equal pay for equal work" and contributed to improvements in pay equity for women in both the public and private sectors. Here, a demonstrator in New York presses for pay equity.

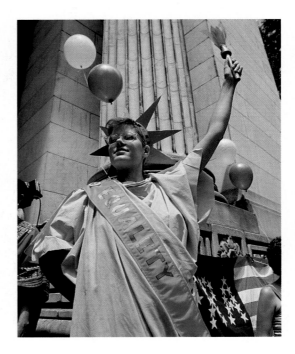

Brennan's compromise, which created a more rigorous scrutiny of gender as a *somewhat* suspect classification. This intermediate scrutiny provided a compromise solution to the problem of choosing between strict and ordinary scrutiny. In the view of the justices, the use of strict scrutiny would endanger traditional sex roles, while the use of ordinary scrutiny would allow blatant sex discrimination to survive. The Burger Court defined a test that it believed to be "just right." Under intermediate scrutiny, government enactments that relied on gender would be constitutional if the use of gender were *substantially related* to an *important objective*. Intermediate scrutiny defines a legal test, then, somewhere between strict and lax. Thus, for example, certain laws protecting pregnant women from dangerous chemicals in the workplace have passed this test.

The improvement of women's rights under the doctrine of intermediate scrutiny is less than what many in the women's movement wanted. While the new standard has allowed the courts to throw out some laws based on degrading stereotypes of women, it was used in *Craig* v. *Boren* to justify invalidating an Oklahoma law that discriminated against young *men*. Similarly, the beneficiaries of intermediate scrutiny decisions in *Wengler* v. *Druggists Mutual Insurance Company* (1980) and *Mississippi University for Women* v. *Hogan* (1982) were also men.

Thus, women's rights have not followed the path of other rights and liberties. The nation has not restructured civil rights for women. Indeed, the Court ruled in 2000 that the Violence Against Women Act, passed in Congress in 1994 with strong bipartisan majorities, was unconstitutional because it was based on a too-strong reading of national powers under the Interstate Commerce clause.

Abortion Rights   One of the most controversial decisions of the Burger Court was *Roe* v. *Wade* (1973). Two recent graduates of the University of Texas Law School, Linda Coffee and Sarah Weddington, were looking for a client who would challenge a Texas statute that prohibited physicians from performing abortions except to save the life of the pregnant woman.[7] They found a client in Norma "Pixie" McCorvey, a 21-year-old divorcee who had already given birth to a child. McCorvey claimed that she had been gang-raped, but her attorneys doubted her story. They argued instead for a general constitutional right to decide not to complete a pregnancy.

For women's rights activists Coffee and Weddington, the federal courts offered an alternative to the Texas legislature. The case transformed abortion from a legislative issue into a constitutional issue, from a matter of policy into a matter of rights. Eleven states had reformed their statutes to allow women abortions when the woman's health, fetal abnormalities, or rape or incest were involved. Four more states (Alaska, Hawaii, Washington, and New York) went further and repealed prohibitions of abortion. In most states, however, progress was slow or nonexistent.

The litigation over abortion reflected changes in public opinion, pressure by interest groups, and persisting inequities against women. Disapproval of abortion decreased and discussion of abortion increased during the 1960s, even among Roman Catholics.[8] Numerous groups worked to reform or to eliminate abortion laws before *Roe* was decided.[9] Norma McCorvey's case relied greatly on the money of supporters of women's rights. The pro-choice team benefited from 42 amicus curiae briefs. The medical profession, which had been instrumental in making abortion a crime in the nineteenth century,[10] supported reform in the 1960s. Justice Harry Blackmun's opinion for the majority prohibited the states from interfering with a woman's decision to have an abortion in the first two trimesters of her pregnancy. He based his opinion on the right to privacy, first given constitutional protection in *Griswold* v. *Connecticut* (1965), even though no such right is mentioned in the Constitution.

The Court's decision hardly resolved matters. Antiabortion groups, energized by the repeal of abortion laws, struck back after *Roe.* Single-issue antiabortion politics surfaced in the 1976 and subsequent elections and became an important pillar of the conservative Reagan movement. The pro-life forces that helped elect Ronald Reagan insisted that he appoint antiabortion judges to the federal courts. He did so with great effectiveness. In the end, the Supreme Court responded to antiabortion politics by deciding two cases, *Webster* v. *Reproductive Health Services* (1989) and *Planned Parenthood* v. *Casey* (1992), that gave considerable latitude to the states in restricting abortions.

Many states have acted. In 1996, nine states enacted 14 measures restricting abortion in one way or another: mandating parental notification, waiting periods, counseling against abortion, and/or prohibiting using public money for the procedure. In 1997, 31 states enacted 44 such measures. In 1998, 22 states passed 46 restrictive bills. And, in 1999, pro-choice New Jersey Gov. Christine Todd Whitman signed a bill requiring teenage girls to notify their parents before getting an abortion.[11] To the surprise of many observers, however, the Court majority, despite the appointment of new justices by Presidents Reagan and Bush, affirmed its support of the basic principles of *Roe* in the *Planned Parenthood* opinion. Also surprising was the Court's decision, in *National Organization for Women* v. *Scheidler* (1994), that abortion clinics could sue antiabortion groups for damages under the federal racketeering law. And, during its 2000 session, the Court ruled that states could not ban so-called late-term abortions and said that state laws and local ordinances keeping anti-abortion demonstrators away from clinic entrances were constitutional.

Abortion has been an important issue in recent judicial confirmations. Judge Robert Bork ascribed his own defeat to the issue,[12] and hearings on Judge David Souter in 1990 and Clarence Thomas in 1992 raised the issue repeatedly. Ruth Bader Ginsburg took a Solomonic position: like conservative pro-lifers, she opposed the reasoning of *Roe* v. *Wade,* but like liberal pro-choicers, she insisted that some abortion rights are essential to women's equality.

Sexual Harassment   Another issue of concern to many women (and men) is sexual harassment in the workplace. One poll reports that 21 percent of women say they have experienced sexual harassment at work.[13] The Equal Employment Opportunity Commission (EEOC) reports that 35 percent of female federal employees have been subjected to unwelcome sexual remarks and that 26 percent have experienced unwelcome touching.[14]

People disagree, of course, about what kinds of behavior constitute sexual harassment, although the courts, regulatory agencies, and legislative bodies are gradually defining the law in this area. In 1980, the EEOC ruled that making sexual activity a condition of employment or promotion violates the 1964 Civil Rights Act, a ruling upheld by the Supreme Court. The EEOC also ruled that creating "an intimidating, hostile, or offensive working environment" is contrary to the law. State courts have begun to fill in the meaning of "intimidating, hostile, or offensive." The Florida Supreme Court ruled in 1991, for instance, that an open display of nude pinups in a mixed-gender workplace fits the definition. A California court ruled that unwelcome love letters from a supervisor constitute harassment. The U.S. Supreme Court took a major step in defining sexual harassment when it ruled unanimously, in *Harris* v. *Forklift Systems, Inc.* (1993), that workers do not have to prove that offensive actions make them unable to do their jobs or cause them psychological harm, only that the work environment is hostile or abusive. In a pair of rulings in June 1998, the Court

Professor Anita Hill's dramatic testimony before the Senate Judiciary Committee considering the nomination of Clarence Thomas to the Supreme Court raised the visibility in American politics of the issue of sexual harassment.

broadened the definition of sexual harassment by saying that companies were liable for the behavior of supervisors even if top managers were unaware of harassing behavior. However, companies were offered a measure of protection by the Court when it ruled that companies with solid and well-communicated harassment policies could not be held liable if victims failed to report harassment in a reasonable period of time.

An increase in public awareness about sexual harassment has triggered an increase in lawmaking by state legislatures to erase sexual harassment in the workplace. Many private companies have also begun to specify appropriate behavior on the job for their employees.

Affirmative Action   Affirmative action guidelines and laws passed by national, state, and local governments have been aimed at rectifying past discrimination against women as well as against racial minorities. The precarious legal and political status of these guidelines and laws, reviewed in the section on racial minorities, means that affirmative action programs for women are in jeopardy across the nation. For this reason, many women's organizations have become increasingly engaged in the struggle over affirmative action. The unsuccessful fight in 1996 against California's Proposition 209 ending all affirmative action programs in the state was spearheaded by women's groups.

Broadening the Civil Rights Umbrella

The expansion of civil rights protections for women and racial minorities has encouraged other groups to press for expanded rights protections.

The Elderly and the Disabled   Interest groups for the elderly have pressed for laws barring age discrimination and have enjoyed some success in recent years. Several federal and state laws, for instance, now bar mandatory retirement. The courts have also begun to strike down hiring practices based on age unless a compelling reason for such age requirements can be demonstrated.

Disabled Americans have also pushed for civil rights and other protections and have won some notable victories, including passage of the Americans with Disabilities Act of 1990. The act prohibits employment discrimination against

LongmanParticipate

CourseCompass

participation
**Statehood for
Puerto Rico
and the District
of Columbia?**

the disabled and requires that reasonable efforts be made to make places of employment and public facilities (such as concert halls, restaurants, retail shops, schools, and government offices) accessible to them. The proliferation of wheelchair ramps and wheelchair-accessible toilet facilities is a sign that the legislation is having an important effect. Several advocates for the disabled, however, claim that the act depends too much on voluntary compliance. In 2001, moreover, the Supreme Court narrowed the reach of the Diabilities Act, arguing that states could not be sued as provided for in the legislation.

Gays and Lesbians   Efforts to secure constitutional rights for gays and lesbians exemplify political exertions in the face of governmental wavering. When the U.S. Supreme Court upheld Georgia's law against sodomy in *Bowers* v. *Hardwick* (1986), the majority opinion declared assertions of a constitutional right to homosexuality to be "facetious." Gay and lesbian activists and their opponents have now shifted the battle to other political arenas, including housing and job discrimination and funding for AIDS research. In the electoral arena, candidate Bill Clinton promised to lift the ban on gay people in the military but was forced to reverse his course in light of the hostile reaction from Congress and the armed services. The resulting "don't ask, don't tell, don't pursue" policy satisfied very few people, and the navy has routinely flouted the policy, as when in 1998 it dismissed a sailor whom it discovered to be gay by tracking down his identity on his America Online profile page. (The sailor eventually won monetary settlements from both the U.S. Navy and AOL.)

The beating death in 1999 of Army Pfc. Barry Winchell, after a long period of harassment by fellow soldiers and noncommissioned officers, again brought the "don't ask, don't tell" policy into the public spotlight. In January 2000, in the midst of the New Hampshire presidential primary campaign, Democrats Bill Bradley and Al Gore both stated that they expected military leaders to soon let

WEB EXPLORATION

The Continuing Struggle for Equality

Issue: The content of the civil rights agenda today has broadened significantly.

Site: Access the Leadership Conference on Civil Rights through the "Course Documents" section of your online course. Go to the "Web Explorations" section for Chapter 16, click on "The Continuing Struggle for Equality," and open "civil rights agenda."

What You've Learned: The Leadership Conference is a coalition of civil rights organizations. By looking at the organizations in the coalition and what they are trying to achieve, you can gain an understanding of what issues remain on the civil rights agenda. Take a sample of organizations (take the first 20 perhaps, or every sixth or seventh one on the list). Select "go to their site" for each, and examine the civil rights issues they believe are most important. From this sampling, define what the civil rights agenda looks like. Are the issues important ones, in your view?

HINT: One of the most interesting developments in American politics over the past several decades has been the transformation of many conventional political issues into "rights" issues.

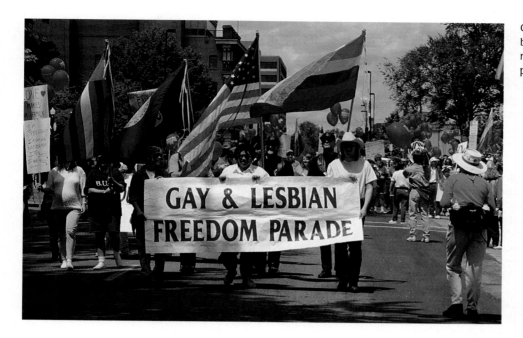

Gay and lesbian Americans have become much more assertive recently in pressing for civil rights protections.

openly gay persons serve in the armed forces; Republicans George W. Bush and John McCain favored the status quo.

Clinton's efforts in 1993 embroiled the White House, the Congress, the Pentagon, and the media in a policy struggle that highlighted the strengths and weaknesses of gay political advocates and their opponents. Although gays and lesbians have recently lost a string of contests in several states and localities to provide protection for gays and lesbians, and while 27 states had passed laws banning same-sex marriages by early 2000, gays and lesbians won some victories as well.

WEB EXPLORATION

Same-Sex Marriage

Issue: Passions run high on the issue of same-sex marriages.

Site: Access two sites that take contrasting positions on the issue of same-sex marriage: the Christian Coalition and TurnOut. Go to the "Course Documents" section of your online course. Go to the "Web Explorations" section for Chapter 16, click on "Same-Sex Marriage," and open "same-sex marriage." At the Christian Coalition site, select "news releases," then "same-sex partners." At the TurnOut site, select "issues" and then "the right to marry."

What You've Learned: Compare the coverage of the issue of same-sex marriage at each site. Is each telling the full story? Are there areas of agreement between the two sides, or is the gap between them a yawning one?

HINT: On issues involving conflicts over fundamental values, agreement and compromise are often very difficult to achieve.

HOW DEMOCRATIC ARE WE?

PROPOSITION: Civil rights was not a prominent feature of the original Constitution nor has the promise of equal citizenship (which goes hand in hand with political equality) been realized over the course of our history.

AGREE: There is no provision in the original Constitution ensuring equality of citizenship for women, African-Americans, and Native Americans. Women were denied the vote well into the twentieth century; most African-Americans were slaves until passage of the Thirteenth Amendment and were not admitted into full citizenship across the nation until at least 1965 after passage of the Civil Rights Act and the Voting Rights Act. Even today, women, racial and ethnic minorities, and gays and lesbians continue to be discriminated against in a wide range of institutions and fail to play a role in the political process commensurate with their numbers in the population.

DISAGREE: While it is true that the framers largely ignored the issue of equal citizenship, the story of the United States is the story of the gradual inclusion of all identifiable groups into the political process as equal citizens. Although the levels of political participation and political power are not the same for all groups, this has more to do with inequalities in the distribution of income, wealth, and education than with formal mechanisms of exclusion.

THE AUTHORS: Political equality is one of the three pillars of democracy, equal in importance to popular sovereignty and political liberty. For most of our history, political equality was not a very high priority in the United States, and the quality of democracy was less than it might have been. The advance of civil rights protections since the end of World War II has enriched American democracy because it has helped make political equality a reality in the United States. It is no longer acceptable, for instance, to deny minorities and women the right to vote, to assemble, to petition the government, or to hold public office, practices widely enforced in this country for most of our history. This is not to say that racial minorities and women have attained full social or material equality; many areas of American life, from wealth holding to representation in the professions and in Congress, remain unequal and unrepresentative. Nor is this to say that all civil rights issues are settled; note the continuing disagreements over same-sex marriages and affirmative action. Nevertheless, the attainment of formal political equality is real and something about which Americans might take great pride.

The Supreme Court ruled in *Romer* v. *Evans* (1996), for example, that Colorado's constitutional provision (known as Amendment 2) prohibiting local communities from passing gay antidiscrimination ordinances is unconstitutional. As Justice Anthony Kennedy put it in his opinion, "a state cannot so deem a class of persons a stranger to its laws." Gay rights advocates can also point to some successes in winning protections of privacy and sexual orientation in *state* laws: Eight states and many localities ban discrimination against gay people, and seven other states operate under executive orders that prohibit such discrimination.[15] Vermont has granted same-sex couples the same legal rights, protections, and benefits as heterosexual married couples (regarding matters such as joint tax returns, property ownership, insurance benefits, and medical decisions involving a spouse). Many local governments and private companies have instituted domestic partner benefit programs for same-sex couples. Perhaps most importantly, opinion surveys show that public attitudes about gays and lesbians are growing steadily more tolerant. Fewer Americans today than in the past think that gay and lesbian relationships are wrong. Substantial majorities, moreover, favor ending discrimination against gays and lesbians in jobs, housing, and education and favor passing hate-crime legislation. The portrayals of gays and lesbians in the mass media and culture have also become steadily more positive.[16]

It is evident that the struggle over gay and lesbian rights will remain an important part of the American political agenda for a long time to come, the eventual outcome being very much in doubt.[17] Several important cases on gay and lesbian civil rights await action by the Supreme Court, including the constitutionality of bans on same-sex marriages.

LongmanParticipate

CourseCompass

simulation
**You Are
the Mayor**

Summary

The Constitution and the Bill of Rights are relatively silent on political equality, other than providing for equality before the law. Important advances for civil rights were the passage of the Thirteenth, Fourteenth, and Fifteenth Amendments after the Civil War. The Fourteenth Amendment, with its specification that all persons born or naturalized in the United States are citizens of both the nation and the states in which they live and that federal and state governments must provide for "equal protection of the laws," was a particularly important civil rights milestone, even though the Supreme Court was slow to act on its promise.

The Court paid little attention during the nineteenth century to the issue of political equality for racial minorities and women. Under the pressure of structural changes in society, the transformation of attitudes about race and gender, and the political efforts of racial and ethnic minority group members and women of all races, the Court slowly began to pay attention by the middle of the twentieth century. Important advances toward equality have been made by both racial minorities and women. Although constitutional law now fully protects both racial minorities and women against discrimination sanctioned by law or government action, the status of affirmative action programs meant to rectify past wrongs and to compensate for institutional barriers to equality remains unsettled. The question of whether lesbians and gay men can be discriminated against in housing, employment, and education has been largely settled, although the issues of gays and lesbians in the military and same-sex marriages remain the subject of considerable political debate.

Suggestions for Further Reading

Bowen, William G., and Derek C. Bok. *The Shape of the River: Long-term Consequences of Considering Race in College and University Admissions.* Princeton: Princeton University Press, 1998.
   Based on surveys of more than 60,000 white and African-American students at highly selective colleges and universities, Bowen and Bok argue that affirmative action in college and university admissions has had substantial and widespread positive effects on American society.

Burns, James MacGregor, and Stewart Burns. *A People's Charter: The Pursuit of Rights in America.* New York: Knopf, 1991.
   A magisterial survey of the history of civil rights and liberties in the United States.

Chavez, Lydia. *The Color Bind: California's Battle to End Affirmative Action.* Berkeley, CA: University of California Press, 1998.
> *A readable and revealing look at the political and legal forces that fought over California's Proposition 209 ending affirmative action.*

Evans, Sarah M. *Born for Liberty: A History of Women in America.* New York: Free Press, 1997.
> *A compelling history of women's struggle for civil rights.*

Kahlenberg, Richard D. *The Remedy: Class, Race, and Affirmative Action.* New York: Basic Books, 1996.
> *A history of the changing meaning of affirmative action and an examination of its effects.*

Sniderman, Paul M., and Edward G. Carmines. *Reaching Beyond Race.* Cambridge, MA: Harvard University Press, 1997.
> *A brilliant examination of what Americans really mean when they answer survey questions about race.*

Thernstrom, Stephan, and Abigail Thernstrom. *America in Black and White.* New York: Simon & Schuster, 1997.
> *An exhaustive scholarly treatment of the gains made by the traditional civil rights movement in the United States and an argument on how affirmative action threatens this progress.*

Internet Sources

Cornell Law Library/Civil Rights   **http://www.law.cornell.edu**
> *Links to the Constitution, landmark and recent Supreme Court civil rights decisions, international treaties on human rights, the Civil Rights Division of the Justice Department, and more.*

Martin Luther King Jr. Home Page   **http://www.seattletimes.com/mlk/**
> *Created by the* Seattle Times, *the site includes study guides on King and the civil rights movement, interactive exercises, audios of King speeches, and links to other King and civil rights Web sites.*

Yahoo/Civil Rights
http://www.yahoo.com/Society_and_Culture/Issues_and_Causes/Civil_Rights/
> *Linkages to a vast compendium of information on civil rights and to organizations devoted to the protection and expansion of rights, domestic and international.*

Notes

1. James MacGregor Burns and Stewart Burns, *A People's Charter: The Pursuit of Rights in America* (New York: Knopf, 1991), p. 37.

2. This section is based on Richard D. Kahlenberg, *The Remedy: Class, Race, and Affirmative Action* (New York: Basic Books, 1996).

3. Sam Howe Verhovek, "In Poll, Americans Reject Means But Not the Ends of Racial Diversity," *New York Times* (December 14, 1997), p. A1; Martin Gilens, Paul M. Sniderman, and James H. Kuklinski, "Affirmative Action and the Politics of Realignment," *British Journal of Political Science* 28 (January 1998), pp. 159–184.

4. Ibid.

5. Paul M. Sniderman and Edward G. Carmines, *Reaching Beyond Race* (Cambridge, MA: Harvard University Press, 1997).

6. Seymour Martin Lipset, *American Exceptionalism* (New York: Norton, 1996), ch. 4.

7. See Marian Faux, *Roe v. Wade* (New York: Macmillan, 1988).

8. Ibid., p. 45.

9. Eva R. Rubin, *Abortion, Politics, and the Courts* (Westport, CT: Greenwood Press, 1982), ch. 2.

10. Kristen Luker, *Abortion and the Politics of Motherhood* (Berkeley: University of California Press, 1984), ch. 2.

11. Katharine Q. Seelye, "Advocates of Abortion Rights Report a Rise in Restrictions," *New York Times* (January 15, 1998), p. A1; and David Kocieniewski, "Abortion Rights Movement Stunned by Whitman," *New York Times* (June 15, 1999), A29.

12. Robert Bork, *The Tempting of America: The Political Seduction of the Law* (New York: Free Press, 1990), p. 281.

13. *Newsweek* (October 21, 1991), p. 34.

14. Ibid., p. 36.

15. Lisa Keen, "Referendums and Rights: Across the Country, Battles over Protection for Gays and Lesbians," *Washington Post* (October 31, 1993), p. C3.

16. Kenneth Sherrill and Alan Yang, "From Outlaws to In-Laws," *Public Perspectives* (January/February 2000), pp. 20–23.

17. See Aart Hendriks, Rob Tielman, and Evert van der Veen, eds., *The Third Pink Book* (Buffalo, NY: Prometheus Books, 1993); Louis Diamant, ed., *Homosexual Issues in the Workplace* (Washington, D.C.: Taylor & Francis, 1993).

CHAPTER 17

Domestic Policy: The Economy and Social Welfare

IN THIS CHAPTER

- Why government is involved in the economy and social welfare

- What tools government uses to manage the economy

- The federal budget, the deficit, and the national debt

- Why government subsidizes some business activities and regulates others

- The American welfare state and how it is changing

- How interest groups, parties, social movements, and public opinion affect economic and social welfare policy

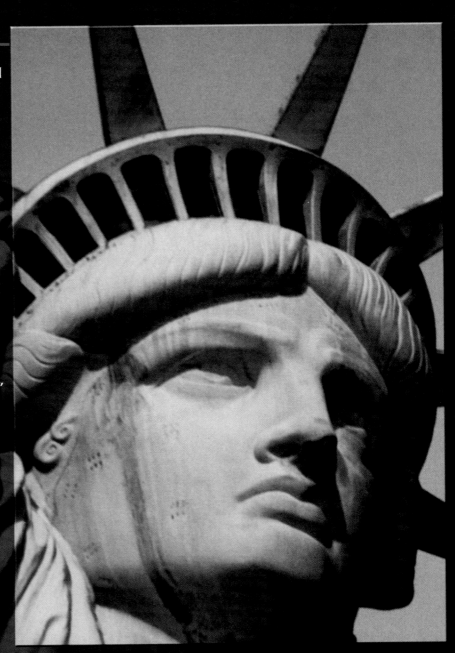

Budget Chaos in the 104th Congress, Compromise in the 105th

Fresh from their landslide victory in the 1994 election, House Republicans in the 104th Congress were eager to cut down the federal government to what they considered its proper size and role. Their tool would be the federal budget. The budget revolutionaries, as they came to be called, were willing to go to the brink to force President Clinton to accept their conservative agenda, vowing to shut down the government if the president refused to sign on the dotted line.

The budget bill fashioned in the House of Representatives was unprecedented in several respects. Normally, budget bills simply decide what the overall level of government spending will be for a single year. The 1995 bill was far more ambitious. It not only aimed for a balanced budget over the course of seven years but also included many provisions about specific federal programs ordinarily left to congressional committees. These provisions included drastic cutbacks in the regulatory responsibilities of the federal government (especially in banking and securities, environmental protection, consumer protection, and workplace safety), a slowdown in Medicare funding, a capital gains tax cut, and the transformation of welfare and Medicaid into block grants run by the states. Senate Republicans eventually signed on.

Having seen Bill Clinton waver and fold on important issues in the past, congressional leaders were confident that the threat to close down the government in the absence of a budget would be too much for the president to resist. Much to their surprise, Clinton refused to be intimidated and vetoed two successive budget bills. After each veto, the federal government shut down, with only "essential" services, such as national defense and air traffic control, permitted to operate under temporary funding measures.

For four weeks in December and January, the government shutdown dominated the news. Stories of people turned away at passport and Social Security offices, national parks, and national museums filled the airwaves. News broadcasts showed government workers on picket lines pleading to go back to work or with their families trying to cope without paychecks. Newscasts also reported air- and water-polluting activities going unregulated, meat inspections not being carried out, and the cleanup of toxic waste sites being suspended. Behind the scenes, members of

Congress were hearing complaints from large government contractors about their inability to finish their work or to collect for work already completed. Exporting companies were stymied by the absence of federal inspectors to certify cargoes. The National Institutes of Health stopped processing applications for biomedical research grants. Financial leaders were angry about the mere mention of the possibility of the government defaulting on its debt payments for fear of sparking economic chaos.[1]

Republican leaders were unprepared for the firestorm of criticism. Much to their chagrin, they, not the president, took most of the public blame. They decided, in the end, to abandon the effort to pass a radical budget bill. The House and the Senate voted instead for a resolution to reopen the government with slightly reduced budgets for most federal programs. Somewhat dispiritedly, House and Senate Republicans turned their attention to other legislative matters, many of them feeling that a historic opportunity had been missed.

The battle had electoral consequences in 1996. Using the budget radicals and Speaker Newt Gingrich as their campaign whipping boys, Democrats increased their numbers in the House and reelected Bill Clinton to the presidency. Somewhat chastened but also aware that President Clinton had announced his support for a balanced budget during the campaign, the GOP leadership pushed aside the budget radicals and entered into serious bipartisan negotiations with Clinton in the opening months of the 105th Congress. Much to the surprise of Washington observers, especially after the bloodletting just a year earlier, a landmark compromise budget emerged from the negotiations, one that promised a balanced budget, increased spending in several areas favored by the president (children's health insurance and restoration of some cuts in welfare assistance to legal immigrants), and decreased capital gains and estate taxes favored by the Republicans.

The annual decision about the budget is one of the most important that the president and Congress make. It is important because it determines in broad outline what activities and programs will be carried out by the federal government and how the government will go about paying for them. In this chapter and the next, we turn our attention to an examination of a broad range of these federal government activities and programs and the effect they have on the American people.

Obviously, we cannot cover every policy area in the allotted space. We focus, instead, on policy areas we consider most important for protecting the security of American citizens and ensuring their economic and social well-being. In the next chapter, we look in detail at U.S. foreign and military policy. In this chapter, we look at two broad areas of domestic policy: (1) federal government activities related to the U.S. economy, including the budget, fiscal and monetary policies, subsidies, and regulation; and (2) social welfare programs, including Social Security, Medicare, and public assistance.

Thinking Critically About This Chapter

Using the Framework. You will see in this chapter how the framework can be used to explain why government does what it does in the areas of economic and social welfare policies. You will use what you learned in previous chapters about structural, political linkage, and government factors to better understand what government does in terms of spending, taxing, regulating, and providing income support and social services.

Using the Democracy Standard. In previous chapters, you used the democracy standard to examine the extent to which American political and government institutions enhanced popular sovereignty, political equality, and liberty. You will use the democracy standard in this chapter to ask whether the American people get the sorts of policies and performance they want from government. ▶

Why Government Is Involved in the Economy and Social Welfare

Governments in all modern capitalist societies play a substantial role in managing their national economies and providing social welfare for their citizens. Let's see why they do so.

Economic Management

No government today would dare leave problems such as stagnant economic growth, unemployment, international trade imbalances, or inflation to work themselves out "naturally." Citizens and political leaders in the Western democracies have learned that free market economies, left to themselves, are subject to periodic bouts of **inflation** and unemployment, as well as occasional collapses of employment and economic output (called **depressions**). The worldwide trauma of the Great Depression in the 1930s was the event that etched this lesson into the minds of virtually everyone and forever changed the role of government in economic affairs.

inflation

A condition of rising prices.

depression

A severe and persistent drop in economic activity.

The inclination to use the federal government to manage the national economy has been enhanced by the relative success of this endeavor since the end of World War II. Although many economic troubles are still with us, government has proved surprisingly effective in easing the swings of the business cycle (see Figure 17.1) and stimulating steady economic growth.

The federal government must also pay attention to economic policy because its purchases of goods and services are so substantial—the federal government is the largest customer in the United States, the biggest borrower, and the biggest employer—that its actions inevitably have an effect on the economy. It would be difficult, therefore, for government leaders to deny responsibility for what is happening in the national economy.[2]

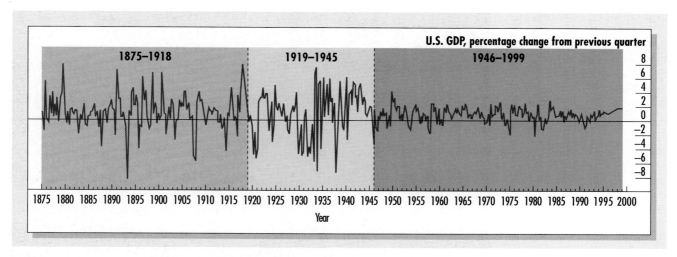

Figure 17.1 ● **Gaining Control of the Business Cycle**

This graph shows changes in the U.S. gross domestic product (GDP) from the previous quarter. Several things are immediately apparent. First, there were frequent deep plunges in GDP—representing depressions—before the early 1940s but none after that. Particularly noteworthy are the economic collapses in 1893, 1907, 1915, 1920, and 1921 and the Great Depression years of the 1930s; the postwar years have periods of economic slowdown but no crises. Second, the earlier period is characterized by a wild roller-coaster, boom-and-bust pattern; this pattern disappears in the later period. Third, the earlier period shows as many down years as up years; since World War II, there have been more up than down years. These indicators suggest that government management of the economy, which began only after World War II, has had an important stabilizing effect.

Source: "Taking the Business Cycle Pulse," *The Economist* (October 28, 1995), p. 89; and *The Economic Report of the President, 2000* (Washington, D.C.: Council of Economic Advisors, 2000).

WEB EXPLORATION

Demographic Change and Government Response

Issue: As society changes, new needs are often created among the population that bear on the responsibilities of government. One of the most important changes in recent American history is the steady increase in how long people live.

Site: Access Public Agenda Online through the "Course Documents" section of your online course. Go to the "Web Explorations" section for Chapter 17, click on "Demographic Change and Government Response," and open "life expectancy." Select "Health Care," then "Fact File," then "increasing life expectancy."

What You've Learned: How would you characterize the trend in life expectancy in the United States since 1940? How much has life expectancy changed in percentage terms in this period? What are aging Americans most likely to ask of their government in the future, and how effective are they likely to be?

HINT: Health care and income maintenance are what older Americans worry about most, and they vote in great numbers.

Industrial work is often dangerous to life and limb. To cope with industrial illness, disability, and death, most industrial societies have created government medical and financial support programs to help victims and their families.

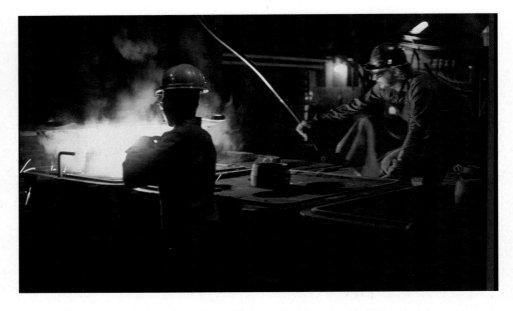

Government responsibility for the state of the national economy is now so widely accepted that national elections are often decided by the voters' judgment of how well the party in power is carrying out this responsibility. When times are good, the party or president in power is very likely to be reelected; when times are bad, those in power have an uphill battle staying in office.

Social Welfare

All rich democracies have programs that protect the minimum standards of living of families and individuals against loss of income due to economic instability, old age, illness and disability, and family disintegration.[3] Nations that provide such a range of programs are often called **welfare states**. All rich democracies are also social welfare states, and the reason is simple: their citizens have demanded it. They have apparently recognized that market economies, even when working at peak efficiency, do not guarantee a minimum decency of living for all or offer protection against economic dislocations even for people making their best efforts.[4]

welfare state

The set of government programs that protects the minimum standard of living of families and individuals against loss of income.

Economic Policy

Government economic policies have a number of objectives; all have consequences for the American people.

The Goals of Economic Policy

What are political leaders trying to accomplish when they fashion economic policies? You will see that economic policy goals sometimes conflict and that important trade-offs are involved whenever economic policies are selected.[5]

gross domestic product (GDP)

Monetary value of all goods and services produced in a nation each year, excluding income residents earn abroad.

Economic Growth   Sustained economic growth—defined here as an annual increase in the **gross domestic product (GDP)**—is the "holy grail" of economic policymakers. Although some environmentalists have argued for the long-term benefits of a smaller, less technologically driven economy, Americans generally want an economy in which each year brings more jobs, more products, and higher incomes. Economic growth is also the basis for increased profits, so business tends to support this goal. For political leaders, economic growth, accompanied by rising standards of living, brings public popularity and heightened prospects for reelection, as well as more revenues for government programs.

Low Unemployment   Americans want to be working. To a very great extent, this depends on a growing economy with high labor force participation rates and low unemployment. Economic **recessions** bring slower job growth and rising unemployment rates. Depressions bring a collapse of the job market (during the Great Depression, the U.S. unemployment rate twice reached 33 percent) and often in its wake social unrest and political instability. It is no wonder, then, that public officials try to keep unemployment levels from rising too high.

recession

A period of decline in overall economic activity.

Stable Prices   Most people want to avoid inflation, a condition in which the purchasing power of money declines. With serious inflation, people's wages, salaries, savings accounts, and retirement pensions are worth less. So, too, are the holdings of banks and the value of their loans. Economists point out that inflation also brings uncertainty and erratic economic behavior as consumers and businesses try to shape their behavior to protect themselves from the effects of future price changes. To nobody's surprise, political leaders seek policies that dampen inflation and provide stable prices. Their problem is that such policies often require slower economic growth, with lower wages and higher levels of unemployment.

A Positive Balance of Payments   The **balance of payments** is the difference between the value of a nation's imports and the value of its exports, including both manufactured goods and services such as insurance and banking. All nations, including the United States, strive to keep the balance positive,

balance of payments

The annual difference between payments and receipts between a country and its trading partners.

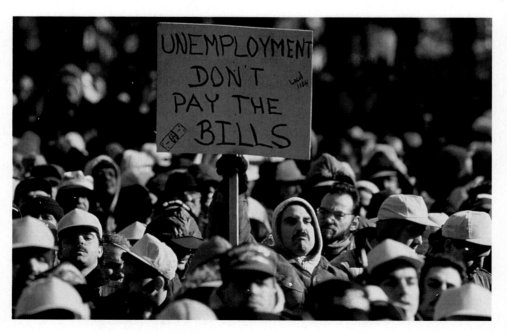

The government is regularly held accountable for economic hardships such as inflation and unemployment. Here demonstrators protest what they believe to be President George Bush's unwillingness to take strong fiscal measures to stimulate the economy. Many analysts believe that these economic difficulties cost Bush his reelection bid in 1992.

Before government regulation, industries were allowed to dump hazardous wastes into the environment without threat of financial or legal repercussions.

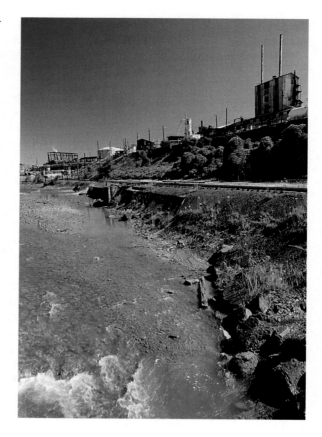

that is, to export more than they import. They do so because sustained negative trade balances lead to a decline in the value of a nation's currency in international markets, as more money leaves the country than is brought in. In this situation, businesses and consumers find that their dollars buy less, and they must either do without or borrow to make up the difference.

Minimizing Negative Externalities   A growing free enterprise economy always produces, in addition to rising living standards, a range of negative side effects, such as air and water pollution, toxic wastes, and workplace injuries and health hazards. These side effects of economic activity—called **negative externalities**—have generated enormous public pressure for compensatory government action. Much of the regulatory activity of the federal government is designed to decrease the incidence of diseconomies.

negative externalities

The positive and negative effects of economic activities on third parties.

Supporting Key Economic Sectors   Certain economic activities are important for the general health of the national economy but are unlikely to be provided by private firms. Almost without exception, governments in the Western democracies, including the United States, have stepped into the breach and provided support for such vital activities and services, either by direct subsidy and tax incentives or by public ownership (although not in the United States). All European countries and the United States, for example, subsidize farmers. The federal government tries to encourage business activity in America's inner cities by using enterprise zone tax incentives; supports the defense industry by direct purchases of weapons systems and subsidization of research; and pays for essential infrastructure such as airports, harbors, and highways.

The Tools of Macroeconomic Policy

Government actions affect (but do not determine) the rate of inflation, the level of unemployment, and the growth of income and output in the national economy. This always has been so. What is new since World War II is that government leaders, economists, and citizens know this to be true and insist that government use whatever means it has available to ensure good economic outcomes.

Government efforts to encourage economic growth, low unemployment, and stable prices fall under the heading of **macroeconomic policy**, or policy that affects the performance of the economy as a whole. The main tools of macroeconomic policy are **fiscal policy** (having to do with government spending and taxes) and **monetary policy** (having to do with the supply and cost of money).

Fiscal Policy   In theory, fiscal policy is a flexible tool for stimulating the economy when it is under-performing and for slowing the economy down when things are getting too hot. Government leaders can increase government spending or decrease taxes when economic stimulation is required (one of the arguments George W. Bush made in favor of his proposed tax cut in 2001); they can cut spending or increase taxes when the economy needs a cooling-off period.

Fiscal tools are not easy to use, however. Decisions about how much government should spend or what level and kinds of taxes ought to be levied are not made simply on the basis of their potential effects on economic stability and growth. The elderly want Social Security and Medicare benefits to keep pace with inflation, for example, regardless of the effect on the overall economy.

Monetary Policy   Fiscal policy is made by the president and Congress when they determine the annual federal government budget. The Federal Reserve Board (commonly known as the Fed) is responsible for monetary policy, decisions that affect how much money is available to businesses and individuals from banks, savings and loans, and credit unions. The more money that is available and the lower the interest rates at which money can be borrowed, the higher overall consumer and business spending are likely to be. If the Fed wants to increase total spending in the economy (called *aggregate demand*), it increases the money supply (by having its *open market committee* buy back government securities from the private sector) and lowers interest rates (by lowering the **discount rate**, or the cost of money to member banks to borrow from the Fed). If it wants to slow the economy down, it decreases the money supply and increases interest rates.

The Debate About the Proper Role of Government in the Economy

People may agree that government has a role to play in the management of the economy, but they disagree about how it should be done. **Keynesians**—who trace their roots to English economist John Maynard Keynes's classic work, *The General Theory of Employment, Interest, and Money*—believe that in an economy where the tools of production (labor, tools, factories, and the like) are not being used to full capacity, which they believe is the case most of the time, government must stimulate economic activity by increasing government spending or by cutting taxes (or both). Most Keynesians have come down on the spending side of the equation and are associated with an activist conception of the role of government most favored by liberal Democrats.

Monetarists, such as Nobel Prize–winning economist Milton Friedman, believe that government (the Federal Reserve in particular) should confine its

macroeconomic policy

Having to do with the performance of the economy as a whole.

fiscal policy

Government's actions affecting spending and taxing levels; affects overall output and income in the economy.

monetary policy

Government's actions affecting the supply of money and the level of interest rates in the economy.

discount rate

The interest rate the Federal Reserve charges member banks to cover short-term loans.

Keynesians

Advocates of government programs to stimulate economic activity through tax cuts and government spending.

monetarists

Advocates of a minimal government role in the economy, limited to managing the growth of the money supply.

activity to managing the growth in the supply of money and credit so that it closely tracks the growth in productivity in the economy as a whole. In the monetarist view, this will allow slow but steady economic growth without inflation through private investment. Balanced federal budgets are essential in the monetarist position because unbalanced budgets, in their view, make it difficult for central banks to control the money supply properly. Monetarism is the economic policy, then, of those who believe in a minimal federal government and the virtues of the free market most associated with conservatives and Republicans.

The Federal Budget and Fiscal Policy

Decisions by the president and Congress on spending and taxes in the federal budget constitute America's fiscal policy.

Spending, Taxes, and Debt

Government Spending   The federal government spent a little more than $1.8 trillion in 1999. This represents a more than fourfold increase since 1960 (in constant dollars) and an expansion of federal outlays as a proportion of GDP from about 18 percent to about 19 percent. (It reached its post–World War II high point of 24 percent of GDP in 1983.) Figure 17.2 shows the change over time in federal outlays as a percentage of GDP. Several things are immediately apparent.

First, the most dramatic increases in federal government spending are associated with involvement in major wars; note the big spikes in the graph for the years associated with World War I, World War II, and the Korean War. Second, the relative spending level of the federal government increased steadily from the early 1930s to the early 1980s. Third, and finally, from the early 1980s to the present, the relative scale of federal spending first leveled off and then declined. This decrease has, in large part, been caused by a substantial decrease in the relative size of the national defense budget in the post–Cold War environment, some cuts in domestic programs instituted by presidents Ronald Reagan and George Bush, and the Clinton–Republican Congress budget agreement in 1995.

Almost 16 percent of federal government expenditures was for *national defense* in 1999[6] (see Figure 17.3), considerably higher than that of other rich democracies but much lower than it was in 1980, when it accounted for almost 23 percent of federal spending. (In 1960, it accounted for more than half of all federal government spending!)

Outlays as a proportion of total federal expenditures for *human resources,* including welfare, health, veterans' benefits, and education and training, have grown considerably since 1980 and now account for around 61 percent of federal spending. Most of the growth is accounted for by just two programs, Social Security and Medicare. Outlays for *physical resources,* including transportation, energy, and the environment, account for about 6 percent of federal dollars, a considerable drop from 1980. Other federal non-defense outlays, which support programs ranging from housing to agriculture, national parks, science and technology, international affairs, and the administration of justice, now attract 6 cents of every federal dollar spent. Interest payments on the national debt are substantial, accounting for 11.0 percent of federal expenditures in 1999 (down from its modern high point in 1996 of 15.9 percent).

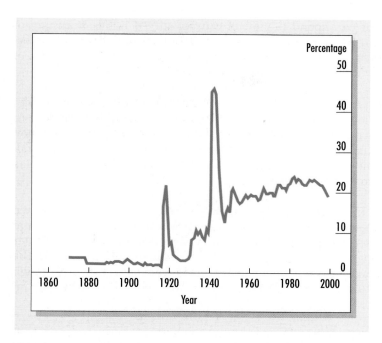

Figure 17.2 ● **Federal Government Spending as a Percentage of GDP, 1869–1999**

This graph shows the scale of federal government spending relative to the size of the U.S. economy. We see that the increase in the relative size of the federal government is a twentieth century phenomenon. We also see that involvement in major wars has been an important factor in the growth in federal spending, with the major spikes coming during World Wars I and II. The permanent change in the role of the federal government in American society is also seen in the steady rise in spending triggered by the Great Depression during the 1930s. Also noteworthy is the recent decline of federal spending as a proportion of U.S. economic activity.

Source: U.S. Bureau of the Census, *Statistical Abstract of the United States, 2000*.

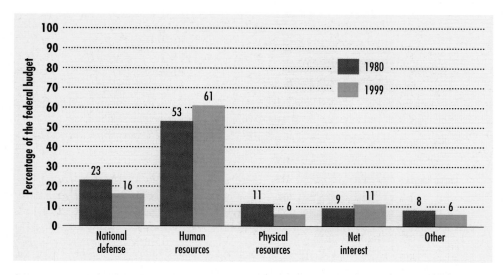

Figure 17.3 ● **Major Categories of Federal Government Spending, 1980 and 1999**

Federal government spending has changed substantially over the past two decades. Most notable is the shift from national defense spending to human resources spending, mainly for Social Security, Medicare, and Medicaid.

Source: Office of Management and Budget, *Budget of the United States, Fiscal 2001*.

Taxes Government can spend money, of course, only if it has a stream of revenues coming in. Such revenues are raised by various kinds of taxes. Although the American system of taxation shares some features with those of other countries, it is unique in a number of ways.

Size of the Tax Bite Although Americans from all walks of life report feeling squeezed by taxes, the total of all taxes levied by all government jurisdictions in the United States as a proportion of GDP is relatively low, at 34 percent, when compared with the tax bite in the other rich democracies (see Figure 17.4). And, on average, what Americans pay in taxes as a percentage of their incomes has stayed about the same for the past 25 years.[7]

Forms of Taxation In our federal system, states and localities levy their own taxes. The national government depends primarily on income taxes (personal and corporate) and payroll taxes to fund its activities (see Figure 17.5). Other rich democracies depend more on national sales and consumption taxes. In the United States, the states get most of their revenues from sales taxes, although many have income taxes as well. Local governments depend most heavily on property taxes.

Complexity of Our Tax System The American tax system is unique in its complexity and particularism. The U.S. Tax Code is a very thick document, filled

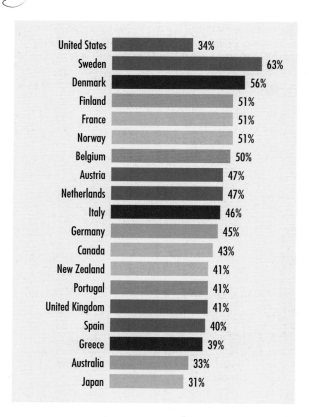

Figure 17.4 ● **Tax Receipts as a Percentage of GDP in the United States and the OECD Countries, 1999**

The tax burden of the United States is much lighter than that of most other rich democracies.

Source: U.S. Bureau of the Census, *Statistical Abstract of the United States, 1999.*

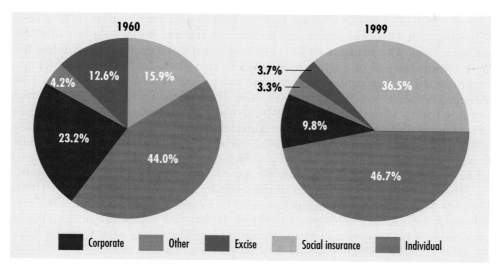

1960
1999

4.2% 12.6% 15.9%
23.2% 44.0%

3.7%
3.3%
9.8% 36.5%
46.7%

| ■ Corporate | ■ Other | ■ Excise | ■ Social insurance | ■ Individual |

Figure 17.5 ● **Sources of Federal Tax Revenues, 1960 and 1999**

The source of federal tax receipts has shifted over the years. Most notable have been the increase in the share of taxes accounted for by social insurance payroll taxes and the shrinking share shouldered by corporations.

Source: Office of Management and Budget, *Budget of the United States, Fiscal 2001.*

with endless exceptions to the rules and special treatment for individuals, companies, and communities. These range from the tax deductibility of home mortgage interest to special treatment of capital gains (income from the sale of property). Often called *tax expenditures,* these shortfalls in what government would collect on income in the absence of these devices amount to a great deal of money, about $500 billion in 1999.

WEB EXPLORATION

Balancing the Budget

Issue: Balancing the government's budget has become an important objective in all of the rich democracies.

Site: Access the Budget of the United States through the "Course Documents" section of your online course. Go to the "Web Explorations" section for Chapter 17, click on "Balancing the Budget," and open "budget." Select "The Citizens Guide," then "List of Charts and Tables," then "Past and Future Budget Deficits or Surpluses."

What You've Learned: What would you conclude about the budgetary performance of the United States compared with other rich democracies? Have we performed significantly better or worse than the others in regard to balancing our government budget?

HINT: Although the United States only managed to balance its budget quite recently, economists predict that the budget will be in surplus for the foreseeable future.

budget deficit

The amount by which annual government expenditures exceed revenues.

national debt

The total outstanding debt of the federal government.

The Deficit and the National Debt   Few issues received more attention over the past two decades than the annual federal budget deficit and the national debt. The **budget deficit** is the annual difference between what the government spends and what it receives in revenues. Like any other person, organization, or institution that spends more than it makes, the federal government must borrow from others to cover the shortfall and must pay interest to those from whom it borrows. The total of what government owes in the form of treasury bonds, bills, and notes to American citizens and institutions (financial institutions, insurance companies, corporations, etc.), foreign individuals and institutions (including foreign governments and banks), and even to itself (that is, to units such as the Social Security Trust Fund) is the **national debt**.

The national debt was much in the news in the late 1980s and early 1990s because persistent annual budget deficits had caused the debt to increase significantly over a very short period of time. Before the 1980s, the national debt grew mainly because of deficit spending to wage war. After each war, the debt, relative to GDP, gradually declined.[8] This pattern changed dramatically during the 1980s, however, when the size of annual federal budget deficits escalated, despite the absence of a major war (see Figure 17.6). The national debt as a

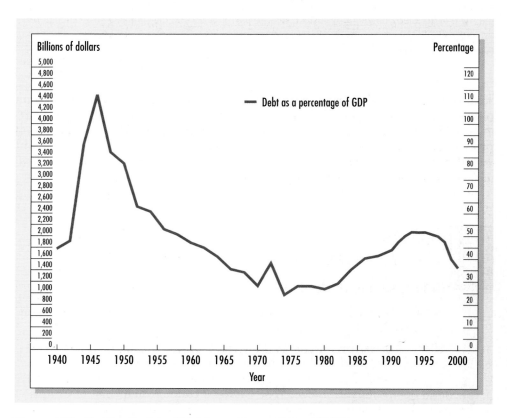

Figure 17.6 ● The National Debt as a Percentage of GDP

In strictly dollar terms, the national debt grew steadily from the early 1970s until 1997, when it began to shrink. The relative national debt—that is, the debt compared with the total size of the American economy (GDP)—also grew from the early 1970s, but it reached its high point in 1993 and has been declining ever since. With recent annual budgets of the federal government in surplus and the economy growing at a brisk pace, the debt is shrinking rapidly. Even at its worst, however, the size of the relative national debt in recent decades was nowhere near the historic high point it reached during World War II.

Source: Office of Management and Budget, *The Budget of the United States, 2001.*

percentage of GDP began to decline in the 1990s as annual budget deficits turned into annual (and growing) surpluses caused by changes in federal fiscal policies and by the tax windfalls from a booming economy. Most economists now believe that the federal budget will be in surplus for a long time and generate a total surplus over 15 years of at least $1.3 trillion. The size of the national debt will continue to shrink as will the relative level of annual interest payments on the debt.

This good news has dramatically changed the political agenda in Washington. Rather than battling over ways to balance the federal budget, Democrats and Republicans have been battling over what to do with the extra money: grant tax cuts, fund prescription drug costs for the elderly, pay down the debt more quickly, or fund new education programs.

Subsidizing Business

Government also supports a range of economic activities considered important to society but unlikely to occur without taxpayer help. *Tax incentives*, for example, encourage home ownership and home building, help manufacturing firms pay for new plants and equipment, and provide incentives for companies to locate in inner-city "enterprise zones." *Loan guarantees* have been used to help troubled but important firms when the need arises, as happened for the Chrysler Corporation in the 1980s.

Regulation

Regulation is one of the most visible and important things the federal government does. Federal agencies issue rules that private businesses must follow. These rules may involve how a company treats its toxic wastes, what hiring procedures it practices, or how it reports its profits and losses.

Why Government Regulates The level of government regulation of private business activities has grown substantially. Scholars disagree on why this has happened.

The Democratic Explanation A free market economy, even when it is working optimally, produces a range of negative externalities that cannot be or are unlikely to be solved by private businesses on their own. These problems include, among others, air and water pollution, inadequate information for investors, unsafe products, unsafe and unwholesome workplaces, toxic wastes, and reckless financial practices. The American people have demonstrated on a number of occasions and consistently in public opinion surveys that they want government to do something about these problems. In a democracy, of course, politicians must respond to such popular pressures on pain of losing office.

The Business Power Explanation Not all scholars are convinced, however, that regulation is solely the product of democratic politics. The *economic theory of regulation* holds that regulation is caused by the political efforts of powerful businesses that turn to government for protection against competitors. Regulation allows firms, it is argued, to restrict overall output, to deny entry to business competitors, and to maintain above-market prices.[9]

A History of American Regulation A brief review of the history of regulation illustrates how the interaction of democratic and nondemocratic factors has produced the regulatory agencies and policies that we have today.[10]

LongmanParticipate

CourseCompass

visual literacy
Evaluating Federal Spending and Economic Policy

LongmanParticipate

CourseCompass

participation
Dealing with a Surplus: Having a Say

regulations
The issuing of rules by government agencies with the aim of reducing the scale of negative externalities produced by private firms.

The stock market crash in 1929 convinced many Americans, including the financial community, that the federal government had an important role to play in regulating and protecting the securities industry against some of its worst excesses. The result was creation of the Securities and Exchange Commission.

Progressive Era Regulation   Between 1900 and World War I, laws were passed to regulate some of the activities of powerful new corporations. Reform was pushed by labor unions, the Populists, and middle-class Americans anxious about the conditions reported by muckraking journalists. Landmark regulatory measures included the Federal Trade Commission Act, the Meat Inspection Act, the Pure Food and Drug Act, and the Federal Reserve Act. These measures dealt with such problems as monopolies, unstable financial institutions, unwholesome products, and unsafe working conditions.

Some scholars believe, however, that large corporations were major players in the conception, formulation, and enactment of regulatory legislation.[11] Seen in this light, the Federal Reserve Act was primarily a government response to the entreaties of the American Bankers Association, which worried about financial panics.

New Deal Regulation   The next wave of regulatory reform occurred in the 1930s when the New Deal turned its attention to speculative and unsafe practices in the banking and securities industries that had contributed to the onset of the Great Depression. Legislation included federal bank inspection, federal deposit insurance, the prohibition of speculative investments by banks, and the creation of the Securities and Exchange Commission to regulate stock market operations.

Again, the political sources of New Deal regulation were mixed. Some came from popular pressures,[12] but some also came from the business community seeking stability in its various industries. Large companies, as we saw in Chapter 7, eventually gained considerable control over regulatory commissions.[13]

The 1960s and 1970s   The successes of the consumer, environmental, and civil rights movements from the late 1960s to the late 1970s resulted in a substantial increase in the federal government's regulation of business, with provisions encouraging broad public participation and accountability. Under the authority of new laws, agencies such as the Environmental Protection Agency, the Equal Opportunity Employment Agency, and the Federal Drug Administration issued numerous rules that affected business operations and

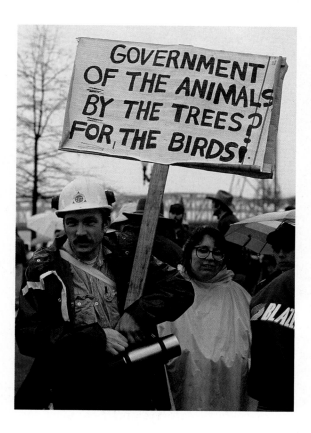

While strong environmental policies are supported by a majority of Americans, business and industry as well as their employees often exert strong pressure to reduce government action in this area.

decisions. It was one of the only times in our history when business was almost entirely on the defensive, unable to halt the imposition of laws and regulations to which it was strongly opposed.[14]

Deregulation By the end of the 1970s, the mood of opinion leaders both inside and outside the government had turned against regulation. Many blamed excessive regulation for forcing inefficient practices on American companies, contributing to the poor performance of the United States in the global economy. Many began to find fault with government imposition on companies of uniform national standards, strict deadlines for compliance with regulations, and detailed instructions.[15] The deregulatory mood was spurred by a business political offensive that took the form of funding for think tanks, journals of opinion, and foundations favorable to the business point of view, as well as funding for the electoral campaigns of sympathetic candidates.[16] From then until today, the watchword has been *deregulation,* loosening the hand of government in a variety of economic sectors including banking and finance, transportation, and telecommunications.

The Future of Regulation While especially egregious, unfair, and inefficient regulations may be erased from the books (or at least we can hope so), it is likely that the regulatory state is here to stay, mainly because the public supports most existing regulatory programs, especially those aimed at environmental and consumer protection. Even at the height of President Reagan's popularity, for example, the Roper Poll reported that only 21 percent of Americans believed that "environmental protection laws and regulations have gone too far," while 69 percent believed that "they are about right or haven't gone far enough."[17]

Should the government try to control children's access to certain content on the Internet? Some Americans think that children can be hurt by things such as pornography, which is freely available on the Net. Others believe that controls, no matter how well intentioned, would violate the freedom of adults.

The regulatory state is here to stay, moreover, because economic activity and technological change bring new problems and demands for government intervention. The ready availability of pornography on the Internet, for example, has triggered efforts by Christian conservatives and others to regulate its content. Unraveling the human genome has led to calls for regulating how this new knowledge will be used. When mergers threaten competition, most consumers welcome government intervention.

Making Economic Policy: The Main Players

Many influences shape American economic policies.

Political Linkage Factors   *Interest groups,* particularly those representing business, but also labor, consumer, and environmental groups, take a keen interest in economic policy, and their permanent representatives in Washington are a constant presence in the halls of Congress and at regulatory agencies. *Voters* and *public opinion* are also important. The public is attuned to overall economic conditions and generally pays attention to what its elected leaders are doing to curb inflation and avoid unemployment and to stimulate growth. We saw in Chapter 10 that the general state of the economy is one of the most important factors in the outcome of national elections. Knowing this, elected leaders do what they can to ensure steady economic growth with low inflation and to prevent economic downturns at election time.

Political parties also play a role in economic policymaking. Because each has its own electoral and financial constituency, made up of groups with identifiable economic interests, the two parties tend to support different economic policies. Democrats talk more about "fairness" when they are making economic policy; Republicans talk more about financial stability, economic efficiency, and government waste. Over many decades, Democrats in office have tended to favor economic policies that decrease unemployment and disparities in income and to worry less about inflation, whereas Republicans have tended to favor policies that control inflation, despite the resulting higher unemployment and greater inequality. The policies matter. Inequality decreases slightly when Democrats control the presidency and increases slightly when Republicans control it.[18]

Governmental Factors   The president, Congress, and the Federal Reserve Board are particularly important in fashioning economic policies.

The President   When things go wrong in the economy, it is the president to whom we usually turn for action. This role is recognized formally in the Employment Act of 1946, which requires that the president report on the state of the economy and recommend action to ensure maximum employment and economic stability. At the center of every modern president's legislative program are proposals for spending, taxing, and regulation that usually have broad macroeconomic effects.

Congress is a full partner in economic policymaking, so presidents must always attend to relations with that body. Presidents must also be skillful at affecting the behavior of the Federal Reserve Board if they want the Fed to regulate the money supply and interest rates in ways that are consistent with the president's program. This is not easy to accomplish because the president has virtually no control over the people he nominates once they are on the board.

Congress   Nearly everything that Congress does has macroeconomic consequences, especially its decisions about the annual federal budget. The decisions it makes about the overall balance of government spending and taxes are, as we have seen, a powerful fiscal instrument, either stimulating or retarding the economy. Taxes levied by Congress shape the incentives for individual and company economic decision making. Laws that regulate, grant subsidies, or supply loan guarantees influence private-sector economic behavior, and trade bills and treaties affect the fortunes of American consumers and many companies.

The Federal Reserve Board   The Federal Reserve Board makes monetary policy for the nation. It is made up of seven members (called governors) who serve overlapping 14-year terms and a chair who serves a renewable four-year term. Each is appointed by the president. The Fed is closely connected with, and very solicitous of, the needs of commercial and investment bankers and generally prefers to control inflation as a first order of business to protect the value of financial assets.

Alan Greenspan, here testifying before the House Banking Committee, has exercised enormous influence over the U.S. and world economies by his skillful use of monetary policy tools as chairman of the Federal Reserve Board.

Federal Reserve Chairman Alan Greenspan has been credited, correctly or incorrectly, as the guiding monetary hand behind the economic boom and low inflation of the 1990s. He more modestly credits the effects of tax cuts, deregulation, and technology-driven productivity gains.

The Fed is relatively independent. Aggressive actions by Congress or the president to pressure the Fed would surely trigger adverse reactions on Wall Street and in the financial community at home and abroad—reactions that neither the president nor Congress is eager to confront.

Social Welfare

Another important domain of domestic policy in the United States is social welfare, a broad range of programs that protects the minimum standards of living of families and individuals against some of life's unavoidable circumstances: unemployment, income loss and poverty, physical and mental illness and disability, family disintegration, and old age. Such programs account for the largest share of the annual federal budget.

Outline of the American Welfare State

Social welfare in the United States is provided by a complex mix of programs.

Types of Programs   There are two basic kinds of welfare state programs in the United States. The first is **social insurance** in which individuals contribute to an insurance trust fund by way of a payroll tax on their earnings and receive benefits based on their lifetime contributions. Social Security is an example. The second kind is **means-tested**, meaning that benefits are distributed on the basis of need to those who can prove that their income is low enough to qualify. These programs are funded by general income tax revenues, rather than by payroll taxes. The food stamp program is an example.

Some social welfare programs are administered directly from Washington, while others are jointly administered by federal and state governments. Social Security is an example of a program run from the nation's capital. Taxes for Social Security are levied directly on wages and salaries by the federal government, and benefit checks are issued to the elderly and the disabled by the Social Security Administration. By contrast, Medicaid is jointly funded and administered. One result of such mixed programs is wide variation in benefit levels across the states.

Some welfare state programs are **entitlement** programs; payments are made automatically to people who meet certain eligibility requirements. All Americans over the age of 65 are covered by Medicare, and most citizens whose income is under a certain limit are entitled to food stamps. Because payments are made automatically, much of the federal budget is locked in, and Congress can only tinker around the margins of the budget. In 1999, about 53 percent of the federal budget went to various entitlements

Cost of the Social Welfare State   The federal government spends a great deal of money supporting the welfare state (state and local governments add to the total); outlays for Social Security, Medicare, Medicaid, and means-tested entitlement programs account for almost one-half of federal spending. Of this total, social insurance programs account for the lion's share, a bit more than one-third of federal government expenditures. As Figure 17.7 shows, these programs

social insurance

Government programs that provide services or income support in proportion to the amount of mandatory contributions made by individuals to a government trust fund.

means-tested

Meeting the criterion of demonstrable need.

entitlements

Government benefits that are distributed automatically to citizens who qualify on the basis of a set of guidelines set by law; for example, Americans over the age of 65 are entitled to Medicare coverage.

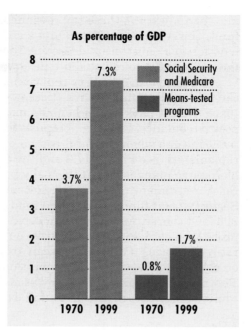

Figure 17.7 ● **Comparing the Size of Social Insurance and Means-Tested Programs**

Social insurance programs, such as Social Security and Medicare, receive many more federal dollars than means-tested programs, such as public assistance, food stamps, and Medicaid. Recently, the relative advantage of social insurance over means-tested programs has become even more pronounced.
Source: Office of Management and Budget, *The Budget of the United States, 2001.*

have grown dramatically over the past three decades relative to means-tested programs. And in a turnabout from the situation that existed in the 1950s and 1960s, they dwarf spending for national defense.

Several things result from this pattern of expenditure. First, and perhaps contrary to common belief, most benefits of the American welfare state do not go to the poor. The lion's share of social insurance benefits go to Americans who were fully employed during their working lives, had the highest incomes, and paid the maximum level of Social Security taxes. Second, because social insurance benefits go mainly to those who are retired, the elderly fare much better than the young. One result is a significant decrease in the poverty rate among the elderly over the past two decades and an increase in the poverty rate among children.[19] (The child poverty rate fell, however, in 1998 and 1999.)

Social Security and Other Social Insurance Programs

Social insurance programs that guard against loss of income due to old age, disability, and illness are the largest, most popular, and fastest-growing parts of the American welfare state.[20]

Components of Social Insurance   There are a number of social insurance programs designed to meet different contingencies.

Old Age, Survivors, and Disability Insurance (OASDI)   This is the largest of the social insurance programs and the full, technical name of Social Security. OASDI is funded by a payroll tax on employees and employers under the Federal Insurance Contributions Act (the familiar FICA on your weekly or monthly pay stub); these tax revenues are deposited in a Social Security trust fund. The self-employed pay into a similar trust fund. Because the program is paid for to a substantial degree by those who are currently working, however, the net effect is to redistribute income across generations.

Many Americans worry that Social Security funds will run out before they can begin collecting benefits. Presently, Social Security takes in more in payroll taxes than it pays out in benefits each year, so its trust fund shows a strong positive balance. However, because the population is aging, there will come a point in time when the fund will be paying out at a faster clip than it is being replenished (see Figure 17.8 and the discussion in Chapter 4). Especially troublesome to many is the sizable baby-boom generation, whose first members will reach retirement age in 2010. Recent estimates by the actuary of the Social Security trust fund say that the fund will not move into the red until the year 2037. Of course, Americans can decide long before then to solve the trust fund problem by raising payroll taxes, cutting back benefit levels, or raising the retirement age.[21] Policymakers can also decide, as some have suggested, to fully or partially privatize the system, thus depending more on the stock market. The public supports this innovation in principle but seems less sure when reminded that stock prices can fall as well as rise.

Medicare Medicare pays for a substantial portion of the hospital and doctor bills of retirees and the disabled. Since Medicare was created in 1965, it has

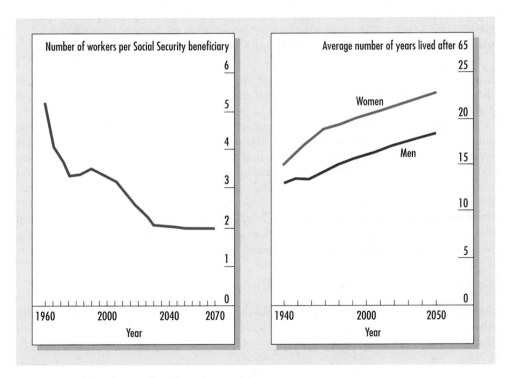

Figure 17.8 ● The Social Security Problem

Demographic trends in the United States (and in the other rich democracies) point to potential problems in financing Social Security in the future: there will be fewer workers supporting more retirees. The financing problem can be solved by raising payroll taxes, cutting benefits, and/or raising the retirement age, or by, in the view of some, privatizing all or part of the system.

Source: Social Security Administration.

grown into one of the largest federal programs in total dollar expenditures; more than $205 billion was spent in 1999, about 12 percent of the federal budget.

Paying for Medicare is a recurring problem. Outlays have been growing at about 10 percent a year for the past 15 years, much faster than those for other federal programs and much faster than Medicare revenues are coming in. And waiting in the wings, again, is the baby-boom generation. It is no wonder, then, that the issue of controlling Medicare costs has become one of the constants of recent American politics. Recent budget surpluses, however, have helped lower the political temperature on this issue. In fact, Al Gore proposed adding prescription drug coverage to Medicare during his 2000 presidential campaign.

Unemployment Insurance Unemployment insurance is administered by the states under federal guidelines, assisted by federal subsidies. It is financed by federal and state taxes on employers for each of their employees. Studies show that the program is not very popular with Americans (unlike other social insurance programs, such as Medicare), perhaps because employees do not contribute to the fund and perhaps because of the importance of work in American culture. Physically able people who are not working do not seem "deserving" to many Americans.[22] The level of benefits is set by the states, and there are wide variations among them.

Do Social Insurance Programs Work?
In an era when it is fashionable to deride the ability of government to do anything well, it is important to know about the relative success of America's social insurance programs.

Successes Social Security and Medicare work beyond the wildest dreams of their founders. Although the benefits do not allow people to live luxuriously, they provide an income floor for the retired and pay for costly medical services that, before 1965, were as likely as not to impoverish those who had serious illnesses and long hospital stays.

Their effectiveness is shown in a 1989 Census Bureau study on the effects of government taxing and spending programs on income inequality and poverty.

WEB EXPLORATION

Reforming Social Security

Issue: There has been a great deal of talk lately about reforming, even "saving" Social Security.

Site: Access Public Agenda Online through the "Course Documents" section of your online course. Go to the "Web Explorations" section for Chapter 17, click on "Reforming Social Security," and open "proposals." Select "Social Security" from the list on the left side of the page, then select "framing the debate." Read the "Perspectives in Brief."

What You've Learned: Which of the competing proposals for reforming Social Security appeals to you the most? Why?

HINT: Your answer will probably depend on how much confidence you have in the present system and how much risk you can tolerate in the stock market.

The principal finding was that Social Security (including Medicare) "is the Federal government's most effective weapon against poverty and reduces the inequality of Americans' income more than the tax system and more than recent social welfare [means-tested] programs."[23] In fact, Social Security and Medicare reduce the elderly poverty rate from about 48 percent to just under 12 percent.[24]

Problems   Despite these successes, many problems remain. Social Security and Medicare have remained viable, for instance, only because Congress has steadily raised payroll taxes to pay for them. FICA and Medicare taxes now take a larger bite out of the paychecks of a majority of Americans than the personal income tax. For those who generally oppose taxes, this trend is cause for concern. Whether taxes are too high cannot be answered objectively or scientifically, of course, although it is worth repeating that our overall effective tax rates remain well below those of most other Western countries.

Many also worry about the fiscal viability of Social Security and Medicare. The problem is serious, to be sure, but it is certainly solvable, as we suggested earlier.

Means-Tested Programs (Welfare)

Means-tested programs, often referred to as *welfare,* account for only a small part of the annual federal budget but have attracted more popular discontent than virtually anything else government does. While Social Security and Medicare enjoy widespread support, means-tested welfare programs have long been an object of scorn.

While most Americans say they want government to help the poor, almost everybody disliked the now-defunct Aid to Families with Dependent Children (AFDC) program—not just conservatives, but liberals as well; not just average citizens, but also welfare recipients; and not just voters and political leaders, but people who work for welfare agencies. A consensus long existed that something was wrong with AFDC.[25]

For most Americans, the traditional welfare program (we will talk about the new form of welfare later) seemed to contradict such cherished cultural values as independence, hard work, stable families, and responsibility for one's own actions. Public opinion polls consistently showed that Americans believed that welfare kept people dependent; didn't do a good job of helping people stand on their own two feet; and encouraged divorce, family disintegration, and out-of-wedlock births.[26]

The government offers several means-tested programs designed to assist low-income Americans. Let us look at the five most important ones.

Food Stamps   This program is available to most Americans who fall below a certain income line. About 8 percent of Americans presently receive food stamps. Food stamp benefit levels are set by the individual states under general federal guidelines, and states vary substantially in their generosity. Stamps can be used only for food; they cannot be used for alcohol, cigarettes, or gambling, despite rumors to the contrary. The program seems to have made a significant dent in the prevalence of malnutrition in the United States, even though the average benefit has never exceeded 80 cents per person per meal.[27]

Medicaid   The federal government allocates matching funds to the states to provide medical assistance for their indigent citizens in this rapidly growing program (expenditures grew from $30 billion in 1988 to $103 billion in 1999). Except for the requirement that they provide Medicaid for all public assistance recipients, the states formulate their own eligibility requirements and set their own benefit levels. The eligibility rules are complex and tend to exclude those who are not extremely poor, blind, disabled, or children of out-of-work parents. The problem of noninclusion is serious; only about 40 percent of the nation's officially designated poor are covered by Medicaid, and the remainder are without medical benefits or protection.

Supplemental Security Income   Supplemental Security Income (SSI) is a program created in 1974 that provides cash benefits to the elderly, blind, and disabled poor when social insurance programs are insufficient to elevate them above the poverty line. The program is relatively small and getting smaller.

Head Start   This is by far the most popular means-tested social welfare program. It reaches about 300,000 children per year (only about 20 percent of those who are technically eligible) in an effort to prepare poor preschool children for entrance into public schools.

Welfare Block Grants   In 1996, the Republican-controlled 104th Congress passed a bill to refashion welfare in the United States (see the vignette that

WEB EXPLORATION

Making It on Welfare

Issue: Is it possible to live a decent life under the new welfare system? Find out by preparing your own family budget and comparing it with the welfare benefits available in your state.

Site: Access the Green Book of the House Ways and Means Committee, and look at the maximum TANF family payment for your state through the "Course Documents" section of your online course. Go to the "Web Explorations" section for Chapter 17, click on "Making It on Welfare," and open "benefits." In Section 7, look carefully at Table 7.9 on "maximum benefits" for each state.

What You've Learned: Imagine you are a welfare recipient living in your present community. Pretend that you have two children. Prepare a budget for what it would cost you to live at a minimum level of decency. Be sure to account for housing costs, including utilities, food (you will pay about half, with food stamps covering the other half), transportation (used car, with insurance and gas) or public transportation, school supplies for your children, some modest entertainment, some clothes, personal hygiene and beauty care products, and whatever else you believe to be essential. Don't worry about medical care; you'll be covered by Medicaid.

How does your budget compare with the maximum benefit paid in your state? Do you believe a life of decency is possible for you and your hypothetical family under TANF? Is there anything you could eliminate from your budget to make it leaner?

HINT: Most students find that what they consider to be necessary for minimum decency is far above what is allowed to welfare families.

opens Chapter 3). Having run in the 1992 presidential election on a pledge to "change welfare as we know it" and having vetoed two previous welfare bills, President Clinton felt compelled to sign the bill, the Temporary Assistance to Needy Families Act (TANF), which created a new system of public assistance, despite some personal reservations about it.

The new welfare system is extremely complex and only in its earliest stages, so how it will eventually develop or how effective it will be is unknown at this time. Its major features are as follows:

- The status of welfare assistance as a federal entitlement has been ended. The families of poor children are no longer guaranteed assistance by the federal government.

- The design and administration of welfare programs have been turned over to the individual states. In the end, the United States will have 50 different welfare systems.

- States receive block grants from the federal government to help them finance the welfare systems they devise. States can use up to 30 percent of the grants on noncash benefit programs for the poor (such as child care, training, transportation, and the like).

- The head of every family receiving welfare is required to work within two years of receiving benefits and is limited to a total of five years of benefits. States are allowed to impose even more stringent time requirements. Connecticut, for example, has set the limit at 21 months. States are also allowed to use their own funds (not federal block grant money) to extend the two-year and five-year limits.

- Unmarried teenage parents can receive welfare benefits only if they stay in school and live with an adult.

- Future legal immigrants are ineligible for benefits during their first five years in the United States.

- States must provide Medicaid to all who qualify under current law.

- The eligibility of poor people who are not raising children to receive food stamps is severely restricted.

Proponents of the legislation suggest that the new welfare system will end welfare dependence, reestablish the primacy of the family, improve the income situation of the poor as they enter the job market, and help balance the federal budget. Opponents of the legislation say that the new system will lead to more poverty, homelessness, and hunger, especially among children once recipients use up their time limits.

Only time will tell which of these scenarios will prevail over the long run. In the short run, however, the results have been surprisingly good,[28] probably because of the spectacular performance of the American economy in the 1990s. For one thing, the welfare rolls have declined dramatically almost everywhere: 38 percent nationally between 1994 and 1998. Moreover, about two-thirds of those people who left welfare during this period now work at least 20 hours per week. Additionally, there is as yet no evidence that homelessness has increased. And, a study in Massachusetts reports that 86 percent of former welfare recipients say they are at least as well off as they were under AFDC.[29]

On the other hand, about 20 percent who left the welfare roles during these years eventually returned, an option that will not be open in the future when the two-year and five-year limits kick in. And, because pay levels for entry-level jobs are so low, only a handful of former welfare recipients have been able to cross the official **poverty-line** threshold.

poverty line

The federal government's calculation of the amount of income families of various sizes need to stay out of poverty.

USING THE FRAMEWORK

Why Did Our Welfare System Change So Suddenly in 1996?

America's traditional welfare system, created in 1935 almost as an afterthought to Social Security, had grown to the point that it provided cash payments to families of one in nine children in the United States by 1995. Although it did not pay very much to individual families, and represented but a tiny portion of the federal government's budget, the program was never very popular with the public, grew even less popular in recent decades, and was replaced by a radically new program in 1996. Examining structural, political linkage, and governmental factors that contributed to a dramatic change in welfare policy will make the story clearer.

Governmental Action

The Temporary Assistance to Needy Families Act becomes law in 1996.

Governmental Level

- The Republican-controlled Congress delivered on its promise in the Republican Contract with America to pass a bill to radically transform welfare.

- President Clinton, himself a believer in welfare reform (he had promised to "end welfare as we know it"), signed the bill into law near the beginning of the 1996 presidential campaign.

Political Linkages Level

- Conservative intellectuals and think tanks attacked the AFDC welfare system during the 1980s on the grounds that it killed individual initiative and created dependency, destroyed families, and rewarded immorality.

- "New Democrats" also embraced welfare reform.

- The Republican Party used the "welfare mess" issue with great effect in election campaigns, winning the presidency in 1980, 1984, and 1988 and the Senate for much of the 1980s.

- Public opinion became more critical of welfare in the 1970s and 1980s.

- Republican conservatives won control of the House and Senate in the 1994 elections.

- The Democratic Party lost a substantial number of blue-collar, unionized workers, concerned about "wasteful spending" on welfare, from their electoral base.

Structural Level

- The American political culture celebrates competitive individualism, small government, and self-reliance and denigrates handouts to the "undeserving" poor.

- Competitive pressures from the global economy in the 1990s pushed governments in all of the rich democracies to make their welfare states more efficient.

- The fall of communism and the post–Cold War boom in the United States enhanced the attractiveness of conservative ideas in America.

- Federalism allowed states to experiment with alternative modes of welfare delivery, gaining valuable information.

The Earned Income Tax Credit   The working poor benefit greatly from a provision in the U.S. Tax Code that allows low-income individuals with at least one child to claim a credit against taxes owed or, for some, to receive a direct cash transfer from the IRS. This provision of the Tax Code benefits more than 50 million low-income Americans without much bureaucratic fuss.[30]

How the American Welfare State Compares with Others

Although all of the industrialized democracies are also social welfare states, not all social welfare states are alike. Welfare states range from low-benefit types, where beneficiaries are narrowly targeted (e.g., the poor and the elderly), to high-benefit types, where beneficiaries include most people in the society. The former are sometimes called *minimal* or *liberal* (in the free market, limited-government sense of the word *liberal*) welfare states; the latter are called *developed* or *social democratic* welfare states.[31] The United States is very close to the minimal end of the spectrum. How you feel about where the United States fits on the spectrum depends on your values. For those who believe that small government is always better than big government, it is a very good thing. Others may disagree, believing that government should play a more significant role in protecting and sustaining its citizens.

How the United States Differs   How does our welfare state compare with those of the other rich democracies?

- *The U.S. welfare state developed later than the others.* Generally, social insurance programs were introduced in America much later than elsewhere.[32] National health insurance was introduced in Germany in the late nineteenth century; it was available in almost all Western European nations by 1950. Medicare for the elderly and Medicaid for the indigent didn't happen in the United States until the 1960s.

- *The American welfare state is smaller than most.* Despite complaints about its size and cost, ours is one of the smallest of the social welfare states.[33] Among the rich democracies, only Japan and Australia spend relatively less than we do on social welfare, and the former is well known for the generosity of company benefits to workers.

- *The American welfare state covers fewer people than other welfare states.* Welfare states near the developed end of the spectrum blanket their entire populations with benefits. Family allowances in such places as Austria, the Netherlands, Norway, and Sweden, for instance, go to all citizens who have children. Medical coverage is universal in most of the OECD nations. In the United States, in contrast, social welfare provision is a patchwork, and many citizens are not protected or covered. More than 40 million Americans, for example, have no health insurance coverage at all.

- *The elderly do considerably better than the young in the American welfare state.* Medicare and Social Security, already the largest parts of social welfare in the United States, continue to outstrip the rate of growth of programs that benefit the nonelderly poor, especially children.[34] In most other welfare states, family allowances and universal medical coverage keep benefit distributions more balanced.[35]

- *The American welfare state is less redistributive.* The degree of income equality in the OECD nations (with the exception of Japan) is a function

Medicare pays for a substantial portion of the health care costs of elderly Americans. Before Medicare, those over 65 depended on private health insurance or paid out-of-pocket for medical care.

of the amount of money they spend on social welfare programs and the degree to which program coverage is universal. The United States ranks very low on both, so our social welfare state does not make much of a dent in the degree of income and wealth inequality in comparison with those of other nations.[36]

- *The American welfare state requires less of private employers.* All Western European welfare states require that employers help employees with their parenting obligations. All require employers to offer maternity and parenting leaves (now required for workers in firms with 50 or more employees in the United States under the Family and Medical Leave Act), with pay (not required here); all require that work schedules be adjusted for parenting needs. German mothers receive six weeks' paid leave before giving birth and eight weeks' after. All Western European governments mandate four to six weeks of paid vacation.

- *The American welfare state does not include universal health care.* The OECD countries either provide health services directly (the National Health Service in Great Britain is an example), offer universal health insurance coverage (e.g., the Canadian system), or use some combination of the two. In the United States, Medicare provides health insurance coverage for the elderly, Medicaid provides coverage for the poor, and the Veterans Administration covers costs for veterans of the military and their dependents. Other Americans must depend on private insurance, pay out-of-pocket, or do without.

Are the Western European Welfare States Becoming More Like Us?

Competitive pressures in the global economy are forcing even very rich nations to become more concerned about the high taxes and budget deficits that seem to be associated with highly developed welfare states. These conditions adversely affect the international competitiveness of countries and their business enterprises. In response, several nations with highly developed welfare states, such as France, Finland, and the Netherlands, have stopped the growth of social welfare spending as a proportion of their GDP, and several have increased the retirement age.

Nevertheless, Western European political leaders have not been able to do much more than chip away at the edges of the welfare state. The reason is that the vast majority of people in Western Europe, including powerful labor unions, support the welfare state and are willing to fight to keep it. Few European leaders, therefore, have tried wholesale reform. Those who have tried have paid the price. When French Prime Minister Jacques Chirac attempted to make major cuts in welfare state benefits in 1995, massive demonstrations and prolonged public employee strikes forced him to withdraw his proposals.

Why the American Welfare State Is Different

How to explain the special character of the American welfare state? Here we identify structural and political linkage factors that influence the kind of social welfare state we have.

Constitutional Rules   Federalism is one of the reasons social welfare programs were introduced here so late. Until the 1930s, it was not clear where the main responsibility for social welfare was constitutionally lodged. It was not generally accepted that the national government had any authority at all on social welfare matters until the U.S. Supreme Court belatedly relented and accepted the New Deal. Federalism is also responsible for the incredible administrative complexity of our social welfare state and for the great unevenness in program coverage. Our system takes into account the needs and interests of each of the states. The result is great variation among the states in benefits, eligibility requirements, and rules. The only large-scale programs that are universal in the European sense (uniform, comprehensive, and administered and funded by the national government) are Social Security and Medicare.

Racial and Ethnic Diversity   It is often argued that Europe's greater propensity toward welfare states with universal coverage is a result of the ethnic and racial homogeneity of their societies. In homogeneous societies, the argument goes, voters are willing to support generous welfare programs because recipients are felt to be very much like themselves, neighbors, down on their luck.[37]

Whether or not this argument is valid—the growing diversity within European countries will eventually allow us to test this idea—it is apparent that racial and ethnic tensions influence the shape of the American welfare state. Some of the hostility toward AFDC, for instance, was probably related to the fact that African-Americans made up a disproportionately large share of AFDC recipients (although less than a majority of all recipients). Politicians such as Jesse Helms in North Carolina have demonstrated considerable skill in weaving together the racial and welfare themes in their electoral campaigns.

Political Culture   Almost every aspect of the American political culture works against a generous and comprehensive welfare state. The belief in competitive individualism is especially important. Voters who believe that people should stand on their own two feet and take responsibility for their lives are not likely to be sympathetic to appeals for help from able-bodied, working-age people.[38]

Antigovernment themes in the political culture also play a role. Generous and comprehensive welfare states, such as those in Europe, are almost always large and centralized states supported by high taxes. Being deeply suspicious of politicians, centralized government, and taxes, Americans are strongly resistant to welfare state appeals.

Business Power   Business plays a disproportionately powerful role in American politics (see Chapter 7). Almost without exception, the business community has opposed the creation of a welfare state along European lines. It has been a voice for low taxes and limited benefits and for voluntary efforts over government responsibility. We can see this stance in the area of medical care. Ours is a patchwork quilt that combines social insurance for the elderly (Medicare), a means-tested program (Medicaid) for *some* of the poor, private insurance (Blue Cross/Blue Shield, Prudential, etc.) for many Americans, and a multitude of for-profit hospitals and nursing homes. Doctors, hospital corporations, insurance companies, and nursing home owners are major players in the American system of interest group politics, and they continuously press politicians to maintain this system of mixed government–private enterprise medical care.

Weak Labor Unions   Countries in which the working class is organized and exercises significant political power have extensive welfare states; countries in which the working class is not well organized and fails to exercise significant political power have minimal welfare states.[39] American labor unions have never been very strong or influential when compared with labor unions in other Western capitalist societies as you learned in Chapter 7. The proportion of American workers who join labor unions has always been lower in the United States than in other capitalist countries. Moreover, neither one of our political parties defines itself as a working-class or labor party committed to using government as an instrument of equality. We have no party equivalent, for example, to the labor-backed Social Democratic party that has dominated Swedish politics since the mid-1930s.

LongmanParticipate

CourseCompass

timeline
**The Evolution of
Social Welfare Policy**

Summary

The federal government plays an important role in national economic affairs and in providing social welfare for its citizens. Both roles arise from problems created by a dynamic free enterprise market economy and the demand by people in a democratic society that government lend a helping hand.

With respect to macroeconomic policy, the government uses both fiscal and monetary tools to try to encourage economic growth and low inflation. The annual budget fashioned by the president and Congress is the main tool of fiscal policy; decisions by the Federal Reserve Board that affect the supply of money in the economy serve as the main tool of monetary policy. Monetary policy has become increasingly important as problems in controlling the budget deficit have made fiscal policy less effective and less attractive.

The federal government also subsidizes essential infrastructure that would otherwise not be made available by private enterprise and plays an important regulatory role. The origins of the government's role may be found in market failures and diseconomies that triggered popular and business pressures on government. Despite the deregulation efforts of recent years, the regulatory responsibilities of the federal government are likely to remain substantial.

Economic policies are fashioned by the president, Congress, and the Federal Reserve Board. But others are involved as well. Interest groups play a particularly central role. Political parties are also important: Democrats and Republicans take different approaches to economic questions and support different policies when in power.

The social welfare commitment of the federal government has grown substantially since the 1930s, with the most important recent growth occurring in social insurance programs such as Social Security and Medicare. Public

LongmanParticipate

CourseCompass

visual literacy
**Where the
Money Goes...**

HOW DEMOCRATIC ARE WE?

PROPOSITION: The economic and social policies that the government in Washington produce are very far from what the people want. Americans don't get the kinds of economic and social policies that satisfy them.

AGREE: The discontent expressed by the public about government—it's too big, spends and taxes too much, and cannot be trusted to do the right thing—is largely related to the fact that government actions do not come very close to what the public wants it to do. Elected leaders are largely unaffected by elections and mainly pay attention to what special interests want, so our economic and social policies are tilted in ways that satisfy them. The tax law, for instance, is riddled with provisions that reward powerful interests.

DISAGREE: In broad outline, the American public gets what it wants from government in terms of economic and social policy, although, to be sure, they continue to complain about government. Even though these policies do not satisfy many conservative and liberal critics, democracy is served to the extent that policies closely match what the majority wants from government. For example, Americans want a level of government spending and taxing that is lower than that of the other rich democracies, which it gets. It wants a government that provides only minimal cash support and services for people who seem able but unwilling to help themselves, which it also gets. In the post–Cold War area, it wants funds shifted from the defense sector to domestic needs, which elected leaders have done. It has demanded that the federal budget be balanced, which happened. The public wants a government that mostly allows the free market to operate on its own, but that also pays attention to issues of consumer safety and environmental protection. Economic policies reflect these seemingly contradictory desires.

THE AUTHORS: It is certainly the case that in broad outline, economic and social policies match what the majority of Americans want. In this sense, popular sovereignty is served. However, we would hasten to add that the hand of special interests may be found in abundance in the details of many of our economic and social policies. This is the case for spending, for example, where commitments to specific priorities and projects, from weapons systems procurement to direct business subsidies, are hammered out in a legislative process in which special interests dominate. This is the case for taxation, where the detailed provisions of the Tax Code are the outcome of the efforts of special interests—who are also the main beneficiaries. This is also the case in regulatory policy, where far too many regulatory agencies remain "captured" or heavily influenced by those they are charged with regulating. This is the case as well in social welfare policy, where business and interest groups representing the professions and the elderly play a prominent role, while the poor play almost no role at all. And, finally, it is the case in monetary policy, where the Federal Reserve Board is especially sensitive to the needs of large investors and financial institutions.

assistance grew less slowly and accounted for a much smaller portion of the federal government's social welfare budget. Public assistance was unpopular, however, and in 1996, it was replaced by a block grant program in which the states were given wide latitude to design their own programs.

The American welfare state is very different from others. Ours is smaller, less comprehensive, less redistributive, and more tilted toward the benefit of the elderly. Structural and political linkage factors explain most of the differences.

Suggestions for Further Reading

Cantril, Albert H., and Susan Davis Cantril. *Reading Mixed Signals.* Washington, D.C.: Woodrow Wilson Center Press, 1999.
> *A report on public ambivalence about the role and responsibilities of government in managing the economy and providing social welfare.*

Harris, Richard, and Sidney Milkis. *The Politics of Regulatory Change.* New York: Oxford University Press, 1989.
> *A history of regulation organized around the idea that different kinds of "regulatory regimes" follow one another.*

Kuttner, Robert. *Everything for Sale: The Virtues and Limits of Markets.* New York: Knopf, 1997.
> *A careful examination of areas where free enterprise and free markets advance human welfare and where they do not and why government has a role to play in compensating for the latter.*

Noble, Charles. *Welfare as We Know It: A Political History of the American Welfare State.* New York: Oxford University Press, 1997.
> *A comprehensive, sophisticated, and lively discussion of why we have the kind of welfare state we have in the United States and why the establishment of a European-style welfare state remains out of the question here.*

Page, Benjamin I., and James R. Simmons. *What Government Can Do: Dealing with Poverty and Inequality.* Chicago: University of Chicago Press, 2000.
> *A passionate, articulate, and empirically supported argument in favor of a larger role for government in alleviating poverty and making the United States a more equal society.*

Peters, Guy B. *American Public Policy: Promise and Performance,* 5th ed. New York: Chatham House/Seven Bridges Press, 1999.
> *A comprehensive examination of the formation and content of American public policies.*

Internet Sources

American Enterprise Institute   **http://www.aei.org/**
> *A prominent conservative think tank with information about social policy.*

Budget of the United States   **http://www.access.gpo.gov/usbudget/**
> *The budget of the United States, with numbers, documentation, and analyses.*

Electronic Policy Network   **www.epn.org/**
> *Reports from liberal think tanks on social welfare issues.*

Fedstats   **http://www.fedstats.gov**
> *Links to statistics and data from a broad range of federal government agencies, including those most relevant for economic and social welfare policy in the United States. These include the Federal Reserve Board, the Bureau of Labor Statistics, the Social Security Administration, the Bureau of the Census, the Bureau of Economic Analysis, and Administration for Children and Families.*

Public Agenda Online   **www.publicagenda.org/**
> *A nonpartisan site with comprehensive information about government policies, alternative proposals to solve societal problems, and what the public thinks about existing and alternative policies.*

Notes

1. Michael Weisskopf and David Maraniss, "Endgame: The Revolution Stalls," *Washington Post National Edition* (January 29, 1996), p. 6.

2. Arnold J. Heidenheimer, Hugh Heclo, and Carolyn Teich Adams, *Comparative Public Policy: The Politics of Social Choice in America, Europe, and Japan,* 3rd ed. (New York: St. Martin's Press, 1990), p. 137.

3. Fred C. Pampel, *Age, Class, Politics, and the Welfare State* (New York: Cambridge University Press, 1989), p. 16; Harold Wilensky, *The Welfare State and Equality* (Berkeley, CA: University of California Press, 1975).

4. Robert E. Goodin, "Reasons for Welfare," in J. Donald Moon, ed., *Responsibility, Rights, and Welfare: The Theory of the Welfare State* (Boulder, CO: Westview Press, 1988); and Wilensky, *The Welfare State and Equality.* See also Clark Kerr, John T. Dunlop, Fredrick H. Harbison, and Charles A. Myers, *Industrialism and Industrial Man* (New York: Oxford University Press, 1964).

5. This discussion is based largely on B. Guy Peters, *American Public Policy: Promise and Performance,* 5th ed. (New York: Chatham House, 1999), pp. 187–199.

6. The budget figures in this section are all from *The Budget of the United States, 2001* (Washington, D.C.: Office of Management and Budget, 2000).

7. *The Budget of the United States, Fiscal 2001.*

8. Benjamin Friedman, *Day of Reckoning: The Consequences of American Economic Policy Under Reagan and After* (New York: Random House, 1989), p. 90.

9. George J. Stigler, "The Theory of Economic Regulation," *Bell Journal* 2 (Spring 1971), pp. 3–21. Also see Gabriel Kolko, *The Triumph of Conservatism* (Chicago: Quadrangle, 1967); James Weinstein, *The Corporate Ideal in the Liberal State* (Boston: Beacon Press, 1968).

10. See Richard Harris and Sidney Milkis, *The Politics of Regulatory Change* (New York: Oxford University Press, 1989).

11. See G. William Domhoff, *The Higher Circles* (New York: Random House, 1970); Edward S. Greenberg, *Capitalism and the American Political Ideal* (Armonk, NY: Sharpe, 1985); Kolko, *The Triumph of Conservatism;* Weinstein, *The Corporate Ideal in the Liberal State.*

12. Frances Fox Piven and Richard A. Cloward, *Poor People's Movements* (New York: Vintage, 1979).

13. Marver Bernstein, *Regulation by Independent Commission* (Princeton, NJ: Princeton University Press, 1955); Grant McConnell, *Private Power and American Democracy* (New York: Vintage Books, 1966); Theodore J. Lowi, *The End of Liberalism,* 2nd ed. (New York: Norton, 1979).

14. David Vogel, *Fluctuating Fortunes: The Political Power of Business in the United States* (New York: Basic Books 1989), pp. 59, 112.

15. James Buchanan and Gordon Tullock, "Polluters, Profits and Political Responses: Direct Control versus Taxes," *American Economic Review* 65 (1975), pp. 139–147; L. Lave, *The Strategy of Social Regulation* (Washington, D.C.: Brookings Institution, 1981); Murray Weidenbaum, *The Costs of Government Regulation of Business* (Washington, D.C.: Joint Economic Committee of Congress, 1978).

16. See Thomas Byrne Edsall, *The New Politics of Inequality* (New York: Norton, 1984); Vogel, *Fluctuating Fortunes;* Kevin P. Phillips, *The Politics of Rich and Poor: Wealth and the American Electorate in the Reagan Aftermath* (New York: Random House, 1990); Thomas Ferguson and Joel Rogers, *Right Turn: The Decline of the Democrats and the Future of American Politics* (New York: Farrar, Straus & Giroux, 1986).

17. As reported in Vogel, *Fluctuating Fortunes,* pp. 262–263, 278–279.

18. Ibid., ch. 7.

19. Eugene Smolensky, Sheldon Danziger, and Peter Gottschalk, "The Declining Significance of Age in the United States: Trends in the Well-Being of Children and the Elderly Since 1939," in John L. Palmer, Timothy Smeedling, and Barbara Boyle Torrey, eds., *The Vulnerable* (Washington, D.C.: Urban Institute, 1988); and *Poverty in the United States, 1998,* U.S. Bureau of the Census.

20. See Merton C. Bernstein and Joan Brodshaug Bernstein, *Social Security: The System That Works* (New York: Basic Books, 1988), pp. 13–14; Peters, *American Public Policy,* ch. 11.

21. Benjamin I. Page and James R. Simmons, *What Government Can Do: Dealing with Poverty and Inequality* (Chicago: University of Chicago Press, 2000), ch. 3.

22. Fay Lomax Cook and Edith J. Barrett, *Support for the American Welfare State: The Views of Congress and the Public* (New York: Columbia University Press, 1992), ch. 7.

23. "U.S. Pensions Found to Lift Many of the Poor," *New York Times* (December 28, 1989), p. A1. See also Theodore R. K. Marmor, Jerry L. Mashaw, and Philip L. Harvey, *America's Misunderstood Welfare State* (New York: HarperCollins, 1990), ch. 4.

24. U.S. Bureau of the Census, 1999.

25. Hugh Heclo, "The Political Foundations of Anti-Poverty Policy," in Sheldon Danziger and Daniel Weinberg, eds., *Fighting Poverty: What Works and What Doesn't?* (Cambridge, MA: Harvard University Press, 1986); and Cook and Barrett, *Support for the American Welfare State.*

26. David T. Ellwood, *Poor Support: Poverty in the American Family* (New York: Basic Books, 1988).

27. John E. Schwarz, *America's Hidden Success: A Reassessment of Public Policy from Kennedy to Reagan* (New York: Norton, 1988), p. 37.

28. Robert Pear, "White House Releases Glowing Data on Welfare," *New York Times* (August 1, 1999), p. 12; Jason DeParle, "States Struggle to Use Windfall Born of Shifts in Welfare Law," *New York Times* (August 28, 1999), p. 1.

29. Carey Goldberg, "Most Get Work After Welfare," *New York Times* (April 16, 1999), p. 1.

30. Peters, *American Public Policy,* p. 207; Christopher Howard, *The Hidden Welfare State* (Princeton, NJ: Princeton University Press, 1997), ch. 3.

31. Gosta Esping-Andersen, "The Three Political Economies of the Welfare State," *Canadian Review of Sociology and Anthropology* 26 (1989), pp. 10–36; Norman Furniss and Timothy Tilton, *The Case for the Welfare State* (Bloomington, IN: Indiana University Press, 1977); Walter Korpi, *Democratic Class Struggle* (New York: Routledge, 1983).

32. Christopher Pierson, "The 'Exceptional' United States: First New Nation or Last Welfare State," *Social Policy and Administration* 24 (1990), p. 188.

33. Vincent A. Mahler and Claudio J. Katz, "Social Benefits in Advanced Capitalist Countries: A Cross-National Assessment," *Comparative Politics* 21 (1988), pp. 37–50. See also Heidenheimer, Heclo, and Adams, *Comparative Public Policy;* Stein Ringen, *The Possibility of Politics: A Study in the Political Economy of the Welfare State* (New York: Clarendon Press, 1987).

34. Smolensky, Danziger, and Gottschalk, "The Declining Significance of Age in the United States."

35. Fred C. Pampel and Paul Adams, "Demographic Change and Public Support for Children: Family Allowance Expenditures in Advanced Industrial Democracies," working paper, Department of Sociology, University of Colorado, Boulder, 1990.

36. Mahler and Katz, "Social Benefits in Advanced Capitalist Countries"; John Freeman, *Democracy and Markets* (Ithaca, NY: Cornell University Press, 1989); Ringen, *The Possibility of Politics,* ch. 7.

37. Nathan Glazer, *The Limits of Social Policy* (Cambridge, MA: Harvard University Press, 1988), pp. 187–188. See also W. Sombart, *Why There Is No Socialism in the United States* (Armonk, NY: Sharpe, 1976).

38. See Louis Hartz, *The Liberal Tradition in America* (New York: Harcourt Brace, 1955); G. V. Rimlinger, *Welfare Policy and Industrialization in Europe, America and Russia* (New York: Wiley, 1971); Marmor, Marshaw, and Harvey, *America's Misunderstood Welfare State;* Wilensky, *The Welfare State and Equality.*

39. See David Cameron, "Social Democracy, Corporatism, Labor Quiescence, and the Representation of Interests in Advanced Capitalist Society," in John H. Goldthorpe, ed., *Order and Conflict in Contemporary Capitalism* (New York: Clarendon Press, 1984); Francis G. Castles, *The Impact of Parties: Politics and Policies in Democratic Capitalist States* (Newbury Park, CA: Sage, 1982); Gosta Esping-Andersen, *Politics Against Markets* (Princeton, NJ: Princeton University Press, 1985); Korpi, *Democratic Class Struggle;* John Stephens, *The Transition from Capitalism to Socialism* (London: Macmillan, 1979).

Foreign Policy and National Defense

The Senate Defeats the Nuclear Test Ban Treaty

Late in the evening of October 13, 1999, the Senate of the United States refused to ratify the Nuclear Test Ban Treaty that President Bill Clinton had signed in 1996. The treaty, designed to slow the spread of nuclear weapons, not only fell short of the two-thirds required for ratification, but failed to win even a simple majority. It was the most important treaty rejected by the Senate since President Woodrow Wilson's Versailles Treaty was defeated in 1920 and the first time an arms control treaty had ever gone down to defeat.

The defeat of the treaty came as a shock to both allies and erstwhile enemies and generated a flood of criticism from governments and foreign commentators. Friends of the United States abroad worried that the United States had lost its moral leadership on the issue of nuclear proliferation and any leverage it might have in trying to persuade India, Pakistan, and North Korea to sign the treaty and China, Russia, Egypt, and Israel (all of whom have signed the treaty) to ratify it. Many Americans worried about the same things. As Republican Senator John Chafee of Rhode Island put it after the vote, "I don't know how we can lecture other countries to stop their testing after this has occurred. We've lost a very valuable platform."

Several things struck journalistic, political, and scholarly observers of the proceedings in the Senate. First, compared with other major pieces of legislation and treaties, the Senate's consideration of the Test Ban Treaty was exceedingly brief. This stands in marked contrast to the extensive testimony and debates surrounding the defeat of the Versailles Treaty. Second, the treaty was brought to a vote on the floor of the Senate even after 52 senators from both parties signed a plea to Majority Leader Trent Lott to postpone the vote. Bowing to the Republican caucus majority, Lott reneged on his promise to Democratic leaders to hold off the vote. Third and finally, the debate was conducted in an atmosphere of bitter partisanship, with both Democrats and Republicans treating the treaty as yet another tool with which to score points against their opponents. The low point in the floor debate came when Jesse Helms (R–NC), the Chair of the Senate Foreign Relations Committee, contemptuously dismissed British Prime Minister Tony Blair's public request that the Senate vote in favor of the treaty, posing an imaginary

conversation between Blair and President Clinton in which Blair's final words were "Give Monica my regards."

Why was the treaty defeated? A number of possibilities have been offered. It may well be the case that the treaty was fatally flawed, as its opponents claimed, diminishing U.S. sovereignty and threatening the usefulness of our nuclear arsenal, without doing much about the proliferation of nuclear weapons. It may also have been the case, as some have observed, that President Clinton and Senate Democrats made important tactical mistakes, such as not including Republicans in the original treaty negotiations, not acting in a bipartisan manner in the Senate process, and insisting on Senate consideration of the treaty when the Republicans were in the majority. Additionally, the treaty may have been defeated as a way for Republicans to embarrass Bill Clinton and damage his historical legacy. Unable to remove him from office through the impeachment process, and frustrated by his continuing popularity, so the argument goes, many in the GOP were not about to allow President Clinton a significant foreign policy achievement in the final years of his administration and an honorable place in the history books. There is also reason to believe, finally, that what happened to the treaty is simply a reflection of the fact that, without the Cold War or the serious threat of a large-scale shooting war, the office of president has lost some of its power and prestige in foreign and military affairs (see Chapter 12), and Congress has become increasingly willing and anxious to flex its muscles in these areas, much as it has always done in domestic affairs (see Chapter 11).

There is yet another possibility. In the end, the treaty may well have been the victim of America's ambivalence about what role it wants to play in the post–Cold War world. While it is clear (as we shall describe in this chapter) that the United States is the last remaining superpower, it is not entirely self-evident to elected leaders, citizens, journalists, or scholars how we ought to behave at this moment in history when our survival is no longer at issue, as it was for much of the period from the mid-1950s to the collapse of the Soviet Union in 1989. We examine this possibility in more detail later in the chapter.

▶Thinking Critically About This Chapter

This chapter is about American foreign and military policies, how these policies are made, and how they affect Americans and others.

Using the Framework. You will see in this chapter how foreign and military policies are the product of the interaction of structural factors (such as American economic and military power, the collapse of the Soviet Union, and "globalization"), political linkage level factors (such as the choices the media make about foreign news coverage, public opinion about what the U.S. role in the world ought to be, and what various interest groups want the government to do), and governmental factors (such as the objectives and actions of presidents, members of Congress, and important executive branch agencies such as the Central Intelligence Agency and the Joint Chiefs of Staff).

Using the Democracy Standard. Using the evaluative tools you learned in Chapter 1, you will see that foreign policy is not always made with the public as fully informed or as involved as in domestic affairs. You will see why this is so, ask whether policies would be better if they were made more democratically, and investigate how the public might play a larger role. ▶

Foreign Policy and Democracy: A Contradiction in Terms?

Making U.S. foreign policy has traditionally been different from making domestic policy. For one thing, presidents and the executive branch tend to play a much more important part than they do on domestic issues. In the perpetual tug-of-war between presidents and Congress on international matters, presidents usually prevail in the midst of diplomatic or military crises. Also, the ordinary political factors, such as public opinion and interest groups, are sometimes set aside in favor of considerations of the **national interest**, as defined by a small number of national security advisers and other executive branch officials.

national interest

What is of benefit to the nation as a whole.

Foreign policy is not always purely the result of democratic processes, as we understand democracy. Public opinion, for example, is sometimes reshaped or ignored. In crisis situations, the public often "rallies 'round the flag," accepting the president's actions, at least as long as the results seem good and there is little dissent among political leaders. (When things go wrong, however, domestic politics can return with a vengeance, as it did in the case of the Vietnam War.) Also, much of foreign policy is influenced by *structural* factors, such as the power and resources of the United States, its economic interests abroad, and the nature and behavior of other nations.

Several features of foreign affairs tend to limit the role of ordinary citizens in policymaking. The sheer complexity of international matters, their remoteness from day-to-day life, and the unpredictability of other countries' actions all tend to make the public's convictions about foreign policy less certain and more subject to revision in the light of events. In military matters, the need for speed, unity, and secrecy in decision making and the concentration of authority in the executive branch mean that the public may be excluded and that government policy sometimes shapes public opinion rather than being shaped by it.

At the same time, however, the exclusion of the public is far from total. The American public has probably always played a bigger part in the making of foreign policy than some observers have imagined, and its role appears to be increasing as foreign policy becomes directed more at issues such as trade, immigration, and corporate global behavior and less at strictly military affairs. Note, for example, the very high involvement of the public in general, and interest groups in particular—labor unions, environmental organizations, corporations, business trade associations, and the like—in the struggle over ratification of the North American Free Trade Agreement (NAFTA) and in the debate over granting China normal trade status and membership in the WTO. Public involvement was high because what was decided in these cases was certain to have important effects on jobs, wages, and environmental quality. Just how big the role of the public should be is a matter of dispute, an object of the ongoing struggle for democracy.

The United States as a Superpower: History and Structure

In the autumn of 1990, the United States sent more than half a million troops, 1,200 warplanes, and six aircraft carriers to the Persian Gulf region to roll back Iraq's invasion of Kuwait. In 1996, U.S. troops were deployed in Bosnia as part of a NATO peacekeeping operation. The warring parties signed the peace agreement only after the United States consented to be the guarantor of the agreement, backed by troops on the ground in Bosnia. In 1999, the United States supplied almost all of the pilots, airplanes, ordinance, supplies, and intelligence for the NATO bombing campaign to force the Serb military out of Kosovo province (although the other NATO members supplied the bulk of peacekeeping forces on the ground after the bombing ended). These examples reflect the status of the United States as a **superpower**, a nation armed with nuclear weapons and strong enough militarily and economically to project its power into any area of the globe. Indeed, since the collapse of the Soviet Union, the United States is the world's *only* military superpower and its preeminent economic power.

superpower

A nation armed with nuclear weapons and able to project force anywhere on the globe.

During the Cold War, the United States and the Soviet Union were locked in a nuclear stalemate in which each side had the power to destroy the other, even after absorbing a first strike from its adversary. Here Soviet nuclear missiles are prominently displayed in a military parade in Moscow during the height of the Cold War.

The Cold War

When World War II ended with Japan's surrender on August 15, 1945, Germany and Japan, devastated by the bombing of their cities and industries, found themselves occupied by Allied forces. Britain and France, great powers of the past, had also suffered severe damage and were losing their world empires to nationalist revolutions. But the United States emerged with its homeland intact, its economy much larger than before the war (accounting for more than half the manufacturing production of the entire world), its military forces victorious around the globe, and—for a few years, at least—with monopoly control of nuclear weapons.[1]

The only serious challenge to the power of the United States came from the Soviet Union, which had been terribly damaged in the war (suffering perhaps 20 to 25 million deaths) but which retained a large population and military and occupied most of Eastern Europe. The United States and the Soviet Union soon found themselves in a series of confrontations.

American foreign and military policy was focused, for more than 40 years, on the **Cold War** struggle against the Soviet Union (so-called because the adversaries never actually fought each other during these years). In an odd sort of way, this made matters relatively simple for policymakers both here and in the Soviet Union. Relationships with allies; efforts to win the support of newly independent poor countries in Africa, Asia, and Latin America; and what weapons systems to develop were all measured against what the other side was doing or likely to do.

American policy was based on the doctrine of **containment**, meaning that foreign and military policy was designed to halt the spread of the Soviet state and the influence of communism.[2] The policy was first put into effect when the United States agreed to give military aid to the Greek government so that it could prevent a communist takeover. President Truman invoked what came to be known as the **Truman Doctrine**—the idea that the United States would help "free peoples" resist "armed minorities or outside pressures"—when he introduced the Greek-Turkish Aid bill to Congress.

In the decades that followed, the struggles between the United States and the Soviet Union, and between liberal capitalism and communism, played themselves out in alliance-building by each side (see Figure 18.1), small but hot wars fought by surrogates, counterinsurgency and terror directed against the opposing alliance, and efforts to win over Third World nations. The United States began with **Marshall Plan** aid to rebuild Europe, the formation of the Federal Republic of Germany out of the parts of the old Germany controlled by the United States, Britain, and France, and the creation of NATO (the North Atlantic Treaty Organization), an anti-Soviet military alliance. For its part, the Soviets installed puppet governments in the Eastern European countries, and with them, formed the **Warsaw Pact** to oppose NATO on the military front. Sharply drawn boundaries divided Eastern from Western Europe.[3]

In retrospect, we can see that the Cold War essentially stalemated or stabilized in the early 1950s after the Korean War—in which the United States and South Korea fought North Korea and China—with most of the world divided into two opposing camps that had fairly fixed boundaries and a reasonably stable balance of power. For some 35 years afterward, both sides spent immense resources—perhaps $12 trillion—on huge armies that faced each other across the stable boundaries in Europe, never fighting but deterring attack and helping keep their own countries' allies in line. Elsewhere in the world, the many covert operations, skirmishes, and civil wars between pro- and anticommunist forces had important (sometimes devastating) effects on the local people

Cold War

The period of tense relations between the United States and the Soviet Union from the late 1940s to the late 1980s.

containment

The policy of resisting expansion of the Soviet Union's influence by diplomatic, economic, and military means.

Truman Doctrine

President Truman's policy that the United States should defend noncommunist countries from outside pressure and internal rebellion from communists.

Marshall Plan

The program of U.S. economic aid set up to rebuild Europe after World War II.

Warsaw Pact

An alliance of the Soviet Union and Eastern European communist countries.

Figure 18.1 ● U.S. Alliances and Overseas Bases, 1959

Many regional alliances against the Soviet Union and Communist China were established in the 1950s.

Source: Robert D. Schulzinger, *American Diplomacy in the Twentieth Century,* 2nd ed. (New York: Oxford University Press, 1990), p. 249.

involved, but they had little real impact on the great powers or on the shape of the Cold War world.

One crucial reason for this stalemate was the presence on both sides of powerful nuclear weapons. Both the United States and the Soviet Union built large numbers of strategic bombers that could drop nuclear warheads on the other country, and both began ballistic missile programs. Eventually, both sides attained a sort of nuclear parity, or rough equality. A surprise attack by either side would result in the devastation of both countries. This situation, which came to be called **mutually assured destruction (MAD)**, deterred either side from launching a nuclear attack. The balance of terror was threatened only once, during the Cuban Missile Crisis in 1962, when President Kennedy forced the Soviet Union to remove intermediate-range missiles from Cuba. Sobered by the threat of mutual nuclear destruction, the United States and Soviets eventually agreed to a Strategic Arms Limitation Treaty (SALT I).

Vietnam was the great exception to the relative peace that Americans enjoyed for more than three decades after the Korean War. As we saw in Chapter 5, the Vietnam War, fought in an effort to prevent a communist

mutually assured destruction (MAD)

A situation of nuclear balance in which either the United States or the Soviet Union could respond to a surprise attack by destroying the other country.

These casualties from the 1968 Tet Offensive added to the total of more than 45,000 Americans killed and 150,000 wounded during the Vietnam War.

takeover of South Vietnam, was a major setback for American foreign policy. The war's cost (about $179 billion, in 1990 dollars) and casualties (47,355 battle dead, 153,303 wounded),[4] as well as the social disruption and moral unease that accompanied it and the economic difficulties that followed it, discouraged intervention abroad for a while. Nervousness about military involvement in Somalia, Bosnia, Kosovo, and Haiti in the 1990s stemmed from memories of the Vietnam War and its effects.

CourseCompass

WEB EXPLORATION

Understanding the Cold War

Issue: The great danger for most of the Cold War period was that minor incidents and military actions between the United States and the Soviet Union might escalate to a nuclear confrontation between the two superpowers.

Site: Access the Cold War Virtual Museum through the "Course Documents" section of your online course. Go to the "Web Explorations" section for Chapter 18, click on "Understanding the Cold War," and open "the Cold War." Examine their materials on the history of the Cold War. Read the materials for each decade.

What You've Learned: How close did we come to a disastrous confrontation? Which incidents almost brought the world to the brink of disaster? What do you think explains why the worst never happened?

HINT: Some credit sheer blind luck; others say that mutually assured destruction forced leaders on both sides to act responsibly.

The End of the Cold War

The Cold War ended with unexpected suddenness in 1989, symbolized by the fall of the Berlin Wall. The Soviet Union, demoralized by military failure in Afghanistan, weakened and humbled by the failure of its economy (especially when compared with the booming economies of the United States, Western Europe, Japan, and the so-called Asian Tigers, including Hong Kong, Taiwan, and Singapore), unable to compete in military technology, and unable to keep up with renewed American spending on defense, was ready for radical reform when Mikhail Gorbachev came to power in 1985. He introduced policies to foster greater use of the "market" in economic affairs (*perestroika,* or "restructuring") and more political freedom (*glasnost,* or "openness"). He also refused to intervene militarily, as the Soviet Union had done on numerous occasions in the past, when anticommunist regimes came to power in Poland, Czechoslovakia, and Hungary and asked the Soviets to withdraw behind their own borders. In November 1989, Berliners tore down the wall that had long separated them from their friends, family, and countrymen, and the process was under way that would eventually lead to the absorption of the former communist East Germany into the German Federal Republic.

The final collapse of the Soviet Union followed a failed coup against Gorbachev in August 1991 by hard-line communists. Boris Yeltsin, president of the Russian Republic—the first popularly elected official in Russian history—led the resistance to the coup in Moscow and Leningrad. The coup plotters, winning little popular or military support, quickly gave up. Gorbachev was restored to office. But the central government rapidly disintegrated. The Communist party, which Gorbachev had tried to reform, lost all legitimacy and was temporarily banned in most of the Soviet Union. The Soviet Union itself fell apart as the Baltic republics (Estonia, Latvia, and Lithuania) became completely independent, and virtually all the other 12 republics, even the crucial Ukraine and Russia, then insisted on independence. Power passed to Yeltsin and other leaders of the republics.

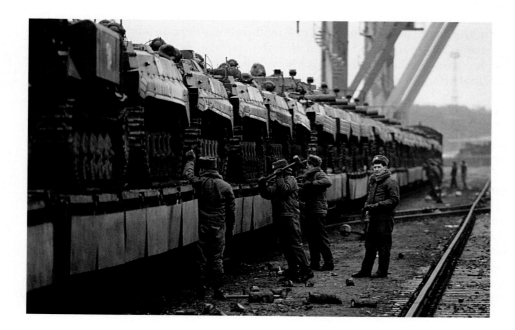

With the reunification of Germany after the collapse of communism in Eastern Europe, there was no longer a reason to garrison Soviet troops in East Germany. Here, Soviet tanks are loaded on a train for shipment out of Germany.

North Atlantic Treaty Organization (NATO)

An alliance of the United States, Canada, and Western European countries for defense against the Soviet Union.

In 1997, the Russian Republic reluctantly agreed to the inevitable: the eastward expansion of the **North Atlantic Treaty Organization (NATO)**. In that year, former Soviet bloc members Poland, Hungary, and the Czech Republic formally applied to join the alliance formed originally to guard against Soviet and Russian expansion into Western Europe; by 1998, their applications were approved. Although many Russians saw NATO expansion as a threat to their struggling nation, President Yeltsin saw no way to stop it.

The Structural Bases of American Superpower Status

A nation's place in the international system is largely determined by its relative economic, military, and cultural power. At the beginning of the new century, the United States is particularly advantaged in all three areas.

Economic Power   By the end of the 1990s, the United States had a population of about 275 million people—considerably fewer than China's 1.25 billion or India's roughly 1 billion—but enough to support the world's largest economy, with an annual gross domestic product (GDP) of more than $8.5 trillion. The GDP of the United States is almost twice that of China (but nine times larger on a per capita basis); almost three times that of Japan; almost five times that of Germany or India; six times that of Great Britain; and 14 times that of Russia.

By all indications, the relative strength of the American economy is increasing. While Asia, Japan, and Europe's economic performance at the end of the twentieth century and beginning of the twenty-first have been inconsistent and uncertain, the U.S. economy has boomed as its companies have established their dominance in the economic sectors that count the most in the new global economy: telecommunications, mass entertainment, biotechnology, software, finance, e-commerce, business services, transportation, and computer chips. The worries about the coming economic challenges of Japan, China, or Asia, often heard from commentators and political and business leaders in the 1980s and early 1990s, now seem far off the mark.

American corporations are increasingly global. For the largest of them, a substantial portion of their revenues comes from sales abroad, much of their manufacturing takes place in other countries, and many of the parts for items manufactured domestically are imported. And in industries such as oil and petrochemicals, many of the sources of raw materials are outside our borders. Because American businesses can be found almost anywhere, American national interests can be said to be found almost anywhere as well. It follows that American officials must be attentive to potential trouble spots around the globe.

intercontinental ballistic missiles (ICBMs)

Guided missiles capable of carrying nuclear warheads across continents.

Military Power   This enormous economic strength enables the United States to field the most powerful armed forces in the world. The United States spent roughly $289 billion in 1999 on its military (5 times more than Russia, 7 times more than China and Britain, and 26 times more than India) and has almost 1.4 million men and women on active military duty. It has just under 2,500 **intercontinental ballistic missiles (ICBMs)** and 159 strategic bombers, each carrying multiple nuclear warheads. The U.S. Navy has 12 aircraft carriers; 17 nuclear missile submarines; and many other warships, amphibious assault ships, and tactical aircraft. The army is organized into ten active divisions, backed by large numbers of tanks, artillery, and tactical missiles with many tactical nuclear warheads. The U.S. armed forces have been downsized somewhat from their Cold War peak, but force levels have now stabilized.[5] And, the United States is currently unchallenged in its ability to wage high-technology warfare, and may even develop and deploy a strategic missile defense system.

The F-117A Stealth fighter-bomber, a star of the Persian Gulf War and the air war in Kosovo, represents just a small part of U.S. military strength.

No other country in the world comes close to matching the power of the U.S. armed forces. Russia, after the breakup of the Soviet Union, with its economy and once-proud military in disarray, has renounced most foreign adventures, reluctantly agreed to the eastward expansion of NATO, and proceeded to cut their nuclear and conventional arms under international treaties. Although it retains a formidable nuclear arsenal, Russia's ability to use force abroad (except on its immediate periphery, in former Soviet republics) is now very much in doubt.

China has a fast-growing economy, millions of military personnel, and some strategic nuclear missiles, but it is much weaker than it looks on paper. Most of China's arms consist of old Soviet-style weapons that the Iraqis found inadequate when they were decisively defeated by U.S. airpower, **smart bombs**, and missiles in the Persian Gulf War. China's recent efforts at modernizing its weapons have not yet gotten very far (this may change as its economy becomes richer and more sophisticated).

smart bombs

Bombs capable of being guided precisely to their targets.

WEB EXPLORATION

American Military Power

Issue: It is often said that the United States is the world's last remaining superpower.

Site: Access the Web site of the U.S. Arms Control and Disarmament Agency, and look at the report on "World Military Expenditures and Arms Transfers" through the "Course Documents" section of your online course. Go to the "Web Explorations" section for Chapter 18, click on "American Mitlitary Power," and open "military power." Look at the tables for the most recent year.

What You've Learned: Select two or three countries you think are also military powers—Russia, China, Germany, Britain, and so on— and compare the relative military power of each. Collect data on various measures of military strength on each country as well as on the United States. Does the United States have a serious military rival?

HINT: Future rivals might conceivably include a unified Europe and/or a modernized Chinese military.

The rich countries of Western Europe (Great Britain and France) have relatively small military establishments and a relatively small number of nuclear weapons. They do produce, deploy, and operate very sophisticated military technologies, however, usually under the umbrella of NATO in which the United States plays the leading role. During the Kosovo bombing campaign, European military and political leaders became uncomfortably aware, however, that they were heavily dependent on the United States for laser-guided bombs, strategic reconnaissance, and aircraft, and they began to talk publicly about the need for a new, joint European military command, bolstered by substantially enhanced defense spending by the European states.[6] How vigorously the Europeans will move in this direction remains to be seen.

No other nation, moreover, has anything like the scores of U.S. military bases abroad (with about 100,000 troops stationed in Europe and another 100,000 in Asia), the ports and ships that control the Atlantic and Pacific Oceans, the high-tech attack aircraft and missiles, the satellite surveillance capabilities, or the rapid-deployment ships and planes that can project force anywhere, any time, on any continent.

"Soft Power"   Although the effect of "Americanization" is often decried by critics here and abroad—the spread of McDonald's, Kentucky Fried Chicken, Disney theme parks, Hollywood movies, and television sitcoms and dramas take the brunt of the criticism—we should not underestimate the influence of what some have called "soft power," the attractiveness of a nation's culture, ideology, and way of life for people living in other countries. As political scientist Joseph Nye has pointed out, it is important for the U.S. position in the world that more than half a million foreign students study in American colleges and universities; that people in other countries flock to American entertainment and cultural products; that English has become the language of the Internet, business, science, and technology; and that the openness and opportunity of American society is admired by more than would perhaps care to admit it.[7] And, if it is this very openness and opportunity that allows the United States to be in the best position to prosper in the new global, information-based economy—which many believe to be the case—then the United States's soft power enhances its harder economic and military powers.[8]

LongmanParticipate

CourseCompass

timeline

The Evolution of Foreign and Military Policy

Problems of the Post–Cold War World

While the United States is the world's preeminent superpower, it is not entirely clear what the American public and its leaders want to do with this power. The Cold War is over and with it have gone the clarity and coherence that the bipolar conflict lent to policymaking. As suggested earlier in the chapter, three stances are evident in public discourse about America's role in the world:

isolationists

Those who believe the United States should defend itself behind formidable defensive walls and avoid foreign military and diplomatic entanglements.

unilateralists

Those who believe the United States should vigorously use its military and diplomatic power to pursue American national interests in the world, but on a "go it alone" basis.

 ● The **isolationists** would have the United States arm itself for self defense, avoid getting ensnared in "entangling alliances" (as suggested by George Washington), and let other countries solve their own problems. Senator Arlen Specter (R–PA) thought that this yearning for a "fortress America" was what most of his party colleagues were doing when they voted against the Nuclear Test Ban Treaty, as did President Clinton.

 ● The **unilateralists** would have the United States actively engage the world, based on their belief that what goes on elsewhere around the world cannot help but affect American interests, but would have the

United States do so on its own terms, without asking the permission of others or binding itself under restrictive international treaties. The existence of such a theme in American foreign policy may better explain the defeat of the Nuclear Test Ban Treaty, as well as the United States's unwillingness to sign treaties on the establishment of an international criminal court and on the banning of land mines.

- The **multilateralists** would vigorously protect American interests in the world but, recognizing that the United States is not all-powerful, would seek to work in cooperation and collaboration with other nations. This theme in our foreign policy can be seen in our participation in NATO operations in Kosovo and in our participation in the international agreement that created the World Trade Organization.

multilateralists

Those who believe the United States should use its military and diplomatic power in the world in cooperation with other nations and international organizations.

Even as Americans grapple with the problem of what stance to take toward the world, a whole series of new foreign policy problems has arisen.

New Security Issues

The most frightening possibility of the past—a Soviet-led invasion of Western Europe that could lead to a nuclear Armageddon between the superpowers—has completely vanished. But security issues remain.

Russia and the Former Soviet Union   The collapse of the centralized communist regime threw into question the fate of the vast Russian and former Soviet armed forces, with their millions of troops and many nuclear weapons—more than 10,000 of them. Could these weapons fall into the hands of warring ethnic factions, criminal organizations, terrorist groups, or rogue states such as Iraq, creating new dangers and instability? The United States worked out agreements for drastic reductions in Russian, Ukrainian, and Kazakh nuclear weaponry. Ukraine and Kazakhstan have renounced nuclear weapons altogether, but their stockpiles of weapons remain large, and central control appears shaky. There is some evidence of Russian nuclear materials showing up

Bitter ethnic conflicts are one legacy of the collapse of communism in Eastern Europe, raising new issues for American foreign and military policymakers. Here ethnic Albanians flee brutal Serbian military and paramilitary forces in Kosovo. Similar scenes of desperate refugees on television helped spur U.S. and NATO military intervention.

nuclear proliferation

The spread of nuclear weapons to additional countries or to terrorist groups.

on the international black market, raising dangers of **nuclear proliferation**, or the spread of nuclear weapons. A high-priority task for American foreign policy has been to prevent proliferation.

The United States avoided entanglement in the bloody ethnic strife that broke out in the former Soviet republics of Armenia, Azerbaijan, and Georgia and between Russians and rebels in the province of Chechnya. But ethnic strife in the border areas of the Russian Republic as well as civil unrest within Russia itself are likely in the future. Will this lead to military adventures or to waves of refugees heading west? Will the United States be drawn into ethnic conflicts as it was in the Balkans?

Another long-term problem is knowing what to do about democracy and free enterprise in Russia. What can we do to encourage the institutionalization of democracy? What can we do to encourage economic development? The IMF (International Monetary Fund), in which the United States plays the preeminent leadership role, has given very large loans to Russia, but the results have not been encouraging.

The Balkans   What about the countries of the Balkans? Bitter ethnic and national tensions have arisen in this area, most notably among the Serbs, Croats, and Muslims of the former Yugoslavia. The United States brokered a peace agreement between the warring factions in Bosnia and sent troops to help enforce it. In Kosovo, the United States and NATO waged an air campaign to get the Serb military and paramilitary out of the province. American policymakers are struggling still, however, on what role we should play in the Balkans. Some say that the Balkans are a European problem, and the European powers should worry about the area. Others believe the Balkans to be a problem of world order that only the world's single remaining superpower can handle.

Japan, China, and the Pacific   With the end of the Cold War, how much reduction can or should there be in the vast U.S. naval forces in the Pacific Ocean or in the nearly 75,000 troops stationed in Japan and South Korea?

WEB EXPLORATION

What Direction for U.S. Foreign Policy?

Issue: Although the United States is unequaled in military and economic power, Americans are not entirely sure how they want to use that power.

Site: Access Public Agenda Online through the "Course Documents" section of your online course. Go to the "Web Explorations" section for Chapter 18, click on "What Direction for U.S. Foreign Policy?," and open "U.S. role." Select "America's global role," then look in the section "Major Proposals."

What You've Learned: See what the public thinks about the United Nations, humanitarian intervention, and foreign assistance. After looking at the poll results, would you conclude that Americans are isolationists, unilateralists, or multilateralists?

HINT: You might be surprised to learn how many Americans lean in a multilateral direction.

Does North Korea, a militarized state suffering mass starvation, pose a threat to South Korea? What about China, with its huge population, fast-growing economy, and modernizing military? Some Americans have warned of a great "clash of civilizations" between the West and "Confucian" China.[9] Disputes over fair trade, alleged nuclear spying, threats against Taiwan, and human rights disputes periodically cloud U.S.–Chinese relations.

The Developing World   Can regional conflicts be resolved, for example, between the Israelis and the Palestinians (where the United States has played an active diplomatic role) or between nuclear-armed India and Pakistan? Can or should regional powers such as Iraq and Iran be restrained or disarmed and kept from acquiring nuclear weapons, as U.S. policy has sought to do? Will the United States have to keep sending troops abroad from time to time, or might the United Nations or regional alliances be strengthened for peacekeeping and humanitarian purposes?

What about humanitarian intervention? When the government of a country is violating the basic human rights and taking the lives of segments of its own population—Rwanda, Kosovo, and Chechnya come to mind—should the United States intervene or stay out? If it intervenes, should it do so on its own or under the auspices of the United Nations or NATO?

Does the enormous gap between rich and poor nations pose a long-term security threat to the United States in terms of illegal immigration, terrorism, or armed conflicts? How can or should the United States encourage economic growth and democracy in poor countries?

Economic and Social Dilemmas

It is apparent, then, that America's exalted status as the world's only military superpower and its preeminent economic power has not made U.S. foreign policy problems go away. In fact, national security has taken on new and broader meanings and encompasses new problems.

International Trade   At the peak of its economic dominance after World War II, the United States presided over a world regime of free trade in which many countries negotiated lower tariff barriers through the **General Agreement on Tariffs and Trade (GATT)**. Tariffs, duties, quotas, and other means of keeping out foreign exports were reduced in much of the world. Because the United States was the world's most powerful trading state, this reduction was very advantageous for U.S. exports and investments, which continued to grow.

By the late 1960s, however, the rebuilt economies of Germany and Japan began to turn out goods that challenged American products abroad and in the United States, beginning with automobiles and moving on to consumer electronics. Additional competition came from newly industrialized countries (NICs), such as South Korea, Taiwan, Singapore, and Hong Kong, and from the increasingly integrated Economic Community (EC) of Europe. By the mid-1980s, Americans were importing many more goods than they were exporting, creating a multibillion-dollar **trade deficit**. The trade deficit meant that many goods were cheaper in the United States but also that many goods formerly produced in America by American workers were now being produced elsewhere.

Reacting to this competitive pressure, the United States during the 1980s pressured other countries—especially Japan and the EC, now known as the **European Union (EU)**—to lower hidden barriers and subsidies that hurt American exports while at the same time arranging voluntary quotas and other

General Agreement on Tariffs and Trade (GATT)

An international agreement that requires the lowering of tariffs and other barriers to free trade.

trade deficit

An excess of the value of the goods a country imports over the value of the goods it exports.

European Union (EU)

A common market formed by Western European nations, with free trade and free population movement among them.

North American Free Trade Agreement (NAFTA)

An agreement among the United States, Canada, and Mexico to eliminate nearly all barriers to trade and investment among the three countries.

World Trade Organization (WTO)

An agency designed to enforce the provisions of the General Agreement on Tariffs and Trade and to resolve trade disputes between nations.

policies to control imports to the United States. Next, U.S. policymakers negotiated the **North American Free Trade Agreement (NAFTA)** with Canada and Mexico, which was finally implemented after a 1993 vote in Congress resolved a bitter political conflict over its implications for U.S. jobs.[10] Many worried that the agreement would lead to a wholesale migration of American companies to Mexico from where goods would be shipped back to the United States and to other countries. Experts disagree whether this has happened; it is still too early to tell. The Clinton administration also concluded a comprehensive free trade agreement with 116 countries, under the Uruguay Round of GATT. The agreement, signed in 1994, set up the **World Trade Organization (WTO)** for enforcement. It cut already low tariffs by about an additional one-third and, for the first time, reduced restrictions on trade in agricultural products and financial services. U.S. negotiators hoped that the new agreement would open more markets to American agricultural products and halt the piracy of patented and copyrighted goods such as software and films. The massive anti-WTO demonstrations in Seattle in late 1999 and other demonstrations in Washington, D.C., and Prague in 2000, helped focus public attention on the WTO.

A crucial question about rapidly growing international trade, and about the increased ability of U.S. and other firms to produce goods cheaply abroad, is whether it brings prosperity to all Americans or tends to push American workers' wages down while wages in the newly industrializing countries rise toward equilibrium. If free trade hurts U.S. wages—a matter about which economists are deeply divided[11]—what can be done, short of inefficient protectionism? Could enforceable worldwide agreements on working conditions and environmental protection soften the pressure against wages?

Foreign Aid   The world is divided rather starkly into rich nations and poor nations. Rich nations, whether for humanitarian or security reasons, have given assistance to poor countries in an effort to improve living standards. Although the U.S. has programs such as Food for Peace, the Peace Corps, and technical and educational assistance programs and contributes to World Bank developmental loans for poor countries, our spending for foreign aid is very low and has been declining—to $11.2 billion, or less than 0.1 percent of U.S. GDP in 1998.[12] In relative terms, what we spend on foreign assistance is much lower than that of such countries as Denmark, Norway, Sweden, and France (see Figure 18.2). Moreover, only about two-thirds of U.S. foreign aid goes for assistance for economic development and humanitarian relief; the remainder is linked to military and security objectives or to encourage sale of American goods and services abroad.

Since the end of the Cold War, the total amount of U.S. aid and the portion devoted to military purposes have both declined, and the pattern of recipients has changed somewhat. As it has for quite a while, Israel tops the list of aid recipients, with Egypt second. Substantial money is now given to Russia and Ukraine, with some for development, but mostly for the destruction of nuclear weapons.[13] Some funds for development, population programs, and the environment are disbursed through the World Bank, the United Nations, and other international agencies. Of course, some money is always reserved for humanitarian crises such as the Rwandan refugee disaster of 1994.

Arms Sales   The United States sells many weapons to other countries. During the Cold War, we shared dominance of the international arms market with the Soviet Union, which in 1989 sold $11.7 billion worth of arms abroad, a bit more than the United States' $10.8 billion. After the war with Iraq and the

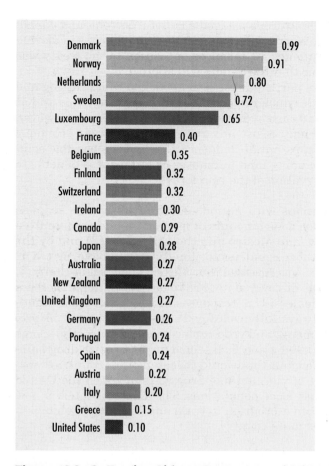

Figure 18.2 ● **Foreign Aid as a Percentage of GDP, 1998**

Although Americans often complain about how much aid we give to other countries, a comparison with other donor countries shows that we give very little as a percentage of GDP.

Source: Organization for Economic Cooperation and Development.

breakup of the Soviet Union, however, Russian arms sales fell sharply, and most countries clamored to buy American weapons. Now we are by far the biggest arms exporter in the world, with $31.8 billion in sales in 1999, much more than runner-up Britain's $6.6 billion or Russia's $2.3 billion.[14]

The Global Environment   Increasingly, Americans realize that environmental problems cross national borders. The United States and Canada have worked out a joint approach to reduce acid rain; many nations have tried to negotiate agreements on oil spills, the exploitation of Antarctica, the protection of the ozone layer, and the prevention of global warming. In some of these cases, the United States initially took a go-slow attitude, insisting, for example, that the evidence of global warming was not yet sufficient to justify reducing the consumption of fossil fuels in order to cut carbon dioxide emissions. The Clinton administration moved ahead somewhat more rapidly, agreeing to sign the biodiversity treaty and to plan to limit greenhouse gas emissions. And in December 1997, the Clinton administration signed the Greenhouse Gases Emissions Treaty in Kyoto, Japan, pledging the United States to cut emissions to a level 7 percent lower than that of 1990 (Europe pledged a cut of 8 percent, and Japan, 6 percent). Because cutting emissions will require important changes in driving habits, manufacturing, and auto design, business opposition to the treaty was intense, and it is not at all clear that the Senate will approve it.

Environmentalists express particular concern about the rapid cutting and burning of tropical rain forests, which removes oxygen-producing trees and at the same time pours smoke and carbon dioxide into the atmosphere. However, such countries as Brazil strongly resist any restrictions on their economic development unless they get substantial compensation. Various possible solutions have been discussed, including land purchases or forgiveness of debts to U.S. banks in return for preservation of the rain forests.

The Drug Trade   U.S. relations with nations south of its border are also complicated by the flow of enormous amounts of marijuana and cocaine from Peru, Bolivia, Haiti, Colombia, and Mexico into the United States and by the inability or unwillingness of those countries to stop the profitable drug trade. It was not encouraging when it was revealed that Mexico's general in charge of suppressing the drug trade was discovered in 1998 to have been in partnership with leading Mexican drug dealers. U.S. responses have included assistance with law enforcement (not always fully welcomed), crop eradication (bitterly resented by poor peasant farmers), and crop replacement (very costly). Some military strategists have proposed using U.S. armed forces to seize drug shipments and eradicate production, but that would threaten other countries' sovereignty and raise the specter of Vietnam-like drug wars in which the United States might be pitted against local populations. The United States is now heavily involved, for example, in a program to train and equip the Colombian military to wage war on drugs in its country.

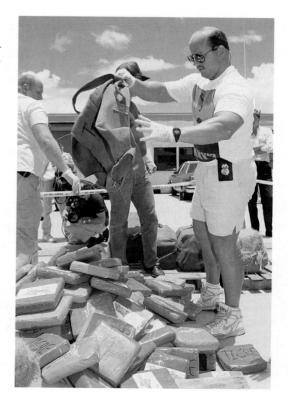

An official dumps cocaine seized on a freighter from Latin America. Stopping the flow of illegal drugs, which brings huge profits to exporting countries, is a major U.S. foreign policy challenge.

Part of the problem in eradicating the drug trade is that demand for drugs is very high in the rich countries, including the United States. Additionally, many of the technologies and organizational strategies that make it possible for corporations to operate on a global scale also help criminal drug organizations do the same thing. Such organizations have easy access to e-mail, express package service, air freight, global banking services, and high-speed telecommunications to enhance the efficiency of their operations.

Immigration   Throughout history, people have migrated to other lands, seeking a better way of life for themselves and their families. In the emerging global economy, where manufacturing and associated jobs are highly mobile, and where the revolution in transportation makes movement of people easier, cheaper, and more efficient, people in search of improvements in their standards of living are increasingly mobile. Especially noteworthy is the migration of people from poor Third World countries to the rich democracies of the West. Where poor countries lie adjacent to rich countries—for example, Mexico and Central America are close to the United States, the world's richest country— immigration pressures are especially strong.

In recent years, immigration from abroad—especially illegal immigration— has become a major political issue in the United States, because many Americans perceive pressure on their jobs, wages, and tax-supported social benefits, as well as worries about cultural conflict. Government leaders have responded by tightening the borders, denying government benefits to illegal immigrants, and making it harder to hire illegal aliens. See Chapter 4 for more on the political response to immigration.

LongmanParticipate

CourseCompass

visual literacy
**Evaluating
Defense Spending**

WEB EXPLORATION

What Does the Future Hold?

Issue: A number of new and serious challenges are emerging in the post–Cold War world that will command the attention of the American public and its political leaders.

Site: Access the *Which World?* site on our Web site at **www.ablongman.com/greenberg**. Go to the "Web Explorations" section for Chapter 18 and open "challenges." Select "Explore the Site," then "Trends," then "scenarios."

What You've Learned: Which problems are emerging as the most important ones in the new century? Is it population growth? Increasing inequality of living standards? Environmental degradation? Arms proliferation? Are you optimistic or pessimistic about the future? Do you think that the United States can help alleviate the major problems you have identified, or should we leave that to others?

HINT: What you think can and should be done about emergent problems will probably depend on whether you are an isolationist, a unilateralist, or a multilateralist.

Who Makes Foreign Policy?

The president and members of the executive branch are the chief governmental decision makers on most foreign policy issues most of the time, particularly those involving crisis situations or covert operations. But Congress has always been involved in decisions about international trade, foreign aid, military spending, immigration, and other matters that clearly and directly touch constituents' local interests, and it is seeking a larger voice in diplomatic and military affairs. Public opinion, the mass media, and organized interest groups affect what both Congress and the executive branch do.

Different types of foreign policy are made in very different ways. Crisis decision making, for example, involving sudden threats, high stakes, and quick action, or **covert operations**, belongs mostly to the executive branch—often, just a small, unified group of top national security officials. Congress, the public, interest groups, and others usually do not play much part, except to the extent that executive decision makers consult a few key members of Congress and try to anticipate the public's reactions.

Broader issues of defense policy, including treaties on arms control or military alliances, participation in major wars, and the amount of money spent on defense, involve much greater participation by Congress, the general public, interest groups, and others. Here, too, the executive branch ordinarily takes the lead, but it must either respond to domestic political forces or change those forces. Decisions about military bases and procurement contracts involve congressional committees and interest groups, especially local businesspeople dependent on bases and weapon-producing corporations. Foreign trade, international economic policy, and immigration also sometimes provoke substantial political conflict.

covert operations

Secret or semisecret activities abroad, often involving intelligence gathering, influence on other countries' politics, or the use of force.

The President and the Executive Branch

Because the Constitution gives the principal diplomatic and war powers to the president—the power to appoint and receive ambassadors, to negotiate treaties, and to be commander in chief of the armed forces—the president is the top decision maker on foreign policy and military issues. He has help from many people and government units. In the Bush administration, Vice President Dick Cheney plays an especially important role in foreign policy.

One of the president's most important White House staff members is the *national security adviser,* head of the *National Security Council (NSC),* who meets with the president nearly every day on matters of defense and foreign policy. The NSC can brief the president on any part of the world or on any military or intelligence matter at a moment's notice.[15]

The *State Department,* headed by the Secretary of State, is the president's chief arm for carrying out diplomatic affairs. The Department is organized along both functional lines—economic affairs, human rights, counterterrorism, and refugees—and geographic lines with "country desks" devoted to each nation of the world. There are 270 embassies and missions that carry out policy abroad and advise the department on new developments.[16] Attached to the State Department are the Arms Control and Disarmament Agency, the U.S. Information Agency, and the Agency for International Development, which oversees foreign economic aid. As issues of trade, U.S. corporate investment in other countries, and protection of intellectual property rights (patents and copyrights) become more important in the global economy, both the *Department of Commerce* and the *Office of the U.S. Trade Representative* have become more important.

The president remains the most important maker of foreign policy in the federal government. Here President Clinton welcomes Chinese Premier Jiang Zemin in an elaborate ceremony at the White House in 1997, signaling the important place of China in American foreign policy.

The *Department of Defense (DOD),* housed in the **Pentagon**, is also influential in shaping foreign and military policies. The DOD is headed by a civilian *secretary of defense,* who has authority over the entire department and reports directly to the president. Civilian secretaries are in charge of the Departments of the Army, Navy, and Air Force and report to the secretary of defense. Each service also has a military command structure headed by people in uniform: the army and air force chiefs of staff, the chief of naval operations, the commandant of the marine corps, and their subordinates. The uniformed chiefs of each branch serve together in a body called the **Joint Chiefs of Staff (JCS)**, headed by the chairman of the Joint Chiefs, who reports not only to the secretary of defense but also directly to the president. The organization of the Defense Department often leads to a certain degree of tension between civilian control and military hierarchy and rivalries between the services over missions, weapons systems, and budgets.

A large intelligence community is also involved in the fashioning and implementation of foreign and military policy, despite an apparent decline in direct military threats to the United States. This community is made up of a number of specific agencies. The **National Security Agency (NSA)** is responsible for intercepting and monitoring electronic messages from around the world, and the **National Reconnaissance Office (NRO)** is responsible for satellite reconnaissance. Each of the armed services has a separate tactical intelligence unit. Most important is the **Central Intelligence Agency (CIA)**, which was established in 1947 to advise the National Security Council, to coordinate all U.S. intelligence agencies, to gather and evaluate intelligence information, and to carry out such additional functions as the NSC directs.

Pentagon

The building in Arlington, Virginia, that contains the offices of the military chiefs and top officials of the Defense Department.

Joint Chiefs of Staff (JCS)

The military officers in charge of each of the armed services.

National Security Agency (NSA)

The federal government agency that intercepts and decodes electronic messages and secures U.S. communications around the world.

National Reconnaissance Office (NRO)

The government agency in charge of surveillance by satellite photography and other technological means.

Central Intelligence Agency (CIA)

The organization that coordinates all U.S. intelligence agencies; it also gathers and evaluates intelligence itself and carries out covert operations.

These B-52 bombers, destroyed by the United States as part of the Strategic Arms Limitations Treaty, must be left in their dismembered state for 90 days so that Russia can confirm their destruction with satellite photos. Satellite photography is used by the United States and other nations to confirm arms control measures and as a strategic device to monitor activities around the world.

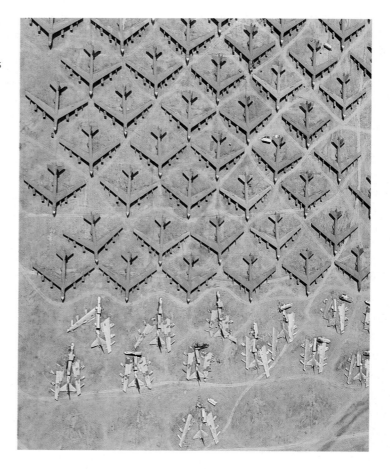

Although the CIA mostly gathers information from public sources, spies on the ground, and electronic intercepts, it has also been historically associated with covert operations designed to influence and sometimes overthrow other governments. CIA operations overthrew the Mossadeq government of Iran in 1953 and the Arbenz government of Guatemala in 1954, and during the 1950s and 1960s the agency assisted revolts in Indonesia, Cuba, Congo (Zaire), the Dominican Republic, Vietnam, Cambodia, and other places. In the 1980s, the Agency conducted covert actions in Afghanistan, Angola, and Nicaragua. Some of these target governments were allied with the Soviet Union, but others were simply too leftist or too nationalistic to suit U.S. officials' tastes.[17]

Covert operations are supposed to be secret, or at least officially "deniable." Direct supervision is confined to small groups of executive branch officials. Neither Congress nor the public is much involved; since 1980, only the two intelligence committees of the House and the Senate—with limited staffs and bound by secrecy—must be informed of major operations.

Congress

Congress has generally played a less active role in foreign than in domestic policy. Members of Congress believe that their constituents care more about policies that are close to home than those that are far away. Moreover, the executive branch, with its vast intelligence and national security apparatus, has far more information, expertise, and control of events. Still, Congress shows signs of more activity since the end of the Cold War. Because the military threat to the United States has declined with the collapse of the Soviet Union, members of Congress no longer feel as compelled as before to defer to the commander-in-chief on any but the most dangerous situations; because many foreign policy issues (such as immigration, drug trafficking, and corporate investment abroad) now directly affect the everyday lives of their constituents, members of Congress are less willing to leave matters to the president. In addition, animosity was so deep between the Republican-dominated Congress and President Clinton during his second term that Congress felt even freer to try to place its stamp on foreign and military policy. The House of Representatives, for instance, passed a bill in early 2000 that mandated more direct ties between the U.S. and Taiwan military, much to the dismay of President Clinton, who was trying to forge stronger relations with China and whose leadership sees Taiwan as one of its own provinces.

The Constitution gives Congress the power to declare war and to decide about any spending of money. It also gives the Senate the power to approve or disapprove treaties and the appointment of ambassadors. Each of these powers can make a difference. Many of President Clinton's appointments of ambassadors, for example, were held up for months as a result of his dispute with Senator Jesse Helms over the organization of the State Department. The United States was left with no ambassador in several important countries, including India and China. At times, Congress has used its treaty or spending powers to challenge the president on important issues: trying to force an end to the Vietnam War, creating difficulties over the Panama Canal treaty and the SALT II arms control treaty, defeating the Nuclear Test Ban Treaty, resisting the Reagan administration's aid to the Nicaraguan Contras, and barely acquiescing to military and peacekeeping operations in Bosnia and Kosovo.

Congress has probably exerted its greatest influence on issues that involve spending money, which must pass through the regular congressional appropriations process. Foreign aid appropriations, for example, tend to be cut in Congress. Military bases and contracts are a special focus of attention because each has a great economic effect on congressional districts and powerful interest groups. Because of congressional pressure, for example, the commission on base closings and the Clinton administration decided to keep open several bases that the military said it did not need.

The Senate has substantial influence on foreign policy. Senator Jesse Helms (R–NC), former chairman of the Foreign Relations Committee, blocked a number of Clinton administration ambassadorial appointments in a struggle over the organization of the State Department and U.S. dues payments to the United Nations.

Public Opinion and the Mass Media

It was once thought that public opinion on foreign policy was so uninformed, unstable, and weak that it could not possibly have much effect on policymaking. As we saw in Chapter 5, however, that picture is not correct. It is now clear that public opinion does, in fact, have substantial effects. Historical studies of such issues as arms control and foreign aid indicate that policymakers have often taken public opinion into account in making their decisions.[18] About two-thirds of the time, too, *changes* in public opinion on foreign policy are followed within a year or so by policy changes moving in the same direction.[19]

Still, the executive branch has considerable leeway. Seldom does public opinion demand that particular actions be taken abroad. More often, the public more or less goes along with what the president does, at least until the results begin to come in. If the results look bad (as in the Vietnam War), the public tends to punish the administration with low popularity ratings and rejection at the polls. If the results look good (as the Persian Gulf War did, at least initially), the public rewards the administration.

electoral reward and punishment

The tendency to vote for the incumbents when times are good and against them when times are bad.

As indicated in Chapter 10, this system of **electoral reward and punishment** creates incentives for presidents to do things that will please the public in the long run, but there is leeway in the short run, and presidents sometimes miscalculate how things will work out. Moreover, with many foreign policies that are secret or barely visible, the moment for reward or punishment never comes, and the administration can act without being called to account. On some issues, however, the public is so clear about its preferences that a president must tread carefully. For example, the public's apparent reluctance to accept combat casualties (except when the security threat to the United States is tangible) convinced President Clinton to rule out the use of ground forces to drive Serb troops out of Kosovo and end "ethnic cleansing." (See the "Using the Framework" feature.)

According to political scientist V. O. Key Jr., public opinion mainly sets up "dikes" that confine policy to certain broad channels. Within those channels, the president and the executive branch largely determine the flow.[20] This view may have to be altered slightly to take account of the increasingly important role the mass media play in placing issues on the agenda and framing the debate about them. When the plight of Kosovar Muslims at the hands of the Serbs dominated the news broadcasts, the president, the executive branch, and Congress were forced to pay attention. Other human rights tragedies receiving less attention—as in the early stages of the Rwanda atrocities—did not lead to significant U.S. intervention.

Corporations, Interest Groups, and Social Movements

American corporations are among the most active players in the global economy, producing, marketing, and selling goods and services around the world. Naturally, these corporations with a considerable global presence have good reasons to care about U.S. foreign policy. Companies such as Microsoft want the government to aggressively fight software piracy in places such as China and Russia. Many multinational firms seek free trade policies and diplomatic or military protection abroad. Other firms, especially those relying on U.S. markets but threatened by foreign competition (e.g., in automobiles, steel, clothing, and consumer electronics), have sought government subsidies, tariffs, or quotas against foreign goods.

The defense budget involves big money as well. Arms manufacturers such as Lockheed Martin, Boeing, Raytheon, and General Dynamics play a

USING THE FRAMEWORK

Why Did We Depend Entirely on Air Power in Kosovo? Why No Ground Forces?

Announcing his plan to rely solely on an air bombing campaign to try to halt the Serb "ethnic cleansing" campaign in the Yugoslavian province of Kosovo, President Clinton renounced the use of ground combat troops. Many critics, including several of our NATO allies, believed that only troops on the ground could protect Kosovar Muslims from being forced from their homes. In fact, once the bombing campaign began, the Yugoslav military and Serb irregular units increased the pace and intensity of their "cleansing." Air power eventually prevailed, forcing a Serb withdrawal, but it took time, and the human toll was high. Why, then, did President Clinton avoid sending ground troops? Taking a broader look at how structural, political linkage, and governmental factors affected President Clinton's decision to only use air power in Kosovo will help explain the situation.

Governmental Action

President Clinton orders air strikes against Serb forces in Yugoslavia and Kosovo.

Governmental Level

- The president and his advisors believed that Serb aggression threatened the stability of the Balkans and that some form of military intervention in Kosovo was essential.

- Congress was uneasy about the use of ground troops and voted a (nonbinding) resolution against their use.

- The Joint Chiefs and other military leaders did not want to get bogged down in a Balkan quagmire.

Political Linkages Level

- Recently, the mass media have "individualized" and "personalized" American military action so that virtually every American combat death receives extensive coverage.

- The public was not inclined to accept American casualties in humanitarian interventions where the perceived threat to the United States was low.

- The public came to believe that air power was both effective and saved American lives.

Structural Level

- As commander-in-chief, the president had the constitutional power to put American military forces into action.

- As the leading military power in the world, the United States had the resources to wage any form of military campaign in Kosovo it wished.

- The United States had, near at hand, especially at various locations in Europe, sufficient air assets to wage a bombing campaign.

significant part in decisions about the development and selection of weapons systems.

Ethnic groups also can affect U.S. foreign policy. This is most obvious in the case of U.S. policy toward Israel, in which widespread public sympathy toward that country is reinforced by the efforts of the American-Israel Public Affairs Committee (AIPAC) and by various organized groups representing Jewish Americans. Palestinian-American organizations are becoming more active in an effort to counteract this tendency in U.S. foreign policy. Similarly, African-American groups strongly opposed apartheid in South Africa and military rule in Haiti, and Cuban-American groups have insisted on tough policies against Fidel Castro's Cuba.

HOW DEMOCRATIC ARE WE?

PROPOSITION: Foreign and military policymaking is not and should not be very democratic.

AGREE: Americans care more about what is going on in the United States that affects them directly than they do about issues and developments in distant places. They also know more about what is going on in the United States—whether health care, living standards, or the environment—than they do about what is happening elsewhere, particularly in the poor countries that get very little media news coverage. Additionally, to be effective, many foreign and military policies must be made in secret, so citizens often do not have the information that is necessary to be politically effective. Given all of this, it is clear that Americans are more competent as citizens when faced with domestic matters than with military and foreign affairs. Therefore, for the most part, Americans give political, diplomatic, and military leaders a relatively free hand in making foreign and military policy.

DISAGREE: While it is true that citizens play a smaller role in deciding foreign policies compared with domestic policies, they are not powerless. Citizens do, in fact, give their leaders a great deal of freedom in deciding what to do in foreign and military affairs, but these leaders are ultimately answerable to the people, and they know it. Presidents and members of Congress pay very close attention to public opinion and worry about the next election, so they are careful to avoid actions that may eventually prove unpopular. In addition, if Americans play a lesser role than required by democratic theory, it is something we ought to work on improving. If we are to be a democracy at all, citizens must be engaged in helping to decide all important policies, whether these policies are about health care or nuclear proliferation.

THE AUTHORS: It is true that Americans know less and care less about foreign affairs than they do about domestic affairs. It is also true that some secrecy is required in fashioning and conducting foreign and military policies and that speed is sometimes of the essence. However, it is also probably the case that Americans are becoming more informed about other places, whether through the mass media or the Internet, and are coming to recognize the interconnectedness of our fate with the fates of others. Americans are paying increasing attention to and learning more about international trade and competitiveness, human rights violations abroad, and global warming and other environmental problems, to take only a few examples. They are becoming more competent as citizens and seem to be paying closer attention to what our political leaders do in these policy areas and holding them accountable. This is all to the good, in our view, because democracy involves popular control of government leaders and the policies they make.

As the single-minded focus on the Cold War has receded and other foreign policy issues with domestic implications come to the fore, an increasing number of public and private interest groups have been drawn into the politics of foreign policymaking. Labor unions, for example, have become very active in the politics of trade agreements, pushing hard for wage guarantees and worker safety provisions so that jobs at home are not lost to cheap labor abroad. Farm organizations in 2000 successfully lobbied Congress to allow food exports to Cuba. Conservative religious groups and human rights organizations became involved in the fight over the trade status of China because of that regime's ill-treatment of Christians (see the Chapter 7 opening vignette). The incipient antiglobalization movement made its presence felt in the streets of Seattle in late 1999 where it clashed with police during demonstrations against the World Trade Organization, causing President Clinton and some other world leaders to consider including labor standards and environmental protections in global trading rules.

LongmanParticipate

CourseCompass

simulation
**The China
Dilemma**

Summary

The United States has become the world's only military superpower, with a much larger economy and much more powerful armed forces than any other nation. It grew into this role during roughly 200 years of westward expansion and settlement, industrialization, and then active involvement in World War I and World War II.

For more than 40 years, American foreign policy was focused around the tense Cold War with the Soviet Union, competing for influence in Europe, fighting Soviet allies in Korea and Vietnam, and skirmishing over the Third World. When the Soviet Union collapsed, attention turned to other issues, including regional and ethnic conflicts, international economic competition, efforts at transition to democracy and free markets in Russia and Eastern Europe, problems of world poverty, and the global environment.

Foreign policy has traditionally been made mostly in the executive branch, where the president is assisted by a large national security bureaucracy, including the National Security Council, the Department of Defense, the Department of State, and various intelligence agencies. Congress has been little involved in crises or covert actions and has generally gone along with major decisions on defense policy; it has asserted itself chiefly on matters of foreign trade and aid, military bases, and procurement contracts. Recently, Congress has shown signs that it wants to play a bigger role. Public opinion affects policy, perhaps increasingly so, but this influence is limited by the executive branch's centralization of decision making, secrecy, and control of information. How large a part interest groups and corporations play is disputed, but it is probably substantial. Structural factors, including U.S. economic and military strength and the nature of the international system, strongly affect what policies seem feasible or desirable.

Suggestions for Further Reading

Ambrose, Stephen. *Rise to Globalism,* rev. ed. New York: Penguin Books, 1997.
  Describes the rise of the U.S. military, economic, and political power in the twentieth century.

Greider, William. *One World, Ready or Not: The Manic Logic of Global Capitalism.* New York: Simon & Schuster, 1997.
  A pessimistic analysis of trends in global capitalism; describes the future as one of economic instability, growing inequality, and corporate control.

Huntington, Samuel P. *The Clash of Civilizations: Civilizations and the Remaking of World Order*. New York: Simon & Schuster, 1997.
> *Suggests that the post–Cold War world will be organized along the lines of competing civilizations and that one of these civilizations, Islam, presents the greatest danger to a stable world order.*

Kegley, Charles W., Jr., and Eugene R. Wittkopf. *American Foreign Policy: Pattern and Process*, 5th ed. New York: St. Martin's Press, 1995.
> *Thoroughly describes the institutions and processes of foreign policymaking.*

La Feber, Walter. *America, Russia, and the Cold War, 1945–1990*. New York: McGraw-Hill, 1991.
> *A clear, brief history of the Cold War.*

Mann, James. *About Face: A History of America's Curious Relationship with China, Nixon to Clinton*. New York: Knopf, 1999.
> *An examination of how China has used its rather meager resources to gain political, diplomatic, and military advantages in its relationship with the United States.*

Russett, Bruce M. *Controlling the Sword: The Democratic Governance of National Security*. Cambridge, MA: Harvard University Press, 1990.
> *Argues that public opinion is much more important in making foreign policy than was previously thought.*

Sen, Amartya Kumar. *Development as Freedom*. New York: Knopf, 1999.
> *The Nobel Prize winner in economics argues that freedom is the basis for the development of poor countries, a fact that should inform the foreign policies of the rich countries.*

Internet Sources

Amnesty International **http://www.amnesty.org/**
> *Reports and documents from the international human rights organization.*

Defense Link **www.defenselink.mil/**
> *The home page of the Department of Defense.*

Fedworld **http://www.fedworld.gov/**
> *Links to the home pages of all federal departments and agencies involved in foreign affairs and national defense, including the State Department, the Central Intelligence Agency, the Commerce Department, and the Defense Department.*

International Herald Tribune Online **http://www.iht.com/**
> *Complete international news with a much broader perspective than that found in most U.S. newspapers and other media outlets.*

National Security Website **www.nationalsecurity.org/spons.html**
> *Essays and news about foreign and military policy, sponsored by the Heritage Foundation, from a conservative point of view.*

Peacenet **http://www.peacenet.apc.org/peacenet/**
> *A Web site devoted to peace, social and economic justice, and human rights; information on all of these subjects as well as links to organizations working in these fields.*

Statistical Resources on the Web: Military and Defense
www.lib.umich.edu/libhome/Documents.center/stats.html
> *A vast statistical and information compendium on military and national security issues; covers the United States and other countries.*

United Nations **http://www.un.org/**
> *Home page of the United Nations; links to a wealth of statistics, documents and reports, UN departments and conferences, and information on reaching UN officials.*

Notes

1. Paul Kennedy, *The Rise and Fall of the Great Powers* (New York: Random House, 1987).

2. "X" (George F. Kennan), "The Sources of Soviet Conduct," *Foreign Affairs* 25 (1947), pp. 566–582; Lawrence S. Wittner, *American Intervention in Greece, 1943–1949* (New York: Columbia University Press, 1982).

3. Walter La Feber, *America, Russia, and the Cold War, 1945–1990* (New York: McGraw-Hill, 1991).

4. U.S. Bureau of the Census, *Statistical Abstracts of the United States, 1992* (Washington, D.C.: U.S. Government Printing Office, 1992), pp. 341, 344. Some authorities give a figure of 58,000 for total U.S. *war-related* deaths in Vietnam.

5. Office of Management and Budget, *Budget of the United States, Fiscal 2001* (Washington, D.C.: U.S. Government Printing Office, 2000), table 9.1.

6. Roger Cohen, "Europe Seeks a New Parity," *New York Times* (June 15, 1999), p. A1.

7. Joseph S. Nye, Jr., "Redefining the National Interest," *Foreign Affairs* (July/August, 1999), pp. 22–35.

8. Thomas L. Friedman, *The Lexus and the Olive Tree* (New York: Farrar, Straus, Giroux, 1999).

9. Samuel P. Huntington, "The Clash of Civilizations," *Foreign Affairs* 72 (1993).

10. Mario F. Bognanno and Kathryn J. Ready, eds., *The North American Free Trade Agreement: Labor, Industry, and Government Perspectives* (Westport, CT: Praeger, 1993).

11. Jagdish Bhagwati and Marvin H. Kosters, eds., *Trade and Wages: Leveling Down Wages?* (Washington, D.C.: AEI Press, 1994).

12. *Budget of the United States, 2001.*

13. Organization for Economic Cooperation and Development (OECD), *International Development Statistics, 1999.*

14. Department of State, *Bureau of Arms Control Annual Report, 2000.*

15. Charles W. Kegley Jr. and Eugene R. Wittkopf, *American Foreign Policy: Pattern and Process,* 4th ed. (New York: St. Martin's Press, 1991), p. 387.

16. Donald M. Snow and Eugene Brown, *Puzzle Palaces and Foggy Bottom: U.S. Foreign and Defense Policy-Making in the 1990s* (New York: St. Martin's Press, 1994), p. 96.

17. David Wise and Thomas B. Ross, *The Invisible Government* (New York: Random House, 1964); Twentieth Century Fund, *The Need to Know: The Report of the Twentieth Century Fund Task Force on Covert Action and American Democracy* (New York: Twentieth Century Fund, 1992); Victor Marchetti and John D. Marks, *The CIA and the Cult of Intelligence* (New York: Knopf, 1974).

18. Bruce M. Russett, *Controlling the Sword: The Democratic Governance of National Security* (Cambridge, MA: Harvard University Press, 1990); Richard Sobel, ed., *Public Opinion in U.S. Foreign Policy: The Controversy over Contra Aid* (Lanham, MD: Rowman & Littlefield, 1993).

19. Alan D. Monroe, "Consistency Between Public Preferences and National Policy Decisions," *American Politics Quarterly* 7 (1979), pp. 3–19; Benjamin I. Page and Robert Y. Shapiro, "Effects of Public Opinion on Policy," *American Political Science Review* 77 (1983), pp. 175–190.

20. V. O. Key Jr., *Public Opinion and American Democracy* (New York: Knopf, 1961), p. 552.

Appendix

- The Declaration of Independence
- The Constitution of the United States
- The Federalist Papers, Nos. 10, 51, and 78
- Presidents and Congresses, 1789–2001

The Declaration of Independence

When in the Course of human events, it becomes necessary for one people to dissolve the political bands which have connected them with another, and to assume among the Powers of the earth, the separate and equal station to which the Laws of Nature and of Nature's God entitle them, a decent respect to the opinions of mankind requires that they should declare the causes which impel them to the separation.

We hold these truths to be self-evident, that all men are created equal, that they are endowed by their Creator with certain unalienable Rights, that among these are Life, Liberty and the pursuit of Happiness. That to secure these rights, Governments are instituted among Men, deriving their just powers from the consent of the governed, That whenever any Form of Government becomes destructive of these ends, it is the Right of the People to alter or to abolish it, and to institute new Government, laying its foundation on such principles and organizing its powers in such form, as to them shall seem most likely to effect their Safety and Happiness. Prudence, indeed, will dictate that Governments long established should not be changed for light and transient causes; and accordingly all experience hath shown, that mankind are more disposed to suffer, while evils are sufferable, than to right themselves by abolishing the forms to which they are accustomed. But when a long train of abuses and usurpations, pursuing invariably the same Object evinces a design to reduce them under absolute Despotism, it is their right, it is their duty, to throw off such Government, and to provide new Guards for their future security.—Such has been the patient sufferance of these Colonies; and such is now the necessity which constrains them to alter their former Systems of Government. The history of the present King of Great Britain is a history of repeated injuries and usurpations, all having in direct object the establishment of an absolute Tyranny over these States. To prove this, let Facts be submitted to a candid world.

He has refused his Assent to Laws, the most wholesome and necessary for the public good.

He has forbidden his Governors to pass Laws of immediate and pressing importance, unless suspended in their operation till his Assent should be obtained; and when so suspended, he has utterly neglected to attend to them.

He has refused to pass other Laws for the accommodation of large districts of people, unless those people would relinquish the right of Representation in the Legislature, a right inestimable to them and formidable to tyrants only.

He has called together legislative bodies at places unusual, uncomfortable, and distant from the depository of their Public Records, for the sole purpose of fatiguing them into compliance with his measures.

He has dissolved Representative Houses repeatedly, for opposing with manly firmness his invasions on the rights of the people.

He has refused for a long time, after such dissolutions, to cause others to be elected; whereby the Legislative Powers, incapable of Annihilation, have returned to the People at large for their exercise; the State remaining in the mean time exposed to all the dangers of invasion from without, and convulsions within.

He has endeavoured to prevent the population of these States; for that purpose obstructing the Laws of Naturalization of Foreigners; refusing to pass others to encourage their migration hither, and raising the conditions of new Appropriations of Lands.

He has obstructed the Administration of Justice, by refusing his Assent to Laws for establishing Judiciary Powers.

He has made Judges dependent on his Will alone, for the tenure of their offices, and the amount and payment of their salaries.

He has erected a multitude of New Offices, and sent hither swarms of Officers to harass our People, and eat out their substance.

He has kept among us, in times of peace, Standing Armies without the Consent of our legislature.

He has affected to render the Military independent of and superior to the Civil Power.

He has combined with others to subject us to a jurisdiction foreign to our constitution, and unacknowledged by our laws; giving his Assent to their acts of pretended legislation:

For quartering large bodies of armed troops among us:

For protecting them, by a mock Trial, from Punishment for any Murders which they should commit on the Inhabitants of these States:

For cutting off our Trade with all parts of the world:

For imposing taxes on us without our Consent:

For depriving us in many cases, of the benefits of Trial by Jury:

For transporting us beyond Seas to be tried for pretended offences:

For abolishing the free System of English Laws in a neighbouring Province, establishing therein an Arbitrary government, and enlarging its Boundaries so as to render it at once an example and fit instrument for introducing the same absolute rule into these Colonies:

For taking away our Charters, abolishing our most valuable Laws, and altering fundamentally the Forms of our Governments:

For suspending our own Legislature, and declaring themselves invested with Power to legislate for us in all cases whatsoever.

He has abdicated Government here, by declaring us out of his Protection and waging War against us.

He has plundered our seas, ravaged our Coasts, burnt our towns, and destroyed the lives of our people.

He is at this time transporting large armies of foreign mercenaries to compleat the works of death, desolation and tyranny, already begun with circumstances of Cruelty & perfidy scarcely paralleled in the most barbarous ages, and totally unworthy the Head of a civilized nation.

He has constrained our fellow Citizens taken Captive on the high Seas to bear Arms against their Country, to become the executioners of their friends and Brethren, or to fall themselves by their Hands.

He has excited domestic insurrections amongst us, and has endeavoured to bring on the inhabitants of our frontiers, the merciless Indian Savages, whose known rule of warfare, is an undistinguished destruction of all ages, sexes and conditions.

In every stage of these Oppressions We have Petitioned for Redress in the most humble terms: Our repeated Petitions have been answered only by repeated injury. A Prince, whose character is thus marked by every act which may define a Tyrant, is unfit to be the ruler of a free People.

Nor have We been wanting in attention to our British brethren. We have warned them from time to time of attempts by their legislature to extend an unwarrantable jurisdiction over us. We have reminded them of the circumstances of our emigration and settlement here. We have appealed to their native justice and magnanimity, and we have conjured them by the ties of our common kindred to disavow these usurpations, which, would inevitably interrupt our connections and correspondence. They too have been deaf to the voice of justice and of consanguinity. We must, therefore, acquiesce in the necessity, which denounces our Separation, and hold them, as we hold the rest of mankind, Enemies in War, in Peace Friends.

We, therefore, the Representatives of the united States of America, in General Congress, Assembled, appealing to the Supreme Judge of the world for the rectitude of our intentions, do, in the Name, and by Authority of the good People of these Colonies, solemnly publish and declare, That these United Colonies are, and of Right ought to be Free and Independent States; that they are Absolved from all Allegiance to the British Crown, and that all political connection between them and the State of Great Britain, is and ought to be totally dissolved; and that as Free and Independent States, they have full Power to levy War, conclude Peace, contract Alliances, establish Commerce, and to do all other Acts and Things which Independent States may of right do. And for the support of this Declaration, with a firm reliance of the Protection of Divine Providence, we mutually pledge to each other our Lives, our Fortunes and our sacred Honor.

John Hancock,
Josiah Bartlett, Wm Whipple, Saml Adams, John Adams, Robt Treat Paine, Elbridge Gerry, Steph. Hopkins, William Ellery, Roger Sherman, Samel Huntington, Wm Williams, Oliver Wolcott, Matthew Thornton, Wm Floyd, Phil Livingston, Frans Lewis, Lewis Morris, Richd Stockton, Jno Witherspoon, Fras Hopkinson, John Hart, Abra Clark, Robt Morris, Benjamin Rush, Benja Franklin, John Morton, Geo Clymer, Jas Smith, Geo. Taylor, James Wilson, Geo. Ross, Caesar Rodney, Geo Read, Thos M:Kean, Samuel Chase, Wm Paca, Thos Stone, Charles Carroll of Carrollton, George Wythe, Richard Henry Lee, Th. Jefferson, Benja Harrison, Thos Nelson, Jr., Francis Lightfoot Lee, Carter Braxton, Wm Hooper, Joseph Hewes, John Penn, Edward Rutledge, Thos Heyward, Junr., Thomas Lynch, Junor., Arthur Middleton, Button Gwinnett, Lyman Hall, Geo Walton.

The Constitution of the United States

We the people of the United States, in Order to form a more perfect Union, establish Justice, insure domestic Tranquility, provide for the common defence, promote the general Welfare, and secure the Blessings of Liberty to ourselves and our Posterity, do ordain and establish this constitution for the United States of America.

Article I

Section 1 All legislative Powers herein granted shall be vested in a Congress of the United States, which shall consist of a Senate and House of Representatives.

Section 2 The House of Representatives shall be composed of Members chosen every second Year by the People of the several States, and the Electors in each State shall have the Qualifications requisite for Electors of the most numerous Branch of the State Legislature.

No person shall be a Representative who shall not have attained to the Age of twenty-five Years, and been seven Years a Citizen of the United States, and who shall not, when elected, be an Inhabitant of that State in which he shall be chosen.

Representatives and direct Taxes shall be apportioned among the several States which may be included within this Union, according to their respective Numbers, which shall be determined by adding to the whole Number of free Persons, including those bound to Service for a Term of Years, and excluding Indians not taxed, three fifths of all other Persons. The actual Enumeration shall be made within three Years after the first Meeting of the Congress of the United States, and within every subsequent Term of ten Years, in such Manner as they shall by Law direct. The Number of Representatives shall not exceed one for every thirty Thousand, but each State shall have at Least one Representative; and until such enumeration shall be made, the State of New Hampshire shall be entitled to chuse three, Massachusetts eight, Rhode-Island and Providence Plantations one, Connecticut five, New-York six, New Jersey four, Pennsylvania eight, Delaware one, Maryland six, Virginia ten, North Carolina five, South Carolina five, and Georgia three.

When vacancies happen in the Representation from any State, the Executive Authority thereof shall issue Writs of Election to fill such Vacancies.

The House of Representatives shall chuse their Speaker and other Officers; and shall have the sole Power of Impeachment.

Section 3 The Senate of the United States shall be composed of two Senators from each State, chosen by the Legislature thereof, for six Years; and each Senator shall have one Vote.

Immediately after they shall be assembled in Consequence of the first Election, they shall be divided as equally as may be into three Classes. The Seats of the Senators of the first Class shall be vacated at the Expiration of the second Year, of the second Class at the Expiration of the fourth Year, and of the third Class at the Expiration of the sixth Year, so that one-third may be chosen every second Year; and if Vacancies happen by Resignation, or otherwise, during the Recess of the Legislature of any State, the Executive thereof may make temporary Appointments until the next Meeting of the Legislature, which shall then fill such Vacancies.

No Person shall be a Senator who shall not have attained to the Age of thirty Years, and been nine Years a Citizen of the United States, and who shall not, when elected, be an Inhabitant of that State in which he shall be chosen.

The Vice President of the United States shall be President of the Senate, but shall have no vote, unless they be equally divided.

The Senate shall chuse their other Officers, and also a President pro tempore, in the absence of the Vice President, or when he shall exercise the Office of the President of the United States.

The Senate shall have the sole Power to try all Impeachments. When sitting for that purpose, they shall be on Oath or Affirmation. When the President of the United States is tried, the Chief Justice shall preside: And no person shall be convicted without the Concurrence of two thirds of the Members present.

Judgment in Cases of Impeachment shall not extend further than to removal from Office, and disqualification to hold and enjoy any Office of honor, Trust, or Profit under the United States: but the Party convicted shall nevertheless be liable and subject to Indictment, Trial, Judgment, and Punishment, according to Law.

Section 4 The Times, Places and Manner of holding Elections for Senators and Representatives, shall be prescribed in each state by the Legislature thereof; but the Congress may at any time by Law make or alter such Regulations, except as to the Places of Chusing Senators.

The Congress shall assemble at least once in every Year, and such Meeting shall be on the first Monday in December, unless they shall by Law appoint a different Day.

Section 5 Each House shall be the Judge of the Elections, Returns and Qualifications of its own Members, and a Majority of each shall constitute a Quorum to do Business; but a smaller number may adjourn from day to day, and may be authorized to compel the Attendance of absent Members, in such Manner, and under such Penalties, as each House may provide.

Each House may determine the Rules of its Proceedings, punish its Members for disorderly Behavior, and, with the Concurrence of two thirds, expel a Member.

Each House shall keep a Journal of its Proceedings, and from time to time publish the same, excepting such Parts as may in their Judgment require Secrecy; and the Yeas and Nays of the Members of either House on any question shall, at the Desire of one fifth of those Present, be entered on the Journal.

Neither House, during the Session of Congress, shall, without the Consent of the other, adjourn for more than three days, nor to any other Place than that in which the two Houses shall be sitting.

Section 6 The Senators and Representatives shall receive a Compensation for their Services, to be ascertained by Law, and paid out of the Treasury of the United States. They shall in all Cases, except Treason, Felony, and Breach of the Peace, be privileged from arrest during their Attendance at the Session of their respective Houses, and in going to and returning from the same; and for any Speech or Debate in either House, they shall not be questioned in any other Place.

No Senator or Representative shall, during the Time for which he was elected, be appointed to any civil Office under the Authority of the United States, which shall have been created, or the Emoluments whereof shall have been increased, during such time; and no Person holding any Office under the United States shall be a Member of either House during his continuance in Office.

Section 7 All Bills for raising Revenue shall originate in the House of Representatives; but the Senate may propose or concur with Amendments as on other bills.

Every Bill which shall have passed the House of Representatives and the Senate, shall, before it become a Law, be presented to the President of the United States; If he approve he shall sign it, but if not he shall return it, with his Objections, to that House in which it shall have originated, who shall enter the Objections at large on their Journal, and proceed to reconsider it. If after such Reconsideration two thirds of that House shall agree to pass the bill, it shall be sent, together with the objections, to the other House, by which it shall likewise be reconsidered, and if approved by two thirds of that House, it shall become a Law. But in all such Cases the Votes of both Houses shall be determined by Yeas and Nays, and the Names of the Persons voting for and against the Bill shall be entered on the Journal of each House respectively. If any Bill shall not be returned by the President within ten Days (Sundays excepted) after it shall have been presented to him, the Same shall be a Law, in like Manner as if he had signed it, unless the Congress by their

Adjournment prevent its Return, in which Case it shall not be a Law.

Every Order, Resolution, or Vote to which the Concurrence of the Senate and House of Representatives may be necessary (except on a question of Adjournment) shall be presented to the President of the United States; and before the Same shall take Effect, shall be approved by him, or being disapproved by him, shall be repassed by two thirds of the Senate and House of Representatives, according to the Rules and Limitations prescribed in the Case of a Bill.

Section 8 The Congress shall have Power

To lay and collect Taxes, Duties, Imposts and Excises, to pay the Debts and provide for the common Defence and general Welfare of the United States; but all Duties, Imposts and Excises shall be uniform throughout the United States;

To borrow money on the credit of the United States;

To regulate Commerce with foreign Nations, and among the several States, and with the Indian Tribes;

To establish a uniform Rule of Naturalization, and uniform Laws on the subject of Bankruptcies throughout the United States;

To coin Money, regulate the Value thereof, and of foreign Coin, and fix the Standard of Weights and Measures;

To provide for the Punishment of counterfeiting the Securities and current Coin of the United States;

To establish Post offices and post Roads;

To promote the Progress of Science and useful Arts, by securing for limited Times to Authors and Inventors the exclusive Right to their respective Writings and Discoveries;

To constitute Tribunals inferior to the Supreme Court;

To define and punish Piracies and Felonies committed on the high Seas, and Offences against the Law of Nations;

To declare War, grant Letters of Marque and Reprisal, and make Rules concerning Captures on Land and Water;

To raise and support Armies, but no Appropriation of Money to that Use shall be for a longer Term than two Years;

To provide and maintain a Navy;

To make Rules for the Government and Regulation of the land and naval forces;

To provide for calling forth the Militia to execute the Laws of the Union, suppress Insurrections and repel Invasions;

To provide for organizing, arming, and disciplining the Militia, and for governing such Part of them as may be employed in the Service of the United States, reserving to the States respectively, the Appointment of the Officers, and the Authority of training the Militia according to the discipline prescribed by Congress;

To exercise exclusive Legislation in all Cases whatsoever, over such District (not exceeding ten Miles square) as may, by Cession of particular States, and the acceptance of Congress, become the Seat of Government of the United States, and to exercise like Authority over all Places purchased by the Consent of the Legislature of the State in which the Same shall be, for the Erection of Forts, Magazines, Arsenals, dock-Yards, and other needful Buildings;—And

To make all Laws which shall be necessary and proper for carrying into Execution the foregoing Powers, and all other Powers vested by this Constitution in the government of the United States, or in any Department or Officer thereof.

Section 9 The Migration or Importation of such Persons as any of the States now existing shall think proper to admit, shall not be prohibited by the Congress prior to the Year one thousand eight hundred and eight, but a tax or duty may be imposed on such Importation, not exceeding ten dollars for each Person.

The privilege of the Writ of Habeas Corpus shall not be suspended, unless when in Cases of Rebellion or Invasion the public Safety may require it.

No Bill of Attainder or ex post facto Law shall be passed.

No capitation, or other direct, Tax shall be laid unless in Proportion to the Census or Enumeration herein before directed to be taken.

No Tax or Duty shall be laid on Articles exported from any State.

No Preference shall be given by any Regulation of Revenue to the Ports of one State over those of another: nor shall Vessels bound to, or from, one state, be obliged to enter, clear, or pay Duties in another.

No Money shall be drawn from the Treasury, but in Consequence of Appropriations made by Law; and a regular Statement and Account of the Receipts and Expenditures of all public Money shall be published from time to time.

No Title of Nobility shall be granted by the United States: And no Person holding any Office of Profit or Trust under them, shall, without the Consent of the Congress, accept of any present, Emolument, Office, or Title, of any kind whatever, from any King, Prince, or Foreign State.

Section 10 No state shall enter into any Treaty, Alliance, or Confederation; grant Letters of Marque and Reprisal; coin Money; emit Bills of Credit; make any Thing but gold and silver Coin a Tender in Payment of Debts; pass any Bill of Attainder, ex post facto Law, or Law impairing the Obligation of Contracts, or grant any Title of Nobility.

No State shall, without the Consent of the Congress, lay any Imposts or Duties on Imports or Exports, except what may be absolutely necessary for executing its inspection Laws: and the net Produce of all Duties and Imposts, laid by any State on Imports or Exports, shall be for the Use of the Treasury of the United States; and all such Laws shall be subject to the Revision and Control of the Congress.

No State shall, without the Consent of Congress, lay any duty of Tonnage, keep Troops, or Ships of War in time of Peace, enter into any Agreement or Compact with another State, or with a foreign Power, or engage in War, unless actually invaded, or in such imminent Danger as will not admit of delay.

Article II

Section 1 The executive Power shall be vested in a President of the United States of America. He shall hold his Office during the Term of four years, and, together with the Vice President, chosen for the same Term, be elected, as follows:

Each State shall appoint, in such Manner as the Legislature thereof may direct, a Number of Electors, equal to the whole Number of Senators and Representatives to which the State may be entitled in the Congress; but no Senator or Representative, or Person holding an Office of Trust or Profit under the United States, shall be appointed an Elector.

The Electors shall meet in their respective States, and vote by Ballot for two persons, of whom one at least shall not be an Inhabitant of the same State with themselves. And they shall make a List of all the Persons voted for, and of the Number of Votes for each; which List they shall sign and certify, and transmit sealed to the Seat of the Government of the United States, directed to the President of the Senate. The President of the Senate shall, in the Presence of the Senate and House of Representatives, open all the Certificates, and the Votes shall then be counted. The Person having the greatest Number of Votes shall be the President, if such Number be a Majority of the whole Number of Electors appointed; and if there be more than one who have such Majority, and have an equal Number of Votes, then the House of Representatives shall immediately chuse by Ballot one of them for President; and if no Person have a Majority, then from the five highest on the List the said House shall in like Manner chuse the President. But in chusing the President, the votes shall be taken by States, the Representation from each State having one Vote; a quorum for this Purpose shall consist of a Member or Members from two-thirds of the States, and a Majority of all the States shall be necessary to a Choice. In every Case, after the Choice of the President, the Person having the greatest Number of Votes of the Electors shall be the Vice President. But if there should remain two or more who have equal votes, the Senate shall chuse from them by Ballot the Vice President.

The Congress may determine the time of chusing the Electors, and the Day on which they shall give their Votes; which Day shall be the same throughout the United States.

No person except a natural-born Citizen, or a Citizen of the United States, at the time of the Adoption of this Constitution, shall be eligible to the Office of President; neither shall any Person be eligible to that Office who shall not have attained to the Age of thirty-five years, and been fourteen Years a Resident within the United States.

In Case of the Removal of the President from Office, or of his Death, Resignation, or Inability to discharge the Powers and Duties of the said Office, the same shall devolve on the Vice President, and the Congress may by

Law provide for the Case of Removal, Death, Resignation, or Inability, both of the President and Vice President, declaring what Officer shall then act as President, and such Officer shall act accordingly, until the disability be removed, or a President shall be elected.

The President shall, at stated Times, receive for his Services a Compensation, which shall neither be increased nor diminished during the Period for which he shall have been elected, and he shall not receive within that Period any other Emolument from the United States, or any of them.

Before he enter on the execution of his Office, he shall take the following Oath or Affirmation:—"I do solemnly swear (or affirm) that I will faithfully execute the Office of President of the United States, and will, to the best of my Ability, preserve, protect, and defend the Constitution of the United States."

Section 2 The President shall be Commander in Chief of the Army and Navy of the United States, and of the Militia of the several States, when called into the actual Service of the United States; he may require the Opinion, in writing, of the principal Officer in each of the executive Departments, upon any subject relating to the Duties of their respective Offices, and he shall have Power to Grant Reprieves and Pardons for Offences against the United States, except in Cases of Impeachment.

He shall have Power, by and with the Advice and Consent of the Senate, to make Treaties, provided two thirds of the Senators present concur; and he shall nominate, and by and with the Advice and Consent of the Senate, shall appoint Ambassadors, other public Ministers and Consuls, Judges of the supreme Court, and all other Officers of the United States, whose Appointments are not herein otherwise provided for, and which shall be established by Law: but the Congress may by Law vest the Appointment of such inferior Officers, as they think proper, in the President alone, in the Courts of Law, or in the Heads of Departments.

The President shall have Power to fill up all Vacancies that may happen during the Recess of the Senate, by granting Commissions which shall expire at the End of their next Session.

Section 3 He shall from time to time give to the Congress Information of the State of the Union, and recommend to their Consideration such Measures as he shall judge necessary and expedient; he may, on extraordinary occasions, convene both Houses, or either of them, and in Case of Disagreement between them, with respect to the Time of Adjournment, he may adjourn them to such Time as he shall think proper; he shall receive Ambassadors and other public Ministers; he shall take Care that the Laws be faithfully executed, and shall Commission all the Officers of the United States.

Section 4 The President, Vice President and all civil Officers of the United States, shall be removed from Office on Impeachment for, and Conviction of, Treason, Bribery, or other high Crimes and Misdemeanors.

Article III

Section 1 The judicial Power of the United States, shall be vested in one supreme Court, and in such inferior Courts as the Congress may from time to time ordain and establish. The Judges, both of the supreme and inferior Courts, shall hold their Offices during good Behaviour, and shall, at stated Times, receive for their Services, a Compensation, which shall not be diminished during their Continuance in Office.

Section 2 The judicial Power shall extend to all Cases, in Law and Equity, arising under this Constitution, the Laws of the United States, and treaties made, or which shall be made, under their Authority;—to all Cases affecting ambassadors, other public ministers and consuls;—to all cases of admiralty and maritime Jurisdiction;—to Controversies to which the United States shall be a Party;—to Controversies between two or more States;—between a State and Citizens of another State;—between Citizens of different States,—between Citizens of the same State claiming Lands under Grants of different States, and between a State, or the Citizens thereof, and foreign States, Citizens or Subjects.

In all Cases affecting Ambassadors, other public Ministers and Consuls, and those in which a State shall be Party, the supreme Court shall have original Jurisdiction. In all the other Cases before mentioned, the supreme Court shall have appellate Jurisdiction, both as to Law and Fact, with such Exceptions, and under such Regulations as the Congress shall make.

The trial of all Crimes, except in Cases of Impeachment, shall be by Jury; and such Trial shall be held in the State where the said Crimes shall have been committed; but when not committed within any State, the Trial shall be at such Place or Places as the Congress may by Law have directed.

Section 3 Treason against the United States, shall consist only in levying War against them, or in adhering to their Enemies, giving them Aid and Comfort. No Person shall be convicted of Treason unless on the testimony of two Witnesses to the same overt Act, or on Confession in open Court.

The Congress shall have power to declare the Punishment of Treason, but no Attainder of Treason shall work Corruption of Blood, or Forfeiture except during the Life of the Person attained.

Article IV

Section 1 Full Faith and Credit shall be given in each State to the public Acts, Records, and judicial Proceedings of every other State. And the Congress may by general Laws prescribe the Manner in which such Acts, Records and Proceedings shall be proved, and the Effect thereof.

Section 2 The Citizens of each State shall be entitled to all Privileges and Immunities of Citizens in the several States.

A Person charged in any State with Treason, Felony, or other Crime, who shall flee from Justice, and be found in another State, shall on demand of the executive Authority of the State from which he fled, be delivered up, to be removed to the State having Jurisdiction of the crime.

No Person held to Service or Labour in one State, under the Laws thereof, escaping into another, shall, in Consequence of any Law or Regulation therein, be discharged from such Service or Labour, but shall be delivered up on Claim of the Party to whom such Service or Labour may be due.

Section 3　New States may be admitted by the Congress into this Union; but no new State shall be formed or erected within the Jurisdiction of any other State; nor any State be formed by the Junction of two or more States, or parts of States, without the Consent of the Legislatures of the States concerned as well as of the Congress.

The Congress shall have Power to dispose of and make all needful Rules and Regulations respecting the Territory or other Property belonging to the United States; and nothing in this Constitution shall be so construed as to Prejudice any Claims of the United States, or of any particular State.

Section 4　The United States shall guarantee to every State in this Union a Republican Form of Government, and shall protect each of them against Invasion; and on Application of the Legislature, or the Executive (when the Legislature cannot be convened) against domestic Violence.

Article V

The Congress, whenever two-thirds of both Houses shall deem it necessary, shall propose Amendments to this Constitution, or, on the Application of the Legislatures of two-thirds of the several States, shall call a Convention for proposing Amendments, which, in either Case, shall be valid to all Intents and Purposes, as part of this Constitution, when ratified by the Legislatures of three-fourths of the several States, or by Conventions in three-fourths thereof, as the one or the other Mode of Ratification may be proposed by the Congress; Provided that no Amendment which may be made prior to the Year One thousand eight hundred and eight shall in any Manner affect the first and fourth Clauses in the Ninth Section of the first Article; and that no State, without its Consent, shall be deprived of its equal Suffrage in the Senate.

Article VI

All Debts contracted and Engagements entered into, before the Adoption of this Constitution, shall be as valid against the United States under this Constitution, as under the Confederation.

This Constitution, and the Laws of the United States which shall be made in Pursuance thereof; and all Treaties made, or which shall be made, under the Authority of the United States, shall be the supreme Law of the Land; and the Judges in every State shall be bound thereby, any Thing in the Constitution or Laws of any State to the Contrary notwithstanding.

The Senators and Representatives before mentioned, and the Members of the several State Legislatures and all executive and judicial Officers, both of the United States and of the several States, shall be bound by Oath or Affirmation to support this Constitution; but no religious Test shall ever be required as a qualification to any Office or public Trust under the United States.

Article VII

The Ratification of the Conventions of nine States shall be sufficient for the Establishment of this Constitution between the States so ratifying the same.

Done in Convention by the Unanimous Consent of the States present the Seventeenth Day of September in the Year of our Lord one thousand seven hundred and Eighty seven, and of the Independence of the United States of America the Twelfth. In Witness whereof We have hereunto subscribed our Names.

Go. Washington, President and deputy from Virginia; Attest William Jackson, Secretary; Delaware: Geo. Read,* Gunning Bedford, Jr., John Dickinson, Richard Basset, Jaco. Broom; Maryland: James McHenry, Daniel of St. Thomas' Jenifer, Danl. Carroll; Virginia: John Blair, James Madison, Jr.; North Carolina: Wm. Blount, Richd. Dobbs Spaight, Hu Williamson; South Carolina: J. Rutledge, Charles Cotesworth Pinckney, Charles Pinckney, Pierce Butler; Georgia: William Few, Abr. Baldwin; New Hampshire: John Langdon, Nicholas Gilman; Massachusetts: Nathaniel Gorham, Rufus King; Connecticut: Wm. Saml. Johnson, Roger Sherman,* New York: Alexander Hamilton; New Jersey: Wil. Livingston, David Brearley, Wm. Paterson, Jona. Dayton; Pennsylvania: B. Franklin,* Thomas Mifflin, Robt. Morris,* Geo. Clymer,* Thos. FitzSimons, Jared Ingersoll, James Wilson, Gouv. Morris.

Articles in Addition to, and Amendment of, the Constitution of the United States of America, Proposed by Congress, and Ratified by the Legislatures of the Several States, Pursuant to the Fifth Article of the Original Constitution.

Amendment I [1791]

Congress shall make no law respecting an establishment of religion, or prohibiting the free exercise thereof; or abridging the freedom of speech, or of the press; or the right of the people peaceably to assemble, and to petition the Government for a redress of grievances.

Amendment II [1791]

A well regulated Militia, being necessary to the security of a free State, the right of the people to keep and bear Arms shall not be infringed.

Amendment III [1791]

No Soldier shall, in time of peace, be quartered in any house, without the consent of the Owner, nor in time of war, but in a manner to be prescribed by law.

Amendment IV [1791]

The right of the people to be secure in their persons, houses, papers, and effects, against unreasonable searches and seizures, shall not be violated, and no Warrants shall issue, but upon probable cause, supported by Oath or affirmation, and particularly describing the place to be searched, and the persons or things to be seized.

Amendment V [1791]

No person shall be held to answer for a capital or otherwise infamous crime, unless on a presentment or indictment of a Grand Jury, except in cases arising in the land or naval forces, or in the Militia, when in actual service in time of War or public danger; nor shall any person be subject for the same offence to be twice put in jeopardy of life or limb; nor shall be compelled in any criminal case to be a witness against himself, nor be deprived of life, liberty, or property, without due process of law; nor shall private property be taken for public use, without just compensation.

Amendment VI [1791]

In all criminal prosecutions, the accused shall enjoy the right to a speedy and public trial, by an impartial jury of the State and district wherein the crime shall have been committed, which district shall have been previously ascertained by law, and to be informed of the nature and cause of the accusation; to be confronted with the witnesses against him; to have compulsory process for obtaining witnesses in his favor, and to have the Assistance of Counsel for his defence.

Amendment VII [1791]

In suits at common law, where the value in controversy shall exceed twenty dollars, the right of trial by jury shall be preserved, and no fact tried by a jury, shall be otherwise reexamined in any Court of the United States, than according to the rules of the common law.

Amendment VIII [1791]

Excessive bail shall not be required, nor excessive fines imposed, nor cruel and unusual punishments inflicted.

Amendment IX [1791]

The enumeration in the Constitution, of certain rights, shall not be construed to deny or disparage others retained by the people.

Amendment X [1791]

The powers not delegated to the United States by the Constitution, nor prohibited by it to the States, are reserved to the States respectively, or to the people.

Amendment XI [1798]

The Judicial power of the United States shall not be construed to extend to any suit in law or equity, commenced or prosecuted against one of the United States by Citizens of another State, or by Citizens or Subjects of any Foreign State.

Amendment XII [1804]

The Electors shall meet in their respective States and vote by ballot for President and Vice President, one of whom, at least, shall not be an inhabitant of the same State with themselves; they shall name in their ballots the person voted for as President, and in distinct ballots the person voted for as Vice President, and they shall make distinct lists of all persons voted for as President, and of all persons voted for as Vice President, and of the number of votes for each, which lists they shall sign and certify, and transmit sealed to the seat of the government of the United States, directed to the President of the Senate;—The President of the Senate shall, in the presence of the Senate and House of Representatives, open all the certificates and the votes shall then be counted;—The person having the greatest number of votes for President, shall be the President, if such number be a majority of the whole number of Electors appointed; and if no person have such majority, then from the persons having the highest numbers not exceeding three on the list of those voted for as President, the House of Representatives shall choose immediately, by ballot, the President. But in choosing the President, the votes shall be taken by states, the representation from each state having one vote; a quorum for this purpose shall consist of a member or members from two-thirds of the states, and a majority of all the states shall be necessary to a choice. And if the House of Representatives shall not choose a President whenever the right of choice shall devolve upon them, before the fourth day of March next following, then the Vice President shall act as President, as in the case of the death or other constitutional disability of the President.—The person having the greatest number of votes as Vice President, shall be the Vice President, if such number be a majority of the whole number of Electors appointed, and if no person have a majority, then from the two highest numbers on the list, the Senate shall choose the Vice President; a quorum for the purpose shall consist of two-thirds of the whole number of Senators, and a majority of the whole number shall be necessary to a choice. But no person constitutionally ineligible to the office of President shall be eligible to that of Vice President of the United States.

Amendment XIII [1865]

Section 1   Neither slavery nor involuntary servitude, except as a punishment for crime whereof the party shall have been duly convicted, shall exist within the United States, or any place subject to their jurisdiction.

Section 2   Congress shall have power to enforce this article by appropriate legislation.

Amendment XIV [1868]

Section 1   All persons born or naturalized in the United States, and subject to the jurisdiction thereof, are citizens of the United States and of the State wherein they reside. No State shall make or enforce any law which shall abridge the privileges or immunities of citizens of the United States; nor shall any State deprive any person of life, liberty, or property, without due process of law; nor deny to any person within its jurisdiction the equal protection of the laws.

Section 2   Representatives shall be apportioned among the several States according to their respective numbers, counting the whole number of persons in each State, excluding Indians not taxed. But when the right to vote at any election for the choice of electors for President and Vice President of the United States, Representatives in Congress, the Executive and Judicial officers of a State, or the members of the Legislature thereof, is denied to any of the male inhabitants of such State, being twenty-one years of age, and citizens of the United States or in any way abridged, except for participation in rebellion, or other crime, the basis of representation therein shall be reduced in the proportion which the number of such male citizens shall bear to the whole number of male citizens twenty-one years of age in such State.

Section 3   No person shall be a Senator or Representative in Congress, or elector of President and Vice President, or hold any office, civil or military, under the United States, or under any State, who, having previously taken an oath, as a member of Congress, or as an officer of the United States, or as a member of any State legislature, or as an executive or judicial officer of any State, to support the Constitution of the United States, shall have engaged in insurrection or rebellion against the same, or given aid or comfort to the enemies thereof. But Congress may by a vote of two-thirds of each House, remove such disability.

Section 4   The validity of the public debt of the United States, authorized by law, including debts incurred for payment of pensions and bounties for services in suppressing insurrection or rebellion, shall not be questioned. But neither the United States nor any State shall assume or pay any debt or obligation incurred in aid of insurrection or rebellion against the United States, or any claim for the loss or emancipation of any slave; but all such debts, obligations, and claims shall be held illegal and void.

Section 5   The Congress shall have the power to enforce, by appropriate legislation, the provisions of this article.

Amendment XV [1870]

Section 1   The right of citizens of the United States to vote shall not be denied or abridged by the United States or by any State on account of race, color, or previous condition of servitude—

Section 2   The Congress shall have power to enforce this article by appropriate legislation.

Amendment XVI [1913]

The Congress shall have power to lay and collect taxes on incomes, from whatever source derived, without apportionment among the several States, and without regard to any census or enumeration.

Amendment XVII [1913]

The Senate of the United States shall be composed of two Senators from each State, elected by the people thereof, for six years; and each Senator shall have one vote. The electors in each State shall have the qualifications requisite for electors of the most numerous branch of the State legislatures.

When vacancies happen in the representation of any State in the Senate, the executive authority of such State shall issue writs of election to fill such vacancies: Provided, That the legislature of any State may empower the executive thereof to make temporary appointments until the people fill the vacancies by election as the legislature may direct. This amendment shall not be so construed as to affect the election or term of any Senator chosen before it becomes valid as part of the Constitution.

Amendment XVIII [1919]

Section 1   After one year from the ratification of this article the manufacture, sale, or transportation of intoxicating liquors within, the importation thereof into, or the exportation thereof from the United States and all territory subject to the jurisdiction thereof for beverage purposes is hereby prohibited.

Section 2   The Congress and the several States shall have concurrent power to enforce this article by appropriate legislation.

Section 3   This article shall be inoperative unless it shall have been ratified as an amendment to the Constitution by the legislatures of the several States, as provided in the Constitution, within seven years from the date of the submission hereof to the States by the Congress.

Amendment XIX [1920]

The right of citizens of the United States to vote shall not be denied or abridged by the United States or by any State on account of sex.

Congress shall have power to enforce this article by appropriate legislation.

Amendment XX [1933]

Section 1   The terms of the President and Vice President shall end at noon on the 20th day of January, and the terms of Senators and Representatives at noon on the 3d day of January, of the years in which such terms would have ended if this article had not been ratified; and the terms of their successors shall then begin.

Section 2   The Congress shall assemble at least once in every year, and such meeting shall begin at noon on the 3d day of January, unless they shall by law appoint a different day.

Section 3   If, at the time fixed for the beginning of the term of the President, the President elect shall have died, the Vice President elect shall become President. If a President shall not have been chosen before the time fixed for the beginning of his term, or if the President elect shall have failed to qualify, then the Vice President elect shall act as President until a President shall have qualified; and the Congress may by law provide for the case wherein neither a President elect nor a Vice President elect shall have qualified, declaring who shall then act as President, or the manner in which one who is to act shall be selected, and such person shall act accordingly until a President or Vice President shall have qualified.

Section 4   The Congress may by law provide for the case of the death of any of the persons from whom the House of Representatives may choose a President whenever the right of choice shall have devolved upon them, and for the case of the death of any of the persons from whom the Senate may choose a Vice President whenever the right of choice shall have devolved upon them.

Section 5   Sections 1 and 2 shall take effect on the 15th day of October following the ratification of this article.

Section 6   This article shall be inoperative unless it shall have been ratified as an amendment to the Constitution by the legislatures of three-fourths of the several States within seven years from the date of its submission.

Amendment XXI [1933]

Section 1   The eighteenth article of amendment to the Constitution of the United States is hereby repealed.

Section 2   The transportation or importation into any State, Territory, or possession of the United States for delivery or use therein of intoxicating liquors, in violation of the laws thereof, is hereby prohibited.

Section 3   This article shall be inoperative unless it shall have been ratified as an amendment to the Constitution by conventions in the several States, as provided in the Constitution, within seven years from the date of the submission hereof to the States by the Congress.

Amendment XXII [1951]

No person shall be elected to the office of the President more than twice, and no person who has held the office of President, or acted as President, for more than two years of a term to which some other person was elected President shall be elected to the office of the President more than once.

But this Article shall not apply to any person holding the office of President when this Article was proposed by the Congress, and shall not prevent any person who may be holding the office of President or acting as President, during the term within which this Article becomes operative from holding the office of President or acting as President during the remainder of such term.

Amendment XXIII [1961]

Section 1   The District constituting the seat of Government of the United States shall appoint in such manner as the Congress may direct:

A number of electors of President and Vice President equal to the whole number of Senators and Representatives in Congress to which the District would be entitled if it were a State, but in no event more than the least populous State; they shall be in addition to those appointed by the States, but they shall be considered, for the purposes of the election of President and Vice President, to be electors appointed by a State; and they shall meet in the District and perform such duties as provided by the twelfth article of amendment.

Section 2   The Congress shall have power to enforce this article by appropriate legislation.

Amendment XXIV [1964]

Section 1   The right of citizens of the United States to vote in any primary or other election for President or Vice

President, for electors for President or Vice President, or for Senator or Representative in Congress, shall not be denied or abridged by the United States or any State by reason of failure to pay any poll tax or other tax.

Section 2   The Congress shall have the power to enforce this article by appropriate legislation.

Amendment XXV [1967]

Section 1   In case of the removal of the President from office or his death or resignation, the Vice President shall become President.

Section 2   Whenever there is a vacancy in the office of the Vice President, the President shall nominate a Vice President who shall take the office upon confirmation by a majority vote of both houses of Congress.

Section 3   Whenever the President transmits to the President pro tempore of the Senate and the Speaker of the House of Representatives his written declaration that he is unable to discharge the powers and duties of his office, and until he transmits to them a written declaration to the contrary, such powers and duties shall be discharged by the Vice President as Acting President.

Section 4   Whenever the Vice President and a majority of either the principal officers of the executive departments, or of such other body as Congress may by law provide, transmit to the President pro tempore of the Senate and the Speaker of the House of Representatives their written declaration that the President is unable to discharge the powers and duties of his office, the Vice President shall immediately assume the powers and duties of the office as Acting President.

Thereafter, when the President transmits to the President pro tempore of the Senate and the Speaker of the House of Representatives his written declaration that no inability exists, he shall resume the powers and duties of his office unless the Vice President and a majority of either the principal officers of the executive departments, or of such other body as Congress may by law provide, transmit within four days to the President pro tempore of the Senate and the Speaker of the House of Representatives their written declaration that the President is unable to discharge the powers and duties of his office. Thereupon Congress shall decide the issue, assembling within 48 hours for that purpose if not in session. If the Congress, within 21 days after receipt of the latter written declaration, or, if Congress is not in session, within 21 days after Congress is required to assemble, determines by two-thirds vote of both houses that the President is unable to discharge the powers and duties of his office, the Vice President shall continue to discharge the same as Acting President; otherwise, the President shall resume the powers and duties of his office.

Amendment XXVI [1971]

Section 1   The right of citizens of the United States, who are 18 years of age or older, to vote shall not be denied or abridged by the United States or any state on account of age.

Section 2   The Congress shall have the power to enforce this article by appropriate legislation.

Amendment XXVII [1992]

No law varying the compensation for the service of Senators and Representatives shall take effect until an election of Representatives shall have intervened.

The Federalist Papers

The Federalist Papers is a collection of 85 essays written by Alexander Hamilton, John Jay, and James Madison under the pen name Publius. They were published in New York newspapers in 1787 and 1788 to support ratification of the Constitution. Excerpts from Federalist Nos. 10, 51, and 78 are reprinted here.

JAMES MADISON:
Federalist No. 10

Among the numerous advantages promised by a well constructed Union, none deserves to be more accurately developed than its tendency to break and control the violence of faction. The friend of popular governments never finds himself so much alarmed for their character and fate as when he contemplates their propensity to this dangerous vice. He will not fail, therefore, to set a due value on any plan which, without violating the principles to which he is attached, provides a proper cure for it. The instability, injustice, and confusion, introduced into the public councils, have, in truth been the mortal diseases under which popular governments have everywhere perished; as they continue to be the favorite and fruitful topics from which the adversaries to liberty derive their most specious declamations. The valuable improvements made by the American constitutions on the popular models, both ancient and modern, cannot certainly be too much admired; but it would be an unwarrantable partiality, to contend that they have as effectually obviated the danger on this side, as was wished and expected. Complaints are everywhere heard from our most considerate and virtuous citizens, equally the friends of public and private faith, and of public and personal liberty, that our governments are too unstable; that the public good is disregarded in the conflicts of rival parties; and that measures are too often decided, not according to the rules of justice, and the rights of the minor party, but by the superior force of an interested and overbearing majority. However anxiously we may wish that these complaints had no foundation, the evidence of known facts will not permit us to deny that they are in some degree true. It will be found, indeed, on a candid review of our situation, that some of the distresses under which we labor, have been erroneously charged on the operation of our governments; but it will be found, at the same time, that other causes will not alone account for many of our heaviest misfortunes; and, particularly, for the prevailing and increasing distrust of public engagements, and alarm for private rights, which are echoed from one end of the continent to the other. These must be chiefly, if not wholly, effects of the unsteadiness and injustice, with which a factious spirit has tainted our public administrations.

By a faction, I understand a number of citizens, whether amounting to a majority or minority of the whole, who are united and actuated by some common impulse of passion, or of interest, adverse to the rights of other citizens, or to the permanent and aggregate interests of the community.

There are two methods of curing the mischiefs of faction: The one, by removing its causes; the other, by controlling its effects.

There are again two methods of removing the causes of faction: the one, by destroying the liberty which is essential to its existence; the other, by giving to every citizen the same opinions, the same passions, and the same interests.

It could never be more truly said, than of the first remedy, that it was worse than the disease. Liberty is to faction what air is to fire, an aliment, without which it instantly expires. But it could not be a less folly to abolish liberty, which is essential to political life because it nourishes faction, than it would be to wish the annihilation of air, which is essential to animal life, because it imparts to fire its destructive agency.

The second expedient is as impracticable, as the first would be unwise. As long as the reason of man continues fallible, and he is at liberty to exercise it, different opinions will be formed. As long as the connection subsists between his reason and his self-love, his opinions and his passions will have a reciprocal influence on each other; and the former will be objects to which the latter will attach themselves. The diversity in the faculties of men, from which the rights of property originate, is not less an insuperable obstacle to a uniformity of interests. The protection of those faculties is the first object of government. From the protection of different and unequal faculties of acquiring property, the possession of different degrees and kinds of property immediately results; and from the influence of these on the sentiments and views of the respective proprietors, ensues a division of the society into different interests and parties.

The latent causes of faction are thus sown in the nature of man; and we see them everywhere brought into different degrees of activity, according to the different circumstances of civil society. A zeal for different opinions concerning religion, concerning government, and many other points, as well of speculation as of practice; an attachment to different leaders, ambitiously contending for preeminence and power; or to persons of other descriptions, whose fortunes have been interesting to the human passions, have, in turn, divided mankind into parties, inflamed them with mutual animosity, and rendered them much more disposed to vex and oppress each other, than to cooperate for their common good. So strong is this propensity of mankind, to fall into mutual animosities, that where no substantial occasion presents itself, the most frivolous and fanciful distinctions have been sufficient to kindle their unfriendly passions, and excite their most violent conflicts. But the most common and durable source of factions has been the various and unequal distribution of property. Those who hold, and those who are without property, have ever formed distinct interests in society. Those who are creditors, and those who are debtors, fall under a like discrimination. A landed interest, a manufacturing interest, a mercantile interest, a moneyed interest, with many lesser interests, grow up of necessity in civilized nations, and divide them into different classes, actuated by different sentiments and views. The regulation of these various and interfering interests forms the principle task of modern legislation, and involves the spirit of party and faction in the necessary and ordinary operations of government.

No man is allowed to be a judge in his own cause; because his interest will certainly bias his judgment, and, not improbably, corrupt his integrity. With equal, nay, with greater reason, a body of men are unfit to be both judges and parties at the same time; yet what are many of the most important acts of legislation, but so many judicial determinations, not indeed concerning the rights of single persons, but concerning the rights of large bodies of citizens? And what are the different classes of legislators, but advocates and parties to the cause which they determine? Is a law proposed concerning private debts? It is a question to which the creditors are parties on one side, and the debtors on the other. Justice ought to hold the balance between them. Yet the parties are, and must be, themselves the judges; and the most numerous party, or, in other words, the most powerful faction, must be expected to prevail. Shall domestic manufactures be encouraged, and in what degree, by restrictions on foreign manufactures? are questions which would be differently decided by the landed and the manufacturing classes; and probably by neither with a sole regard to justice and the public good. . . .

It is in vain to say, that enlightened statesmen will be able to adjust these clashing interests, and render them all subservient to the public good. Enlightened statesmen will not always be at the helm; nor, in many cases, can such an adjustment be made at all, without taking into view indirect and remote considerations, which will rarely prevail over the immediate interest which one party may find in disregarding the rights of another, or the good of the whole.

The inference to which we are brought is, that the causes of faction cannot be removed; and that relief is only to be sought in the means of controlling its effects.

If a faction consists of less than a majority, relief is supplied by the republican principle, which enables the majority to defeat its sinister views, by regular vote. It may clog the administration, it may convulse the society; but it will be unable to execute and mask its violence under the forms of the constitution. When a majority is included in a faction, the form of popular government, on the other hand, enables it to sacrifice to its ruling passion or interest, both the public good and the rights of other citizens. To secure the public good, and private rights, against the danger of such a faction, and at the same time to preserve the spirit and the form of popular government, is then the great object to which our inquiries are directed. Let me add, that it is the great desideratum, by which alone this form of government can be rescued from the opprobrium under which it has so long labored, and be recommended to the esteem and adoption of mankind.

By what means is this object attainable? Evidently by one of two only. Either the existence of the same passion or interest in a majority, at the same time must be prevented; or the majority, having such coexistent passion or interest, must be rendered, by their number and local situation, unable to concert and carry into effect schemes of oppression. If the impulse and the opportunity be suffered to coincide, we well know, that neither moral nor religious motives can be relied on as an adequate control. They are not found to be such on the injustice and violence of individuals, and lose their efficacy in proportion to the number combined together; that is in proportion as their efficacy becomes needful.

From this view of the subject, it may be concluded, that a pure democracy, by which I mean a society consisting of a small number of citizens, who assemble and administer the government in person, can admit of no cure from the mischiefs of faction. A common passion or interest will, in almost every case, be felt by a majority of the whole; a communication and concert, results from the form of government itself; and there is nothing to check the inducements to sacrifice the weaker party, or an obnoxious individual. Hence it is, that such democracies have ever been spectacles of turbulence and contention; have ever been found incompatible with personal security, or the rights of property; and have, in general been as short in their lives, as they have been violent in their deaths. Theoretic politicians, who have patronized this species of government, have erroneously supposed that by reducing mankind to a perfect equality in their political rights, they would, at the same time, be perfectly equalized and assimilated in their possessions, their opinions, and their passions.

A republic, by which I mean a government in which the scheme of representation takes place, opens a different prospect, and promises the cure for which we are seeking. Let us examine the points in which it varies from pure democracy, and we shall comprehend both the nature of the cure and the efficacy which it must derive from the union.

The two great points of difference, between a democracy and a republic, are, first, the delegation of the government, in the latter, to a small number of citizens elected by the rest; secondly, the greater number of citizens, and greater sphere of country, over which the latter may be extended.

The effect of the first difference is on the one hand, to refine and enlarge the public views, by passing them through the medium of a chosen body of citizens, whose wisdom may best discern the true interest in their country, and whose patriotism and love of justice, will be least likely to sacrifice it to temporary or partial considerations. Under such a regulation, it may well happen, that the public voice, pronounced by the representatives of the people, will be more consonant to the public good, than if pronounced by the people themselves, convened for the purpose. On the other hand, the effect may be inverted. Men of factious tempers, of local prejudices, or of sinister designs, may by intrigue, by corruption, or by other means, first obtain the suffrages, and then betray the interests, of the people. The question resulting is, whether small or extensive republics are most favorable to the election of proper guardians of the public weal; and it is clearly decided in favor of the latter by two obvious considerations.

In the first place, it is to be remarked, that however small the republic may be, the representatives must be raised to a certain number, in order to guard against the cabals of a few; and that however large it may be, they must be limited to a certain number, in order to guard against the confusion of a multitude. Hence, the number of representatives in the two cases not being in proportion to that of the constituents, and being proportionally greatest in the small republic, it follows that if the proportion of fit characters be not less in the large than in the small republic, the former will present a greater option, and consequently a greater probability of a fit choice.

In the next place, as each representative will be chosen by a greater number of citizens in the large than in the small republic, it will be more difficult for unworthy candidates to practice with success the vicious arts, by which elections are too often carried; and the suffrages of the people being more free, will be more likely to center in men who possess the most attractive merit, and the most diffusive and established characters. . . .

The other point of difference is, the greater number of citizens, and extent of territory, which may be brought within the compass of republican, than of democratic government; and it is this circumstance principally which renders factious combinations less to be dreaded in the former, than in the latter. The smaller the society, the fewer probably will be the distinct parties and interests composing it; the fewer the distinct parties and interests, the more frequently will a majority be found of the same party; and the smaller the number of individuals composing a majority, and the smaller the compass within which they are placed, the more easily they will concert and execute their plans of oppression. Extend the sphere, and you take in a greater variety of parties and interests; you make it less probable that a majority of the whole will have a common motive to invade the rights of other citizens; or if such a common motive exists, it will be more difficult for all who feel it to discover their own strength, and to act in unison with each other. . . .

Hence, it clearly appears, that the same advantage, which a republic has over a democracy, in controlling the effects of faction, is enjoyed by a large over a small republic—is enjoyed by the union over the states composing it. Does this advantage consist in the substitution of representatives, whose enlightened views and virtuous sentiments render them superior to local prejudices, and to schemes of injustice? It will not be denied, that the representation of the union will be most likely to possess these requisite endowments. Does it consist in the greater security afforded by a greater variety of parties, against the event of any one party being able to outnumber and oppress the rest? In an equal degree does the increased variety of parties, comprised within the union, increase this security? Does it, in fine, consist in the greater obstacles opposed to the concert and accomplishment of the secret wishes of an unjust and interested majority? Here, again, the extent of the union gives it the most palpable advantage. The influence of factious leaders may kindle a flame within their particular states, but will be unable to spread a general conflagration through the other states; a religious sect may degenerate into a political faction in a part of the confederacy; but the variety of sects dispersed over the entire face of it, must secure the national councils against any danger from that source; a rage for paper money, for an abolition of debts, for an equal division of property, or for any other improper or wicked project, will be less apt to pervade the whole body of the union, than a particular member of it; in the same proportion as such a malady is more likely to taint a particular country or district, than an entire state.

In the extent and proper structure of the union, therefore, we behold a republican remedy for the diseases most incident to republican government. And according to the degree of pleasure and pride we feel in being republicans, ought to be our zeal in cherishing the spirit, and supporting the character of Federalists.

JAMES MADISON: Federalist No. 51

To what expedient then shall we finally resort, for maintaining in practice the necessary partition of power among the several departments, as laid down in the constitution? The only answer that can be given is, that as all these exterior provisions are found to be inadequate, the defect must be supplied, by so contriving the interior structure of the government, as that its several constituent parts may, by their mutual relations, be the means of keeping each other in their proper places. . . .

In order to lay a due foundation for that separate and distinct exercise of the different powers of government, which, to a certain extent, is admitted on all hands to be essential to the preservation of liberty, it is evident that each department should have a will of its own; and consequently should be so constituted, that the members of each should have as little agency as possible in the appointment of the members of the others. . . .

It is equally evident, that the members of each department should be as little dependent as possible on those of the others, for the emoluments annexed to their offices. Were the executive magistrate, or the judges, not independent of the legislature in this particular, their independence in every other would be merely nominal.

But the great security against a gradual concentration of the several powers in the same department, consists in giving to those who administer each department, the necessary constitutional means, and personal motives, to resist encroachments of the others. The provision for defense must in this, as in all other cases, be made commensurate to the danger of attack. Ambition must be made to counteract ambition. The interest of the man must be connected with the constitutional rights of the place. It may be a reflection on human nature, that such devices should be necessary to control the abuses of government. But what is government itself, but the greatest of all reflections on human nature? If men were angels, no government would be necessary. If angels were to govern men, neither external nor internal controls on government would be necessary. In framing a government, which is to be administered by men over men, the great difficulty lies in this: You must first enable the government to control the governed; and in the next place, oblige it to control itself. A dependence on the people is, no doubt, the primary control on the government; but experience has taught mankind the necessity of auxiliary precautions.

This policy of supplying by opposite and rival interests, the defect of better motives, might be traced through the whole system of human affairs, private as well as public. We see it particularly displayed in all the subordinate distributions of power; where the constant aim is, to divide and arrange the several offices in such a manner, as that each may be a check on the other; that the private interest of every individual, may be a sentinel over the public rights. These interventions of prudence cannot be less requisite to the distribution of the supreme powers of the state.

But it is not possible to give to each department an equal power of self-defense. In republican government, the legislative authority necessarily predominates. The remedy for this inconvenience is, to divide the legislature into different branches; and to render them by different modes of election, and different principles of action, as little connected with each other, as the nature of their common functions, and their common dependence on the society will admit. It may even be necessary to guard against dangerous encroachments, by still further precautions. As the weight of the legislative authority requires that it should be thus divided, the weakness of the executive may require, on the other hand, that it should be fortified. An absolute negative on the legislature, appears, at first view, to be the natural defense with which the executive magistrate should be armed. But perhaps it would be neither altogether safe, nor alone sufficient. On ordinary occasions, it might not be exerted with the requisite firmness; and on extraordinary occasions, it might be perfidiously abused. May not this defect of an absolute negative be supplied by some qualified connection between this weaker department, and the weaker branch of the stronger department, by which the latter may be led to support the constitutional rights of the former, without being too much detached from the rights of its own department?

There are, moreover, two considerations particularly applicable to the federal system of America, which place that system in a very interesting point of view.

First. In a single republic, all the power surrendered by the people is submitted to the administration of a single government, and the usurpations are guarded against by a division of the government into distinct and separate departments. In the compound republic of America, the power surrendered by the people is first divided between two distinct governments, and then the portion allotted to each subdivided among distinct and separate departments. Hence a double security arises to the rights of the people. The different governments will control each other, at the same time that each will be controlled by itself.

Second. It is of great importance in a republic not only to guard the society against the oppression of its rulers, but to guard one part of the society against the injustice of the other part. Different interests necessarily exist in different classes of citizens. If a majority be united by a common interest, the rights of the minority will be insecure. There are but two methods of providing against this evil: the one by creating a will in the community independent of the majority—that is, of the society itself; the other, by comprehending in the society so many separate descriptions of citizens as will render an unjust combination of a majority of the whole very probable, if not impracticable. The first method prevails in all governments possessing an hereditary or self-appointed authority. This, at best, is but a precarious security; because a power independent of the society may as well espouse the unjust views of the major, as the rightful interests of the minor party, and may possibly be turned against both parties. The second method will be exemplified in the federal republic of the United States. Whilst all authority in it will be derived from and dependent on the society, the society itself will be broken into so many parts, interests and classes of citizens, that the rights of individuals, or of the minority, will be in little danger from interested combinations of the majority. In a free government the security for civil rights must be the same as that for religious rights. It consists in the one case in the multiplicity of interests, and in the other in the multiplicity of sects. The degree of security in both cases will depend on the number of interests and sects; and this may be presumed to depend on the extent of country and number of people comprehended under the same government. This view of the subject must particularly recommend a proper federal system to all the sincere and considerate friends of republican government, since it shows that in exact proportion as the territory of the Union may be formed into more circumscribed Confederacies, or States, oppressive combinations of a majority will be facilitated; the best security, under the republican forms, for the rights of every class of citizens, will be diminished; and consequently the stability and independence of some member of the government, the only other security, must be proportionately increased. Justice is the end of the government. It is the end of civil society. It ever has been and ever will be pursued until it be obtained, or until liberty be lost in the pursuit. In a society under the forms of which the stronger faction can readily unite and oppress the weaker, anarchy may as truly be said to reign as in a state of nature, where the weaker individual is not secured against the violence of the stronger; and as, in the latter state, even the stronger individuals are prompted, by the uncertainty of their condition, to submit to a government which may protect the weak as well as themselves; so, in the former state, will the more powerful factions or parties be gradually induced, by a like motive, to wish for a government which will protect all parties, the weaker as well as the more powerful. It can be little doubted that if the State of Rhode Island was separated from the Confederacy and left to itself, the insecurity of rights under the popular form of government within such narrow limits would be displayed by such reiterated oppressions of factious majorities that some power altogether independent of the people would soon be called for by the voice of the very factions whose misrule had proved the necessity of it. In the extended republic of the United States, and among the great variety of interests, parties, and sects which it embraces, a coalition of a majority of the whole society could seldom take place on any other principles than those of justice and the general good; whilst there being thus less danger to a minor from the will of a major party, there must be less pretext, also, to provide for the security of the former, by introducing into the government a will not dependent on the latter, or, in other words, a will independent of the society itself. It is no less certain than it is important, notwithstanding the contrary opinions which have been entertained, that the larger the society, provided it lie within a practical sphere, the more duly capable it will be of self-government. And happily for the republican cause, the practicable sphere may be carried to a very great extent, by a judicious modification and mixture of the federal principle.

ALEXANDER HAMILTON: Federalist No. 78

We proceed now to an examination of the judiciary department of the proposed government.

In unfolding the defects of the existing confederation, the utility and necessity of a federal judicature have been clearly pointed out. It is the less necessary to recapitulate the considerations there urged; as the propriety of the institution in the abstract is not disputed; the only questions which have been raised being relative to the manner of constituting it, and to its extent. To these points, therefore, our observations shall be confined.

The manner of constituting it seems to embrace these several objects: 1st. The mode of appointing the judges; 2nd. The tenure by which they are to hold their places; 3rd. The partition of the judiciary authority between courts, and their relations to each other.

First. As to the mode of appointing the judges: This is the same with that of appointing the officers of the union in general, and has been so fully discussed . . . that nothing can be said here which would not be useless repetition.

Second. As to the tenure by which the judges are to hold their places: This chiefly concerns their duration in office; the provisions for their support; the precautions for their responsibility.

According to the plan of the convention, all the judges who may be appointed by the United States are to hold their offices during good behavior; which is conformable to the most approved of the state constitutions. . . . The standard of good behavior for the continuance in office of the judicial magistracy is certainly one of the most valuable of the modern improvements in the practice of government. In a monarchy, it is an excellent barrier to the despotism of the prince; in a republic, it is a no less excellent barrier to the encroachments and oppressions of the representative body. And it is the best expedient which can be devised in any government, to secure a steady, upright, and impartial administration of the laws.

Whoever attentively considers the different departments of power must perceive, that, in a government in which they are separated from each other, the judiciary, from the nature of its functions, will always be the least dangerous to the political rights of the constitution; because it will be at least in a capacity to annoy or injure them. The executive not only dispenses the honors, but holds the sword of the community. The legislature not only commands the purse, but prescribes the rules by which the duties and rights of every citizen are to be regulated. The judiciary, on the contrary, has no influence over either the sword or the purse; no direction either of the strength or of the wealth of the society; and can take no active resolution whatever. It may truly be said to have neither force nor will, but merely judgment; and must ultimately depend upon the aid of the executive arm for the efficacious exercise even of this faculty.

This simple view of the matter suggests several important consequences: It proves incontestably, that the judiciary is beyond comparison, the weakest of the three departments of power, that it can never attack with success either of the other two: and that all possible care is requisite to enable it to defend itself against their attacks. It equally proves, that, though individual oppression may now and then proceed from the courts of justice, the general liberty of the people can never be endangered from that quarter; I mean so long as the judiciary remains truly distinct from both the legislature and executive. For I agree, that "there is no liberty, if the power of judging be not separated from the legislative and executive powers." It proves, in the last place, that as liberty can have nothing to fear from the judiciary alone, but would have everything to fear from its union with either of the other departments; that, as all the effects of such a union must ensue from a dependence of the former on the latter, notwithstanding a nominal and apparent separation; that as, from the natural feebleness of the judiciary, it is in continual jeopardy of being overpowered, awed or influenced by its coordinate branches; that, as nothing can contribute so much to its firmness and independence as permanency in office, this quality may therefore be justly regarded as an indispensable ingredient in its constitution; and, in a great measure, as the citadel of the public justice and the public security.

The complete independence of the courts of justice is peculiarly essential in a limited constitution. By a limited constitution, I understand one which contains certain specified exceptions to the legislative authority; such, for instance, as that it shall pass no bills of attainder, no ex post facto laws, and the like. Limitations of this kind can be preserved in practice no other way than through the medium of the courts of justice, whose duty it must be to declare all acts contrary to the manifest tenor of the constitution void. Without this, all the reservations of particular rights or privileges would amount to nothing.

Some perplexity respecting the right of the courts to pronounce legislative acts void, because contrary to the constitution, has arisen from an imagination that the doctrine would imply a superiority of the judiciary to the legislative power. It is urged that the authority which can declare the acts of another void, must necessarily be superior to the one whose acts may be declared void. As this doctrine is of great importance in all the American constitutions, a brief discussion of the grounds on which it rests cannot be unacceptable.

There is no position which depends on clearer principles than that every act of a delegated authority, contrary to the tenor of the commission under which it is exercised, is void. No legislative act, therefore, contrary to the constitution, can be valid. To deny this would be to affirm, that the deputy is greater then his principal; that the servant is above his master; that the representatives of the people are superior to the people themselves; that men, acting by virtue of powers, may do not only what their powers do not authorize, but what they forbid.

If it be said that the legislative body are themselves the constitutional judges of their own powers, and that the construction they put upon them is conclusive upon the other departments, it may be answered, that this cannot be the natural presumption, where it is not to be collected from any particular provisions in the constitution. It is not otherwise to be supposed that the constitution could intend to enable the representatives of the

people to substitute their will to that of their constituents. It is far more rational to suppose that the courts were designed to be an intermediate body between the people and the legislature, in order, among other things, to keep the latter within the limits assigned to their authority. The interpretation of the laws is the proper and peculiar province of the courts. A constitution is, in fact, and must be, regarded by the judges as a fundamental law. It must therefore belong to them to ascertain its meaning, as well as the meaning of any particular act proceeding from the legislative body. If there should happen to be an irreconcilable variance between the two, that which has the superior obligation and validity ought, of course, to be preferred; in other words, the constitution ought to be preferred to the statute, the intention of the people to the intention of their agents.

Nor does this conclusion by any means suppose a superiority of the judicial to the legislative power. It only supposes that the power of the people is superior to both; and that where the will of the legislature declared in its statutes, stands in opposition to that of the people declared in the constitution, the judges ought to be governed by the latter, rather than the former. They ought to regulate their decisions by the fundamental laws, rather than by those which are not fundamental. . . .

It can be of no weight to say, that the courts, on the pretense of a repugnancy, may substitute their own pleasure to the constitutional intentions of the legislature. This might as well happen in the case of two contradictory statutes; or it might as well happen in every adjudication upon any single statute. The courts must declare the sense of the law; and if they should be disposed to exercise will instead of judgment, the consequence would equally be the substitution of their pleasure to that of the legislative body. The observation, if it proved anything, would prove that there ought to be no judges distinct from the body.

If then the courts of justice are to be considered as the bulwarks of a limited constitution, against legislative encroachments, this consideration will afford a strong argument for the permanent tenure of judicial officers, since nothing will contribute so much as this to that independent spirit in the judges, which must be essential to the faithful performance of so arduous a duty.

This independence of the judges is equally requisite to guard the constitution and the rights of individuals, from the effects of those ill-humors which are the arts of designing men, or the influence of particular conjunctures, sometimes disseminate among the people themselves, and which, though they speedily give place to better information, and more deliberate reflection, have a tendency, in the meantime, to occasion dangerous innovations in the government, and serious oppressions of the minor party in the community. . . . Until the people have, by some solemn and authoritative act, annulled or changed the established form, it is binding upon themselves collectively, as well as individually; and no presumption, or even knowledge of their sentiments, can warrant their representatives in a departure from it, prior to such an act. But it is easy to see, that it would require an uncommon portion of fortitude in the judges to do their duty as faithful guardians of the constitution, where legislative invasions of it had been instigated by the major voice of the community.

But it is not with a view to infractions of the constitution only, that the independence of the judges may be an essential safeguard against the effects of occasional ill-humors in the society. These sometimes extend no farther than to the injury of the private rights of particular classes of citizens, by unjust and partial laws. Here also the firmness of the judicial magistracy is of vast importance in mitigating the severity, and confining the operation of such laws. It not only serves to moderate the immediate mischiefs of those which may have been passed, but it operates as a check upon the legislative body in passing them; who, perceiving that obstacles to the success of an iniquitous intention are to be expected from the scruples of the courts, are in a manner compelled by the very motives of the injustice they meditate, to qualify their attempts. . . .

That inflexible and uniform adherence to the rights of the constitution, and of individuals, which we perceive to be indispensable in the courts of justice, can certainly not be expected from judges who hold their offices by a temporary commission. Periodical appointments, however regulated, or by whomsoever made, would, in some way or other, be fatal to their necessary independence. If the power of making them was committed either to the executive or legislature, there would be danger of an improper compliance to the branch which possessed it; if to both, there would be an unwillingness to hazard the displeasure of either; if to the people, or to persons chosen by them for the special purpose, there would be too great a disposition to consult popularity to justify a reliance that nothing would be consulted but the constitution and the laws.

There is yet a further and a weighty reason for the permanency of judicial offices, which is deducible from the nature of the qualifications they require. It has been frequently remarked, with great propriety, that a voluminous code of laws is one of the inconveniences necessarily connected with the advantages of a free government. To avoid an arbitrary discretion in the courts, it is indispensable that they should be bound down by strict rules and precedents, which serve to define and point out their duty in every particular case that comes before them; and it will readily be conceived, from the variety of controversies which grow out of the folly and wickedness of mankind, that the records of those precedents must unavoidably swell to a very considerable bulk, and must demand long and laborious study to acquire a competent knowledge of them. Hence it is, that there can be but few men in the society, who will have sufficient skill in the laws to qualify them for the stations of judges. And making the proper deductions for the ordinary depravity of human nature, the number must be still smaller, of those who unite the requisite integrity with the requisite knowledge. . . .

Presidents and Congresses, 1789–2001

Year	President and Vice-President	Party of President	Congress	Majority Party — House	Majority Party — Senate
1789–1797	**George Washington** John Adams	None	1st 2nd 3rd 4th	Admin. Supporters Federalist Democratic-Republican Federalist	Admin. Supporters Federalist Federalist Federalist
1797–1801	**John Adams** Thomas Jefferson	Federalist	5th 6th	Federalist Federalist	Federalist Federalist
1801–1809	**Thomas Jefferson** Aaron Burr (to 1805) George Clinton (to 1809)		7th 8th 9th 10th	Democratic-Republican Democratic-Republican Democratic-Republican Democratic-Republican	Democratic-Republican Democratic-Republican Democratic-Republican Democratic-Republican
1809–1817	**James Madison** George Clinton (to 1813) Elbridge Gerry (to 1817)	Democratic-Republican	11th 12th 13th 14th	Democratic-Republican Democratic-Republican Democratic-Republican Democratic-Republican	Democratic-Republican Democratic-Republican Democratic-Republican Democratic-Republican
1817–1825	**James Monroe** Daniel D. Tompkins	Democratic-Republican	15th 16th 17th 18th	Democratic-Republican Democratic-Republican Democratic-Republican Democratic-Republican	Democratic-Republican Democratic-Republican Democratic-Republican Democratic-Republican
1825–1829	**John Quincy Adams** John C. Calhoun	National-Republican	19th 20th	Admin. Supporters Jacksonian Democrats	Admin. Supporters Jacksonian Democrats
1829–1837	**Andrew Jackson** John C. Calhoun (to 1833) Martin Van Buren (to 1837)	Democratic	21st 22nd 23rd 24th	Democratic Democratic Democratic Democratic	Democratic Democratic Democratic Democratic
1837–1841	**Martin Van Buren** Richard M. Johnson	Democratic	25th 26th	Democratic Democratic	Democratic Democratic
1841	**William H. Harrison** (died a month after inauguration) John Tyler	Whig			
1841–1845	**John Tyler** (VP vacant)	Whig	27th 28th	Whig Democratic	Whig Whig

Year	President and Vice-President	Party of President	Congress	Majority Party	
				House	**Senate**
1845–1849	**James K. Polk** George M. Dallas	Democratic	29th 30th	Democratic Whig	Democratic Democratic
1849–1850	**Zachary Taylor** (died in office) Millard Fillmore	Whig	31st	Democratic	Democratic
1850–1853	**Millard Fillmore** (VP vacant)	Whig	32nd	Democratic	Democratic
1853–1857	**Franklin Pierce** William R. King	Democratic	33rd 34th	Democratic Republican	Democratic Democratic
1857–1861	**James Buchanan** John C. Breckinridge	Democratic	35th 36th	Democratic Republican	Democratic Democratic
1861–1865	**Abraham Lincoln** (died in office) Hannibal Hamlin (to 1865) Andrew Johnson (1865)	Republican	37th 38th	Republican Republican	Republican Republican
1865–1869	**Andrew Johnson** (VP vacant)	Republican	39th 40th	Unionist Republican	Unionist Republican
1869–1877	**Ulysses S. Grant** Schuyler Colfax (to 1873) Henry Wilson (to 1877)	Republican	41st 42nd 43rd 44th	Republican Republican Republican Democratic	Republican Republican Republican Republican
1877–1881	**Rutherford B. Hayes** William A. Wheeler	Republican	45th 46th	Democratic Democratic	Republican Democratic
1881	**James A. Garfield** (died in office) Chester A. Arthur	Republican	47th	Republican	Republican
1881–1885	**Chester A. Arthur** (VP vacant)	Republican	48th	Democratic	Republican
1885–1889	**Grover Cleveland** Thomas A. Hendricks	Democratic	49th 50th	Democratic Democratic	Republican Republican
1889–1893	**Benjamin Harrison** Levi P. Morton	Republican	51st 52nd	Republican Democratic	Republican Republican
1893–1897	**Grover Cleveland** Adlai E. Stevenson	Democratic	53rd 54th	Democratic Republican	Democratic Republican

Year	President and Vice-President	Party of President	Congress	Majority Party	
				House	**Senate**
1897–1901	**William McKinley** (died in office) Garret A. Hobart (to 1901) Theodore Roosevelt (1901)	Republican	55th 56th	Republican Republican	Republican Republican
1901–1909	**Theodore Roosevelt** (VP vacant, 1901–1905) Charles W. Fairbanks (1905–1909)	Republican	57th 58th 59th 60th	Republican Republican Republican Republican	Republican Republican Republican Republican
1909–1913	**William Howard Taft** James S. Sherman	Republican	61st 62nd	Republican Democratic	Republican Republican
1913–1921	**Woodrow Wilson** Thomas R. Marshall	Democratic	63rd 64th 65th 66th	Democratic Democratic Democratic Republican	Democratic Democratic Democratic Republican
1921–1923	**Warren G. Harding** (died in office) Calvin Coolidge	Republican	67th	Republican	Republican
1923–1929	**Calvin Coolidge** (VP vacant, 1923–1925) Charles G. Dawes (1925–1929)	Republican	68th 69th 70th	Republican Republican Republican	Republican Republican Republican
1929–1933	**Herbert Hoover** Charles Curtis	Republican	71st 72nd	Republican Democratic	Republican Republican
1933–1945	**Franklin D. Roosevelt** (died in office) John N. Garner (1933–1941) Henry A. Wallace (1941–1945) Harry S. Truman (1945)	Democratic	73rd 74th 75th 76th 77th 78th	Democratic Democratic Democratic Democratic Democratic Democratic	Democratic Democratic Democratic Democratic Democratic Democratic
1945–1953	**Harry S. Truman** (VP vacant, 1945–1949) Alben W. Barkley (1949–1953)	Democratic	79th 80th 81st 82nd	Democratic Republican Democratic Democratic	Democratic Republican Democratic Democratic
1953–1961	**Dwight D. Eisenhower** Richard M. Nixon	Republican	83rd 84th 85th 86th	Republican Democratic Democratic Democratic	Republican Democratic Democratic Democratic
1961–1963	**John F. Kennedy** (died in office) Lyndon B. Johnson	Democratic	87th	Democratic	Democratic

Year	President and Vice-President	Party of President	Congress	Majority Party	
				House	**Senate**
1963–1969	**Lyndon B. Johnson** (VP vacant, 1963–1965) Hubert H. Humphrey (1965–1969)	Democratic	88th 89th 90th	Democratic Democratic Democratic	Democratic Democratic Democratic
1969–1974	**Richard M. Nixon** (resigned office) Spiro T. Agnew (resigned office) Gerald R. Ford (appointed vice-president)	Republican	91st 92nd	Democratic Democratic	Democratic Democratic
1974–1977	**Gerald R. Ford** Nelson A. Rockefeller (appointed vice-president)	Republican	93rd 94th	Democratic Democratic	Democratic Democratic
1977–1981	**Jimmy Carter** Walter Mondale	Democratic	95th 96th	Democratic Democratic	Democratic Democratic
1981–1989	**Ronald Reagan** George Bush	Republican	97th 98th 99th 100th	Democratic Democratic Democratic Democratic	Republican Republican Republican Democratic
1989–1993	**George Bush** J. Danforth Quayle	Republican	101st 102nd	Democratic Democratic	Democratic Democratic
1993–2001	**Bill Clinton** Albert Gore Jr.	Democratic	103rd 104th 105th 106th	Democratic Republican Republican Republican	Democratic Republican Republican Republican
2001–2005	**George W. Bush** Richard Cheney	Republican	107th	Republican	Republican

Notes

1. During the entire administration of George Washington and part of the administration of John Quincy Adams, Congress was not organized in terms of parties. This table shows that during these periods the supporters of the respective administrations maintained control of Congress.

2. This table shows only the two dominant parties in Congress. Independents, members of minor parties, and vacancies have been omitted.

Glossary

affirmative action   Programs of private and public institutions favoring the hiring of certain minorities in an attempt to compensate for past discrimination.

agenda setting   Influencing what people consider important.

amicus curiae   Latin for "a friend of the court"; describes a brief in which individuals not party to a suit may have their views heard.

anarchist   A political philosophy which holds that government is both inherently coercive and unnecessary for the provision of public order and services.

Anti-Federalists   Opponents of the Constitution during the fight over ratification.

appellate courts   Courts that hear cases on appeal from other courts.

appropriation   Legal authority for a federal agency to spend money from the U.S. Treasury.

balance of payments   The annual difference between payments and receipts between a country and its trading partners.

beat   The assigned location where a reporter regularly gathers news stories.

bias   Deviation from some ideal standard, such as representativeness or objectivity.

bicameral   As applied to a legislative body, consisting of two houses or chambers.

bill of attainder   A governmental decree that a person is guilty of a crime that carries the death penalty, rendered without benefit of a trial.

Bill of Rights   The first ten amendments to the U.S. Constitution, concerned with basic liberties.

block grants   Federal grants to the states to be used for general activities.

blue-collar worker   A skilled, semiskilled, or unskilled worker in industry.

briefs   Documents setting out the arguments in legal cases, prepared by attorneys and presented to courts.

budget deficit   The amount by which annual government expenditures exceed revenues.

capital crime   Any crime for which death is a possible penalty.

capitalism   An economic system based on private ownership and the existence of markets to coordinate most economic activities.

capture   A situation in which a regulated industry exercises substantial influence on the government agency regulating it.

casework   Services performed by members of Congress for constituents.

categorical grants   Federal aid to states and localities clearly specifying what the money can be used for.

caucus   A meeting of party activists to choose delegates to a national presidential nominating convention.

Central Intelligence Agency (CIA)   The organization that coordinates all U.S. intelligence agencies; it also gathers and evaluates intelligence itself and carries out covert operations.

checks and balances   The constitutional principle that government power shall be divided and that the fragments should balance or check one another to prevent tyranny.

chief of staff   A top adviser to the president who also manages the White House staff.

circuits   The 12 geographical jurisdictions and 1 special court that hear appeals from the federal district courts.

civil disobedience   Intentionally breaking a law and accepting the consequences as a way to publicize the unjustness of the law.

civil liberties   Freedoms protected from government interference.

civil rights   Guarantees of equal citizenship to all social groups.

civil servants   Government workers employed under the merit system; not political appointees.

civil service   Federal government civilian employees, excluding political appointees.

class action suit   A suit brought on behalf of a group of people who are in a situation similar to that of the plaintiffs.

cloture   A vote to end a filibuster or a debate; requires the votes of three-fifths of the membership of the Senate.

Cold War   The period of tense relations between the United States and the Soviet Union from the late 1940s to the late 1980s.

collective public opinion   The political attitudes of the public as a whole, expressed as averages, percentages, or other summaries of many individuals' opinions.

concurring opinion   The opinion of one or more judges who vote with the majority on a case but wish to set out different reasons for their decision.

conditions   Provisions in federal assistance requiring that state and local governments follow certain policies in order to obtain the money.

confederation   A loose association of states or territorial divisions formed for a common purpose.

conference committees   Ad hoc committees, made up of members of both the Senate and the House of Representatives, set up to reconcile differences in the provisions of bills.

Connecticut Compromise   Also called the *Great Compromise*; the compromise between the New Jersey and Virginia plans put forth by the Connecticut delegates at the Constitutional Convention; called for a lower legislative house based on population and an upper house based on equal representation of the states.

conservative   The political position that holds that the federal government ought to play a very small role in economic regulation, social welfare, and overcoming racial inequality.

constituency   The district of a legislator.

constituent   A citizen who lives in the district of an elected official.

constitutional courts   Federal courts created by Congress under the authority of Article III of the Constitution.

containment   The policy of resisting expansion of the Soviet Union's influence by diplomatic, economic, and military means.

contract clause   The portion of Article I, Section 10, of the Constitution that prohibits states from passing any law "impairing the obligation of contracts."

convention   A gathering of delegates who nominate a party's presidential candidate.

conventional participation   Political activity related to elections (voting, persuading, and campaigning) or to contacting public officials.

cooperative federalism   Federalism in which the powers of the states and the national government are intertwined like the swirls in a marble cake.

cost-benefit analysis   A method of evaluating rules and regulations by weighing their potential costs against their potential benefits to society.

Council of Economic Advisers (CEA)   An organization in the Executive Office of the President made up of a small group of economists who advise on economic policy.

covert operations   Secret or semisecret activities abroad, often involving intelligence gathering, influence on other countries' politics, or the use of force.

dealignment   A gradual reduction in the dominance of one political party without another party supplanting it.

delegate   According to the doctrine articulated by Edmund Burke, an elected representative who acts in perfect accord with the wishes of his or her constituents.

democracy   A system of rule by the people, defined by the existence of popular sovereignty, political equality, and political liberty.

depression   A severe and persistent drop in economic activity.

devolution   The delegation of power by the central government to state or local bodies.

direct democracy   A form of political decision making in which the public business is decided by all citizens meeting in small assemblies.

discharge petition   A petition signed by 218 House members to force a bill that has been before a committee for at least 30 days while the House is in session out of the committee and onto the floor for consideration.

discount rate   The interest rate the Federal Reserve charges member banks to cover short-term loans.

dissenting opinion   The opinion of the judge or judges who are in the minority on a particular case before the Supreme Court.

disturbance theory   A theory that locates the origins of interest groups in changes in the economic, social, or political environment that threaten the well-being of some segment of the population.

divided government   Control of the executive and the legislative branches by different political parties.

dual federalism   Federalism in which the powers of the states and the national government are neatly separated like the sections of a layer cake.

due process clause   The section of the Fourteenth Amendment that prohibits states from depriving anyone of life, liberty, or property "without due process of law," a guarantee against arbitrary or unfair government action.

economic conservatives   People who favor private enterprise and oppose government regulations or spending.

economic liberals   People who favor government regulation of business and government spending for social programs.

elastic clause   Article I, Section 8, of the Constitution, also called the *necessary and proper clause*; gives Congress the authority to make whatever laws are necessary and proper to carry out its enumerated responsibilities.

electoral college   Representatives of the states who formally elect the president; the number of electors in each state is equal to the total number of its senators and congressional representatives.

electoral competition   The process by which parties seeking votes move toward the center of the political spectrum.

electoral reward and punishment   The tendency to vote for the incumbents when times are good and against them when times are bad.

electors   Representatives who are elected in the states to formally choose the U.S. president.

entitlements   Government benefits that are distributed automatically to citizens who qualify on the basis of a set of guidelines set by law; for example, Americans over the age of 65 are entitled to Medicare coverage.

enumerated powers   Powers of the federal government specifically mentioned in the Constitution.

equal protection clause   The section of the Fourteenth Amendment that provides equal protection of the laws to all citizens.

Equal Rights Amendment (ERA)   Proposed amendment to the U.S. Constitution stating that equality of rights shall not be abridged or denied on account of a person's sex.

equal time provision   The former requirement that television stations give or sell the same amount of time to all competing candidates.

establishment clause   The part of the First Amendment to the Constitution that prohibits Congress from establishing an official religion; the basis for the separation of church and state.

European Union (EU)   A common market formed by Western European nations, with free trade and free population movement among them.

ex post facto law   A law that retroactively declares some action illegal.

exclusionary rule   A standard promulgated by the Supreme Court that prevents police and prosecutors from using evidence against a defendant that was obtained in an illegal search.

Executive Office of the President (EOP)   A group of organizations that advise the president on a wide range of issues; includes the Office of Management and Budget, the National Security Council, and the Council of Economic Advisers.

executive privilege   A presidential claim that certain communications with subordinates may be withheld from Congress and the courts.

faction   Madison's term for groups or parties that try to advance their own interests at the expense of the public good.

fairness doctrine   The former requirement that television stations present contrasting points of view.

federal   Describing a system in which significant governmental powers are divided between a central government and smaller units, such as states.

federalism   A system in which significant governmental powers are divided between a central government and smaller units, such as states.

Federalists   Proponents of the Constitution during the ratification fight; also the political party of Hamilton, Washington, and Adams.

filibuster   A parliamentary device used in the Senate to prevent a bill from coming to a vote by "talking it to death," made possible by the norm of unlimited debate.

fiscal policy   Government's actions affecting spending and taxing levels; affects overall output and income in the economy.

framing   Providing a context for interpretation.

franchise   The right to vote.

franking privilege   Public subsidization of mail from the members of Congress to their constituents.

free exercise clause   That portion of the First Amendment to the Constitution that prohibits Congress from impeding religious observance or impinging on religious beliefs.

free rider   One who gains a benefit without contributing; explains why it is so difficult to form social movements and noneconomic interest groups.

General Agreement on Tariffs and Trade (GATT)   An international agreement that requires the lowering of tariffs and other barriers to free trade.

general revenue sharing   Federal aid to the states without any conditions on how the money is spent.

gerrymandering   Redrawing electoral district lines to give an advantage to a particular party or candidate.

grand juries   Groups of citizens who decide whether there is sufficient evidence to bring an indictment against accused persons.

grandfather clause   A device that allowed whites who had failed the literacy test to vote anyway by extending the franchise to anyone whose grandfather had voted.

grass roots   The constituents, voters, or rank-and-file of a party.

Great Depression   The period of economic crisis in the United States from the stock market crash of 1929 to America's entry into World War II.

gross domestic product (GDP)   Monetary value of all goods and services produced in a nation each year, excluding income residents earn abroad.

habeas corpus   The legal doctrine that a person who is arrested must have a timely hearing before a judge.

hearings   The taking of testimony by a congressional committee or subcommittee.

hopper   The box in the House of Representatives in which proposed bills are placed.

ideology   A system of interrelated attitudes and beliefs.

in forma pauperis   Describing a process by which indigents may file a suit with the Supreme Court free of charge.

incorporation   The gradual use of the Fourteenth Amendment by the Supreme Court to make the Bill of Rights and other constitutional protections binding on the states.

independent expenditures   Money spent on behalf of candidates by interest groups and individuals who are not connected to a candidate's campaign organization.

Industrial Revolution   The period of transition from predominantly agricultural to predominantly industrial societies in the Western nations in the nineteenth century.

inflation   A condition of rising prices.

infotainment   The merging of hard news and entertainment in news presentations.

institutional presidency   The permanent bureaucracy associated with the presidency, designed to help the incumbent of the office carry out his responsibilities.

integration   Policies encouraging the interaction of different races, as in schools or public facilities.

intercontinental ballistic missiles (ICBMs)   Guided missiles capable of carrying nuclear warheads across continents.

interest group   Any private organization or association that seeks to influence public policy as a way to protect or advance some interest.

interest group liberalism   A political regime in which interest groups help formulate and carry out government policies.

intermediate scrutiny   A legal test falling between ordinary and strict scrutiny relevant to issues of gender; under this test, the Supreme Court will allow gender classifications in laws if they are *substantially* related to an *important* government objective.

iron triangle   An enduring alliance of common interest among an interest group, a congressional committee, and a bureaucratic agency.

isolationism   The policy of avoiding involvement in foreign affairs.

isolationists   Those who believe the United States should defend itself behind formidable defensive walls and avoid foreign military and diplomatic entanglements.

Jim Crow   Popular term for the system of legal racial segregation that existed in the American South until the middle of the twentieth century.

Joint Chiefs of Staff (JCS)   The military officers in charge of each of the armed services.

joint committees   Congressional committees with members from both the House and the Senate.

judicial activism   Actions by the courts that go beyond the strict role of the judiciary as interpreter of the law and adjudicator of disputes.

judicial review   The power of the Supreme Court to declare actions of the other branches and levels of government unconstitutional.

Keynesians   Advocates of government programs to stimulate economic activity through tax cuts and government spending.

laissez-faire   The political-economic doctrine that holds that government ought not interfere with the operations of the free market.

legislative courts   Highly specialized federal courts created by Congress under the authority of Article I of the Constitution.

liberal   The political position that holds that the federal government has a substantial role to play in economic regulation, social welfare, and overcoming racial inequality.

literacy test   A device used by the southern states to prevent African-Americans from voting before the passage of the Voting Rights Act of 1965, which banned its use; usually involved interpretation of a section of a state's constitution.

lobby   An interest or pressure group that seeks to convey the group's interest to government decision makers.

macroeconomic policy   Having to do with the performance of the economy as a whole.

majority-minority districts   Districts drawn to ensure that a racial minority makes up the majority of voters.

majority rule   The form of political decision making in which policies are decided on the basis of what a majority of the people want.

majority tyranny   Suppression of the rights and liberties of a minority by the majority.

mandate   A formal order from the national government that the states carry out certain policies.

markup   The process of revising a bill in committee.

Marshall Plan   The program of U.S. economic aid set up to rebuild Europe after World War II.

mass mobilization   The process of involving large numbers of people in a social movement.

means-tested   Meeting the criterion of demonstrable need.

monetarists   Advocates of a minimal government role in the economy, limited to managing the growth of the money supply.

monetary policy   Government's actions affecting the supply of money and the level of interest rates in the economy.

multilateralist   The stance toward foreign policy that suggests that the United States should seek the cooperation of other nations and multilateral institutions in pursuing its goals; those who believe the United States should use its military and diplomatic power in the world in cooperation with other nations and international organizations.

mutually assured destruction (MAD)   A situation of nuclear balance in which either the United States or the Soviet Union could respond to a surprise attack by destroying the other country.

national debt   The total outstanding debt of the federal government.

national interest   What is of benefit to the nation as a whole.

National Reconnaissance Office (NRO)   The government agency in charge of surveillance by satellite photography and other technological means.

national security adviser   A top foreign policy and defense adviser to the president who heads the National Security Council.

National Security Agency (NSA)   The federal government agency that intercepts and decodes electronic messages and secures U.S. communications around the world.

National Security Council (NSC)   An organization in the Executive Office of the President made up of officials from the State and Defense Departments, the CIA, and the military, who advise on foreign and security affairs.

nationalizing   The process by which the provisions of the Bill of Rights become incorporated. See *incorporation.*

nativist Antiforeign; applied to political movements active in the nineteenth century.

necessary and proper clause Article I, Section 8, of the Constitution, also known as the *elastic clause*; gives Congress the authority to make whatever laws are necessary and proper to carry out its enumerated responsibilities.

negative externalities The positive and negative effects of economic activities on third parties.

New Deal The programs of the administrations of President Franklin D. Roosevelt.

New Deal coalition The informal electoral alliance of working-class ethnic groups, Catholics, Jews, urban dwellers, racial minorities, and the South that was the basis of the Democratic party dominance of American politics from the New Deal to the early 1970s.

New Jersey Plan Proposal of the smaller states at the Constitutional Convention to create a government based on the equal representation of the states in a unicameral legislature.

newsworthy Worth printing or broadcasting as news, according to editors' judgments.

normal vote The proportion of the votes that each party would win if party identification alone affected voting decisions.

North American Free Trade Agreement (NAFTA) An agreement among the United States, Canada, and Mexico to eliminate nearly all barriers to trade and investment among the three countries.

North Atlantic Treaty Organization (NATO) An alliance of the United States, Canada, and Western European countries for defense against the Soviet Union.

nuclear proliferation The spread of nuclear weapons to additional countries or to terrorist groups.

nullification An attempt by states to declare national laws or actions null and void.

objective news News reported with no evaluative language and with any opinions quoted or attributed to a specific source.

obscenity As defined by the Supreme Court, the representation of sexually explicit material in a manner that violates community standards and is without redeeming social importance or value.

Office of Management and Budget (OMB) An organization within the Executive Office of the President that advises on the federal budget, domestic legislation, and regulations.

open-seat election An election in which there is no incumbent officeholder.

opinion The explanation of the majority's reasoning that accompanies a Supreme Court decision.

opinion of the Court The majority opinion that accompanies a Supreme Court decision.

ordinary scrutiny The assumption that the actions of elected bodies and officials are legal under the Constitution.

original intention The doctrine that the courts must interpret the Constitution in ways consistent with the intentions of the framers rather than in light of contemporary conditions and needs.

original jurisdiction The authority of a court to be the first to hear a particular kind of case.

participation Political activity, including voting, campaign activity, contacting officials, and demonstrating.

partisan A committed member of a party; seeing issues from the point of view of the interests of a single party.

party caucus An organization of the members of a political party in the House or Senate.

party identification The sense of belonging to one or another political party.

party platform A party's statement of its positions on the issues of the day.

Pentagon The building in Arlington, Virginia, that contains the offices of the military chiefs and top officials of the Defense Department.

petit (trial) juries Juries that hear evidence and sit in judgment on charges brought in civil or criminal cases.

plaintiff One who brings suit in a court.

pluralist A political scientist who views American politics as best understood in terms of the interaction, conflict, and bargaining of groups.

plurality More votes than any other candidate but less than a majority of all votes cast.

pocket veto Rejection of a bill if the president takes no action on it for ten days and Congress has adjourned during that period.

policy preferences Citizens' preferences concerning what policies they want government to pursue.

political action committee (PAC) A private organization whose purpose is to raise and distribute funds to candidates in political campaigns.

political efficacy The sense that one can affect what government does.

political equality The principle that says that each person carries equal weight in the conduct of the public business.

political liberty The principle that citizens in a democracy are protected from government interference in the exercise of a range of basic freedoms, such as the freedoms of speech, association, and conscience.

poll tax A tax to be paid as a condition of voting.

popular sovereignty The basic principle of democracy that the people ultimately rule.

pork Also called *pork barrel;* projects designed to bring to the constituency jobs and public money for which the members of Congress can claim credit.

poverty line The federal government's calculation of the amount of income families of various sizes need to stay out of poverty.

precedents Rulings by courts that guide judicial reasoning in subsequent cases.

preemption Exclusion of the states from actions that might interfere with federal legislation.

presidential approval rating A president's standing with the public, indicated by the percentage of Americans who tell survey interviewers that they approve a president's "handling of his job."

presidential popularity The percentage of Americans who approve a president's handling of his job.

pressure group An interest group or lobby; a group that brings pressure to bear on government decision makers.

primary elections State elections in which delegates to national presidential nominating conventions are chosen.

prior restraint The government's power to prevent publication, as opposed to punishment afterward.

privatization The process of turning over certain government functions to the private sector.

privileges and immunities clause The portion of Article IV, Section 2, of the Constitution that states that citizens from out of state have the same legal rights as local citizens in any state.

proportional representation The awarding of legislative seats to political parties to reflect the proportion of the popular vote each party receives.

public goods Products and services that citizens want but the private sector does not provide, such as national defense and pollution control.

public opinion Political attitudes expressed by ordinary citizens.

pundits Somewhat derisive term for print, broadcast, and radio commentators on the political news.

random sampling The selection of survey respondents by chance, with equal probability, to ensure their representativeness of the whole population.

ranking minority member The minority party member with the greatest seniority on a committee.

realignment The process by which one party supplants another as the dominant party in a political system.

reapportionment The redrawing of congressional district boundaries to account for changes in population.

recession A period of decline in overall economic activity.

reciprocity Deferral by members of Congress to the judgment of subject-matter specialists, mainly on minor technical bills.

red tape Overbearing bureaucratic rules and procedures.

regulations The issuing of rules by government agencies with the aim of reducing the scale of negative externalities produced by private firms.

remedy An action that a court determines must be taken to rectify a wrong.

representative democracy Indirect democracy, in which the people rule through elected representatives.

republicanism A political doctrine advocating limited government based on popular consent, protected against majority tyranny.

reservation clause The Tenth Amendment to the Constitution, reserving powers to the states or the people.

responsible party A political party that takes clear, distinct stands on the issues and enacts them as policy.

retrospective voting Voting on the basis of past government performance.

rule of four An *unwritten* practice that requires at least four justices of the Supreme Court to agree that a case warrants review by the Court before it will hear the case.

sample survey An interview study asking questions of a set of people who are chosen as representative of the whole population.

scope of conflict The number of groups involved in a political conflict; few groups mean a narrow scope of conflict, and many groups mean a wide scope of conflict.

secularization The spread of nonreligious values and outlooks.

select committees Temporary committees in Congress created to conduct studies or investigations. They have no power to report bills.

selective incorporation The U.S. Supreme Court's gradual and piecemeal making of the protections of the Bill of Rights binding on the states.

senatorial courtesy The tradition that judicial nominations for federal district court appointments be cleared by the senior senator of the president's party from the relevant state.

seniority Length of service.

separate but equal doctrine The principle articulated in *Plessy* v. *Ferguson* (1896) that laws prescribing *separate* public facilities and services for nonwhite Americans are permissible if the facilities and services are *equal* to those provided for whites.

separation of powers The distribution of government legislative, executive, and judicial powers to separate branches of government.

sit-down strike A form of labor action in which workers stop production but do not leave their job site.

smart bombs Bombs capable of being guided precisely to their targets.

social conservatives People who favor traditional social values; they tend to support strong law-and-order measures and to oppose abortion and gay rights.

social insurance Government programs that provide services or income support in proportion to the amount of mandatory contributions made by individuals to a government trust fund.

social liberals People who favor civil liberties, abortion rights, and alternative lifestyles.

soft money Expenditures by political parties on general public education, voter registration, and voter mobilization.

spillover effects Policy effects that go outside the boundaries of the governmental unit making the policy.

spoils system The practice of distributing government offices and contracts to the supporters of the winning party; also called *patronage*.

standing Authority to bring legal action because one is directly affected by the issues at hand.

standing committees   Relatively permanent congressional committees that address specific areas of legislation.

stare decisis   The legal doctrine that says precedent should guide judicial decision making.

stay acts   Enactments postponing the collection of taxes or mortgage payments.

strict construction   The doctrine that the provisions of the Constitution have a clear meaning and that judges must stick closely to this meaning when rendering decisions.

strict scrutiny   The assumption that actions by elected bodies or officials violate constitutional rights.

suffrage   The right to vote.

Sun Belt   States of the Lower South, Southwest, and West, where sunny weather and often conservative politics prevail.

superpower   A nation armed with nuclear weapons and able to project force anywhere on the globe.

supremacy clause   The provision in Article VI of the Constitution that the Constitution itself and the laws and treaties of the United States are the supreme law of the land, taking precedence over state laws and constitutions.

suspect classification   The invidious, arbitrary, or irrational designation of a group for special treatment by government.

test case   A case brought to force a ruling on the constitutionality of some law or executive action.

think tanks   Nonprofit organizations that do research on public policy issues and distribute their findings through a variety of outlets. Although formally nonpartisan, most have an identifiable ideological stance.

trade deficit   An excess of the value of the goods a country imports over the value of the goods it exports.

Truman Doctrine   President Truman's policy that the United States should defend noncommunist countries from outside pressure and internal rebellion from communists.

trustee   According to Edmund Burke, a representative who believes that his or her own best judgment, rather than instructions from constituents, should be used in making legislative decisions.

trusts   Large combinations of business corporations.

turnout   The proportion of eligible voters who actually vote in a given election.

tyranny   The abuse of power by a ruler or a government.

unanimous consent   Legislative action taken "without objection" as a way to expedite business; used to conduct much of the business of the Senate.

unconventional participation   Political activity in the form of demonstrations or protests.

unilateralist   The stance toward foreign policy that suggests that the United States should "go it alone," pursuing its national interests without seeking the cooperation of other nations or multilateral institutions; those who believe the United States should vigorously use its military and diplomatic power to pursue American national interests in the world, but on a "go it alone" basis.

unitary system   A system in which a central government has complete power over its constituent units or states.

veto   Presidential disapproval of a bill that has been passed by both houses of Congress. The president's veto can be overridden by a two-thirds vote in each house.

Virginia Plan   Proposal by the large states at the Constitutional Convention to create a strong central government with power in the government apportioned to the states on the basis of population.

Warsaw Pact   An alliance of the Soviet Union and Eastern European communist countries.

watchdog   The role of the media in scrutinizing the actions of government officials.

welfare state   The set of government programs that protects the minimum standard of living of families and individuals against loss of income.

whip   A political party member in Congress charged with keeping members informed of the plans of the party leadership, counting votes before action on important issues, and rounding up party members for votes on bills.

whistle-blowers   People who bring official misconduct in their agencies to public attention.

white-collar worker   A person working at a service, sales, or office job.

white primaries   Primary elections open only to whites.

World Trade Organization (WTO)   An agency designed to enforce the provisions of the General Agreement on Tariffs and Trade and to resolve trade disputes between nations.

writ of certiorari   An announcement that the Supreme Court will hear a case on appeal from a lower court; its issuance requires the vote of four of the nine justices.

writ of mandamus   A court order that forces an official to act.

yellow journalism   Sensational newspaper stories with large headlines and, in some cases, color cartoons.

Credits

Text, Figures, and Tables

Page 71: Figure 3.2, *Statistical Abstract of the United States,* 1997, Tables 506 and 536; **p. 60:** Boxed figure, used with the permission of the Center for American Women and Politics (CAWP), Eagleton Institute of Politics, Rutgers University; **p. 61:** Boxed figure, Copyright © 1997 by *The New York Times Co.* Reprinted by permission; **p. 88:** Figure 4.2, Copyright © 1991, *The Washington Post.* Reprinted with permission; **p. 90:** Figure 4.3, U.S. Census Bureau, 1991; **p. 95** Figure 4.7, © *The Economist Newspaper Group, Inc.* Reprinted with permission. Further reproduction prohibited. **www.economist.com**; **p. 99** Figure 4.9, Copyright © 1995 by *The New York Times Co.* Reprinted by permission; **p. 186:** Figure 7.1, From Edward S. Greenberg, *The American Political System,* Fifth Edition. Copyright © 1989. Reprinted by permission of Addison Wesley Educational Publishers; **p. 219:** "Mary Beth Tinker Protests the War," Reprinted with the permission of The Free Press, a Division of Simon & Schuster, Inc., from *The Courage of Their Convictions* by Peter Irons. Copyright © 1988 by Peter Irons; **p. 222:** Table 8.1, reprinted with the permission of Simon & Schuster from *America in Black and White* by Stephan Thernstrom and Abigail Thernstrom. Copyright © 1997 by Stephan Thernstrom and Abigail Thernstrom; **p. 319:** Figure 11.5, from *The Congressional Quarterly,* November 1992. Reprinted by permission; **p. 325:** Figure 11.7, from Roger H. Davidson and Walter J. Oleszek, *Congress and Its Members,* Seventh Edition, p. 268. Copyright © 2000 *Congressional Quarterly Inc.*; **p. 354:** Table 12.1, The Public's list is from The Gallup Poll, 1991. The Expert's list is from a poll conducted by *The New York Times* and reported in Arthur M. Schlesinger, Jr., "The Ultimate Approval Rating," *The New York Times Magazine,* December 15, 1996, pp. 48–49; **p. 421:** Figure 14.3, from *Storm Center: The Supreme Court in American Politics,* Fourth Edition by David M. O'Brien. Copyright © 1996, 1993, 1990, 1986 by David M. O'Brien. Used by permission of W. W. Norton Company, Inc.; **p. 467:** Figure 15.1, Louis Harris and Associates as reported in *The Public Perspective,* a publication of the Roper Center for Public Opinion Research, University of CT, October/November 1999, p. 42. Reprinted by permission; **p. 483:** Figure 16.1, Source: Survey by Washington Post/Harvard/Kaiser Family Foundation, July 20–September 28, 1995. As published in *Public Perspective,* February/March 1996, p. 28. Reprinted with permission, The Roper Center for Public Opinion Research, University of CT, Storrs, CT; **p. 499:** Figure 17.1, © The Economist Newspaper Group, Inc. Reprinted with permission. Further reproduction prohibited. **www.economist.com**; **p. 516:** Figure 17.8, from *The Washington Post National Edition,* January 13, 1997, p. 19 from The Social Security Administration; **p. 537:** Figure 18.1, from *American Diplomacy in the Twentieth Century,* Second Edition by Robert D. Schulzinger. Copyright © 1984 by Robert D. Schulzinger. Used by permission of Oxford University Press, Inc.

Photos

Page abbreviations are used as follows: **(T)** top, **(C)** center, **(B)** bottom, **(L)** left, **(R)** right.

Page 4 (T): AP/Wide World Photos; **p.4 (C):** Archive Photos; **p. 7:** The Granger Collection; **p. 8:** The Image Works; **p. 10:** The Granger Collection; **p. 12:** The Granger Collection; **p. 16:** AP/Wide World Photos; **p. 25:** The Granger Collection; **p. 28 (L):** The Granger Collection; **p. 28 (R):** Courtesy of the Library of Congress; **p. 32:** Folio, Inc.; **p. 35:** Art Resource, N.Y.; **p. 37:** © The Illustrated London News/February 16, 1861; **p. 47:** Impact Visuals Photo & Graphics, Inc.; **p. 53:** New York Times Pictures; **p. 55:** AP/Wide World Photos; **p. 59:** The Image Works; **p. 64:** Stephen Ferry/Liaison Agency, Inc.; **p. 67:** Corbis; **p. 68:** Pearson Education U.S. ELT/Scott Foresman; **p. 74:** Lyndon Baines Johnson Library Collection; **p. 75:** Corbis/Sygma; **p. 76:** The Cartoon Bank; **p. 77:** Corbis/Sygma; **p. 78:** Corbis; **p. 79:** Unicorn Stock Photos; **p. 85:** Corbis/Sygma; **p. 89:** S. Kelly: © 1995 San Diego Union-Tribune, Copley News Service; **p. 90:** Folio, Inc.; **p. 92:** The Image Works; **p. 98:** Unicorn Stock Photos; **p. 102:** Liaison Agency, Inc.; **p. 106:** Corbis/Sygma; **p. 108:** Corbis/Sygma; **p. 117:** Corbis/Sygma; **p. 120:** The Image Works; **p. 121:** Corbis; **p. 125:** Corbis/Sygma; **p. 126:** Corbis; **p. 131:** Liaison Agency, Inc.; **p. 134:** SABA Press Photos, Inc.; **p. 136:** Corbis; **p. 137:** PhotoEdit; **p. 138 (T):** Black Star; **p. 138 (B):** David R. Frazier Photolibrary, Inc.; **p. 149:** SABA Press Photos, Inc.; **p. 151:** © Reprinted by permission Tribune Media Services; **p. 153 (L):** © New York Journal, February 7, 1898; **p. 153 (R):** Colorado Historical Society; **p. 155 (T):** Liaison Agency, Inc.; **p. 155 (B):** AP/Wide World Photos; **p. 158:** Corbis/Sygma; **p. 161:** Folio, Inc.; **p. 162:** Kobal Collection; **p. 164:** Ben Van Hook; **p. 167:** Corbis/Sygma; **p. 172:** Creators Syndicate, Inc.; **p. 173:** The Image Works; **p. 175:** Darren McCollester/Newsmakers/Liaison Agency;

Index